# ETHICAL
# LEADERSHIP

# ETHICAL LEADERSHIP

## A PRIMER

### SECOND EDITION

EDITED BY

ROBERT M. MCMANUS

*Executive Director of Applied Leadership and Professor of Leadership, Muskingum University, Ohio, USA*

STANLEY J. WARD

*Principal, Influence Coaching LLC, Texas, USA*

ALEXANDRA K. PERRY

*Clinical Ethicist, OhioHealth and Dean of the McDonough Center, Marietta College, Ohio, USA*

Edward Elgar
PUBLISHING

Cheltenham, UK • Northampton, MA, USA

Cover image: Beth Nash.
Cover design: Tina Ullman.

The Five Components of Leadership Model was first developed by Gama
Perruci and appeared in 'Leadership education across disciplines: The
Social science perspective,' *Journal of Leadership Studies*, vol. 7 no. 4,
2014, 43–7. The model was further refined and developed in McManus
and Perruci's *Understanding Leadership: An Arts and Humanities
Perspective*, New York: Routledge, 2015 and again in the second edition
of the book published in 2020.

Published by
Edward Elgar Publishing Limited
The Lypiatts
15 Lansdown Road
Cheltenham
Glos GL50 2JA
UK

Edward Elgar Publishing, Inc.
William Pratt House
9 Dewey Court
Northampton
Massachusetts 01060
USA

Companion website material can be found at:
https://www.e-elgar.com/textbooks/mcmanus-ethical-leadership-2ed

A catalogue record for this book
is available from the British Library

Library of Congress Control Number: 2023941677

Printed on elemental chlorine free (ECF)
recycled paper containing 30% Post-Consumer Waste

ISBN 978 1 80220 863 4 (cased)
ISBN 978 1 80220 864 1 (eBook)
ISBN 978 1 80220 865 8 (paperback)

Printed and bound in the USA

# CONTENTS IN BRIEF

## SECTION II

# FULL CONTENTS

**SECTION I**

# TABLES

# CONTRIBUTORS

## EDITORS

**Robert M. McManus** is the Executive Director of Applied Leadership and Professor of Leadership at Muskingum University (Ohio). His previous institutions include the McDonough Center for Leadership and Business at Marietta College (Ohio) and Claremont Lincoln University (California). He is the co-author of *Understanding Leadership: An Arts and Humanities Perspective* (Routledge, 2015/2020). McManus is an active member of the International Leadership Association. He is an award-winning educator and has travelled extensively teaching on leadership in global contexts. He is also a highly trained leadership coach and consultant. McManus holds a Ph.D. in Communication as well as a Master of Business Administration.

**Alexandra K. Perry** is currently the Dean and an Associate Professor of Leadership and Ethics at the McDonough Center at Marietta College. Alex is also a clinical ethicist with a decade of experience in ethics consultation and serves as a trustee on the board of the Bioethics Network of Ohio. She is the author or editor of six books and is currently working on a book that examines leadership and ethics in end-of-life care in the American hospital.

**Stanley J. Ward** holds a Ph.D. in leadership studies and has years of experience as an administrator and instructor of ethical leadership and business communication. He is also the founder and principal at Influence Coaching LLC. His coaching practice helps driven and thoughtful leaders create sustainable positive changes that include reducing unproductive conflict and avoiding burnout. Since 2011, he has coached clients through major transitions and leadership challenges, helped them address root causes, and partnered with them to create positive results both at work and home. Besides his work as a writer, he is also an active member of the International Coaching Federation and volunteers on a variety of boards.

## CONTRIBUTORS

**J. Michael Cervantez** is a professor of philosophy and religious studies at Crafton Hills College. In this role, he also serves as the chair for the Social Sciences. He holds a Ph.D. in philosophy and an M.A. in philosophy and ethics. He has published articles in journals and books on topics in ethics, political philosophy, leadership, and religion. In addition to teaching and writing, he has worked as a clinical ethicist and chaplain. Most recently he was elected to City Council where he works to promote civility and community in local government.

**Benjamin P. Dean** serves as Head of the Management & Entrepreneurship Department and associate professor of management in the Tommy and Victoria Baker School of Business at The Citadel, a public university in Charleston, South Carolina. He also is the former head of the Department of Leadership Studies. He holds a Ph.D. in organizational leadership, and teaches in organizational development, human resources, and business law and ethics. His certifications include Senior Professional in Human Resources (SPHR), and the Senior Certified Professional certification by the Society of Human Resources Management (SHRM). He is a licensed attorney and certified mediator, having actively practiced in business law and civil litigation, and served on the White House staff as Assistant Counsel to the President. He has extensive organizational and global experience, and has worked in over thirty countries. Dr. Dean has authored journal articles and textbook chapters on organizations, leadership, law, and online education. He speaks and consults in leading organizational change and in human capital development.

**Amy Elliott** (instructor ancillaries) is the Director of the Office of Community Engagement and a professor of Leadership Studies in the McDonough Center for Leadership and Business. She enjoys teaching courses in leadership, organizational leadership, board governance, social change leadership, and civil discourse. She provides facilitation for organizations and individuals in transition and consults with philanthropists struggling to ensure responsible, sustainable, positive impact.

**Sabrina B. Little** is an Assistant Professor in the Department of Leadership and American Studies at Christopher Newport University. She holds a doctorate in Philosophy from Baylor University, a Masters in Philosophy of Religion from Yale University, and a Bachelor of Arts in Philosophy and Psychology from The College of William and Mary. Her research is in virtue ethics, moral psychology, and leadership and the emotions.

**Stephanie E. Raible** is an Assistant Professor of Social Innovation and Entrepreneurship at the Alfred Lerner College of Business and Economics' Department of Business Administration and Horn Entrepreneurship at the University of Delaware. She also serves as UD's faculty director of the Social Entrepreneurship Initiative. Prior to her position with the Lerner College, she held a joint appointment between University of Delaware's Department of Human Development and Family Sciences and Horn Entrepreneurship and another role as an instructor of cultural entrepreneurship with the University of Minnesota Duluth. She possesses an Ed.D. in organizational leadership from Northeastern University, as well as an M.A. in lifelong learning policy and management from UCL Institute of Education and University of Deusto, a M.S.Ed. in higher education management from the University of Pennsylvania, and a B.A. in Italian studies from the University of Delaware.

**Molly Reed-Waters** is a Senior Lecturer of Leadership Studies in the Department of Leadership and American Studies at Christopher Newport University. She holds a doctorate in Philosophy from Regent University, a Masters of Organizational Leadership and Healthcare Administration from Regent University, and a Bachelor of Arts in Communication and Leadership Studies from Christopher Newport University. Her research is in healthcare leadership, bioethics, and leadership in crisis situations and mass-casualty events.

**Jon Rogers** is an Assistant Professor of Leadership Studies at Marietta College. Jon holds a doctorate in Pedagogy and Philosophy from Montclair State University and Master's degrees in Education from Montclair State and Applied Ethics from Bowling Green State University.

He has also worked in various positions in the energy industry including both the midstream and land management sectors. Jon's research interests are around leadership in the fields of energy and sustainability.

**Maribeth Saleem-Tanner** currently serves as Executive Director of Community Food Initiatives (CFI), a community-based nonprofit in Athens, Ohio, that works to foster communities where everyone has equitable access to healthy, local food. Prior to her work at CFI, Maribeth directed the Office of Civic Engagement at Marietta College, teaching courses within the McDonough Leadership program, overseeing co-curricular programs and community outreach, and supporting regional nonprofit capacity-building through the Nonprofits LEAD program. Maribeth formerly worked at High Rocks, an award-winning youth leadership program in West Virginia. She holds an M.A. in conflict transformation with a concentration in peacebuilding and development from the Center for Justice and Peacebuilding at Eastern Mennonite University in Harrisonburg, Virginia, as well as a B.A. in English and creative writing from Pomona College. Her research at EMU focused on understanding differing perspectives on community development in Appalachia.

**Phyllis H. Sarkaria** is a master certified executive coach, facilitator, and trusted adviser. She has held executive roles in government affairs and human resources in energy and life science industries. Before founding The Sarkaria Group, Sarkaria served as VP, HR for Quidel Corporation (now QuidelOrtho), a leading medical diagnostics manufacturer, where she was responsible for global HR strategy and people programs. Sarkaria is the author of *Courageous Clarity: Navigating the way forward on your leadership journey*. She works with individual clients and leadership teams in a wide range of industries to gain fresh perspective, communicate more clearly, and elevate their performance by increasing their leadership effectiveness. Sarkaria holds a BBA, Finance and an MBA from Texas Tech University and an M.A., Ethical Leadership from Claremont Lincoln University. Her coaching certifications are from the Berkeley Executive Coaching Institute, Marshall Goldsmith's Stakeholder Centered Coaching, and Peter Hawkins' Systemic Team Coaching through the Academy of Executive Coaching.

**Emily Schuck** is a professor of Leadership Studies at the McDonough Center for Leadership and Business at Marietta College, Ohio. Emily teaches undergraduate courses in organizational leadership, theories and models of leadership and leadership for the arts and humanities. She is also the Vice President for Enrollment Management at Furman University. She has worked in higher education administration for over twenty years at both public and private institutions. Emily holds a master's degree in education from Marietta College and is a doctoral student at Concordia University of Chicago. Her current research concentration is on the topic of complex problem-solving strategies of higher education leaders within the framework of adaptive leadership.

**Lavina Sequeira** is the Associate Dean for Humanities and Associate Professor of Philosophy at Felician University, New Jersey. She is the co-editor of *Inclusion, Diversity, and Intercultural Dialogue in Young People's Philosophical Inquiry* published by Sense Publishers. Her main research interests are in the field of Educational Philosophy and Immigrant Education. Her current interdisciplinary research projects focus specifically on the intersections between best teaching practices, racial/ethnic/academic identities, and the dialogical self of immigrant and minority youth in higher education. She teaches courses in the areas of educational foundations, ethics, and critical reasoning. She holds an Ed.D. in Pedagogy and Philosophy from Montclair State University.

**Keren Tanguay** is assistant professor of Religion and Bioethics in the Humanities Department at Kettering College and Director of Clinical Ethics at Kettering Health. She holds a Masters in Divinity from Fuller Theological Seminary and a doctorate from the The Ohio State University. Dr. Tanguay formally trained in Clinical Ethics at OhioHealth in Columbus, Ohio and is Healthcare Ethics Consultant-Certified through the American Society for Bioethics and Humanities. Her areas of research interest include the intersect of narrative medicine and medical chart documentation in addition to ethical dilemmas related to standards of care for substance use patients with infective endocarditis.

**James N. Thomas** is the Senior Pastor at First Baptist Church in Fayetteville, Georgia. His fields of interest include evangelical theology, servant leadership, and Christian discipleship. He currently serves on the teaching faculty of The Bonhoeffer Project, an international multi-denominational Christian ministry challenging pastors and ministry leaders to become disciple-making leaders in their organizations and serves as Director of Bonhoeffer Press. He is also a teaching member of Project 70, a Brazilian Church Planting Partnership in southern Brazil. He has taught master's level leadership courses in Brazil and has been a guest lecturer at the Korean Baptist theological University/Seminary in Daejeon, South Korea. He holds a Bachelor of Arts in Religion from Baylor University, a Master of Arts in Religious Education from Southwestern Baptist Theological Seminary in Fort Worth, Texas, and a Ph.D. in Leadership Studies from Dallas Baptist University.

**Stephen C. Trainor** is Founder and Chief Explorer for Expeditionary Leadership, a learning & leadership consultancy based in Bentonville, AR and also serves as a faculty lead for Walton College of Business Executive Education. Most recently, he was Global Head of Curriculum and Faculty Strategy in The Google School for Leaders. Trainor's extensive military career includes operational leadership in Naval Aviation, executive talent management, and service as the U.S. Naval Academy's first Permanent Military Professor of Leadership. As Director of Leadership Education and Development at the U.S. Naval Academy, he transformed the approach to leadership education and development and created the first 'School' of leadership at a U.S. Service Academy. Trainor currently serves on the editorial board of *The Journal of Character and Leadership Development* at the U.S. Air Force Academy and holds a Ph.D. in Sociology as well as master's degrees in International Affairs and National Security Studies.

**Stephanie Varnon-Hughes**, Ph.D., is the Dean of Teaching, Learning & Leadership at Claremont Lincoln University, an award-winning public-school teacher and community educator, and the author of *Interfaith Grit: How Uncertainty Will Save Us.* Varnon-Hughes was a co-founder and editor-in-chief of the *Journal of Inter-Religious Studies*, a peer-reviewed journal, and its sister publication *State of Formation*, an online forum for emerging ethical leaders. She holds a Ph.D. in inter-religious education from Claremont Lincoln University, an M.A. and STM from Union Theological Seminary, and her undergraduate degrees are in

English and Education, from Webster University. Her research interests include mindfulness, resilience, and equipping communities to build programs and policies that promote justice and flourishing.

# ACKNOWLEDGMENTS

No book has ever been published without a number of gracious people lending their support. That is *especially* true of this book. First, we must acknowledge our contributors. They grasped our vision for developing an accessible text that truly merged the fields of leadership and ethics. In many ways, producing a book of this kind *is an act of leadership*. We could not have asked for a group of more dedicated followers who truly came along side us as partners as we sought to reach the common goal of delivering the book you now hold in your hands.

We want to be sure to mention a few other folks that helped us along the way: David Brown for his helpful comments on the early drafts of the manuscript; Beth Nash, Tina Ullman and Ryan Zundell for their outstanding art and design work; and the manuscript reviewers at Edward Elgar and Alan Sturmer, the Executive Editor at Edward Elgar, for believing in our vision.

Finally, we must thank our friends and family who supported us in countless ways as we toiled to bring this project to completion. To all of these kind and generous people, we offer our deepest gratitude.

While completing the second edition of this book, Dr. Gama Perruci passed away. We are forever grateful to his leadership and mentorship in our lives.

# FOREWORDS

## FOREWORD FOR THE FIRST EDITION OF *ETHICAL LEADERSHIP: A PRIMER*

*Gama Perruci*

As the world becomes increasingly interconnected, our leaders face complex challenges that do not have simple answers. Figuring out solutions requires ethically grounded leadership. It is always surprising (at least, to me) to see that amid so many books on ethics, and even more on leadership, there are few of them that actually bring the two together in an intentional way.

Ethics and leadership are often presented as separate tracks. Introductory texts on ethics may make references to ethical dilemmas that leaders face, but these books tend to focus primarily on the ethical models (such as utilitarianism, ethical egoism, and other such theories). Conversely, leadership texts may make references to ethical challenges, but they are still focused mainly on leadership. It is left up to the aspiring leader to glean the golden nuggets of wisdom from one or the other, at times accidentally.

This book is actually about "ethical leadership," merging *ethical thinking* and *ethical doing*. When we look at the leadership theories through the lens of ethical models, we can see that the separateness of the two tracks is actually artificial. They are part of the same process. We want our leaders to not only think about ethics, but also engage in the practice of ethical conduct.

I particularly like the word 'primer' in the title – from the Latin word (*primus*) for 'first.' If you are getting ready to do something, a primer becomes your first step in the process. In this case, before you go out into the world and practice ethical leadership, it will serve you well to explore how these two tracks intersect.

In 2015, Robert McManus and I published a book entitled *Understanding Leadership*, in which we offered the Five Components of Leadership Model. The model was developed through many years of teaching at the McDonough Leadership Program at Marietta College. It helps our students see leadership as a *process*. The model focuses on the relationship between leaders and followers as they pursue common goals. Many leadership definitions focus on those three components, as if the relationship takes place in a vacuum, but our model adds two other critical components – context and cultural norms.

Context can be understood both at the organizational and societal levels. Human activities shape structures that can either constrain or enable certain types of human relations. The classical gathering at the water cooler is a reference to the way an object can bring people together and foster information exchange and dialogue. The fifth component was added as a circle around the other four to express the idea that cultural norms affect the leader–follower relationship, the types of goals that are pursued, and the organizational/societal context. In other words, the values that we hold dear shape the leadership process.

McManus and I then took the five components and connected them to leadership theories, using an arts and humanities approach. I am delighted to see that the Five Components of Leadership Model can be applied so effectively to the study of ethical leadership, as well. Each component of the model – leaders, followers, goals, context, and culture – provides the ethical lens through which we can evaluate leadership theories – such as authentic leadership, follow-ership, as well as the other leadership theories and models contained in this book.

In our book *Understanding Leadership*, McManus and I drew attention to the wise words of John W. Gardner, who counsels against acting without first understanding. The same applies here. Before our leaders go out and practice ethical leadership, they must first think deeply about the way ethical models connect to leadership perspectives. This is not solely an intellectual exercise. It should be grounded in the desire to be thoughtful when choosing an ethical path.

Another great benefit of this primer is the use of a liberal-arts approach to ethical leadership. As we see the value of a liberal-arts education being contested in the halls of government, particularly at the national level, it is reassuring to see how a liberal-arts approach can enhance our understanding of complex issues. Practitioners – including the political leaders who have questioned the value of the liberal arts – will be well served by integrating the approach used by the authors in their own thinking about ethical leadership.

This volume builds on the tradition of the Humanities. It provides a holistic approach, exploring ethical leadership as 'a way of being,' as opposed to the utilitarian approach of seeing ethical leadership merely as a means to an end. The former invites a deeper understanding of ethical leadership as an ongoing challenge that merits a more sophisticated perspective, which is adroitly presented in the coming pages.

Every chapter ends with the question – 'What does this mean?' That is an invitation for the reader to explore the ways in which each chapter connects to their personal experiences in the field. This book serves, therefore, as an accessible resource that can be used by both students of leadership, as well as practitioners, who seek to understand how ethical approaches connect to leadership theories. Enjoy it!

Gama Perruci
Dean, McDonough Leadership Center
Marietta College
Marietta, Ohio

# FOREWORD FOR THE SECOND EDITION OF *ETHICAL LEADERSHIP: A PRIMER*

*Ronald E. Riggio*

For anyone researching, teaching, or studying leadership, the topic of ethical leadership is the single most complex and difficult to wrap our minds around. In order to understand ethical leadership, one needs to first have a solid foundation in philosophy and ethics. Ethics, however, needs to be placed into the leadership context, and that requires a thorough knowledge of leadership theories, group/team dynamics, and the contexts in which leadership takes place. Which brings me to this book – the second edition of *Ethical Leadership: A Primer*.

The first half of this edited volume provides an authoritative review of major schools of thought in ethics, ranging from virtue ethics, through Kantianism, utilitarianism, cultural values, cultural relativism, and into social contract theory and a review of justice and the common good. In essence, this is an entire course on ethics, and a very good one. The second half of the book looks at modern theories of leadership, ranging from authentic and servant leadership, and transformational and adaptive leadership, and explores how each of these theories deals with the issue of ethics – what does *good* leadership look like through the lenses of these various, and popular, theories. Of course, a thorough review of ethical leadership also needs a focus on the role of followers and followership, and the contrast of *bad*, or toxic, leadership. This last addition to this text is critically important – making an excellent book even better.

There are several features included in each chapter that assist in learning the material. Each chapter begins with a "Framing Question," that asks the reader to consider the main theme of each topic. An historical timeline is also at the beginning of each chapter which allows the leader to see the history and evolution of the topic, with reference to major works in the area. Each chapter also contains a detailed case study that helps illustrate ethical leadership as portrayed through the lens of the theory or construct. Each chapter ends with provocative discussion questions to review and deepen the reader's understanding, and additional resources for exploration.

Many years ago, we offered courses in ethical leadership as part of our program, but these were not comprehensive review courses. They tended to focus on one or more theoretical or philosophical perspectives and then integrated leadership theories into those. Teaching a fuller range of ethical leadership was difficult because readings needed to be cobbled together from a variety of sources. What was missing then was an all-inclusive approach that allowed the student to understand the full landscape of ethical leadership. This textbook has provided that.

Leadership ethics cannot be truly understood from one disciplinary perspective. The best approach, and I am biased here (but I believe correctly so), is to provide a liberal arts-based understanding of leadership ethics. A quick review of the disciplinary orientation of the various chapter authors, as well as their credentials, lets us know that this book does indeed provide a diverse, interdisciplinary (perhaps "transdisciplinary" is a better word) treatment of leadership ethics. Finally, kudos to the Editors in making an already stellar book even better.

Ronald E. Riggio, Ph.D.
Henry R. Kravis Professor of Leadership and Organizational Psychology
Kravis Leadership Institute
Claremont McKenna College

# SECTION I

In Section I, readers will find the five components of leadership applied to 11 different ethical models. We selected these models based on what we believed to be their influence – either explicit or not – on how leaders think today. We also chose models we believed were necessary primary material for students who wished to go deeper into the literature surrounding ethics and leadership.

Our discussion starts with Kantianism and utilitarianism because of their influence on the other ethical models we discuss. We then go into discussions of virtue ethics, egoism, care ethics, universal cultural values, relativism, divine command theory, social contract theory, justice as fairness, and the common good. As readers progress through the chapters, we ask that they keep in mind how these different models often have similar fundamental concerns, yet they have different implications for the five components of leadership.

Readers will also find a variety of case studies in this section. We will take a look at leadership examples from social media, museums, the military, athletics, medicine, international relations, religion, higher education, and law. Readers may also want to refer to the book's online companion site at Edward Elgar to find more case studies. Our hope is that by drawing from such a broad selection of settings, readers can appreciate how the phenomena of 'ethical leadership' can be expressed in a variety of public, private, and social sectors.

# 1
# Introduction to *Ethical Leadership: A Primer*

*Robert M. McManus, Stanley J. Ward and Alexandra K. Perry*

You are likely reading this book as a class assignment. Please indulge the authors by allowing us to suggest an even more important reason: To learn how to distinguish between 'right' and 'wrong.'

The first edition of Ethical Leadership: A Primer was released in 2018, and since that time people around the world have witnessed how leaders have chosen to define right and wrong in the ways they have responded to the pandemic, waged war, contested elections, made laws, and reacted to other crises large and small for organizations and nation states. We've also observed the *consequences* of those choices. Sometimes those consequences have been deadly. That's one of the reasons that we decided to add a chapter on 'toxic leadership' to the second edition you are now reading. We also added a chapter on the ethics of care and updated the case studies in the book. Finally, we added some general guidelines in the last chapter to help leaders make decisions more ethically.

So why read this updated book with its new case studies and added material on ethical decision-making? Because how you define right and wrong matters. For what it's worth: since you are reading this book, the authors believe you are already a leader or on your way to becoming one. You hold or have the potential to hold a great deal of power. You would be wise to learn how to handle that power responsibly.

## WHAT IS LEADERSHIP?

Academic work and the life of the mind are not merely about recording and transmitting information. Rather, they also include asking critical questions and doing our best to find answers to those questions. Sometimes the answer to those questions may be 'I don't know' or 'I need to find more information.' Yet, even while arriving at an inconclusive answer, the learner benefits by discovering new information and perspectives. Similarly, readers will note that we use a series of framing questions to move through each of the models we cover in the book. In a sense, the overarching question for the book is 'What is ethical leadership?' In the broadest terms, we propose a two-pronged answer to this question. *Ethical leadership is (1) the practice of leaders using various approaches of ethics to make ethically sound decisions, and (2) using one's position of leadership to bring about positive change.*

One might object to this definition and argue that it does not provide sufficient clarity for ethical dilemmas and that leaders and followers desperately desire such clarity. We respond by suggesting ethical decision-making requires leaders and followers to have a sufficient knowledge of ethics to be able to apply the concepts to their particular problem. Only then can the leader begin to answer the age-old ethical question, 'What is the right thing to do?' By the time readers have worked through our text, they may not have a definitive answer to all their questions. Still, they will be able to formulate a robust response that considers many of the nuances of leadership across a variety of situations. Furthermore, because leadership is a 'practical' art, we hope that learners will put their new insights to work so that their organizations and communities will benefit from their leadership.

If we are going to discuss questions about ethical leadership, we should probably start with a fundamental question – what exactly is 'leadership'? Leadership is more than just stellar individual performance. One might be a 'leader' in a particular field (meaning a top performer), but that does not mean the individual exhibits positive 'leadership.' We can make an argument that leaders can unquestionably produce impressive quantities or qualities of work; yet, the way they get those results, and sometimes the secondary consequences of those results, are utterly disastrous. Our book defines leadership as a *process* that includes the work of leaders and followers accomplishing a goal in a particular context, all the while being influenced by cultural values and norms. This model encourages a broader perspective regarding the many elements of the leadership experience – components that extend far beyond just the individual leader. That is not to diminish the importance of individual leaders, as our case studies include examples of individual excellence and failures as such, but the excellence in question involves much more than just individual leaders accomplishing their personal goals.

Here is a metaphor that may help. Think of 'leadership' as a powerful train engine that can take us almost anywhere. Some of these destinations can benefit us and maybe even our descendants; other destinations can cause harm to both us and future generations. With an engine that powerful, the question 'where are we heading' becomes urgent and vital. In effect, our book will demonstrate how each of these five components of leadership can step forward to influence the direction of the train rather than just the engineer alone. A team of engineers is at work – so let's better understand which ones have the most influence in any particular situation.

The original impetus for this project is from Robert and Stan's teaching together in the Master of Ethical Leadership program at Claremont Lincoln University. Stan observed that the course texts often focused primarily on ethics *or* primarily on leadership, and he wanted a text that could provide a solid bridge between the two. He was looking for a text with a robust mix of ethical thinking and ethical doing, written in such a way that students who were new to ethics and leadership could come away with a framework that would support future study, reflection, and above all, action. In short, he wanted a text that would help students appreciate how different ethical models worked, provide guidelines for applying those models, and illustrate what that looked like in the 'real world.' Further, because questions related to ethics and leadership have been part of the human experience for millennia, he wanted a text that explicitly drew on the history of the ideas that impacted ethics.

Those motivations carried forward into the creation of Ethical Leadership: A Primer. Here we offer our readers – presumed to be upper-level undergraduate or graduate students – an introductory text that is intended to be learner-friendly while still rooted in the history of ideas. By linking the concepts with case studies and specific action recommendations, our book combines *ethical thinking* and *ethical doing* for leaders. As Robert and Stan began to work on the text, they realized the need for additional expertise in ethics. That's when Robert's colleague, Alex Perry, joined the team of editors. So, for every chapter, Alexandra, Robert, and Stan attempted to edit with an eye for ethics, leadership studies, and practitioner concerns.

For professors reviewing our text, we suggest it could work as a singular text for an ethical leadership class or complement other introductions to leadership such as McManus and Perruci's *Understanding Leadership or* Northouse's *Leadership: Theory and Practice*. Likewise, it would pair well with Craig Johnson's *Meeting the Ethical Challenges of Leadership* and Terry Price's *Leadership Ethics: An Introduction*. We hope that this textbook represents the best parts of a liberal arts education, with its emphasis on the history of ideas, critical exploration, and application to human problems. Given how the liberal arts continue to look for ways to prove their relevance in higher education, we believe that we have drawn from that approach to create a resource for leadership programs in technical schools and state universities as well as liberal arts colleges.

## THE FIVE COMPONENTS OF LEADERSHIP

To provide a consistent reference point in our discussion of ethics and leadership, we will use McManus and Perruci's Five Components of Leadership Model (Figure 1.1), which they present in their book *Understanding Leadership: An Arts and Humanities Perspective*.

### Understanding Leadership[1]

In their text, McManus and Perruci present leadership as a *process* – instead of simply the heroic ability of leaders[2] – and that leadership should be viewed as a *purposeful interaction*.[3] Such an approach is especially beneficial in an ethical leadership text because it does not place the entire emphasis for moral success or failure on the individual leader, but rather by emphasizing the *leadership process* we can consider the many layers of a leadership event. As leadership studies grow in its appreciation for factors outside of the individual leader, this model becomes even more helpful. Let's briefly consider each component of the model.

### The Leader

As one would expect in a leadership text, we start our model and consideration with the individual leader. Though in some cases, we find several people or even an entire organization may engage in the role of 'leader.'

## The Follower

It has been observed that if a leader does not have followers, that person is simply 'going on a walk.' So, followers are a crucial part of the leadership equation. Here we consider those working with the leader (and sometimes *against* the leader) to accomplish a specific goal.

## The Goal

The third component of a leadership system is what the leaders and followers are trying to achieve – the goal. In its purest expression, leadership 'success' or 'failure' has been viewed as 'goal achievement.' Here we will go beyond a definition of leadership that is just about getting things done by also looking at *how* those goals are accomplished.

## The Context

Leadership does not occur in a vacuum, and it is not a thought experiment. Instead, leadership is tied to an actual location in both time and space, and that context includes considerations that are part of a leadership event. We will find that behaviors viewed as ethical in one context may not work directly in another context.

## The Culture

Leaders must also be aware of the forces at work that goes beyond the immediate interactions of leaders, followers, and goals within a specific location. Cultural values, norms, *zeitgeists*, and larger belief systems also impact the leadership process. Discussing ethics and distinguishing between the five components can be tricky because all ethical systems are making claims about values and norms, thus tapping into what we label as 'culture.' Yet, as we review different ethical and leadership models, we will find that some systems seem to judge the appropriateness of a leadership event with a particular emphasis on factors such as the actions of the leader, the relationship with followers, the 'rightness' of a goal, or sometimes the demands of a particular context or culture.

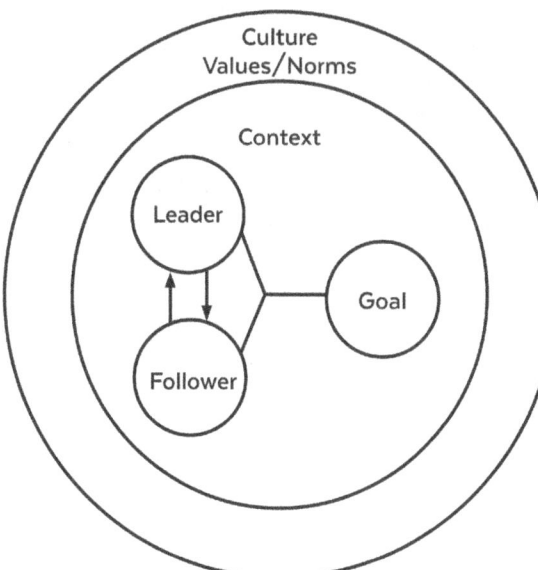

**Figure 1.1** The Five Components of Leadership Model

Considering all of these components, the definition of leadership that we will be using throughout this book then is this: '*Leadership is the process by which leaders and followers work together toward a goal (or goals) within a context shaped by cultural values and norms.*'[4]

## THE NUANCES OF 'ETHICAL LEADERSHIP'

To appreciate the complexities of a question like 'What is ethical leadership,' let's consider the disbanding of The President's Club in Great Britain in 2018. The organization was famous for its all-male, black-tie charity dinner, which required the servers to be attractive females in revealingly short black dresses. Guests at the event included prominent members of British society who were raising funds for children's hospitals in London. Over the 33 years of the organization's existence, The President's Club raised over 20 million pounds for charity (28 million USD).[5] However, these esteemed guests engaged in fondling servers, asking servers to sit in their laps and dance on the table, and sometimes even propositioned sex. When an undercover reporter posed as a server and recorded the event, then released video footage and described her experiences, the news of the event – especially during the exact historical moment of the #MeToo movement – resulted in such public outcry that the club permanently disbanded. In the meantime, charities that had received money from the group rushed to return it and distance themselves from the organization.[6]

Simply put, the President's Club was an example of men behaving badly while raising money for a good cause. Now for some ethical analysis: a strictly utilitarian approach might argue the behavior was part of charity work – so while the behavior might seem reproachable, it's the results that matter most. A counter-argument would say 'how' you get the results is just as important as the results themselves. Thus, no matter how much money was raised for charity, there was no excuse for these men's behavior, and the entire event was ethically reprehensible.

Who is right? Both are making an ethical claim about how wealthy and powerful men are allowed to behave. Our text asks similar questions about behavior, but we are expanding our concept and examples of leadership to include more than just wealthy and powerful men.

So if we use our five-component model to analyze the President's Club example, we find an organization where the goal is to raise money for charities. The 'leaders' in this case seem to be the event organizers, and the 'followers' are the attendees and servers. So far, so good. We have a group of people working together to raise money for a good cause.

The problem arises when we look at the context and cultural values at work in the event. The specific context is an event where women are objectified and sexually harassed. To make this more problematic, all this occurred during a time when customs of sexual behavior were being challenged by the #MeToo movement, and powerful men were being called out for just such poor behavior. So, while a strict utilitarian might argue that the good done by the President's Club outweighed the bad behavior of the men present at the dinner, the Kantian perspective – which emphasizes the importance of respect for persons – would quickly dismiss such thinking as sophistry and balderdash. As we later consider other examples of what is good for the institution itself versus what is good for the institution's members, we will again see clashes of this nature.

The President's Club example is also helpful because it demonstrates that one doesn't need the formal title of 'leader' to demonstrate 'leadership.' Here, a reporter endured hours of crude behavior to bring a harmful situation to light. In doing so, she worked with her newspaper and the readers of that paper to accomplish a goal – and the impact of her work became increasingly significant as her article spread.[7]

## EXPLAINING OUR STRUCTURE

Although we have several contributors to our text, we adopted a consistent structure throughout the book. *Ethical Leadership: A Primer* is divided into two major sections. The first section focuses on ethical models and uses the five components of leadership as a lens for understanding and applying the ethical model in a leadership setting. The second section then looks at popular leadership models that include ethical implications and views those models through the lens of the Five Component Model.

### Section I: Ethical Models

The first section of our book focuses on ethics models: Kantianism, utilitarianism, virtue ethics, egoism, ethics of care, universal ethics, cultural relativism, divine command, social contract, justice as fairness, and the common good. For those who wish to preview the contents of those chapters, we suggest they look at Table 19.2 in the conclusion of our book. That table lists the ethical models, the questions we use to frame each chapter, which parts of the five components of leadership we believe are emphasized in those models, and the case study that accompanies the chapter.

Because we don't assume our readers have previous training in ethics, we keep the discussion focused at an introductory level appropriate for university work. We chose ethical models based on what we observed as standard models both in the study of ethics that what we see being applied in the world of leadership. We hope our selected models represent both a thoughtful and practical selection process. By exploring these models and their impact on different components of leadership, we believe leaders can be more intentional with how they approach ethical thinking and ethical doing.

### Section II: Leadership Models

We then take a look at some popular leadership models that claim an intentional ethical component: authentic leadership, servant leadership, followership, transformational leadership, adaptive leadership, and toxic leadership. Like Section I, we don't assume prior knowledge of these leadership models. So, our hope here is to help readers become more intentional in how they approach their own leadership challenges, with an emphasis on being ethical leaders.

At the end of Section II, we offer a summary overview of the ideas in our text, present some helpful guidelines for leaders to apply the information in the book, and make some final observations of the themes raised. After reading our text, readers should be well prepared to dive into more nuanced discussions of ethical leadership and take intentional action in their own leadership roles. To return to our train metaphor, readers will leave the book with an improved sense of what different leadership engines offer and where they can take us. They will also better understand the team of engineers driving the train. Most importantly, they will know some of their options when the train seems off course.

For Sections I and II, we follow a similar outline where each chapter contains the following elements.

### Framing questions

We start each chapter with a framing question. The question highlights what the ethical or leadership model asks those practicing leadership to consider. Our goal for the question is to provide an introductory hook that brings forward the key concerns of each ethical or leadership model. As leadership educators, we hope these rudimentary questions will help with the scaffolding process needed when learning new content. The chapter then attempts to answer that question, essentially hanging information on that introductory hook. Direct questions promote new levels of both self- and situational awareness for leaders. We hope these basic questions do the same for students reading our text.

### Timelines

We hope that readers will sense the 'gravitas' of ethics and leadership by seeing how humanity has been wrestling with many of these questions for centuries (if not millennia) and how leaders are still grappling with them today. We provide a visual representation of significant works addressing the ethical or leadership model alongside the events of our case studies. Our timelines purposefully connect the history of ideas and the historical events of case studies, showing how these ideas still matter.

### History and major concepts

The history and major concepts we provide here are not an exhaustive discussion by any means. Instead, we have asked ourselves, 'What are the essential concepts that would benefit leaders when applying ethics models in leadership?' This section offers a literature trail as well as a more practice-oriented discussion. We also define key terms in this section.

### Five components analysis

When we initially considered writing a primer for ethical leadership, we wanted to find a bridge that helped connect the ethical models and leadership models. To help ethics and leadership 'speak' with each other, we consider the implications of a particular ethical or leadership model for the component parts of leadership. To help readers sort out the differences between these models, we also asked ourselves which components seemed to receive particular attention in each model. For example, in our discussion of the President's Club, as perceived by utilitarian or Kantian views, we saw that both perspectives emphasized the goal. However, they had different conclusions of what those goals should be – the overall benefit of a leadership event versus how people should be treated. We admit to simplifying concepts here for the sake of accessibility, yet we strove to do so in a way that did not simplify to the point of total absurdity.

Part of what makes this text a contribution to the field of leadership studies is our attempt to provide a visual representation of how ethics and leadership engage each other, where we consider the interplay of multiple factors. When visualized this way, we hope that readers will gain a renewed appreciation for why ethical leadership is so demanding and a better sense of where they need to direct their energies when engaging in ethical leadership.

### Case studies
Because we are concerned with both 'ethical thinking' and 'ethical doing,' each chapter describes a real-world event and analyzes that event against the concerns of a particular ethical or leadership model. We start with a narrative about the case and then consider the issue through the lens of the Five Components of Leadership Model.

### Summary and concluding remarks
As we close each chapter, we will return to the framing question and attempt to provide a summary response that includes some action steps. Those suggestions will be broad enough to apply in various circumstances but still actionable and measurable, emphasizing behaviors.

### Discussion questions
True to our intent of creating a teaching text, we include questions designed for either personal reflection or classroom discussion.

### Additional resources
Consistent with the fact that our book is a 'primer' that can only offer a 'first word' in the conversation between ethics and leadership, we also provide suggestions for additional resources that students can use as they continue to study these topics. Instructors may also obtain additional resources from the publisher. The publisher also has additional case studies, PowerPoints, and a test bank available for instructors.[8]

## THE PROBLEM OF PRONOUNS

The presence of women, people of color, and members of the LGBTQ+ community serving as leaders in a variety of fields has increased in the last 50 years. Likewise, leadership studies continue to grow beyond exclusively Western perspectives. While our text strives to provide a variety of leadership examples, our cases were chosen because of their ability to illustrate the ethical or leadership models rather than cases that would offer a complete representation of gender and ethnic diversity in leadership. Similarly, readers will find masculine and feminine singular pronouns referencing individual leaders, as well as the use of the singular 'they.' This is at the discretion of our contributors. Please know that the decisions were pragmatic and grammatical and not intended as a slight against leaders of any gender or ethnic identity.

## N.B.: NOT THE LAST WORD

The abbreviation N.B. stands for the Latin phrase, *nota bene*, which we can translate as 'note well.' The initials highlight important information, though not necessarily the focus of the issue being discussed.

So here we offer our *nota bene* at the end of our introduction. Once again, we return to the fact that our text is offered as a 'primer.' By definition, the book is not an exhaustive source for leadership ethics. And its opinions are limited to the perspectives and skills of the individual writers and the team of editors who compiled the text. Because we represent a diversity of backgrounds and organizations, not all the contributors necessarily agree with each other's conclusions. And because we are filtering all our cases through a particular ethical or leadership lens, not all the nuances of a specific case will be expressed. With that in mind, we offer only a 'first word' in the conversation about ethics and leadership. Knowing that much more work is needed, we invite reviewers and researchers to continue the work by returning to these cases with additional resources and viewpoints. Thus, we offer *Ethical Leadership: A Primer* to our readers as a tool for launching their own conversations about ethical leadership. We hope that the material herein empowers meaningful conversations that lead to vital leadership action.

As a final comment, we return to what we think makes the humanities tradition so helpful – it focuses on the constant challenges we face as human beings. So we hope that, if nothing else, our readers come away with this marked conclusion: ethical leaders *and followers* who read this text – our world continues to need both your ideas and your practice.

### DISCUSSION QUESTIONS

1. Before reading this introduction, how did you define leadership?
2. How does that definition compare to what the authors of this text suggest about leadership?
3. In your understanding of leadership, how important are factors outside the leader?
4. How do you recognize when leadership is 'ethical'?

### ADDITIONAL RESOURCES

R.M. McManus and G. Perruci, *Understanding Leadership: An Arts and Humanities Perspective* 2nd edn., New York: Routledge, 2020.

McManus and Perruci provide a representative work both for the Five Component Model and for how a liberal arts approach to leadership studies can be beneficial to further understanding the leadership process.

J.T. Wren, R. Riggio, and M.A. Genovese (eds.), *Leadership and the Liberal Arts: Achieving the Promise of a Liberal Education*, London: Palgrave Macmillan, 2009.

This collection of chapters from different contributors examines the contributions that leadership studies can make to general education and how the liberal arts contribute to leadership studies.

K. Grint, *Leadership: Very Short Introduction*, Oxford: Oxford University Press, 2010.

S. Blackburn, *Ethics: A Very Short Introduction*, Oxford: Oxford University Press, 2010.

These short books offer an accessible starting point for studying leadership and ethics.

## NOTES

1. The Five Components Model was initially referred to as 'The McDonough Model' in reference to its origins at the McDonough Center for Leadership and Business at Marietta College. Gama Perruci presented the model in 'Leadership education across disciplines: The Social science perspective,' *Journal of Leadership Studies*, vol. 7 no. 4, 2014, 43–7. The model was further refined and developed in McManus and Perruci's *Understanding Leadership: An Arts and Humanities Perspective* in the first edition of the book published in 2015 and again in the second edition published in 2020.
2. R.M. McManus and G. Perruci, *Understanding Leadership: An Arts and Humanities Perspective* 2nd edn. New York: Routledge, 2020, p. 16.
3. McManus and Perruci, *Understanding Leadership*, p. 19.
4. McManus and Perruci, *Understanding Leadership*, p. 17.
5. R. Pérez-Peña, 'Britain's "most un-p.c. charity" will shut down,' *New York Times*, January 24, 2018. https://www.nytimes.com/2018/01/24/world/europe/uk-presidents-club-dinner.html (accessed July 4, 2022).
6. Pérez-Peña, 'Britain's "most un-p.c. charity".'
7. M. Marriage, 'Men only: Inside the charity fundraiser where hostesses are put on show,' *Financial Times*, January 23, 2018. https://www.ft.com/content/075d679e-0033-11e8-9650-9c0ad2d7c5b5 (accessed July 4, 2022).
8. See https://www.e-elgar.com/textbooks/mcmanus-ethical-leadership-2ed.

# 2
# Kantianism

*J. Michael Cervantez*

## FRAMING QUESTION

What is the moral duty of leaders and followers?

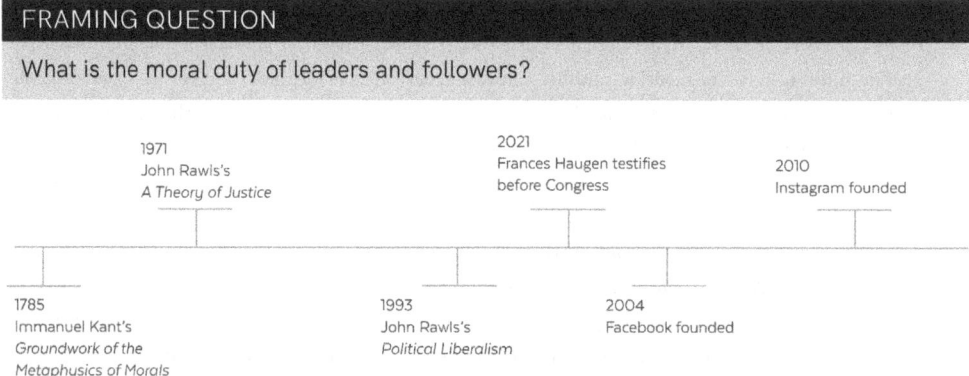

| 1971 | | 2021 | | 2010 |
| John Rawls's | | Frances Haugen testifies | | Instagram founded |
| *A Theory of Justice* | | before Congress | | |

| 1785 | | 1993 | 2004 | |
| Immanuel Kant's | | John Rawls's | Facebook founded | |
| *Groundwork of the* | | *Political Liberalism* | | |
| *Metaphysics of Morals* | | | | |

**Figure 2.1**    Timeline of major works on Kantian ethics in relation to the chapter case study

Unlike most other ethical theories, Kantian ethics owes its name and reputation to one thinker. Sometimes referred to as Kantian moral theory or simply Kant's ethics, Kantian ethics takes its name from the influential eighteenth-century Prussian philosopher Immanuel Kant.[1] Kant is regarded as one of the foremost theorists in the Western intellectual tradition. His work remains prominent to this day (Figure 2.1). His many philosophical contributions are frequently esteemed alongside significant thinkers such as Plato, Aristotle, René Descartes and David Hume. Though Kant was interested in many areas of philosophical and scientific inquiry, his unique contributions to ethics are the most enduring aspects of his work. In this chapter, we will examine Kantian ethics and position them within the Five Components of Leadership Model. We will then apply them to a case study surrounding Meta (Facebook and Instagram) and its business practices.

## HISTORY

Kantian moral philosophy originated with the publication of Kant's *Groundwork of the Metaphysics of Morals* and, to a lesser extent, the publication of the *Metaphysics of Morals*. It should be noted, however, that the *Metaphysics of Morals* was first published separately in two parts as the *Doctrine of the Right* and the *Doctrine of Virtue*. Both appeared as separate publications sometime in 1797 before being compiled into one volume at a later date.[2] In any event, Kant's *Groundwork* has proven the more influential of the two.

In addition to the texts mentioned here, *The Critique of Practical Reason*, *Anthropology from a Pragmatic Point of View* and various other essays have also contributed to and provided augmentations of Kant's ethics. However, the *Groundwork of the Metaphysics of Morals* remains the most widely read and studied text on Kant's moral philosophy. Since the publication of *Groundwork*, the influence of Kantian ethics has been remarkable. To this day, Kant's ethics, along with utilitarianism and virtue ethics, continues to dominate contemporary debates around ethical theory and remains one of the leading moral theories among academics.

In recent years, the most noteworthy champion of Kant's ethics has been the late moral and political philosopher John Rawls, whom we will discuss later in Chapter 11. Rawls' *A Theory of Justice* and *Political Liberalism* are replete with allusions to Kant's moral philosophy. Most importantly, Rawls' emphasis on justice as fairness seems, to some extent, inspired by Kant's emphasis on personal autonomy and moral agency. Samuel Freeman points out a clear Kantian interpretation of justice as fairness. It 'relies upon the Kantian conception of moral personality' and 'interprets the principles of justice as an expression of the moral powers of agency and practical reasoning. It plays a central role in [Rawls'] congruence argument.'[3] A survey of Rawls' work will demonstrate the importance of Kant's philosophy to the development of his ideas. In particular, many Kantian conceptions will ultimately provide the basis for Rawls' Kantian Constructivism, which is prominent throughout his work.

## MAJOR CONCEPTS IN KANTIAN ETHICS

Turning our attention back to Kant's ethics, we find several concepts deserving attention. This section begins with a discussion of good will and what Kantians mean by 'acting out of duty'. After this, we will undertake an essential introduction to Kant's categorical imperative. Together, these ideas form the foundation of a Kantian moral framework.

### Good Will and Acting Out of Duty

At the core of Kant's ethics is an important question: 'What gives an action moral value?' Why is an action a moral action as opposed to another sort of action? Is there something that makes an action morally significant?

The Kantian answer to this question can be clarified by contrasting it with the utilitarian response.[4] According to the utilitarian – or consequentialist – views of morality, it is the consequences of our actions that are morally significant. An action is morally good when it produces a good outcome. Mark Timmons puts it this way: right actions should be understood primarily in terms of the value and utility of an action's consequences when compared to alternative actions. In short, 'An action is right if and only if (and because) its consequences would be at least as good as the consequences of any alternative action that the agent might instead perform.'[5] So, when two or more potential actions are considered, the morally good action is the one that produces the most utility (utilitarianism) or the more desirable consequences (consequentialism).

In this view, an individual's motives are irrelevant. Why one chooses to act as they do is unimportant. Morality is not a matter of moral motives, but favourable outcomes. Per John Stuart Mill, 'He who saves a fellow creature from drowning does what is morally right whether his motive be duty, or his hope is being paid for his trouble.'[6] So, while utilitarian ethicists hold this view, this attitude is misguided according to Kantian moral philosophy.

Kant maintains that an action is morally praiseworthy only when it is done with the right motive. Kant refers to this as 'good will'. Good will, he maintains, is the only thing that is good without limitation.[7] In Kant's language, 'a good will is good not because of what it effects or accomplishes [not] because of its fitness to attain some proposed end, but only because of its volition, that is, it is good in itself.'[8] That is to say, the good will (that is, a good motive or intention) is primary. Why? Because our 'good will' is in our control. The consequences of our actions are out of our control. What will happen because of our actions is not something we can reasonably foresee at the time. Tying morality to something outside our control is to take morality out of a person's hands and make it a matter of chance. This idea is what Bernard Williams and Thomas Nagel have famously dubbed 'moral luck'. If an action produces good results, it is morally good. If it turns out that our actions generated bad results, then those actions were immoral.[9] For Kant, this is fundamentally mistaken. Unpacking the reasons is essential for a complete and accurate picture of Kantian ethics.

First and foremost, morality comes down to our motives. Did we act with good will? Did our actions have good intentions? We might summarize Kant on this point, saying that having a good will is doing what is right just because it is right and for no ulterior motives. Kant famously refers to this as 'acting out of duty' or 'acting from duty'. It is our *duty* to do the right thing simply because it is the right thing.

To illustrate, consider Kant's well-known example of a shopkeeper who always charges her customers a fair price. In such a case, Kant imagines three possible reasons the shopkeeper might always act fairly. First, the shopkeeper might always charge a fair price because it's good business. Most people would likely agree that there is nothing wrong with this rationale. At the same time, we might say that something is not quite right about it either. There should be something more to ethics than merely good business.

Second, Kant considers the possibility of the shopkeeper being a naturally fair-minded individual. Being a fair person is just their moral temperament. Cheating a customer would keep them up at night. So, they do the right thing because they do not want an immoral action on their conscience. Again, there is nothing wrong with this rationale. In fact, having a moral conscience is a good thing. However, Kantian ethics challenges us at this point by insisting that ethical principles are more than merely the way I happen to feel about something. Kantians insist that ethics must be more than what happens to be good for an individual or organization.

This idea brings us to Kant's third consideration. He contends that the shopkeeper could choose to be fair to their customers not merely because it's good business and because they happen to be so inclined but because being fair is their moral imperative. For Kant, therefore, leaders and organizations ought to be motivated to do good not merely because it is good for their bottom line and not simply because they like to help people, but because this is their moral duty.

In sum, a moral agent ought to have the right motivation when acting. Kant's right motivation is acting according to one's duty as our moral imperatives dictate. This demand raises another critical question: 'How can we determine our moral imperatives?' When can we be sure that we are acting out of duty? The answer to this question lies in what Kantians call the 'categorical imperative'.

## The Categorical Imperative

Central to Kant's ethics is the idea of a categorical imperative. The term 'categorical' refers to something unconditional or unqualified and without exception. The meaning behind 'imperative' is, of course, a rule, requirement, or command of some kind. Thus, putting these two concepts together, a categorical imperative is an absolute moral requirement. For Kant, therefore, morality is best understood as a moral law or rule that must be performed and to which there is no exception. In short, ethics is an absolute moral law. As such, Kant preferred to characterize the categorical imperative 'as an objective, rationally necessary and unconditional principle that we must always follow despite any natural desires or inclinations we may have to the contrary'.[10]

Kantian ethics maintains that our moral duties are derived from these absolute moral imperatives. There are several formulations of Kant's categorical imperative. The two most essential formulations equip Kantians with their most important moral principles. The first moral principle underscores the moral duty always to respect humanity. The second moral principle is equivalent to a moral test for determining when any proposed action becomes a moral duty. We will now briefly consider each of these principles.

### Always respect humanity

One formulation of the categorical imperative is sometimes called the Respect for Humanity Principle. Kant asks us to consider what constitutes proper treatment of persons. He concludes that we ought to 'Act in such a way that you always treat humanity, whether in your own person or in the person of any other, never simply as a means, but always at the same time as an end.'[11] This principle suggests that morality, at the most fundamental level, is about treating human beings with respect.

With this moral principle, Kant brought the notion of respect to the centre of moral philosophy for the first time. Respect, per Kantian ethics, amounts to respecting a person's autonomy. It is honouring a person's ability to set his or her own goals and be self-governing. As such, human beings should never be regarded as objects to be used or exploited. Humans are autonomous moral agents and must be treated as 'ends in themselves' and not as a mere means to an end.[12] Kant believed that 'it is the presence of the self-governing reason in each person that … offered decisive grounds for viewing each as possessed of equal worth and deserving of equal respect.'[13]

### Always act in accordance with the universal law

Another formulation of the categorical imperative is referred to as the Universal Law Principle. Kantian ethics holds that we should 'always act in such a way that the maxim of your action can be willed as a universal law of humanity'. Or, put otherwise, 'Act as though the maxim of your action were by your will to become a universal law of nature.'[14] The heart of Kant's language here is that individuals must only act in a way that they could will for everyone. In other words, before making a moral decision, one should ask, could (or should) my action be a universal law for everyone to follow. By 'maxim' Kant means an action we are putting to the test. If a leader was considering sidestepping an inconvenient organizational policy, for example, they should formulate a maxim: it is permissible to circumvent the policy in question. To determine the morality of the maxim, ask if it could be universalized for all to follow. Could the action in question become a universal moral law?

This principle is a way to test whether our actions or choices are morally coherent and consistent. We typically think that everyone has the same moral obligations. No one should cheat. We all should keep our word. It's never right to steal from your employer and so forth. Following these ethical norms is the right thing to do. No exception. So, making an exception for yourself or justifying an exception to a moral requirement is fundamentally wrong. What's fair for one person, morally speaking, is fair for everyone. Saying that everyone else ought to adhere to company policy but that this requirement doesn't apply to you is unfair. In this way, Kantian ethics gives us a handy moral principle. Just ask yourself, would I want my action or behaviour in this situation to become a universal law for others to follow?

## CRITIQUES OF KANTIAN ETHICS

Kantian ethics is not without its problems or its critics. Two central problems must be addressed. First, there is the relevance of consequences in moral decision-making. Second, there is the question of moral exceptions. Each of these critiques is briefly explored in this section.

### What About the Consequences?

One significant critic of Kantian ethics was John Stuart Mill. Mill and his predecessor Jeremy Bentham are regarded as the founding fathers of modern utilitarianism (see Chapter 3).[15] Utilitarianism has proven to be one of the most formidable challenges to Kant's ethics. For this reason, the debate between Kantianism and Utilitarianism has allowed Kantian moral philosophers to clarify their ideas. Kantian ethics typically emphasizes human dignity and is, thus, often pitted against the utilitarian ideal of maximizing utility. Utilitarians typically criticize Kantians because Kantians do not worry enough about the consequences of their actions.

This argument is a longstanding critique of Kant's ethics. It goes as far back as Bentham and Mill and is clearly expressed in the classic text *The Definition of the Good* by A.C. Ewing. Ewing maintains, 'it is hard to believe that it could ever be a duty deliberately to produce less good when we could produce more.'[16] Ewing is essentially invoking the utilitarian principle of maximizing utility. When it is feasible for a moral agent to do more good rather than less, it is an agent's duty to produce the better outcome. In other words, Ewing wonders whether it is ever morally justified to intentionally produce less good than we could have as a result of our actions.

As a duty-based moral system, Kantian ethics emphasizes moral obligations over utility. Kantians are primarily interested in identifying and acting in accordance with our moral imperatives. There is no significance given to the results of our actions. In fact, Kantians concede that following our moral duties could generate less desirable consequences and, thus, less good as a result. Nevertheless, adhering to our moral duties, as identified by the categorical imperative, is the essence of morality for Kantians. This conclusion might be difficult for some.

Notwithstanding, Kantian ethics insists that morality is not about maximizing utility. As such, Kantian ethics precludes moral agents from engaging in certain actions. Some actions – such as torture or exploitation – are so morally appalling that they should never be morally permissible. This is true even if they could generate better consequences. It is certainly conceivable that torture might maximize utility under the right circumstances. Think of a case in which a terrorist, if tortured, would reveal vital information – information that could save thousands of lives. Even still, Kantians insist that we ought to draw moral lines and never cross them. Torture, for example, crosses a moral line by treating a human being as a means to an end; it is, thus, off the table as a moral option no matter how favourable the outcome. Adherents of Kantian ethics insist that Kant's categorical imperative provides the necessary moral safeguards we need to protect people and their fundamental rights.

## No Exceptions?

Kantian ethics is sometimes referred to as an 'absolutist' moral theory. This is because Kant's ethics follows from his categorical imperative. As noted, the categorical imperative generates absolute moral duties. Consequently, the nature of Kant's categorical imperative is such that moral duties are unconditional requirements. This raises the question: 'Are there no exceptions to these moral requirements?'

For Kantian ethics, the answer is 'no'. Ethics imposes on the moral agent absolute moral rules that must be followed without exception. Leaders always ought to tell the truth. Managers should never mistreat their employees. Cheating is under no circumstances a good idea. These are unquestionable moral duties and thus, cannot be side-lined for the sake of convenience, expedience, or the greater good. As some Kantians say, 'Being a moral agent, then, means guiding one's conduct by "universal laws" – moral rules that hold, without exception, in all circumstances.'[17]

It is sometimes believed, however, that every good rule has an exception. Moral rules, therefore, should be no exemption. As a rule, leaders should tell the truth and not cheat, for example. However, there will undoubtedly be occasions where lying or cheating may seem necessary in the course of leading others and guiding a successful organization. In combat situations, military leaders, for example, are regularly confronted with difficult moral dilemmas. Obvious examples of this involve saving a subordinate's life. If a lie could save a subordinate, shouldn't the moral rule to *always tell the truth* be suspended?

To be sure, this is a difficult challenge for Kantians. Perhaps, there are resources within Kantian ethics to deal with this worry. It seems plausible to suppose that Kantian ethics could universalize moral exceptions. For instance, if there is a genuine circumstance where lying or cheating is morally conceivable, then we ought to be able to universalize those examples. That is to say, as a moral rule, when moral duties conflict – such as telling the truth versus saving a life – moral agents ought to adhere to the greater duty. W.D. Ross' duty-based moral theory would refer to such actions as one's 'all-things-considered-duty.' It is unclear whether Kantians would permit such a moral rule, but it is not unreasonable to think that they could.

## FIVE COMPONENT ANALYSIS

Now that we have a better understanding of Kantianism let's look at it in light of the Five Components of Leadership Model presented in Chapter 1.

Kant's categorical imperatives provide a highly practical and effective strategy for determining the morally right action. Adhering to Kant's moral principles ensures that leaders maintain a healthy respect for all stakeholders. Therefore, the respect for humanity principle will safeguard leaders and their organizations against inadvertently exploiting followers, partners or other interests. Figure 2.2 offers an illustration of the Five Components of Leadership Model when viewed through the lens of Kantian ethics.

As illustrated in the model depicted here (Figure 2.2), *Kantian ethics focuses on the goal of leaders and followers upholding their moral duty to behave ethically regardless of the surrounding contextual and cultural factors.* Kant's universal law principle can ensure that leaders and followers hold fast to their integrity when making difficult moral decisions. By putting proposed actions to the test, leaders and followers can practise critical self-reflection. This sort of moral reasoning will act as a check on one's intended decisions and actions. By carefully thinking about and testing our proposed actions, leaders and followers can mitigate moral shortcomings by removing

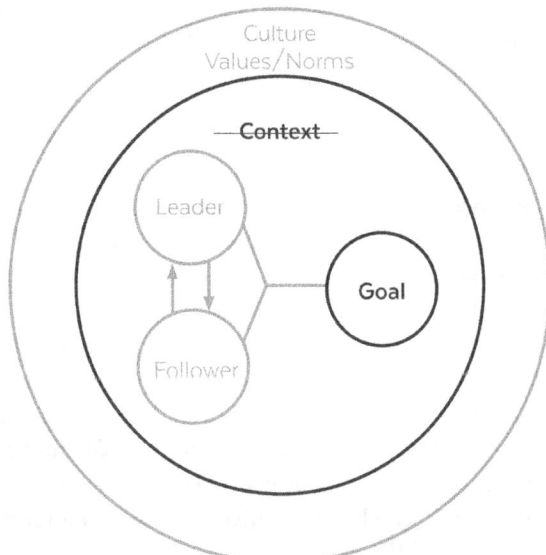

**Figure 2.2**     The Five Components of Leadership Model applied to Kantian ethics

possible moral blind spots, confronting biases, and otherwise compelling people to examine their actions. Here are five practical ways Kantian ethics can help leaders and followers make morally sound decisions.

First, leaders and followers must understand that they have moral duties. Their duties do not change as a matter of position or power. Whether one is in a position of influence or in a support role, we all have absolute moral requirements. Kantian ethics expects individuals to perform and honour their duties without deviation. In doing so, leaders and followers will fulfil Kant's universal law principle. For example, leaders have the moral duty always to be forthright and honest to their subordinates. Consider a situation where it is in the personal interest of a leader to misrepresent the truth. Suppose, for example, that one's organization is anticipating a downturn and jobs are at stake. Undoubtedly, some leaders will want to sidestep this issue with their subordinates. But what's their moral duty? If it is relevant to their followers' well-being, leaders should disclose this information to them as a matter of respect. A Kantian ethical framework implies that leaders, among other things, have the responsibility always to demonstrate deference for others. This responsibility includes being forthright with leaders and followers even when doing so is difficult. Recall that moral duties are, according to Kantian ethics, categorical imperatives – absolute, unchanging moral requirements.

Kant's universal law formulation of his categorical imperative implies that leaders and followers ought to see it as their moral duty to honour their professional responsibilities and obligations. For example, this would imply not calling in sick when this is only a ploy; not taking items from their organizations for personal use without permission; not violating company policies for the sake of convenience; not handling company time inappropriately, and so forth. In short, it is imperative for leaders and followers to always adhere to their moral duties even when it is not in their personal interest to do so. The universal law formulation of Kant's categorical imperative mandates that persons only act in a way they can consistently will for others. So, since neither leaders nor followers could consistently will a lack of professionalism for others, it is their duty to always act with professional integrity as well.

Second, neither leaders nor their followers are, morally speaking, superior to the other. Kantian ethics coheres with McManus and Perruci on this point (see Chapter 1). Understanding followers as equally important as leaders in one's conception of leadership is a significant moral advancement. For example, leaders ought to respect the rights of followers, while followers must take moral responsibility for their actions. In this way, the respect for humanity principle applies equally to those in authority and subordinates. This means that the well-being of followers matters as much as that of leaders. This point has obvious application when considering the issues of recognition, individual worth, compensation, working conditions and so on.

Third, to the point of working conditions, Kantian ethics has practical implications for organizational working environments. To the extent that it is the responsibility of leaders to care about the working conditions of their organizations, leaders should strive for safe and healthy working conditions for their followers. Why? Applying Kant's respect for humanity principle entails that the dignity and value of workers are upheld. Workers are not mere commodities or machines. They are persons and must be treated as such. Thus, followers should not be subjected to physically or psychologically hazardous working conditions. Leaders are primarily responsible for regulating working conditions. Consequently, leaders must ensure that working environments are safe, healthy and well regulated.

Fourth, the leader–follower relationship is built upon reciprocal respect. Followers, as well as leaders, deserve deference and equal consideration. In some industries, managers may tend to exploit their subordinates. They might pressure them to work longer hours or perform extra duties not specified in their job description. The balance of power certainly leans in favour of leaders in these circumstances. Thus, rather than pressure or intimidate employees into additional responsibilities, Kantian ethics demands that leaders be sensitive to their subordinates' needs and expectations. Leaders should engage in more relational building efforts rather than resort to tactics involving fear, ridicule or shame. For example, leaders ought to treat followers as persons who appreciate (and deserve) a little consideration and courtesy. Accolades and recognition go a long way in fostering mutual respect. In their book *The Leadership Challenge*, James Kouzes and Barry Posner suggest that recognition should be personalized. In their words, recognition is about stepping into other people's shoes and asking yourself, 'what do I wish other people would do to celebrate and recognize my contribution? Let your answer to this question guide your own behaviour with others.'[18] Such actions are consistent with the respect for humanity formulation of Kant's categorical imperative.

Finally, leaders and followers should see it as their moral duty to work toward the mutual benefit of the other. As stated above, the relationship between leader and follower is reciprocal. Each works for the mutual benefit of both leader *and* follower (and, of course, other stakeholders). To be sure, leaders should receive proper benefits for their contributions. Moreover, as a matter of consistency, followers ought to receive a proportional benefit for their labours. Consider the issue of CEO compensation. According to some studies, the average CEO pay is over 300 times that of the average employee. In some cases, this disparity is over 800 times more than workers.[19] This dynamic is not healthy for the leader–follower relationship in any organization, nor is it morally justified under a Kantian analysis.[20] It clearly fails to value subordinates as an end in themselves. Instead, it seems to use workers only as a means to an end. This leads us to the goal.

Leaders and followers inevitably work toward some end or goal. The best-case scenario is for leaders and followers to work together to develop and achieve organizational goals. To be sure, leaders and followers each play distinct roles in developing and achieving goals. However, the point is that organizational goals are what Kouzes and Posner call 'finding a common purpose'.[21] Leaders and followers need to see their work as a joint endeavour. 'What this requires is finding common ground among those people who have to implement the vision [of the organization. A leader's] constituents want to feel part of the process.'[22] Kouzes and Posner go on to say, 'nobody really likes being told what to do or where to go, no matter how right it might be. People want to be a part of the vision development process.'[23] The idea of 'a common goal' speaks to the Kantian notion of autonomy. Leaders and followers want to have ownership when pursuing and implementing goals. Thus, leaders honour the personal autonomy of their followers by finding ways for their constituents to work towards a shared vision and common goal.

A separate point related to goals needs to be stressed. A Kantian moral framework insists that formulating organizational goals must cohere with absolute moral duties and not deviate from these morals to maximize utility. If an organization's goal requires justifying immoral means for the sake of some desired end, such an action must be deemed impermissible. For example, consider the issue of sweatshops. Some multinational corporations consider it morally justified to outsource their labour to developing countries. Outsourcing labour cuts costs and often sidesteps cumbersome regulations and policies. Notwithstanding, if outsourcing labour means treating people like human cogs in a machine, then it is morally unacceptable. For example, if compensation is not fair, safety conditions are inadequate, or human rights are violated in the process, then the practice is not morally justified regardless of the economic benefits. Again, consistent with Kantian ethics, the formulation and implantation of organizational goals must (1) be for the mutual benefit of leaders and followers; and (2) always demonstrate respect for humanity. Thus, leaders should ensure the fair treatment of their followers and never exploit or take advantage of them.

There is a growing trend among businesses to see ethical practices as an essential part of their financial success. Good ethics is often seen as good business. To be sure, to some degree, this is a good thing. Social and environmental responsibility should be essential to any organization's model. Nevertheless, Kant's ethics would invite us to question the motive behind this growing trend.

There might be an ulterior motive behind much of corporate social responsibility and philanthropy – particularly 'green' campaigns. For example, some companies are putting pressure on their customers to 'go paperless' and no longer receive paper bills in the mail. Why? Some corporations contend that their customers should go paperless because it's good for the environment. But is that their true motive? Indeed, going paperless would save more trees, and in some ways, this is acting socially responsible. However, do these companies actually care about the environmental impact of using so much paper? Or is the real incentive to go paperless their bottom line? Paperless bills will save their company money. Is this their real motivation? If so, then why be disingenuous and play the ethical card? The answer is that good ethics is often seen as good business. However, Kant reminds us that organizations should be driven not just by the bottom line but also by good will. To be sure, environmental considerations are important. The point is not that we shouldn't 'go green'; rather, the idea is that my motive to 'go green' ought to be sincere.

Finally, Kantian ethics maintains that the specific context or cultural values and norms do not alter one's moral duties. Morality is a matter of categorical imperatives. As such, ethical norms are not changed due to particular situations or cultural circumstances. Both the respect for humanity and the universal law principles hold fast. Their application is the same for leaders and organizations in business and the non-profit sector. It is the same in Europe, South America, the Middle East, or anywhere else in the world.

Cultural relativism argues that morality is determined by cultural context. It is the culture that decides what is moral. (We will feature this ethical approach in Chapter 8.) For example, many cultures forbid same-sex relationships and discriminate against gay men and women in employment. If cultural relativism is correct, then there is nothing, in principle, morally wrong with this discriminatory policy. After all, in this view, the culture decides moral principles. Notwithstanding, Kantian ethics disagree. Kant's theory has the moral resources to oppose discriminatory policies. Again, according to Kant's respect for humanity principle, everyone deserves to be treated with dignity and respect no matter their sexual orientation and, for that matter, regardless of their gender, ethnicity, religion or age. The implications of Kant's ethics are emphatic on this point. Leaders have a moral duty to treat all persons fairly, justly and deferentially.

Having discussed the core concepts of a Kantian ethical framework and provided examples of how these moral ideals apply in the context of leadership, it is time to turn our attention to a case study. The case study will contextualize Kantian ethics within a real-world situation and focuses on a tragic leadership failure. The subject of the case study is Meta (Facebook and Instagram) and its operating practices. As we will see, the primary moral failure, in this case, was not putting the interests and welfare of others over and above profits. Individuals, it would seem, were used as a means to an end rather than treated as ends in themselves. There are essential leadership principles to gain from this unfortunate case.

## CASE STUDY: KANTIAN ETHICS APPLIED TO META (FACEBOOK AND INSTAGRAM)

The pace of technological innovations can be morally alarming. Technology is moving forward at an ever-increasing rate. So much so that human understanding cannot always keep pace with the speed at which new technologies appear. The swift rise of new technologies has created challenges for articulating the moral complexities associated with humanity's newfound obsession with computers and many other electronic devices. The pervasive place of technological devices in our lives raises many pressing ethical considerations, questions we struggle to articulate, let alone answer. For example, what are computer technologies' short-term and long-term impacts on public health or safety? There are also concerns surrounding individual privacy and data storage and the growing addictions associated with compulsively using mobile devices and the internet. To be sure, the growing relationship between technology and human well-being is morally complicated, and the final word on this matter is still a long way off. Whether or not this relationship will prove good for humanity is a matter of ongoing debate.

As an example of the moral challenges raised by new technologies, consider how in the autumn of 2021, Facebook, Inc. (now Meta) came under fire for some alleged moral shortcomings connected to their popular social media platforms. (Instagram is a social media platform owned and operated by Meta - formerly Facebook, Inc. So, any references to Meta, Facebook and Instagram are speaking of the same corporation.)

Meta's business practices started to be scrutinized after a whistle-blower leaked internal documents. The internal documents contained serious information from the company's employees and executives about the many social problems that Meta's products potentially exacerbate. According to leaked documents, Meta has become a place of rampant misinformation. There has allegedly been, for instance, the promotion of misinformation associated with current events, like recent elections, race relations and vaccines. It has also been claimed that Meta has seen a rise in many so-called deep fake videos being used to manipulate people's impressions of political leaders, among other prominent figures. These were among the many societal problems mentioned in the leaked documents and by the subsequent whistle-blower who drew attention to them. However, this case study focuses on an altogether different social worry connected to Facebook - the apparent connection between Instagram usage and the mental health of teenagers.

In September of 2021, *The Wall Street Journal* published a story claiming that Meta's executives have known that Instagram is connected to various mental health issues in teens. Jeff Horwitz, a *Wall Street Journal* reporter, was one of the first to go public with his findings, claiming that leadership at Meta has chosen to focus on increasing usage of its products and largely ignore the problems it creates for some of its most vulnerable stakeholders.[24]

The internal documents reveal how Meta's own research on Instagram uncovered that their popular social media technology has troubling ramifications for young users, particularly young teenage girls. In short, the internal research conducted by Meta demonstrates a connection between Instagram usage and an increase in negative mental health issues. I will have more to say about what these mental health issues are shortly.

The Meta whistle-blower went public on 5 October 2021 revealing her identity. Testifying before a Senate subcommittee, the public discovered that she was a former Facebook product manager named Frances Haugen. Among her many accusations was that Meta's products 'harm children'. According to an NPR report on Haugen's testimony, 'one [leaked] Facebook study found that 13.5% of U.K. teen girls in one survey say their suicidal thoughts became more frequent after starting on Instagram. Another leaked study found that 17% of teen girls say their eating disorders got worse after using Instagram. About 32% of teen girls said that when they felt bad about their bodies, Instagram made them feel worse.'[25] Haugen claims that according to those familiar with Meta's internal workings, it is evident that 'Facebook exploited teens using powerful algorithms.'[26] These claims are morally troubling. Facebook and Instagram are ubiquitous parts of our culture. People, especially teenagers, spend countless hours on these platforms, which is why these accusations are potentially problematic.

Some might claim that the connection between Instagram usage and the reported negative mental health issues for young users has not been scientifically proven. So, making a hard connection between using Instagram (or Facebook) and these poor outcomes for young users is premature. Maybe so. However, making a hard connection between the two is not necessary for this case study. Suppose that the negative consequences for young children using Instagram are, in fact, inconclusive or that Meta unintentionally caused the adverse outcomes. Even still, the findings were serious enough to warrant considerable public scrutiny and lead to robust internal investigations by Meta executives into the safety of their products. At the very least, these findings should have given an organization committed to social responsibility pause. Internal reflection and systematic oversight should have followed to ensure the safety and well-being of everyone. Yet, this does not seem to be what happened. Haugen's testimony before Congress was even more damning for Meta's executives on this point.

Haugen claims that Meta's own research into its products demonstrates that executives knew that its products were 'potentially' harmful to children and did nothing about it. Haugen says, 'The choices being made inside Facebook are disastrous for our children.'[27] She claims that she has witnessed Facebook leadership 'consistently resolve conflicts with its products in favor of its own profits'. In a powerful statement before Congress, she said, 'The company's leadership knows how to make Facebook and Instagram safer but won't make the necessary changes because they have put their astronomical profits before people.'[28] To be sure, these allegations would be morally alarming for any corporation. What makes all of this most troubling is that it comes from a company like Facebook and highlights the apparent neglect of its leadership. Users trust Facebook. They spend countless hours on the company's platform. In so doing, they believe that Facebook's social media platforms will, if not improve their quality of life, at least not harm them. The company's website pledges, as one of its core principles, to 'keep people safe'. They claim, 'We have a responsibility to promote the best of what people can do together by keeping people safe and preventing harm.'[29] If this was indeed the company's pledge to its user, then any serious allegations to the contrary must have been heeded, or so you would think.

Below you can find a modified version of the Five Components of Leadership Model to illustrate the leadership process in relationship to our case study.

## FIVE COMPONENT ANALYSIS

In Figure 2.3, we can see how Kant might place this case on the Five Components of Leadership Model. In this instance, the leaders are the Meta executives. The followers are the adolescent users. The goal in the safe consumption of Instagram. Kant would say that the context of the drive for more users and profits should be ignored in favour of the cultural value of safeguarding youth and their ability to safely consume content on Instagram.

The following quote from Haugen's testimony before Congress is worth citing in its entirety. It seems to directly undermine Facebook's commitment to 'keep people safe'.

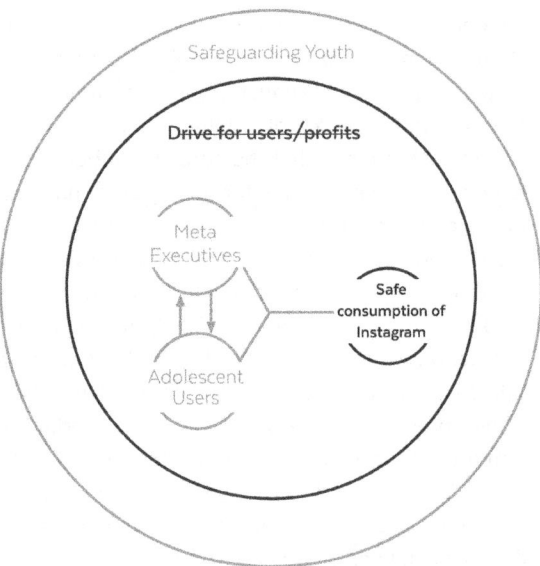

During my time at Facebook, I came to realize a devastating truth: Almost no one outside of Facebook knows what happens inside of Facebook. The company intentionally hides vital information from the public, from the U.S. government and from governments around the world. The documents I have provided to Congress prove that Facebook has repeatedly misled the public about what its own research reveals

**Figure 2.3**    The Five Components of Leadership Model applied to the Meta case study

about the safety of children ... Not only does the company hide most of its own data, my disclosure has proved that when Facebook is directly asked questions as important as how do you impact the health and safety of our children, they choose to mislead and misdirect.[30]

If correct, these charges demonstrate an egregious failure of leadership. It would mean that not only has Meta failed to protect vulnerable stakeholders, but it has also potentially put them into harm's way to increase revenues and then purposefully misled the public about its motivations.

This case study does not intend to put Meta on trial. Nor does it claim to know whether Meta's products actually cause the harm that Haugen claims they do. The jury is still out as to the extent to which her claims are accurate. However, for the purposes of this case study, suppose it is only a reasonable possibility that Meta's products cause the harms Haugen, and others, claim they do. There seems to be sufficient evidence from appropriate experts to justify this more modest assumption.

Let us briefly apply a Kantian moral framework to this case study. Looking at this social dilemma through the lens of a Kantian perspective will provide some moral clarity about the missteps made by Facebook executives in this case. In what follows, we will consider three aspects of Kantianism: first, Kant's idea of a good will; second, the Respect for Humanity Principle; and finally, the Universal Law Principle.

First, Kant's ethics are helpful when considering the basic requirements of morality. Recall that for Kant, first and foremost, morality comes down to having the right motive. So, the first thing we can ask when considering the decisions of Meta's leadership is, did they act with a good motive? Did their actions have good intentions? Did they intend to do well by all morally relevant stakeholders, or did they intend to 'mislead and misdirect'? If Haugen's claims are correct, it is clear that Meta's motivations were less than moral.

When confronted with the potential negative consequences of their products, Meta's leadership should have immediately turned their attention to considering the welfare of their stakeholders. Instead, in the immediate aftermath of the allegations, CEO Mark Zuckerberg turned his attention to attacking Haugen's credibility and insisting that Meta was blameless.[31] Suppose Zuckerberg sincerely believes that he is right about this. Even so, is this the appropriate response of ethical leadership? Kant famously refers to 'acting out of duty' or 'acting from duty'. That is, it is our duty to do the right thing simply because it is the right thing. Rather than immediately discounting serious health and safety concerns, the correct response, according to Kant, should be motivated by the immediate concern for the safety of others.

This moral sentiment is strengthened when considering Kant's principle to Respect Humanity. For example, Kant maintains that there is a minimum moral requirement to always act in ways that constitute the proper treatment of persons. He says that we ought to 'Act in such a way that you always treat humanity, whether in your own person or in the person of any other, never simply as a means, but always at the same time as an end.' So, following Kant here, organizational goals must include provisions for respecting the welfare and rights of all stakeholders.

This organizational goal is strengthened by considering Meta's financial success. When we consider the financial means at Meta's disposal, it becomes evident that leaders in positions of influence not only ought to do more to ensure they are mitigating potential harms, but they, in fact, can also do more. That is to say, given the vast resources at Meta's fingertips, it would be a moral outrage for the welfare of vulnerable stakeholders not to be given sufficient attention. Kantian ethics compels leaders to protect human persons, but especially vulnerable human persons. Consequently, if Meta's products jeopardize the welfare of its young users, it is the moral responsibility of leaders to redress this concern.

Furthermore, you might remember that Kant's Universal Law Principle holds that we should 'always act in such a way that the maxim of your action can be willed as a universal law of humanity'. Or, put differently, 'Act as though the maxim of your action were by your will to become a universal law of nature.' Could Meta's leaders universalize their approach to this problem? It is not likely that Meta could universalize a policy that permits a disregard for vulnerable stakeholders. Instead, if properly applied, Kant's moral principle would ensure that leaders and organizations are mindful of their impact upon everyone, not least of which those who are children. This principle is true whether or not local laws or policies require doing so. Why? Protecting and maintaining human welfare is in everyone's interest. As a matter of moral principle, therefore, Meta ought to go beyond the requirements of the law to ensure human well-being and safety. Consequently, it is not enough for leaders and their corporations to simply make following the law their goal; they must also be mindful of other important moral considerations.

Turning our attention once again to the Five Components of Leadership Model, we must start by looking at leaders and followers and see what we can learn from the Meta case.

In this case, the leaders would be represented by Meta executives, and the followers could be any number of stakeholders. For simplicity, I will suppose that a follower, in this case, is best understood as the many young people that are using Meta's social media platforms. The relationship at work between the leaders and followers, in this case, is one that is marked by trust. For example, followers can and should make informed decisions or decide to protest some feature when it is appropriate to do so – as when their rights or safety are in jeopardy. Nevertheless, the followers must be able to trust that leadership is being transparent with them. In this case, followers should be able to trust that Meta's executives have their well-being in mind. If there are potential risks or vulnerabilities, then these must be disclosed. Followers (i.e. users) must maintain the right to make informed decisions about using a product. Whether some product or service is worth the risk is entirely up to the user, buyer or customer. However, making an informed decision requires a full disclosure of the facts, something that was apparently withheld from users by Meta's leadership. If, instead, leadership at Meta decided to disclose their findings to users, then the two might have been able to work together to find a better outcome for everyone.

Of course, this is entirely relevant to the goals and context of leadership. To be adequately prepared for any possible 'known' and 'unknown' future outcome, ethical leadership must be guided by proper organizational motivation. This includes a moral motivation to do well by all an organization's stakeholders – not just shareholders. In the end, the Meta case demonstrates why it is especially critical for leaders to know and appreciate Kantian ethics. In particular, Kant's Respect for Humanity Principle, which, if properly applied, should provide leaders with the moral outlook for properly treating other people in any context. At a minimum, this means that leaders, if necessary, ought to put the welfare of others over and above their own profits.

## SUMMARY AND CONCLUDING REMARKS

What, then, is the moral duty of leaders and followers? For those who wish to follow Kant's ethics, the leader's actions must first be motivated by 'good will'. To qualify as acting out of 'good will', leaders must ensure they always respect humanity and act in a way consistent with universal law. The moral requirement to always 'act out of duty' was explained with reference to two crucial Kantian principles. First, leaders must, without exception, respect humanity. Additionally, leaders should act in accordance with the universal law. In so doing, leaders will ensure that they adhere to their moral duties.

So how can this perspective work practically in an organization? Both leaders and followers must be clear on what is required for 'respect' and the values that are non-negotiable and represent universal law. In sum, it may be helpful to return to the framing question at the outset of this chapter. In introducing Kant's ethics, we asked: what is a leader's moral duty? According to a Kantian moral framework, the answer to this question is now clear. The leader's actions and decisions ought to be motivated by 'good will', where 'good will' is the guiding intention to always act out of duty – always to do the right thing. Why? Because it is a leader's absolute moral imperative.

## DISCUSSION QUESTIONS

1. How would you apply Kant's Universal Law formulation of his categorical imperative to the Meta case study?
2. Is Kant's Respect for Humanity principle relevant to the Meta case study? How? Explain.
3. Briefly consider the case study from the perspective of Kantian ethics and utilitarianism. Which moral assessment do you find most compelling? Explain?
4. Suppose you are a leader at Meta; what steps would you take to mitigate potential problems for vulnerable stakeholders?

## ADDITIONAL RESOURCES

R. Audi, *Business Ethics and Ethical Business*, New York: Oxford University Press, 2009.

This book is an introductory level assessment of ethics and ethical issues related to business practices.

N. Bowie Norman, *Business Ethics: A Kantian Perspective*, New York: Cambridge University Press, 2017.

This book applies Kantian ethical principles to contemporary business practices. It aims to demonstrate how corporations can maintain institutional integrity and professional success.

C.M. Korsgarrd, *Creating the Kingdom of Ends*, Cambridge: Cambridge University Press, 1996.

This text outlines a compelling reading of Kantian ethics. This interpretation of Kant's philosophy emphasizes his ethics' teleological and practical nature.

O. O'Neil, *Acting on Principle: An Essay on Kantian Ethics*, Cambridge: Cambridge University Press, 2013.

This book takes Kant's idea of a categorical imperative seriously and aims to guide the reader toward a proper application and understanding of this concept in practical ethical decision-making.

## NOTES

1.  Kantian ethics is a type of deontological ethical system. Deontological ethics (or deontology) is a rule- or duty-based ethical system. Though Kant's ethics is rightly classified as a form of deontological ethics, it is by no means the only form.

2.  See I. Kant, 'Groundwork of the Metaphysics of Morals', in Mary Gregor (ed.), *Cambridge Texts in the History of Philosophy*, Cambridge: Cambridge University Press, 1785/1997, p. xxxii.

3.  S. Freeman, *Rawls*, New York: Routledge, 2007, p. 474.

4.  It has become standard in the academy to compare and contrast utilitarianism (or consequentialism) with Kantian ethics. The dissimilarities between the two are striking. Thus, it is informative to distinguish one from the other. A complete introduction to utilitarianism is discussed elsewhere in this volume.

5.  M. Timmons, *Disputed Moral Issues*, New York: Oxford University Press, 2014, pp. 6–7.

6.  J.S. Mill, *Utilitarianism*, 2nd edn, Indianapolis, IN: Hackett Publishing Company, Inc., 2002, p. 18.

7.  Kant/Gregor, *Cambridge Texts in the History of Philosophy*, p. 7.

8.  Kant/Gregor, *Cambridge Texts in the History of Philosophy*, p. 8.

9.  For more about the concept of 'moral luck,' see the following influential sources: B. Williams, *Moral Luck*, Cambridge: Cambridge University Press, 1981; and T. Nagel, 'Moral Luck,' in Daniel Statman (ed.), *Moral Luck*, Albany, NY: State University of New York Press, 1993, pp. 57–71.

10. R. Johnson and A. Cureton, 'Kant's moral philosophy', *The Stanford Encyclopedia of Philosophy*, Spring 2017 edn. https://plato.stanford.edu/archives/spr2017/entries/kant-moral/ (accessed 14 October 2022).

11. Kant/Gregor, *Cambridge Texts in the History of Philosophy*, p. 37.

12. Kant/Gregor, *Cambridge Texts in the History of Philosophy*, p. 37.

13. Johnson and Cureton, 'Kant's moral philosophy'.

14. Kant/Gregor, *Cambridge Texts in the History of Philosophy*, p. 31.

15. As stated above, utilitarianism and key figures associated with this theory are explored in greater detail elsewhere in this volume (see Chapter 3).

16. A.C. Ewing, *The Definition of Good*, London: Macmillan, 1947, p. 188.

17. J. Rachels and S. Rachels, *The Elements of Moral Philosophy*, 8th edn, New York: McGraw-Hill Education, 2014, p. 131.

18. J. Kouzes and B. Posner, *The Leadership Challenge*, San Francisco, CA: Wiley, 2012, p. 286.

19. See, for example, M. Krantz, '9 CEOs paid 800 times more than their workers', *USA Today*, 5 August 2015. http://www.usatoday.com/story/money/markets/2015/08/05/ceos-paid-many-times-more/31148137/ (accessed 14 October 2022).

20. With respect to organizational health, see C. O'Reilly, T. Pollock and J. Wade, 'Overpaid CEOs and underpaid managers: fairness and executive compensation', *Organization Science*, vol. 17 no. 5, 2006, 527–44.

21. Kouzes and Posner, *The Leadership Challenge*, p. 116.

22. Kouzes and Posner, *The Leadership Challenge*, p. 116.

23. Kouzes and Posner, *The Leadership Challenge*, pp. 116–17.

24. G. Wells, J. Horwitz and D. Seetharaman, 'Facebook knows Instagram is toxic for teen girls, company documents show', *The Wall Street Journal*, 14 September 2021. https://www.wsj.com/articles/facebook-knows-instagram-is-toxic-for-teen-girls-company-documents-show-11631620739 (accessed 14 October 2022).

25. B. Allyn, 'Here are 4 key points from the Facebook whistle-blower's testimony on Capitol Hill,' *NPR*, 5 October 2021. https://www.npr.org/2021/10/05/1043377310/facebook-whistleblower-frances-haugen-congress (accessed 14 October 2022).

26. Allyn, 'Here are 4 key points'.

27. Allyn, 'Here are 4 key points'.

28. Allyn, 'Here are 4 key points'.

29. Company info: Meta. Company Info Meta (n.d.). https://about.facebook.com/company-info/ (accessed 15 March 2022).

30. United States Senate Committee on Commerce, Science and Transportation Sub-Committee on Consumer Protection, Product Safety, and Data Security (n.d.). Statement of Frances Haugen. https://www.commerce.senate.gov/services/files/FC8A558E-824E-4914-BEDB-3A7B1190BD49 (accessed 27 October 27).

31. L. Cathey, 'Zuckerberg breaks silence, denies Facebook whistle-blower's claims', *ABC News*, 6 October 2021https://abcnews.go.com/Politics/mark-zuckerberg-breaks-silence-denies-facebook-whistleblowers-claims/story?id=80432492 (accessed 5 January 2022).

# 3
# Utilitarianism

*Alexandra K. Perry*

## FRAMING QUESTION

How do leaders create the greatest good for the greatest number?

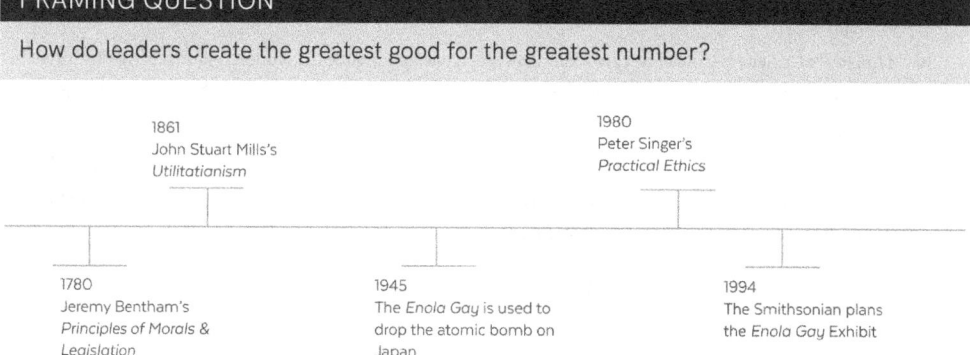

1861
John Stuart Mills's
*Utilitarianism*

1980
Peter Singer's
*Practical Ethics*

1780
Jeremy Bentham's
*Principles of Morals &*
*Legislation*

1945
The *Enola Gay* is used to
drop the atomic bomb on
Japan

1994
The Smithsonian plans
the *Enola Gay* Exhibit

**Figure 3.1**    Timeline of major works on utilitarian ethics in relation to the chapter case
study

Each moral act can be divided into two parts: action (or inaction), and the consequences
brought about by the action. Ethical theories use different evaluative tools to judge the relative
morality of action and inaction. Utilitarianism takes a distinct approach; the subject of its
evaluation is the consequences of various actions, and its evaluative tool is utility. At its core,
utilitarianism asks the question: Which action maximizes utility and minimizes harm for the
greatest number of people?

Throughout this chapter, we will examine utilitarian ethics and the implication the
approach has upon leadership. We will consider major utilitarian philosophers and the various
ways they have approached and refined the idea, as well the investigate utilitarianism's major
concepts and critiques. After we apply the Five Components of Leadership Model to utilitarian
ethical theory, we will 'put the theory on its feet' by applying it to the debate regarding the way
museums preserve history and the controversy surrounding the Smithsonian's display of the
*Enola Gay* – the plane that released the atomic bomb on Hiroshima at the end of the Second
World War. Throughout our time together, we hope to see the benefits, liabilities, and implications for leaders using this popular approach to ethical practice.

## HISTORY

In his book *An Introduction to the Principles of Morals and Legislation*, Jeremy Bentham first proposed utilitarianism as a moral principle. However, utilitarianism's roots can be traced to the ancient world. Aristippus, a student of Socrates and a contemporary of Plato, first popularized hedonism – the ancient Greek principle that individual happiness ought to be the primary aim of human life.

Aristippus' view of hedonism was epistemological scepticism at its core. He believed all knowledge was sensory; therefore, there was no universal truth or knowledge. For this reason, the individual's goal should be to maximize pleasurable sensations and minimize painful sensations.[1] The challenge, Aristippus believed, was for each individual to be in control of their own pleasure and avoid those pleasures that would lead to pain in the long run. From this challenge unfolded the hedonistic ethical view: follow the law so as not to experience the consequences of law-breaking; act justly so as to reap the pleasures that result; be good to friends because of the friendliness you will likely experience in return. Like utilitarianism, Aristippus' hedonism evaluated the consequences of each action in order to assess its moral worth; however, the evaluative tool was not utility, but rather immediate individual pleasure. Epicurus, an ancient Greek philosopher who lived in the third century BCE, popularized the idea of hedonism by shifting its focus to moderation. To Epicurus, maximizing happiness meant that happiness must be sustained, and therefore the individual's goal should be to live a peaceful life free from fear.[2]

### Non-Western Roots

While the ancient Greeks were developing schools of hedonism, non-Western thinkers were also developing early forms of utilitarianism. Chinese Mohist thinkers, whose work is traced back to the fifth century BCE, developed an ethical view that also sought to maximize happiness.[3] Unlike hedonism, the Mohist's focus was not on the individual but on the happiness of the community writ large. Mohist consequentialism held that the most important factors for human welfare were population growth, material goods, and social 'order', which referred to times of peace and the avoidance of warfare.

Maximizing these goods, the Mohists believed, would improve the welfare of all humans. This benefit to the individual by way of the collective offers a glimpse of utilitarian theories that were to come later. However, the emphasis on the welfare of the collective sets Mohism apart from other consequentialist theories.

Some scholars have argued that Buddhism is the converse of utilitarianism.[4] While utilitarianism focuses on the maximization of pleasure, Buddhism aims to reduce or eliminate suffering. Both goals end up roughly in the same place: A world where pleasure outweighs pain, and an ethical appraisal system that calculates pleasure over pain to assess its efforts toward a goal (maximizing pleasure in utilitarianism and minimizing suffering in Buddhism).

## Utilitarianism

Utilitarianism certainly has roots in ancient Greek philosophy and non-Western thought, but its approach is distinct from these ethical frameworks because its goal is much further reaching. The aim of utilitarianism is two-fold: maximize utility for the greatest number of people. When Jeremy Bentham wrote *An Introduction to the Principles of Morals and Legislation*, he argued that the second part of this goal, that utility has to be maximized for the greatest number of people, made it important to be both an ethical framework and a legal framework.[5] Bentham believed that his 'greatest happiness principle', which he called his utilitarian calculus, would eventually be a complete legal system. He wrote, 'nature has placed mankind under the governance of two sovereign masters, pain and pleasure. It is for them alone to point out what we ought to do, as well as to determine what we shall do.'[6]

Bentham developed a calculus to determine an ethical course of action, which he called the felicific calculus. The felicific calculus included circumstances that ought to be considered when determining the moral value of any specific action. These circumstances included duration, purity, extent, certainty, remoteness, and fecundity. The units of currency in felicific calculus were hedons (positive ethical worth) and dolors (negative ethical worth). In addition to being a philosopher, Bentham was an economist whose work focused on improving social welfare, so it is no surprise that his ethical framework borrowed from the language and theory of economics.

Jeremy Bentham became close friends with the British historian James Mill in the early nineteenth century. Bentham's work influenced Mill, who wrote on utilitarianism in publications such as the *Philanthropist* between 1808 and 1818 before his most famous book, *The History of British India*, was published. At the time, Mill had a young son, John Stuart Mill, who would grow up under the influence of his father and Bentham. Mill was taught exclusively at home in his early years and learned Greek, Latin, economics, science, and mathematics from Bentham and his contemporaries. It would be J.S. Mill who would propel the development of Bentham's utilitarianism forward.

In 1863 J.S. Mill published his work *Utilitarianism*, in which he outlined a clear and concise development of Bentham's ethical theory. Responding to critics of Bentham who claimed that utilitarianism was unrefined, or simply a form of hedonism, Mill made a distinction between lower levels of pleasure, which are typically derived from physical stimuli, and higher-level pleasures, which were more intellectual or moral by nature. Mill's most famous quote in utilitarianism reads:

> It is better to be a human being dissatisfied than a pig satisfied; better to be Socrates dissatisfied than a fool satisfied. And if the fool, or the pig, are of a different opinion, it is because they only know their own side of the question.[7]

Mill's utilitarianism maintained the foundation of ethical appraisal that Bentham laid. However, his distinction between levels of pleasure is what contemporary utilitarians have argued sets the theory apart from its hedonistic predecessors.

Over the past century, two philosophers have been fundamental to the continued evolution of utilitarianism, R.M. Hare and Peter Singer. Hare, whose career spanned the mid-to-late twentieth century, continued the work of Mill but with an eye towards the growing emphasis on language in philosophical theory. Hare's work included *The Language of Morals* and *Moral Thinking*, and in both, he outlined the underpinning linguistic and cognitive conventions of moral thinking. Hare developed the term preference utilitarianism, which considers both the universalizability and prescriptive nature of moral terms, and leads to a form of utilitarianism that maximizes the satisfaction of the preferences of the majority of people.

Singer, a student of Hare at Oxford, did not make significant contributions to the theory of utilitarianism but rather to its application. Singer's career began as the field of applied ethics was beginning to formalize. While philosophers had a long tradition of contributing to ethical theory, there had been a separation of philosophical theory and application for much of the twentieth century. Applied ethicists began getting involved in various rights movements and contributing to areas such as medicine, art, and business. Singer quickly became the most prominent utilitarian voice in applied ethics and sought to live a lifestyle consistent with a utilitarian framework in order to serve as an example of the theory's practicality. His work is controversial for the boundaries he draws around his appraisal's scope. Singer has been an outspoken advocate of animal rights, arguing that if animals can feel pain, they ought to be considered in a strict utilitarian calculus.[8] Singer has also taken controversial positions on subjects such as donating most of one's money to the poor, giving up cars, and euthanizing disabled infants on utilitarian grounds.[9]

## MAJOR CONCEPTS IN UTILITARIAN ETHICS

The idea that what is ethical is what maximizes good for the greatest number of people is quite intuitive and has certainly gained traction since Bentham first popularized utilitarianism. Actually measuring the consequences of an action in order to determine whether it is moral, however, is quite complicated. Calculating the scope of those consequences is yet more complicated, as is understanding how those consequences are best weighted to appraise the relative harms and benefits an action brings. Bentham, Mill, and the contemporary utilitarians each approached these questions in slightly different ways. This section will highlight these major concepts in utilitarianism with an eye towards the value of utilitarianism for leaders before discussing the major challenges to utilitarianism in the following section.

### Utilitarian Calculus

The fundamental question of utilitarianism is daunting: How can a leader measure the consequences of an action in order to determine whether it is right or wrong? Bentham's felicific calculus was the first formalized attempt at addressing this question.

The felicific calculus attempted to quantify the moral value of an action by assigning each hedon (pleasure value) and dolor (pain value) a worth of 1. Ultimately, a leader's assessment should be based on whether the number of hedons outweighs the number of dolors. For each hedon and dolor, the leader is told to consider its duration, certainty, and intensity, in addition to the number of those who will be affected, the probability that the sensation is pure and will not lead to a sensation of the opposite kind, and the timeframe in which the result will occur. If that sounds like an overwhelming task, Bentham has a device intended to make it easier to remember:

> Intense, long, certain, speedy, fruitful, pure – Such marks in pleasures and in pains endure. Such pleasures seek if private be thy end: If it be public, wide let them extend. Such pains avoid, whichever be thy view: If pains must come, let them extend to few.[10]

The attempt to quantify moral value was not a central theme in John Stuart Mill's work on utilitarianism. Mill instead turned his sights to the differences in quality between different pleasures. Mill believed that lower-level pleasures and pains included those actions that brought about primarily physical sensations. For example, eating or taking a walk would be considered lower-level pleasures primarily, while the experience of falling in love or saving a life would be higher-level pleasures because they have intellectual and moral qualities to them. Likewise, stubbing a toe would be a lower-level pain, while heartbreak would be a higher-level pain.

Though Mill and Bentham emphasized different elements of the evaluative process, they both agreed that the most ethical course of action is the one that brings about the greatest amount of good for the greatest number of people.

For example, the leader of a corporation might use a utilitarian calculation when trying to decide which supplier to award a contract to when building a new office space. Using Bentham's calculus, the leader might consider all of the people who might be affected by her decision. She would likely consider the cost of each bid, the time each supplier might take, the effect on her employees, the implications for her stockholders, and so on. Weighing the options, she would likely select the supplier whose product would maximize the happiness of the greatest number of people. In doing so, Bentham would argue that she has done what is morally correct.

Mill would want the leader to take her consideration a step further by balancing not just the potential happiness with the potential unhappiness, but also by deliberating over the weight that she gives to each consideration in her calculus. For Mill, the temporary inconvenience of employees who are anxious to move into their new office space would be far outweighed by a consideration of the social practices of the supplier that the leader chooses. Mill would want her calculus to consider each company's environmental policies, whether the bids have come from businesses with a history of discriminatory practices, and so on. Because these factors have an intellectual and moral element, Mill would say that they are higher-level pleasures than the factors relating to the employees' immediate comfort. How is one to distinguish lower- from higher-level pleasures? Mill's advice is to watch educated citizens and concern ourselves with the pleasures they focus on, using the things they consider as 'good' to be the standard that guides our actions.

## Defining the Scope of Evaluation in Utilitarianism

A more difficult question for utilitarians is where the boundaries of evaluation should fall. Bentham and Mill both emphasized that their ethical framework was not akin to the Mohist's hedonism in that the goal of utilitarianism is not the overall well-being of society or even all individuals. Still, utilitarian boundaries are not drawn as narrowly as the ancient hedonists might have drawn them, with the individual residing by his or her lonesome within their confines. Utilitarian thinkers have consistently maintained that the scope of utilitarian consideration should be all individuals the decision will affect.

Utilitarianism is inherently non-discriminatory. Bentham's famous decree, 'each to count for one and none for more than one', is the true goal of utilitarianism. Each individual affected by a particular decision should count as one, regardless of his or her status or standpoint. Still, utilitarianism struggles to define which individuals are worthy of inclusion. How is one to know at the outset of a decision how far the effects of that decision will be felt?

More recent utilitarians like Peter Singer often consider just this question in their evaluation of contemporary moral issues. For Singer, the most salient example of this dilemma is the question of animal rights.[11] Singer has argued extensively that non-human animals ought to be considered as humans are in the appraisal of any ethical question of which they are the subject. For Singer, this means that it is unethical to consume animal products, to warehouse animals in zoos or other facilities designed for human entertainment, or to hunt for sport. If animals can feel pain, why shouldn't they be considered in an ethical system that measures levels of discernible pleasures and pains? Singer coined the term 'speciesism' in response to this concern. He argues that ignoring the pain of animals based on their species is discriminatory in the same way that someone might be racist, sexist, or homophobic. Would the leader in the example above also need to consider the possible harm to animals that might come from her choosing one supplier over another? Or would she act ethically as long as she considered her employees, their families, her stockholders, and the customers her business serves?

## CRITIQUES OF UTILITARIAN ETHICS

Utilitarianism can be a very practical way for leaders to make ethical decisions. The theory prompts the leader to consider his followers and the goal they are working towards to decide what is right. Ideally, it also prompts the decision-maker to engage those who might be impacted by the decision at hand in order to determine which option will maximize happiness for those impacted. Still, utilitarianism faces some unique challenges and critiques.

Recent elections in many democratic countries worldwide illustrate what might be the most pressing challenge for leaders attempting to use utilitarianism to guide their ethical decision-making. Many of these elections highlighted the incongruent desires of citizens within the same political boundaries. With many elections resulting in poll numbers close to 50 per cent for each candidate, it is fair to ask how a leader might act ethically according to utilitarianism. How can a leader maximize happiness for the greatest number of his or her followers if those followers each want very different things? The happiness that some followers feel as a result of a moral decision will always come at the expense of the happiness of other followers. Does the happiness of the majority always outweigh the suffering of the minority? This section will look at some of these challenges to utilitarianism and highlight the differences between utilitarianism and deontology, which are commonly viewed as contrasting theories.

## The Role of the Minority

The most pressing challenge to utilitarianism is the question of the rights of the minority. As a theory, utilitarianism aims to maximize happiness for the greatest number of people. However, this aim, at best, ignores the desires of the minority and, at worst, allows for the moral permissibility of actions that directly cause harm to the minority.

In his lectures on justice, moral philosopher Michael Sandel uses the example of organ donation to highlight this point. Imagine there are five patients, Sandel asks the audience, and each one is in need of a different organ transplant. It might take years for each of these individuals to become transplant recipients if they are listed on the organ transplant waitlist and subject to the same lottery methods as other organ recipients. It's likely that most of the five, if not all five, would not survive the wait. Sandel then asks the audience to imagine that there is a healthy person in the next room. Why couldn't we simply sedate that person, procure their organs, and provide transplants to each of the other five?[12]

A straightforward and simple utilitarian calculus might allow for this. Five people benefit from the action, while one suffers. Clearly, the appraisal would have to be more complex than this: there are families to consider, the likelihood of each organ's suitability, the chance for failure, and other factors. The details can be shifted in thousands of different ways in order to influence the calculation and weigh the relative harms and benefits.

The criticism is simple, however: Why doesn't that healthy patient have the right to keep his own organs and his life? The fact that he is in the minority does not seem to negate the fact that he has the right to remain free from harm. At an intuitive level, something just seems wrong about allowing someone to die for the sake of the majority. Furthermore, it need not be a matter of life and death to serve as a hefty criticism of utilitarian theories. Don't all individuals deserve happiness, whether they fall in the majority or the minority?

## Limits to the Consideration of Consequences

A second major criticism of utilitarianism is that it is impossible to understand all of the potential consequences of an action and that it is undoubtedly impossible to consider each one before making an ethical decision. If I am driving down the highway tonight and see a family struggling to get their car to start on the side of the road, I will quickly have to decide whether or not to stop to help them. It seems insensible for me to consider the effect that this might have on my own family, my ability to sleep well tonight, and the implications for my colleagues if I am late arriving for work. In the time I have to make that decision, I will likely consider my safety and the safety of the family stuck on the side of the road. My ability to consider more than that is limited by my lack of time and ability to truly understand how far-reaching the effects of my action might be.

Axel Gosseries, a Belgian moral philosopher, uses the example of baby food production to illustrate this point. Manufacturers often produce baby food that has a shelf life of a few years.[13] This timetable means that children not even born at the point of production – perhaps not even conceived – will consume much of the baby food in those jars. Still, we regulate the safety and quality of baby food even though those who might be harmed by it are simply hypothetical beings. We likely consider the rights of these future humans because of the immediacy of their future existence and our manufacturing norms, but how often do we have to consider harms to future generations? How often do we have to consider harms to the deceased? Do we need to consider those on the periphery of our decisions? Utilitarianism has trouble addressing these questions.

Mill anticipates this challenge by limiting our obligation to the consideration of only those immediately and actually affected by our decision at hand. Still, even this qualification raises questions as it tries to address them.

## Inherent Moral Value

Deontology, the moral theory most commonly viewed as the contrast to utilitarianism, takes as its central tenet the idea that actions have inherent moral value without regard to their consequences. Immanuel Kant, the eighteenth-century German philosopher whose work is viewed as the foundation of deontology, used a principle called the 'Categorical Imperative' to determine whether an action is right or wrong. (For more on Kant, see Chapter 2.) This principle holds that moral laws are intrinsically good and that all reasonable people will agree on their worth.

The deontological challenge to utilitarianism is that it disregards this intrinsic moral value of certain actions, favouring an ends-justify-the-means appraisal instead. Utilitarianism leaves room for actions such as lying, stealing, and even murder to be viewed as ethical as long as they maximize the happiness of the greatest number of people. Bentham and Mill dismiss this criticism. Both theorists argue that certain actions will always be unethical in a society that follows utilitarian moral principles because they will not maximize happiness overall. This means that murder, for example, would always be unethical under utilitarianism because it is theoretically impossible for it to maximize happiness overall.

## FIVE COMPONENT ANALYSIS

Considering utilitarianism's major concepts and critiques, let's now see how the theory applies to the Five Components of Leadership Model.

As we see in Figure 3.2, utilitarian ethics focuses directly on the goal and context highlighted in the Five Components of Leadership Model. However, that does not mean that utilitarian ethics does not also speak to the other leadership components. Utilitarian ethics places a great deal of responsibility on leaders and their decision-making. Unlike ethical egoism, introduced in Chapter 5, in which a leader makes a decision based upon what is best for him or her personally, utilitarianism forces the leader to consider himself or herself as only one of many stakeholders. Unlike Machiavelli's famous 'ends/means' calculus that states the ends justifies the means if it preserves the individual's position and power,[14] utilitarian ethics forces the leader to consider the greatest good for the greatest number of people. The 'greatest good' may not be beneficial for the leader personally. Likewise, the leader may not find himself or herself in the company of the 'greatest number of people'; indeed, the leader may be a part of the minority. Thus, utilitarian ethics forces leaders to hold to a high ethical standard for themselves and carefully consider their motivations and reasoning when making a decision.

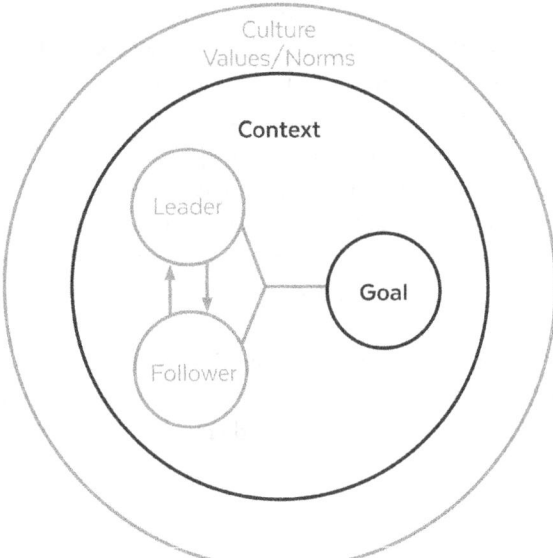

**Figure 3.2**    The Five Components of Leadership Model applied to utilitarian ethics

For example, consider an American politician who receives a large donation from the National Rifle Association (NRA) for his political campaign. (The NRA is an advocacy group for gun owners.) Let's say the politician is from a district that has witnessed a large number of gun-related deaths – perhaps even a mass shooting. Let's also say a bill is introduced to the legislature that would place new restrictions on the purchase of guns in the politician's district. Should the politician vote for the proposed measure? What is the greatest good? What is the greatest number of people? Some may argue that the politician should vote for the bill to protect the lives of the people in his district. They would argue that this is the greatest good for the greatest number of people. Contrarily, others may argue that the politician should vote against the bill to protect the rights of the people in his district to purchase and own guns. They may argue that even if some people use guns to commit murder and terrible crimes, to deny people a right guaranteed by the Unites States' constitution would be detrimental to their other freedoms in the long run. If the politician votes for the bill, he runs the risk of alienating one of his key donors and a portion of his constituents, which may mean he might lose in the next election. If he votes against the bill, he may be accused of succumbing to special interests and the protection of his own career rather than serving his constituents, in which case he may also lose the next election. What is he to do? Utilitarian ethics would say the politician must take himself out of the equation and only consider what he believes to be the greatest good for the greatest number of people regardless of his personal consequences. This is a tall order, but it is required if the politician truly follows the mandate utilitarian ethics stipulates.

Followers must also consider their motivations when considering what is the greatest good for the greatest number of people. They must also be able to look past their immediate interests and immediate gratification to consider what may be right for the larger majority. Consider recycling. We all enjoy the benefits of petroleum products, from the petrol we use in our vehicles to get us from one place to another to the water bottles we use to quench our thirst on a hot summer's day. These conveniences are simply a part of our modern society. However, rarely do we consider the impact these little conveniences have upon others – including the natural environment, non-human animals, and even future generations. Don't we have an ethical obligation to consider these aspects and the impact our actions have on others?

For a more specific example, consider the great pacific garbage patch between the West Coast of the United States and Japan. This area of the ocean contains billions of pieces of debris and plastic, much of which cannot even be seen by the naked eye. These particles float in the top portion of the water column and are ingested by marine life, often leading to their death. Many of these particles are used to produce exfoliating soaps and scrubs so popular in the West – little particles of plastic that give us softer and smoother skin. Is it really necessary to have softer skin at the expense of marine life and the ability of future generations to enjoy the benefits and beauties of the sea? Even if our leaders do not provide the regulation to prohibit such particles from being used in our beauty and hygiene products, isn't it incumbent upon the vast majority of followers to consider the impact their actions will have on others and the environment? Utilitarianism answers this question unequivocally – yes! Followers must also consider the greatest good for the greatest number, even at the expense of their own convenience and comfort.

Perhaps the most relevant aspect of the Five Components Model as it relates to utilitarian ethics is the goal. Utilitarian ethics falls under the umbrella of teleological ethics – that is, that branch of ethics that considers the ends – or the consequences – of actions. From a normative perspective, what is right or what is wrong is dependent upon the outcome of our actions. For example, consider Second World War Germany. Nazi soldiers come knocking at your door and ask if you are hiding Jewish people in your attic – and indeed you are. Some interpretations of Kantian ethics would say that you are obligated to tell the truth; you must act upon the maxim that you would want to be the law. If you don't want other people to lie to you, you must not lie to others; that is your duty. Thus, Kantian ethics falls under the umbrella of deontological or duty-based ethics. According to Kantianism, if the Nazis find and harm the people hiding in your attic, they are morally responsible for their actions – not you. However, utilitarianism looks at the ends rather than the means to that end. If telling the truth would mean that the people hiding in your attic would be taken to concentration camps and face torture and death, then the morally correct thing would be to lie. In this case, the greatest good – saving a life – far outweighs one's moral obligation to tell the truth. From a normative perspective, what is right or wrong depends upon the outcomes of an action. This is the core of utilitarian ethics as it relates to the Five Components Model – the goal is of utmost importance.

Although the goal is essential to understanding how utilitarian ethics relates to leadership, the context is also very important. What might be morally honourable in one situation may be morally reprehensible in another. Again, we might use a wartime example to understand this aspect of the theory. In a time of war, killing the enemy is considered the right thing to do. If your commanding officer (in this case, your leader) gives you the order to shoot – you shoot. This is especially true if you and your fellow soldiers are in immediate danger of being killed and if the cause for which you are fighting is just. However, what should the soldiers do if the context changes and there is no immediate danger? This is precisely what happened in the My Lai Massacre during the war between the United States and Vietnam.

In 1968, during the Vietnam police action, the US Charlie Company came across the village of My Lai in Northern Vietnam. Although there was no threat to the soldiers in the village, and no enemy was ever found, Lieutenant William Calley gave orders to his company to shoot and kill the civilians in the village, including the elderly, pregnant women, children, and even infants. The soldiers raped an untold number of young girls and women, opened machine gun fire on trapped children, and burned the village to the ground. In the end, more than 500 Vietnamese civilians were killed.[15] All is not fair in love and war. Even though the soldiers may have been given orders to shoot 'the enemy', in the context of the peaceful village, the leader and the followers committed an atrocity. This piece of history is a horrible reminder that context matters. Utilitarianism does not give its proponents a license to act unscrupulously.

Finally, we consider cultural values and norms. As we will see in Chapter 8, different cultures may hold various values and norms that may deem certain actions ethical in one culture and unethical in others. However, this is not to say that no guiding principles are valued across cultures, as we will see in Chapter 7, where we discuss universal human values. Just because racial discrimination is permitted in one culture does not make it permissible for a person to take a laissez-faire 'when in Rome' attitude to racial discrimination when travelling abroad. Ethicists also note that some cultures may have better reasons than others for their practices and ethical concerns.[16] Regardless, the motivating considerations for utilitarianism are what is the greatest good for the greatest number of people, regardless of cultural customs and mores. That is why its primary concerns are placed in the domains of the goal and the context on the Five Components of Leadership Model. Let's now see how utilitarian ethics play out in a specific situation. For that, we turn to our case study.

## CASE STUDY: THE SMITHSONIAN'S ENOLA GAY CONTROVERSY[17]

The mid-1990s saw a great deal of controversy over what history ought to make of Hiroshima, a half-century after the city became the target of the world's first use of nuclear weapons. This controversy arose in debates over how best to commemorate the fiftieth anniversary of the bombings of Hiroshima and Nagasaki, Japan, in the Second World War and, more precisely, how the artefacts of the bombings ought to be preserved. The question of how to best memorialize Hiroshima would be of great significance to debates over heritage ethics and historical preservation. As historians and ethicists continue to grapple with the problem of preservation, it becomes clear that the answer to this question is still quite elusive.

The debate over Hiroshima caught the public's attention when the Smithsonian National Air and Space Museum (NASM) announced that it would display the fuselage of the *Enola Gay*. This B-29 heavy bomber aircraft dropped the atomic bomb Little Boy over Hiroshima on 6 August 1945. NASM planned to display the *Enola Gay* in an exhibit that would open during the summer of 1995 to commemorate the fiftieth anniversary of Hiroshima and Nagasaki. Draft scripts of the planned Smithsonian exhibit were circulated during the summer of 1994, and quickly the NASM designers were being maligned for their efforts to revise history and advance a 'victimology thesis' that 'lay embedded in the structure of the exhibition'.[18] The editor of the *Air Force Magazine*, John Correll, was outraged at the NASM's proposed approach to preserving the *Enola Gay*, which he claimed 'depicted the Japanese as defenders of their homeland and Emperor but provided little background on Japan's earlier aggression, which had made such a defence necessary. In this telling of it, the Americans were cast as ruthless invaders, driven by revenge.'[19] As the summer 1994 Op-Ed pages of the *New York Times*, *Washington Post*, and *Wall Street Journal* show, many historians and political commentators agreed with Correll's impression of the exhibit.[20]

Charles Krauthammer wrote a 1994 editorial in *The Washington Post* where he described the exhibit and offered alternative approaches to preserving Hiroshima artefacts:

> The Air and Space commemoration of Hiroshima promises to be an embarrassing amalgam of revisionist hand-wringing and guilt. What to do? General Paul Tibbets, the man who commanded the *Enola Gay*, has the right idea: Hang the plane in the museum without commentary or slanted context. Display it like Lindbergh's plane, with silent reverence and a few lines explaining what it did and when. Or forget the whole enterprise and let the Japanese commemorate the catastrophe that they brought upon themselves.[21]

Eugene Meyer echoed Krauthammer's views almost one year later as debates over the exhibit continued to rage. Meyer described the proposed exhibit as 'an anti-nuke morality play in which Americans are portrayed as ruthless racists hell-bent on revenge for Pearl Harbor, with the Japanese as innocent, even noble victims'.[22]

Many commentators were reacting to the designers' inclusion of the following statement that was included in the draft: 'For most Americans, this war was fundamentally different than the one waged against Germany and Italy – it was a war of vengeance. For most Japanese, it was a war to defend their unique culture against Western imperialism.'[23]

Some of the artefacts to be included in the exhibit were also up for debate. The draft script proposed the inclusion of a child's lunch pail with 'the carbonized remains of sweet green peas and polished rice, a rare wartime luxury'.[24] In addition, critics of the exhibit were enraged at the preservation of photographs of the corpses of Japanese victims, mainly because the number of photographs depicting Japanese suffering was far greater than the number of photographs depicting American suffering.

Of course, some historians thought that the Smithsonian draft script proposed an ethical way to preserve the *Enola Gay*. Historian Mike Wallace points out, 'any exhibition focused on the *Enola Gay* and its bombing run would, almost by definition, depict more Japanese than American casualties.'[25] He claimed that those who opposed the proposed *Enola Gay* exhibit were raising an objection 'to problematizing something deemed utterly unproblematic. Truman dropped the bomb to shorten the war and save lives, period.'[26]

The draft of the exhibit shows plans to include a section about the atomic bombs labelled 'Historical Controversies' in which copy accompanying the artefacts would tell of debates over the number of American lives spared through the use of the atomic bombs and over the legitimacy of claims that the bombings were necessary to bring about Japanese surrender. One of the controversies included in the draft included the question of whether the Japanese would have surrendered if the USA had presented terms in which the security of the Japanese Emperor's position had been guaranteed rather than calling for unconditional surrender. Winston Churchill, General MacArthur, and others claimed that this provision would have ended the war without the use of nuclear force. Historians in favour of the exhibit claimed that the indication that such claims were controversial ought to have been enough to pacify critics. This view that using nuclear weapons could be justified on utilitarian grounds provides a good context for the utilitarian debate over the exhibit itself.

The Smithsonian controversy illustrates how deeply philosophical debates over preservation and display are. Such debates raise questions such as whether and when it is appropriate to preserve, how things ought to be preserved, and who should be permitted to make decisions about preservation. The preservation debates range from artefacts to heritage, art to the environment, documents to languages, and embryos to human bodies. These debates span different disciplines, from art to archaeology, literature to library science, museum studies to medicine. Their roots run particularly deep in history, however, where arguments over preservation often raise questions about who owns the past and how it ought to be used.

Preservation and display in museums or exhibits is especially complicated, however, because these spaces often influence public opinion about history. The Smithsonian controversy illustrates this: critics of the exhibit's plans were not simply offended by the proposed content; they were alarmed by the story that the exhibit space might tell museum-goers. The story of Hiroshima could be told in two ways: the heroic and tragic last resort of a military desperate for an end to the war, or an unnecessary display of power with many innocent victims. The way that the NASM exhibit space was used would determine which of these stories was told 50 years after Hiroshima.

Utilitarian questions about the Smithsonian Controversy abound: Who will be affected by the exhibit? What framing of the exhibit will bring about the greatest amount of good for the greatest number of people? Should good be defined as compelling for viewers, educational for those who engage, or instructive and helpful to prevent future atrocities?

The debate over the display of *Enola Gay* at the NASM illustrates how museums exist as political spaces and how their displays influence how history is told in moral and political terms. Debates in history about whether and how to preserve the past include not only the consideration of artifacts but of heritage, historical narratives, viewpoints, and practices. We aim to preserve paintings, artefacts, manuscripts, and the life of someone seriously ill: all tangible things. But often, we also aim to preserve intangible things such as the rights of prisoners through concepts like restorative justice, the autonomy of those who have a mental illness that leaves them irrational, marriages that seem to be in disrepair, religious freedom for the devout, or the memory of a child who has died.

In history, the impulse to preserve is undoubtedly strong. The controversy over the *Enola Gay* exhibition was not simply about whether it was appropriate to preserve the fuselage of the plane but also about whether it was appropriate to preserve the memory of the bombing of Hiroshima or the moral sentiments towards the bomb held by those who thought the bombing was essential to the end of the Second World War, on one side of the issue, and those who thought of Hiroshima as a ferocious display of power on the other. Some critics argued that the *Enola Gay*, forever a symbol of evil, should be destroyed altogether.

Debates over preservation often centre on how to best preserve those artefacts, narratives, and practices that are regarded as worth preservation. The debate over the preservation of the *Enola Gay* was not simply a matter of whether it ought to be preserved but also whether to display and offer access to it, what the exhibit should look like if it were displayed, and where it might be best preserved. Who would benefit from its display? Who would be harmed? Essentially, it was a utilitarian debate over space and the political knowledge that would be produced as a result of its use.

Decisions over preservation and display must consider who might have the right to make decisions about preserving an archive, historical narrative, or counter-narrative. In the case of the *Enola Gay*, a variety of conflicting views on whether to preserve the plane's fuselage and whether and how to display it led to debates over who might hold the right to determine such things. Should the decision be left up to Air Force Veterans? To the Smithsonian? Should Japanese views on the atomic bomb be considered at all? It is necessary to consider precisely how the right to a particular historical narrative might be determined because the answer to this question will be critical to any assessment of whether or how to preserve a particular artefact or narrative.

## FIVE COMPONENT ANALYSIS

From a utilitarian perspective, the question of how the *Enola Gay* and other artefacts from Hiroshima should be displayed should be answered by looking at how the exhibition might bring about the greatest amount of good to the greatest amount of people. As we apply this scenario to the Five Components of Leadership Model, we can see that, in this case, the leaders are identified as the exhibition designers. The followers are the people who view (or will view) the display. The goal is to educate viewers about Hiroshima. The context is the controversy over how the story of Hiroshima should be told. The cultural values and norms are the American values of conquest and concord, often at odds with one another. In this case, they post a question that lives in tension: Is Hiroshima a story of concord in terms of ending the war and preventing future casualties or unjustified conquest against a cultural group?

For the leaders of the Smithsonian exhibit, engagement was the central consideration in arguments over the preservation and display of the *Enola Gay*. The curators who developed the original draft of the exhibit believed

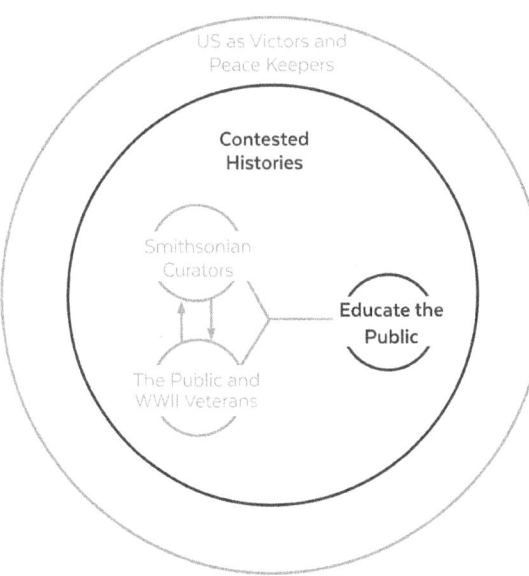

**Figure 3.3**    The Five Components of Leadership Model applied to the Enola Gay exhibit

that if the *Enola Gay* was to be preserved and displayed, then the goal ought to be that viewers who engaged with it were prompted to consider the magnitude of Hiroshima and Nagasaki. In this context, they argued, those who viewed the exhibit would be encouraged to reflect on the weight of the decision that the USA had to make. The curators aimed to emphasize the heroic actions of the Air Force and the melancholy with which President Truman decided to drop the bomb, the suffering of the victims in Hiroshima and Nagasaki, and the views of those who thought that the bomb was unnecessary.[27]

The followers are also an important factor in applying a utilitarian calculus to this case. Followers who disagreed with the way that the proposal for how the *Enola Gay* was to be preserved and displayed cited the need to respect the veterans of the Second World War. Many argued that the exhibit was offensive to veterans and would be a dishonourable way to remember their efforts, an exhibit to which they could not be proud to bring their grandchildren.[28] Still, many argued that the *Enola Gay* should not be preserved at all and that its preservation would be disrespectful to the thousands of Japanese victims of the atomic bomb. For the utilitarian leader, these are all factors to consider in assessing how the display might bring about the greatest good for the greatest number while reducing the overall harm it might cause.

The goal, in this case, to educate viewers about Hiroshima must be considered in terms of what will bring about the greatest good for the greatest number. Will an honest appraisal of the harm caused by the atomic bomb warn future generations about the use of nuclear weapons? Or will this emphasis on the death toll discourage people from seeing the exhibit and ultimately lead to less engagement overall?

The context here, which is the controversy over how educators ought to engage with the Hiroshima artefacts, is important. Determining the right way to engage with history is particularly complicated in cases where historical artefacts or narratives represent a morally contentious period. Preservation debates often centre on so-called artefacts of evil, such as the *Enola Gay*, the sites of prison or concentration camps, or the relics of colonialism. The cultural values and norms inform these debates on American military history. They include seemingly conflicting expressions of value in striving to be victorious and peace-keeping all at once. The stakes are high in such debates because, often, how these artefacts are displayed and viewed will go a long way towards determining how they are interpreted and understood. Janet Malcolm writes, 'time heals all wounds, smooths, cleanses, obliterates; history keeps the wound open, picks at it, makes it raw and bleeding.'[29] Contested histories such as that of Hiroshima suggest that this metaphor might ring true. Determining how to engage with and preserve the artefacts of Hiroshima meant determining how the museum space might influence the views of the bomb for generations to come.

## SUMMARY AND CONCLUDING REMARKS

This chapter has explored the ethical theory of utilitarianism and the framing question: 'How can leaders create the greatest good for the greatest amount of people?' Generally speaking, utilitarian theories answer this question by determining which action can maximize happiness and minimize harm for the greatest number. For leaders, this approach to ethical leadership would entail being reflective about the choices they might make to analyse which choice might bring about the greatest good for their followers. Applying utilitarianism to the issue of displaying the *Enola Gay* has highlighted some of the challenges that leaders might face in taking this approach to leadership.

How do leaders create the greatest good for the greatest number? Utilitarian leaders consider both their immediate actions and the consequences of those actions. Similar to the common good, the area of concern for these leaders goes beyond themselves and their immediate circle of concern to how the secondary consequences of their actions affect all whom their organization influences. To make this happen, leaders must look beyond the immediate goal and consider the positive and negative consequences of that goal for their larger communities. In the end, leaders considering a utilitarian approach to understand the ethical dilemmas they face must first consider their ultimate goal and the surrounding context to know how to act to bring about the greatest good for the greatest number of their followers.

## DISCUSSION QUESTIONS

1. Is it ever ethical to display objects in museums that helped to create untold horror?
2. Consider the Kantian critique of utilitarianism. Is there a danger to defining 'right' and 'wrong' based on the happiness of the majority?
3. How does utilitarianism differ from hedonism, the theory that everyone should do what makes them happy?
4. The case study presents museum curators as leaders in the *Enola Gay* case. How would the case differ if we defined the US military as having a leadership role? What would that role look like, and what obligations would the military have?

## ADDITIONAL RESOURCES

P. Singer, *The Most Good You Can Do: How Effective Altruism is Changing Ideas About Living Ethically*, New Haven, CT: Yale University Press, 2015.

Singer offers an analysis of the application of utilitarianism to contemporary ethical challenges such as vegetarianism and charitable giving.

M. Sandel, *Justice: What's the Right Thing to Do?*, New York: Farrar, Straus and Giroux, 2008.

Sandel considers utilitarianism as an approach to ethical decision-making and compares it to alternatives such as Kantianism and Virtue Ethics.

# NOTES

1. K. Lampe, *The Birth of Hedonism: The Cyrenaic Philosophers and Pleasure as a Way of Life*, Princeton, NJ: Princeton University Press, 2014.

2. Lampe, *The Birth of Hedonism*.

3. C. Fraser, *The Philosophy of the Mòz?: The First Consequentialists*, New York: Columbia University Press, 2016.

4. B. Contestabile, 'Negative utilitarianism and Buddhist intuition', *Contemporary Buddhism: An Interdisciplinary Journal*, vol. 15 no. 2, 2014, 298–311.

5. J. Bentham, *The Collected Works of Jeremy Bentham: An Introduction to the Principles of Morals and Legislation*, ed. J.H. Burns and H.L.A Hart, New York: Oxford/Clarendon Press 1789/1996.

6. Bentham, *Collected Works*, p. 11.

7. J.S. Mill, *Utilitarianism*. Originally published in 1861. See J.S. Mill, *Utilitarianism*, Project Gutenberg, 22 February 2004. https://www.gutenberg.org/files/11224/11224-h/11224-h.htm (accessed 30 September 2020).

8. P. Singer, *Animal Liberation*, New York: Harper Collins, 1975.

9. For example, see P. Singer, 'Voluntary euthanasia: a utilitarian perspective', *Bioethics*, vol. 17 no. 5–6, 2003, 526–41.

10. Bentham, *Collected Works*, p. 38.

11. Singer, *Animal Liberation*.

12. M. Sandel, *Justice: What's the Right Thing to Do?* New York: Farrar, Straus and Giroux, 2008.

13. A. Gosseries, *Intergenerational Justice*, Oxford: Oxford University Press, 2009.

14. N. Machiavelli, *The Prince*, trans. N.H. Thompson, New York: Dover Thrift, 1532/1992, pp. 20–23.

15. For more information, see My Lai massacre, History.com, 2009, A+E Networks. http://www.history.com/topics/vietnam-war/my-lai-massacre (accessed 30 September 2022).

16. M. Velasquez, C. Andre, T. Shanks and M.J. Meyer, 'Ethical relativism', Markkula Center for Applied Ethics, 1 August 1992. https://www.scu.edu/ethics/ethics-resources/ethical-decision-making/ethical-relativism/ (accessed 30 September 2022).

17. This case study was originally featured in A.K. Perry, *Paper Cranes and Mushroom Clouds*, Newcastle upon Tyne: Cambridge Scholars Publishing, 2016. Used by permission of Cambridge Scholars and the author.

18. M. Wallace, *Mickey Mouse History and Other Essays on American Memory*, Philadelphia, PA: Temple University Press, 1996.

19. J. Correll, 'The last act at air and space,' *Airforce Magazine*, vol. 77 no. 9, 1994, 58–64, p. 58.

20. R. Kohn, 'History and the culture wars: the case of the Smithsonian institution's *Enola Gay* exhibition', *The Journal of American History*, vol. 82 no. 3, 1995, 1036–63.

21. C. Krauthammer, 'World War II, revised. Or, how we bombed Japan out of racism and spite', *The Washington Post*, 19 August 1994, p. A-27.

22. E. Meyer, 'Smithsonian sifts debris of *Enola Gay* plan', *The Washington Post*, 20 August 1995. https://www.washingtonpost.com/archive/lifestyle/1995/04/20/smithsonian-sifts-debris-of-enola-gay-plan/0c265c07-2f97-4b51-968b-6e21e0a224be/ (accessed 30 September 2022).

23. National Air and Space Museum, Smithsonian Institution Exhibition Planning Committee, 'The Crossroads: The End of World War II, The Atomic Bomb, and The Onset of the Cold War', 1993. http://secure.afa.org/media/enolagay/07-93.asp (accessed 30 September 2022).

24. J. Correll, 'Revisionism gone wrong', *Air Force Magazine*, April 2004. https://www.airforcemag.com/article/0404revision/ (accessed 30 September 2022).

25. Wallace, *Mickey Mouse History*, p. 318.

26. Wallace, *Mickey Mouse History*, p. 319.

27. J. Dower, 'The politics of memory', *Technology Review*, August/September 1995, 48–51.

28. Dower, 'The politics of memory', 1.

29. J. Malcolm, 'The silent women', *The New Yorker*, August 1993, pp. 8–9.

# 4
# Virtue ethics

*Sabrina B. Little and Molly Reed-Waters*

## FRAMING QUESTION

What virtues should a leader possess to act ethically?

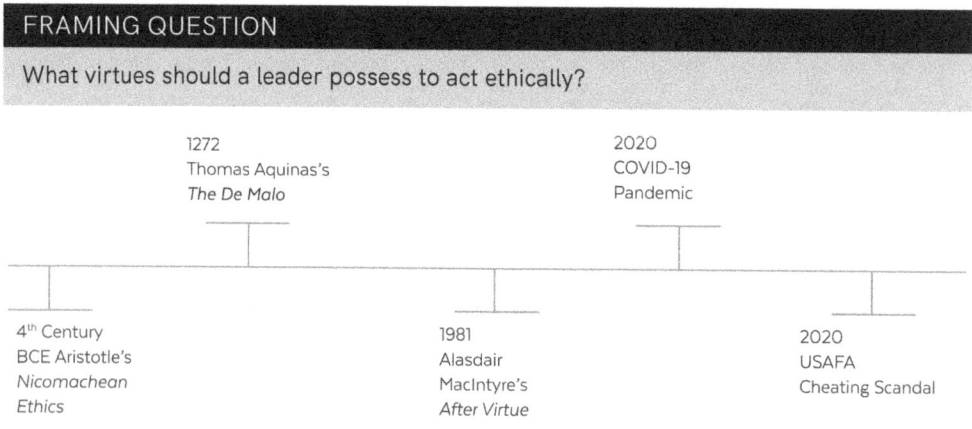

1272
Thomas Aquinas's
*The De Malo*

2020
COVID-19
Pandemic

4th Century
BCE Aristotle's
*Nicomachean
Ethics*

1981
Alasdair
MacIntyre's
*After Virtue*

2020
USAFA
Cheating Scandal

**Figure 4.1**     Timeline of major works on virtue ethics in relation to the chapter case study

Virtue ethics is an approach to ethics that describes morality primarily in terms of virtues and vices of one's character. It offers a vocabulary for naming good and bad qualities and a way to identify what is praiseworthy or blameworthy. As such, it benefits our understanding of ourselves and others and thus protects us. If we cannot name what we find admirable or detestable in our leaders, we are vulnerable to 'unreflectively conform' to those who may not have our best interests at heart.[1] Since most leadership infractions are described as failures of character, virtue ethics has high explanatory power and practical value for those interested in the ethics of leadership. This chapter will examine virtue ethics and position it within the Five Components of Leadership Model. We will then apply virtue ethics to a case study surrounding a recent cheating scandal at the Air Force Academy in the United States.

## HISTORY

The field of ethics has three branches: metaethics, normative, and applied.

Metaethics involves questions about the meaning of moral language or what it means to say that one 'ought' to *do* or to *be* one thing rather than another. On what grounds, or for what reasons, should we do anything at all? Normative ethics is the branch of ethics concerned with what makes actions right and wrong. Virtue ethics is one of three rival normative ethical systems, alongside consequentialism and deontology, which were highlighted in Chapters 2 and 3. The final branch of ethics is applied ethics, which involves specific moral problems, such as abortion, end-of-life issues, climate change, and how one should comport oneself with others. We delve into applied ethics throughout this textbook when we apply the ethical and leadership theories we are exploring to specific case studies.

While these are three separate branches of ethics, they are not separable in practice. Normative systems are informed by what one supplies as the answer to the metaethical question on the nature of 'ought'. This is called metaethical grounding. For example, a Kantian needs to answer the question of what makes an action obligatory. Relevant to virtue ethics, we may wonder whether the goodness of certain traits is grounded in human nature – that having particular virtues (like honesty or temperance) is suitable for the kind of beings we are. Additionally, we might wonder whether certain traits are good because a god recognizes them as such. Without first supplying an answer to the metaethical questions – about the source of the norm – a virtue ethicist is at a loss for naming which qualities are, in fact, good.

Likewise, how one answers an applied ethical question is contingent upon the normative system assumed. An example is that a deontologist may describe the obligations one has to other humans and non-human animals to decide about environmental ethics. A utilitarian may compare the predicted results of different actions, pursuing the greatest good for the greatest number of people. In contrast, a virtue ethicist may wonder 'what kind of person' would recycle or save paper or inquire about what follows from particular virtues. For example, how might a responsible or respectful citizen act in a situation?

To summarize, virtue ethics is a normative system concerned with virtue and character. It is a theory (alongside deontology and consequentialism) by which applied ethical decisions can be made. These decisions will also depend on one's metaethical commitments. Throughout this chapter, we will explore concerns relevant to these three branches – metaethics, normative ethics, and applied ethics.

In the Western tradition, Plato and Aristotle are the founders of virtue ethics, whereas, in the East, the founders are considered to be Mencius and Confucius.[2] In the West, virtue ethics was the dominant moral theory throughout the medieval period, sustained and adapted by voices such as the Roman Stoics and Scholastic theologian Thomas Aquinas. Subsequently, Western moral philosophy was dominated by consequentialism and deontology – presenting mainly the rival views of Bentham and Mill versus Kant, as we saw in Chapters 2 and 3.[3] Recently there has been a revived interest in virtue ethics in the West, led by philosophers such as Anscombe, Foot, MacIntyre, McDowell, and Slote.[4]

When many Westerners think of virtue, they think of the Greek and Roman roots of the virtue theory. However, virtue and vice, as concepts integral to discussions of the good life, are traceable to Islamic, Buddhist, Chinese, Hindu, and Jewish cultures.[5] Virtue ethicists propose accounts of virtue that differ in many ways, such as in the set of virtues named. For example, Buddhists, like Christian virtue ethicists, include humility as an excellence, whereas Aristotle does not. The definitions of common virtues differ among virtue theorists as well. For example, Aristotle and Aquinas depart substantially on the virtue of magnanimity. For Aristotle, the magnanimous person 'deems himself worthy of great things and *is* worthy of them'.[6] He knows his relative value as an agent, is aware of his capacity for doing great things, and does those great things.[7] According to Aquinas, Aristotelian magnanimity commits an error of valuing. It has an 'inordinate desire for pre-eminence'.[8] Contra Aristotle, Aquinas redescribes magnanimity as a kind of excellence that is not maliciously proud. A more substantial difference is that Aquinas lists three theological virtues – faith, hope, and love – which Aristotle does not include. These three theological virtues are also called infused virtues, and we address what makes them 'infused' a bit later in this chapter. An additional difference among virtue theorists is the goal of the good life. Whereas Aristotle describes our greatest good as flourishing, Aquinas describes our greatest good as communion with God, and Buddhists describe our greatest good as Nirvana – a kind of awakened life constituted by virtues and characterized by the ability to see the world as it really is.

In the interest of focusing our attention in the space we have here, we will examine Aristotle's take on virtue ethics. Thus, this chapter focuses on a broadly Western explanation of virtue ethics for brevity and clarity. However, it is important to remember that virtue has broader relevance than exclusively Western voices.

## MAJOR CONCEPTS OF VIRTUE ETHICS

Chances are, you can already name several virtues. If we asked you to name the qualities you admire in a best friend or a favourite teacher, you would probably list a few examples of virtues – honest, trustworthy, humorous, or wise.

### Function

By definition, a virtue is the kind-specific excellence of a thing. The Greek word for virtue, *arete*, literally means excellence. By 'kind-specific', we mean that there are particular excellences proper to different things. A good cat is fluffy, for example. A good tree is not fluffy since this quality is irrelevant to what makes trees excellent. Aristotle investigates the virtues of a thing by asking what something's *ergon*, or function, is. This is called Aristotle's Function Argument. For example, the function of a knife is to cut well. The qualities that permit it to fulfill that function (or to be a good knife) include a sharp blade and a sturdy handle. These are two of the knife's virtues. It would be odd if the good qualities one sought in a pet cat, for example, included a sharp blade or a strong handle. These are not excellences suited to that thing.

However, the question of function becomes complicated when it comes to people. This is because it depends on what kind of thing a human is or what one thinks people are *for*. Are humans *for* amassing power and wealth, maximizing pleasure, or acquiring knowledge? These are answers often supplied by popular culture, sometimes explicitly in advertisements or implicitly in terms of cultural values. For Aristotle, humans are *for* pursuing our greatest good, and our greatest good is *eudaimonia*.

## Eudaimonia

For Aristotle, *eudaimonia* is happiness. Happiness is a plausible candidate for our greatest good because happiness is a goal we seem to hold in common. It is also a good that is an end in itself, rather than a means to some other end. It is good in itself and for its consequences. But what does *eudaimonia* involve?

*Eudaimonia* is not happiness in the sense of a steady stream of happy feelings, which Julia Annas refers to as the 'smiley-face account' of happiness.[9] Some of the self-reported happiest moments of our lives are not smiley moments. Consider climbing mountains or giving birth. Happiness as *eudaimonia* is also not happiness in the sense of desire-satisfaction.[10] First, not all desires are good ones. Some desires, for example, are selfish or unjust. Second, if happiness were desire-satisfaction, this would mean that wealthy, powerful people, such as celebrities – people better positioned to fulfill their desires – would be happier overall. This is not the case.[11] Rather, Aristotle defines *eudaimonia* as a kind of activity of the soul in accordance with virtue and suited to our rational natures.[12] Flourishing is constituted by virtues, albeit not exclusively. (Aristotle also states that there are some accidental conditions of a flourishing life, such as long life and reasonably good health.) Accounts like Aristotle's, wherein happiness is defined as our greatest good, are called *eudaimonist* virtue theories. *Eudaimonism* is the most common form of virtue theory.

We might also apply the function argument to humans in narrower terms than the human life in total, asking about social roles or vocations. Consider a football player. A football player's virtues include speed, strength, and grit. These are not the same virtues relevant for a university professor because being fast and gritty are not qualities conducive to helping professors fulfill their teaching and research functions. These qualities are beside the point.

It can be helpful to think about leadership virtues and eudaimonia in relationship to Aristotle's function argument. We might consider the position we have (e.g. leader of a major corporation or an assistant youth soccer coach) and what would make one successful in that role. In knowing one's function, we are better able to consider how the agent should act and the virtues relevant to develop to excel in that role.

## Moral and Intellectual Virtues

According to Aristotle, one can acquire two kinds of virtues – moral and intellectual. In broad terms, moral virtues are primarily excellences of emotions, whereas intellectual virtues are excellences of reason. Examples of moral virtues include courage (an excellence with respect to the emotion of fear) and temperance (an excellence with respect to pleasure). Examples of intellectual virtues include wisdom (an excellence of knowing what is of value) and practical wisdom (right thinking plus action).

Moral virtues involve hitting a balance, or a middle ground, with respect to emotion. This middle ground is Aristotle's 'golden mean'. Every virtue is a mean between two vices – a vice of excess and a vice of deficiency. For example, a courageous person is not without fear. She has a suitable amount of fear for the situation. Her fear is neither excessive (cowardice) nor deficient (rashness).

A second example is the virtue of wittiness. Wittiness involves taking fitting pleasure in jokes, neither too little pleasure as to be a boor nor too much as to be a buffoon. Unlike moral virtues, intellectual virtues do not have a virtue mean. For example, there is no such thing as being *too* wise. There is no excess of intellectual virtues. There is only a deficiency. It is one thing to be able to identify virtues, but how does one attain them?

## Acquiring Virtues

Both moral and intellectual virtues are acquired rather than a consequence of a person's biology. We are not born with a particular virtue. Instead, to be a virtue, a trait 'must be possessed by someone who has cooperated in its formation'.[13] A virtue is a kind of achievement.

While both moral and intellectual virtues are acquired, they are acquired in different ways. Intellectual virtues, such as practical wisdom, are developed through teaching and experience. Moral virtues develop as habits do – by repeated practice. The focus on personal agency is one of the most helpful features of virtue ethics. There is no mystery about how to develop a good character. We practise in the same way we practise in other domains. Aristotle writes, 'For the things we have to learn before we can do them, we learn by doing them, e.g., men become builders by building and lyre players by playing the lyre; so too we become just by doing just acts, temperate by doing temperate acts, brave by doing brave acts.'[14] If you would like to become a more just person, a more courageous person, or a person who better modulates his or her appetites, you cannot just learn about these qualities or recognize their absence. You have to practise them, too.

We often think about practice in the context of skill acquisition – soccer, running, computer coding, or playing the violin – but we rarely think of character development in this way. We should. In the same way that it is challenging to learn to play an instrument or develop good school habits, we may struggle at first to speak honestly or act justly. Nevertheless, if we stick with it, it starts to feel natural and becomes almost easy. Virtues can become second nature.

One clarification in virtue practice is that this practice is not merely external. In practising virtuous actions, we must also develop the appropriate *motivations* for good actions. A common intuition of virtue is that not all virtue-tracking actions are virtuous if done for the wrong reasons. For example, imagine a wealthy donor who gives a large sum of money to a children's hospital. If we were later to find out that he did so out of a narcissistic hero complex rather than from a genuine concern for the children, we might cease to think he is generous. Part of what is admirable in a virtuous action is the internal state that generates the action – the motivation.

While moral and intellectual virtues are two distinct types of virtues, they have a relationship of mutual dependence upon one another. For example, becoming too angry makes a person less responsive to reason. Another example is that, since we are embodied creatures, if we are intemperate in our desires, this can make it challenging to think clearly. Moreover, certain fallacies, or failures of reason, are actually failures of *moral* virtues. Consider the *ad hominem* fallacy – in which a person attacks an opponent rather than addressing the argument. This is a moral issue, best described as a failure of justice or humility, resulting in an intellectual mistake. We need moral virtues in place in order to reason well.

Additionally, moral virtues depend on intellectual virtues. For example, to take proper pleasure in food (temperance) means one appropriately values food among other goods, and this requires wisdom, or *sophia*. Furthermore, *all* moral virtues rely upon practical wisdom, or *phronesis*. This is because virtues require sensitivity to situations. Consider bravery. Being brave on the soccer field requires different actions than being brave in a classroom or a courtroom. In order to act excellently relative to a given trait requires that we can navigate the conventions of each situation suitably. This demands practical wisdom. Moral virtues depend on intellectual virtues, and intellectual virtues depend on moral virtues.

This is a brief introduction to Aristotelian-informed virtue ethics. We now turn our attention to personality and character.

## PERSONALITY AND CHARACTER

Again, we ask you to name the qualities you admire in a best friend or a favourite teacher. You would probably name virtues, such as patience, wit, or wisdom. However, what if we asked you to describe your best friend (let's call her Sally) in more general terms than only the qualities you admire? You might name some of Sally's physical characteristics, such as being short, athletic, or brunette. These are her non-personality traits. You might also name Sally's personality traits – her psychological or dispositional qualities or how she is inclined to think, feel, and act. When speaking about virtues, we refer to a particular subset of one's personality. Virtues are special because they are normative. Normative means there is an implied 'ought' or 'ought not' to these qualities. We *ought* to be kind. We *ought not* to be deceptive. An example of a *non*-normative personality trait is introversion. It is neither good, bad, right, nor wrong that a person is an introvert. Still, introversion is descriptive of Sally's personality, and this trait disposes her to act in certain ways. An example of a *normative* aspect of personality is generosity. Another is recklessness. Virtues and vices are normative aspects of a person's personality. We are accountable for these qualities, and they are within our control to change.

Thus far, we have used the term 'aspect' of personality because there is some disagreement about what kind of thing a virtue or a vice is. Aristotle uses the word *hexis*, which means an active disposition. A *hexis* is a kind of active habit involving inclinations of thinking, acting, and feeling. For example, a person with the *hexis* of courage may be disposed to *think* courageous thoughts, *feel* suitable fear, and *act* courageously when that person ought. Conversely, some philosophers have characterized virtues as skills, or skill-like.[15] In part, this seems to be because many virtues develop the way skills do, by repeated practice. Another popular characterization of virtues is as traits – specifically, normative traits. A trait involves an 'enduring tendency or disposition'[16] to do or to be one way rather than another, which is how we would also be inclined to describe virtues. Virtues are lasting features of a person's character and are constituted by a set of dispositions to think, act, and feel in ways relevant to that virtue.[17]

So, what does it mean for a virtue to be a trait or an enduring aspect of one's character? It means that a person is reliably or predictably excellent in a given way. To be virtuous means consistently acting well in a given respect, over an extended period of time, across different situations, for the right motivation.[18] For example, if your best friend were honest *once*, you would unlikely consider her honest. Virtues define a person in a stable way – that is, over an extended period of time. Furthermore, if your best friend is honest only when speaking to her friends, and you are aware that she regularly lies to her parents, cheats on quizzes, or evades taxes, you would not be inclined to attribute to her the virtue of honesty either. This is because virtues are cross-situational.[19] A common intuition of virtue is that we should exhibit the virtue in all, or nearly all, areas of life in which the virtue is relevant, rather than just one or two (like only when speaking to friends or exclusively while paying taxes). Lastly, on many accounts of virtue, a good action must be done with proper motivation.[20] Part of what is admirable in a virtuous action is the internal state that generates the action – the motivation.

If you think about it, these are tough requirements. Not only must a person consistently act well in a certain respect and across situations, but that person must also do it for the right reasons to count as virtuous. For Aristotle, virtues are exceedingly rare. Most people do not possess them. Contemporary virtue ethicists have responded to this assumed rarity in different ways. Some lower the standards for virtues in various ways. Others make space for developmental virtues. For example, Christine Swanton describes two kinds of virtues. The first is mature virtues, which are exceedingly difficult to achieve. The second is what she calls 'basic' virtues. These are developmental virtues. They are stage- and ability-specific.[21] The category of basic virtues helps to make sense of how widely we apply the language of virtue, such as towards children, even when they do not meet the high standards of classical virtue. Philosopher Christian Miller provides another alternative. He affirms that most people do not meet the high standards for virtue (or the low standards for vice). Still, we act predictably for the good in some ways, for some of the right reasons, and not for others. He describes the moral majority as having what he calls 'mixed traits' to describe the varying sets of trait-relevant dispositions that people have.[22]

## VARIATIONS AMONG THEORIES

In the preceding sections, we described several critical features of an Aristotelian-informed virtue theory account, introducing some places where there is variation among theories. Some of these variations include the set of virtues named, what aspects of character virtues are best defined as (habits, skills, dispositions, or traits), how rare virtues are, and what flourishing consists of. Earlier in this chapter, we also described how virtue theories are contingent upon one's metaethical commitments.

Thus far, we have explored a *eudaimonist* account of virtue, wherein virtues are constitutive features of the good life. This widely held account of virtues leaves us with an important question: What exactly does it mean to flourish? While flourishing is the kind of thing where we might be inclined to say, 'You know it when you see it,' this seems not to be the case. People often build their lives around the wrong things – such as money, beauty, and power – assuming these things will make them happy. Realistically, these goods are incomplete. Money, for example, is only a means to some *other* good. The same is true of power. Power and money are not goods in themselves. Moreover, beauty fades. It is only a short-term good. In any case, the answer to the question of what flourishing is largely depends on what human nature is or – as we phrased it earlier – what people are *for*.[23] If we can answer that question well, particularly in a pluralistic society where people have different political, theological, and sociological assumptions about humanity, virtue ethics gains more traction.

Setting *eudaimonism* aside, there are alternative forms of virtue ethics. Two alternatives are (a) agent-based accounts of virtue and (b) hybrid virtue ethical accounts.

## Agent-based Accounts

An agent-based account of virtue answers the question of how we know what the virtues are differently from a *eudaimonist*. A *eudaimonist* looks at the features that constitute a good life. The agent-based theorist points to moral exemplars – excellent people. Two prominent agent-based virtue theorists are Michael Slote and Linda Zagzebski. Slote describes his theory as 'treat[ing] the moral or ethical status of acts as entirely derivative from independent and fundamental aretaic (as opposed to deontic) ethical characterizations of motives, character traits, or individuals'.[24] Zagzebski likewise argues that our reflective admiration of morally excellent people is the means by which we encounter what virtues are. Moreover, on an agent-based account, there is no independent grounding for the virtues (such as, perhaps, reflection on human nature).

Indeed, we often learn about virtues through good people. An example is that we learn about wisdom from Gandhi and honesty from Abraham Lincoln. We might learn about courage from Martin Luther King, Jr and patience from our caretakers. These people are our moral exemplars. Furthermore, people not only teach us what goodness looks like; our admiration of them motivates us to do likewise. We are inclined to put on those qualities for ourselves or to emulate these people. Emulation offers us practice in these virtues. Still, a separate theoretical question is whether or not virtues are solely grounded in excellent others, without some additional account for what makes virtues *good* and vices *bad*.

## Hybrid Accounts

Earlier, we described three rival normative ethical systems – deontology, consequentialism, and virtue ethics. It is possible to combine these systems in specific ways. An example is the consequentialist virtue theory proposed by Julia Driver. For Driver, virtues are just character traits that consistently produce good consequences, regardless of the agent's internal condition.[25] Consequentialist virtue ethics is a position that is *not* concerned with moral motivation. It assumes that for a person to consistently act in such a way that they regularly produce good consequences, they likely have suitable motivations to sustain those actions. Driver makes the interesting claim that, sometimes, achieving adequate self-understanding, part of what is often deemed an appropriate internal condition for being virtuous, can impede success in virtue. She names modesty as a virtue for which accurate making accurate self-assessments can impede virtue. However, Driver's position is a minority view in virtue ethics.

A second hybrid account is deontological virtue ethics. An example is Immanuel Kant's account of virtue. For Kant, virtue is 'the moral strength of a man's will in fulfillling his duty.'[26] Virtue is a kind of duty-driven resolve. This definition could not be more different from Driver's proposal. Driver's virtues need not include good motives, whereas Kant's virtues need not yield good results.

Counter Driver and Kant, on most virtue ethical accounts, both motivation and consequence matter for virtue. Good actions should be done with a suitable motivation. A virtuous person will (in general) reliably bring about good results because virtues require practical wisdom in successfully performing good actions.


## VIRTUES AND VICES OF LEADERSHIP

Imagine an excellent student body president. What makes this person excellent? We might be inclined to name intellectual virtues, such as *phronesis* (practical wisdom), fair-mindedness, and attentiveness. These qualities are undoubtedly important. Another crucial intellectual virtue in a leader is *sophia* (wisdom). A wise leader knows what is *truly* of value. This is important because a leader often has many practical skills and can lead effectively, but he or she leads people in the wrong direction. An example is Adolf Hitler. Adolf Hitler's wrongful devaluation of humanity (evidence of a lack of wisdom) exhibited itself in his racism, megalomania, and xenophobia, among his myriad vices. Leadership has to account for both virtues and vices.

### Virtues of Leadership

In considering good leadership, we may be inclined to name *moral* virtues. Temperance will be necessary since our leaders ought to be able to self-govern well. If a leader cannot self-govern effectively, the leader is unlikely to govern others effectively. It is also unlikely that an intemperate leader can think clearly and make good decisions. We might also name fortitude (or courage), patience, and tenacity. Humility is valuable in leaders because it makes a person teachable and adaptable. Humility enables us to act on behalf of one another rather than prioritizing our own interests. It permits us to own up to our mistakes, apologize, and make amends. Humility is an invaluable trait in a leader. It is an invaluable trait in all of us.

In part, the virtues of leadership depend on the specifics of the leadership position. This is because what is required of a leader depends on the situation's particulars, the collaborators' character, and the followers' level of participation. For example, collaboration may be an excellence in a student body president, but it is less excellent in a monarch. In a monarch, it may be a source of vulnerability and signal a lack of resolve. This is because, traditionally, monarchs have been required to act autonomously, or, at least more so than a student body president. Also, consider a leader working among associates or followers who have flawed moral characters. In this situation, it may be better for the leader to act independently rather than collaboratively.

Often, leaders need to be good listeners. Rarely, such as when a leader possesses unique expertise, listening to others might make a leader less successful. For example, it would not benefit a master electrician to listen to the masses about how to wire an attic successfully. Another example is the quarterback on the football field. As he calls the plays, the quarterback needs to be decisive. To pause and ask for feedback while in action would impede the team's performance. Being in the habit of welcoming insights in both situations would be unhelpful to leaders. However, in most instances, listening to followers is vital to the leadership process. Nonetheless, it is important to consider what virtues are called for in the particular leadership position a person is inhabiting.

## Vices of Leadership

In the previous section, we stated that Adolf Hitler was (unsurprisingly) a bad leader. He was bad in many ways, broadly characterized by many as evil. This observation is a crucial point about leadership. Someone may be an effective initiator of actions, highly motivating, and command attention. However, insofar as this person is not leading others in ethical ways, this is not a *virtuous* leader. It is a bad, or unvirtuous, leader. Joseph Stalin, the Soviet dictator, and Atilla the Hun, dubbed the 'Scourge of God', are additional examples. In these three cases, 'bad' leadership refers in a general sense to their moral character. All three men were broadly unvirtuous, and this led to unspeakable harm and human death.

However, there is another way to be a bad leader. It is by being ineffective in that role. For example, a person can be wise, love all the right things, and be disorganized. A disorganized leader will fail to mobilize people suitably. Timidity may make a leader ineffective, too. Lack of practical wisdom is a vice difficult to overcome in a leadership capacity. Another example of a potential vice is spontaneity. This is an interesting vice. In other contexts, such as friendship or artistry, spontaneity can be an asset. Yet, in the context of leadership, spontaneity can seem impetuous or abrupt. It makes a leader seem less trustworthy or dependable. Recall Aristotle's Function Argument as a means of discerning which qualities count as excellences and defects of a thing. Thinking in terms of 'function' is often a helpful way to discern which qualities make one a good or a bad leader. For example, it may be the case that spontaneity enriches friendship, but spontaneity can impede fulfilling one's function as a leader. In this sense, it is a vice, not a virtue of leadership.

In her text on failures of leadership, appropriately entitled *Bad Leadership*, Barbara Kellerman lists several additional vices of leaders. Examples include intemperance, callousness, and rigidity.[27] We might also add pride, laziness, and impatience. There are many ways to fail in positions of authority, and we are sure you can name several examples of vices by thinking about the bad characteristics of leaders we have observed over the years.

A final thought about virtues and vices is this: we often cannot anticipate when we will find ourselves in positions of leadership, and because the development of virtues takes time, experience, education, and practice, virtue ethics emphasizes the point that it is essential to develop a good character now, rather than assume we can shift gears and act like someone else later.

Now that we have a better understanding of virtue ethics let's take a moment to explore some of the criticisms of the theory.

## CRITIQUES OF VIRTUE ETHICS

There are a few common objections to virtue ethics. To clarify, these are not objections to the idea that we should have good characters or exhibit virtues. The objections are to the explanatory value and practical use of a theory based on the concept of virtues. Four common objections regard action-guidingness, egoism, situationism, and moral luck.

### Action-guidingness

The action-guidingness objection goes like this: Virtue theory is framed in terms of what we ought *to be* rather than what we ought *to do*.[28] Virtue theory is concerned with norms of character rather than norms of action. In that sense, it is not a helpful guide for moral actions. Or, put less harshly, virtue theory is a *less* helpful guide than either consequentialism, for which we can weigh results to decide what to do, or deontology, which is codifiable as a set of rules or principles from which to act.

This is a persistent critique of virtue ethics. Virtue ethics is a normative theory often excluded from applied ethical discussions about the environment, for example. Discussions about the environment are often framed in terms of the *rights* of certain beings – plants, animals, humans – or the *duties* humans have to do one thing rather than another (deontology). Other discussions are framed in terms of weighing goods – often economic goods, such as convenience or money versus competing interests (consequentialism). However, the exclusion of virtue ethics seems to be a mistake. As Thomas E. Hill, Jr points out, our intuitions about what makes a person *selfish* or *proud* (two vices) are often stronger than what (for example) is *owed* to the local deer or a grassy field.[29] Regarding strip mining of the Appalachian Mountains, Hill points out that it can be clarifying to ask the question, 'What sort of person would do a thing like that?'[30] In this way, virtue ethics *is* action-guiding. It offers an alternative perspective to what can sometimes be heady, theoretical conversations about rights and duties or consequentialist conflicts about which result has higher utility.

### Egoism

The egoist critique of virtue ethics is as follows: A theory of goodness and badness should not be rooted in a person's happiness. That's selfish! A good person should act for others.

In part, this critique seems to be founded on a misunderstanding. Rosalind Hursthouse points out that while the virtuous person is indeed likely to be happy, this does not mean the virtuous person's *motivation* for virtuous actions is to be happy. It is a mistake to assume that a virtuous person 'acts as she does because she believes that acting thus on this occasion will help her to achieve *eudaimonia*'.[31] Acting with the motivation to secure one's happiness is not a suitable motivation for being charitable, for example. This motivation would disqualify the action as virtuous. A suitable motivation would be something like love for others.

Furthermore, the virtuous person is a better instance of her kind than the non-virtuous person. Considering humans are social animals, developing the virtues (or excellences) of that social nature is a means by which people become better citizens, family members, and friends.

Honest, just, patient people are not egoistic in how they inhabit the world. Rather, they are more likely to be altruistic.

## Situationism

The situationist critique of virtue ethics was a movement at its peak in the 1960s and 1970s.[32] The main idea is that the *situation* one is in, rather than a person's *character*, is the salient factor in how a person behaves. Some philosophers, such as Doris and Harman, put it more strongly: No character traits exist.[33] Our actions are a function of the situations in which we find ourselves.

For example, in the infamous Stanley Milgram experiment, participants were asked to administer shocks to students who gave the wrong answers on a test. The participants were not genuinely administering shocks, but they did not know this. While they heard students screaming with increasing intensity in the next room, most participants were willing to administer deadly levels of shock to the students simply because the proctor asked them to. The takeaway of the experiment was that people are willing to do *surprising* things (even things that oppose human decency) in certain situations, such as while under the guidance of authority figures. While many people described themselves as humane and compassionate, they failed to act in terms of these qualities when prompted to do otherwise in the laboratory. So, maybe these traits do not really exist.

At this point, the debate is largely settled, with virtue theorists satisfied to have answered the critique. There are a few different responses virtue ethicists have supplied over the years. Some have argued that virtue is, as Aristotle described, exceedingly rare. Therefore, we should not expect that it will be common for people to exhibit virtues in the laboratory. Virtue is the exception, not the empirical norm. Others point out that, in the original transcript from the Milgram experiment, many participants expressed severe internal turmoil during the task, feeling compelled to press on against their better judgment in the odd empirical setting. Others have pointed out that laboratory settings are short-term, singular experiences, and virtues are qualities that are dispositional trends across a person's lived experience. Failing to act in terms of a virtue in a singular, staged scenario in a laboratory is not a threat to the existence of traits. It is not indicative of much at all.

Other contemporary virtue ethicists have gone the empirical route, engaging in psychological work to refine our understanding of virtues and their expression. For example, as we introduced earlier, Christian Miller proposed 'mixed traits' to explain the varying sets of trait-relevant dispositions that people have, which do not usually meet the high threshold of traditional virtue and vice. Miller also points out that people seem to have, what he calls, 'surprising dispositions'.[34] These are situational forces that activate certain mental dispositions, allowing us to act in particular, surprising ways. Examples include inclinations to harm others in the face of legitimate authority and inclinations against helping when we think we will be disapproved of.[35] In becoming sensitive to these surprising dispositions, we can better 'see' and anticipate the expression of traits as they really are.

## Moral Luck

A final objection to virtue ethics is moral luck. The problem of moral luck, as it pertains to virtue ethics, is this: We are praiseworthy and blameworthy for our good and bad character, but our character may not be entirely *up to us*. This seems unfair.

For example, suppose a person is biologically constituted such that she has a hot temper. In that case, it may be more difficult for her to develop virtuous anger – being angry at the right things, in the right ways, to a suitable intensity – than for someone who is naturally more measured in her responses to things. It can seem unfair that the second person has a disposi-tional head start or fewer roadblocks to developing virtue.

A second example is early education and caretaker exposure.[36] Aristotle writes of the impor-tance of early moral habituation: 'It makes no small difference to be habituated this way or that way straight from childhood, but an enormous difference, or rather *all the difference*.'[37] For Aristotle, if someone does not have good early moral training and habituation, then we have missed a critical window of time for that person to form virtue. Most contemporary virtue ethicists do not share Aristotle's severe conclusion about a window closing altogether. However, it does seem true that it is *easier* to develop good habits in childhood when we are actively forming habits for the first time than to redirect oneself from bad habits later in life.

The question of moral luck is important and, in part, an empirical question. Is it, in fact, the case that certain people are biologically or developmentally disadvantaged for developing good characters? Or do we *all* have a say in improving our characters to some degree? If moral luck is a significant part of what makes us good and bad people, how does this change the way we extend praise and blame? If nothing else, the problem of moral luck should turn us to gratitude for any goodness we see in ourselves and perhaps help us to extend more grace or humanity toward those who are morally blameworthy.

## FIVE COMPONENT ANALYSIS

Virtue ethics provides a helpful blueprint for determining how to behave morally. The vocab-ulary of virtue ethics helps us understand what traits we should look for in leader behaviour. Naming excellence is crucial as it allows us to decipher between good and bad character. This is particularly important from a leadership perspective as character strongly impacts the leader/ follower relationship and how ethical decisions are made. Virtue ethics provides a beneficial strategy for determining good leadership character (Figure 4.2).

McManus and Perucci define leadership as 'the process by which leaders and followers develop a relationship and work together toward a goal (or goals) within a context shaped by cultural values and norms'.[38] As shown in the Five Components of Leadership Model, virtue ethics focuses on the leader's character and how it impacts every area of the leadership process. The Model highlights this relationship with the arrows pointing outwards from the leader. There is a clear need to account for virtue ethics in the leadership process. Isolating each com-ponent of the Model shows the importance of having a virtuous leader who consistently does the right thing at the right time for the right reasons. It is pivotal to develop leaders of character

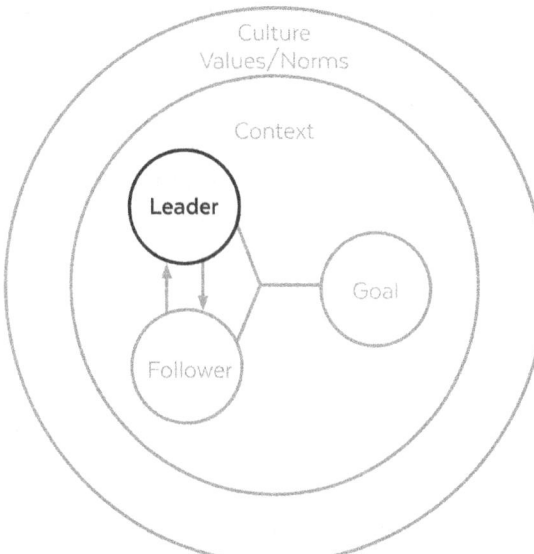

**Figure 4.2**   The Five Components of Leadership Model applied to virtue ethics

who understand not just what leadership is but what it means actually *to be* a good leader and how this impacts more than just the follower.

How do we judge a good leader? Can we hold them to a higher ethical standard than we hold ourselves? Surely we cannot expect them to be perfect; that would be an unreliable assessment of goodness. Good leadership should be measured by a leader's intention, values, beliefs, and what they stand for – this is also known as character.[39] The word 'character' is rooted in Greek to mean an engraved mark, a symbol, or an imprint on the soul. When a leader's character makes an engraved mark on a follower, we could consider this an influential process.

When the leader influences a group of followers, they are responsible for doing so ethically. Leaders are uniquely positioned to have power and control over various elements of the leadership process, as depicted in the Model. With increased power comes increased responsibility and ethical burdens. Leaders should make every effort to act in a virtuous way to benefit rather than damage the leadership process. As we can see in the Model, the influence goes beyond the leader/follower relationship. The process of leadership influences all the layers of a leadership event. In his book *Leadership*, James McGregor Burns focuses on ethics and morality by asking, 'what is a good leader?'[40] Understanding the virtues tied to leadership is essential as they help answer Burns' question. A leader's 'goodness' is inextricably tied to virtue – good character happens through practice. This practice happens by engaging in virtuous behaviours (he refers to them as modal values), specifically in how they treat followers.[41] To get a complete understanding of this relationship, we must pay close attention to the follower.

The Five Components of Leadership Model highlights the importance of virtuous behaviour because of the leader's impact on multiple areas of the leadership process – beginning with the follower. The effect of virtuous leadership on the follower's moral action is vital. A leader's virtuous behaviours can motivate followers to perpetuate the virtuous spiral and enhance their followers' lives.[42] Such behaviours serve as a buffer against dysfunction and illness at the individual and group level by encouraging resilience, hardiness, and even protection from trauma and stress. Both leaders and followers have a moral duty to act ethically. This duty is consistent regardless of positional power and influence. A commitment to ethical values and the daily practice of such commitment meets the functionality of virtue ethics. It allows leaders and followers to act honourably in the workplace while fulfillling their obligations and meeting organizational goals, which can be seen in the Model's centre alongside the leader and follower.

Leadership is not just about the relationship between leader and follower but also the pursuit of a goal. For goals to be achieved, the leaders and followers must work together. James MacGregor Burns believed that a leader's job should be to mobilize followers towards a goal.[43] The virtuous behaviour of leaders can influence goal achievement through several mechanisms. Firstly, and as previously stated, the ethical behaviour of a leader has a considerable impact on followers' well-being and motivation. In some situations, the leader can act as a teacher, showing them how to achieve a goal and motivating them in the process. After all, goal achievement is the result of the combined efforts of many individuals. Secondly, goals are achieved when a follower trusts the leader. A virtuous leadership style enhances trust more than other leadership styles.[44] Trust is also a key player in the process of empowerment. Empowerment helps followers tackle hardships and achieve the unachievable. Thus, a virtuous leader helps to create a context in which followers can trust their leader and feel empowered to reach the desired goal. Finally, the leader and follower's behaviour mutually influences the context, as well as the cultural values and norms. A leader's virtues can amplify the organizational experience, positively impacting the leader/follower relationship and the larger context. Likewise, vices can have the inverse effect, negatively impacting the leader/follower relationship and context. Contrarily, the context and culture in which the leader and followers are embedded helps to establish the virtues the leader is expected to emulate and the vices the leader is expected to shun.

Having discussed the core concepts of virtue ethics and its application to the Five Components of Leadership Model, it is time to place it into a case study. The following case takes an in-depth look at how people can choose to act unethically and not virtuously. The case focuses on failures of character: United States Air Force Academy Cadets cheating on exams. Cheating often symbolizes the failings and failures of people we would otherwise assume to be trustworthy. It is a classic example of moral failure. This case asks the age-old question, 'who are you when no one is looking?'

## CASE STUDY: COVID-19 AND THE UNITED STATES AIR FORCE CHEATING SCANDAL

*We will not lie, steal, or cheat, nor tolerate among us anyone who does. Furthermore, I resolve to do my duty and to live honorably, (so help me God).*
–Honour Code of the United States Air Force Academy.

The Covid-19 pandemic in March of 2020 turned the higher education system in the United States upside down. Universities across the country quickly shifted their courses online. Virtual education was unfamiliar to many institutions, and faculty were thrust into online learning without instruction and experience in the new platform. Students, however, familiar with all things technological and social, were more confident in their ability to navigate a complex learning system.

Few institutions were prepared for the challenges that came with online learning, and specifically cheating. Academic cheating typically falls into three categories: conscious deception, self-deception, and ignorant deception. Each category focuses on intentional deceit in which the student is consciously and voluntarily engaged. Many students used the distance from peers and instructors as an opportunity to cheat. They became creative in their ability to game the proverbial system to earn high marks on tests and assignments. As it became increasingly evident that there had been an increase in cheating amongst college students, faculty members struggled with dealing with the situation. Educational institutions were unaware of the measure students took to get an easy, high grade. Take, for example, a 'student' who logged in to take a pre-med chemistry test at a well-known mid-Atlantic university.[45] This student, however, was no student at all. Instead, he was a hired ringer being paid to take the test. A proctor hired by the university discovered this by reviewing video recordings of students taking exams. They noticed that this person had taken tests for at least ten different students enrolled at universities across the country.[46] The ringer had a spreadsheet on his wall that indicated student names, schedules, and course login information.

This case was far from unique. The problem is that many believe that what they were doing is not, in fact, dishonest. For example, websites such as Course Hero, Chegg, and Quizlet (to name a few) provide students with copies of tests from students who have already taken them.[47] The sites typically require an account and subscription fees. As students upload old tests and answers, they can receive 'credits' for answers on other exams provided by 'tutors' who work for the websites. Many students do not believe this behaviour is cheating but rather another way to prepare for an exam.

Usage on testing sites exploded during the pandemic. Chegg is perhaps the most significant facilitator of academic dishonesty and has become synonymous with cheating. Students refer to this as 'chegging'.[48] For a fee, students have access to millions of textbooks and exams. Students across the country have indicated that if they do not want to study for an exam or learn the material, 'they can chegg it' – in other words, they can cheat. A study by *Forbes* showed that out of 52 students interviewed, 48 said they regularly used Chegg to cheat.[49]

While it seems easy to blame Chegg or other online sites for the increase in cheating, the problem is character. Although many students believe 'the ends justify the means', they fail to realize that the process devalues any degree they obtain. Rather than doing the right thing of due diligence in studying and work, they are taking the easy way out and rooting their character in dishonesty, imprudence, and a lack of integrity.

In January 2021, the Air Force Academy announced a scandal in which 249 cadets were implicated in academic cheating. Examples of their infractions included using online tutoring websites to receive exam solutions, failing to cite sources on papers appropriately, and collaborating with peers on exams. The infractions occurred in the spring of 2020, following the Academy's quick transition from in-person classes to virtual learning for most of the student body due to the Covid-19 pandemic.

The Air Force Academy has an honour code like all military and other academic institutions. Cadets pledge to 'not lie, steal, or cheat, nor tolerate among us anyone who does', and they are held accountable for infractions. At the time of the Academy's announcement, two cadets were dismissed from the Academy. At the same time, the vast majority were placed on probation and sentenced to participate in remediation, dedicating themselves to additional honour code training and instruction.

Why should we care about good character? The short answer is that we are in great need of it. The recent surge in academic cheating is one example. The transition from in-person to online instruction saw unprecedented increases in cheating behaviours, and the Air Force Academy was not unique in this predicament. In 2021, the military academy West Point likewise reported its worst cheating scandal in over 40 years, and colleges and universities throughout the United States experienced similar phenomena.[50]

These increases in cheating are attributable to increased web access and student autonomy in the virtual classroom, alongside waning academic motivation and waxing pandemic anxieties. Students are stressed. Moreover, it is easier, in some ways, to cheat in the virtual classroom than in the in-person classroom, with the internet at one's disposal and removal from the supervision of professors. However, while institutions saw a rapid increase in academic infractions during the recent pandemic, this new problem was not new. Rather this marked the continuation of an upward trend institutions have seen for decades. Students cheat now more than ever. For example, in 2012 a study reported that more than two-thirds of university students admitted to cheating over the previous year.[51] This finding is an increase from just 23 per cent of students self-reporting cheating in 1940.[52]

Academic cheating undermines a student's ability to learn in the classroom. Cheating subverts classroom justice for everyone in the classroom (not just for the person cheating) and destabilizes relationships among students and with their professors. Cheating also offers a student practice in building the wrong sorts of habits, which will very likely translate into how the student participates in society and the workplace. For these reasons, these statistics should be worrying.

It can be valuable to examine the institutional and systemic features of a situation that incline groups toward unethical actions. In the current rise of academic cheating, one might wonder about deficiencies in the virtual classroom, social pressures, and an incentive structure in academia that leaves students preoccupied with securing good grades over genuinely learning. It is also valuable to examine individual accountability and the qualities of persons that incline one to cheat or not.

Few institutions take their honour code more seriously than military academies in the United States. Even with strict adherence to a robust honour education system, these academies were not spared from the increased cheating seen at non-military affiliated institutions. Like many institutions, the USAFA has a judiciary process run by fellow cadets. As such, the Academy waited for students to return to campus during the fall 2020 semester before taking punitive measures.[53] Due to Covid restrictions, the process was slow, but the Academy was committed to the process. In all, 249 cadets were found guilty of violating the honour code.[54] Two cadets were dismissed from the Academy, while the remaining 247 were placed on probation and remediation. The USAFA received criticism for how it handled the cheating scandal. USAFA Superintendent Lt Gen. Richard M. Clark defended the process but recognized the ramped cheating highlighted the need to evaluate and refresh the policies. They have sought help from consultants to review the honour programme and see how processes can be improved, as well as examine internal processes, structures, and activities associated with the honour programme, according to the Academy. However, they remain adamant that peer-to-peer accountability is a crucial part of the process that will continue throughout their military career.

According to virtue ethics, every person possesses the disposition to behave virtuously.[55] It is human nature to strive for goodness. Cheating is not virtuous and is considered to be far from an admirable trait. In Aristotle's words, being virtuous is a 'capacity to judge and do the right thing in the right place at the right time in the right way'.[56] Among the classical seven virtues, honesty is particularly relevant to the cheating phenomenon. Many students would consider themselves to live a virtuous life, which is contrary to the nature of cheating. Academic dishonesty can be viewed from several ethical perspectives. Reviewing the case study elements from an ethical lens, one can easily see why students were tempted to cheat and justified their actions. Cheating has become commonplace and somewhat of an expected phenomenon in institutions of higher learning. Academic dishonesty is found in morally bankrupt students and the overall campus climate. Regardless, no one can be blamed for the increase in cheating but the student themselves. The question is, how do we consider virtue ethics when evaluating the cheating crisis? The underlying cause of cheating is a change in what is considered right and wrong. Ethically virtuous behaviour, however, is acquired and demonstrated through practice. Moral character that focuses on virtues of honesty, trust, and excellence of character would not tolerate any form of deception and dishonesty. Developing virtuous habits strengthens character and the desire to resist temptations to do what is not consistent with virtuous behaviour. Aristotle recognized the need for rules like honour codes to prohibit specific actions and provide recommendations for related judicial consequences to maintain consistency in virtuous habits.[57]

## FIVE COMPONENT ANALYSIS

We can now turn our attention to the way McManus and Perruci's five components of leadership relate to the Air Force Academy cheating scandal (Figure 4.3). In this case, we see a collapse in ethically virtuous behaviour. Virtue ethics states that a person should do the right thing, at the right time, and for the right reasons. When this is not adhered to, there is a ripple effect, and many things are impacted. Looking at the Model, we can note how intertwined the leadership process is. If a leader, in this case, a cadet, acts unethically, the message sent to fellow cadets – the followers – is that such behaviour is acceptable. It sends the message that straying from morality to reach a goal is acceptable if no one notices – cheating is only a problem if you get caught.

The cadets failed to realize the negative impact their decision to cheat would have on the Academy, the military, and higher education as a whole. Not only was their character damaged, but the future of their career as military officers was also placed in jeopardy. The Model highlights how the cheating behaviour of a leader and follower would undoubtedly derail goals, in this case, to follow the Honour Code. In this case, many cadets were placed on probation, required to do extra service, and, in some cases, expelled from the Academy. Regardless of the consequence, the decision to cheat left a permanent mark on their academic record – a Scarlett letter symbolizing the question of character.

We previously noted that the ethical decisions of leaders and followers in their pursuit of goals impact the context and culture. The Air Force Academy had a long history of being respectable and honourable – a reputation that came into question when the Academy moved to online education due to the Covid-19 pandemic. Many argued that the trust they had in the USAFA had been dismantled. The culture of the USAFA was challenged, and as a result, it was changed. USAFA leadership decided the honour code needed to be revamped and that an emphasis should be placed on why it is important to live ethically.

The cheating scandal at the USAFA impacted the higher education community. This particular scandal was only a manifestation of a larger cheating culture that is a part of many colleges and universities. If cheating could happen at such a prestigious institution, it could happen

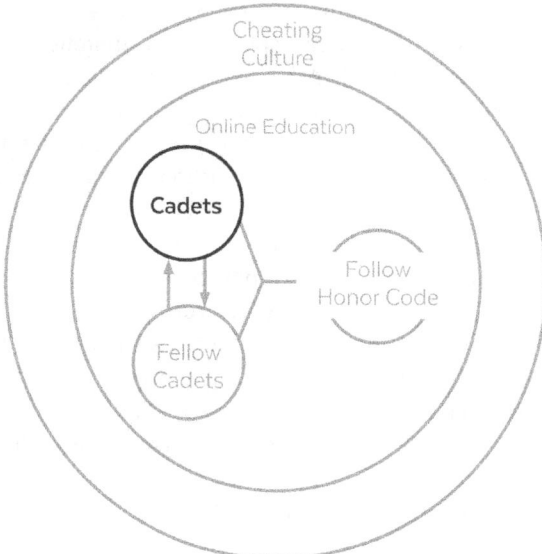

**Figure 4.3**    The Five Components of Leadership Model applied to the Air Force cheating scandal

anywhere. Institutions worldwide are implementing safeguards to prevent cheating scandals on campus. More universities are developing stricter honour codes and stricter punishments for violating the honour codes. A university's culture is created by those within it, their actions, and their decisions.

## SUMMARY AND CONCLUDING REMARKS

To summarize what has been discussed in this chapter, we refer back to the original framing question: What virtues should a leader possess to act ethically? While there is not a solidified answer to this question, we have argued in this chapter that when a leader acts virtuously, they are focused on living a life in a morally good way. Doing so requires daily practice and commitment.

It is crucial to develop leaders who understand not just what leadership is but what it means to *be* a good leader. This development impacts the entirety of the leadership process. Behaviour is often rooted in who the person is. If we look back at the case study on cheating at higher education institutions, we can conclude that the cheating behaviour is rooted in the kind of person each student is. One could easily assume that what motivates each student is not virtuous behaviour but rather a desire to succeed at any cost. While the students know what it means to follow the honour code rules, they fail to make ethically sound decisions when faced with the opportunity to cheat. These situations are not isolated to higher education but rather permeate various factions of society. Evaluating and understanding how one develops into an ethical person is fundamental. By providing a contemporary and historical overview of the components of virtue ethics and how they fit in the larger Five Components of Leadership Model, we hope you will begin to look at virtuous leadership as not something that is mastered but something that is practised daily.

## DISCUSSION QUESTIONS

1. How would you define 'virtuous behaviour', and what does that look like in a leader?
2. Virtue is the disposition to do the right thing for the right reason, in the appropriate way – honestly, courageously, and so on. What is the role of the leader in this process?
3. Aristotle claims virtues are fixed by our human nature. Do you agree? Can the virtues be relative to a specific culture and time? Are they fixed or absolute?
4. Can you think of any historical or contemporary leaders who leaned into their vices rather than virtues? What impact did this have on their followers?
5. Think of a time when you were in a situation that had an 'easy way out' that required less than virtuous behaviour. How did you respond? Why did you respond that way?
6. Think of a time when you responded virtuously to a challenging situation. Why did you choose to behave as you did?

## ADDITIONAL RESOURCES

B. George, *Discover Your True North*, Hoboken, NJ: John Wiley & Sons, 2015.

Bill George's authentic leadership theory focuses on leaders behaving in a way that is consistent with their positive values.

J. Ciulla, *Ethics, the Heart of Leadership*, 3rd edn, Westport, CT: Praeger, 2014.

This book is often used in the field of leadership studies when studying leadership character and values.

R. Hursthouse, *On Virtue Ethics*, New York: Oxford University Press, 1999.

This text is helpful for those interested in learning about virtue ethics from an introductory standpoint.

C. Johnson, *Meeting the Ethical Challenges of Leadership: Casting Light or Shadow*, Thousand Oaks, CA: Sage, 2019.

This book allows for a look at what happens when leaders choose not to act virtuously and its impact on various areas, including followers.

# NOTES

1. K. Kristjánsson, 'Emulation and the use of role models in moral education', *Journal of Moral Education*, vol. 35 no 1, 2006, 37–49.

2. R. Hursthouse and G. Pettigrove, 'Virtue ethics', *The Stanford Encyclopedia of Philosophy*, Winter 2018 edn, ed. Edward N. Zalta. https://plato.stanford.edu/archives/win2018/entries/ethics-virtue/ (accessed 18 July 2022).

3. R. Hursthouse, *On Virtue Ethics*, New York: Oxford University Press, 1999, pp. 1–3.

4. Hursthouse, *On Virtue Ethics*.

5. J. Frey, 'What is virtue and why does it matter?', *Fordham Institute*, 18 November 2021. https://fordhaminstitute.org/national/commentary/what-virtue-and-why-does-it-matter (accessed 18 July 2022).

6. Aristotle, *Nicomachean Ethics*, trans. R. Bartlett and S. Collins, Chicago, IL: Chicago University Press, 2011, p. 1123a35.

7. C.A. Boyd, 'Pride and humility', in K. Timpe and C.A. Boyd (eds), *Virtues and Their Vices*, Oxford: Oxford University Press, 2014, p. 248.

8. Aquinas, *De Malo* VIII.2.ad.16.

9. J. Annas, 'Happiness as achievement', *Daedalus*, vol. 133 no. 2, Spring 2004, 45.

10. Annas, 'Happiness as achievement', 45.

11. Annas, 'Happiness as achievement', 45–8.

12. Aristotle, *Nicomachean Ethics*, I.13.

13. R. Roberts, 'Humor and the virtues', *Inquiry*, vol. 31 no. 2, 1988, 127–49, p. 142.

14. Aristotle, *Nicomachean Ethics*, II.2.4.

15. See J. Annas, 'Virtue as skill', *Philosophical Studies*, vol. 3 no. 2, 1995, 227–43; and M. Stichter, 'Ethical expertise: the skill model of virtue', *Ethical Theory and Moral Practice*, vol. 10 no. 2, March 2007, 183–94. See also Aristotle when talking about constitutive goods early in *Nicomachean Ethics*.

16. C. Miller, *Moral Character: An Empirical Theory*, New York: Oxford University Press, 2013, p. 5.

17. See C. Miller, *Character and Moral Psychology*, New York: Oxford University Press, 2014, pp. 31–8 for more information regarding virtues and traits.

18. Miller, *Moral Character*, pp. 16–19.

19. Miller, *Moral Character*, pp. 16–19.

20. Miller, *Moral Character*, p. 24.

21. C. Swanton, 'Developmental virtue ethics', in J. Annas, D. Narvaez and N.E. Snow (eds), *Developing the Virtues: Integrating Perspectives*, New York: Oxford University Press, 2016, p. 125.

22. A better (earlier) source would be as follows: Miller, C.B. *Character and Moral Psychology*. Oxford University Press, 2014, pp. 43–61.

23. American author, Wendell Berry, has a collection of essays by this name. W. Berry, *What are People For?: Essays by Wendell Berry*, New York: North Point Press, 1990.

24. M. Slote, *Motives from Morals*, New York: Oxford University Press, 2001, p. 5.

25. J. Driver, 'Modesty and ignorance', *Ethics*, vol. 109 no. 4, 1999, 827–34.

26. I. Kant. *Metaphysics of Morals*, 6.390.

27. B. Kellerman, *Bad Leadership: What It Is, How It Happens, Why It Matters*, Cambridge, MA: Harvard Business School Press, 2004.

28. Hursthouse, *On Virtue Ethics*, p. 25.

29. T.E. Hill, Jr, 'Ideals of human excellence and preserving natural environments', in Louis P. Pojman, Paul Pojman and Katie McShane (eds), *Environmental Ethics: Readings in Theory and Application*, Boston, MA: Cengage Learning, 2017, pp. 26–36.

30. Hill, 'Ideals of human excellence', pp. 26–7.

31. Hursthouse and Pettigrove, 'Virtue ethics'.

32. Miller, 2014, op. cit., p. 85.

33. J.M. Doris, 'Persons, situations and virtue ethics,' *Nous*, vol. 32 no. 4, 1998, pp. 504–530. See also G. Harman, 'Moral philosophy meets social psychology: Virtue ethics and the fundamental attribution error,' *Proceedings of the Aristotelian Society*, vol 99 no 1, 1999, pp. 316–31.

34. C. Miller, 'On Kristjánsson on Aristotelian character education,' *Journal of Moral Education*, vol. 45 no. 4, 2016, pp. 490–501, p. 498.

35. Miller, *Moral Character*, pp. 498–9.

36. Hursthouse, *On Virtue Ethics*, p. 116.

37. Aristotle, *Nicomachean Ethics*, 1103b, 23–5.

38. R.M. McManus and G. Perruci, *Understanding Leadership: An Arts and Humanities Perspective*, 2nd edn, New York: Routledge, 2020.

39. J. Gardner, *On Leadership*, New York: The Free Press, 1990.

40. J.M. Burns, *Leadership*, New York: Harper, 1978.

41. Burns, *Leadership*, p. x.

42. D. DeGraaf, C. Tilley and L. Neal, 'Servant-leadership characteristics in organizational life', in L.C. Spears and M. Lawrence (eds), *Practicing Servant Leadership*, Indianapolis, IN: Jossey-Bass, 2004, pp. 133–65.

43. Burns, *Leadership*.

44. M. Hendricks, M. Burger, A. Rijsenbilt, E. Pleeging and H. Commandeur, 'Virtuous leadership: a source of employee well-being and trust', *Management Research Review*, vol. 43 no. 8, 2020, 951–70.

45. D. Newton, 'Another problem with shifting education online: a rise in cheating', *The Washington Post*, 7 August 2020. https://www.washingtonpost.com/local/education/another-problem-with-shifting-education-online-a-rise-in-cheating/2020/08/07/1284c9f6-d762–11ea-aff6–220dd3a14741_story.html (accessed 18 July 2022).

46. Newton, 'Another problem'.

47. Newton, 'Another problem'.

48. Newton, 'Another problem'.

49. S. Adams, 'This $12 billion company is getting rich off students cheating their way through COVID', *Forbes*, 31 March 2021. https://www.forbes.com/sites/susanadams/2021/01/28/this-12-billion-company-is-getting-rich-off-students-cheating-their-way-through-covid/?sh=6298c87b363f (accessed 18 July 2022).

50. M. Hill, '51 West Point cadets caught cheating must repeat a year', *Associated Press*, 18 April 2021. https://www.armytimes.com/news/your-army/2021/04/18/51-west-point-cadets-caught-cheating-must-repeat-a-year/ (accessed 15 October 2022).

51. E. Collins, 'Harvard cheating scandal sheds light on culture of cheating', *USA Today*, 2 September 2012. https://www.usatoday.com/story/college/2012/09/02/harvard-cheating-scandal-sheds-light-on-culture-of-cheating/37396983/ (accessed 15 October 2022).

52. D.L. McCabe, L.K. Treviño and K.D. Butterfield, 'Cheating in academic institutions: a decade of research', *Ethics & Behavior*, vol. 11 no. 3, 2001, 219–32.

53. H.H. Seck, 'Dismissals and discipline at Air Force Academy after 249 cadets investigated for cheating', *Military News*, 29 January 2021. https://www.military.com/daily-news/2021/01/29/dismissals-and-discipline-air-force-academy-after-249-cadets-investigated-cheating.html (accessed 18 July 2022).

54. Seck, 'Dismissals and discipline'.

55. T. Bretag and M. Green, 'The role of virtue ethics principles in academic integrity breach decision-making', *Journal of Academic Ethics*, vol. 12 no. 3, September 2014, 165–77.

56. A.C. MacIntyre, *After Virtue: A Study in Moral Theory*, Notre Dame, IN: University of Notre Dame Press, 1984.

57. MacIntyre, *After Virtue*.

# 5
# Ethical egoism

*Jon Rogers and Robert M. McManus*

## FRAMING QUESTION

What is self-interested leadership??

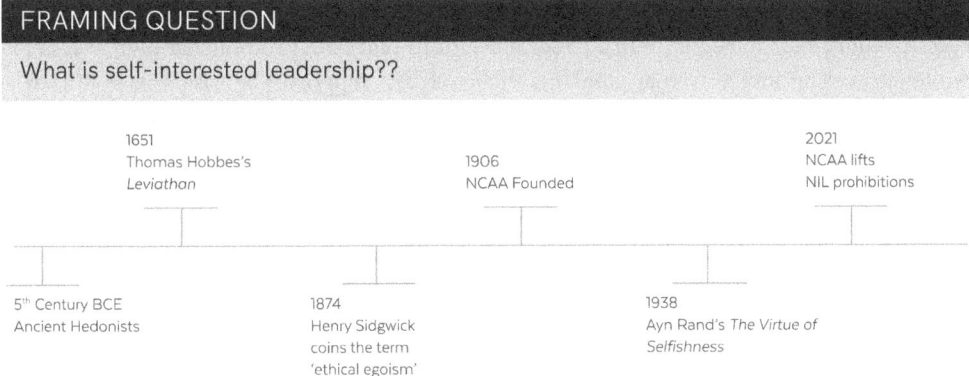

**Figure 5.1**    Timeline of major works on ethical egoism in relation to the chapter case study

Considering the appropriate way for leaders to act in a morally fraught situation is relatively straightforward when the outcomes of the situation will only affect the leader. A leader deciding whether to tell the truth about something they have done can make this decision far more easily if they only assess the benefits and risks of various courses of action for how they will be impacted. If we can tease out our interests from the interests of others who stand to be affected by our decisions, it is far simpler to come to conclusions about how to act. This ability to untangle the leader's interests from the interests of their followers is rare, however, and in most ethical dilemmas will not be straightforward.

Ethical egoism is the moral framework that suggests that each person should act in a way that best maximizes their self-interest. Often, when we hear of egoism, it is in the context of self-interest that is at odds with the interest of the followers: a CEO who thwarts the efforts of her stakeholders in order to build a platform to better her own interests, or a politician who focuses on his standing in the next election rather than the concerns of his constituents. Ethical egoism can also be a moral approach to leadership, however. It can also look like the CEO balancing her work life with her time for family and her own well-being, thereby empowering her employees to do the same. It can look like the politician focusing on re-election because of all of his progress in addressing his constituents' concerns, allowing the results to speak for themselves.

Ethical egoism differs significantly from the ethical theories introduced earlier in this book because it does not focus directly on others. Kantianism asks leaders to think categorically about what the right thing to do is in terms of what should be obligatory for all. Utilitarianism asks leaders to do the thing that brings about the greatest amount of good for the greatest number of people. Ethical egoism could appear hedonistic because it does not require leaders to consider others first, but instead asks them to promote their own well-being.

This tension does not create quite as wide a divide as it seems. For example, the CEO in our example can't simply act any way that she would like, treating employees poorly, neglecting to pay invoices, or not listening to her board's advice. If she does, she will not ultimately achieve what is in her own self-interest, to remain CEO. To act as an ethical egoist, she needs to acknowledge that her well-being is tied up with the well-being of her stakeholders. Ethical egoism would encourage her to make moral decisions that both promote her own well-being while also acting in a way that gains her stakeholders' support. Likewise, the politician is required as an ethical egoist to work in a self-interested way. Still, if concentrating on winning the upcoming election is what serves his best interest, then he is forced to consider the interests of his constituents to gain their votes. This chapter will assess ethical egoism as a way for leaders to consider what is in their best interests and apply the theory to a case study highlighting student-athletes in the National Collegiate Athletic Association (NCAA) profiting from their name, image, and likeness to understand the idea in action.

## HISTORY AND MAJOR CONCEPTS OF ETHICAL EGOISM

Like virtue ethics, ethical egoism traces its roots to Aristotle. Aristotle proposed that all human activity aims to maximize what he called *eudemonia*, or human flourishing. Though Aristotle believed that being a virtuous person was the ticket to maximizing flourishing, it could be argued that his emphasis on flourishing also lays the foundation for ethical egoism.[1]

### Ancient Hedonism

Aristotle's concept of *eudaimonia* is perhaps the most well-known in the ancient world, but other theorists proposed a similar emphasis on self-interest. Yangzi, a Chinese philosopher who lived around 400 BCE, wrote about the concept of *wei wo*, which translates roughly to acting for oneself, or valuing the self over rulers or government.[2]

The ancient hedonists also are sometimes considered to be ethical egoists. Hedonists believed that pleasure should always be maximized while pain should always be minimized. Ethical hedonism is the theory that the right thing to do is to maximize pleasure.[3] Utilitarianism gets its roots from this idea, but ethical hedonism lacks the emphasis on others that utilitarianism highlights. Without focusing on maximizing the good for the greatest number of people, ancient ethical hedonism begins to resemble ethical egoism in its focus on self-interest.

However, this relatively reductive view of ethical hedonism does have one significant difference from modern ethical egoism. Hedonism emphasizes maximizing pleasure over pain, but pursuing pleasure and pursuing self-interest do not ultimately yield the same results. The politician might take a great deal of money from donors involved in lobbying that his followers would find distasteful to expedite his campaign. This money could maximize his pleasure in the short term because it would allow him to spend the campaign funds. Taking a longer-term view of self-interest, however, might prompt the politician to decline the funds to maintain the integrity of his campaign and the trust of his followers in order to win the re-election. Egoism mandates that the focus is on self-interest, which sometimes means suppressing desire in order to work towards what is ultimately in one's best interest.

Epicurus is perhaps the ancient Hedonist whose philosophy most closely resembles ethical egoism. Epicurus did not follow the theories of many other hedonists who sought to maximize pleasure in all ways. Instead, Epicurus advocated for a more moderate and sustainable version of pleasure that resembled freedom from anxiety or worry. He rejected the pursuit of pleasure that could lead to distress or tension.[4] In this way, Epicurus advocated for a self-interested view of ethics that is nearer to ethical egoism than his contemporaries.

## The State of Nature

Thomas Hobbes, whose theories we will come across later in this book in our discussion of Social Contract theory (Chapter 10), introduced a view of the state of nature that created the conditions by which ethical egoism arises.[5] Hobbes proposed that humans are, by nature, in conflict with one another. He advocated that humans must become communal in order to protect their self-interest. Imagine, Hobbes urged, that you are living in a society of hunter-gatherers. If you must leave your house daily to hunt and gather food, and your neighbours need to do the same, it will quickly become necessary to come to some communal agreements. It would be in my self-interest to avoid stealing the food my neighbour leaves behind as she goes hunting and gathers food to have her agree to leave my food alone when I leave my home. It doesn't benefit me for us to enter into a back-and-forth of food stealing, and it doesn't benefit my neighbour either. Though our interests are separate, agreeing to cooperate and avoid stealing from one another shows that we can enter into a social contract that benefits both of us. Returning to our CEO, this means that she might want to steal the trade secrets of her competitor's company but refrains from doing so to avoid years of litigation over intellectual property. She doesn't treat her competitor well because she is altruistic; she does it out of an ethical framework grounded in self-interest.

It is important to note that *ethical egoism is not psychological egoism*. Psychological egoism is a *descriptive claim* that human motivations for action are based on self-interest. Ethical egoism differs from psychological egoism because it makes a *normative claim* in the domain of morally right or wrong actions. Ethical egoism maintains that to act morally, a person *ought to* behave in their own self-interest. Outside of morality, ethical egoism makes no claims about human motivations for action. Table 5.1 summarized the different approaches to egoism.

**Table 5.1**  Summary of different approaches to egoism

| Concept | Authors | Summary |
| --- | --- | --- |
| Psychological egoism | Thomas Hobbes | Human judgment is easily misguided, so we must focus on our self-interest (Descriptive) |
| Rational egoism | Ayn Rand | Since the basis of morality is self-interest and reason defines a person's self-interests, a person has a rational responsibility to pursue those interests |
| Ethical egoism | Also seen in Hobbes | A person *should* act in his or her own self-interest (Normative) |
| Consequentialism | John Stuart Mill | A person should promote, increase, or create the best state of affairs for the greatest number of people |
| Deontology | Immanuel Kant | Regardless of the possible benefits, a person's actions must be constrained by certain considerations |

## Henry Sidgwick

Henry Sidgwick, a philosopher who was definitively *not* an ethical egoist, would eventually name ethical egoism in his 1874 book *The Methods of Ethics*.[6] Sidgwick was a staunch utilitarian who wrote about ethical egoism to contrast its methods to those employed by utilitarians. Sidgwick aimed to address the critique of utilitarianism as being hedonistic or only focused on pleasure. He argued that utilitarianism is not self-interested because of its emphasis on maximizing the greatest good *for the greatest number*, which could ultimately lead to the subjugation of self-interest in favour of amplifying what is good for the majority. In contrast, ethical egoism, a term he coined, would focus simply on maximizing self or individual interest. Sidgwick also proposed a third method of ethics, Intuitionism, which is the idea that some moral truths are self-evident and universally agreed upon. This idea is similar to the concept of universal ethics, which is explored later in this book (see Chapter 7).

Sidgwick viewed ethical egoism as problematic, not because it was immoral, but because he saw it as incompatible with utilitarianism. He considered the ethical mandates of acting in a way that promotes your self-interest and operating in a way that advances the interests of the community to be both intuitive and contradictory. For leaders, this might be said to be especially true. Leaders cannot ignore their self-interest, or for most there would be very little motivation to lead. But leaders who neglect the interests of the community of followers they lead may begin to slide down the slippery slope toward a form of leadership that closely resembles a dictatorship. Sidgwick offered little resolution to this conflict, only a hope that leader and follower interests would magically align.

## Ayn Rand

Ayn Rand was not so sure that Sidgwick should be so hopeful. Rand described her version of ethical egoism as selfishness rather than self-interest.[7] Rand's book, *The Virtue of Selfishness*, outlined a theory of laissez-faire leadership that proposed that people ought to act selfishly without the interference of rules and regulations. Rand believed that all interaction, including that between leader and follower, must be free of coercion or control. If everyone is truly free to act selfishly, Rand says, it is likely that most would come to realize that the well-being of others is an advantage even to the most self-interested. For example, if I am self-interested, I would likely want to be educated. Education is not as effective in isolation – I need other educated people to discuss ideas, develop a curriculum, and teach it effectively. If I want to live in an educated community, I also likely want it to contain good schools, transportation, and adequate infrastructure such as roads. Rand identified as a radical individualist, but this does not mean that she believed ethical egoists should be isolated or reclusive.

Now that we have a bit of a better understanding of ethical egoism, let's hear some of its criticisms.

## CRITIQUES OF ETHICAL EGOISM

The primary criticism of ethical egoism is the idea that it could actually lead to unethical action. There is, perhaps justifiably, a concern that any moral theory rooted in self-interest is bound to lead people to ignore the rights and interests of others. Self-interest might lead people to steal, lie, or cheat without regard for the effects this may have on others.[8] This criticism is a good reminder of the importance of distinguishing between maximizing pleasure, as the hedonists strived to do, and acting out of self-interest. Self-interest will often coincide with the interests of others, given the inevitability of community. The threat of consequence or punishment for universally unethical action would be enough to deter the ethical egoist if they are genuinely self-interested.

A second criticism of ethical egoism is that it provides no mechanism for resolving conflict between two self-interested parties. As Sidgwick pointed out, self-interest will often align with the self-interest of others, and when this happens, ethical egoism works well. When there are conflicts between two self-interested leaders or the interests of the leader versus the interest of the group, then this criticism must be taken seriously.[9] Even resolving conflicts between two occurrences of self-interest within the same person can be difficult. Maybe the politician wants to go to bed early after a long week of campaigning and acknowledges that he will be able to think and speak more clearly in a debate scheduled for the next day if he is well-rested. On the other hand, staying awake would give him more time to prepare to represent his constituents better. What is the right thing to do? There is no clear answer for the ethical egoist. Both options are grounded in self-interest of the sort that ethical egoism requires.

A final criticism of ethical egoism might be its rootedness in the Western world view. Egoism certainly is intertwined with individualistic values that promote and allow for self-interest. It would be an unfamiliar concept in groups that value collectivism, though not unheard of, as seen in the philosophy of Yangzi, as outlined earlier. Yangzi's thoughts were developed in the context of ancient China, which on the whole valued collectivism. His ideas rejected the government and the collectivist notion of ethics that dominated ancient Chinese thought.[10] Thus, although self-interest may be a hallmark of individualist cultures, it is certainly found in more collectivist cultures as well.

Now that we have a better understanding of ethical egoism and its various forms and implications, we can apply it to the Five Components of Leadership Model.

## FIVE COMPONENT ANALYSIS

For leaders, ethical egoism is a complex moral theory. The mandate that leaders make ethical decisions based on what best maximizes their self-interest can look very different depending on the leader's perspective. Narcissism and radical self-care can both be viewed as extreme applications of ethical egoism. In reality, the purest application of ethical egoism is likely somewhere in the middle and could be summarized by the old cliché that you can't pour from an empty cup. Ethical egoism mandates that leaders first serve themselves so that they can lead effectively. This section will explore how ethical egoism relates to the Five Components of Leadership Model.[11]

Returning to the idea of the politician seeking re-election, if we assume that the politician is running for a position in representative government, it is easy to assume that the politician is ethically obligated to represent their constituents' interests fully. But what if this means that the politician loses re-election? This loss could be a failure for the politician and constituents if the candidate is genuinely the best one to advocate for their needs. The politician must get past the hurdle of being re-elected before she is ever in a position to represent and advocate for the followers in her district. In this case, an ethical egoist would recommend that the leader focus on her own self-interest and do what it takes to win re-election but also consider the fact that her self-interest is bound to the interests of her followers. She cannot compromise herself so much in the service of winning the election that she loses their support.

For the purposes of the Five Components Model, the leader is the component that is emphasized above all else (Figure 5.2). Though the leader must work with followers in some capacity, the leader is responsible for setting the goal based on their self-interest. This raises a question for the third component of the model: the goal. Is it possible to have a common goal when the leader is motivated by self-interest? It is; however, this would essentially be a coincidence or out of the leader's need to satisfy the followers to serve the leader's own self-interest.

To revisit the cliché that you cannot pour from an empty cup, the leader must take care of her needs in

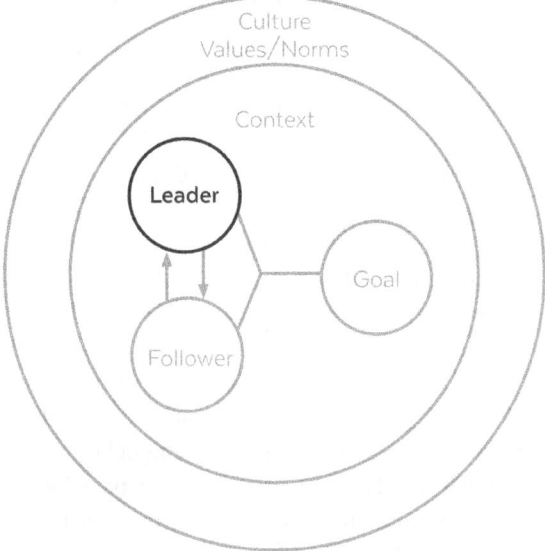

**Figure 5.2**    The Five Components of Leadership Model applied to ethical egoism

order to take care of her follower's needs. The politician must be elected before she can begin to address the failing school system in her district. In this instance, the leader's goal to be elected coincides with the followers' goal to have her elected in order to address their needs; therefore, their goal is a common one. In fact, in this case, the leader's ability to reach her goal actually rests on the follower's goal because without addressing the followers' goal, the leader cannot reach her own.

It would be easy to interpret this to mean that for ethical egoism, self-interest is instrumental. Filling one's own cup so that you can pour into others implies that the reason behind acting in a self-interested way is because it ultimately allows you to serve your followers more effectively. Though this is sometimes a positive outcome of ethical egoism, this is not actually its intent. *Ethical egoism's focus on leaders acting out of self-interest is the end; it is not merely a means to serve followers.*

The context of any situation in which a leader acts self-interestedly will inform how self-interest is defined, just as the cultural values and norms that inform the leadership moment will. For ethical egoism, however, they are more explanatory than instructive. Egoism focuses so heavily on the leader's interests that it largely ignores these other components.

Now that we have seen how ethical egoism relates to the Five Components of Leadership Model let's see how the theory works in a particular situation. For that, we turn to our case study that features collegiate athletes profiting from their name, image, and likeness.

## CASE STUDY: THE NATIONAL COLLEGIATE ATHLETIC ASSOCIATION (NCAA) AND STUDENT-ATHLETES PROFITING FROM THEIR NAME, IMAGE, AND LIKENESS (NIL)

College athletics have long been a staple of universities and colleges across the United States. Considered the front porch of the institution, football, basketball, and other athletic teams are often the primary means by which the public identifies and interacts with an educational institution of higher learning. And collegiate sports are big business. In 2019, college athletics accounted for more than 18 billion dollars in revenue for institutions belonging to the NCAA.[12] These proceeds may come in the form of government and institution support, ticket sales, media rights, donor funding, and other more minor or tangential sources.[13] Athletics is also an essential recruitment tool for US colleges and universities. Athletic teams are a vital part of an institution's brand. They are a compelling factor in a student's desire to attend a particular college or university, whether they even play on a team, translating to billions of dollars in tuition and fees.

Until recently, the student-athletes powering these economic engines were forbidden from profiting from their contribution to these institutions except for receiving scholarships to attend school. Players were prohibited from receiving any sort of financial compensation or gifts in kind from their institution, boosters, or outside companies. Breaking these rules resulted in stiff penalties for student-athletes and their universities. However, in 2021 the NCAA lifted the ban on players profiting from their name, image, or likeness (NIL). Many saw this as a matter of fairness to allow athletes a piece of the pie they themselves had baked.

Nevertheless, the NCAA ruling also opened a Pandora's box of other ethical implications. This case study examines the issue of college athletes profiting from their NIL from the standpoint of ethical egoism and further explores the ethical implications of the NCAA's policy. We will also place this leadership situation on the Five Components of Leadership Model to better understand this issue through this ethical lens. But first, we need to examine the background surrounding this situation.

The NCAA's roots date back to 1905 when President Theodore Roosevelt convened the athletic leaders from top universities to confront football players' severe injuries and deaths in collegiate programmes. However, the official founding of the NCAA dates to 1906 and the 62 charter members of the Intercollegiate Athletic Association of the United States (IAAUC), whose mission was to 'regulate the rules of college sports and protect young athletes'.[14] The IAAUC was renamed the National Collegiate Athletic Association in 1910 and expanded its role to provide national championships to member schools. Throughout the decades since its inception, the NCAA has grown and has increased its focus to incorporate its student-athletes' academic interests. The NCAA also separated into Division I, II, and III and enlarged its mission to address Title IX, which is US federal legislation that prohibits discrimination based on sex in collegiate athletics. Thus, throughout its existence, the NCAA has expanded its focus to include various issues related to regulating collegiate athletics, including student-athlete name, image, and likeness rights.

Prior to 2021, the NCAA prohibited student-athletes from receiving compensation for their participation in collegiate athletics beyond the cost of attendance of the educational institution - essentially tuition and fees, room and board, books, and a few other limited educational-related costs. The NCAA's primary argument was that student-athletes were amateurs and, thus, by definition, could not be paid for their participation in sports. However, in 2021, in the *NCAA vs. Alston* case, the United States Supreme Court struck down the NCAA's rules restricting the number of education-related benefits schools could provide to their athletes. The plaintiffs in the case claimed that the NCAA violated the Sherman Act, a US 1890 anti-trust law protecting free trade.[15] The Supreme Court agreed. In response, the NCAA temporarily lifted its rules against players profiting from their NIL in July 2021.[16] Before this time, NCAA athletes were prohibited from receiving compensation for advertising or endorsing products while playing for their school. With the NCAA's lifting of their policy, players could now capitalize on their fame by selling merchandise that displayed their name, appearing in media advertisements, and endorsing products. Players could now also use a lawyer or marketing agent to help oversee and advocate for their financial affairs, which would have previously resulted in a loss of eligibility to play for their team before the NCAA lifting its policy. The NCAA's temporary ruling allowed the organization to comply with the Supreme Court decision until a more permanent solution could be offered. In the meantime, student-athletes must adhere to a patchwork of NIL laws within the states where their college or university is located.

Of note, the Supreme Court's ruling and the NCAA's current policy *does not affect* the prohibitions on colleges and universities paying athletes to play for their teams or offering improper recruiting incentives. However, in practice, NIL rights may prove to be a bit more of a slippery slope in this regard. We will return to this later in the case study.

Our case illustrates some of the essential components of ethical egoism. First, as stated above, ethical egoism is the moral framework that suggests that each person ought to act in a way that best maximizes their own self-interest. In our case, players can now pursue their financial self-interests while pursuing their education and playing sports. Second, rather than being opposed to the interests of their universities and teams, the students' self-interests are compatible with the colleges and universities they attend and the teams on which they play. After all, the better their team performs, the more likely their own continued financial success.

Contrarily, although the NCAA's lifting of players' NIL prohibitions allows players to pursue their financial self-interests, it may also open the door for potential unethical behaviour. For example, although the NCAA has reaffirmed its commitment to avoid pay-for-play and improper inducements tied to choosing to attend a particular school,[17] in practice, it would seem that the NCAA's change in NIL policy has opened to door for some parties to skirt these rules with lucrative NIL contracts to incentivize athletes to attend their institutions. *Sports Illustrated* reported that head coaches at prominent institutions have bragged about the NIL opportunities their institutions offer players who attend their schools. Louisiana State University coach Ed Orgeron recently declared, 'We're paying players now: name, image, and likeness, So if you guys wanna start paying our players, you can go ahead!'[18] Alabama coach Nick Saban recently boasted that his sophomore quarterback was approaching one million dollars' worth of endorsements.[19] Ohio State's top prospect quarterback skipped his senior year of high school so he could earn endorsements.[20] And a booster for the Miami Hurricanes promised each player on the team $500 if they endorsed his business.[21] To have equal competition, all parties must abide by the same rules. At this point, colleges and universities, as well as the boosters who support them, are still prohibited from providing financial incentives to players to attend particular schools. But it seems that many are not following the spirit of the NCAA's commitment.[22]

Ethical egoists might suggest that all this competition is actually good for players. Individual players may earn more in NIL deals, but that does not mean that these deals are good for these players and collegiate athletics in the long term. Such a system may create an unethical environment that undercuts fair play. The 1970s and 1980s were rife with scandals throughout NCAA sports programmes, including paying for recruits, point shaving, and academic cheating. Although NIL may be good for individual players in the short term, collegiate athletic coaches, players, and teams that bypass or outright break the rules often do long-term damage to the reputation of the NCAA and everyone involved. It would be counterproductive to collegiate sports to return to these days even if NIL policies were in the short-term best interests of the players. As mentioned earlier in this chapter, the primary criticism of ethical egoism is the idea that it could actually lead to unethical action. This criticism seems to ring true in the NIL controversies swirling around collegiate athletics today.

Likewise, much of the appeal of collegiate sports is based on amateur athletes, the love of the game, and the academic institutions for which they play. Although a few high-profile players go on to very lucrative careers in professional sports, the vast majority of NCAA athletes do not. By skirting the recruiting and pay-for-play rules, collegiate sports look more like professional sports every day. This image seems to be an unintended side effect of the new NIL policies.

Take, for example, the use of the transfer portal. The transfer portal is an NCAA database that allows student-athletes to declare their intent to transfer between colleges and universities. Players are allowed a one-time transfer between schools without sitting out a season. There have already been high-profile cases of athletes moving from one school to another and scoring large NIL contracts.[23] These deals may also be supported by billionaires and collectives who can pool their money to incentivize top athletes to attend their alma maters with big NIL deals.[24]

But so what? Isn't all this competition good for individual players? Isn't that the whole point of ethical egoism? The answer is 'yes' and 'no'. Yes, ethical egoism encourages individuals to prioritize their self-interests, but NIL's thinly veiled pay-for-play incentive often upsets the parity between institutions and harms fair play. In essence, those schools that can offer more financial incentives for high-performance players will always have the advantage on the athletic field. Professional sports leagues have attempted to minimize this through measures such as salary caps and prioritizing draft picks for poorer-performing teams. However, the NCAA's current standards do not seem to provide sufficient regulation. Thus, wealthy teams or teams with access to wealthy boosters or collectives have an unfair recruiting advantage. This lack of parity can also translate to decreased interest in the sport. After all, who wants to watch a game when the winner is essentially determined in advance? These financial incentives can also lead to an increased cynicism about collegiate sports in general, further damaging the NCAA and the educational institutions involved. So, although lucrative NIL deals may be in the short-term interest of particular players, they may not be in the NCAA's long-term interests, the universities they play, the future of collegiate athletics, or the athletes themselves.

Recall that another concern about ethical egoism is that any moral theory rooted in self-interest is bound to lead people to ignore the rights and interests of others. All parties would be wise to remember the importance of distinguishing between maximizing pleasure – the short-term pay-out from a lucrative NIL contract or obtaining a high-performance player – and acting out of self-interest – ensuring a fair and evenly matched contest between rivals. Both of these options are grounded in self-interest of the sort that ethical egoism requires.

## FIVE COMPONENT ANALYSIS

Now let's turn to the Five Components of Leadership model to understand how our case study relates to ethical egoism and leadership (Figure 5.3). In this instance, the leader would be the individual players on collegiate athletic teams. The followers in this case would be the teams and the institutions for which they play. The goal would be for the players and their teams to win games that can lead to prestige and financial gain for both the players and their teams and institutions. The context is the recent lifting of the NCAA's regulations of players profiting from their name, image, and likeness. The cultural values and norms at play are the expectations that individuals profit from within systems of fair play.

For the purposes of the Five Components Model, the leader is the component that is emphasized above all else. In this case, an ethical egoist would recommend that the player obtain the best NIL deal they can in order to serve their own self-interest but also to consider the fact that the player's self-interest is bound to the interests of their team and collegiate sports overall. Neither the player nor the team can compromise so much in the service of winning personally or collectively that the player or the team damages their own reputation or the overall reputation of collegiate athletics and NCAA sanctions for flouting the rules. The goal, in this case, is not a common goal but a mutually beneficial goal to the leader and the followers.

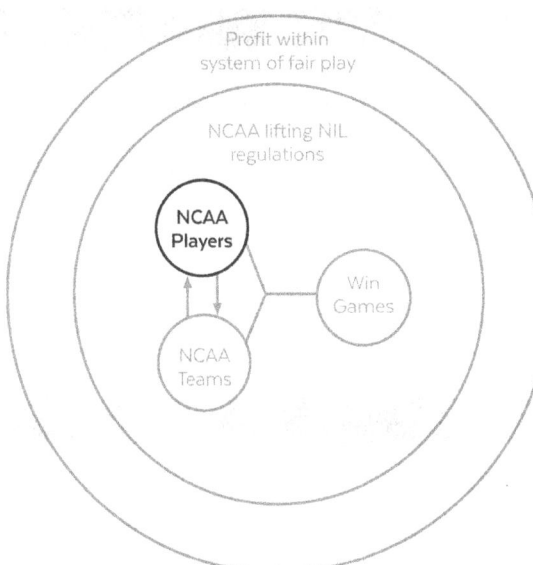

Winning games benefits both parties. The context, in this case, is evolving. The NCAA's prohibition on players profiting from their name, image, and likeness barred players from fully serving their self-interests. However, the current lifting of the NCAA's NIL policy has created an environment that may lead to unfair recruiting practices, pay-for-play, and an overall unethical environment. Ethical egoists in this context must be mindful that their long-term interests may face negative repercussions if they focus solely on short-term economic gains. This leadership situation is set within the cultural values and norms of individuals being able to profit within the bounds of fair play. If the players or the teams or intuitions for which they play profit

**Figure 5.3** The Five Components of Leadership Model applied to the NCAA and NIL case study

unfairly through unethical or illegal recruiting practices and skirting the NIL rules, they risk hurting their long-term goals. As seen here, because egoism focuses so heavily on individual interests, it risks ignoring the other components of the leadership process. Ethical egoism is a helpful way for leaders to consider their self-interests, but they must employ it with thoughtful caution.

## SUMMARY AND CONCLUDING REMARKS

At the beginning of the chapter, we set out to explore the question, 'what is self-interested leadership?' Self-interested leadership can mean many things but, for the ethical egoist, it does not mean that leadership is hedonistic, narcissistic, or selfish. It also does not mean that leadership must be rooted in the sort of self-care that takes the leader away from their long-term priorities. Self-interested leadership, according to ethical egoism, means that the leader sets their goals based on what serves them well and understands that the leader's function within a community means that, more often than not, the leader will address the interests of the followers either coincidentally, or intentionally in cases where the leader needs the followers' goals to be satisfied in order to pursue their own. Finally, it is essential to remember that all of the theories explored in this text are pieces of the larger puzzle of ethical leadership – to use ethics to inform decision-making and to use one's leadership position for positive ends. Leaders must use all the ethical theories at their disposal to make ethically informed decisions lest they run the risk of failing to use their leadership to reach positive purposes for all parties involved.

## DISCUSSION QUESTIONS

1. Think of a recent decision you have made. How much was self-interest a relevant consideration? Should it have played a larger or smaller role in your decision-making? Why?
2. Can ethical egoism be considered a foundation for leadership if it does not always rely on a common goal? If so, how so?
3. With what elements of ethical egoism do you agree? With what elements of ethical egoism do you disagree? Why?
4. How might leaders and followers balance ethical egoism with other approaches to ethics, such as Kantianism, utilitarianism, or the common good?

## ADDITIONAL RESOURCES

A. Rand, *The Virtue of Selfishness*, New York: Signet, 1964.

This book succinctly summarizes Rand's egoist arguments in a more direct form than her fictional novels, such as *Anthem*, *Atlas Shrugged*, and *The Fountainhead*, although her novels are more memorable and are often referenced as testimonies to her objectivist philosophy.

T.L. Price, *Understanding Ethical Failures in Leadership*, Cambridge: Cambridge University Press, 2006.

This is a good resource to explore more about the potential implications of egoist leadership.

# NOTES

1.  T. Nagel, 'Aristotle on eudaimonia', *Phronesis*, vol. 17 no. 3, 1972, 252–9.
2.  E. Fox-Brindley, *Individualism in Early China: Human Agency and the Self in Thought and Politics*, Honolulu: University of Hawaii Press, 2010.
3.  J. Hastings (ed.), 'Hedonism', in *Encyclopedia of Religion and Ethics*, Edinburgh: T&T Clark, pp. 567–8, p. 567.
4.  D. Sedley, 'Epicurus, On Nature, Book XXVIII', 1973.
5.  T. Hobbes, *Leviathan*, ed. Edwin Curley, Indianapolis, IN: Hackett, 1994 (1651/1668).
6.  H. Sidgwick, *The Methods of Ethics*, London: Macmillan and Co., 1874.
7.  A. Rand and N. Branden, *The Virtue of Selfishness: A New Concept of Egoism*, New York: New American Library, 1964.
8.  S. Rachels, 'Nagelian arguments against egoism', *Australasian Journal of Philosophy*, vol. 80 no. 2, 2002, 191–208.
9.  D. Gauthier, *Morals by Agreement*, Oxford: Clarendon Press, 1986.

10. R. Villaver, 'Does *guiji* mean egoism?: Yang Zhu's conception of self', *Asian Philosophy*, vol. 25 no. 2, 2015, 216–23.

11. R. McManus and G. Perruci, *Understanding Leadership: An Arts and Humanities Approach*, New York: Routledge, 2015, p. 15.

12. F. Richter, 'U.S. college sports are billion-dollar game', *Statistic*, 2 July 22021. https://www.statista.com/chart/25236/ncaa-athletic-department-revenue/ (accessed 9 October 2022).

13. Richter, 'U.S. college sports'.

14. NCAA.org, History, 2022. https://www.ncaa.org/sports/2021/5/4/history.aspx (assessed 9 October 2022).

15. T. Witter, 'From "student-athletes" to "players": a review of the 2021 legal developments shaping a new reality of college sports', 6 January 2022. https://www.jdsupra.com/legalnews/from-student-athletes-to-players-a-6189761/#5 (accessed 9 October 2022).

16. M.B. Hosick, 'NCAA adopts interim name, image, and likeness policy', *NCAA Media Center*, 30 June 2021. https://www.ncaa.org/news/2021/6/30/ncaa-adopts-interim-name-image-and-likeness-policy.aspx (accessed 9 October 2022).

17. Hosick, 'NCAA adopts'.

18. R. Dellenger, 'The first thing to understand about NIL is that nobody fully understands NIL', *Sports Illustrated*, Daily Cover, 26 August 2021. https://www.si.com/college/2021/08/26/ncaa-recruiting-name-image-likeness-daily-cover (accessed 9 October 2022).

19. H. Holland, 'Nick Saban of Bryce Young's NIL deals: "It's almost seven figures"', *Sports Illustrated*, Fan Nation, 20 July 2021.
https://www.si.com/college/alabama/bamacentral/bama-central-nick-saban-bryce-young-seven-figures-nil-deal-july-20-2021 (accessed 9 October 2022).

20. R.D. Russo, 'Top QB recruit to skip senior year of HS and join Ohio State', *AP News*, 2 August 2021.
https://apnews.com/article/sports-college-football-ohio-texas-longhorns-football-ohio-state-buckeyes-football-ae3a662b2ab1b2cebf123fcd912c4767 (accessed 9 October 2022).

21. J. Salvador, 'Local gym owner plans to pay Miami football scholarship players $500 a month', *Sports Illustrated*, 6 July 2021. https://www.si.com/college/2021/07/06/gym-owner-pay-university-of-miami-football-players-monthly (accessed 9 October 2022).

22. D. Dodd, 'NCAA aims to crack down on boosters disguising "pay for play" as name, image and likeness payments', 3 May 2022. https://www.cbssports.com/college-football/news/ncaa-aims-to-crack-down-on-boosters-disguising-pay-for-play-as-name-image-and-likeness-payments/ (accessed 9 October 2022).

23. B. Smith, 'NIL and the transfer portal: which schools get caught cheating?', *Sports Illustrated*, Fan Nation, 4 May 2022.
https://www.si.com/college/ucf/college-football-news/nil-transfer-portal-ncaa-cheating-scandel (accessed 9 October 2022).

24. R. Dellenger, 'Sources: NCAA enforcement begins attempted NIL crackdown with Miami inquiry', *Sports Illustrated*, 14 June 2022.
https://www.si.com/college/2022/06/14/miami-nil-inquiry-ncaa-john-ruiz (accessed 9 October 2022).

# 6
# Care ethics

*Keren Tanguay and Alexandra K. Perry*

## FRAMING QUESTION

What obligations do leaders have to care for their followers?

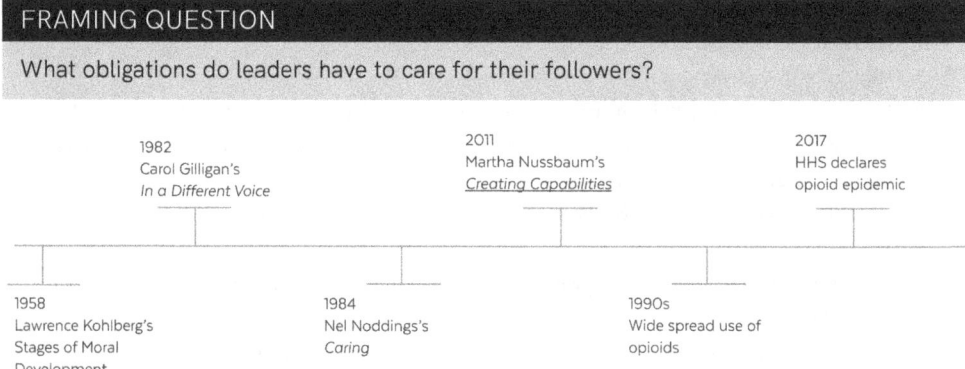

**1982**
Carol Gilligan's
*In a Different Voice*

**2011**
Martha Nussbaum's
*Creating Capabilities*

**2017**
HHS declares
opioid epidemic

**1958**
Lawrence Kohlberg's
Stages of Moral
Development

**1984**
Nel Noddings's
*Caring*

**1990s**
Wide spread use of
opioids

**Figure 6.1**     Timeline of major works on care ethics in relation to the chapter case study

A few months after getting a new cell phone service some fees started showing up on my bill which led me to call the customer service line. As I waited for my inquiry to be connected to a live person, a little phrase was iterated by a recorded voice: 'Please wait as we connect you with your care agent.'

*Care agent.* The verbiage struck me. Presumably, neither I nor my soon-to-be assigned 'care agent' had ever met. But this interaction created a leader–follower relationship. By facilitating the word *care*, a common goal, and perhaps even a set of obligations, had been established. I, the follower, expected this agent to be caring, to take care of me by answering my questions, and maybe by issuing a refund for these fees. By being designated a care agent, this leader now had an obligation to care for a customer they had never met, to do everything in their ability to demonstrate a caring disposition towards me, the follower, to satisfy the goal. Thus, it would seem that the term 'care' can form relationality, even without a previously existing relationship.

The term 'care' is utilized and iterated in numerous and diverse settings. It can be used to refer to ordinary things (e.g. I care about the Green Bay Packers), or it can be used to refer to more weighty things (e.g. I care about healthcare equity among underserved populations). The word 'care' as a vocabulary and a sentiment can be uttered over a vast continuum. However, in this chapter, we will look at 'care' within the discipline of care ethics, which many claim to be capable of guiding moral and ethical action among individuals and society. We will then apply the theory to a case study examining a doctor's obligation to care for patients who are intravenous drug users.

## HISTORY

Unlike many moral theories in the study of ethics, care ethics is one of the newer approaches, only a few decades old. Starting in the early 1980s, several scholars contributed to the development of care ethics as a discipline. Though it had yet to be formulated as a cohesive discipline at the time, care ethics in the 1980s was a feminist response to the pre-existing moralities introduced by male scholars who built the image of 'moral man' on the idea of independent, autonomous, rational individuals.[1] This conception of morality neglected the contribution of women not only as rational beings but also as essential contributors to society. Thus, much of the original work in care ethics was done by female scholars as a feminist rendering of ethics that gave special attention to certain aspects of human life such as child rearing and the psychology of women.

This feminist approach to ethics offered numerous alternatives to the pre-existing moral theories. Instead of focusing on the independent and autonomous man, care ethics emphasized relationality, believing that humans are more necessarily *dependent* on one another than *independent*. Rather than highlighting objective rationality, care ethics highlights expressions of emotions in contextual dilemmas. All these aspects – emotions, contextual sensitivity, dependent relationality – lead individuals to what care ethics scholars believe is the best approach to a moral dilemma, namely a focus on *care*.

As with all newer disciplines and fields of scholarship, many have questioned whether care ethics can reasonably claim to be a distinct field of its own or whether it is merely supplemental to other well-established moral theories. Klaver et al. bring awareness to this concern by offering some helpful criteria on how we might distinguish whether a line of scholarship has developed into a discipline of its own. They write:

A full-grown discipline has (1) a particular object of research, (2) a body of accumulated specialist knowledge which refers to their object of research and is specific to their discipline and not shared generally with other disciplines, (3) theories and concepts that can organize the accumulated knowledge effectively, (4) specific terminologies or language adjusted to their research object, (5) developed specific research methods according to their research requirements, and (6) some institutional manifestation.[2]

These criteria are perhaps a complex deciphering to accomplish for care ethics since, indeed, ever since the beginning of its origin with the work of Gilligan's critique of Kohlberg's model on moral development, care ethics has always been at least multidisciplinary, if not interdisciplinary, in nature.[3] Is care ethics a discipline of its own, or can it be absorbed within existing dominant moral theories?

Some have questioned, for example, whether care ethics is merely an extension of the well-known virtue ethics. Virtue theorist Michael Slote argues that caring *is* 'the primary virtue and that a morality based on the motive of caring can offer a general account of right and wrong action and political justice'.[4] Indeed, there are several overlaps between care ethics and virtue ethics. 'Both examine practices and the moral values they embody. Both understand that the practices of morality must be cultivated, nurtured, shaped.'[5] (See Chapter 4 for a discussion of virtue ethics.)

While many care ethics scholars can agree that there are certainly similarities between care ethics and virtue ethics, other scholars, such as Virginia Held, uphold that care ethics has distinctions entirely of its own that separate it from virtue ethics. Virtue theory, for instance, has not paid sufficient attention to the caring practice women have disproportionately been expected to provide to society. Likewise, while virtue ethics captures virtues as embedded in traditions, care ethics is wary of existing traditions and generally seeks to destabilize existing structures of practices rather than uphold them.[6]

Another ethical theory heavily examined in light of care ethics is the principle of justice. It is perceived that the ethics of justice and the ethics of care are entirely opposed rationales. Those eager to preserve care ethics as a novel approach find this duality appealing. After all, as presented by the principle of justice, a universal understanding of moralities certainly seems to undermine the contextual-specific approach care ethics lends itself to. However, scholars such as Joan Tronto disagree. She writes, 'A theory of justice is necessary to distinguish among more and less urgent needs.'[7] In Tronto's view, justice serves as a critical component to executing an ethic of care, serving as an accountability and assessment tool for prioritizing which needs to care for first or most. Indeed, Tronto is perhaps one of the most unorthodox care ethics scholars in that she also incorporates a necessity for 'universalist moral principles' such as 'one should care for those around one or in one's society.'[8] In this way, Tronto challenges whether strict boundaries truly exist between care ethics and other moral theories in the field of ethics. Even so, whether care ethics is perceived as compatible or in opposition to other moral theories, specific tenants of care ethics do form *some* boundary markers, marking it as a distinct field of inquiry and scholarship. To these, we shall now turn.

## MAJOR CONCEPTS OF CARE ETHICS

Two primary tenets are necessary to speak of an ethics of care: (1) relationship-based morality and, (2) recognition of situatedness and contextuality, which generally means judgments are not universal or generalizable.[9] This section will discuss how each scholar developed and contributed to these two tenets in different ways in the study of ethics and morality.

### Carol Gilligan

In her book *In a Different Voice*, Carol Gilligan sent waves through the field of psychology.[10] Her book challenged the presumptions established by well-known psychologists such as Erik Erikson and Lawrence Kohlberg that men had a higher level of moral thinking than women.

Gilligan was suspicious of this finding and sought to study the matter by interviewing women. She found that while men used an ethic of justice to reason through hypothetical dilemmas, women used an ethic of care to reason through real-life difficulties. Women constructed the moral problem in entirely *different* ways, but not in *inferior* ways. This form of approaching moral issues was a distinct voice that had previously not been studied or acknowledged but had significant implications for addressing ethical dilemmas. While an ethic of justice approaches moral problems by analysing, weighing competing principles, and drawing conclusions objectively in cool deliberation, the ethics of care, in contrast, focuses on problems considering contextual factors and the nature of the relationship between those involved in the dilemma.[11] Later in this chapter, we will talk about physician leaders' obligations in caring for their patient followers. An ethic of justice might be whether physicians treat their patients fairly. An ethic of care would approach the problem by looking at each patient and the circumstances surrounding their care to understand what each patient needs, then assess whether the physician is adequately addressing them.

Gilligan demonstrated how women were 'framing self and morality, and relationships and choices' in ways that didn't deal with abstract moralities but rather 'in ways that focused and prioritized *relationship*'.[12] Referencing her research, she states, '… if women were eliminated from the research sample, care focus in moral reasoning would virtually disappear.'[13] The importance of Gilligan's work is not entirely in its specific distinctions between how men versus women might think, but rather that an altogether different approach to moral thinking is possible. This distinction was one of the most significant contributions care ethics offers. It offered an alternatively to what was seen then as mainstream ethics and moral thinking.

## Nel Noddings

Soon after Gilligan's work was published, Nel Noddings wrote her book *Caring*.[14] In it, Noddings provided one of the first comprehensive theories that argued for caring as a foundation of moral action. Looking closely at the actual activities of care, Noddings demonstrated how care ethics is both a value *and* a practice. Noddings viewed caring as an ontological foundation for humanity and the relationships therein. In any relationship, she identified two specific roles: the carer and the cared-for.[15] She writes,

> As a relational ethic, care ethics recognizes the roles of both carer and cared-for in establishing and maintaining the caring relationship. The carer is attentive, open to the possibility of being affectively moved and experiencing motivational displacement, and responds to meet the needs of the cared-for or, at least, to maintain the caring relationship. The cared-for completes the connection by acknowledging the efforts of the carer.[16]

Noddings' commitment to the importance of relationality in care ethics is so forefront in her work that she makes the rather striking claim that organizations – whether they be schools, hospitals, or any others – are not able to participate in care directly.

Noddings believes only humans can form authentic relationships where caring can be exchanged. This claim is interesting since many leadership models portray organizations as embodying human traits and virtues such as 'care'. Noddings finds this to be a misrepresentation of the 'care' verbiage. Instead, she states that although organizations cannot care, they must 'concentrate on establishing conditions under which caring-for can take place, and under which relations of care and trust are established and maintained'.[17]

Critical within the relational dynamic of carer and cared-for is the process of perceiving needs. The key to a well-practised care ethic is ensuring that needs are not *assumed* but *expressed* by the cared-for. This step, Noddings states, needs to happen in the *caring-about* stage, in which we ensure that the needs being met by caring are indeed ones expressed by the care-for and not those by the carer. Noddings provides a compelling example of this common occurrence. Giving the example of global-aid projects in which organizations swoop in to provide disaster relief in developing countries, she discusses how organizations will assume the needs of countries offering food and clothes when what the locals actually need are funds to reconstruct schools and roads or vice or versa.[18] This illustration emphasizes her stance that humans, not organizations, can form care relationships and thus ascertain expressed needs. Additionally, she states, 'Too often, it is supposed that what has been decided as the caring-about stage is definitive.'[19] Instead, she encourages an iterative process that is context specific and, most importantly, flexible and adaptable for change when new or different needs emerge.

Noddings' work continues to be a crucial contribution to care ethics, refining not only to who are the essential actors in caring – namely humans and not organizational powers made up by humans – and the necessity for context-specific caring that is adaptable and meets *expressed* needs. For leadership, this means that leaders have an obligation to know their followers and understand the contextual elements of their followership. It also implies that followers are obligated to adequately express their needs and explain their context as they work toward the common goal of addressing their needs.

## Martha Nussbaum

In a more recent contribution to the field of care ethics, Martha Nussbaum's work has served to reorient the application of care ethics to new domains of thinking, namely political spheres. Perhaps Nusbaum's most notable contribution to care ethics is her conception of the *capabilities approach*. Though originally developed by Amartya Sen, the capability approach became most influential through Nussbaum's application to assessing human well-being and quality of life.[20] 'Nussbaum has helped to shift developmental thinking away from focusing only on economic growth towards more holistic conceptions of what it would take to ensure human flourishing.'[21] Nussbaum's capabilities approach includes ten capacities that she argues ungird the 'basic constitutional principles that should be respected and implemented by the governments of all nations'.[22] These capabilities are life; bodily health; bodily integrity; senses, imagination, and thought; emotion; practical reason; affiliation; other species; control over one's environment; and play.[23] All this talk of governments and economic growth may seem like a striking detour to the core tenet of relationality central to care ethics. However, Nussbaum's ten capabilities are purposed to demonstrate how 'a human personality can acquire the capacity for concern, for responsibility, and for mutuality in love, giv[ing] ethics an essential information, without which its normative proposals are incomplete'.[24] In other words, Nussbaum's ten capabilities approach can also be understood as the ten capabilities of *care*.

As described by Nussbaum, the ten capabilities approach takes some clear alternate routes from the care ethics described early on by Gilligan and Noddings. For example, Nussbaum's capabilities approach has served as a political assessment of development and human agency across various nations, forming a somewhat universalness to what human flourishing should look like. This universal application of human development and human agency flies in the face of the contextual, site-specific priorities expressed by early care ethics scholars. However, at the same time, Nussbaum's approach has been praised for making care ethics accessible to multitudes of individuals and especially in adding a more human, relational-based approach to assessing governmental obligations towards their citizens.[25]

Unsurprisingly then, with its universal applications, Nussbaum's capabilities approach also lends itself to the principle of justice: 'The basic idea behind the capabilities approach is dignity and equality of opportunity for a human being. A society that does not guarantee these to all its citizens at some threshold level falls short of being a fully just society.'[26] Of note, Nussbaum's conceptions of care ethics also destabilize Nodding's original prioritization of strictly *human* care relationships. Number eight of Nussbaum's ten capabilities include 'Other Species. Being able to live with concern for and in relation to animals, plants, and the world of nature.'[27] In this way, Nussbaum finds a concern for other species, 'extending capabilities within self-experience to the experience of the interpersonal world to experience of ourselves with nature,' as an important obligation of human flourishing and care.[28]

Martha Nussbaum's contribution to care ethics certainly served to problematize some of the earlier tenants central to care ethics, both in its expansion of who are the viable actors in caring relationships (e.g. governments, animals, nature) and the universal – even political – elaboration of care obligations. However, one tenet of care ethics remains unwavering in Nussbaum's approach: a consistent priority on relationality. '[The] ten essential points remind us that we are all incomplete, requiring others' recognition, response, witness, and clarifying presence.'[29] Organizations and systems, built for efficiency, often deprioritize relationality in favour of an emphasis on outcomes. A corporation that monitors employees' time on task is not prioritizing the needs of the employees but instead prioritizing the efficiency of work towards a goal. Because ethics of care is so closely related to virtue ethics, a question might arise about which approach is most likely to cause each employee to flourish.

Now that we have a better understanding of care ethics, we can move to its critiques.

## CRITIQUES OF CARE ETHICS

Like many moral theories, many of the tenets that are expressed as strengths by some are argued to be weaknesses by others. Much of what propelled care ethics as an alternative moral theory was its feminist take on morality that displaced the normative, primarily masculine, conceptions of ethics that had prevailed until that point. However, care ethics' preoccupation with feminism is also argued by some to be one of its most significant setbacks. Carol Gilligan's work offered a voice that exemplified the feminist struggle and was intended to rectify gender inequality in moral reasoning. However, scholars such as MacKinnon argue that this preoccupation between women versus men, this duality we might call it, is not helpful to women and merely serves to reify stereotypes of women.[30] Rather than liberate women, some argue that care ethics places women in a position where they only have two choices: be the same as men or different from them. This essentialism alienates an entire population of women who may not resonate with either of those strict dualities.[31]

MacKinnon indicates that many feminist scholars are ambivalent to this restrictive, essentialist position of care ethics due to much of care ethics historically emerging within circles associated with maternalism, housekeeping, and childcare. This position not only limits what 'femaleness' is but restricts female contribution to the private life instead of what should be the equally accessible public and political life.[32] Instead of relying so heavily on gender differences, Linda Nicholson believes that more attention should be given to how 'race, class, and the sheer specificity of historical circumstances also profoundly affect social life and thus a moral perspective'.[33]

For this reason, many argue that care ethics *alone* is not sufficient to guide moral action. Other scholars argue for the necessity of other moral theories to 'come along with' next to care ethics, such as '… the values of justice to ensure a balanced and reasoned resolution of practical issues and social problems'.[34] In this way, care ethics' novelty as its own discipline, in its own right, is challenged by critiques. As a moral theory, care ethics requires the implementation of *other* theories to provide filters, boundaries, and clarification on what things *should* be cared about and when.

The lack of boundaries in care ethics as seen within in tenants surrounding relational obligations, has also been critiqued and serves as yet another point of contention. 'The ethics of care promotes total engrossment and displacement of one's own values in another individual, which is a risky act.'[35] Other critics find that suggestions of care ethics as the sole foundation of moral principles are dangerous.[36] Various other virtues must accompany care ethics to lead to moral action. Hassan gives the illustration of a wife that has been instructed by her husband not to vote in favour of legislation that lends itself to equality among the LGBTQ+ community. The wife's engrossment with her husband and her obligation to not break her caring relationship with her husband thus impairs her moral action. In situations like this and others, more is needed than just care ethics. Other virtues need to be considered to lead to moral action; virtues such as the idea of justice and all humans being equal.[37]

Critics also argue the lack of boundaries within care ethics places women in a vulnerable position. 'Adult relationships should be based on reciprocity, not one-way caring. This idea of one-caring entraps a woman into the role of permanent caretaker, with her ethics based on her ability to care.'[38] There are many ways this entrapment could make women susceptible to abuse and manipulation – all in the name of caring. This observation again contributes to the critique's belief that additional moral theories, separate from care ethics, are needed to discern moral action. For example, considerations of autonomy and agency would be important to prevent this engrossment and the potential abuse it can lend itself to. As Davion writes, 'I believe that what is missing from Noddings' account [of care ethics] is an account of the individuals within caring relations as important in themselves.'[39]

Lastly, much of the critique of care ethics revolves around its perceptions as ambiguous. 'Caring ethicists can tell us nothing about "what" and the "how" which underlies the judgement [of action].'[40] Noddings believed that ethics are motivated by a sense of duty, with that duty being to care. She split up care into two categories: 'natural caring' and 'ethical caring'. However, she believed that ethical care depended on natural care.[41] This split feels problematic to critics who point out that this distinction between natural care and ethical care says nothing about motive or intent; indeed, the motive and intent behind caring are often so difficult to decipher.[42] Is it an innate compulsion to care? Is it an ethical duty? Or is it something else that motivates caring action?

Additionally, although Noddings' pretext of care ethics is based on her belief that caring is a natural, innate trait of humans, why single out caring? Surely there are other sentiments and inclinations of feelings, such as hate, sadness, or jealousy. Why not choose those as ideals for leading moral action? The argument that care is innate to humans ultimately obscures more than it clarifies.[43] A distinct gap within care ethics is an explanation of assessing care as appropriate and good care. As Peter Allmark points out, 'It is not necessary for the core definition of care that people's cognitive values be in good order.'[44] Thus, a pitfall of care ethics is that it assumes all care is good and gives little assessment tools on how to identify otherwise. There are plenty of things people care about that may not be worth caring for. How do we assess which have moral gravity or are moral failing? This is a question that many feel care ethics has mistakenly left unanswered:

> In the core sense, almost all of us care about different things to different degrees. Without such care, our lives would be directionless and psychopathic. The ethics of care says we should care, that caring is a moral quality and that we should encourage conditions that create care. It means that we should care about the right things in the right way and promote the required qualities. But by focusing on care as a moral quality in itself, something it is not, the ethics of care can tell us nothing of what those right things are.[45]

Though new generations of care ethics scholars seek to remedy some of this ambiguity, care ethics' relatively recent development means that it has a long way to go until it has addressed some of these gaps. Additionally, this remedy should steer the discipline away from essentialist views of feminism and offer additional tools to assess the qualities of care.

## FIVE COMPONENT ANALYSIS

How does care ethics come to weigh in on leadership? Care ethics implores leaders to utilize their platform (however large or small it may be) as a catalyst for offering care and concern to followers. Care ethics sees concern and care for others as a moral obligation and responsibility of all humans, particularly for leaders and their followers. In alignment with the Five Component Model, in which leadership is not an *event* but rather a *process*,[46] care ethics encourages a purposeful interaction between leaders and followers through the *caring-about* engagement that takes place within the carer and cared-for relationship. As expressed by

Noddings, this means having leaders that are adaptive listeners – leaders who do not assume what caring looks like but rather listen to those being cared-for for *their* expressed needs. It also means being flexible and adapting to what those cares might be and how to accomplish caring based on specific and unique situations or individuals. In this way, care ethics creates an obligation for mutual reliability between leaders and followers, carer and cared-for. This is expressed in the Five Components of Leadership Model with a focus on the leader and the arrow pointing from the leader to the follower (Figure 6.2).

The focus on relationality in care ethics challenges traditional paradigms in organizational leadership where one person is designated leader over numerous followers. For example, a director of human resources may have over 20 or more employees that report to her. However, the kind of leadership care ethics supports is time-consuming, requires one-on-one sit-downs to develop personal knowledge and relationships, and requires significant adaptability and flexibility. Doing that with 20 or more employees may be challenging, if not impossible. Thus, a care ethics approach requires a leadership approach that multiplies the number of leaders, producing leaders out of followers themselves, and nurturing humans who can reflect and recognize the

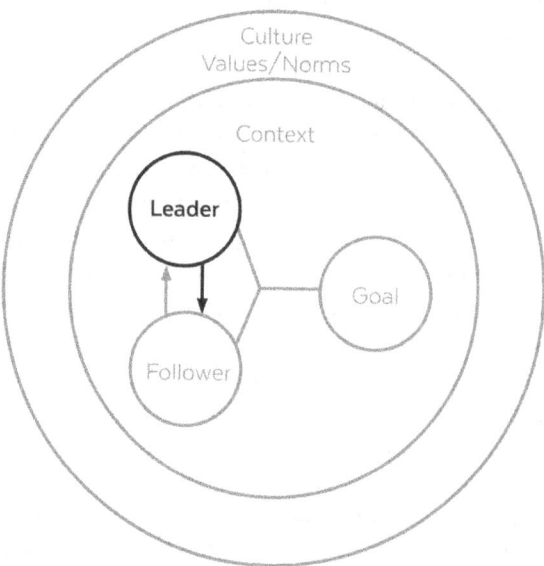

**Figure 6.2**      The Five Components of Leadership Model applied to care ethics

mutual dependency all members have on one another, whether a leader or a follower. In other words, care ethics is preoccupied with an equitable agency that views the categorization of 'leader' or 'follower' as interchangeable, depending on the department's specific care needs. This interchange allows for improved equitable access to being cared for, a kind of 'cared-for' that wouldn't exist with the typical ratio of corporate leadership of 1 to 20.

The goal must be one that both the leader and follower hold in common. The goal cannot be dictated by the leader, but rather, must be negotiated in consultation with the follower. The leader must ask the follower what they need and what they want to accomplish. Likewise, the follower must express their needs and wants to the leader for the leader and the follower to reach the goal together.

For an ethic of care to be successful, the context must allow the leader to adapt to the needs of the follower. This may or may not be fully possible given the mitigating factors that may enable or prohibit the leader to fully adapt to the needs of the follower. We will see the influence of the context on this process in more detail in our case study.

Finally, the cultural values and norms, as many feminist scholars have pointed out, may also enable or prohibit a leader from fulling embracing an ethic of care. Those cultures which value a care ethic may be more willing to adapt to the unique needs of particular followers; whereas those cultures that hold more of a logic of care may not so readily adapt to a follower's unique needs. This tension is one of the primary criticisms many feminist scholars hold of cultures that embrace a logic rather than an ethic of care as we have seen in this chapter.

In the next section, we will outline a care ethics approach to leadership by using a case study on substance use patients who present to an acute care hospital requiring hospital resources such as heart valves to replace their own after infections develop because of substance abuse. After presenting the historical background to the case, we will discuss the challenges patients with substance use disorder present to leadership and look at how care ethics might approach this issue using the Five Components Model of leadership to work toward an ethical outcome.

## CASE STUDY: PHYSICIAN CARE-GIVING AND PATIENTS WITH SUBSTANCE USE DISORDER

In healthcare, we often refer to physicians as 'caregivers'. But what does an ethic of care actually look like in this context? It might look like physician leaders investing time in listening to the patient's expressed needs instead of assuming needs that are standard following a specific diagnosis. It also means altering or experimenting with options that may or may not be the 'standard of care' but nonetheless meet the specific circumstances of a particular patient with an illness. Some considerations include access to transportation, a primary care provider, or stable housing. All of these psychosocial considerations that *should* impact patient care plans must emerge in the caring-about stage between carer and cared-for, leader and follower.

One of the most complex issues in healthcare in terms of the convergence of physical and psychosocial factors is addiction or substance use disorder. Between a patient's physical dependence on a substance(s) and the correlation of substance use disorder with psychosocial factors (e.g. mental illness, housing instability, child welfare involvement, alienation from friends and family, unemployment), patients with substance use disorder often require a great deal of care. The complicated understanding of addiction as a nonbinary choice or disease sometimes means that this population of patients is also difficult to care for. If you view addiction as a choice, caring for an addict leads to frustration with the patient's unwillingness to comply with their treatment. If you view addiction as a disease, then you are treating a patient who is part of a population that statistically has a very poor prognosis and for whom end-of-life care is not always appropriate. Addiction, as a disease, holistically consumes patient's lives making medical care extremely challenging and often perplexing.

For physicians (leaders) who are treating patients (followers) with substance use disorder, there is a clear foundational (common) goal: treat the patient in a way that is curative and promotes healing. Sometimes this means treating physical dependence or physical symptoms resulting from addiction. Sometimes this means treating the underlying addictive behaviours. Sometimes this means both.

The question that frames care ethics is illuminated here: what obligation do leaders have to care for the needs of their followers? This idea of an obligation to care is particularly complicated in the context of patients who often do not seem to be engaging in goal-oriented behaviour or who might work toward sobriety and physical health for some time and then relapse. The physician leader's definition of addiction and their values surrounding addiction treatment will often define the sort of obligation they have to care. Leaders might struggle with the chronic destabilizing condition of substance use disorder. Unlike many other diagnoses, more care will often not result in better outcomes.

For patient followers, hospital stays can be torturous. Aside from physical dependence on a substance that is no longer accessible, hospitalization often destabilizes the patient further in terms of psychosocial factors. Receiving care that addresses the follower's needs can often result in the creation of new needs or the non-fulfillment of existing ones. This situation becomes increasingly complicated when the patient contracts other diseases as a result of their substance abuse.

One of the common physical consequences of intravenous (IV) drug use is endocarditis – an inflammation of the heart's chambers and valves caused by bacteria, fungi, or germs. Endocarditis is a serious condition that frequently results in the patient needing a heart valve replacement. Endocarditis occurs when a person who injects drugs utilizes unsterilized needles that carry an infection into the bloodstream. When infectious bacteria travel through the bloodstream and attach to the heart valves or chambers, they can cause severe effects like blocking blood flow to the heart, heart failure, or sepsis. Part of the complexity of detecting, diagnosing, and treating endocarditis is that the presentation of the disease can indicate any number of conditions. Symptoms can include fever, night sweats, fatigue, weight loss, or loss of appetite, to name a few. Often, replacing the affected valve is the only way to treat endocarditis.

Decades ago, this was a very serious undertaking that involved open-heart surgery. Since 2011, however, a procedure called a trans-aortic valve replacement (TAVR) has allowed physicians to use a catheter to replace a heart valve with a relatively non-invasive procedure. This procedure is so low-risk that it has become the standard of care for people with endocarditis.

However, infective endocarditis is often not a one-time occurrence for substance users. This infection can occur numerous times in patients who continue to utilize IV drugs with many patients requiring repeat valve replacements. Valve replacements usually are done with artificial or animal valves, so they are not a limited resource the way that human organs for transplant might be. This essentially means they can be repeated without any strain on tangible resources. Still, there are often ethical questions about IV drug users who need multiple valve replacements. The ethical complexity surrounding the treatment of endocarditis centres on the fact that patients who struggle with addiction and patients who do not use substances but who both have infective endocarditis are often cared for in very different ways.

As a condition, endocarditis is a fairly unremarkable infection. It is extremely common in hospitalized patients and yet it continues to be the source of significant distress among providers. The underlying conditions leading to infective endocarditis can range from kidney disease or diabetes to increased age or rheumatic heart disease. In these ways, infective endocarditis is characterized by a great deal of ambiguity but also constitutes an expansive portfolio affecting a large population of hospitalized patients. However, only one instance of this disease seems to cause contention within medicine and to create distress

for providers – namely infective endocarditis which is acquired as the result of IV drug use.
   Though infective endocarditis was discovered centuries ago, the opioid epidemic in the United States over the last few decades has changed the landscape of this condition, making patients who inject drugs one of the most prominent patient demographics for the disease. Infective endocarditis accounts for up to 20 per cent of substance users' hospitalizations and up to 10 per cent of their deaths.[47] Both in discourse within medical journals and among providers, infective endocarditis has become uninformedly connected with this *one* patient demographic, substance users.

## FIVE COMPONENT ANALYSIS

For our case study we can consider the physicians as the leaders while their patients with infective endocarditis who are IV drug users are the followers (Figure 6.3). The goal is to manage the patient's infected heart valves. The context is what complicates this issue. The context is one in which the harm is often caused by various forms of patient-follower non-compliance, including continual drug use. The culture is one in which there are two primary models of drug use: one social (a choice) and another medical (a disease).

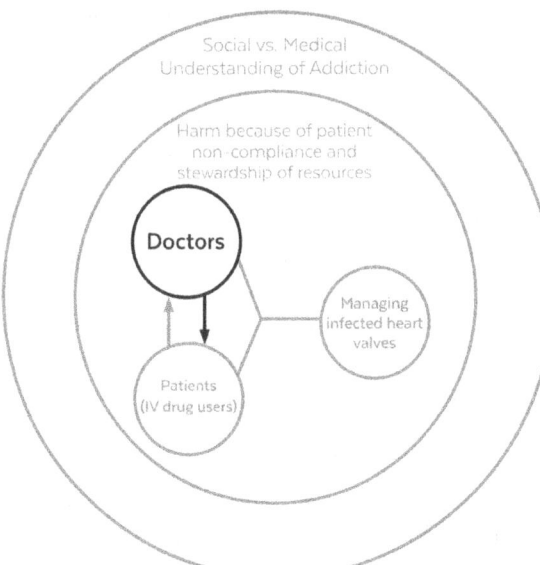

   The unique contention around this patient population is not about its diagnosis per se but rather its treatment. As mentioned earlier, the standard of care treatment for patients with infective endocarditis typically consists of replacing the infected heart valve and an intensive regime of numerous weeks of inpatient antibiotic treatments. However, patients who have acquired endocarditis due to their intravenous drug use and are admitted to the hospital with an infection of their heart valve are often denied a valve replacement or any surgical intervention. The heightened risk of reoccurrence of infection that continued drug use poses makes surgical intervention for *only* this patient population appear

**Figure 6.3**     The Five Components of Leadership Model applied to physicians treating IV drug users with infective endocarditis

futile and inadvisable. This hesitation in applying the standard of care that other patients with IE receive is less about care for the patient and more about the frustration of the medical providers.

Many articles and journals that debate the efficacy of valve procedures in intravenous drug uses have titles that read, 'When is enough enough? The dilemma of valve replacement in a recidivist intravenous drug user', 'or 'Doctors consider ethics of costly heart surgery for people addicted to opioids.'[48] These titles give evidence of the two primary ways in which arguments for withholding life-sustaining interventions are made: (1) a distinct disapproval and disdain for what is believed to be a self-destructive, socially undesirable behaviour that has both moral and legal dimensions, and (2) an argument to be good stewards of medical care and preserve what are perceived to be limited resources for more deserving patients.

One key way of understanding this phenomenon is to look closely at the decision-making process between clinicians and substance use patients with endocarditis. Care ethics can weigh in on alternatives to traditional approaches to medical decision-making that can lead to improved ethical outcomes.

Seemingly at odds in healthcare practice is how to reconcile the principle of autonomy with the expertise of clinicians. In the age of twenty-first-century American healthcare, where patient autonomy is articulated as the foundation of modern medicine, providing patients with choices and honouring those choices is the pinnacle of the patient–provider relationship. However, it's worth assessing whether our modern claim and right to *choose* are all that helpful within the context of healthcare. Particularly among intravenous drug users with endocarditis, whose shortcomings in treatment compliance are reduced to the failings of individual *choice*, it is worth asking whether prioritizing patient choice is actually beneficial and leads to valuable ends.

Traditionally medicine's prioritization of autonomy and patient choice has placed clinicians and patients at two completely separate sides of the spectrum, leaving the search for a middle ground hard to find. In her book, *The Logic of Care: Health and the Problem of Patient Choice*, Annemarie Mol seeks to destabilize the centrality of patient choice in modern healthcare by proposing a new logic, the logic of *care*. She argues that mobilizing the logic of choice only shifts the weight of everything that goes wrong onto the patient, resulting in poor care.[49] Instead, the logic of care should be enacted in healthcare in which decisions and explorations of 'next steps' begin at 'the fleshiness and fragility of life', not solely beginning at the juncture of patient choice.[50] In essence, Mol's argument can be understood as comparing the principle of autonomy with an ethic of care.

In the day-to-day practice of endocarditis among substance users, patients are expected to make many choices. Patients must decide whether they will remain in the hospital for an extended stay of up to eight weeks for intravenous antibiotic therapy, knowing that this extended stay may create complications for their responsibilities outside the hospital. Their medical providers expect them to choose between abstaining and continuing the use of illicit drug use. In medical practice, clinicians find that one of their obligations is to provide patients with enough information to make informed decisions.

At one end, the provider's role and responsibility start and end with providing factual, value-free information and then implementing whatever decision is made by the patient. On the other end, patients are solely responsible for making the decision at hand. This continuum is not so in the logic of care and an ethic of care. Providers and patients are *partners* in treatment. One cannot accomplish health or treatment goals without the other. The provision of 'value-free information' passed at the bedside is not what is called for. As Mol indicates, patients are not 'students who need to acquire knowledge about [their disease], but rather a person who has to learn how to live with it'.[51] *Living* with disease versus merely *learning* about the disease is what the logic of care is about. Living with the disease requires problem-solving, trial and error, and flexibility for real-life complexities that do not come to mind within the clinic walls and yet become evident in the community. Only in an ethics of care, in which mutual dependency and relationality are prioritized, can this kind of adaptability be succeeded.

Unfortunately, the primary approach of a logic of *choice*, or respecting a patient's autonomy, does not make room for such flexibility. Rather than creating space for patients, it alters daily practices in ways that do not fit well with the intricacies and unknowability of disease.[52] By providing everyone a choice, clinicians assume they are being equitable and just. They assume they are honouring patient autonomy and preserving the dignity of a patient's values. This assumption is because the logic of choice supposes everyone has the luxury of choice. It treats everyone as if they were equal, as if one size fits all, and as if everyone had the same options available. Yet, this could not be further from the truth.

Addicted patients with endocarditis often lack support and resources, such as a primary care physician, transportation, and a stable home, that would otherwise assist them in their journey of health. The logic of choice assumes that 'the way we live already follows from the choices that we make.'[53] Yet lived realities, particularly among substance users, demonstrate that much of their present lives are entirely outside of the domain of individual choice. Understanding this reality problematizes whether it is truly just to withhold valve replacements in substance use patients with infective endocarditis.

Looking at the case of physicians (leaders) trying to care for patients (followers) with substance disorders within the organizing frame of the Five Components of Leadership model helps to understand this problem a bit more clearly. Physicians and patients share a goal, to address the patient's medical needs. Care ethics suggests that part of what constructs the obligation between leader and follower is the elements of relationality and mutual dependence in working towards a common goal. Patients need providers to care for them and make recommendations about their health. Providers need patients to do their job. Because of this mutual dependence, relationality is created.

The relationship between providers and patients can feel tenuous when the patient is not compliant with their treatment plan. It might feel to the leader that the follower is not adequately engaged in working towards the common goal of patient recovery or health. When a patient refuses to stay in the hospital, relapses, or seems unconcerned with the long-term effects of not following their physician's recommendations, it can seem like the follower is not engaged in working towards a common goal. Care ethics prompt us to look into the 'why?' as a piece of the context. For example, a patient who won't stay in fear of losing housing should be addressed differently from a patient who simply refuses to comply.

The values and norms around a patient's treatment will also influence how the patient is treated. Culturally, if the physician managing the patient's care believes that addiction is a disease, the physician will be more likely to empathize with the patient and recommend a valve replacement. Likewise, a physician who values autonomy to an extreme degree and values explanations of addiction that promote the narrative that addiction is a *choice* would approach their care for the patient in a more judgmental way and might begin to care less if it feels like the patient is not engaging or maintaining their sobriety. Care ethics addresses the question of 'how can a leader best help to meet their followers' needs?' in this case, by pointing leaders to the context and the values and norms components of the Five Components of Leadership Model. This would mean asking questions to define the context a bit better, asking, 'why is this patient disengaging?'

In an approach that considers both justice and autonomy, it may be easy to withhold valve replacements as a treatment option. After all, the patient made a choice. Being the sixth admission with endocarditis, they have chosen to continue drug use. The patient decided not to complete their eight weeks of inpatient antibiotics in the prior admission. The patient chose to leave against medical advice from the nursing facility. Thus, following such choices, clinicians seemingly have good ground to stand on not to offer a valve replacement. As the belief goes, patients' autonomy is honoured by allowing patients to make poor choices.

An ethics of care, however, does not arrive at such conclusions so quickly. Instead, an ethics of care stops to interject the question of, 'Why?' An ethics of care stops long enough to have compassion, curiosity, and care about what barriers might exist that prevent this patient from completing care plans that are purposed within the sterile walls of the hospital but are somehow incompatible with real-life living. Why did the patient leave before his eight weeks of antibiotics were up? Why did the patient leave the nursing facility against medical advice? Was it because the nursing facility doesn't provide medically assisted therapies for substance use, and thus the patient was enduring withdrawal that the nursing facility was unwilling to treat? Was it because after five weeks of trying to ensure childcare for their four-year-old daughter, that child care had fallen through, and now the patient needed to return home to watch his child? When drawn out, there could be numerous reasons that are entirely understandable but that, most importantly, can be navigated. An ethic of care believes that getting to that point of navigation, in which barriers of care are identified, is a moral obligation of care providers at all levels of healthcare. An ethics of care creates the space for such navigations to occur and for the outcome of such navigations not to be homogeneous but rather reflect the specific needs of each particular patient. In this way, care ethics challenges normalized standards of care.

## SUMMARY AND CONCLUDING REMARKS

This chapter began by asking if a focus on relationality can direct moral obligations and lead to ethical actions. Care ethics makes the focus of leadership follower-centric while also creating awareness around the mutual dependency between leader and follower. Not only do leaders have an obligation to care for their followers, but they must care for one another. The journey is one of companionship, not isolation. Acknowledgment and living out the reciprocal care and dependency between leader and follower allow for both sides to contribute to learning from one another. In our case study, physicians have much to learn from substance use patients on what it's like to live with endocarditis. Patients have much to learn from clinicians on what steps can lead to health and recovery. In providing optimal care, autonomous leadership is not what is called for, but rather mutual caring in which both sides acknowledge and understand one another to reach an expressed goal.

## DISCUSSION QUESTIONS

1. In what ways is care ethics compatible with other dominant moral theories outlined in this book?
2. In what ways does care ethics distinguish itself from other dominant moral theories?
3. Is care ethic's preoccupation with relationality a strong enough priority to guide moral actions in leadership? If yes, explain why? If not, what other tenets would be necessary?
4. How does one reconcile, or make sense, the deviations that exist among care ethics scholars themselves on who can be considered an actor capable of forming caring relationships?
5. Do you find the ethics of care a compelling approach to ensuring equality among citizens in different nations? Why or why not?

## ADDITIONAL RESOURCES

C. Gilligan, *In a Different Voice: Psychological Theory and Women's Development*, Cambridge, MA: Harvard University Press, 1982.

Gilligan's book championed the need for a variety of fields to listen to the unique voices of women. It is a pivotal work in an ethics of care and all-feminist scholarship.

V. Held, *The Ethics of Care: Personal, Political, and Global*, Oxford: Oxford University Press, 2006.

Held's work summarizes the ethics of care and its implications for a variety of fields and contemporary issues.

N. Noddings, *Caring: A Relational Approach to Ethics and Moral Education*, 2nd edn, Berkeley: University of California Press, 2013.

Noddings builds a philosophical argument for caring as the foundation for human interaction.

# NOTES

1. V. Held, *The Ethics of Care: Personal, Political, and Global*, New York: Oxford University Press, 2006, p. 19.
2. K. Klaver, E. van Elst and A.J. Baart, 'Demarcation of the ethics of care as a discipline: discussion article', *Nursing Ethics*, vol. 21 no. 7, November 2014, 755–65, p. 756.
3. Klaver et al., 'Demarcation'.
4. Held, *The Ethics of Care*.
5. Held, *The Ethics of Care*.

6.   Held, *The Ethics of Care*.

7.   J. Tronto, *Moral Boundaries: A Political Argument for an Ethic of Care*, New York: Routledge, 1993, p. 138.

8.   Tronto, *Moral Boundaries*, p. 178.

9.   Klaver et al., 'Demarcation', 757.

10.  C. Gilligan, *In a Different Voice: Psychological Theory and Women's Development*, Cambridge, MA: Harvard University Press, 1982.

11.  S.D. Edwards, 'Three versions of an ethics of care', *Nursing Philosophy*, vol. 10 no. 4, October 2009, 231–40, p. 232.

12.  Gilligan, *In a Different Voice*, p. 25.

13.  Gilligan, *In a Different Voice*, p. 25.

14.  N. Noddings, *Caring: A Relational Approach to Ethics and Moral Education*, Berkeley: University of California Press, 1984. See also N. Noddings, 'Care ethics and "caring" organizations', in D. Engster and M. Hamington (eds), *Care Ethics and Political Theory*, New York: Oxford University Press, 2015.

15.  Noddings, *Caring*, p. 73.

16.  Noddings, *Caring*, p. 73.

17.  Noddings, *Caring*, p. 73.

18.  Noddings, *Caring*, p. 73.

19.  Noddings, *Caring*, p. 77.

20.  J. Jaarsveld, 'Nussbaum's capability approach and African environmental ethics: is the African voice heard?', *Oxford Development Studies*, vol. 48 no. 2, 3 May 2020, 135–47.

21.  Jaarsveld, 'Nussbaum's capability approach', 135.

22.  M. Nussbaum, *Women and Human Development: The Capabilities Approach*, Cambridge: Cambridge University Press, 2000, p. 5.

23.  M. Nussbaum, 'Nature, function, and capability: Aristotle on political distribution', in J. Annas and R.H. Grimm (eds), *Oxford Studies in Ancient Philosophy*, Supplementary Volume, Vol. 6, 1988, Oxford: Clarendon Press, pp. 145–84.

24.  I.S. Miller, 'The relevance of Martha C. Nussbaum's human rights capabilities approach for today's psycho-analytic inquiry', *American Jounal of Psychoanalysis*, vol. 81 no. 4, December 2021, 527–33, p. 527.

25.  Jaarsveld, 'Nussbaum's capability approach', 137.

26.  N. Bhasin and P. Jain, 'Anuradha and anupama: gender issues through Nussbaum's capabilities approach', *Visual Anthropology*, vol. 34 no. 3, 27 May 2021, 257–63, p. 258.

27.  Quoted in Jaarsveld, 'Nussbaum's capability approach', 137.

28.  Miller, 'The relevance', 529.

29.  Miller, 'The relevance', 531.

30.  Y. Okano, 'Why has the ethics of care become an issue of global concern?', *International Journal of Japanese Sociology*, vol. 25, no. 1, 2016, 85–99.

31.  Okano, 'Why has the ethics of care'.

32.  Okano, 'Why has the ethics of care'.

33.  Okano, 'Why has the ethics of care', 88.

34.  Okano, 'Why has the ethics of care', 88.

35.  T. Hassan, 'An ethic of care critique', *Quest Proceedings*, 2008, 159–62. https://dspace.sunyconnect.suny.edu/handle/1951/43954 (accssed 22 October 2022).

36.  Hassen, 'An ethic of care critique', 159.

37. Hassan, 'An ethic of care critique', 160.

38. Hassan, 'An ethic of care critique', 160.

39. Hassan, 'An ethic of care critique', 160.

40. P. Allmark, 'Can there be an ethics of care?', *Journal of Medical Ethics*, vol. 21 no. 1, February 1995, 19–24, p. 19.

41. Hassan, 'An ethic of care critique', 159.

42. Hassan, 'An ethic of care critique'.

43. Allmark, 'Can there be an ethics of care?'.

44. Allmark, 'Can there be an ethics of care?', 21.

45. Allmark, 'Can there be an ethics of care?', 23.

46. R.M. McManus and G. Perruci, *Understanding Leadership: An Arts and Humanities Perspective*, New York: Routledge, 2020.

47. Y. Ji, L. Kujtan and D. Kershner, 'Acute endocarditis in intravenous drug users: a case report and literature review', *Journal of Community Hospital Internal Medicine Perspective*, vol. 2 no. 1, 2012, 1–4.

48. S.R. Baldassarri, I. Lee, S.R. Latham and G. D'Onofrio, 'Debating medical utility, not futility: ethical dilemmas in treating critically ill people who use injection drugs', *The Journal of Law, Medicine & Ethics: A Journal of the American Society of Law, Medicine & Ethics*, vol. 46 no. 2, 2018, 241–51.

49. A. Mol, *The Logic of Care: Health and the Problem of Patient Choice*, New York: Routledge, 2008.

50. Mol, *The Logic of Care*, p. 13.

51. Mol, *The Logic of Care*, p. 48.

52. Mol, *The Logic of Care*.

53. Mol, *The Logic of Care*, p. 67.

# 7
# Universal ethics

*Stephanie E. Raible and Alexandra K. Perry*

## FRAMING QUESTION

How can universal standards guide leaders and followers in any context?

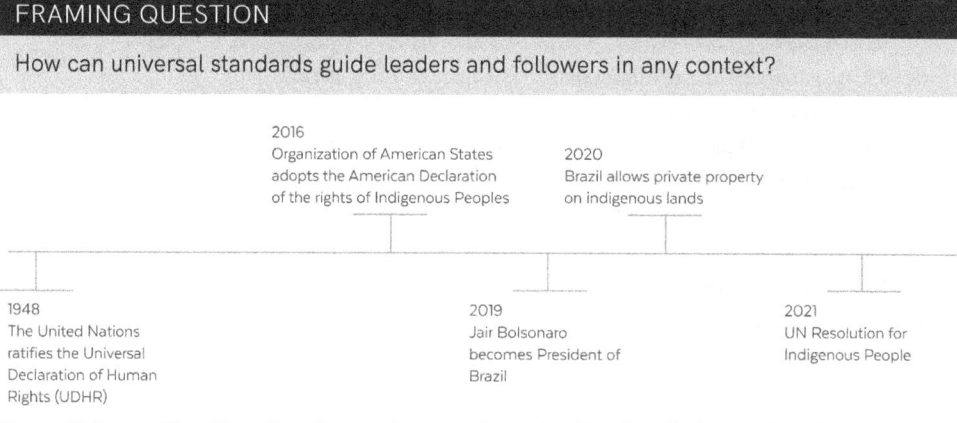

**Figure 7.1**     Timeline of major works on universal ethics in relation to the chapter case study

Both universal ethics and relativism (Chapter 8) attempt to answer a common problem: finding ethical standards for leadership in any context. However, they conclude differently just how to do that. Universal ethics asserts the need for widespread dialogue and ethical transparency to find common ground for well-being and survival.[1] Whatever source we may appeal to for our ethics, such as faith, tradition, or culture, the appeal of universal ethics spans beyond national boundaries, fields of scholarship, and industry. The hope is that a universal ethic can provide unity and stability in an increasingly interconnected and globalized world. Universal ethics are not just theoretical because some measure of universal ethical values is already at work today, underpinning our laws, agreements, and behaviours at both individual and collective levels. They help to centre our interactions and engagements on the minimal basic consensus of establishing internal peace, economic and legal order, and institutional frameworks.[2] The concept of universal ethical values assumes common 'truths about humanity, regardless of context, community, or culture'.[3] We might think of these truths as an invisible bridge connecting humanity's institutions and collective frameworks to the underlying beliefs and values that hold them together.

The issue of human history brings us to a primary reason for studying and upholding universal ethical values. One argument is that universal values are necessary for sustaining the future world, as there cannot be 'ordering of the world without a world ethic'.[4] To this end, having a common set of universal ethics at an international level allows for a shared understanding of perceived values and an ability to distinguish right from wrong.[5] For example, the 1997 UNESCO *Declaration on the Responsibilities of the Present Generations to the Future Generations* says that 'at this point in history, the very existence of humankind and its environment are threatened.'[6] And therefore, 'there is a moral obligation to formulate behavioural guidelines for the present generations within a broad, future-oriented perspective.'[7]

Like our chapter on relativism, this chapter returns to questions rooted in culture. The modern study of universal ethical values has arisen from the perceived need to address challenges raised by the intersection of cultures. So, let us take a moment to reflect on what we mean here by 'culture'. Culture is 'the relatively stable set of inner values and beliefs generally held by groups of people in countries or regions and the noticeable impact those values and beliefs have on the peoples' outward behaviours and environment'.[8] Culture includes both visible and covert elements. Visible facets of culture include behaviours, rituals, cultural products (e.g. music, art, craft, literature), and cultural identifiers (e.g. attire, jewellery, tattoos). Beneath the surface are the covert underpinnings of culture, which include perspectives, philosophies, thoughts, and values. We will explore the concept of culture and universal ethics throughout this chapter. We will then consider how one set of universal values addresses a cultural conflict: the right for indigenous people to hold land in Brazil.

## HISTORY

Throughout history, there have been multiple attempts to resolve the question of what universal standards could guide leadership across cultures. This section outlines the history of prescriptive, descriptive, and practical attempts of the philosophers and leaders who have argued for universal ethical values.

### Prescriptive Attempts

First, let's consider prescriptive attempts, which focus on providing rules for how people ought to conduct themselves. These attempts make authoritative claims to establish universal ethics. Several theories in this textbook are underpinned by some effort to establish a universal ethic. Here, we will briefly consider how virtue ethics, divine command, Kant, and the social contract all attempt to dictate what is 'always right' to do, no matter the context.

Although theories of virtue ethics do not define universal values or action,[9] the earliest records of seeking universal ethics could be attributed to its attempts to define a moral philosophy of virtuous character. As detailed in Chapter 4 on Aristotle and virtue ethics, virtuous people, by nature, do the universally right thing at that moment and within that context. Between the extremes of excess and deficiency, the golden mean is understood to be the middle-ground virtuous behaviour given an individual's abilities, available resources, and environmental context. So, the normative prescription here is always to seek the golden mean. Within virtue ethics, it is assumed that a virtuous character is developed through habituation over time. The challenge of this orientation for universal ethics is the presumption that all people would ubiquitously (1) view and judge virtuous action the same way, (2) agree that virtuous behaviour would yield *eudaimonia* (a state of human flourishing), and (3) strive to be virtuous to achieve *eudaimonia*.

Another prescriptive attempt to achieve a universal ethic comes from divine command theory (Chapter 9), which regards religion as the definitive source of morality. Before the twentieth century, much of the Western world expressed confidence in its ability to navigate questions of right and wrong by appealing to ethics rooted in a God-given moral code, as per the divine command theory. The practical dilemma that divine command adherents face is countless interpretations of sacred texts, even by those of the same faith. So, while adherents of the divine command theory may be able to agree on the source of their ethical values, they still struggle with specific practical applications. To this end, divine command theory endeavours to establish universal ethics but has yet to show to be effective at accomplishing this in practice.

While some other philosophers called upon religion to establish universal ethics, others appealed to rationalism's power to reach ethical conclusions, such as Immanuel Kant's use of reason (Chapter 2). Kant's categorical imperative systematically attempts to rationalize that one should respect humanity by acting only in accordance with rules that hold for all others in all contexts. Only those reflections that pass the categorical imperative can be willed to become a universal law. For Kant, 'only a universal law can provide a rational person with a sufficient reason to act in good faith.'[10]

Social contract theory (Chapter 10) also offers a prescriptive attempt toward a universal value. In its assertion that free and rational people think that social contracts benefit them, social contracts are cooperatively formed and enforced. Contracts help to create shared expectations, securities, rules, and freedoms. When developed among cultures, social contracts help find common ground and universal points of agreement for conduct. However, there are remaining challenges in practice using social contract theory. It struggles to resolve issues of distrust, repression, coercion, cultural imperialism, threats, and contextually driven difficulties in applying amendments and enforcement. Social contract theory falls short of achieving a fair and sustainable universal ethic, especially when one or more parties feel un- or under-represented.

## Descriptive Attempts

Beyond the prescriptive attempts towards universalism, there have also been several descriptive attempts to accomplish the same aim. Descriptive attempts chronicle behaviours, patterns, and beliefs. To draw a straightforward distinction between descriptive and prescriptive ethics, prescriptive ethics focuses on what we 'ought' to do, and descriptive ethics focuses on describing what is already being done. For this section, we will review how care ethics and egoism describe universal ethical practices.

When looking at the universal foundations of the ethics of care (see Chapter 6), its central pillars of care and belonging, as well as a sense of community, kinship, and family (biological or otherwise), are all considered universal traits shared across cultures.[11] Think of this as a relational approach to addressing moral obligations. Care ethics builds upon this universal to delineate our moral obligations and actions to our loved ones, as established through the various philosophical lenses offered within the ethics of care. Care encompasses 'everything we do to maintain, contain, and repair our "world" so that we can live in it as well as possible'.[12]

Egoism (Chapter 5) observes only one universal aspect of human nature: individuals are programmed to act in their own interest. Thus, all voluntary acts are motivated by self-interest. Although this may seem to challenge most ethical approaches that centre on some level of responsibility to others, ethical egoism, a prescriptive side of egoism, settles this by stating that acting in one's best interest is a moral good. For an individual to be able to act in their own interest, egoism depends on the individual being free and having free will. When looking to its universal roots, egoism can be seen as sourcing from human nature's interest in survival through balancing one's own needs and interests with other practical realities like the possibility of retribution or conflict.[13]

## Policy-based Attempts

The catalyst to engage in policy-based attempts towards universal ethics comes from human-kind's history of experiencing the pains of operating without a common ground for values. Social and political conflicts, unrest, chaos, power struggles, and the loss of economic opportunity have been regarded as an chance for reflection and discussion.[14] The following attempts to establish universals through practical means represent only a small selection of the agencies, declarations, and agreements formed to formalize common, universal values.

The catastrophic devastation of the Second World War was the driving force behind the establishment of the United Nations to create a forum for global dialogue. In 1945, the United Nations Charter was drafted by 50 countries.[15] Over 70 years since its founding, the United Nations comprises 193 member states, serving as the central forum for global discussion. Among the United Nations' most significant achievements was the drafting of two universal human rights declarations: the Universal Declaration of Human Rights (UDHR) and the Convention on the Rights of the Child. The two declarations have served to frame universal understandings of human rights. With only a few but noteworthy exceptions, the two declarations have served as a foundational backbone through which countries have put in place further protections and regulations to support their recommendations.

At the international level, the United Nations Environment Programme serves in a coordinating and advisory role. In addition, many countries have their own agencies that help set standards for protecting the environment. When looking at the national level, the Environmental Protection Agency (USA), Environment Agency (UK), Ministry of Environmental Protection (China), and Federal Environment Agency (Germany), among many others, operate to lead efforts, promote research, and provide access to information to the public on matters that relate to the environment and the protection of human health from environmental risks. One of the most significant global attempts to find common ground on environmental policy was the Paris Agreement, which was ratified by 179 of the 197 Parties to the Convention.[16] The

Paris Agreement represents a practical attempt to solidify common standards and expectations to combat climate change and improve environmental conditions worldwide.

Another prominent example of leadership using universal ethical values is within the field of medicine. Beyond the UN's World Health Organization (WHO), voluntary professional organizations also help to set universal ethics of practice. The World Medical Association (WMA) is a voluntary organization of over eight million doctors spanning the globe. The WMA's International Code of Medical Ethics was adopted in 1949, with amendments in 1968, 1983, and 2006.[17] This document helps set common standards for physicians, including their responsibilities as a practitioner in the field and their behaviours with patients and colleagues.

As mentioned previously, relativism (Chapter 8) also attempts to bridge gaps in shared values, laws, and conduct. Relativism positions all cultural practices, moralities, and beliefs as being of equal validity and worth. When looking at one branch of relativism, cultural relativism, morality is contextually bound, culturally defined, and equally privileged. Therefore, what one culture may consider a moral practice, another culture might regard as dishonourable. Cultural relativism also recognizes multiple circles of culture, which can overlap or conflict. Within a particular context, leaders can be pulled from one cultural circle to another, which can cause confusion and paralysis in decision-making. As a positive, relativism can present a leader with a simple model from which to accept other moral positions and orientations. However, from the universalist perspective, a strong relativistic practice might put leaders in a compromising position and risk experiencing instability, uncertainty, and unpredictability.[18] In this respect, universalism helps leaders move past a point of paralysis and towards clarity, a common foundation, and to make ethical decisions confidently.

One primary example stands out when making the argument for universal ethics: Nazi atrocities during the Second World War. After all, if all cultural values are equal, how could we condemn acts like the Holocaust? During the international dialogue following the devastations of the Second World War, there was a strong impetus to discuss universal ethical values in the form of establishing a common understanding of human rights, or the 'innate, inalienable rights of all human beings in virtue of being human'.[19] Born from the concept of natural rights, human rights are relevant to the discussion of universal ethics because they form a common foundation of human values and ethics.

In response to the war, the Universal Declaration of Human Rights (UDHR) was adopted by the UN General Assembly in December 1948.[20] The UDHR aimed to serve as a universal standard applied to all human beings across national boundaries and all cultures. The declaration serves as a framework and guide that protects and promotes common respect, rights and freedoms. UDHR established a standard set of human rights for all people, as detailed within 30 Articles, with each identifying a different facet of human rights. This framework has been a lasting attempt to structure a set of common understandings for ethical behaviour.

Although UDHR is the most recognizable global declaration on universal ethics, there followed other attempts to represent better the unique voices and concerns of different cultures, religions, and nations. These include, but are not limited to, the International Covenant on Civil and Political Rights;[21] International Covenant on Social, Economic, and Cultural Rights;[22] Declaration Toward a Global Ethic;[23] Universal Islamic Declaration of Human Rights;[24] Cairo Declaration on Human Rights in Islam;[25] The Bangkok Declaration;[26] and Asian Human

Rights Charter: A People's Charter,[27] among others. Readers will find a summary of these in Table 7.1.

**Table 7.1** Summary of human rights documents

| Document | Date and issuing group | Basic content |
| --- | --- | --- |
| International Covenant on Civil and Political Rights (ICCPR) | Ratified in 1966 by the United Nations | Along with UDHR and ICESCR, serves as foundational text for international human rights. Addresses physical integrity, liberty and security of persons, procedures and rights for the accused, specific individual liberties and political rights |
| International Covenant on Economic, Social, and Cultural Rights (ICESCR) | Ratified in 1966 by the United Nations | Along with UDHR and ICCPR, serves as foundational documents for International Bill of Human Rights. Addresses rights for labour, health, education, and adequate standard of living |
| Declaration Toward a Global Ethic | Ratified in 1993 by Parliament of World Religions | Interfaith document that calls for commitments to cultures of nonviolence and respect for life, solidarity and just economic order, tolerance and a life of truthfulness, equal rights and partnership between men and women |
| Universal Islamic Declaration of Human Rights | Ratified in 1981 by Islamic councils in Paris and London | Based on both the Qur'an and Sunnah, outlines human rights from an Islamic perspective |
| Cairo Declaration of Human Rights in Islam | Ratified in 1990 by the Organization of the Islamic Conferences | Guarantees many of the same rights as the UDHR and does this based on Islamic Law (Sharia) |
| Bangkok Declaration | Ratified in 1993 by Ministers and Representatives of the Asian States | Focuses on commitments of the Asian region to human rights in preparation for the World Conference on Human Rights. Reaffirms commitments to UDHR and adds that terrorism has become a threat to human rights |
| Asian Human Rights Charter: A People's Charter | Produced in 1998 by NGOs in South Korea | Endorses UDHR, ICCPR, ICESR as 'an affirmation of the desire and aspirations of the people of Asia to live in peace and dignity' (Preamble) |

## MAJOR CONCEPTS OF UNIVERSAL ETHICS

The primary assumption of universal ethics is the existence of some common values consistent across cultures, thus 'universal'. These universals identify the core nature and essential characteristics of humanity itself.[28] Scholarship across disciplines has identified the following, among others, to be common threads across all cultures: dualistic thought (existence of binary opposites); religions, belief, or rituals; kinship, community, and family; reciprocity; conflict and war; frameworks of public, government, or social affairs and regulation; law and rules (including a sense of right and wrong); etiquette.[29]

One of the critical facets of universal ethics is the attempt to form a common set of moral rules to which we can all appeal. This attempt recognizes a common human need to create a sense of ethics.[30] But, of course, rules need an application to be meaningful. The United Nations' Universal Declaration of Human Rights is one attempted application of common morals. For example, UDHR's Article 15 states the following regarding citizenship rights: (1) Everyone has the right to a nationality; (2) No one shall be arbitrarily deprived of his nationality nor denied the right to change his nationality. Underpinning Article 15 is a common belief that community affiliation is a universal value. Building upon this assumption, the article declares all human beings have the right to national citizenship. Nevertheless, every country has its own laws and regulations as to the rights corresponding to nationality and naturalization processes. To this point, universals are intentionally broad in order to best represent the common ground among cultures without prescribing specific rules and rights that would be considered inappropriate or unsuitable for any one culture.

## CRITIQUES OF UNIVERSAL ETHICS

There are significant criticisms when seeking to frame universal ethics. These critiques align in two overarching categories – (1) ethics cannot be universally established fairly, and (2) universal ethics are not worth establishing.[31] We will now consider these two objections.

### Challenges from Relativism

One conceptual criticism of universal ethics stems from relativism, which argues that ethical disagreements among cultures are more significant than their areas of agreement.[32] From a relativist point of view, universals should be secondary to showing respect for the values and customs of other cultures. Because universalism can be viewed as promoting one culture's values over another's, universal values are not considered a worthwhile pursuit. For example, the 'universal' concept of individual rights and freedoms has been a contested concept from some Eastern cultures that would favour a more collectivist orientation of obligations and responsibility toward a larger group. Rights are seen as the Western, individualistic complement to freedoms, whereas obligations and responsibility are the Eastern, collective equivalents.[33] From a relativist perspective, promoting the Western versions over the Eastern is not universalism but imperialism.

Ethical imperialism presumes the superiority of a specific culture's values, ethics, and perspectives. Consequently, this ideal culture should serve as the universal standard across contexts and cultures. Historically, ethical imperialism has been a critique against Western societies in their historical colonialism and modern global leadership.[34] Because ethical imperialism typically favours the dominant power's cultural orientation, the established common values lack the voices of underrepresented global powers.[35] Thus, imperialism has favoured 'Western' values under the guise of finding universal space. As a consequence, what some view as universal values, others would critique as being oppressively Western. There have been criticisms of the UDHR for this very orientation.[36]

As mentioned earlier, a rule is only as good as its enforcement. So, besides the conceptual critique of universalism, practical criticism is that there is no consistent universal mechanism to hold leaders and followers accountable for their commitment to common values. For example, despite declarations like the UDHR, human rights violations can be seen worldwide. Despite the movements to draft and ratify international declarations and agreements, issues such as child labour, sex trafficking, genocide, and discrimination continue to be present and pervasive globally.

## Representation of Values

One of the greatest challenges of attempting to establish universals is to be representative of all global cultural stakeholders. Thus, another practical critique of universalism questions how representative any established common values can be. With only national-level leadership negotiating common ethics, there are populations of people who may feel unrepresented or underrepresented by their leaders. Indigenous and minority populations worldwide may feel that their cultures and voices do not appear in the discussions on universal morals. What makes this event more complicated is that there are so many global cultures. How, then, do leaders ensure that all voices are accurately and equally represented in the final representation of values?

## FIVE COMPONENT ANALYSIS

Having discussed the features, benefits, and challenges of universal ethics, we next examine how universalism plays out for the five components: the leader, follower, goal, context, and culture.

Under a universal ethical values model, leaders help establish, maintain, and enforce a universal standard of values. Because 'universal' ethics cut across contexts, leaders at international, national, regional, local, organizational, and community levels can all encounter challenges relevant to universal ethics. Leaders must look to the common ground among cultural norms, behaviours, and ethics to find universals among all their stakeholders. Further, once a common standard of ethical practices and values is established, leaders must share, abide by, and enforce these common moral values. For this to work, leaders must share the common basis of ethical values with their followers. Here, leaders across contexts and fields are charged with safeguarding follower rights and freedoms. In order for leaders in both the public and private spheres to safeguard and enforce human rights within all areas of their purview, it is critical to have a foundational framework of universal human rights. Beyond establishing, maintaining, and enforcing universal ethical values, leaders also set an example for followers. Because universal ethics are greater than any one person, leaders not upholding universal values can be accountable to their followers and forced to resign, go to trial, or be usurped.

A universal ethical standard is only helpful to followers if they know about it (Figure 7.2). The perspective of universal moral values requires followers to be informed about their rights and how the universal values impact their practices. Followers should be trained on how to conduct themselves within the parameters of shard ethics. This training includes common values established by international declarations, such as the UDHR, and the established national, regional, industry, and organizational standards. For example, the workers within a community health clinic should be aware of ethical standards set about human rights broadly, as well as established standards set forth by their relevant medical associations, governmental agencies, and medical affiliates or system. In this mode of thought, it is crucial to ensure that followers are well-informed and trained on how to act in line with these universal values.

As we will see in our followership chapter (Chapter 15), followers also play a critical role in holding their

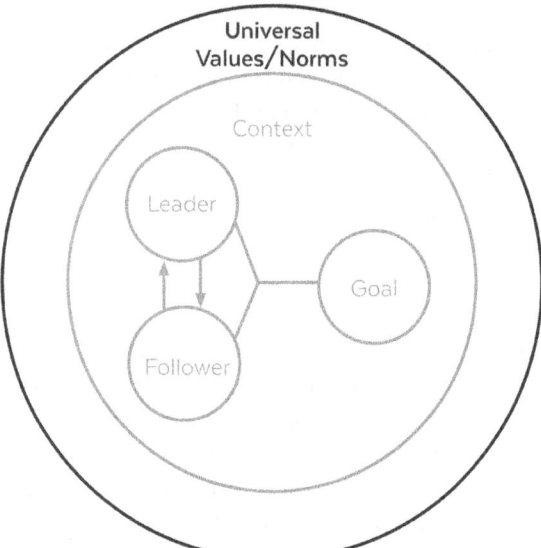

**Figure 7.2**    The Five Components of Leadership Model applied to universal ethics

leaders accountable for their practices and enforcing universal ethical values. Followers can promote universal ethics by having clear expectations for how those universal ethics are drafted, monitored, and enforced by their leaders. Followers are empowered when they are informed to monitor and hold leaders' actions to a common, formalized standard. Having an external set of universal ethical values also helps followers to be able to point to common standards to set their expectations and justify any of their concerns.

The goal of universal ethics is to find enough common ground in behaviours, social norms, and ethics to co-exist peacefully and successfully communicate, collaborate, and practise. Küng's basic minimal consensus of internal peace, economic and legal order, and institutional frameworks helps to set the essential baseline for why universal ethics are needed at an international and societal level.[37] When paring this down to the organizational level, universal ethical values aim to establish ethical transparency. The goal is to have universals in place to guide practice following a baseline of ethical practices, regardless of the cultural makeup of the organization. One of the central goals of universal ethical values is to help deliver on the promise of a common standard of treatment of other human beings, regardless of cultural orientation. Consequently, this goal is meant to protect the rights of both leaders and followers who may come from different cultures.

From the perspective of universal ethics and the UDHR, the validity of the leader's actions and legislation should be judged as to the leader's respect for human rights.[38] This rule applies in any context. So, leaders outside of the public sector should also be held accountable for their commitment to protecting human rights, even though they are not the ones granted the power to prosecute cases of human rights violations.[39]

As discussed within the goal portion of the analysis, universal ethical values aim to establish a baseline for common rights. In some contexts, this might be a measure to ensure equality regardless of cultural orientation, but it does not necessarily mean equal treatment of all regardless of culture.

Within the context of universal ethical values, the weight of power centres within the cultural component. Where we find agreement in this larger cultural context plays a critical role in determining how leaders and followers relate to each other and what goals are appropriate. Within a globalized world, with those of different cultures interacting with greater frequency, the common standards set and upheld by the United Nations and its agencies, governmental agencies, and industry organizations serve as the foundations for organizational ethical strategy. There have been many challenges to establishing common standards for ethical practices and behaviours, but that is to be expected from the intersection of different cultures and their beliefs, attitudes, and convictions.

Now that we have a better understanding of universal ethics, we can turn to our case study to see how the concept can be applied.

## CASE STUDY: UNIVERSAL ETHICS APPLIED TO INDIGENOUS LAND RIGHTS IN BRAZIL

The challenges indigenous peoples face on most continents around the globe serve as a natural case study for universal ethics and codes of human rights like the UDHR. Indigenous groups have a long history of being the subject of colonization, land appropriation, and a myriad of other human rights violations in many countries.

This case study will explore indigenous land rights, an issue that has often gone unaddressed. One of the reasons that human rights violations against indigenous peoples are often so complex is that they frequently occur alongside or as a part of new development when there is not yet a set of mature human rights instruments to address such atrocities. This is certainly true insofar as it relates to indigenous land. History illustrates numerous examples of homelands being stolen from indigenous peoples by more powerful groups. This topic will be explored in the case, focusing specifically on the concerns about indigenous land rights in Brazil under President Jair Bolsonaro.

The Universal Declaration of Human Rights was one of the first initiatives that centred land rights and the right to ownership as a Human Rights issue. Article 17 of the UDHR says, 'Everyone has the right to property alone as well in association with others. No one shall be arbitrarily deprived of his property.'[40] This resolution was welcome for indigenous groups in many countries but came far too late. For centuries indigenous groups faced land appropriation through the settlement efforts of non-indigenous groups. Because no formal structure around land ownership existed in most indigenous communities for centuries, there was typically no mechanism for resolving conflicts over land. This lack of mechanism allowed for land appropriation to occur and for the outcomes to be determined based on who was able to maintain power or wield force. In largely peaceful indigenous communities, this meant that the arrival of European settlers often meant susceptibility to forces that author Jared Diamond terms 'guns, germs, and steel' in his book by the same title.[41] The 'guns' component is obvious and refers to the fact that indigenous communities were easily overpowered by settlers and often violently forced from their land. 'Germs' such as smallpox and influenza hit hard in indigenous communities which had not developed any immunity to them, and weakened communities were more easily moved off of their native lands. 'Steel', or the mining of indigenous lands for resources to serve scientific and technological innovation, served as a primary motivation for land appropriation. In many cases, indigenous lands were stripped of the materials to build railroads and the industrial infrastructure of modern cities.

Because the 1948 UDHR did not apply specifically to indigenous groups, it did not address many of the unique human rights violations facing these communities. In 2006, the United Nations considered a more specific resolution, The United Nations Declaration on the Rights of Indigenous Peoples, which, after initial deferral, was adopted on 13 September 2007.[42] The General Assembly of the United Nations expressed a concern 'that indigenous peoples have suffered from historic injustices as a result of, inter alia, their colonization and dispossession of their lands, territories, and resources, thus preventing them from exercising, in particular, their right to development in accordance with their own needs and interests'.[43]

To address this concern, the UN resolution put forward a series of articles outlining the rights of indigenous groups and the obligations of the communities occupying the lands that once belonged to them. Article 8 (part 2) of the resolution outlines an obligation for states to 'provide effective mechanisms for the prevention of, and redress for: (b) any action which has the aim or effect of dispossessing them of their lands, territories, or resources'.[44] The resolution also asserts that indigenous peoples must be compensated for the use of their land and that it should only be sold or utilized with the informed consent of the communities impacted. Specifically, Article 10 of the resolution states that 'Indigenous peoples shall not be forcibly removed from their lands or territories. No relocation shall take place without the free, prior and informed consent of the indigenous peoples concerned and after agreement on just and fair compensation and, where possible, with the option of return.'[45]

The resolution continues to elaborate on the rights of indigenous communities, with Article 26 of the resolution most directly addressing the right to land ownership. That article states:

> (1.) Indigenous peoples have the right to the lands, territories and resources which they have traditionally owned, occupied or otherwise used or acquired; (2.) Indigenous peoples have the right to own, use, develop and control the lands, territories and resources that they possess by reason of traditional ownership or other traditional occupation or use, as well as those which they have otherwise acquired; (3.) States shall give legal recognition and protection to these lands, territories and resources. Such recognition shall be conducted with due respect to the customs, traditions and land tenure systems of the indigenous peoples concerned.[46]

About a decade after the UN Resolution, the Organization of American States (OAS) adopted the American Declaration on the Rights of Indigenous Peoples. The OAS was formed in the same year that the Universal Declaration of Human Rights was published, in 1948. The goal of the organization is to unite its member states to achieve 'an order of peace and justice, to promote their solidarity, to strengthen their collaboration, and to defend their sovereignty, their territorial integrity, and their independence'.[47] The OAS member states include all 35 independent states of the Americas. Both Brazil and the United States are members of the OAS, along with many Latin American countries, Canada, and some island nations.

The OAS's American Declaration on the Rights of Indigenous Peoples was made in June 2016. It took a significant step of involving members of indigenous communities in drafting the declaration, and recognized the contribution that they made, and also recognized that indigenous communities could be multicultural, multiracial, and otherwise not homogeneous. Like the previous UN resolution, the OAS declaration denounced the dispossession or appropriation of native lands but also introduced a discussion of conservation and sustainability. Article XIX of the Declaration, which is titled, 'Right to Protection of a Healthy Environment', reads:

1. Indigenous peoples have the right to live in harmony with nature and to a healthy, safe, and sustainable environment, essential conditions for the full enjoyment of the rights to life and to their spirituality, cosmovision, and collective well-being.
2. Indigenous peoples have the right to conserve, restore, and protect the environment and to manage their lands, territories and resources in a sustainable way.
3. Indigenous peoples have the right to be protected against the introduction, abandonment, dispersion, transit, indiscriminate use, or deposit of any harmful substance that could adversely affect indigenous communities, lands, territories and resources.
4. Indigenous peoples have the right to the conservation and protection of the environment and the productive capacity of their lands or territories and resources. States shall establish and implement assistance programs for indigenous peoples for such conservation and protection, without discrimination.[48]

In 2018 the UN Permanent Forum on Indigenous Issues recognized that indigenous land rights aren't only necessary in terms of addressing harm to indigenous peoples based on resource theft but also as the ethical thing to do to promote the common good. They wrote:

> There is growing recognition that advancing indigenous peoples' collective rights to lands, territories and resources not only contributes to their well-being but also to the greater good, by tackling problems such as climate change and the loss of biodiversity. Indigenous lands make up around 20 per cent of the earth's territory, containing 80 per cent of the world's remaining biodiversity – a clear sign that indigenous peoples are the most effective stewards of the environment.[49]

Given the dual ethical benefit of restorative justice when lands are returned to those who have been dispossessed and the common good when considering conservation and biodiversity, why has it historically been so difficult to protect indigenous land rights? This disconnect highlights one of the challenges of universal declarations of human rights, enforceability. Many human rights initiatives or universal declarations or resolutions prohibit or warn against land dispossession, but enforcement must happen at a much more local level. Often, the probability of local or regional gain outweighs the potential for universal sanctions for governments whose sphere of power overlaps with indigenous lands.

This emphasis on conservation and preservation is critical not simply because of the need to safeguard the physical environment against threats but also because of the role that indigenous land plays in maintaining the traditions and preserving the history of indigenous peoples. Emphasis needs to be put on why indigenous land rights are central to conserving biodiversity and the natural environment and preserving indigenous culture.

The UN resolution expressed concern about the dispossession of indigenous lands in terms of the theft of resources that was occurring, but also shared that they were 'convinced that control by indigenous peoples over developments affecting them and their lands, territories and resources will enable them to maintain and strengthen their institutions, cultures and traditions, and to promote their development in accordance with their aspirations and needs'.[50] This point is important given the loss of heritage that indigenous communities have experienced due to land dispossession.

Indigenous groups tend to face extremely high rates of poverty compared to regionally similar non-indigenous communities. The book *Indigenous Peoples, Poverty, and Development* presented longitudinal data on indigenous groups throughout the globe.[51] The research demonstrated that indigenous groups comprise 10 per cent of the globe's poverty while only making up 5 per cent of the world's population. The book looked at the well-being of indigenous communities in Africa, Latin America, North America, and Asia. It looked at the nations and compared indigenous poverty to poverty in the same regions in non-indigenous communities. Using five of the Millennium Development Goals as indicators for economic development, the study explored poverty in terms of infant mortality, water deprivation, malnutrition, literacy, and primary school enrolment. Importantly, it found that indigenous communities were moving more predictably towards development in Asian countries where systematic efforts had been made to increase access to and the quality of propellers of human development. The authors attributed this to long-term policy initiatives that promoted economic growth. In contrast, Latin American indigenous communities saw almost no change in poverty rates despite some efforts to target development such as healthcare and education reform. The authors attributed this to 'the absence of broad-based policy and growth'.[52] In fact, indigenous populations in countries like Brazil are actually facing higher levels of poverty over time despite development efforts.

Poverty rates are directly tied to land dispossession in indigenous communities. Land rights allow for economic security through access to food, jobs, housing stability, and the potential for development. Dispossession of land leads to instability in governance and a loss of tradition and heritage that dilutes indigenous tradition and community. In places like Latin America, where indigenous groups are rapidly losing land and the ability to have communities that aren't reliant on external groups, indigenous culture is at risk of complete erasure.

Indigenous land rights in Brazil are under serious threat from governmental policies that do not recognize the status of lands traditionally belonging to indigenous peoples and which weaken environmental protections as well as the agencies tasked with environmental regulation in the country. It is perhaps one of the most extreme cases of the challenge that the *Indigenous Peoples, Poverty, and Development* book recognized in its analysis of the development of global indigenous communities almost a decade ago.

Jair Bolsonaro became the thirty-eighth president of Brazil in 2019. A long-time military leader, Bolsonaro's first political position was as the Councillor of Rio de Janeiro in the early 1990s. Bolsonaro then joined the Brazilian National Congress as the Federal Deputy for Rio de Janeiro, and over 27 years in that role, his political positions and affiliations evolved significantly.[53] By the time Bolsonaro launched his presidential campaign, he had promoted socially and economically conservative views. His motto was, 'Brasil acima de tudo, Deus acima de totos!' which translates from Portuguese as 'Brazil above everyone, God above everyone!' During his campaign, political scientists raised concerns over the future of Brazil's democracy based on Bolsonaro's alarming nationalist and anti-democratic rhetoric, which journalists compared to that of the Nazis.[54]

Bolsonaro holds extreme far-right views and is anti-abortion, anti-environmental regulation, and against same-sex marriage while being a big supporter of gun rights, the integration of Church and state, and many controversial foreign policy positions.[55] Perhaps one of the most controversial moments of Bolsonaro's campaign was his victory speech, in which he threatened to purge the nation of the party of his political opponent, the Worker's Party, sometimes nicknamed the 'red' party. Bolsonaro said, 'These red outlaws will be banished from our homeland. It will be a cleanup the likes of which has never been seen in Brazilian history, either they go overseas or they go to jail,' and he promised to use any method necessary to purge Brazil of dissenters.[56]

Bolsonaro has also focused much of his campaigning and policy on loosening environmental regulations to allow for easier use of Amazonian resources. Before taking office, Bolsonaro promised to eliminate indigenous lands in order to 'remove barriers to agribusiness'. He declared that if he became president, 'not one centimetre of land will be demarcated for indigenous reserves or quilombolas' (descendants of runaway enslaved peoples).[57]

According to the International Work Group for Indigenous Affairs, a global human rights organization, indigenous peoples in Brazil belong to about 305 distinct groups, some of which are so small that their members are considered to be living in isolation. As of the 2010 census, the population was 896,917 indigenous persons, and about 274 distinct dialects are spoken in indigenous communities. The largest Brazilian indigenous ethnicity is the Tikúna, and most Brazilian indigenous communities live in the Amazon.[58]

Each of these groups is at risk under new national policies and shifts in leadership in Brazil. This risk highlights the complexity of universal ethics attempts, which are typically implemented through declaration or resolution. The UDHR, the UN Declaration on Indigenous Rights, and the Organization of American States' policy make it clear that land dispossession must be halted, and efforts towards restorative justice must be made to counteract centuries of historical injustice. However, Brazilian national policies are changing in a way that jeopardizes the enactment of these resolutions, and it is unclear how they might be enforced.

One challenge to enforcing protections for indigenous peoples is that the organizations that resolve to safeguard them against human rights violations are multinational. Associations like the UN or the OAS have strength in their federation of nation states around common policy or resolve. While not all member states will be impacted equally by each resolution, typically, they share an interest in allyship and trade that is strong enough to promote progress towards what is ethical for the common good of the federation. In other words, nations will often put aside their differences or indifference in order to develop shared policy if focusing on the common good allows the government to benefit in terms of allyship or resources. Nations might enter conversations from the standpoint of an ethical egoist (what best serves my interest?) to develop universal ethical declarations that best serve the interest of the commons (what bests serves the common good?).

This approach has been effective historically, particularly in the wake of the two world wars, after which there was a strong desire for countries to make peace and work productively with one another. More recently, however, many countries have seen a turn back towards nationalism and retreated from the multinational organizations that help them see how their interests align with other nation states and the common good. This newfound nationalism in countries like Brazil makes enforcement of instruments like the UDHR difficult. Brazil under Bolsonaro is less interested in democratic engagement and the sort of diplomacy involved in working within a federation and instead is focused on promoting Brazilian interests in a global market. In this specific instance, this means that Bolsonaro is more interested in finding ways to gain financially from the resources found in the Amazon than in implementing protections for indigenous land rights in accordance with the UDHR and instruments that followed it.

Bolsonaro's leadership is threatening indigenous lands in three specific ways: policy changes meant to remove land rights, the defunding of organizations that would once have protected indigenous lands from an environmental and cultural standpoint, and a deliberate ethnocide implemented through a targeted effort to drain indigenous communities of basic human rights.

In terms of policy change, Bolsonaro's government has allowed for several regulations that make it easier for indigenous lands to be developed by non-indigenous peoples. Bolsonaro designated leaders with whom he shares alliances in key agencies such as the FUNAI, the Brazilian federal agency for indigenous affairs. With those alliances in place, policies that breach the human rights of indigenous peoples were far easier to implement. In April 2020, FUNAI issued a policy allowing private properties to be registered on the interior of indigenous lands as long as the specific plot of land is not yet demarcated as belonging to an indigenous group. This policy allowed the Brazilian government to register large swathes of land in the territories of 49 indigenous communities, a total of over 690,000 acres. Though this land is now available to private owners, banks and other lending institutions are hesitant to lend to developers or indigenous groups attempting to buy back their land because of the potential for litigation over land rights. As a result, the federal government has been one of the only groups able to obtain land registration in indigenous territories. Much of it is being used for its natural resources through mining, deforestation, and energy production.[59]

Bolsonaro's administration is also using strategic defunding to breach the indigenous peoples' land rights in Brazil. After taking office, Bolsonaro's administration announced drastic budget cuts to FUNAI, the federal agency for indigenous affairs. FUNAI historically deployed leaders to advocate for the rights of indigenous peoples and to advocate against potential human rights violations. The cuts to agency funding make it impossible for FUNAI to effectively stop legislation that legalizes logging and mining on indigenous lands.[60] Bolsonaro appointed a missionary, Ricardo Lopes Dias, as the head of FUNAI.

Dias's goal was to reach even the most isolated indigenous peoples for the purpose of mission work rather than to safeguard the rights of these communities. The Brazilian congress eventually blocked his appointment.[61]

Bolsonaro's administration has also carried out a plan to 'dismantle the environment ministry from within' by cutting the budget of the Brazilian Institute of Environment and Renewable Natural Resources (IBAMA) and decreasing its enforcement agent numbers from 1,500 to less than 600.[62] Though IBAMA doesn't directly protect the rights of indigenous peoples, it does investigate and fine for environmental violations, which means there is the monitoring of illegal activities such as mining on protected lands.

Finally, Bolsonaro has engaged in an ethnocide that has deprived indigenous peoples not only of their land but also of their culture. Bolsonaro's disdain for indigenous Brazilians is not new. In 1998 he commented that it was a 'shame that the Brazilian cavalry hadn't been as efficient as the American one, which exterminated the Indians'.[63] Since taking office, Bolsonaro has commented that 'the indigenous person can't remain in his land as if he was some prehistoric creature.'[64] To that end, his administration has worked to deprive indigenous communities of necessary resources to decrease populations on protected lands. The federal government stopped paying teacher salaries at indigenous schools and issued threats that led to the withdrawal of 8,300 Cuban physicians working in Brazilian indigenous communities through an international NGO.

Without the essential resources that allowed indigenous peoples to remain in their communities and on their land, many indigenous Brazilians are having to make a difficult choice to move into cities and onto non-indigenous lands. This flight from the community will ultimately cause an ethnocide of many indigenous groups, with more isolated communities at risk of losing their history, dialect, and heritage altogether.

## FIVE COMPONENT ANALYSIS

As a final analysis of the case, this section revisits the Five Components of Leadership Model in light of the presented case. Each subsection will review the role, perspective, and challenges of the case's leader, follower, goal, context, and larger culture under a universal ethics lens (Figure 7.3).

The leader highlighted, in this case, is the former president of Brazil, Jair Bolsonaro. As the question at the outset of the chapter suggests, the obligation of leaders under UDHR is to consider and be guided by codes of ethics. In this case, Bolsonaro, as a leader, failed to look to universal codes like the UDHR or the UN resolution that aimed to protect indigenous people across the globe. Bolsonaro's failure was not simply falling short; though, universal standards are often difficult to apply. Instead, Bolsonaro's unwillingness to comply with existing universal standards highlights the challenge of enforcing universal standards in the face of growing tendencies towards nationalism.

This case treats indigenous peoples in Brazil as the follower group. The followers are charged with working toward a common goal with the leader. In this instance, the followers are not empowered to work toward the goal of preserving indigenous land rights because the leader has failed to enforce universal standards or codes of ethics. In most cases, the leader uses universal codes of ethics as a bare minimum standard for ensuring that the followers do not face human rights violations. Despite this lack of safeguarding on the part of Bolsonaro's administration, indigenous followers are rising up to become leaders in their own right and to enforce the universal ethical standards that have been developed to protect their lands.[65]

The goal of this case is to protect the rights of indigenous peoples to their lands, both because restorative justice efforts need to be made to counteract the effects of land dispossession and because the impact of development on indigenous lands has created an environmental crisis in Brazil. The Amazon was once a thriv-

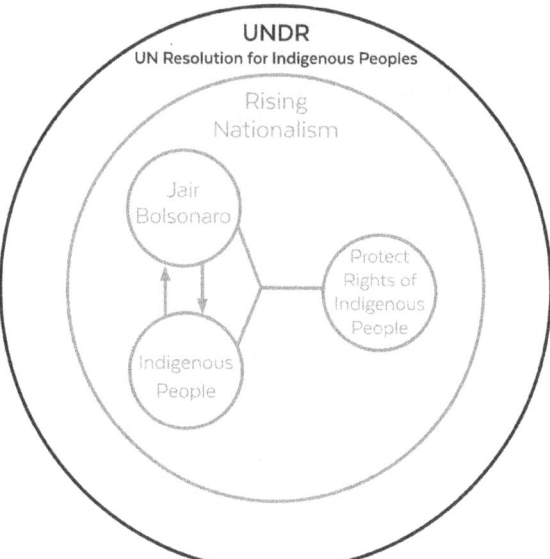

**Figure 7.3**    The Five Components of Leadership Model applied to the indigenous people's land rights in Brazil

ing and biodiverse ecosystem, and it is at increased risk because of deforestation and mining. The loss of biodiversity is keeping pace with the loss of indigenous culture, despite the goal outlined in various universal ethical declarations that indigenous land rights and culture ought to be protected.

The context is Brazil under the authority of Jair Bolsonaro and his administration. The characterization of Bolsonaro as a nationalist who would like to eliminate any minority views in Brazil and isolate it from engagement in global relationships that are not strictly for the purposes of trade is relevant. Many universal ethical standards are challenged when the coalitions that develop them are weakened. As nationalism becomes more widespread, universal ethical standards that are developed by a coalition will ultimately become weaker.

As mentioned in the context discussion, multiple cultural forces are at work in the larger culture. The competing norms and values existing within the Brazilian indigenous land rights case include the protections of indigenous communities, the rights guaranteed by UDHR, and the competing values of nationalism and capitalism, which Bolsonaro and his administration prioritize.

A lack of agreement on the goal, which has been set by groups like the UN or the OAS, and which is memorialized in documents like the UDHR or resolutions on indigenous rights, can lead to egregious violations of human rights. In a more optimistic light, the UDHR offers leaders and followers a place to look for guidelines on how they engage with each other. These guidelines can empower NGOs and indigenous communities to mobilize to protect native lands.

## SUMMARY AND CONCLUDING REMARKS

Our chapter identifies both challenges and opportunities for its response. First, the criticisms of universal ethical values point out the difficulties of identifying truly universal values, especially because 'universals' can be more representative of groups with greater relative power and privilege (e.g. 'Western'). Another challenge for universal values is enforcement. However, suppose leaders and followers can work together to find broad common values and have the patience to continually revisit the practical applications of those values – especially when they may appear contradictory. In that case, universal ethics can be a model for providing guidance in any context.

Let's return to the opening question of the chapter, 'How could universal standards guide leaders and followers in any context?' The short answer is: 'it's tricky'. The guidelines offered must be broad enough that they can be applied in any context, and both leaders and followers will need to revisit how those guidelines are being applied continually. They will need to ensure a 'universal' value as a check and balance. Also, they will need to find a way to enforce these values when they are violated.

### DISCUSSION QUESTIONS

1. How might universal ethics influence your personal life, organization, or academic institution?
2. When considering the regulations within your organization, institution, or region, what policies support the individual rights identified within UDHR? What policies might be regarded as infringing on these rights?
3. What are the ways in which you see bias on all levels (from the individual up to the local cultural context) affecting a leader's ability to uphold universal ethical values in their organization's daily business processes?
4. Is it the responsibility of leaders to uphold observation of the UDHR within their practice, or are local laws, regulations, and customs more critical to uphold?
5. When reflecting on the case study, what are the limits of the UDHR? How might the open interpretation of the UDHR's Articles be problematic?

### ADDITIONAL RESOURCES

H. Küng, *Global Responsibility: In Search Of A New World Ethic*, New York: Crossroad Publishing Company, 1991.

Küng's work makes the case that a global ethic is necessary for the survival of the human race. He is a significant figure in the discussion of global ethics, and his work has been influential for both the Parliament of the world's religions and the United Nations.

Rushworth M. Kidder, 'Universal human values: finding an ethical common ground', *Public Management*, vol. 77 no. 6, 1995, 500–508.

Though written in the 1990s, Kidder's article still provides helpful insights through interviewing two dozen 'men and women of conscience' and determining eight common values that can sustain humanity as it moves into the twenty-first century.

UN General Assembly, 'Universal Declaration of Human Rights', 217 (III) A. Paris, 1948. http://www.un.org/en/udhrbook/pdf/udhr_booklet_en_web.pdf.

For those who wish to understand the UDHR better, the UN provides an easily downloadable PDF copy of the declaration in its entirety. This booklet version is easy to read, and its accompanying illustrations can be helpful for those who wish to explain these concepts to a younger audience.

## NOTES

1. H. Küng, *Global Responsibility: In Search of a New World Ethic*, New York: Crossroad, 1991, p. 32.
2. Küng, *Global Responsibility*, p. 28.
3. K. Hutchings, *Global Ethics: An Introduction*, Malden, MA: Polity Press, 2010, p. 231.
4. Küng, *Global Responsibility*, p. 34.
5. A global imperative and adjoining justification for this is suggested in the 1997 UNESCO Declaration on the Responsibilities of the Present Generations Towards the Future Generations, which asserts 'the necessity for establishing new, equitable and global links of partnership and intragenerational solidarity, and for promoting inter-generational solidarity for the perpetuation of humankind', UNESCO *Declaration on the Responsibilities of the Present Generations to the Future Generations* 1997 (resolution 44), adopted 12 November 1997. https://en.unesco.org/about-us/legal-affairs/declaration-responsibilities -present-generations-towards-future-generations#:~:text=The%20present%20generations%20have%20the %20responsibility%20to%20identify%2C%20protect%20and,common%20heritage%20to%20future %20generations (accessed 25 October 2022).
6. UNESCO, *Declaration*.
7. UNESCO, *Declaration*.
8. B. Peterson, *Cultural Intelligence: A Guide to Working with People from Other Cultures*, London: Nicholas Brealey, 2004, p. 17.
9. N. Athanassoulis, 'Virtue ethics', *Internet Dictionary of Philosophy*. www.iep.utm.edu/virtue/ (accessed 25 October 2022).
10. M.D. Hauser, *Moral Minds: How Nature Designed Our Universal Sense of Right and Wrong*, New York: Ecco, 2006, p. 13.
11. D.E. Brown, *Human Universals*, Philadelphia, PA: Temple University Press, 1991.
12. B. Fisher and J. Tronto, 'Toward a feminist theory of caring', in E.K. Abel and M.K. Nelson (eds), *Circles of Care: Work and Identity in Women's Lives*, Albany: State University of New York Press, 1990, p. 40.
13. Brown, *Human Universals*.
14. Küng, *Global Responsibility*.
15. See United Nations, 'History of the United Nations'. http://www.un.org/en/sections/history/history-united -nations/ (accessed 25 October 2022).

16. See United Nations, 'United Nations climate change'. http://unfccc.int/paris_agreement/items/9485.php (accessed 25 October 2022).

17. World Medical Association, 'WMA International Code of Medical Ethics'. https://www.wma.net/policies-post/wma-international-code-of-medical-ethics/ (accessed 25 October 2022).

18. C.J. Sanchez-Runde, L. Nardon and R.M. Steers, 'The cultural roots of ethical conflicts in global business', *Journal of Business Ethics*, vol. 116 no. 4, 2013, 689–701.

19. Hutchings, *Global Ethics*.

20. United Nations General Assembly, *Universal Declaration of Human Rights* 1948 (resolution 217 A), adopted 10 December 1948. http://www.ohchr.org/EN/UDHR/Documents/UDHR_Translations/eng.pdf (accessed 25 October 2022).

21. Office of the United Nations High Commissioner for Human Rights (OHCHR), *International Covenant on Civil and Political Rights* 1966 (resolution 2200A; XXI), adopted 16 December 1966. Entered into force 23 March 1976. http://www.ohchr.org/EN/ProfessionalInterest/Pages/CCPR.aspx (accessed 25 October 2022).

22. Office of the United Nations High Commissioner for Human Rights (OHCHR), *International Covenant on Economic, Social and Cultural Rights* 1966 (resolution 2200A; XXI), adopted 16 December 1966. Entered into force 3 January 1976. http://www.ohchr.org/EN/ProfessionalInterest/Pages/CESCR.aspx (accessed 25 October 2022).

23. H. Küng and Council for a Parliament of the World's Religions, *Declaration Toward a Global Ethic 1993*, adopted 4 September 1993. https://parliamentofreligions.org/global-ethic/towards-a-global-ethic-an-initial-declaration/ (accessed 25 October 2022).

24. Islamic Council of Europe, *Universal Islamic Declaration of Human Rights* 1981, adopted 19 September 1981. http://www.alhewar.com/ISLAMDECL.html (accessed 25 October 2022).

25. Organization of Islamic Cooperation, *Cairo Declaration on Human Rights in Islam* 1990, adopted 5 August 1990. http://hrlibrary.umn.edu/instree/cairodeclaration.html (accessed 25 October 2022).

26. Ministers and representatives of Asian States, *Final Declaration of the Regional Meeting for Asia of the World Conference on Human Rights* 1993, adopted 29 March to 2 April 1993. https://www.hurights.or.jp/archives/other_documents/section1/1993/04/final-declaration-of-the-regional-meeting-for-asia-of-the-world-conference-on-human-rights.html#_ednref1 (accessed 25 October 2022).

27. Asian Human Rights Commission, *Asian Human Rights Charter: A Peoples' Charter* 1998, adopted 17 May 1998. http://www.refworld.org/pdfid/452678304.pdf (accessed 25 October 2022).

28. W.H. Goodenough, *Description and Comparison in Cultural Anthropology*, Chicago, IL: Aldine, 1970.

29. Brown, *Human Universals*.

30. Küng, *Global Responsibility*, p. 29.

31. G. Demuijnck, 'Universal values and virtues in management versus cross-cultural moral relativism: an educational strategy to clear the ground for business ethics', *Journal of Business Ethics*, vol. 128 no. 4, 2015, 817–35.

32. C. Gowans, 'Moral relativism', in Edward N. Zalta (ed.), *The Stanford Encyclopedia of Philosophy*, Winter 2016 edn. https://plato.stanford.edu/archives/win2016/entries/moral-relativism/ (accessed 25 October 2022).

33. O.A. Sanchez, 'Some contributions to a universal declaration of human obligations', in T.S. Axworthy (ed.), *Bridging the Divide: Religious Dialogue and Universal Ethics*, Montreal: McGill-Queen's University Press, 2008, pp. 187–95, p. 188.

34.  C. Kleist, 'Global ethics', *Internet Encyclopedia of Philosophy*. http://www.iep.utm.edu/ge-capab/#SH4b (accessed 25 October 2022). See also N.L. Roth, T. Hunt, M. Stavropoulos and K. Babik, 'Can't we all just get along: cultural variables in codes of ethics', *Relations Review*, vol. 22 no. 2, 1996, 151–61.

35.  Roth et al., 'Can't we all just get along'.

36.  Sanchez, 'Some contributions'.

37.  See 'Towards a Global Ethic: An Initial Declaration', Parliament of the World's Religions, Chicago, 1993.

38.  T. Pogge, *World Poverty and Human Rights: Cosmopolitan Responsibilities and Reforms*, Cambridge: Polity Press, 2002.

39.  B. Fasterling and G. Demuijnck, 'Human rights in the void? Due diligence in the UN Guiding Principles on Business and Human Rights', *Journal of Business Ethics*, vol. 116 no. 4, 2013, 799–814, p. 802.

40.  United Nations, *Universal Declaration of Human Rights, Article 17*, 1948. https://www.un.org/en/about-us/universal-declaration-of-human-rights#:~:text=Article%2017,arbitrarily%20deprived%20of%20his%20property (accessed 25 October 2022).

41.  J. Diamond, *Guns, Germs, and Steel: The Fates of Human Societies*, New York: Norton, 2005.

42.  United Nations, *Declaration on the Rights of Indigenous Peoples*, 13 September 2007. https://www.ohchr.org/en/indigenous-peoples/un-declaration-rights-indigenous-peoples (accessed 25 October 2022).

43.  United Nations, *Declaration on the Rights of Indigenous Peoples*.

44.  United Nations, *Declaration on the Rights of Indigenous Peoples*.

45.  United Nations, *Declaration on the Rights of Indigenous Peoples*.

46.  United Nations, *Declaration on the Rights of Indigenous Peoples*.

47.  Organization of American States (OAS), *Charter of the Organization of American States*, 30 April 1948. https://www.refworld.org/docid/3ae6b3624.html (accessed 25 October 2022).

48.  OAS, *Charter*.

49.  United Nations, Permanent Forum on Indigenous Issues, 19 April 2018. https://www.un.org/development/desa/indigenouspeoples/wp-content/uploads/sites/19/2018/04/Indigenous-Peoples-Collective-Rights-to-Lands-Territories-Resources.pdf (accessed 25 October 2022).

50.  United Nations, *Universal Declaration of Human Rights*, Preamble.

51.  G. Hall and H.A. Perkins, *Indigenous Peoples, Poverty, and Development*, New York: Cambridge University Press, 2012.

52.  P. Horn, 'Book review of Indigenous peoples, poverty, and development', *The Journal of Development Studies*, vol. 50 no. 11, 2014, 1588–90.

53.  R. Lapper, *Beef, Bible, and Bullets: Brazil in the Age of Bolsanaro*, Manchester: Manchester University Press, 2022.

54.  'Jair Bolsonaro hopes to be Brazil's Donald Trump', *The Economist*, 9 November 2017. https://www.economist.com/the-americas/2017/11/09/jair-bolsonaro-hopes-to-be-brazils-donald-trump (accessed 25 October 2022).

55.  G. Casarões, 'Brazilian foreign policy under Jair Bolsonaro: far-right populism and the rejection of the liberal international order', *Cambridge Review of International Affairs*, vol. 35 no. 4, 2021, 1–21.

56.  T. Phillips, 'Brazil's Jair Bolsonaro threatens purge of leftwing "outlaws"', *The Guardian*, 22 October 2018. https://www.theguardian.com/world/2018/oct/22/brazils-jair-bolsonaro-says-he-would-put-army-on-streets-to-fight (accessed 25 October 2022).

57. M. Mendes and N. Pontes, 'Indigenous land, culture at stake in Brazil election – experts", Reuters, 26 October 2018.
https://www.reuters.com/article/us-brazil-election-landrights-deforestat/indigenous-land-culture-at-stake-in-brazil-election-experts-idUSKCN1N0241 (accessed 25 October 2022).

58. International Work Group for Indigenous Affairs, 'Indigenous peoples in Brazil'. http://www.iwgia.org/en/brazil.html (accessed 26 October 2022).

59. R. Anzolin Begotti and C.A. Peres, 'Brazil's indigenous lands under threat', *Science*, 8 February 2019. https://www.science.org/doi/10.1126/science.aaw3864 (accessed 26 October 2022).

60. C. Rocha, M. Reverdos and R. Pedroso, 'Deforestation is accelerating in Brazil as Bolsonaro's first term ends, experts say', CNN, 20 September 2022.
https://www.cnn.com/2022/09/20/americas/brazil-bolsonaro-deforestation-term-intl-latam (accessed 25 October 2022).

61. M. Savarese, 'Former evangelical missionary to lead Brazil's isolated indigenous unit', Associated Press, 5 February 2020.
https://www.pbs.org/newshour/world/former-evangelical-missionary-to-lead-brazils-isolated-indigenous-unit (accessed 25 October 2022).

62. M. Rodrigues, 'Bolsonaro's troubled legacy for science, health and the environment', *Nature*, 27 September 2022. https://www.nature.com/articles/d41586-022-03038-3 (accessed 25 October 2022).

63. E. Londoño and L. Casado, 'As Bolsonaro keeps Amazon vows, Brazil's indigenous fear "ethnocide"', *New York Times*, 19 April 2020.
https://www.nytimes.com/2020/04/19/world/americas/bolsonaro-brazil-amazon-indigenous.html (accessed 25 October 2022).

64. M. Schuch, 'Indigenous people cannot stay in their land like prehistoric human beings, says Bolsonaro', *Valor*, 18 February 2020. https://valor.globo.com/politica/noticia/2020/02/18/indio-nao-pode-ficar-na-sua-terra-como-ser-pre-historico-diz-bolsonaro.ghtml (accessed 25 October 2022).

65. P. Villegas, 'Besieged and ignored, Brazil's indigenous women are running for office', *The Washington Post*, 30 September 2022.
https://www.washingtonpost.com/world/2022/09/30/brazil-election-indigenous-women/ (accessed 25 October 2022).

# 8
# Cultural relativism

*Stephanie Varnon-Hughes, Stanley J. Ward and Alexandra K. Perry*

## FRAMING QUESTION

How do culture and context impact leadership?

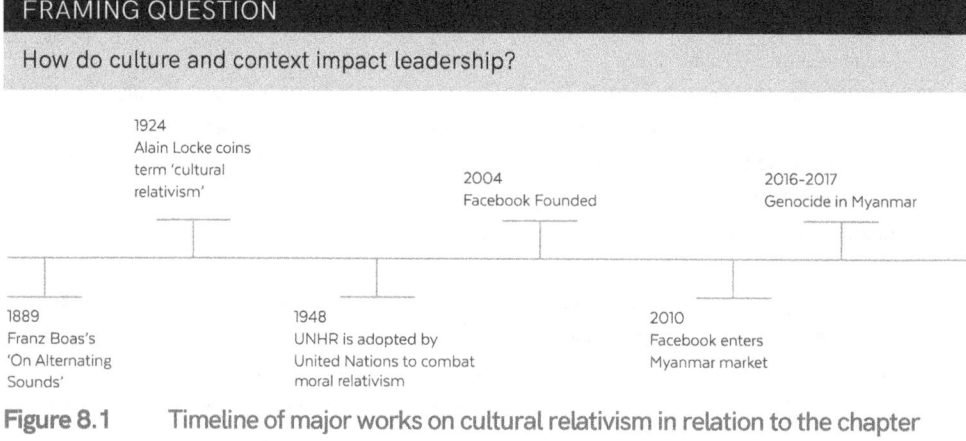

1924
Alain Locke coins
term 'cultural
relativism'

2004
Facebook Founded

2016-2017
Genocide in Myanmar

1889
Franz Boas's
'On Alternating
Sounds'

1948
UNHR is adopted by
United Nations to combat
moral relativism

2010
Facebook enters
Myanmar market

**Figure 8.1**   Timeline of major works on cultural relativism in relation to the chapter
case study

In 2019, U.S. multinational enterprises employed 43.9 million workers.[1] In some of these
countries, giving gifts is how business gets done; in other countries, giving gifts is viewed as
a bribe. When organizations interact with diverse populations – across nations or even within
their own national borders – culture and context make a difference. Based on cultural differences, relativism highlights the impact of culture and context on ethical decisions.

For as long as leaders have engaged with communities outside their own, questions of different values have challenged notions of what it means to lead ethically. Within various cultures,
different values dictate different perceptions of what is 'moral', 'right', 'good', and 'just'. Ethical
relativism is a challenge for any leader, regardless of leadership style or a leader's relationship
with followers. And yet, despite being a challenge, the critical and creative thinking skills developed by grappling with relativism are also essential for responsive, culturally sensitive leadership.

A variety of factors can contribute to the challenges of relativism in a leadership setting:
sometimes, issues come from the community of followers; sometimes, they come from cultural
differences; and sometimes they come from the specific context. Occasionally – and most chal-

lenging for leaders – the same goal can be ethically correct in one setting but unethical in another. A minefield of potential 'improper' ethical decisions exists for organizations and endeavours that work and collaborate across cultures. However, by virtue of their very position, leaders must not become mired in relativism. Rather than surrender to 'paralysis by analysis', leaders must act – even in the midst of differing ethical opinions. Those who choose to express leadership must use their cultural intelligence to make informed decisions and take action. In this chapter, we'll trace the factors that have converged to construct our current understanding of 'ethical relativism', the key ideas essential for leaders to understand and navigate the concept, and the model's critiques. We will then apply the Five Components of Leadership Model to explore how relativism can be both a challenge and an advantage for any diverse organization. We will then use a recent case study to examine relativism's essential themes.

Some criticize higher education because they perceive it as presenting relativism as the only philosophical 'truth'. Our chapter is not making that argument but rather trying to unpack the implications of relativism for leadership. First, let's define what we mean by 'relativism' for our chapter. It may be helpful to define relativism by way of contrast. Where 'absolutism' tells us that some things are always ethically correct and can be independently verified as such, relativism says that the context must always be taken into account. Relativism is a widely used term in philosophical discussions and can be variously defined, as indicated in Table 8.1.[2] To narrow our focus, we will focus on cultural relativism. Leaders frequently confront challenges related to diverse cultural perspectives thanks to the ubiquity of international media, the Internet, and multinational corporations and organizations.

A favourite way to express the ethics of cultural relativism is to assert, 'When in Rome, do as the Romans'. The struggle here is that the Romans allowed for certain forms of infanticide and human slavery. Can leaders from one culture that condemns these practices simply allow for them when in the Roman context? While our Roman illustration may seem dated, it's relevant because when we look at our case study, we will consider the implications of failing to consider the cultural implications of the way a product or service may be used in another culture. But first, let's consider the history of relativism as a philosophical concept.

Table 8.1   Types of relativism

| Type | Major concepts |
| --- | --- |
| Cultural relativism | Norms and values of right and wrong are based on the conventions of a particular location, group, or culture |
| Conceptual relativism | We determine the categories by which we interpret our experience. There is no pre-determined reality |
| Alethic relativism | Objective truth does not exist. What is true for one person may not be true for another |
| Epistemic relativism | What counts as 'knowledge' is determined by the context which produces it. No one system of knowledge can be proven superior to another |

Note: The Stanford Encyclopedia of Philosophy lists 'moral relativism' as the fifth type but also explains that moral relativism, if seen as culturally dependent, can be seen as a sub-type of cultural relativism. That is how we use it here.

Source: Typology adapted from M. Baghramian and J.A. Carter, 'Relativism', Stanford Encyclopedia of Philosophy, 11 September 2015.

## HISTORY

Cultural relativism has a long and rich history in ethics literature. As early as the fourth century, Herodotus recognized that when faced with multiple cultural perspectives, humans prefer their own way of doing things rather than trying to find what is 'true'. As a philosophical theory, relativism dates back to the eighteenth-century moral philosopher Immanuel Kant, the subject of Chapter 2. Kant's theory of knowledge was that there are structures that exist *a priori*, meaning that knowledge of them is independent of any experience. Mathematical facts, the movement of time, or tautologies (such as, 'all men are human') are all examples of *a priori* truths. Beyond these *a priori* truths, Kant believed that all knowledge was derived from experience, making it relative to each person so that those with shared experiences would also share more of a knowledge base than those without shared experiences.[3] Though Kant did not use the term 'cultural relativism', the theory was articulated in his epistemological work.

Cultural anthropologists picked up on the ideas Kant and his students laid out during the period that spanned both world wars. With increasing exposure to other places and cultures during the wars, academics struggled to make sense of how the different cultures they encountered could have such diverse and seemingly incommensurate value systems. Cultural relativism was a way of making sense of conflicting values. Linguists, especially, felt that this theory had a lot of explanatory power. Given that language has such a clear impact on the way that we understand our world, it was no wonder that people who spoke different languages might also have different value systems. This idea expanded on an earlier study by Franz Boas, a nineteenth-century anthropologist who studied Native American language and began to notice idiosyncrasies in the linguistic convention between groups that he first believed to be meaningless. The longer he studied these groups, he began to realize that these idiosyncrasies in pronunciation actually carried great significance.[4] A half-century later, during the Second World War, anthropologists began to go back to Boas' work and to use the term 'cultural relativism', which he had coined.

However, the challenge with cultural relativism as studied by anthropologists is that it doesn't offer a solution to competing values. Anthropology might describe the radical views of the Nazis as compared to the opposition of the Allied forces, but when both sides aggressively assert that they are correct, how can such a conflict be resolved? According to cultural relativism, there may not be a way to resolve it. The Allied forces believed they were right based on their values; so, too, the Nazis believed that they were right based on their own cultural ideals. Without moral absolutes, there is no way to determine which group is right.

Cultural relativism hit its peak in the United States during the Vietnam War. In this case, the competing 'cultures' were actually based on generation and class. The war was one that many didn't understand and believe in, and it spurred protests and anti-government movements. Again, academics turned to cultural relativism to describe the vastly different values held by Vietnam opponents and those in favour of the war.[5] While cultural relativism reached its zenith as an ethical construct in the 1970s, most ethical scholars now temper its claims. Now that we have a basic understanding of the definition and history of relativism, we can more closely examine the idea's fundamental assumptions.

## MAJOR CONCEPTS IN CULTURAL RELATIVISM

As we try to understand cultural relativism and its impact on leaders, we should first consider five key claims and implications for relativism in a leadership context:

1. Culture and context necessarily dictate our values;
2. As a consequence, values are based on a particular framework;
3. Therefore, no viewpoint is more correct than others;
4. Yet, relativism should not be confused with nihilism;
5. Thus, values become a crucial part of the conversation on relativism.

Readers should note that our discussion of relativism here is not purely theoretical – because that might lead to nihilism – or a rejection of all moral principles – that leaders cannot and should not abide. Instead, our thoughts are guided by a desire to offer a practical form of relativism. Rather than concentrating on individual claims as we have done in previous chapters, we will focus on these critical arguments beginning with our first premise, 'culture and context necessarily dictate our values', and proceed to relativism's conclusion, 'values become a crucial part of the conversation on relativism'.

If we are raised in a water-rich environment, wasting water is not sinful. If cows are sacred, fast food includes veggie patties and dairy but never meat. Both avowed religious women and mothers are celebrated in the same culture, while the former practice celibacy and the latter do not. So even though values vary widely, we humans are capable of evaluating laws, cultural norms, and individual practices based on factors including human need, issues of scarcity, that which we hold as sacred, and exposure to new technologies or knowledge. That said, even when we are capable of understanding that there are a variety of possible values in a given setting, for the most part, human communities and organizations prefer to operate with one set of predominant values.

For example, in the United States, even while vegetarian and vegan menu items options have become more widely available and normalized in restaurants, specific meals (like Thanksgiving dinner) and certain settings (BBQ picnics, parties celebrating football) remain linked to the consumption of meat. The strands of culture that make 'tradition' in the United States – like our Judeo-Christian background, a privileging of Western European values and food practices, and commercial farming and ranching – set up decisions around hospitality and consumption. Once again, although we might understand that there are different values and norms, we still operate within a predominant paradigm, or a particular way of thinking and doing things.

In some countries, a glass of beer or wine at a working lunch is typical. In others, the same glass of beer or wine would be immoral or even illegal. A 'good' team member might need to adapt to both practices within a career at the same company. To succeed in our careers, to be generous hosts, or to participants in collaborative endeavours, we often leave the comfort zones of our own preferences and bend a bit to the prevailing values of the cultures and contexts in which we interact.

For example, scholars at academic conferences frequently attend formal receptions and informal gatherings at hotel bars and restaurants. As Islamic studies, inter-religious studies, and Muslim scholars have become more represented in academia, many young, practising Muslim academics find themselves challenged. Muslims do not believe in consuming alcohol. Personally, they would prefer not to meet in a bar. Professionally, they know it is appropriate and helpful – they may be left out of critical collaborations and continued joint conversations if they demur.

Here is the point where many of us become paralysed. This equality of views may seem a logical conclusion from 'values and actions are relative to a particular framework'. Further, in the world of philosophy and ideas, it can be instructive to play with this and investigate this concept. The struggle is that it cannot be an operating framework in the real world. At some point, we have to choose whether to go to the bar and have a drink with our colleagues. Also, even for relativists, some viewpoints have much more value than others.

For example, most leaders' decisions prioritize the safety, ongoing security, and conditions for individual human lives to flourish above the needs and rights of other living creatures and other possible factors. Economist Amartya Sen and philosopher Martha Nussbaum call this 'maximum human flourishing' when they evaluate economic systems and how they impact human communities.[6] That is, if a business or government has options that can create opportunities for flourishing (health, autonomy, access to education, economic security, and civil liberties) for a greater number of people, they should pursue those options over those choices that either curtail those rights, or only create opportunities for flourishing for a few.

There are still some values we can agree on, such as the value of respecting life, but we struggle to create cross-cultural definitions that work here. Suppose one follows relativism to the false and unhelpful conclusion that because all values are equal, it is impossible to choose how to act responsibly. In that case, we come to nihilism – the idea that no possible moral choice exists, so life is meaningless. While many of us wrestle with cynicism and doubt from time to time, part of our identity as leaders includes desiring to bring about change. To foster change, we must believe that current conditions and obstacles can be addressed and a 'better' outcome can be created and maintained.

Thus, scholars such as Rorty and Nussbaum argue for 'flourishing' as a guiding moral value.[7] Individual humans can flourish; so too can families, cities, businesses, governments, and economies. Questions related to values go beyond the first questions we often ask about productivity and efficiency: How do we maximize profit? How do we speed up production? How do we beat our competition? How do we cut our losses? Instead, flourishing-related questions should include: How does this decision positively impact the greatest number? Does this policy allow for flexibility and individual choice? Does this budget curtail healthcare access for those in our community? Do the long-term effects of this decision create environmental or economic harm for this region? Now that we have a better understanding of relativism's fundamental principles, let's consider its major critiques.

## CRITIQUES OF RELATIVISM

There are two primary critiques of cultural relativism as an approach to ethical leadership – the first theoretical and the second practical.

The theoretical critique is of the central tenet of the theory itself: if morality is relative – at least to culture – how is it possible to say that morality exists at all? In other words, if the appraisal of what is right can only be done within the confines of the culture in which an action takes place, is it ever possible to condemn actions that seem to be universally worth condemnation or to praise those actions that seem inherently good? Cultural relativists are not uncomfortable with this critique. Morality is similar to currency – its value is tied to the culture within which it is circulated, and yes, this causes challenges when cultures collide. Still, we may find ways to adapt and address these challenges.

It is really in extreme cases that this critique shows its teeth. While some particular values may be shared across and between cultures, other actions seem impossible to understand through the lens of cultural relativism. How can we condemn mass murder, such as that witnessed in Cambodia under Pol Pot, if we subscribe to a view that moral and immoral action can only be assessed within the confines of particular cultures? The critique asserts that although different viewpoints exist, that does not necessarily entail that they are all right. People can be both sincere and fervent and also simply wrong.

The practical critique is of relativism's utility for leaders. It asks: 'How can leaders make ethical decisions when they lead diverse groups?' Critics claim that relativism makes it difficult or even impossible for leaders to be decisive and take action. This claim, in turn, creates distress amongst followers who look to leaders for clarity and moral guidance. Leaders do not have the luxury of indecisiveness.

Take, for example, a college administrator planning for the academic year calendar. The school has a relatively small but present percentage of Jewish students. This year, the Jewish high holy days all fall on Wednesdays. The administrator considers closing the university on those days to allow students to observe the holidays with their families. However, given how small the Jewish population is and the number of classes that meet only on Wednesdays, she decides that this would make it impossible for those courses to offer the number of contact hours necessary for the class. She chooses to implement a policy that allows Jewish students to be absent from classes on these days without any penalty to their grades and without any requirement to make up the work they missed that day. While this solution is sensitive to the cultural significance of the high holy days, it leaves the university's professors in a bind: Does this mean that the students who observe these holidays are now responsible for less material than the students who do not? Does this mean the material present on cumulative exams cannot be taught these days? How are faculty to determine which students can 'legitimately' miss these classes and which students' absences should be deemed unexcused? The truth is, there is no solution to this challenge that will satisfy everyone. Relativists would claim that this is acceptable; respecting all cultural beliefs is the right thing to do. Critics look at the practicality of doing so in a society where we welcome diversity and argue that it is impossible for a leader to truly be decisive enough to embrace cultural relativism. This is just one example of cultural relativism's practical implications for leaders. However, the ethical theory also has implications for the other aspects of the leadership process.

## FIVE COMPONENT ANALYSIS

We now return to our five components of leadership to clarify how relativism impacts leadership as a phenomenon. Similar to our discussion of the pivotal concepts of relativism, we will strive to provide an analysis that is practical and not purely theoretical. As we can see from Figure 8.2, cultural values and norms are the keys to understanding how cultural relativism relates to the Five Components of Leadership Model.

One implication of cultural relativism is that leaders need a kind of cultural humility as well as to develop skills related to cultural intelligence. As part of that cultural intelligence, they must distinguish between what elements of their ethical system are 'core' to who they are and what parts are flexible, depending on the context. This need for self-knowledge resonates with the authentic leadership model described in Chapter 13, where leaders need to know their core values. One difference here is that authentic leadership does not provide much guidance for how leaders can negotiate the 'flex' required when dealing with cultural relativism.

Self-awareness alone will not meet the demands of ethical relativism. Leaders must also be aware of who their followers are and what they hold sacred. This follower-awareness is another example of the humility required by leaders who embrace cultural relativism and how the ideas of 'core' and 'flex' play an important role.[8] What may make this tricky for leaders is that they must balance the needs of the organization to accomplish certain tasks with the belief systems of followers who may be limited in their ability to perform certain tasks. Leaders need discernment to recognize what requests from followers are authentic and bear accommodation, which we will consider further in our discussion of 'context.'

On a practical level, even after identifying their own perspectives and listening to what followers hold sacred, leaders still have work to do. Leaders trying to address cultural relativism are in a precarious situation because if they place too much emphasis on highlighting the different perspectives in the room, there is a risk of creating even more divisions within the group of followers. One

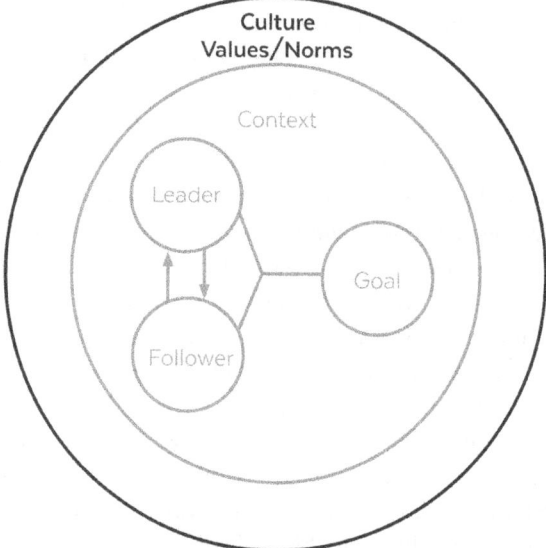

**Figure 8.2**      The Five Components of Leadership Model applied to cultural relativism

way to address these differences while still encouraging unity is to focus on how the group's different cultural perspectives can contribute to achieving the overall goal.[9]

Relativism also impacts the relationships between various followers. Followers must realize that both peers and leaders may hold beliefs that are contrary to their own, yet their peers and leaders hold those beliefs with equal sincerity. So followers, too, must develop a measure of cultural humility and allow for what is most important to others. Readers should note that, once again, awareness of the 'other' and the ability to negotiate critical tasks based on that awareness is a crucial skill set for leaders and followers to accomplish goals within cultural relativism.

A positive consequence of recognizing cultural relativism is that doing so can foster a culture of respect. This culture of respect can be measured to the extent that both leaders and followers are aware of the authentic needs of both each other and the organization, and to the extent that those personal and organizational needs and values are accommodated. In a sense, this accommodation demonstrates an attempt to meet both the task and the relational challenges faced by organizations, where 'task' can be understood as the necessary outputs of an organization and differing personal values are considered part of the 'relationship'.[10]

Determining the validity of a goal and its possible unintended consequences becomes difficult with relativism (as will be seen in our case study). Multiple ethical filters are at play. The possibility for confusion implies a need for leaders and followers to communicate at length about clarifying the goal (like the adage 'measure twice, cut once'). We know that a principal expectation from followers is a desire for clarity, yet ethical clarity can easily be lost here. The good news is that although it is difficult to evaluate a moral stand in settings that experience cultural relativism, once we have negotiated it and found a shared sense of purpose, we can stand there with greater confidence.

Relativism recognizes that even in one specific organization's context, many cultural expectations still make demands on the leader, follower, and goal. As a benefit, relativism draws awareness to what makes people unique even though they share the same immediate context.

Relativism also creates challenges in the context of leadership engagement. One concern is how we honour another's culture without putting undue stress on the organization. For example, consider a circumstance where a worker's religion demands that he not shave, yet the company requires clean-shaven appearances because of the preferences of the company's clientele. Both the religious adherent and the company are sincere in their desire to uphold their values within a specific context, and both are trying to honour demands placed on them by outside forces (religion or the requirements of a particular client base). Indeed, one solution is to say, 'Well, the religious adherent should simply find employment somewhere else.' But what if the 'clean-shaven' positions provide higher income and career advancement opportunities than positions that allow for facial hair? Shouldn't leaders also care about implementing a fair and equitable environment?

As we've already discussed, relativism makes it difficult for leaders and followers to achieve ethical clarity. The temptation then becomes to descend into the abyss of nihilistic cultural values where 'anything goes' or 'might makes right'. That temptation to fall into an unprincipled pragmatism is one more reason that leaders must be intentional in how they choose to engage the cultural values surrounding their context.

More than any other ethical models we've considered, relativism advocates for many cultural spheres that bind leaders, followers, goals, and contexts. Sometimes these spheres integrate neatly, and at other times these spheres conflict with each other harshly. Many human resource programmes today struggle with navigating diversity in the workplace precisely because of how these cultural spheres can come into conflict. Other models may project a more monolithic representation of culture. Relativism acknowledges the flurry of interactions going on in the modern world. Let's now turn to a specific instance to illustrate the way cultural relativism may impact the leadership process. For that, we turn to our case study.

## CASE STUDY: THE USE OF FACEBOOK AS A NEWS SOURCE WITHOUT LOCAL-LANGUAGE MODERATION

'The Facebook' began as a way for college students to see and rank classmates' attractiveness. Later, we used it in the United States to look up high school classmates and play imaginary farming games. According to its mission, Facebook seeks to bring people together. In the early 2000s, it was a website where real-life friends could share information and interact digitally, like 'poking' or 'tagging' in photographs. Originally for students only, thousands more people joined once the requirement to have an .edu email address was removed. It became common to 'friend' acquaintances, people from the gym or workplace, or far-removed family members. Businesses and non-profits created 'pages' users could follow, and news agencies began delivering news designed for social media. Despite the vast amount of information its platform shares, Facebook has steadfastly refused to be categorized as a 'media company'. Such a designation would mean they would have to subject themselves to the same oversight newspapers and journalists have regarding reporting practices, such as not publishing hate speech or inflammatory media.

The United Nations reported that Facebook was a key factor in disseminating information and cultivating behaviours that led to genocide in Myanmar. In 2016, the Burmese military began killing or persecuting the Rohingya people, who are Muslim. Many of these people fled to Bangladesh, which led to the creation of the world's largest refugee camp. In an official statement, US Secretary of State Anthony Blinken labelled the events in 2016 and 2017 as 'genocide' with over 9,000 Rohingya killed in 2017 alone and 700,000 fleeing across the border.[11]

How does a 'social network' go from light-hearted connections between IRL ('in real life') friends to becoming a tool for violence? This case study traces the rapid growth of Facebook (now known as 'Meta') and how that growth brought challenges for the leader and followers. The lack of understanding of context and culture exacerbated those challenges. Certainly, context and culture are part of what makes the Facebook experience immediate and appealing for users. Yet, the lack of preparation to confront issues of ethical leadership with organizational health and functionality threaten the organization.

Its rapid adoption in Myanmar exemplifies what makes the platform so appealing and accessible and how cultural differences would create nearly insurmountable difficulties for the organization. In 2010, Facebook entered the Burmese market, and 'Facebook initially allowed its app to be used without incurring data charges, so it gained rapid popularity. It would come pre-loaded on mobile phones and was a cultural fit.'[12] This occurred in a country where in 2014 less than 1 per cent of the population had internet access.

By 2016, Myanmar had more Facebook users than any other south Asian country, and 'A 2016 report by GSMA, the global body representing mobile operators, found that in Myanmar many people considered Facebook the only internet entry point for information, and that many regarded postings as news.'[13]

At the time of the case of increasing communal violence in 2017, nationalist posts inciting attacks on the Rohingya 'spiked'. For example, in one 55,000-member Facebook group, posts went from below 25 to more than 300 per day during attacks. During this time, Facebook was in a phenomenal growth period. By 2021, more than half the country used Facebook.

While Facebook succeeded in being widely used in Myanmar, its success also became part of a humanitarian crisis. The Republic of the Gambia and Rohingya refugees in the United States and the United Kingdom are bringing separate civil actions against Facebook for its role in the genocide against Rohingya people in Myanmar. The United Nations has specifically cited Facebook for playing a direct role in the humanitarian crisis.[14]

Facebook CEO Mark Zuckerberg and senior leadership expressed dismay that Facebook had a part in the genocide. They hired additional Burmese and other translators in Myanmar and other areas where Facebook became a platform for hate speech, terrorism, and political oppression.

Facebook has also accelerated policies and processes to prevent their participation in atrocities or harm to communities or individuals. It has released an official statement that it had not done enough to prevent Facebook 'from being used to foment division and incite offline violence'.[15] In their admission of complicity, Facebook named 'being a force for good' as their organizational aim. They stated, 'We know we need to do more to ensure we are a force for good in Myanmar and in other countries facing their own crises.'[16]

Increasingly, Facebook utilized artificial intelligence to review and flag problematic content, using automated systems to flag content related to terrorism and hate speech in more than 50 languages. However, real-life usage and language nuance change rapidly and are highly contextual; Facebook insiders share that 'the problem of inferring the semantic meaning of speech with high precision is not remotely close to solved' and artificial intelligence can't help without human trainers.[17]

One thing that did not change was their basic business model. Increasing the number of countries, users, languages, and markets that use Facebook means more advertising revenue. Facebook has long said that they are not responsible for 'user content', and allow users to report content that goes against community standards. This attitude may work in one setting where Facebook is only one of various internet platforms, only a few languages are dominant, and content can be moderated. The situation becomes far more challenging in settings where Facebook becomes synonymous with 'the internet'. What responsibilities do leaders have when growing a market for 'social' media when it becomes used in new (and violent) ways in new geopolitical domains? Is it possible for a multinational company to marry the twin aims of increasing users, clicks, and revenue with being a force for good? Which aim has priority? If users misuse the platform, what responsibility does Meta have?

## FIVE COMPONENT ANALYSIS

In this case, Facebook as an organization is the leader. Its power over the dissemination of information that its users want gives it tremendous global influence (Figure 8.3).

In response to the use of information for violent purposes, Facebook also created an internally sanctioned Human Rights Impact Assessment. They sought in 2018 to hire 'dozens' of Burmese language content reviewers.[18] They also invested in staff with language knowledge in places like Afghanistan and Somalia. Military or insurgent groups in regions with military conflict and civil war were banned from using the platform. Since 2018, Facebook has also begun working with local NGOs to prevent the spreading of hate speech and propaganda. Likewise, they began campaigns in places like Somalia to educate users on disinformation, community standards, and reporting mechanisms for users to report content.[19]

In the case of the use and misuse of the platform by anti-Rohingya criminals in Myanmar, Facebook did address the issue, after the fact. Because of increased scrutiny following the UN investigation, other followers have begun increasing scrutiny, seeking accountability, and offering additional solutions. The success of these actions will depend on Facebook's ability to prevent harm from occurring by considering second- and third-level consequences relating to language and culture. Their platform will also need to be adapted accordingly.

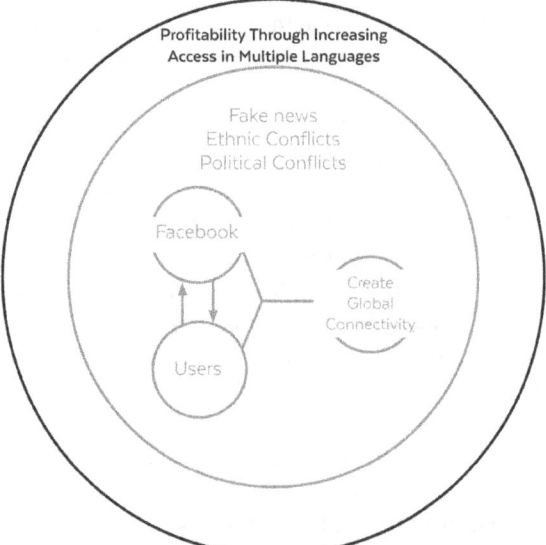

Within the Facebook organization, there are multiple followers. There are managers within the Meta and Facebook organizations; spokespeople who make connections with political leaders to build brand awareness and enter new markets; the market leaders who introduce the platform in new global markets; the advertising specialists who collect

**Figure 8.3**    The Five Components of Leadership Model applied to the Facebook case study

data on users and content to sell customized ad space within the platform; digital specialists who use some cultural knowledge (i.e. understanding a history of censorship and a 'tea shop culture' in Myanmar) to strategically place the platform; local governments who allow and use the platform both for 'news' and ease and affordability of communication and who abuse it; moderators and AI trainers who participate in a corporate culture where the little they can do sometimes fails in the face of millions of users and thousands of instances of disinformation, problematic content, hate speech, or incitement to genocide; advertisers, including universities and publishers, who use the platform to increase revenue; and individual users who are willing to cede privacy for entertainment and a potentially illusory sense of 'connection'.

Facebook's users are also followers. When we examine each follower's actions and level of culpability, we also must bear in mind the mission of Meta and the various cultures in which Facebook as a platform interacts. For example, in regions where political discourse is varied, and democracy is sound, users who share 'fake news' can cause harm by participating in negative discourse without critical thinking. Their impact can be lessened when translators, moderation, and community standards all work robustly with the majority language. However, in cultures with despotic leaders, a history of censorship, internet access or literacy inequities, and multiple political factions and dialects, the ease of rapidly creating and sharing unexamined Facebook content (especially without moderation or community reporting available in those languages) exacerbates and causes harm.

Global connectivity was the goal, empowered by a business model that relied on advertising to its users. All these followers were stakeholders in achieving the overall goal of 'to give people the power to build community and bring the world closer together'.[20] As followers across the globe rapidly participated in that business goal, conflicting cultural values surfaced. Note that context and culture are root causes for cultural relativism struggles because what may work in one cultural setting does not in another. Here, the challenge lies in a hyperconnected context without adequate representation from local cultures to moderate content. The goal of connectivity is a good thing. The problem arose when the goal was applied in a setting where numerous 'bad actors' were present. Connecting them becomes dangerous – especially when there is not a moderating voice that can speak to that group.

Facebook is used by nearly three billion people in more than 100 languages, but moderation is done in only 70, and community standards are only available in 50. Two-thirds of Facebook users are doing so in a language other than English. In many circumstances, hate speech cannot be reported by users. For example, in Afghanistan, at the time this chapter was written, users cannot access community standards in either Dari or Pashto, the two official languages of the country.[21] However, sophisticated threat actors are increasingly adept at generating 'fake news' (specifically, targeted disinformation campaigns) by targeting groups likely to share it and communities likely to fracture because of it. One unintended consequence of seeking to grow communities in new regions and add as many new users as possible (both to build community and increase exposure to advertising) is that the addition of millions of users with varying intentions and thousands of languages and dialects means content cannot be moderated successfully. A team of analysts and scholars from the government, higher education, and the private sector shared in research published in 'Combatting Targeted Disinformation Campaigns: A whole-of-society issue' as part of the 2019 Public–Private Analytic Exchange Program by the US Department of Homeland Security:

> Unlike the publication and distribution of print sources, which require publishing houses, editors, proofreaders, promotional advertisements, and bookstores, online information does not require an intermediary between creator and consumer. As public confidence in mainstream media outlets has waned, interest in social media platforms and other online forums that offer uncensored communication channels to share ideas and commentary has increased.[22]

Moderation may be one tool to prevent harmful content from remaining published and being shared and accessed by users. However, moderation only works if there are staff on the ground in each location who are fluent in each language *and* understand the nuances of local culture and politics. For example, some phrases that an outsider might see as neutral or slightly negative (like 'cockroach')[23] are overt calls to violence for those living within a shared language and political situation.

Facebook has sought to increase paid staff in specific regions and moderators when political pressure asks them to consider their role in political elections, abuses of power, and the use of the platform by military groups to oppress and divide. One ethical dilemma looms large: Is it ethical to accept advertising revenue for 'clicks' that are increased by fake news and hateful rhetoric? A more specific question for this case study is: What responsibility do business owners have when moving into new markets to attend to language and cultural norms? Is it acceptable to leave the responsibility to 'users', or should social media companies be responsible for investing in moderation, reporting, and embedded community participation and understanding?

How much cultural understanding should leaders seek when tasked with providing moderation in geographic regions troubled by military coups, civil wars, corrupt governments, ethnic strife, racism, or hate speech? Is it enough to provide a translation? Ought a company embed and pay local staff? Should we require corporations to become intimately familiar with geopolitical issues and linguistic nuances to better moderate, report, and ban? Should outside governments take civil action to punish companies who allow their products to be misused or remove those companies from regions altogether? Note, some critics of Facebook would not say the product was 'misused' in the genocide, but instead used as designed by like-minded 'friends' who used the application to share news, memes, highlight political ideas, create calls to action, and consolidate action with events and maps.

In this case, the context of the leadership engagement differed from the originating context of the leadership organization. Some initiatives were started reactively in North America after international criticism of an event in the global South. Some initiatives, called for by followers, are slowly coming to fruition in various markets and at business headquarters. These contextual differences are part of what continues to lead to unintended consequences. In one context, the platform's rapid adoption increases access to news and community. In another context, these same tools provide means for harm to come to minorities and for terrorism and hate speech to be perpetuated and amplified.[24]

For nearly 20 years, Meta has sought to make Facebook 'the internet' in as many new locations as possible. Goals related to revenue and increased users may be at odds with the stated goal of creating community. Almost immediately, rapid global adoption into vastly different regions with hundreds of new languages and dialects allowed actors with destructive intentions to use the social media tool for harm. Meta struggled to catch up to the challenges.[25]

Revenue complicates this. In the United States, we work in a capitalist system that encourages businesses and individuals to pursue profit. Ideally, companies like Facebook pay their workers well and contribute to society via taxes. Unfortunately, in places in the world where Facebook 'equals the internet' means that daily and constant usage brings excellent ad revenue. In one way, Facebook as a business should want to be in the very locations where dictators and regimes can abuse it.

As leaders, how do we balance goals of profit and safety that are sometimes in opposition? Facebook's business model – to recruit more users and keep them engaged – requires content that 'stoke[s] the curiosity of users'.[26] As researchers with the US Department of Homeland Security put it, 'The more alluring the content, the greater the time on the platform, and thus the greater potential profit.'[27] Search algorithms provide related results. For example, suppose a young fighter with the Tatmadaw (armed forces in Myanmar) engages with racist anti-immigrant content a few times. In that case, Facebook will serve more related content.

The case illustrates multiple cultural forces and expectations interacting. Some of those cultural forces include access to technology and a variety of unbiased news sources, participation in a majority language versus a more minor dialect, use practices, and different values like revenue and individual responsibility (users have the freedom to post) versus expectations that a business consider how their product might be misused to cause harm.

From the perspective of Western values celebrating profit and individualism, Facebook is successful. However, Mark Zuckerberg expressed regret that his business facilitated real harm. Zuckerberg has publicly committed to making changes and investing in staff and AI to prevent the case of Facebook's involvement in the Rohingya genocide from happening in another circumstance. Additionally, many individual users are beginning to struggle with the conflicting values of 'bring[ing] the world closer' without checks and balances in place to prevent conflict.

None of us (if we are users of these social media platforms) can simply say that all values are equal in resolving these cultural differences. We will have to work together, along with other stakeholders, to determine a way to move forward. All parties must understand the different cultural values and norms that are at play to find a way to reach the goal of participating in tools that make connection free and accessible but can perpetuate dehumanization and destruction if gone unexamined.

The diverse culture accessible to all users is one benefit of accessing Facebook. However, it also creates opportunities for conflict between followers and the leader, as various national identities, ethnic groups, and world views are not only expressed as part of the content for Facebook but also are chafing against Facebook's expressed policies and business practices.

'Culture' also includes an online community co-created by users in ways unexpected by the leader and continuing to evolve. For example, younger users are migrating to new social media platforms, changing the demographics intended by the leader. Business, non-profit leaders, local political leaders, and community organizers use Facebook to speak directly with stakeholders. As current users become disenchanted with the way culture has changed on Facebook, they either leave or ask for changes.

So, our case not only illustrates different cultural values at work but also shows how these values interplay with factors including technological advances and rapid adoption of digital tools, cultural and political beliefs, language differences, and commitments to investors and economic growth – both internationally and within emerging markets. All these factors influence how the goals are perceived and success measured.

Ethical leadership requires us to persist even in complex situations where relationships between leaders, followers, and adjacent stakeholders are fraught and shifting. One benefit of cultural relativism as a lens for evaluation is that it requires leaders to consider both culture and context. This case study crosses geographical, language, ethnic, political, economic, and cultural values. Applying the Five Component Analysis allows us to tease apart the roles and relationships between the leaders, followers, and the complex interactions of context and culture.

One critique of cultural relativism is that it leads to nihilism. If we can make no easy choice, we should give up. In this case, so many of us use the apps created and facilitated by the leader. Here, a Five Component Analysis requires us to seek accurate information, clarity about impact, and equip ourselves to understand how we participate as followers. Just as leaders must behave ethically (and with ethical knowledge), so too must followers. Disinformation, both accidental and malicious, has affected all our lives. Simply scrolling through content without applying critical and creative thinking, or questioning our values and participation, exacerbates the problem.

## SUMMARY AND CONCLUDING REMARKS

To answer the question posed at the beginning of the chapter, 'How do culture and context impact the decisions I make as a leader?' we can assert, to be effective, the leader must develop 'cultural intelligence' and be aware of the ways cultural values and norms affect the leadership process. Leaders must recognize that no matter the current context, there are multiple cultural contexts at work of which one should be aware. Cultural relativism shows that leaders must approach each leadership situation with a certain measure of cultural humility, recognizing that other cultural values may be important for their followers and that a leader's particular cultural assumptions may have unintended and negative consequences. Part of that cultural humility requires leaders to listen to the deeply held values of their followers. Still, leaders need to be decisive. In spite of the fact that there are multiple and often competing cultural contexts at play, leaders must still make decisions. Knowing the difference between a leader's 'core' values and where there might be room to 'flex' can help with this.

So, 'How do culture and context impact the decisions I make as a leader?' According to cultural relativism, leaders must navigate contexts awash in multiple cultural values. Sometimes these values are in harmony with each other, and other times they are not. So, leaders must develop a cultural intelligence that helps them recognize the values in play and a cultural humility that allows them to recognize what other cultural perspectives can add to achieving the goal. Leaders must also be willing to make decisions and take action rather than being paralysed by competing cultural values. To make this happen, leaders will benefit from developing trusted relationships with partners who represent various cultural perspectives and identify what is 'core' and what is 'flexible' to their personal and organizational values.

### DISCUSSION QUESTIONS

1. Share an example where two points of view can be equally 'right' when they are based on a person's cultural values and norms. Follow the outcomes from making a decision from each point of view to their logical end considering consequences, stakeholders, and risks.
2. Think about your position as a leader, paying particular attention to issues of power and privilege. Describe your social context: sex, gender, race, educational attainment,

language skills and access, wealth, property ownership, religion, national identity, and other aspects of identity. How might your identity affect the way you look at the world?

3. Have you ever experienced conflict between professional practice and personal belief? How did you deal with this challenge?

4. When you are participating in a culture unfamiliar to you, how much do you expect that culture to suspend its practices to welcome you as a visitor, and how much are you willing to change to be a gracious visitor? Examples might include: eating or drinking things you normally would not, dancing in public as a performance for esteemed teachers or dignitaries, sitting on the floor, removing your shoes, staying up late or rising especially early, avoiding contact with members of the opposite sex, or giving or receiving gifts (even if prohibited by your organization's policies).

5. In the case of Facebook, what kinds of professional development would you recommend to increase awareness of the impact of decisions that are not always just 'business' decisions?

6. If you were writing a code of conduct for an international organization, from which sources would you draw perspectives and guidance? How will you decide which to adopt if there are two opposing perspectives?

## ADDITIONAL RESOURCES

P.C. Earley and E. Mosakowski, 'Cultural intelligence', *Harvard Business Review*, October 2004.

This is an often-cited article that presents a thoughtful discussion of culture and leadership.

T. Donaldson, 'Values in tension: ethics away from home', *Harvard Business Review*, September–October 1996.

This practical *HBR* article provides guidelines for managers addressing issues related to conflicting economic development and conflicting cultural traditions. As part of his solution, the author suggests the flexible application of an international organization's core values.

H. Miner, 'Body ritual among the Nacirema', in A. Podolefsky, P. Brown and S. Lacy (eds), *Applying Anthropology*, 10th edn, New York: McGraw-Hill, 2012, pp. 503-7.

This chapter presents a memorable and creative treatment of culture and cultural studies.

J. Middleton, *Cultural Intelligence: The Competitive Edge for Leaders Crossing Boundaries*, London: Bloomsbury, 2014.

Middleton presents a compelling case for a leader understanding their 'core' values and where they can 'flex'.

# NOTES

1. Bureau of Economic Analysis, Activities of US multinational companies, 12 November 2021. https://www.bea.gov/news/2021/activities-us-multinational-enterprises-2019 (accessed 26 October 2022).

2. M. Baghramian and J.A. Carter, 'Relativism', *Stanford Encyclopedia of Philosophy*, 11 September 2015, ed. Edward N. Zalta. https://plato.stanford.edu/entries/relativism/ (accessed 26 October 2022).

3. I. Kant, *Critique of Pure Reason*, trans. M. Weigelt, New York: Penguin, 1781/2007.

4. F. Boas. *Race, Language, and Culture*, Chicago, IL: University of Chicago Press, 1940.

5. W. Washburn, *Against the Anthropological Grain*, New Brunswick, NJ: Transaction Publishers, 1998.

6. A. Sen, *Development as Freedom*, Oxford: Oxford University Press, 1999.

7. R. Rorty, *Consequences of Pragmatism: Essays*, Minneapolis: University of Minnesota Press, 1982.

8. J. Middleton, *Cultural Intelligence: The Competitive Edge for Leaders Crossing Boundaries*, London: Bloomsbury, 2014.

9. D. Thomas and R.J. Ely, 'Making differences matter: a new paradigm for managing diversity', in *On Managing Across Cultures*, Boston, MA: Harvard Business Review Press, 2016. Thomas and Ely call this an 'integration' paradigm in contrast to an assimilation or differentiation paradigm.

10. The different perspectives on leaders and followers for the categories of tasks and relationships were part of a classic Ohio State management study in the 1950s. See R.M. Stogdill, O.S. Goode and D.R. Day, 'New leader behavior description subscales', *Journal of Psychology*, vol. 54 no. 2, 1962, 259–69.

11. A. Archie and J. Hernandez, 'U.S. officially says Myanmar's violence against Rohingya was genocide', NPR.org, 21 March 2022. https://www.npr.org/2022/03/16/1086826753/us-rohingya-genocide-myanmar (accessed 25 July 2022).

12. S. Asher, 'Myanmar coup: how Facebook became the "digital tea shop"', BBC News, 4 February 2021. https://www.bbc.com/news/world-asia-55929654 (accessed 25 July 2022).

13. L. Hogan and M. Safi, 'Revealed: Facebook hate speech exploded in Myanmar during Rohingya crisis', *The Guardian*, 2 April 2018. https://www.theguardian.com/world/2018/apr/03/revealed-facebook-hate-speech-exploded-in-myanmar-during-rohingya-crisis (accessed 25 July 2022).

14. United Nations Human Rights Council, report of the independent international fact-finding mission on Myanmar, 12 September 2018. https://www.ohchr.org/sites/default/files/Documents/HRBodies/HRCouncil/FFM-Myanmar/A_HRC_39_64.pdf (accessed 25 July 2022).

15. A. Warofka, 'An independent assessment of the human rights impact of facebook in myanmar', Meta, 5 November 2018. https://about.fb.com/news/2018/11/myanmar-hria/ (accessed 28 October 2022).

16. Warofka, 'An independent assessment'.

17. T. Simonite, 'Facebook is everywhere, but its Arabic moderation is nowhere close', *Wired*, 26 October 2021. https://wired.me/business/facebook-is-everywhere-but-its-arabic-moderation-is-nowhere-close/ (accessed 25 July 2022).

18. 'Facebook "too slow" in combating hate speech in Myanmar', *Taipei Times*, 17 August 2018. https://taipeitimes.com/News/world/archives/2018/08/17/2003698686 (accessed 25 July 2022).

19. Facebook submission to UN Special rapporteur on freedom of opinion and expression for report on disinformation, United Nations Human Rights Office of the High Commissioner, n.d. https://www.ohchr.org/sites/default/files/Documents/Issues/Expression/disinformation/4-Companies/Facebook.pdf (accessed 25 July 2022).

20. Meta, Meta investor relations, n.d. https://investor.fb.com/resources/default.aspx (accessed 25 July 2022).

21. Simonite, 'Facebook is everywhere'.

22. Department of Homeland Security Public–Private Analytic Exchange Program, 'Combatting targeted disinformation campaigns: a whole-of-society issue', October 2019. https://www.dhs.gov/sites/default/files/publications/ia/ia_combatting-targeted-disinformation-campaigns.pdf (accessed 25 July 2022).

23. S. Fyfe, 'Tracking hate speech acts as incitement to genocide in international criminal law', *Leiden Journal of International Law*, 9 January 2017. https://www.cambridge.org/core/journals/leiden-journal-of-international-law/article/abs/tracking-hate-speech-acts-as-incitement-to-genocide-in-international-criminal-law/671620A70B629DDE9C37E774CDEBAC65 (accessed 25 July 2022).

24. E.J. Kennedy, 'Genocide by social media posts: will Facebook be held accountable?', MinnPost, 3 January 2022. https://www.minnpost.com/community-voices/2022/01/genocide-by-social-media-posts-will-facebook-be-held-accountable/ (accessed 25 July 2022).

25. R. Iyengar, 'Facebook has language blind spots around the world allow hate speech to flourish', CNN Business, 26 October 2021. https://www.cnn.com/2021/10/26/tech/facebook-papers-language-hate-speech-international/index.html (accessed 25 July 2022).

26. Department of Homeland Security, 'Combatting targeted disinformation'.

27. Department of Homeland Security, 'Combatting targeted disinformation'.

# 9
# Divine command theory

*James N. Thomas*

## FRAMING QUESTION

What does the divine require from leadership?

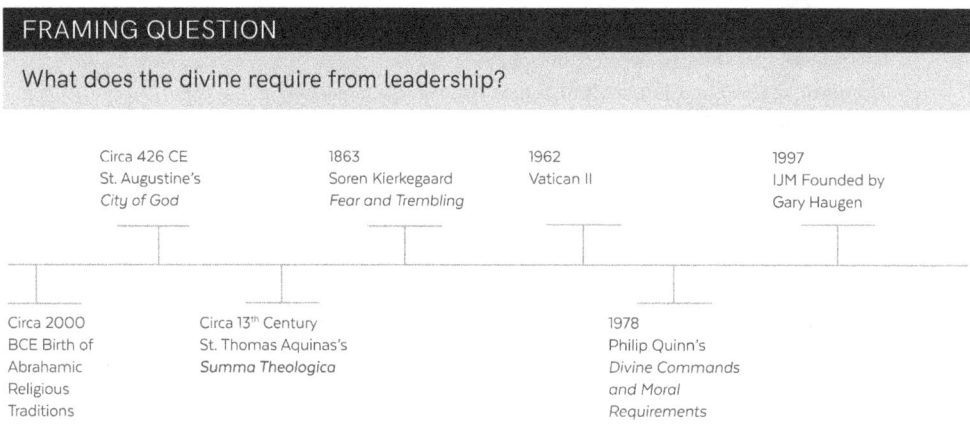

| Circa 426 CE | 1863 | 1962 | 1997 |
| St. Augustine's | Soren Kierkegaard | Vatican II | IJM Founded by |
| *City of God* | *Fear and Trembling* | | Gary Haugen |

| Circa 2000 | Circa 13th Century | 1978 |
| BCE Birth of | St. Thomas Aquinas's | Philip Quinn's |
| Abrahamic | *Summa Theologica* | *Divine Commands* |
| Religious | | *and Moral* |
| Traditions | | *Requirements* |

**Figure 9.1**   Timeline of major works on divine command theory in relation to the chapter case study

One of the oldest and perhaps the most controversial concepts in the field of ethics is the divine command theory of moral obligation. This approach advocates the view that ethics depend, at least in part, on God's will and commands.[1] In other words, what makes something morally obligatory is that God commands it. Religious ethicists generally agree that some or all moral actions depend on God.[3] Such a theory allows leaders to have an objective ethical framework to guide their leadership practices, such as relating to others, daily decision-making, determining motivation, and projecting outcomes and goals. Although this general definition is fairly standard across proponents of the idea, divine command theorists disagree about the specific aspects of the theory and its implications for leaders.

Though the term 'religion' is notoriously broad and covers many world views, most religions have an ethical base. Some polytheistic religions, such as Hinduism, adhere to a high sense of moral duty. For example, the *Bhagavad Gita* teaches that righteous living, or dharma, requires discipline and acting out of a sense of duty to a higher moral law rather than merely concern for the consequences of our actions. Likewise, non-theistic philosophies espouse an ethical base for moral conduct. For instance, Buddhism values unity and interdependency between persons and all living beings. Thus, it teaches that its adherents have a moral responsibility to maintain concern for others and the world in which they live. Confucianism also has prescribed rules of conduct for interactions between people to ensure everyone is treated properly and respectfully.

Religion also plays a part in other areas of human interaction. For example, civil religion is an institutionalized set of beliefs, symbols, and rituals that provide a religious dimension to a nation's collective life.[4] Civil religion claims that morality, at least to some extent, is relative to a particular culture, and religion may even be written into a country's laws. Some examples include Sharia law in the Islamic world, derived from the sacred writings of the Quran and Hadith, and the Judeo-Christian influence on United States jurisprudence. Many Muslim majority countries incorporate Sharia law at some level in their legal framework, with many utilizing it as the highest form of law in their constitution.[5] Likewise, American civil religion is often considered a blend of Judeo-Christian ideas with nineteenth-century enlightenment thinking.[6]

Though we could examine many ethical theories grounded in religion, this chapter will focus on the monotheistic traditions of Judaism, Christianity, and Islam. The idea of moral goodness is so closely tied to these religions that ethics are built into their central doctrines. Their religious texts portray God as instructing humans in what they are and are not to do, such as those decrees found in the Ten Commandments.[7] Consequently, divine command theory has dominated the field of religious ethics.

In this chapter, we will examine the concept of divine command theory and how it relates to leadership ethics. We will study the development of divine command theory, its central concepts, and key critiques of the theory. As we have done in previous chapters, we will then look at the critiques of divine command theory and apply the Five Components of Leadership Model to analyse the theory. We will end our time together with a case study that considers one of the world's most prominent faith-based relief organizations, International Justice Mission.

Throughout the chapter, we will see how the obligation to God's commands compels leaders to hold high ethical standards for their own behaviour in the ways they relate to their followers, in the means through which they pursue their goals, and in the way they influence the broader context surrounding them and the organizations in which they lead. In so doing, leaders must be aware of the larger cultural values in play based on God's commands, the intentional and purposeful interaction between leaders and followers to accomplish these commands, and the shared goals of both leader and follower resulting from these commands. The main lesson from this chapter is that divine command theory is a viable theory of ethics in leadership. This is true as it relates to leadership and its application to an organization's overall context and culture, concerning followers, and achieving shared organizational goals.

## HISTORY

Many Christian thinkers in post-biblical times, including St Augustine, St Bernard of Clairvaux, St Thomas Aquinas, and St Andrew of Neufchateau, claimed that divine commands determined the ethical status of specific actions.[8] For instance, St Augustine proposed that ethics was pursuing the supreme good, which led to human happiness.[9] He argued that humans must love objects that are worthy of human love in the correct order. They are to love God first, which allows them to align their other loves, so they might properly foster their happiness and fulfilment. Pre-Reformation Franciscan philosopher and theologian John Duns Scotus was another early voice proposing a divine command approach to ethics.[10] Scotus argued that the only commands God could not take away were to love God and love others. He proposed that some moral truths are necessary truths, and even God can't change those; they would be true no matter what God willed. (We will explore this point a little later in this chapter.)

The nineteenth-century Danish philosopher Søren Kierkegaard added another defence of divine command theory in the form of his idea of moral obligation.[11] Kierkegaard contended that God's commands are not arbitrary but are directed at human flourishing, leading to genuine happiness, even though obedience requires self-denial and a loss of ego.[12] Kierkegaard argued that those whose moral allegiance is grounded in a religious faith might still participate in a pluralistic society without compromising their faith or elevating a particular religion to any privilege. However, divine command theory is not only found in the area of religion; the concept can also be found in the broader field of ethics, specifically in the work of Immanuel Kant.

As discussed in Chapter 2, eighteenth-century German philosopher Immanuel Kant was traditionally not known as an advocate for divine command theory. Nevertheless, his ethical system may be interpreted as supporting the validity of a divine command theory of moral obligation. Kant's categorical imperative is an absolute, unconditional requirement that must be obeyed in all circumstances and is justified as an end in itself. Kant's imperative becomes a universal law that applies to everyone everywhere. Though Kant does not advocate the concept of moral faith as an argument for divine command theory, a contemporary advocate might argue that the concept of a categorical imperative does lean toward this view of morality.[13]

Though divine command theory fell out of fashion during the nineteenth-century enlightenment when more secular ideas of moral obligation arose to the forefront, there has been a remarkable renewal of divine command theory. This resurgence began with Philip Quinn's book *Divine Commands and Moral Requirements* (1978). Before Quinn's work, there were various references to divine command theory but no sustained working out of the approach in a defensible form. Quinn argues that because God is the source of the moral law, people are obligated to obey this law because it is God who commands it.[14] Since Quinn's book, the argument for divine command theory has continued.

One of the most notable works following in the steps of Quinn's idea of moral obligation is Robert M. Adams' *Finite and Infinite Goods* (1999). Adams contends that the innate goodness of God is the foundation for the obligation to God's commands, which Quinn did not assume.[15] Adams later modified his theory to be accessible to atheists. He does not dismiss the critical thesis of his presupposition of God's goodness as the basis for the ethical obligation to God's commands. However, he modifies it by stating that there are necessary moral truths independently knowable through experience outside of a belief in God – including the nature of ethical wrongness.[16]

Another prominent voice following Quinn's work is Richard Mouw's *The God Who Commands*. Mouw proposes that everyone 'in the drama of life' is called to build a relationship with God.[17] He contends that divine command theory rests upon the central principles of human sinfulness and humility and trust in a sovereign God. Mouw states, 'The proper human response in the context of this will-to-will confrontation [between God and man] is not so much understanding as surrender.'[18] In other words, people are not to respond in blind obedience to a distant sovereign but in faithful submission to divine love in the God who commands. The resurgence in the study and advocacy of divine command theory and its historical precedence merits its consideration as a valid construct for ethical theory.

## MAJOR CONCEPTS OF DIVINE COMMAND THEORY

Since the earliest days of moral reflection, religious philosophy has offered a rich backdrop to answer the fundamental question of ethics – 'What is right and what is wrong?' A central element of religious moral philosophy contends that God is the perfect creator of all things. As a result, right and wrong are derived from God and emerge in two distinct ways: (1) Natural Law, which argues that all humans are imbued with the values of life, procreation, knowledge, and sociability and God's will is reflected in the moral reasoning and ethical behaviour that result; and (2) Divine Command, which declares something morally good or ethically right based on whether or not it conforms to the will of God as revealed in divine commandments and holy texts. Let's take a closer look at the common themes expressed in these ideas.

### Morality Comes from God

Divine command theory provides a mediating moral framework in which theistic philosophers and theologians can find a general, ethical common ground. Divine command theory proposes three principles: (1) morality is dependent upon God; (2) therefore, moral obligation consists of obedience to God's commands; and (3) because morality is ultimately based on God's commands and character, the morally right action is the one that God commands or wills.[19] Though aspects of these divine commands differ according to the particular religion and the specific divine command theorist, all versions claim that morality, rightness and wrongness, and moral obligation ultimately depend on God.

What, then, does it mean for something to be a command from God? God's commands are realized through the general understanding of God speaking, or the 'word' of God. This raises the question of whether God speaks literally or metaphorically. Varying views exist on this subject, but regardless of a person's opinion on the mode of God's commands – literal or metaphorical – either can sustain support for a robust divine command theory.

How then are God's commands communicated? An assumption might be that God's primary mode of communicating commands to people is through a religion's sacred texts, such as Judaism's Tanakh (Hebrew Bible), Christianity's Bible, and Islam's Quran. Muslims, for instance, believe that the One God, or Allah, provided revelations to the Prophet Muhammad and written down in the Holy Quran, which means 'recitation or reading'. It was in this recited form that Allah communicated to his followers.[20] As such, 'All revelations are thus rooted in one transcendent primary source, which becomes articulated to humanity through inspiration. Prophet Muhammad's experience of revelation links the world of transcendence with human affairs, highlighting the sovereignty of God, the reality of the non-material world, and the idea of the accountability of human actions.'[21] Though, for most religious traditions, such a vehicle is accepted and even preferred, there are other ways God's moral commands may be communicated, specifically as they relate to moral obligation.[22] For example, some people might defer to natural law; this is a 'natural' sense of morality given to everyone by God. In fact, natural law theory is presupposed by divine command theory. If God exists as a relational person, creator to creation, then there is a sense in which God is authoritative. Since God has authority over creation, then 'natural laws' have been established based on this authority. As a result, when people act accordingly, they obey God's divine commands. Others might hold that obeying the tenets of a religious organization can result in obeying God's commands. Still, others might respond to God's commands through the dictates of their conscience. Divine command theory accepts that God can communicate in any and all of these ways as long as rational human beings understand God's commands. This brings us to the next major principle in divine command theory – the role of reason.

## Reason

Reason plays a critical role in accessing God's commands within divine command theory. Theological and philosophical ethics demand that God's commands, or any ethical position for that matter, be subject to rational assessment and criticism. Divine command theorists do not advocate a blind or unreasoning approach to ethics but rather expect that any moral obligation associated with God's commands must be measured against God as the standard of goodness. Of course, God's commands, as presented in religious texts, are interpreted through a human lens and are, therefore, open to misunderstanding. An extreme example of this is the case of Deanna Laney.[23] In 2004, Laney killed her two oldest sons by hitting them in the head with a rock because she said God had told her to do so. She believed the world was ending, and God had instructed her to get her house in order. During the investigation, five mental health experts were called to testify to Laney's actions. They all concluded that she suffered from psychotic delusions and could not tell right from wrong. Laney was eventually found not guilty by reason of insanity and committed to a state hospital for eight years. Though this is an extreme example, it illustrates the point that divine command theory requires some sort of reasonable evaluation to avoid misunderstanding and misinterpretation.

According to divine command theory, a command must be evaluated based on the goodness of what is commanded and the appropriate punishment if the command is not obeyed. The objection to God's authority and human autonomy will be addressed later in this chapter. For now, it is important to understand that reason might hinder our understanding of the obligation to God's commands, but not the commands themselves.

A natural question arises: 'What is the moral obligation of the one receiving the commands?' Divine command theory proposes that an action is morally obligatory and consists of being commanded by God. God's commands, by nature of divine goodness, are morally right.

Conversely, those things contrary to God's commands are morally wrong and not morally obligatory. Of course, this assumes that the deity in question is considered the ultimate good. In other words, the nature of the goodness of the command is critical to our obligation to obey it or not. In Islam, the term used to refer to Muslim law is *Shari'a*. The connotation behind this concept is that God intends human beings to follow a divinely ordained path, and that path has been previously revealed to others. In elaborating the *Shari'a*, Muslim scholars sought to ground it in the Qur'an and the example and actions of Prophet Muhammad. However, it was for human beings, through the exercise of moral reasoning and rational tools, to discover and develop the details of the law.[24]

In summary, the study of religious ethics helps answer the questions of 'what is right?' and 'what is wrong?' Divine command theory proposes that morality depends on God and that moral obligation consists of obedience to God's commands based on divine character. The morally right thing to do, then, is to obey God's commands or will. These commands consist of directives from God through a religion's holy texts, and, in a more general sense, through an understanding of natural law, religious organizations, or the dictates of conscience. These commands are not devoid of reason. In fact, reason plays a critical role in discerning what God's command is and what God's command is not. All perceived commands should be measured against the standard of God's goodness and the appropriate punishment for not obeying the command. Therefore, divine command theorists argue that because God is good divine commands are right and should be obeyed.

## CRITIQUES OF DIVINE COMMAND THEORY

As with any major ethical theory, there are objections to divine command theory's claims. Critics of the theory deride its validity based on several factors. They claim weaknesses in the model for both theists and non-theists and propose that these weaknesses make divine command theory ineffective as a framework for ethical morality. In this section, we will examine two primary critiques of divine command theory and rebuttals to those critiques.

### The Euthyphro Dilemma

The primary critique of divine command theory, and any theistic theory of ethics, comes from a conversation between Socrates and Euthyphro written in Plato's *Euthyphro*.[25] This dialogue is the quintessential objection in philosophical circles to the relationship between God and ethics. Plato, a student of Socrates, writes of an encounter between Socrates and Euthyphro in the king's court. Charges have been brought against Socrates by Miletus, who claims that Socrates has corrupted the youth of that generation by leading them away from a belief in the gods. In the course of their discussion, Socrates is surprised to learn that Euthyphro is prosecuting his own father for the murder of a servant. Euthyphro's family is upset with him because of this and believes that what he is doing to his father is wrong. Euthyphro maintains that his family does not see the more significant divine directive in his action. This fosters a conversation between Socrates and Euthyphro on the nature of piety. In the discussion, Socrates asks

Euthyphro the now-famous question that he, and any theistic philosopher, including divine command theorists, must answer: 'Is the pious loved by the gods because it is pious, or is it pious because it is being loved by the gods?'[26] In other words, does God command an action because it is morally right, or is it morally right because God commands it?

This argument, known as the 'Euthyphro Dilemma', is the standard objection to divine command theory. A divine command theorist believes that if God commands an action, it is morally right. However, the Euthyphro Dilemma suggests that if God commands that we inflict suffering or pain on someone else, then in doing so – based on divine command theory – it would be right. We would be obligated to inflict pain because God commanded it. The problem that Socrates brings up is the arbitrary nature of God's commands, which allows for morally deplorable actions to become morally obligatory, and, thereby, morally justified.

One example dominates the discussion of this issue – Abraham's sacrifice of his son Isaac found in the Torah. (The story is also found in the Quran – although, in the Quran, Abraham's son Ishmael is the son to be sacrificed.) In essence, God speaks to Abraham and commands him to sacrifice his beloved son as an offering to God. Since God commanded it, Abraham began to obey. Abraham takes his son to the mountain, binds him, seizes a knife, and prepares to take his son's life. At the last minute, an angel speaks and stops Abraham from killing his son, saying that his willingness to obey was sufficient to please God. Abraham then finds a ram that had become entangled in the bushes and sacrifices the ram to God in place of his son.[27]

Several questions arise from this account. First, was it right or wrong for Abraham to intend to kill, or actually kill, his son before God commanded it? Was God being arbitrary in commanding Abraham to kill his son in light of the other biblical commands not to kill or murder? Would Abraham have been wrong in disobeying God considering the horror of child sacrifice? These questions provide an excellent example of the Euthyphro Dilemma and call into account the viability of divine command theory.

A divine command theorist would counter the argument of the Euthyphro Dilemma in several ways. One possible response is just to accept that if God commands to inflict suffering, as in our example here, then it would be morally obligatory given the fundamental premise of divine command theory – no matter how immoral it might seem. Most people find this to be an unacceptable view of moral obligation on the grounds that any theory of ethics that leaves open the possibility that such actions are morally praiseworthy is fatally flawed.[28]

Another response to the Euthyphro Dilemma is to ask two important questions: (1) should we love one another because God commands us to do so? and (2) does God command us to love one another because it is the right thing to do?[29] A divine command theorist can conceive of God's moral goodness as something distinct from conformity to moral obligations, and so as something distinct from conformity to divine commands. However, if God commands us to love one another because it is the right thing to do, then moral facts stand over God, and divine goodness is subject to them. A way to sidestep this argument is to consider God as the 'supreme standard' of goodness. God does not consult any outside source but acts according to a divine character that defines goodness. In the case of Abraham and his son, God's goodness supersedes the divine command to offer Abraham's son as a sacrifice. Therefore, Abraham has just cause to obey God's command and put his son in harm's way. But doesn't this still breed arbitrariness about God's character? Why should God be the standard and not some other moral character or principle? One could argue that to invoke God as the supreme moral standard is no more arbitrary than to invoke some objective moral principle. Critics contend that the Euthyphro Dilemma is a critical flaw in divine command theory because it forces the divine command theorist to pick and choose which commands to follow. This leads us to the second critique of divine command theory.

## What about Human Free Will?

A second major critique of divine command theory deals with the subject of human autonomy, or free will. The idea of autonomy suggests that 'a human moral agent is, or should be, a (moral) law unto oneself – that one should find the moral law within oneself.'[30] The idea of autonomy means being morally mature, deciding freely which moral principles will govern one's life, and by extension, we can make moral decisions for which we should be held accountable. Divine command theory seems to contradict this idea, as it is not our will that governs our lives but God's will. However, we can counter this argument by stating that divine command theory and moral responsibility are compatible.[31] God commands, and humans are responsible for their response to obeying or not obeying those commands, correctly understanding them, and deciding through self-critical evaluation what God has commanded us to do. Therefore, human beings are autonomous because we rely on our independent judgment about God's goodness and what moral laws are consistent with his commands.

Several traits might lend to a defence of autonomy as a complementary component of divine command theory.[32] The first is that of responsibility. People who hold themselves responsible for their actions do not abdicate that responsibility simply because of their view of autonomy. They are free agents in the sense that they can choose to submit to God's commands or not. The second is moral competence. The morally competent person is able to make decisions on their own, including God's commands, based on their prescribed beliefs, understanding, and feelings. The third is the area of critical thinking. Those who can examine ethical ideas in the light of critical scrutiny exercise autonomy over those claims and beliefs and, therefore, operate autonomously. The fourth is the ability to care about moral issues. When someone cares about the good in and around their life, they will act autonomously to champion that good in their relationships and responsibilities. God's commands provide the foundation for such good because of God's goodness and the motivation to obey or not obey divine commands.

The Euthyphro Dilemma and the question of human autonomy provide two serious critiques of divine command theory. Theistic ethicists should consider and address both to develop a stronger foundation for a working theory. In doing so, divine command theorists will strengthen the theory's underlying assumptions and provide a framework for application in all areas of life, including, as we will see, within the context of leadership.

## FIVE COMPONENT ANALYSIS

If leadership indeed is a process, as defined in the Five Components of Leadership Model described in Chapter 1, then we can apply a divine command theory of ethics to leadership. If we understand ethics as defined by an obligation to God's commands, that God is good, and, therefore, divine commands are for our good and the good of the whole creation, then there is an ethical base from which we can lead. Let's look at each of the five leadership components in light of divine command theory as presented in this chapter. These are represented in Figure 9.2, emphasizing what is essential in divine command theory.

In light of the Five Components of Leadership Model, we might compare the largest circle of 'cultural values and norms' to the divine itself and the next larger circle of 'context' to the commands issued by the divine. These outer circles are accessible to both leaders and followers and become the ultimate criteria by which we judge the rightness of a goal. The leader and follower then work together to accomplish the greater goal from the larger culture and context.

Since ethical rightness is based on God's commands, and a follower's obligation is simply to obey divine commands, there is a relationship between leader and follower. Such

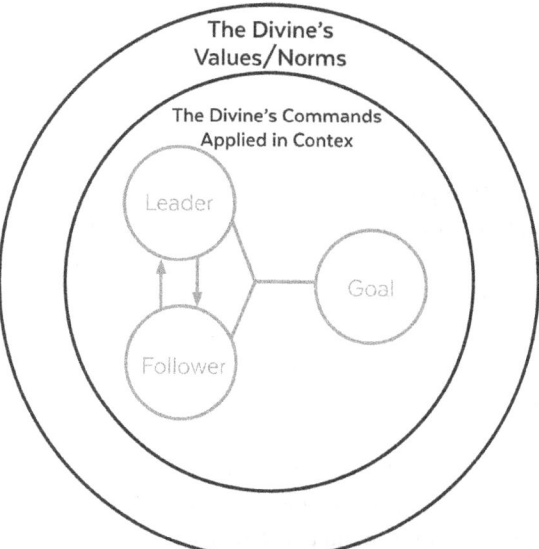

**Figure 9.2**     The Five Components of Leadership Model applied to divine command theory

a relationship corresponds with McManus and Perruci's argument that the central intellectual focus of leadership is *purposeful interaction*. In their book *Understanding Leadership*, McManus and Perruci argue:

> [T]he central intellectual focus [of the study of leadership] revolves around human beings' *purposeful interaction*. The focus invites debates about ethics and power relations. On the ethical side, purposeful interaction suggests choices to be made – forks in the road to be confronted … We can all argue whether the purpose is ethical or not, or who should have the ultimate decision-making authority. However, *purposeful interaction* is the overarching language that organizes our thinking about leadership.[33]

Ethically, purposeful interaction suggests choices to be made that clarify intent. Leaders and followers bring specific values to the relationship, and these values guide their behaviour. Intentionality becomes an expression of their values. As they work together in the relationship, such intentionality helps leaders and followers pursue a common purpose. The follower chooses to accept the leader's commands or directives to attain a greater purpose. As with any ethical theory, the follower must evaluate the adherence or refusal of such commands. The follower's response to the leader's directives has morally positive or negative consequences.

Such a hierarchical structure could also serve as a critique of this theory, potentially leading to the loss of human autonomy or abuse through co-opting the commands or the interpretation of the commands for the leader's personal benefit. However, if the goal of leaders and followers is for some greater purpose, then the leader and follower do not operate out of selfish motives but together for a greater good. In effect, the leader and follower work symbiotically to see the leader's directives related to the greater purpose are accomplished. The model becomes transformative and not merely transactional. As the follower obeys the leader's commands, the leader's purposes are accomplished in the follower's life, organization, and culture.

So, what happens when leaders and followers disagree about what God has commanded? Several lines of thought prove helpful here. First, if God is good and divine commands are good for people, then leaders and followers need to evaluate the potential positive outcome of obeying God's commands. Second, if they disagree with an interpretation of God's commands, they must work together, making their cases and listening to the other to discern the best road forward. Third, if they reach an impasse, common ground must be sought in obedience to God's commands so they can continue working toward desired goals. Finally, if an agreement or common ground cannot be found, they will need to decide whether or not to continue working together.

Now that we have examined the first two components of the Five Components Model, let's look at the next component – the goal. Obedience to the leader's directives leads to success in accomplishing the stated goal. Though divine command theory is highly structured and hierarchical, the benefits of this theory extend beyond the leader. The goal's validity is measured by the nature of the directives as good for both the follower and the organization; therefore, adherence to these directives results in ethical rightness. A follower's acceptance and adherence to the commands legitimize the command's moral rightness. Lack of acceptance and adherence to the commands creates disunity, power struggles, organizational inertia, lack of focus on achieving desired goals, and rejection of the leader's vision, ultimately demonstrating moral wrongness. Since the goal depends on the leader's directives, as a result of the transcendent nature of the context and culture of divine command theory, which is demonstrated in the next section, the goal is important but not as significant as other aspects of the model. We will look at this in a bit more detail in our case study later in this chapter.

The two spheres of context and culture highlighted in the Five Components of Leadership Model are the 'central nervous system' for the divine command theory of moral obligation. As such, when applied in a leadership context, this model should be understood as an ethical leadership model where authority, morality, and ethics transcend both leaders and followers. Of course, a criticism of this theory could be that the leader must interpret God's commands making the leader the most crucial element of the model. Though this model places a high responsibility on the leader to interpret God's commands correctly, it also, by its transformational nature, allows both leaders and followers to access the two outer circles to understand God's will. The leader is vital to the model but becomes subservient to the culture and context and open to input from followers to reach the shared goal. The transcendent nature of the environment of God's commands drives divine command theory-based leadership because the leader, follower, and goals are all subservient to the demands placed on them by the expectations of the divine. God's commands determine what is right and wrong, and so create a moral environment in which leaders, followers, and the goal work together. This process can only happen as leaders and followers demonstrate an attitude of humility and shared vision based on the values and norms established by God's commands.

This environment results in established values and norms that guide ethical behaviour. Leadership, by nature, is situational. The values and norms differ by the leader and by the culture. One strength of a divine command theory-based leadership ethics is that values and norms are established above the leader, follower, and culture. As God establishes moral obligation by divine commands, a moral framework is established to guide leadership practices such as relating to others, daily decision-making, determining motivation, and projecting outcomes and goals across cultural landscapes.

In an ever-changing world, as national borders are blurred and technology links people across the globe, cross-cultural leadership is the new norm of the twenty-first century. Leaders and followers must deal with ever-changing contexts and cultural norms to effectively reach desired goals. Understanding the nature of God's commands, as they establish transcendent values and norms, helps the leader and follower to overcome and go beyond contextual and cultural barriers that might have held them back previously. Adherence to the commands to love, serve, care, share, grow, and be accountable, to name a few, demonstrate the cross-cultural nature of divine command theory as a leadership ethic and establish an objective moral framework for leadership in a global context. As such, the circles of context and culture will be the most noticeable in our graphic model. Now that we have seen how divine command theory relates to the Five Components of Leadership Model in the abstract let's explore how it relates to the model in a specific instance. For that, we turn to our case study.

## CASE STUDY: A FAITH-BASED RESPONSE TO GLOBAL INJUSTICE

The issue of injustice has been a central theme of the human experience throughout history. It continues to be a major topic of discussion and debate into the second decade of the twenty-first century. From the 2020 shootings of George Floyd and Breonna Taylor in the United States to the treatment of men, women, and children under Taliban resurgence in Afghanistan in 2021, issues regarding injustice remain a critical issue in the fight for human rights. Injustice in its broadest form can simply be defined as unfair treatment: a situation in which the rights of a person or group are ignored.[34] Therefore, injustice is the opposite of justice, defined as the maintenance or administration of what is just, especially by the impartial adjustment of conflicting claims or the assignment of merited rewards or punishments.[35]

Many countries and organizations have responded to the global fight against injustice, including faith-based humanitarian organizations. One such organization is International Justice Mission (IJM), founded in 1997 by lawyer Gary Haugen and based in Washington, DC. While serving as director of the United Nations Special Investigations Unit in Rwanda immediately following the genocide in 1994, Haugen led a team of lawyers to investigate over 100 mass graves and massacre sites, gathering evidence against the perpetrators.[36] IJM's mission is to 'partner with local authorities in 24 program offices in 14 countries to combat slavery, violence against women and children, and police abuse of power against people who are poor'.[37] Though a Christian faith-based organization, IJM protects the poor from violence without regard to religion, race, or any other factor. They seek to partner with all people of goodwill. IJM's mission is motivated by the idea that God has called them to seek justice where injustice is prevalent and to work diligently to battle the causes of injustice because God has commanded them to do so.

So, how does International Justice Mission's work demonstrate a leadership expression of divine command theory?

Gary Haugen formed IJM following his mission to Rwanda based on God's command in Isaiah 1:17, which states, 'learn to do good; seek justice, rescue the oppressed, defend the orphan, [and] plead for the widow'.[38] Haugen says,

> We were eager for our little team to be used by God to bring rescue and hope to people suffering violent abuse and oppression. But we were just as eager to invite fellow Christians to join us in God's powerful and passionate work of justice in the world – and to provide local churches with a practical vehicle for partnership in the work ... the struggle against injustice is God's struggle – and we are simply called to do our little part and experience him as he equips his church to do the work ... God's call isn't to *feel bad about injustice* – but to *do justice*! Marvellously, God never gives us a mission without granting us the power to do it. And through the mission, he also promises to change us – to make us more like his Son.[39]

This call to God's divine command has fuelled the work of IJM ever since.

As such, IJM leadership identifies three key areas of response to global injustice: rescue and restore victims, bring criminals to justice, and strengthen justice systems.[40] First, they strive to rescue and restore victims of violence, forced labour, or sex trafficking. IJM reports that there are over 40 million people in some form of slavery globally today, which is more than at any time in human history. They have helped to rescue enslaved people from sex trafficking who have been forced to work in brothels and other mediums, including the Internet. They have also rescued those enslaved to forced labour in brick kilns, fishing boats, tree-cutting facilities, and quarries and mines. All around the world, vulnerable people are taken by oppressors who believe that making money matters more than a person's life. Driven by greed and overlooked by their local legal system, these oppressors steal human beings and intimidate them until they feel too small to fight back. They believe these enslavers should not be allowed to win.[41] One such person is called Mariamma. Mariamma is from India. She and her family, along with many other families from lower castes, work in brick kilns at global poverty levels just to feed their families each day. One day, while working in a kiln where they were paid $6.00 for every 1,000 bricks made, they were approached by a man from another kiln who promised them a higher wage with an advance of $40 per person to pay for moving costs to work at his facility.

Mariamma and the group gladly took the offer, but once they arrived at their new jobs they found themselves in the bonds of slavery. The owner and his son were severely abusive, placed them in debt to pay back their advance, paid them only enough to eat for the day, and would not pay them if they didn't reach their daily quota. At night the owner and his son would tie up the men and take the women to another facility where they would rape them. Mariamma said they would go for as long as seven days without eating. The owner would violently enforce his rules through a gang of thugs who would beat and threaten the people. Though the people eventually escaped, the owner took his thugs to their home-town, captured three men loosely tied to the enslaved people, and threatened to harm them unless the group returned. Eventually, IJM's representative heard of this story, con-fronted the owner and his son, and the hostages were set free.[42] This story illustrates IJM's mission to obey God's command to 'rescue the oppressed'. By intervening in oppressive, broken, and corrupt justice systems and working toward equitable laws, IJM helps to res-cue those who have been held captive in those systems. As such, the divine command is lived out in tangible and life-altering ways.

Second, IJM seeks to bring criminals to justice. IJM makes sure criminals cannot con-tinue to harm vulnerable people. They do this by working with local law enforcement in in-vestigating, arresting, and charging enslavers with crimes. IJM lawyers and partners then continue to fight in courtrooms until those enslavers are put behind bars.[43] Unfortunately, as IJM works with governments around the world, they constantly run into corruption and local laws that keep them from stopping injustice from happening. In the case of Mariamma, the owner and his son fell under 35 counts of criminal activity, including bond-ed labour, labour imprisonment to assault, abduction, rape, extortion, theft, wrongful con-finement, and more.[44] However, in India, these offences are not practically against the law when committed against poor people because the justice system does not strictly enforce the laws. Therefore, no charges were filed against the owner and his son. After two years and relentless pressure from IJM and local attorneys, charges were finally filed against the perpetrators, but they were released on bond. When the case finally came to trial, much of the evidence had been lost, and the wrong son appeared. The case was put off for retrial for another three years. Finally, six years after the enslaved people were freed, the case was assigned to another judge who dismissed it. Though this case, and many others, end in disappointment, IJM continues to work to bring perpetrators to justice because the mis-sion to 'seek justice' is at the core of the divine command that drives IJM from a biblical perspective. Evidence for this clarion call is found in Micah 6:8, which reads, 'He has told you, O man, what is good; and what does the Lord require of you but to do justice, and to love kindness, and to walk humbly with your God?'

Third, IJM helps to strengthen justice systems. IJM contends that slavery still exists because perpetrators can freely exploit those living in poverty. This is possible because police, judges, and other officials are not equipped to enforce the laws. Gary Haugen calls this 'The Locust Effect'. The Locust Effect is the idea that, just like a plague of locusts can destroy the hard work of a farmer, criminals practising everyday violence can devastate the work of the global poor, as well as anti-poverty efforts around the world.[45] Therefore, IJM provides training, mentoring, and support to local law enforcement and community leaders to slow down and stop the cycle of violence and, therefore, the plague of slavery and poverty.

So, how does IJM do this? First, they start by measuring the crime's prevalence and assessing how the justice system responds to it. Second, they track changes in how po-lice, judges, and other actors and institutions in the public justice system respond to the crime being measured and also continue to assess how prevalent the crime is, watching for changes. Third, they ensure people are safer by using this critical information to en-sure that the justice system's response to the crime is genuinely improving and that these improvements are actually making vulnerable people safer from the targeted form of violence – which is the ultimate goal. Finally, they share what they learn with key stakeholders in the communities where they work and with audiences worldwide through talks and published studies and papers.[46]

All of these activities are at the core of how IJM interprets divine command theory. In fact, in the New Testament in Luke 4:18-19, Jesus identifies his own mission by saying, 'The Spirit of the Lord is upon me, because he has anointed me to proclaim good news to the poor. He has sent me to proclaim liberty to the captives and recovering of sight to the blind, to set at liberty those who are oppressed, to proclaim the year of the Lord's favour.' As a Christian-based organization, IJM follows this same pattern because Jesus told his followers in John 14:12, 'Truly, truly, I say to you, whoever believes in me will also do the works that I do; and greater works than these will he do ...'

IJM provides opportunities for others to partner with them in their mission against injustice. They encourage all people of goodwill across religious and cultural lines to join them in helping to bring justice to the poor and marginalized of the world. They encourage people to do this through giving financially to IJM's work, praying for them and those they are rescuing, advocating for justice locally and globally, volunteering, or working for IJM. These opportunities help IJM and their followers 'learn to do good; seek justice, rescue the oppressed, defend the orphan, and plead for the widow'.

As a result, IJM, according to the divine command theory of moral obligation, demonstrates an ethically correct response to the needs of millions who suffer as a result of injustice in the world. As this organization lives out God's commands and actions toward those in desperate need by rescuing and restoring victims, bringing criminals to justice, and strengthening justice systems for victims of injustice, they obey God's command to love their neighbour as themselves.

## FIVE COMPONENT ANALYSIS

In our case study, IJM is the leader and the IJM supporters are the followers. Their unified goal is to respond to global injustice in a context of vulnerable people and corrupt systems. The cultural values and norms encompassing this leadership situation is the Divine's command for justice (Figure 9.3).

The IJM case shows the dependence upon the leader–follower relationship to the broader environment and culture for the greater good. Because divine command theory establishes the overarching cultural values and norms as articulated in a religion's holy texts, the leader and follower work to facilitate the goal through obedience to God's commands – even in a hostile environment. Since God has commanded a life of love, compassion, and justice towards others, IJM works to provide the organizational vision, education, structure, and on-the-ground resources to accomplish this goal. Through partnerships with local churches, empowering local leaders, and providing opportunities for others around the world to help with the global injustice crisis, IJM allows others to join them as they lead out in meeting the needs of those in crisis. International Justice Mission provides numerous local and international touch points where followers and leaders can work together to support their goal of ending global injustice based, which is based on divine command theory. In other words, because God is a God of justice, his followers must demon- strate the same sense of justice they have received.

In our case study, the goal is the result of the Divine's commands. While the goal of meeting the needs of those affected by injustice is the defined mission, it acts as second- ary to the cultural values and norms and the context. The goal is the application of a much larger divine command in a particular situation. Though there are other humanitarian agencies – such as the International Organization for Migration, Madre, Equality Now, and the Human Rights Campaign – that share similar goals for helping end injustice in the world, IJM is different in that the *motive* for the goal is obedience to a divine command.[47] In John 14:15, Jesus says,

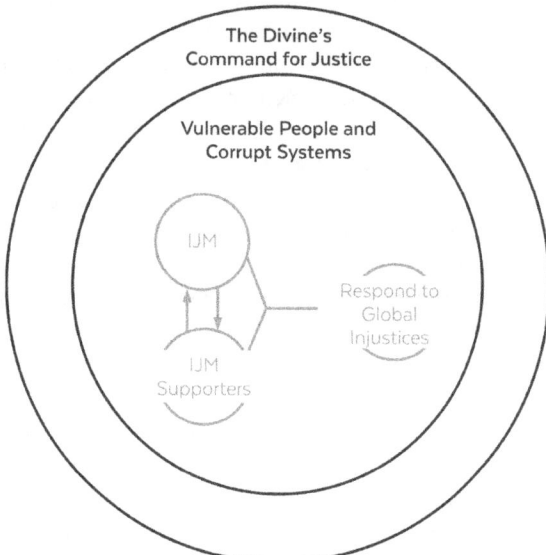

**Figure 9.3**     The Five Components of Leadership Model applied to the IJM case study

'If you love me, you will keep my commandments.' In doing so, IJM empowers its leaders and followers by encouraging them to obey God's commands to love their neighbours and provide for those in need.

This faith forms the outermost cultural values and norms in which International Justice Mission operates. The value is the divine command to 'learn to do good; seek justice, rescue the oppressed, defend the orphan, [and] plead for the widow' and extend compassion and help to those in the greatest need. In this context, leaders and followers work together to accomplish desired goals based on God's commands.

Divine command theory rests on the presupposition that there is a God, who is good, whose commands are the basis for moral rightness and beneficial for those who follow them. Adherents of this theory have an objective moral framework in which to live ethically moral lives as they obey God's command. Divine command theory, then, provides a model for leaders in fostering moral and ethical conduct in their followers and the organizations they lead.

## SUMMARY AND CONCLUDING REMARKS

Our chapter opened with a question for leaders who wish to live by the divine command theory of ethics: What does the divine require from leadership? To answer this question, leaders in a monotheistic tradition look to authoritative sources for guidance, trusting that these sources reflect the character of a divine being who is 'good' and a call to action consistent with that divine being's character. Readers must note that leaders following the divine command tradition do not abnegate responsibility for reasoned consideration of what they perceive as divine dictates. So, while the commands may be divine in nature, their interpretation and application still require a human element. As an example of that human element at work, our chapter considered the case of how a Christian justice organization, IJM, chose to respond to a global injustice crisis. Their response was rooted in an interpretation of commands to do justice found in both Hebrew and Christian scripture.

## DISCUSSION QUESTIONS

1. What is your view of God and ethics? How can a theistic framework help or hinder a better understanding of ethics and leadership?
2. What are the benefits of a divine command theory of moral obligation as an ethical framework? What are its disadvantages? How might these disadvantages be overcome to sustain a viable ethical theory?
3. What role does human autonomy play in the development of divine command theory? How does reason factor into the connection between divine command theory and human independence?
4. What leadership benefits might be obtained from adherence to divine command theory? What leadership challenges might arise from such a theory?
5. How does the leader–follower dynamic in divine command theory speak to a sustainable, ethical framework for leadership? How do context and culture in divine command theory support the leader–follower dynamic in helping them reach their desired goals?
6. What practical applications does divine command theory present in leadership in a case study such as the Syrian refugee crisis?

## ADDITIONAL RESOURCES

C.S. Evans, *God and Moral Obligation*, Oxford: Oxford University Press, 2014.

This text explores the connection between religion and ethics. Evans specifically sets out to address the objections to divine command theory and explores questions about the role of natural disasters and the problem of evil in understanding divine command theory.

D. Baggett and J. Walls, *Good God: The Theistic Foundations of Morality*, Oxford: Oxford University Press, 2011.

Baggett and Walls provide a thorough overview of divine command theory and aim to reinvigorate debates over theology and ethics in contemporary scholarship.

G.A. Haugen and V. Boutros, *The Locust Effect: Why the End of Poverty Requires the End of Violence*, Oxford: Oxford University Press, 2014.

Haugen and Boutros explore the correlation between injustice, violence, and poverty and provide solutions for addressing these issues in eradicating poverty worldwide.

M. Al-Attar, *Islamic Ethics: Divine Command Theory in Arabo-Islamic Thought*, New York: Routledge, 2010.

Al-Attar looks at divine command theory from an Islamic perspective.

## NOTES

1.    P.L. Quinn, 'Divine command theory of ethics', *Encyclopedia of Philosophy*, Detroit, MI: Macmillan Reference, 2005, p. 93.
2.    P.L. Quinn, 'Divine command theory', in H. LaFollette (ed.), *The Blackwell Guide to Ethical Theory*, Chichester: Blackwell Publishing, 2000, p. 54.
3.    P.L. Quinn, 'Divine command theory', in H. LaFollette (ed.), *The Blackwell Guide to Ethical Theory*, Chichester: Blackwell Publishing, 2000, p. 54.
4.    R. Bellah, 'Civil religion in America', *Daedalus*, vol. 96 no. 1, winter 1967, 1–21. http://www.robertbellah .com/articles_5.htm (accessed 1 July 2022).
5.    Bellah, 'Civil religion in America'.
6.    J.A. Boss, *Ethics for Life: A Text with Readings*, New York: McGraw Hill, 2011, p. 146.
7.    Found in both Exodus 20:1–17 and Deuteronomy 5:6–21.
8.    J.M. Idziak, *Divine Command Morality: Historical and Contemporary Readings*, New York: Edwin Mellen Press, 1979.
9.    St Augustine, *The Letters of St. Augustine*, trans. J.G. Cunningham, North Charlotte, SC: Createspace, 2015. See also J.M. Idziak, *Divine Command Morality: Historical and Contemporary Readings*, New York: Edwin Mellen Press, 1979.
10.   J. Hare, *God's Call: Moral Realism, Divine Commands and Human Autonomy*, Grand Rapids, MI: William B. Eerdmans, 2001, p. 50.
11.   S.C. Evans, *Kierkegaard's Ethic of Love: Divine Commands and Moral Obligations*, Oxford: Oxford University Press, 2006, pp. 6–7; and S. Kierkegaard, *Works of Love*, Princeton, NJ: Princeton University Press, 1995, p. 51.
12.   Evans, *Kierkegaard's Ethic of Love*.
13.   I. Kant, *Critique of Pure Reason*, ed. P. Guyer and A.W. Wood, Cambridge: Cambridge University Press, 1999; I. Kant, *Critique of Practical Reason*, trans. A.T. Kingmill, Mineola, NY: Dover Publications, 2004; and I. Kant, *Religion and Rational Theology*, trans. A.W Wood and G. di Giovanni, Cambridge: Cambridge University Press, 2001. Kant had what was called a 'pre-critical' period and a 'critical' period, and his works in the pre-critical period endorse a view of God that is in line with this description. The latter period doesn't fully address the philosophy of religion and has been interpreted as a departure from a theistic world view because Kant himself was anti-religion at that point. It is fair to say that Kant endorsed the necessity of a god, or a divine, insofar as he directly addressed religion. He argued that this entity would be a 'regulator', but there was no endorsement of any specific religious content. See A.W. Wood, *Kant's Moral Religion*, Ithaca, NY: Cornell University Press, 1970.
14.   P. Quinn, *Divine Commands and Moral Requirements*, Oxford: Clarendon Press, 1978.

15. R.M. Adams, *Finite and Infinite Goods: A Framework for Ethics*, Oxford: Oxford University Press, 1999, pp. 42–9.

16. R.M. Adams, 'Divine command metaethics modified again', *Journal of Religious Ethics*, vol. 7 no. 1, 1979, 66–79, p. 71.

17. R.J. Mouw, *The God Who Commands: A Study in Divine Command Ethics*, Notre Dame, IN: University of Notre Dame Press, 1990, p. 73.

18. Mouw, *The God Who Commands*, p. 98.

19. Quinn, *Divine Commands*.

20. Azim Nanji, 'Divine law/divine command: the ground of ethics in Western tradition/Muslim perspectives', *Studies in Christian Ethics*, vol. 23 no. 1, 2010, 35–41. https://journals.sagepub.com/doi/10.1177/0953946809352998 (accessed 31 October 2022).

21. Nanji, 'Divine law/divine command'.

22. Mouw, *The God Who Commands*.

23. 'Mom who said she killed on God's orders acquitted', CNN, 6 April 2004. http://www.cnn.com/2004/LAW/04/03/children.slain / (accessed 1 July 2022).

24. Nanji, 'Divine law/divine command'.

25. Plato, *Five Dialogues: Euthyphro, Apology, Crito, Meno, Phaedo*, trans. J.M. Cooper and G.M.A Grube, Indianapolis, IN: Hackett Publishing Company, 2002, p. 12.

26. Plato, *Five Dialogues*.

27. See Genesis 22.

28. M.W. Austin, 'Divine command theory', *Internet Encyclopedia of Philosophy: A Peer-Reviewed Academic Resource*, 2006. http://www.iep.utm.edu/divine-c/#H3 (accessed 1 July 2022).

29. See W. Alston, 'Some suggestions for divine command theorists', in M.D. Beaty (ed.), *Christian Theism and the Problems of Philosophy*, Notre Dame, IN: University of Notre Dame Press, 1990, pp. 303–26.

30. Adams, *Finite and Infinite Goods*, p. 270.

31. Adams, *Finite and Infinite Goods*, p. 272.

32. Adams, *Finite and Infinite Goods*, pp. 272–4.

33. R.M. McManus and G. Perruci, *Understanding Leadership: An Arts and Humanities Perspective*, New York: Routledge, 2015, p. 17.

34. Merriam-Webster Dictionary. https://www.merriam-webster.com/dictionary/injustice (accessed 1 July 2022).

35. Merriam-Webster Dictionary. https://www.merriam-webster.com/dictionary/justice (accessed 1 July 2022).

36. G.A. Haugen and V. Boutros, *The Locust Effect: Why the End of Poverty Requires the End of Violence*, Oxford: Oxford University Press, 2014, ix.

37. International Justice Mission. https://www.ijm.org/our-work (accessed 1 July 2022).

38. Isaiah 1:17, NRSV.

39. J. Martin, *The Just Church: Becoming a Risk-Taking, Justice-Seeking, Disciple-Making Congregation*, Carol Stream, IL: Tyndale House Publishers, ix, xi.

40. International Justice Mission. https://www.ijm.org/our-work (accessed 1 July 2022).

41. International Justice Mission. https://www.ijm.org/slavery (accessed 1 July 2022).

42. For Mariamma's full story, see Haugen and Boutros, *The Locust Effect*, pp. 20–28.

43. International Justice Mission. https://www.ijm.org/our-work (accessed 1 July 2022).

44. Haugen and Boutros, *The Locust Effect*, p. 24.

45. Dressember. https://www.dressember.org/blog/what-is-the-locust-effect (assessed 1 July 2022).

46. International Justice Mission. https://www.ijm.org/studies (assessed 1 July 2022).

47. IJM also partners with other faith-based organizations working for global justice and the end of poverty. This partnership is called the 'End it Movement' and brings together the leading organizations in the world in the fight for freedom. More information can be found at https://enditmovement.com.

# 10

# Social contract theory

*Lavina Sequeira and Stanley J. Ward*

## FRAMING QUESTION

What obligations do leaders and followers have to each other?

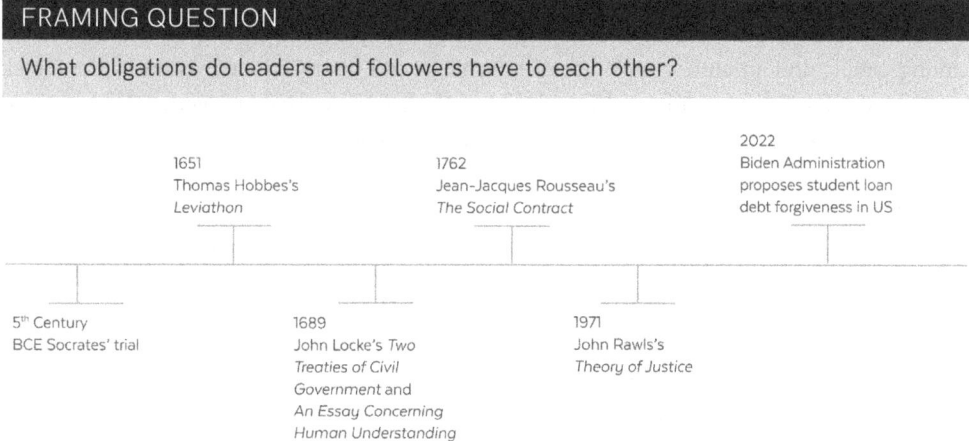

**Figure 10.1**   Timeline of major works on social contract theory in relation to the chapter case study

John Stuart Mill wrote, 'Though society is not founded on a contract, and though no good purpose is answered by inventing a contract in order to deduce social obligations from it, everyone who receives the protection of society owes a return for the benefit.'[1] Mill's statement beautifully encapsulates the concept of social contract theory. Briefly, social contract theory is a moral and political view asserting the notion of a political society resting on the voluntary agreement between a government and the individuals residing in a particular country. This construct defines the rules and duties of the individuals who are part of that society, as well as the obligations of its government. Individuals implicitly agree to give up some of their freedoms for the mutual benefit of others living in that society and to assure their security in a social structure. This perspective asserts that, due to a shared contract, individuals are morally and politically obligated towards each other and to the society of which they are a part. This perspective provides a philosophical framework for understanding the interactions between a society and its members. It also asks, 'What obligations do leaders and followers have to each other?'

In this chapter, we will see how the concept of the social contract has evolved over time and consider the theory's ethical implications. We will also examine how the theory applies to the Five Components of Leadership Model and then apply the theory to our case study. But first, let's delve a bit deeper into the concept of a social contract and its primary proponents, ideas, and critiques.

## HISTORY AND MAJOR CONCEPTS OF SOCIAL CONTRACT THEORY

From a socio-political standpoint, social contract theory asserts that individuals' obligations of morality and participation in political life depend on the agreements and contracts adhered to – implicitly, unwritten, unspoken, or otherwise – between the community and themselves, which help aid the governance of society. Historically, the social contract lends itself to nuanced meanings, one being the contract amongst people in setting a society, and the second among people and an authority. While similar ideas can be traced back as far as the Greek sophists, the modern iteration and popularity of the social contract are generally associated with Thomas Hobbes, John Locke, and Jean Jacques Rousseau. From the lens of morality, the social contract gained momentum in the twentieth century due to Rawls' influential perspectives.[2] Let's take a closer look at each of these perspectives.

In Socrates' time, Athenian society was believed to have established governance. This system is evident in the Platonic dialogues *Euthyphro*, *Crito*, and *Apology*, which mainly focus on a notion of the social contract – a tacit agreement of laws between the government and its citizens. These laws present the citizens' duty toward the State and the State's duty towards its citizens. In choosing to live in Athens, a citizen implicitly endorsed the society's laws. But if the laws were unjust, would one be morally obligated to obey them?

Socrates was charged with breaking the laws of Athens by disobeying the gods of Athens and making up new gods – consequently corrupting the youth of the community. He was found guilty and sentenced to death by drinking hemlock. While in prison, Crito, his friend, offered to help Socrates escape, but he refused. Socrates said it would be unjust for him to flee since he had every opportunity to leave Athens or disagree with the policy, and the government made no effort to deceive him in any way. Thus, in the Platonic dialogue, *Crito*, Socrates alludes to the social contract in asserting that it is immoral for him to escape prison and punishment – even the death penalty – since he entered into a contract with the State and was obligated to the State for raising him and looking after his children. Speaking in Socrates' voice, Plato writes:

[He] who has experience of the manner in which we order justice and administer the State, and still remains, has entered into an implied contract that he will do as we command him. And he who disobeys us is, as we maintain, thrice wrong: first, because in disobeying us he is disobeying his parents; secondly, because we are the authors of his education; thirdly, because he has made an agreement with us that he will duly obey our commands.[3]

Here Socrates asserts that the laws must be obeyed; it is a tacit choice to stay in Athens all these years. Therefore, the implicit agreement made between Socrates and the personified laws stands. If broken, consequences will follow, in this case the death penalty.

In Socrates' view, breaking laws would result in chaos and insecurity, leading to injustice. He maintains that even if one is victimized unjustly, one must not retaliate in an unjust manner. He asserts, '... that neither injury nor retaliation nor warding off evil by evil is ever right'.[4] By escaping, Socrates would be disobeying the law and attempting to challenge the established norms and laws of the State. But Socrates and Plato were not the last to comment upon the social contract. The idea bloomed again during the Renaissance with the thinking of Thomas Hobbes.

Another iteration of the social contract can be found in Hobbes' treatise *Leviathan*. In Hobbes' materialistic conception of the world, human beings are sophisticated mechanical beings with appetites, desires, and aversions. This is the 'natural condition of mankind'. However, the notion of a stateless autonomous condition cannot prevail if a person desires to move beyond a primitive existence. In this condition, human beings will do three things: compete to secure life's necessities, challenge and fight out of fear for personal safety, or challenge and fight for purposes of individual glory and reputation.[5] In this State of Nature, conflict is a real possibility where danger, fear, and violent death prevail. Here, the 'life of man is solitary, poor, nasty, brutish, and short'.[6]

Therefore, a person's natural desire for security will enable them to want self-preservation. People can escape the State of Nature through reason and judgment by creating a civil society and living in peace. In *Leviathan*, Hobbes concluded that rationality demands that humans escape their natural condition for self-preservation. To do this, they must be '... willing to seek peace and follow it' and 'when others are so too, as far forth as for peace and defense of himself he shall think it necessary, to lay down this right to all things'.[7] Thus, men can be expected to enter a social contract in which they agree to establish a civil society by renouncing their rights against one another in the State of Nature. In accepting to live together under shared laws, they submit themselves to the sovereign, the sole political authority and above accountability.

Hobbes posits that civil society arises out of a voluntary agreement, or a social contract. Because rational people desire peace, they would, by mutual consent, appoint a sovereign – an artificial creature. 'For by art is created the great Leviathan called a Commonwealth or State ... which is but artificial man; though of greater stature and strength than the natural for whose protection and defense it was intended.'[8] Since the contract is collectively entered into, the Leviathan would act as an enforcer of peace and justice. This absolute sovereign would guarantee an individual's personal security in return for complete obedience. Humanity must allow its natural rights to transition to the State. The transfer of power to the Leviathan is necessary to ensure peace and move out of a state of destruction and anarchy. In Hobbes' thinking, it is necessary to note that the sovereign retains total liberty and is not a party to the social contract. Since the power has been transferred, the State remains the absolute authority in making laws, receiving the obedience of the citizens in exchange for social order and public welfare.

The Enlightenment thinker John Locke's views on the matter of the social contract differ from Hobbesian absolutism. His opinion of the State of Nature isn't dark, grim, and miserable as that of Hobbes. Locke's State of Nature is one in which '... persons are free to pursue their own interests and plans, free from interference, and, because of the Law of Nature and the restrictions that it imposes upon persons, it is relatively peaceful'; where 'Men [live] together according to reason without a common superior on earth with authority to judge between them.'[9] In this State of Nature, the natural condition of humanity is one of freedom, liberty, and the pursuit of their own interests without interference. The State of Nature does not have a shared authority and is, therefore, pre-political; however, it is certainly not pre-moral. To safeguard this natural condition of freedom in which individuals find themselves, Locke asserts the necessity of individual consent. Through this consent, political societies are created, and individuals join them. One can only become a full member of society by an act of express consent.[10] Locke maintains this is the precondition for the acquisition of private property.

So why is there a necessity for a social contract here? To reiterate, as described by Locke, the State of Nature is a state of equality and perfect freedom. Locke asserts in the State of Nature a person acquires private property by mixing their physical labour with the materials of nature. But rights must be relegated if the person wants to enjoy that property. It is for this property that 'man' may decide to leave the State of Nature. Having done this, people are subject to the will of the majority to make 'one body politic under one government'.[11] While there are restrictions on the accumulation and acquisition of private property, to safeguard one's rights to property a person enters into a social contract with others. Locke asserts:

> [T]he enjoyment of property he has in this State is very unsafe, very unsecure. This makes him willing to quit a condition which, however free, is full of fears and continual dangers: and it is not without reason that he seeks out and is willing to join in society with others who are already united, or have a mind to unite for the mutual preservation of their lives, liberties, and estates, which I call by the general name property.[12]

In Locke's view, laws and individual rights can be violated in the State of Nature. Since there is no political governance, the victims can't enforce the Law of Nature in the State of Nature. This sets the condition for the social contract. For the protection of property, men agree to delegate – or transfer – their rights to the government. The government safeguards the rights and property of its citizens. Therefore, the government has limited powers and obligations to its creators due to the nature of the social contract, and the citizens can thereby modify it at any time.

Another influential Enlightenment philosopher, Jean-Jacques Rousseau, asserted, 'Man was born free; and everywhere he is in chains.'[13] He believed that with their very first breath individuals were shackled by invisible chains – from the State of Autonomy of man being free to the modern condition of inequality and dependency. In *The Social Contract*, Rousseau attempted to find a solution to this problem.

According to Rousseau, man by nature is good, free, wise, and benevolent. But as people come together to form social institutions, they develop vices. The accumulation of private property encourages self-interest. Thus, the good State of Nature degenerates due to the acquisition of private property. Since this original State of freedom, according to Rousseau, is destroyed by inequality due to the corrupting nature of social institutions, it gives rise to the 'right of the strongest'. Rousseau states, 'men reach a point where the obstacles to their preservation in a state of nature prove greater than the strength that each man has to preserve himself in that state.'[14] As uncertainty increases, individuals compare themselves to others leading to public and private values. Since no individual is entitled to have authority over others, it is, therefore, necessary that individuals give their rights to a community. Thus, 'Each of us puts his person and all his power in common under the supreme direction of the general will, and, in our corporate capacity, we receive each member as an indivisible part of the whole.'[15]

The instability of the State of Nature brings people together to form a civil society. Rousseau referred to the agreement among people and the community as the 'Social Contract'. He asserted that the contract must exist between all individual members of the society. A person must agree to surrender their individual rights (or will) to be part of a new moral society and have an equal voice in its laws. Thus, when all members of the State give up their freedoms and liberty, their combined collective individual wills form one 'General Will'. The State and the laws are made by this general will, as it is the will of the people. This general will, therefore, acts as the 'absolute power' or the 'public person'. Additionally, it is actively viewed as the 'body politic' or 'sovereign', and passively the 'state', ensuring individual rights and complete and free participation in state affairs.[16] It guarantees freedom from alienation and individual autonomy.

This General Will unifies society. It derives its existence from the contract between its individual members. Once the multitude is united, any injury towards an injured member is an injury towards the whole. In this sense, the General Will is always in the right as it is delib-erative and resolves differences because it tends to incline itself toward the public good. The General Will demands obedience from every member of its society. As it is a force for good, it is, therefore, inviolable and infallible.

Now we must examine one final view of the social contract proposed by the philosopher you will encounter in Chapter 11, John Rawls.

Rawls holds the view that humans are reasonable, capable of impartiality, and have a capacity for respect and genuine tolerance for 'the other'. He claims that from a hypothetical 'Original Position' the principles of justice and equality are chosen behind a 'Veil of Ignorance'. The original position, although a hypothetical agreement, is a result of moral beliefs possessed by individuals and therefore is obligatory as a real contract after due consideration. In this abstractive view, we can discover humans' State of Nature, the nature of justice – specifically social justice – and the individual requirement for cooperative living.

Rawls states that the social contract 'implies a level of abstraction', in that 'the content of the relevant agreement is not to enter a given society or to adopt a given form of government, but rather to accept certain moral principles.'[17] But why should individuals accept certain moral principles, given that they inevitably hold different world views? What makes such principles 'legitimate' in a diverse society? The idea of justice is based on the perspective that society is grounded in cooperation and mutual advantage between its individual members. While conflicts and shared interests are a part of society, principles of social justice help 'define the appropriate distribution of the benefits and burdens of social cooperation'.[18] From this lens, Rawls asserts 'the principles that free and rational persons concerned to further their own interests would accept in an initial position of equality as defining the fundamental terms of their association.'[19] Even though such principles are based on general considerations, rational individuals would adopt them without knowing their own personal situation – or what Rawls called the Veil of Ignorance.

Since the concept of justice in the original position presupposes a conscious entity – an individual – capable of comprehending its existence and reality, Rawls contends that the most rational choice in the original position is the acceptance of two main principles of justice. The first principle asserts equality and liberty of basic rights, including the pursuance of the good. The second principle asserts that individuals be provided equal opportunities to compete socially and economically as needed to pursue their interests.

In summarizing the above perspectives, it seems clear that Socrates uses the relationship between a patriarchal unit and society as an argument for the social contract. The traditional social contract perspective of Hobbes, Locke, and Rousseau relied heavily on the idea of consent. Hobbes' idea of the social contract is to succumb to fear and force a sovereign through tacit consent. Although Locke asserts express and tacit consent, he also suggests that the social contract will benefit the majority residing in the State. Whereas, for Rawls, making a rational choice based on ignorance helps in the pursuit of social justice (Table 10.1). Now that we have a better understanding of social contract theory let's take a look at some of its critiques.

Table 10.1  Different approaches to social contract theory

| Thinker | Humanity's natural state | The problem | The solution |
| --- | --- | --- | --- |
| Socrates (5th century BCE) | Capable of making rational decisions | The potential for chaos, insecurity, and injustice in society | When one agrees to enjoy the benefits of the state, one must follow the rules of the state |
| Thomas Hobbes (1651) | Human lives are nasty, brutish, and short | People need to go beyond self-preservation and seek peace | Each person transfers their natural rights to the state |
| John Locke (1689) | Freedom, liberty, pursuit of one's own interests without interference | People need to protect laws and individual rights | People express individual consent to the government in order to protect property |
| Jean-Jacques Rousseau (1762) | Born good and free, yet living in shackles created by vices that are driven by self-interest | People need community to protect themselves from the excesses of self-interest | Surrender individual interests in order to form a General Will that unifies society |
| John Rawls (1971) | People are rational, able to show respect and tolerance to 'the other' | Conflicts are caused by a lack of social justice | Accept certain moral principles about cooperation and mutual advantage from the viewpoint of a 'veil of ignorance' |

## CRITIQUES OF SOCIAL CONTRACT THEORY

The influence of the social contract through the ages has been enormous. However, it is not without critique. Two main questions to be asked here are: (1) Can a contract be valid if it hasn't been consented to by the individual members? and (2) If the leader – in this case, the government – does not provide proper protections to its members who have entered into the contract, do the followers (the individual members) have an obligation to uphold the contract? Before we answer these questions, let's first consider critiques of the influential theories summarized.

Rousseau asserts that individuals tacitly consent to the social contract by virtue of taking residence in a civilized society. Residence, however, cannot guarantee that individuals are fully cognizant of the nuanced nature of the social contract. By refusing to leave prison and move to another country, Socrates articulates a tacit approach to the social contract; here, alienation of the will is legitimate. In this perspective, a social contract is an obligation owed to good regimes. For Hobbes, the social contract is an agreement by all persons to abandon their rights to the sovereign, which is the beneficiary of the social contract. It is a contract made under duress and tacit consent. While consent is the distinguishing factor in Locke's view, he also regards tacit consent in accepting benefits. But does the consent of the majority equate to consent for all its citizens? If primacy is allocated to the majority and consent is left to the majority, it is at the expense of individual rights. In Rousseau's case, the body politic is 'sovereign'; therefore, the punishments meted out towards any individual are also to itself. Rousseau completely relies on the tacit consent of the individuals in the State once the political society is instituted.

All these views emphasize individual tacit consent to a certain extent as a way of remaining a member of society. As one author argues, '[Tacit consent] is given by remaining silent and inactive; it is not express or explicit, it is not directly and distinctly expressed by action; rather, it is expressed by the failure to do certain things.'[20] Silence cannot only be interpreted as a form of tacit consent, but also as a form of expressed consent. This raises an ethical concern. If I, as an individual member of a community (a citizen), tacitly agree to follow the rules of the leader (society), and if I reason the leader's rules are unjust, do I still have an obligation to follow society or its rules? Is there a difference in consent between citizens and non-citizens? It would seem that the social contract theory is incompatible with this distinction – specifically the natural rights of the individuals. Indeed, in highlighting this flaw in the social contract, Hume emphasizes that the social contract is speculative, fictional, and attempting to justify a preferred form of rule.[21] Similarly, if the contract or agreement is a hypothetical construct, it cannot be said to represent express agreement.[22] These critiques against the social contract use a philosophical lens, but one can also use a pragmatic lens to critique the concept.

For example, the significance of women was largely ignored in earlier philosophical discussions about the social contract, and women were subjugated to subordinate roles in the political arena. One author asserts that the term 'human nature' used in most articulations 'is intended to refer only to male human nature', which can be problematic as it justifies a male-dominated political view.[23] Likewise, other feminist scholars argue that there has been an implicit contract among men to enforce patriarchy.[24] The ideology of the social contract through the ages may shed light on the patriarchal oppression of women.[25] These perspectives suggest that the social contract can be used as a justification for the exploitation of those who are not considered parties to the contract.

Likewise, pluralism asserts social contract theory is problematic due to its theoretical nature and that the contract is between groups, not an individual and the State. If groups have struggles or conflicting interests, then the decisions made by the State will first represent the interests of the group rather than the individual. Accordingly, another scholar, Charles Mills, notes that in the United States, historically, whites have had an actual, sometimes explicit, but most times implicit contract to enforce white supremacy that led to domination, subordination, and exploitation of other groups.[26] These are practical concerns raised by those critiquing social contract theory. Still, one may also use a historical lens to critique the theory, specifically in the context of the United States.

From a historical perspective, European settlers to the United States were immigrants when considering the Native Americans who already occupied the land. The clashing of two radically different world views lent itself to misconceptions and misgivings, thereby directly contributing to the European–American rationalization of the removal of Native Americans from their land.[27] Indeed, this was not a social contract in which both parties agreed either tacitly or expressly, but rather a 'contract' based on force and violence.

These are some of the major critiques of social contract theory. Nevertheless, the concept continues to highly influence current thinking about the relationship between a country and those residing within its borders. We turn now to consider how social contract theory relates to the Five Components of Leadership Model (Figure 10.2).

## FIVE COMPONENT ANALYSIS

In his influential book *Leadership*, James MacGregor Burns identified the key differences between what he referred to as 'transactional' and 'transforming' forms of leadership. For Burns, transactional leadership was a mere exchange between leader and follower – a quid pro quo between parties – an honest day's pay for an honest day's work, as it were. Burns argued that 'transformational leadership', contrarily, was a form of leadership in which both the leader and the follower challenged each other to 'higher levels of motivation and morality'.[28] For Burns, transformational leadership was leadership at its best. Both the leader and the follower came away from their interaction better for their time together, and they not only reached their goal but exceeded it.

Although Burns obviously preferred transformational leadership, that is not to say that transactional leadership is not useful. We see regular examples of transactional leadership in management by objective (MBO) performance appraisals and in annual bonuses and

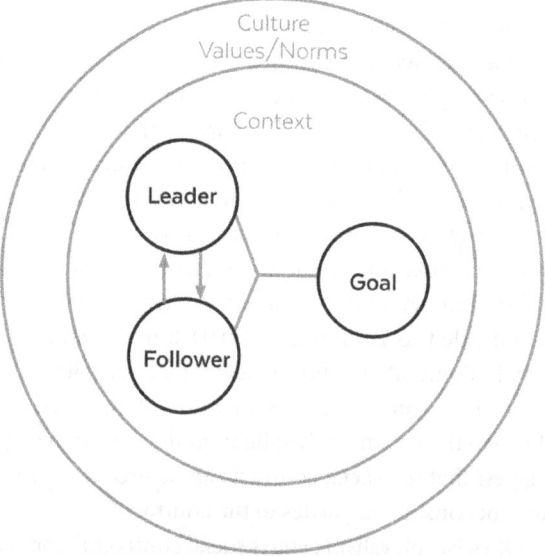

**Figure 10.2** The Five Components of Leadership Model applied to social contract theory

merit-based pay. Such a form of leadership can be efficacious. On a deeper level, transactional leadership is the foundation of social contract theory. Look at Figure 10.2 – notice the circles around the leader, the followers, and the goal. Those three components of the model are the crux of social contract theory as it relates to leadership. The leader and the followers form a relationship – in this case, for mutual benefit – and in so doing, are able to reach a common goal. Notice also the arrows that go both from the leader to the follower and the follower to the leader; it is a mutual process. From the perspective of social contract theory, those two arrows are one of the most important parts of the leadership process. We can think of it this way: if one day your boss came to you and said, 'I would really like you to keep working here, but I can't pay you anymore,' would you stay? Probably not. That is the essence of the leader–follower relationship through the lens of the social contract theory. I will keep my end of the bargain as long as you keep yours, but if that breaks down, all bets are off.

According to social contract theory, the goal is the other vital component of leadership. Remember the first part of the definition of leadership we have been using throughout this book: 'Leaders and followers develop a relationship and work together toward a goal ...' We could then ask the question, 'Do the leader and followers need to have a common goal?' If we apply social contract theory to leadership, the answer might be, 'Not necessarily, but the leader's goal and the follower's goal must be compatible.'

Let's use another employment example. Many people work jobs that they don't neces- sarily enjoy. Why? Are they interested in the mission of the organization? Perhaps, but not necessarily. Are they fulfilled by the work they do? Probably not. Then why go to work? It's simple: they do it for the paycheck they receive at the end of the week. The company wants to offer a product or a service to make money, grow the organization, or meet a need, and the employee wants to be able to put bread on their table. The goals are not necessarily 'common' in that both the company and the employee are merely a means to each other's ends, but those ends (goals) are compatible. The same is true of the goal of the social contract. As we will see later in our case study, we may all want the same goal, but our reasons for wanting this goal and our means for achieving it may be different, but they must be compatible.

Although the context is still important in social contract theory, as in any approach to leadership and ethics, the context is not as important as the relationship established between the leader and the follower and the goal. That is not to say the context is completely irrelevant. Although the social contract stipulates that leaders and followers, specifically within the context of a society, are responsible to each other to hold up their end of the bargain, it does not mean that if one party breaks the social contract, the other party can behave with impunity.

Consider the civil rights protests in the United States in the middle of the twentieth century. The citizens demonstrating were protesting that the State was not fulfilling its end of the bargain – specifically for those of African descent. The scourge of slavery may have been eliminated. However, African Americans still faced discrimination and injustice through the Jim Crow laws that established the 'separate but equal' context that prohibited them from fully participating in society. Dr Martin Luther King, Jr. specifically drew the country's attention to the State's failure to honour the social contract in his 'I Have a Dream' speech in 1963, in which he said:

> In a sense we've come to our nation's capital to cash a check. When the architects of our republic wrote the magnificent words of the Constitution and the Declaration of Independence they were signing a promissory note to which every American was to fall heir. This note was a promise that all men, yes, black men as well as white men, would be guaranteed the 'unalienable Rights' of 'Life, Liberty and the pursuit of Happiness.' It is obvious today that America has defaulted on this promissory note, insofar as her citizens of color are concerned. Instead of honoring this sacred obligation, America has given the Negro people a bad check, a check which has come back marked 'insufficient funds.' But we refuse to believe that the bank of justice is bankrupt. We refuse to believe that there are insufficient funds in the great vaults of opportunity of this nation. And so, we've come to cash this check, a check that will give us upon demand the riches of freedom and the security of justice.[29]

Demonstrations against the State's refusal to honour its promise included civil disobedience, such as refusing to sit in segregated sections on buses, holding sit-ins at lunch counters that refused to serve people of colour, and marching and holding demonstrations despite the State's refusal to grant permits for their assemblies. This form of civil disobedience was disproportionally non-violent when compared to the laws denying African Americans equal rights and the ferocious tactics used to quell protesters, not to mention the beatings and murders of unarmed black people throughout the South. The civil rights activists were wise in their careful use of non-violent resistance. Their leaders knew if their followers responded violently, the State would claim that they were not honouring their part of the social contract, and they would be struck down with impunity. These peaceful and measured responses to the injustices African Americans were enduring drew greater attention to the State's breaking of the social contract to serve and protect all citizens in exchange for citizens obeying the laws of the State. This illustrates the fact that context matters, even within the confines of the social contract.

But how do cultural values and norms relate to the social contract? For this, we need to look at various societies around the world and the way each has set up its unique social contract between its citizens and the State. Communist China, for instance, has a very different social contract with its citizens than capitalist United States, or even the democratic-socialist systems found in Nordic countries. Societies set up various social contracts and their citizens tacitly or expressly enter into these agreements. Whether these agreements hold or not is reliant upon the parties – the State and its citizens – voluntarily supporting the rules of the agreement. When this breaks down, revolution ensues.

But not every breach of the social contract is met with revolution. Citizens and the State often find ways to work around the rules of the social contract, which leads to a breakdown of the contract, but does not completely void it. Consider taxes. Nobody enjoys paying taxes, but those taxes pay for paved roads, clean water, police and fire services, and a wealth of other goods and services on which a civilized society depends. We all enjoy the benefits our collective taxes afford us. Those parties, corporations, or individuals who find ways around paying their fair share of taxes violate the social contract and steal from the State and their fellow citizens. Likewise, those State parties who engage in bribery and graft violate their part of the bargain. But each society has its own values and norms that go into its unique social contract. Swedes may pay a great deal more in taxes in Sweden than Americans in the United States, but they also receive many more benefits, such as state-sponsored healthcare. It is the particular society's cultural values and norms – that is, what a particular society values – that stipulates the terms of the social contract.

Now that we have a better understanding of the social contract and its relationship to the Five Components of Leadership Model let's take a more detailed look at the social contract and its implications found in our case study.

## CASE STUDY: THE NEED FOR A NEW SOCIAL CONTRACT IN HIGHER EDUCATION

The story of higher education in the United States begins with one college, having one purpose, and serving one population. In the nearly 400 years since those origins, higher education has expanded to thousands of institutions serving a wide range of students with different needs and expectations, not to mention the shifting expectations of the public outside of higher education's so-called 'ivory towers'. Current higher education in the USA includes public and private institutions, for-profit and non-profit schools, research universities, liberal arts colleges, junior colleges, and community colleges that serve a wide variety of student populations. In one way or another, nearly all these institutions benefit from state-based financial support – such as the loans and grants that help students pay their tuition and fees – and they are also accountable to follow some measure of federal or State regulation. This case study will provide an overview of how higher education developed in the United States, some of the current pressures it faces, and the opportunity for a new social contract in higher education. Given that this material is primarily written for those currently participating in higher education, we hope this overview will provide them with additional perspective and context for their own experiences and expectations – whether within the US higher education system or not.

Higher education in the United States originated during the colonial era when Harvard College was founded in 1636 to train ministers. Various schools followed as training centres for denominational clergy with a focus on education that included the knowledge of so-called 'dead' languages like Greek and Latin. White men were the presumed student population. By the time of the American Revolution, nine colonial colleges had been founded. All but the University of Pennsylvania had an official religious association.

During the mid-eighteenth century, the focus of higher education began to broaden. For example, Benjamin Franklin founded the University of Pennsylvania with a vision for preparing leaders in areas outside of Church ministry. In the nineteenth century, the focus of higher education expanded significantly with the addition of new programmes and new student populations. For example, the door opened wider to women with the creation of teacher education programmes and all-female seminaries for study.

During the second half of the nineteenth century, the Morrill Act expanded higher education with land-grant colleges offering Bachelor of Science degrees that included mechanical and agricultural studies and no longer required knowledge of Greek and Latin, leading to a significant increase in the number of engineers in the United States. The Morrill Act represented the entrance of the federal government into higher education in 1862. Proceeds from the sales of federally owned land made these agricultural and mechanical schools possible. With this development, higher education entered a new relationship with the State and benefited from greater support.

Before the Civil War, a few colleges in the USA were founded to serve the black population, and this number of schools expanded in the south after the war. The Morrill Act of 1890 required that states establish at least one land-grant college for African Americans in order to benefit from the financial proceeds the act previously made available.

The start of the twentieth century witnessed a new identity for American universities, with a greater emphasis on graduate programmes and degrees specific to various professions. The 1900s also saw the development of junior colleges and community colleges, each with a different sense of mission related to the students they would serve and the programmes they would offer. As of 2020, higher education in the United States included over 3,900 post-secondary schools that granted degrees, with a fall enrolment of 19.4 million students.[30]

Perhaps the greatest transformation to higher education in the twentieth century came through the so-called GI Bill. After the Second World War, the GI Bill created provided a variety of benefits for those who served in the armed forces, including financial aid for education. Education benefits were later expanded to qualifying family members. This development created an influx of higher education students as soldiers returned from the war. Within its first seven years, about eight million veterans took advantage of the programme, which led to more than doubling the number of college and university degree holders in the United States between 1940 and 1950.[31] During the decades that followed, increasingly greater numbers of students attended higher education institutions in the United States as a college degree also became associated with social mobility, economic opportunity, and stability.

We will now consider just a few recent challenges to higher education in the United States. We believe that the challenges, combined with higher education's diversifying stakeholder group, demonstrate the opportunity for a new social contract.

In its nearly 400 years of history, American higher education developed alongside numerous historical challenges. Significant events included the Revolutionary War, the Civil War, the Great Depression, two world wars, and significant social unrest in the 1960s and 1970s. Nonetheless, higher education experienced an overall growth trend – including the number of students participating in higher education, the number of programmes higher education offered, and the growing public support of higher education. However, over the last few decades, higher education seems to be in a time of contraction.

In 2022, over one million fewer college students were enrolled in the USA than before the Covid-19 pandemic's start. The decline in enrolment cannot be blamed on the pandemic alone, as enrolment has been trending downward since 2012. Some of that decline is related to decreases in birth rates at the start of the twenty-first century in the USA. But a decreasing pool of traditional-age college students is not the only factor at work.[32]

Students also appear to be rethinking the value of a college degree. For students who choose to go to work after high school, going to college means having fewer hours available to work, which leads to having less money as well as increased expenses that come with the books, fees, and tuition associated with going to college. Even in 2019, before the pandemic, people who could afford college asked themselves if it was worth it. Previously, universities began marketing to untapped demographic groups to increase enrolment. In the 1970s and 1980s, that meant marketing to women. More recently, that has meant reaching out to under represented populations and first-generation college students.[33]

Currently, we are also witnessing a large population of students with 'some college, no completion', meaning these students have taken college classes, but neither completed a degree programme nor re-enrolled to continue their education. Recent re-enrolment or completion rates for different demographic groups can vary from 51 per cent to 61 per cent, and the six-year graduation rate was 64 per cent, meaning about one-third of the students who started six years previously had not yet graduated.[34]

Not only is the number of enrolled students on the decline. The overall number of institutions has decreased as well. In 2009-10, higher education included nearly 4,500 post-secondary institutions that granted degrees. That number fell to just over 3,900 by 2020.[35] Indeed, given the explosion of online delivery of education brought about by the pandemic in 2019-20, one might even wonder how necessary are the 'ivory towers' and other facilities that we associate with higher education in the public imagination.

While the number of enrolled students may be declining, the cost of going to school is steadily increasing. For public, four-year institutions, average tuition and fees were 10 per cent higher than in 2010-11. For private non-profit four-year schools, tuition increased by 19 per cent. Interestingly, private for-profit schools increased by only 1 per cent from 10 years previous. The average debt of those who completed a bachelor's degree and who had ever received federal loans in the 2017-18 academic year was $20,400. Of those pursuing a bachelor's degree, 68 per cent borrowed federal loans in 2015-16, and the largest percentage per ethnic group was black, not Hispanic or Latino.[36]

So, what about the concerns of those who wonder if a college degree is 'worth it'? On average, possessing a bachelor's degree does have an economic benefit over only having a high school diploma. According to a 2021 report, the median lifetime earnings of someone with a bachelor's degree was $2.8 million versus $1.6 million for a high school diploma or GED. Yet, in some cases (depending on what industries people went to work in), those with only a diploma earned more than those with a bachelor's degree. Overall, those students who go into STEM or healthcare-related fields enjoy better pay.[37]

Notice that these financial considerations highlight the potential economic value of college for those that possess a degree. But what about the value of a degree for society at large? One can easily argue that a larger number of workers earning more money can translate to a larger tax base to support needed public programmes – but what else might be at stake here?

Leadership is about creating needed change. During these challenging years in higher education, there are also opportunities for positive change – such as the creation of a new social contract that clarifies what higher education provides for its student consumers as well as for the general public and how that benefit is worthy of public support.

The call for a new social contract in higher education is not a new idea. US higher education exists in a broader educational context that has called for a new, clear, social contract. For example, The International Association of Universities emphasized the necessity for a new social contract, the goal of which was to revise 'mutual responsibilities, rights and obligations between University and Society so that they may meet the challenges of the new Millennium'.[38]

In a 2005 speech, University of Texas at Austin President Larry Faulkner also called for a new 'social compact' in higher education. Faulkner led the university from 1998 to 2006 and was later recognized as president emeritus. During a public lecture, he first listed several points of what the 'old compact' looked like in higher education.

That compact developed out of the land grant movement, federal funding of scientific research after the Second World War, and the G.I. Bill. That compact could be summarized to include:

opening doors of opportunity to as many as possible rather than serving only an elite class; regional institutions that would be accessible and affordable; state funding to offset costs at these institutions so that tuition stayed affordable

Yet that is not where those expectations have stayed. Faulkner went on to elucidate a plurality of expectations on modern higher education's mission, depending on the group. Those expectations could include undergraduate education; research and some graduate education; a multiplicity of emphases, including 'athletics, arts, agricultural extension, regional economic development, libraries, or cultural preservation'; a growing emphasis on the private economic benefit of a college degree rather than seeing the degree as something that contributes to the public good.[39]

This complexity illustrates the observation of David Labaree that higher education seems to have 'evolved' into something of ever-increasing complexity over the centuries rather than to be something that was designed with a clear and consistent purpose in mind.[40] For some students, the higher education experience is still about expanding their understanding of the world and how they can contribute to it. For many other students, higher education seems to be about associating themselves with a particular 'brand' of experience through participation in extracurricular activities, especially athletics.

Some schools are better positioned to meet a broad set of expectations than others due to the draw of their brand recognition, which leads to increasing enrolments as well as well-funded endowments. As pointed out by Robert Kelchen, 'Flagship public universities and wealthy private colleges experienced record numbers of student applications and strong endowment returns, while the rest of higher education has suffered enrollment declines and has at most modest endowments.'[41]

Over the years, not only have the expectations shifted, but the population having those expectations has changed as well. Faulkner observed that the old social compact was 'rooted in a simpler, less pluralistic America, one with fewer voices, fewer challenges, fewer urgencies, fewer hopes'.[42]

## FIVE COMPONENT ANALYSIS

Let us now apply the five-component model to the opportunity for creating a new social contract in higher education (Figure 10.3).

The leader, in this case, is higher education as a broad institution – like the idea of 'the State' in a political social contract. Higher education is made up of various individual administrators, educators, laws, and regulations at both the local and federal levels. The responsibility for higher education is to provide something of real value to its followers in exchange for their financial support as well as their willingness to work within the systems of higher education to obtain a degree.

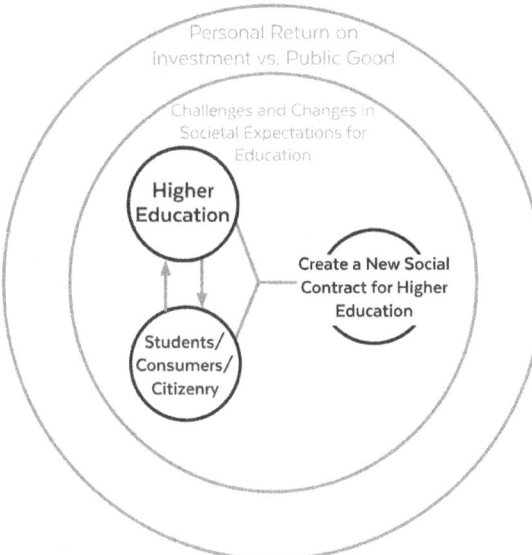

The followers here are the both the student consumers and the larger public who pay tax money that goes to public institutions, along with the politicians who determine how that money is allocated – especially regarding support for student tuition.

The goal here is for higher education leaders and their followers to create a shared understanding of what higher education provides and what students and other stakeholders will give in exchange. The 'value' higher education offers to both the student consumer and the general public must be clarified, as well as some negotiation around student expectations of what their individual institutions provide and how the larger public will support their local

**Figure 10.3**    The Five Components of Leadership Model applied to the higher education case study

institutions.

To purposefully transform the current social contract in higher education into something new would require critically evaluating and exploring established ways of thinking about the role of education and how it can benefit all parties involved. As part of that contract, we also must evaluate the ethical nature of the rights and obligations of the individuals bound by the contract. In effect, all parties must clarify what they expect from each other. This goal provides an opportunity for students and higher education leaders to work together and clarify their expectations of each other, as well as demonstrate to lawmakers the value of higher education in a way that transcends the current political divisiveness in the United States so that higher education can receive broad support. Somehow, higher education must become a trusted partner for creating a better future for a much broader segment of society.

One element that makes this social contract so difficult to establish is the ongoing changes in the context of higher education in the United States. These shifts include ever-increasing costs for both students and their institutions, meeting the needs of a diversity of students and their academic challenges, demographic changes among student populations, changes in the potential student population, and changing expectations of what a college education will provide – both in economic terms of how a college degree will ensure the economic success of its possessor as well as the expectations of the various industries who employ college graduates. This context also includes numerous criticisms about higher education as a place for 'elites' of either financial means or 'intellectual elites' with a certain political viewpoint.

This call for a new social contract also includes a cultural component. Remember that in the Five-Component Model, the cultural sphere is the sphere of 'values'. As discussed earlier, a growing number of people question the value of higher education, but this seems to be primarily in terms of 'return on investment', where consumers question if they will get their money's worth and more. From a leadership lens, the key issue for higher education is how we understand higher education as a 'public good' versus a 'private good'. The International Commission on the Futures of Education was established in 2019 by UNESCO to evaluate the complexity of education due to various global uncertainties. In their summary, the commission placed emphasis on calling for a new social contract, especially in light of 'the power of education to bring about profound change'. In addition, this new social contract 'must strengthen education as a public endeavor and a common good'.[43] Yet so much of the cultural associations around higher education in the United States are about 'private goods' of individual social mobility and economic opportunity.

As observed by Newman and Couturier:

> Higher education has long occupied a special place in society. Viewed as the creator of knowledge, the producer of leaders, and the engine of the economy, higher education's role has been considered critical to society's well-being … In return, higher education has received public support, been exempted from taxation, and often screened from the scrutiny of the public eye. Much of that has changed.[44]

And thus, we find ourselves in a season of tremendous change for higher education; and it is during these seasons of change that we need leadership. Due to the complex and diverse nature of higher education – its many institutions and diverse sense of mission, a single charismatic leader will not suffice to meet the current challenges. Rather, both the leaders of higher education and the broader public will need to work together to create a new social compact of what the university will provide in terms of public and private goods, as well as what student-consumers and State supporters will provide in return.

## SUMMARY AND CONCLUDING REMARKS

What obligations do leaders and followers have toward each other? This question cuts to the heart of leadership – how leaders and followers can work together to achieve a common goal. This case study specifically looked at the social contract in terms of higher education two. The case study works under the assumption that there is a social contract in place, and continues to evolve as the context changes. This necessitates a deeper understanding and validity of the concept of the social contract, given the changing environment.

To do this, both leaders and followers must recognize that because of constant external pressures, they must set aside pure self-interest in their commitment to a system where everyone also does the same. Then they must clarify what they will provide for each other as well as what they expect from each other. In this system, both leaders and followers will have to make their expectations clear – what they are providing and what they are giving up in order to reach a mutually beneficial goal.

## DISCUSSION QUESTIONS

1. The social contract assumes that the leader and follower must hold a mutually compatible goal. In what situations do you think the leader and follower must have a *common* goal?
2. Refer to Table 10.1. Which approach to social contract theory do you find most compelling? Explain your answer.
3. If a society is not treating some of its members justly, are those members obligated still to defer to the rules and obligations of that society? Provide examples to justify your reasoning.
4. Do you believe the primary purpose of higher education should be to train students to contribute to the social good, or do you believe its primary purpose should be to increase the lifetime earning potential of students? Explain your reasoning.
5. If higher education contributes to the public good, should it be free to students? Why or why not?

## ADDITIONAL RESOURCES

J.H. Gittell, *Transforming Relationships for High Performance: The Power of Relational Coordination*, Stanford, CA: Stanford University Press, 2016.

The author uses the social contract as a framework for looking at leveraging relationships in a business context.

J. Douglass, *The Conditions for Admission: Access, Equity, and the Social Contract of Public Universities*, Stanford, CA: Stanford University Press, 2007.

The author explores whether public universities are engaged in a social contract with the public and what obligations might be an artefact of that contract. It is a practical example of the social contract framework being used to analyse leadership in a contemporary context.

## NOTES

1. J.S. Mill, *On Liberty*, Mineola, NY: Dover, 1859/2002, p. 63.
2. T. Reiner, 'Social contract theory', in M. Bevir (ed.), *Encyclopedia of Political Theory*, Thousand Oaks, CA: Sage, 2010, pp. 1288–93.
3. G. Cronk et al. (eds), *Readings in Philosophy: Eastern & Western Sources*, 2nd edn, Plymouth, MI: Hayden-McNeil, 2004, p. 93.

4.   Cronk et al., *Readings in Philosophy*, p. 91.

5.   T. Hobbes, *Leviathan*, ed. C.B. MacPherson, New York: Penguin 1651/1985, p. 185. See also S.M. Cahn and P. Markie, *Ethics: History, Theory, and Contemporary Issues*, 5th edn, Oxford: Oxford University Press, 2012.

6.   Hobbes, *Leviathan*, p. 186.

7.   T. Hobbes, *Leviathan*, in R.M. Hutchins (ed.) *Great Books of the Western World*, vol. 23, Chicago, IL: Encyclopedia Britannica, 1952, p. 87.

8.   Hobbes, *Leviathan* in Hutchins, p. 47.

9.   J. Locke, *Two Treatises of Government and A Letter Concerning Toleration*, trans. G.D.H. Cole, Stilwell, KS: Digireads.com Publishing, 1689/2005, p. 29.

10.  Locke, *Two Treatises*.

11.  Locke, *Two Treatises*, p. 101.

12.  Locke, *Two Treatises*, p. 109.

13.  J. Rousseau, *The Social Contract*, New York: Penguin Group-Great Ideas, 1762/2006, p. 2.

14.  Rousseau, *The Social Contract*, p. 14.

15.  Rousseau, *The Social Contract*.

16   Rousseau, *The Social Contract*; and R.R. Palmer, J. Colton and L. Kramer, *A History of the Modern World*, 10th edn, Boston, MA: McGraw Hill, 2007.

17.  J. Rawls, *A Theory of Justice*, Cambridge, MA: Harvard University Press, 1971, p. 16.

18.  Rawls, *A Theory of Justice*, p. 4.

19.  Rawls, *A Theory of Justice*, p. 11.

20.  J.A. Simmons, 'Tacit consent and political obligation', *Philosophy and Public Affairs*, vol. 5 no. 3, 1976, 274-91, p. 279.

21.  D. Hume, 'Of the original contract', in *Essays: Moral, Political and Literary*, ed. E.F. Miller, Indianapolis, IN: Liberty Classics, 1777/1987.

22.  R. Dworkin, 'The original position', in N. Daniels (ed.), *Reading Rawls*, New York: Basic Books, 1975.

23.  S.M. Okin, *Women in Western Political Thought*, Princeton, NJ: Princeton University Press, 1979, p. 6.

24.  C. Pateman, *The Sexual Contract*, Stanford, CA: Stanford University Press, 1989.

25.  Pateman, *The Sexual Contract*.

26.  C.W. Mills, *The Racial Contract*, Ithaca, NY: Cornell University Press, 1997.

27.  W.R. Polk, *Neighbors and Strangers*, Chicago, IL: The University of Chicago Press, 1997.

28.  J.M. Burns, *Leadership*, New York: Harper & Row, 1978, p. 20.

29.  M.L. King, 'I Have a Dream', 28 August 1963. https://www.archives.gov/files/press/exhibits/dream-speech.pdf (accessed 10 March 2018).

30.  National Center for Education Statistics, 'Fast facts'. https://nces.ed.gov/fastfacts/display.asp?id=372 (accessed 1 November 2022).

31.  US Department of Defense, 'See 75 years of the GI Bill: how transformative it's been', 9 January 2019. https://www.defense.gov/News/Feature-Stories/story/Article/1727086/75-years-of-the-gi-bill-how-transformative-its-been/ (accessed 1 November 2022); and US Department of Veteran's Affairs, 'About GI Bill benefits'. https://www.va.gov/education/about-gi-bill-benefits/ (accessed 1 November 2022).

32.  National Student Clearing House Research Center, 'Some college, no credential student outcomes annual progress report – academic year 2020/2021', 10 May 2022. https://nscresearchcenter.org/some-college-no-credential/ (accessed 1 November 2022); and E. Nadworny, 'More than one million fewer students are in college: here's how that impacts the economy', NPR, 13 January 2022. https://www.npr.org/2022/

01/13/1072529477/more-than-1-million-fewer-students-are-in-college-the-lowest-enrollment-numbers- (accessed 1 November 2022).

33. Nadworny, 'More than one million'; and E. Nadworny, 'Fewer students are going to college: here's why that matters', 16 December 2019. https://www.npr.org/2019/12/16/787909495/fewer-students-are-going-to -college-heres-why-that-matters (accessed 1 November 2022).

34. National Student Clearing House Research Center, 'Some college'.

35. National Center for Education, 'Fast facts'.

36. National Center for Education Statistics, 'Loans for undergraduate students', *Conditions of Education*. U.S. Department of Education, Institute of Education Services, May 2022. https://nces.ed.gov/programs/coe/ indicator/cub (accessed 1 November 2022).

37. A.P. Carnevale, B. Cheoh and E. Wenzinger, Emma, 'The college payoff: more education doesn't always mean more earnings', Georgetown University McCourt School of Public Policy, Policy Center on Education and the Workforce, 2021. https://cew.georgetown.edu/cew-reports/collegepayoff2021/ (accessed 1 November 2022).

38. International Association of Universities (IAU), 'Academic freedom, university autonomy, and social responsibility', 1998, Paris: IAU.

39. L. Faulkner, 'The social compact of higher education and its public', Educause. https://www.educause .edu/research-and-publications/books/tower-and-cloud/social-compact-higher-education-and-its-public (accessed 1 November 2022).

40. D. Labaree, '2013 Dewey Lecture: college – what is it good for?' *Education and Culture*, vol. 30 no. 1, spring 2014, 3–15, p. 5.

41. R. Kelchen, 'Higher education's uncertain financial future: the overall outlook has improved, but there will be winners and losers', *Chronicle of Higher Education*, 8 February 2022. https://www.chronicle.com/article/ higher-eds-uncertain-financial-future (accessed 1 November 2022).

42. Faulkner, 'The social compact'.

43. UNESCO, International Commission on the Futures of Education, 'Reimagining our futures together: a new social contract for education', UNESCO, 2021. https://unesdoc.unesco.org/ark:/48223/pf0000379707.locale =en (accessed 1 November 2022).

44. F. Newman and L. Couturier, 'Training public good in the higher education market', The Observatory on Borderless Higher Education, January 2002, p. 6. https://eu.pravo.hr/_download/repository/Trading_Public _Good_in_the_Higher_Education_Market.pdf (accessed 1 November 2022).

# 11
## Justice as fairness

*Alexandra K. Perry and Emily Schuck*

### FRAMING QUESTION

How can leaders and followers work together to create principles that will guide a just society?

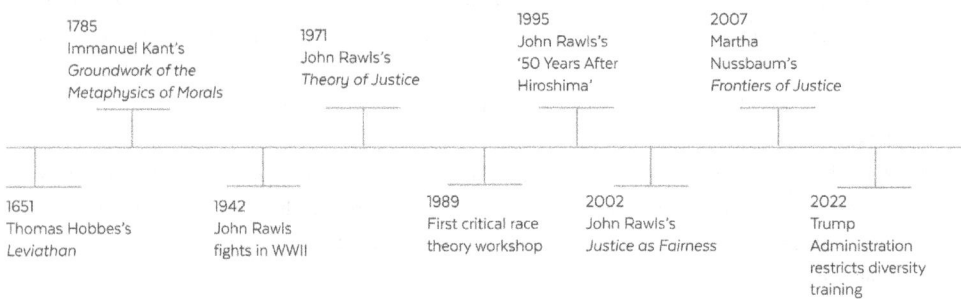

**Figure 11.1**   Timeline of major works on Rawlsian ethics in relation to the chapter case study

Imagine having to establish an entire set of principles and rules to govern a society or organization without any knowledge of its members. What are their strengths and weaknesses? Their habits? Their goals? The catch: you are also a member of this society, but not as you know yourself. All of the factors that you know about yourself might be different. Your race, sex, socio-economic status, age, even your history – there is no way to know what they will be. How would you begin to develop the moral framework for a functioning society without understanding your assigned role within it? You would likely hedge your bets and create a society where you are most likely to thrive no matter who you end up being. What moral principles would form the underpinning of such a society? This is precisely the question that John Rawls asks us to consider.

This thought experiment is titled The Original Position, and Rawls included it in his most notable work, *A Theory of Justice*, published in 1971.[1] In it, Rawls articulates his theory of distributive justice. Rawls roughly attempts to answer the question, 'What would make for a just distribution of the social goods within a society?' He answers this question in one of the longest books in moral philosophy to date, and his answer is – essentially – justice as fairness. For

Rawls, a just society is a fair society. In this chapter, we will explore Rawls' thinking specifically in relation to the Five Components of Leadership Model. We will end with a case analysis that examines the teaching of Critical Race Theory (CRT) in higher education in the United States in light of both of these theories of ethics and leadership. But first, a bit more about John Rawls and his ideas.

## HISTORY

Rawls was a twentieth-century moral and political philosopher who spent much of his career at Harvard. Rawls was a Second World War veteran, and it is often said that his disillusion with war after fighting in the Pacific and seeing the aftermath of Hiroshima strongly influenced his work in moral philosophy.[2] In 1995, Rawls published an article titled, '50 Years after Hiroshima', in which he lamented the nihilistic mindset that many had towards war. He wrote:

> Undoubtedly war is a kind of hell, but why should that mean that all moral distinctions cease to hold? Also, granted that sometimes all or nearly all may be to some degree guilty, that does not mean that all are equally so. There is never a time when we are free from all moral and political principles and restraints.[3]

This notion that there is always a moral framework and a set of logical, moral principles is a common theme in Rawls' work. It is worth noting, given that Rawls' career in philosophy began at the height of the Vietnam War, a time when cultural relativism (discussed in Chapter 8) and moral scepticism were viewed as the prevailing ethical theories. Rawls' work on justice ushered in a new era of moral philosophy that affirmed moral objectivity and focused on the structure of moral and political systems as a source of justice. While the moral relativists and sceptics focused on concepts like anarchy, Rawls and his predecessors concentrated on the role that these social systems and their leaders played in ensuring the health of a society.

Rawls' best-known work is his *A Theory of Justice*. In this book, he outlines his theory in the most detail while introducing what he defines as the two most important principles of justice: the liberty principle and the equality principle. He would expand on the concept of justice as fairness in two other publications. *Political Liberalism*, published in 1993, focused on the question of whether there could be political legitimacy in a society where there was fundamental and irreconcilable disagreement between citizens over matters of significance, such as morality, law, and religion.[4] *The Law of Peoples*, first published as an article in 1993 and later as a book in 1999, focuses on how people ought to live in a just society.[5] It fills in some of the details about life inside of Rawls' just society, for which *A Theory of Justice* built the framework. Rawls also published a final book posthumously in 2002, titled *Justice as Fairness: A Restatement*, which is a response to 30 years of criticism of *A Theory of Justice*.[6]

## The Social Contract

Though Rawls' theory of justice as fairness was a ground-breaking shift from the theories that preceded it, it takes its roots in traditional social contract theory, as well as political liberalism and traditional democratic theory. United States president Bill Clinton famously praised John Rawls for 'helping a whole generation of learned Americans revive their faith in democracy itself'.[7] Rawls certainly was influenced by the social contract theories of Hobbes, Locke, and Rousseau, who are each discussed in Chapter 10 of this book. Rawls' work is similar to the work of these contract theorists, but his goal is different. Rather than defend the social contract, Rawls presupposes its worth and sets out to outline the constraints that should be placed upon it. In other words, Rawls asks what limits there are to our ability to enter into a social contract and what it can morally require of us.

Rawls differs from the other social contract theorists in his view of the power of leaders. While the traditional contract theorists such as Thomas Hobbes and John Locke thought that the social contract primarily served as a mechanism for offering political legitimacy to leaders, Rawls believed that the chief purpose of the social contract was to develop the principles of justice as a group of equal citizens – potential leaders and followers. After these principles were determined, the leader would be obligated to protect them.[8]

Locke probably influenced Rawls' social contract the most because he believed that no leadership could be legitimate unless it originated from a state of equal rights, though his idea of equality was very different from Rawls'. In contrast, Hobbes believed that the most logical thing would be for a group to select one individual and offer them ultimate political authority, as long as that individual was selected under fair conditions.

Other social contract theorists, such as Jean-Jacques Rousseau, believed that the social contract was a way for leaders and followers to decide upon and implement new rules and policies.[9] This idea also influenced Rawls, though he believed that the power of the social contract was in the constraint rather than the negotiation of authority. It would be fair to say that while Rousseau thought of the social contract as a tool for development and construction, Rawls thought of it as a tool for evaluation and analysis.

Rawls' theory makes a very sharp implicit distinction between those goods and liberties that one innately has and those goods and liberties that one acquires through social experience and membership in the community that is being governed. His version of the social contract is designed to protect the innate goods while legitimizing the acquisition of those goods and liberties that are not innate to improve the democratic system as a whole. He uses the original position thought experiment to understand where precisely the distinction between innate and acquired liberties falls and also to determine when the acquisition of liberties and goods is morally permissible.

For leadership, this means that while the traditional social contract theorists outline the contract that the leader and followers might enter into in order to work toward a goal, Rawls' theory of justice tells the leader and followers what conditions can be included in that contract, and what limits there are to what can be considered requisite of that contract. For example, a social contract theorist might argue that the relationship between a consumer and a company is a contractual one. The company has an obligation to produce a quality product that is advertised accurately. The consumer must pay the agreed-upon price and review the product and company fairly. Rawls' theory of justice presupposes this contractual relationship and, instead, defines the moral limits of markets – what can be considered a good for sale? It is common for some goods to be restricted from the market, particularly when there is the potential that someone who is less privileged might be exploited by someone who has privilege. For example, organ donation, the adoption of babies, and military enlistment and conscription are all things that push the moral limits of the market and are therefore subject to immense regulation. Rawls relies on his principle of liberty and principle of equality to make these determinations. Those principles will be outlined later in this chapter.

## Rationality as the Foundation for Justice

Rawls' conception of political liberalism is influenced heavily by Immanuel Kant's work on the human good and rationalism.[10] Both Kant and Rawls define 'the good' as those things that any reasonable person would want, or the way that any reasonable person would act. Rawls defines primary goods as the 'things which a rational man wants, whatever else he wants'.[11] In other words, Rawls defines primary goods as those things that everyone wants, no matter what his or her interests, experience, and lifestyle might be, or those things that humans universally want. This is very similar to Kant's categorical imperative, as discussed in Chapter 2. Kant believed that what made humans unique was their capacity for reason, and therefore reason was the basis for his moral theory. The categorical imperative is the imperative that humans 'act only according to that maxim whereby you can, at the same time, will that it should become a universal law'.[12] This reliance on rationality to determine what is right or good is ultimately the foundation of justice for both Kant and Rawls.

Rawls also includes rationality in his definition of a citizen. In *Theory of Justice*, he defines citizens as those who are able to participate in a social contract developed in the original position as all humans who are capable of rationality and reasonableness. The original position thought experiment uses rationality as its mechanism for developing the principles of justice that Rawls believes are imperative. Essentially the question Rawls asks is, 'What principles of justice would any rational person develop?' If all rational persons would develop the same principles of justice, Rawls considers them to be moral.

## MAJOR CONCEPTS OF RAWLSIAN ETHICS

### The Original Position and the Veil of Ignorance

Rawls' theory has several foundational concepts, but perhaps the most vital aspects of his theory are his concepts of 'the Original Position' and his 'Veil of Ignorance'. Rawls used his original position thought experiment as an exercise in what he calls free choice. The thought experiment is purely hypothetical. Rawls is not arguing that this is how leaders and followers ought to design a society or organization, or even that it might be possible to do so. Instead, Rawls is tasking the thought experiment to support his thesis.

This is what Rawls asks of the reader engaged in his thought experiment: imagine that you are among a group of persons who are entering into a social contract and outlining its terms to provide a moral and political framework to your society or organization. Now, imagine that there is a veil of ignorance in place that makes it impossible for each person to know their own position within the society. Each person enters the original position totally blind to his or her own history, personality, characteristics, strengths, or weaknesses.

The veil of ignorance is an essential feature of Rawls' theory because it sets it apart from other social contract theories. To John Locke, for example, the state of nature in which people enter into the social contract is a state in which all persons are 'free and equal', and a factor of this freedom is complete knowledge of all the facts about themselves. This is central to Locke's theory because he argues that this knowledge will impact the structure of the social contract. In particular, Locke believes that those with power would willingly distribute social and political goods to maintain that power, and that those who do not have power would limit their ability to gain the power to ensure the continued availability of social and political goods.

In contrast, Rawls thought that the veil of ignorance was critical to the development of fair and just principles. This veil ensures that the contract will not be biased in any way, and that the principles of justice that are developed in the original position will be fair and just. Rawls wrote this mandate in his thought experiment assured 'pure procedural justice at the highest level'.[13] Again, this view sets Rawls' social contract theory apart from others. The common understanding of a contract is that it is fair if and only if all parties have access to all pertinent information. To Rawls, a fair agreement can only be entered into if all parties are restricted access to information, thereby making it equal.

The question Rawls asks after setting up the original position and the veil of ignorance is: 'How would any rational person address matters of justice in a society if they did not know their place within it?' The emphasis that Rawls places on rationality in his theory is a nod to the influence of Kant on his thinking. Both Kant and Rawls believe that there is much to be learned by understanding the collective thoughts of rational people. If all rational people value X, then X must be valuable. For Kant, this exercise was used to determine the right thing to do, whereas, for Rawls, the exercise is to determine which principles of justice are ultimately valued by all and to make sure they are not biased by self-interest.[14]

Ultimately Rawls believes that there are two primary principles of justice that all rational persons would agree to in the original position. The first principle, often called the greatest equal liberty principle, states, 'First, each person is to have an equal right to the most extensive basic liberty compatible with a similar liberty for others.'[15] This is similar to the test that Robert Greenleaf requires of servant leadership, as discussed in Chapter 14. Leadership must have a positive impact on the least privileged members of society.[16] The second principle, often called the 'difference principle', states:

> Social and economic inequalities are to be arranged so that they are both: (a) to the greatest benefit of the least advantaged, consistent with the just savings principle, and (b) attached to offices and positions open to all under conditions of fair equality of opportunity.[17]

The second part of the difference principle is sometimes called the 'equal opportunity principle'. In the following sections, I will outline these principles in greater detail and discuss their relevance to leadership.

## The Greatest Equal Liberty Principle

Rawls believes that any rational person in the original position would insist upon what he calls the 'greatest equal liberty' principle. This principle would assure that every citizen is, at the very minimum, afforded all basic liberties in a way that does not infringe upon the basic liberties of others. These liberties include freedom of conscience, freedom of expression, and due process under the law. This principle, Rawls argues, is rational not only because it provides a safeguard for citizens, but also because of the freedom it allows for a democratic government or organization. If all citizens have access to a fully adequate basic scheme of rights, then democracy can remain neutral to competing moral codes. This means that the leader can allow for productive democratic debate and rational disagreement over morality rather than make judgments about goods and values because all citizens will already have access to a set of liberties that is wholly adequate. This principle also allows citizens the freedom to pursue a life that they define as good, as long as it does not restrict another citizen's ability to do so.

In practical terms, this means that all members of a group, according to Rawls' theory, should be afforded all basic liberties in order to then be self-determining. Factors such as race, sex, and socio-economic status should not determine whether a person gets to vote, marry the person they love, hold office, be promoted, or advocate for the causes they care most about. Because these are assured, followers can then focus on pursuing their own conception of the good. Additionally, because the leader does not have to make determinations about such things as who can vote, who can marry, whether women receive equal pay, or what values are acceptable, he or she can then focus on doing what they are obligated to do in the social contract.

The leader's role in Rawls' theory of justice as fairness is described in a section of *Theory of Justice* where he describes the non-ideal theory or the problem of states that are noncompliant or only partially compliant with the theory of justice. To Rawls, a leader's role is mostly political and not moral. The leader should protect democracy, promote the stability of government, work towards international harmony to prevent conflict, preserve and improve society for future generations, and ensure that all citizens have access to their adequate set of liberties. Any leader who ignores the citizens' rights to this set of liberties would be leading a failed state. Followers can also cause a failed state by failing to maintain their end of the social contract.[18]

Rawls argued that the greatest equal liberty principle is the most essential principle, and that it should always take precedence if there is a conflict between principles. However, there is a second principle he believed would also be a rational outcome of the original position: the difference principle.

## The Difference and Equal Opportunity Principles

Rawls' difference principle allows for social and economic inequality as long as all citizens already have access to all basic liberties. Rawls argues that rational persons in the original position would allow for such inequality if the inequality is to 'the greatest benefit of the least-advantaged members of society'.[19] This is because the factors that lead to the benefit of those who are better off are usually not earned, but rather innate. Straight, white, middle-class males might see an advantage that LGBTQ+, minority, lower-class women do not. This advantage is not because they worked to make themselves straight, white, or male, but rather because they were born into this situation. Rawls argues that social stability requires us to benefit those who do not have the same advantage so that they are regarded as equally worthy members of the same society. Removing the veil of ignorance means that the previous state in which all members were equal is now in the past. Allowing for those in privileged positions to, for example, make more money, is fair if it means that those who do not experience the same privilege have more options for employment or a better world in which to live.

The second clause of Rawls' second principle is the principle of equal opportunity. Though this clause comes second in *Theory of Justice*, it is actually conceptually prioritized above the first clause. The equal opportunity principle stipulates that all offices and positions must be open to all citizens through the power of fair equality of opportunity. If there is truly equal opportunity, then and only then are inequalities just.

## CRITIQUES OF THE RAWLSIAN MODEL

Rawls was praised for his restoration of democratic thought in the realm of political theory at a time when the United States faced a great deal of political upheaval. His theory of justice as fairness provides arguably the most important contribution to political philosophy in the twentieth century. However, his theory has unquestionably been subject to critique, as all theories are. Many unsophisticated criticisms of *Theory of Justice* focus on the hypothetical nature of Rawls' original position. There is concern among some scholars that because the original position is impossible to realize, the principles Rawls claims would naturally be developed by all rational citizens are unverifiable. Critiques of this nature are largely not a concern for Rawls because he acknowledges that the original position is intended as a thought experiment or an exercise in freedom of choice.

Nevertheless, there are some critiques of Rawls' theory that are worthy of consideration. In this section, I will discuss the criticism that Rawls relies too heavily on the notion of rationality, and also the critique that capability, rather than equality, needs to be the focus of theories of justice. The latter critique is common in the growing area of care ethics, which has extensively adapted Rawls' theory to respond to the former criticism that his theory is overly reliant on rationality (see Chapter 6).

### Reliance on Rationality

There are two ways in which Rawls has been criticized for his theory's reliance on rationality. The first critique focuses on the validity of his thought experiment when its inclusion in the experiment is so restrictive. Rawls sets out to understand the principles of justice that form the foundation of the social contract, 'between citizens regarded as free and equal, and as normal and fully cooperating members of society over a complete life'.[20] Rawls' language here has been criticized for being both ambiguous and exclusionary. What exactly would it mean for a citizen to be a 'normal and fully cooperating member of society', and why would this have to occur over a whole life for their citizenship to be legitimate? Would this clause exclude those who have spent any time at all in prison (and therefore not been fully cooperative)? Would it exclude those who at some time had been irrational, such as elderly persons with Alzheimer's? And how, when Rawls makes it a goal to allow for wide variations in human flourishing, would one define 'normal'?

The second and more significant criticism about Rawls' reliance on rationality is over the implications that this reliance has for the consideration of citizenship. This understanding of the point and currency of equality has implications for who should count as a citizen. Rawls is explicit: all persons in the social contract must have two qualities to be considered citizens, rationality and reasonableness.[21] A reasonable person will recognize their existence in a social sphere and engage in cooperation in order to improve that sphere for both themselves and the others within it. For example, a reasonable person might want a new car, but they will refrain from stealing someone else's car because they would recognize that the car's owner was also a member of the same society and possessed the same rights. In other words, the reasonable person would limit their own pursuit of the good in order to make sure that their pursuit didn't disregard the fact that all other citizens also have the right to pursue the good.

Rationality is the person's ability simply to pursue the good for himself or herself. A rational person can set proper goals and understand how to work toward those goals appropriately. The rational person will have analytic abilities and the desire and capability to utilize the resources available to them in pursuit of the good.

The assertion that rationality is a necessary condition for citizenship in Rawls' social contract is troublesome given the range of human diversity that the principles developed under the social contract would apply. Who would have the authority to determine which goals were proper, how those goals should be sought after, and whether it is necessary for citizens to have a desire to utilize resources? Further, is restricting the voices that contribute to the development of a theory of justice fair when it will apply to those who have been excluded? As Sophia Wong observed:

> We see that the idea of the person is idealized and simplified, and makes no attempt to capture the full scope of human diversity in the population to which the theory of justice will actually apply.[22]

## Care Ethics: Capability and Human Dignity

Recently, the field of care ethics has started to focus on this challenge to Rawls' theory of justice by adapting it to be more inclusionary. Theorists like Martha Nussbaum and Eva Feder Kittay modify the question that Rawls asks in his inquiry. Rather than ask what is the most equitable way to distribute social goods, care ethicists ask how the social goods that are distributed can be accessed and utilized by the individuals to whom they are distributed. While Rawls uses rationality as a mechanism for ensuring a fair and equal distribution of social goods, Nussbaum and her colleagues focus on the capability that the recipients have to utilize those goods and the function that each good serves.

Nussbaum uses the concept of human dignity as the milepost by which she measures progress in distributive justice.[23] Are resources being allocated in such a way that all persons are able to live a dignified life? This approach de-emphasizes the role of rationality because it allows for a broader acceptance of human diversity. The idea of 'rational goals', which is ambiguous in Rawls' theory, can be replaced with a goal that is set based on the particular individual's capabilities. In essence, the outcomes of this model will be assessed on a scale that can be adapted to suit the capabilities and notion of the good possessed by each citizen, as long as dignity is the ultimate benchmark for each person's flourishing.

The goal of the care ethics adaptation of justice as fairness is not to change Rawls' thesis, but rather to provide more definition to it in order to better employ it and assess it. Rawls didn't intend for his theory to be exclusionary; rationality was simply intended as a mechanism for determining what is just. The care ethicists adapt Rawls' theory so that it focuses on distribution based on capability rather than an equal starting point. In doing so, the theory increases the number of people who can benefit from the distribution of social goods but also brings into focus the necessary societal adaptions that need to be made to best allow individuals to flourish and live a dignified life. Providing equal access to voting does not benefit those who cannot transport themselves to the polling places or navigate their wheelchair through the door. The care ethics approach calls for a consideration of how society might adapt to the range of capabilities in working toward a goal of promoting human dignity. Maybe polling places are open in a wider range of neighbourhoods, and maybe these new polling places include wheelchair ramps. At the very least, it would not just be the individuals' utilization of resources that are examined, but the availability of the resources themselves.

## FIVE COMPONENT ANALYSIS

Rawls' theory of justice as fairness results in a very particular approach to leadership, which we will outline here using the Five Components of Leadership Model. The approach draws influence from the traditional social contract theories, limits the role of leadership in a way that is similar to the laissez-faire approach of Ayn Rand, and relies on rationality to construct moral principles in the way that Kant does, yet it is altogether distinct from these theories.

Rawls' theory of justice as fairness results in two moral principles he claims are universally desirable to all rational individuals. The first principle, the principle of greatest equal liberty, asserts that all citizens should be afforded an adequate scheme of basic liberties such as the right to engage politically, be free from unlawful arrest, and pursue the good however they define it. The second principle emphasizes that the only just unequal distribution of social goods is an inequality that benefits those who do not receive them. For example, a doctor can justly receive more education than those who are not doctors, because, ultimately, having doctors in a society will benefit those who do not receive this level of education.

Rawls claims that all citizens who are rational will agree to a social contract based on these principles. However, in contrast to earlier social contract theorists, Rawls does not believe that the social contract affords a leader full and indiscriminate political legitimacy. Instead, to Rawls, the role of the leader is to safeguard the basic liberties for all citizens, but also to afford them the freedom to pursue the good by protecting them from outside risks and ensuring the continued stability of the organization or society. In a way, the outcome looks roughly like a laissez-faire style of leadership similar to that proposed by Ayn Rand; however, Rawls' leader is much more engaged as a citizen than Rand's leader would be.[24]

The leader (or statesman in Rawls' theory) is supposed to promote peace within the society, ensure that the society is ready to protect itself from outside threats or sources, and work to make the society sustainable for future generations. For the leader of an organization, this translates roughly to providing good stewardship for the organization by promoting peace and democratic discussion among followers; insulating the organization from outside challenges such as the economy, competitors, or legislation that may pose a threat to the success of the organization; and aiming for sustainability both for the ongoing achievements of the organization and also for the community that nurtures it.

The goal of leadership under Rawls' theory is to be developed collaboratively by leaders and followers as an artefact of the social contract. Whatever the goal might be, it needs to respect the two principles of justice developed under the original position and must be rationally deliberated. The addendum to this theory provided by care ethicists such as Martha Nussbaum also necessitates that any goal be considerate of the capability of all citizens to utilize the social goods that are distributed.

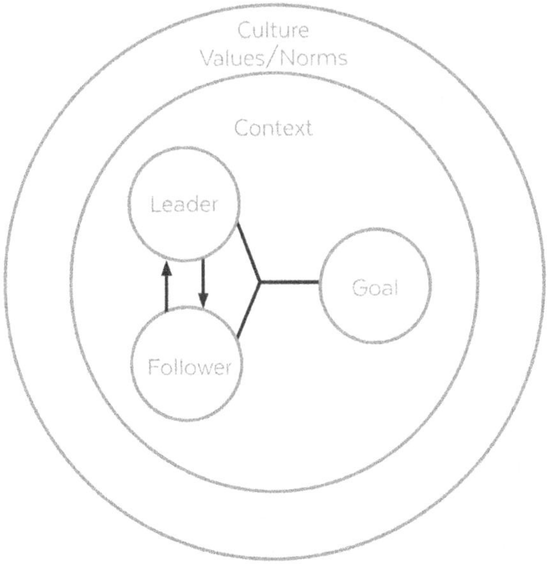

Rawls' theory of justice as fairness focuses on the two-way arrows that go between the leader and followers and the process the leader and followers use to determine and reach the common goal (Figure 11.2). In practical terms, this means that leaders and followers have to engage with one another not only in pursuit of the goal, but also in order to define the goal. Since no leader is afforded absolute political legitimacy, democratic debate must consistently take place in order to set, evaluate, and re-set goals, and also to evaluate whether the leadership is effective in representing all citizens. Justice as fairness requires a collaborative approach to leadership rather than a hierarchical authority-based model. The board of a non-profit is a good example to illustrate the role of the goal in a Rawlsian approach to leadership. The goals of non-profits are typically set through careful deliberation by a board. The president or executive director of a non-profit is often included on the board but does not have the authority to set goals without the input of the board. Once goals have been set, the leader

**Figure 11.2** The Five Components of Leadership Model applied to Rawlsian ethics

and follower's efforts at working toward that goal are consistently evaluated, and there is the option for leadership to change if the current leadership is not effective at meeting the goals.

Non-profit leadership also tends to be distributed, which is very consistent with the way that a Rawlsian would approach working toward goals. There may be a president of the entire non-profit board, but typically there are a number of subcommittees with their own leadership that is formed to focus on specific goals or specific components of an overall goal. This is consistent with Rawlsian leadership because it allows for the goals to be tailored more individually.

The context and culture of the organization or society are also going to be considerations in a Rawlsian approach to ethical leadership. The context or immediate environment will determine the resources available to the group, which will factor into the determination of goals, and the distribution of resources within the environment. For example, one of the most common challenges facing healthcare organizations today is the opioid crisis, among other drug-related challenges. However, the context that the healthcare organization is in is going to determine which goals are set, and how leaders and followers work towards those goals. For example, a healthcare organization in a metropolitan area might have more local resources to help mitigate the effects of the opioid crisis. Maybe they have access to better drug treatment options for discharging patients who have overdosed, or more social workers within their system. However, one of the challenges in a metropolitan area is that many different versions of particular drugs are often much more accessible. Therefore, treatment options and approaches have to be constantly re-evaluated.

In a more rural area, far fewer resources are likely available for the healthcare system to utilize. However, there will be far fewer outlets for drugs to be trafficked into an area, so the patients that the healthcare system sees are likely to respond to treatment similarly. The community is also likely to be culturally more open-minded to grassroots approaches to dealing with the crisis. For example, in rural West Virginia, a group of nurses working in a neonatal intensive care noticed a large number of infants being admitted after being born with drugs in their system. Because the increased number of admissions was causing overcrowding in the NICU, the nurses decided to found a centre in a home-like environment where infants could go through the symptoms of withdrawal while receiving round-the-clock care. This unique fix allowed the NICU nurses and physicians to focus on higher-risk infants, such as those born prematurely or with congenital disabilities.[25] This sort of approach was highly context- and culture-dependent. While a rural area might respond well to this newly developed resource, a more metropolitan area might make this impossible both because of the high costs associated with beginning such a programme and because of the tendency for such areas to be very risk-averse and regulation-driven.

In the next section, the case study outlines a Rawlsian approach to leadership by highlighting the teaching of Critical Race Theory (CRT) in institutions of higher learning in the United States. After presenting the historical background to the case, we will discuss the challenges of policymakers and educators addressing CRT and look at how a Rawlsian might approach this issue using the Five Components of Leadership Model to work towards an ethical outcome.

## CASE STUDY: RAWLSIAN ETHICS APPLIED TO TEACHING CRITICAL RACE THEORY

Education is a hallmark of American democracy and is deemed a basic human right by citizens worldwide.[26] America's public education system makes schooling available to everyone regardless of racial, ethnic, or socio-economic status. Horace Mann even described education as 'the great equalizer', the vehicle to move social class and pay grades based on individual effort and determination.[27] Framed as the remedy for inequality, individuals born with fewer means and opportunities can 'catch up' by accessing and engaging in the educational system that is publicly funded and supported. The principle of education as a common good of society crosses economic, social, and political lines. It is something that, until recently, most people in the United States have been able to agree upon and support.

Historically the noble purpose of education has been viewed as ethically sound; however, today's political climate has put educators on the defensive. The pursuit of truth and knowledge has shifted from a common good for all to experience to a common danger that those in political power must regulate. This is the position educators find themselves in today with the emergence of Critical Race Theory (CRT) as an academic subject that has divided the United States across political lines. In response, individual states have introduced and sometimes passed a spate of laws prohibiting the teaching of CRT.

To fully understand the issue and impacts of this ethical dilemma requires a basic grasp of three key concepts: what CRT is, the role of faculty in determining what students learn, and the external factors that can shape the decision-making process of institutions of higher education.

To understand why CRT has become an ethical challenge in America, it is crucial to understand a little bit more about it. CRT is an intellectual and social framework to identify and critique the causes of social inequality within the structure of American institutions. These institutions include the criminal justice system, the healthcare system, and the education system. CRT was developed in the early 1980s within legal studies as an academic framework to examine social institutions and systems that embed rules and regulations that lead to differential outcomes based on a person's race or gender. The legal scholars who developed CRT identified four primary tenets underpinning the frame.[28] First, the concept of race is a socially constructed idea, not a biological one. The theory views separating people into groups based on physical traits and then attributing specific positive or negative behaviours to a group as an act of social engineering by the majority group. Second, CRT views racism and sexism as the typical experience of people of colour and non-dominant genders. Racism is not the exception but the rule for minority groups in American society. Third, any legal advancements made by minority groups are determined at the will of the dominant group to serve their needs. Fourth, the lived experiences of minority groups are best researched through the qualitative storytelling of its members. The idea is that the voice of the minority must be heard to understand racism and its impact on the disparities created by the inequity of systems. CRT supporters claim that silencing these voices out of fear and what-ifs limits the advancement of knowledge and perpetuates oppression, unconscious bias, and the dominant group mentality, which historically has been white, male, and heteronormative.[29]

Historically, control of the college curriculum has been seated solely with the faculty. The faculty are subject area experts who engage in research and scholarship to stay current on emerging trends and development in the academe. As a result, the curriculum is viewed as fluid and changes as new knowledge is discovered.

A variety of professional organizations and legal precedents support the faculty's role as curators of the curriculum under the auspices of academic freedom. For example, the American Association of University Professors (AAUP) 1940 Statement of Principles on Academic Freedom and Tenure supports the freedom of faculty to conduct research and publish results on their subject areas without fear of retribution or punishment.[30] It is noteworthy that the AAUP drafted the 1940 statement in response to professors at universities in Nazi Germany being persecuted for teaching material that the government deemed unsuitable. The AAUP statement says that faculty have the freedom to teach what they want and how they want in the classroom as long as it relates to their subject area. They are classified as learning professionals who have the right to teach without the fear of censorship or discipline from the institution if it is done within the moral frame of educational purpose.[31]

Likewise, the US Supreme Court has historically supported the right of the institution of higher learning, of which faculty are the central figures, to determine the curricular content it offers. Under the First Amendment Right to Academic Freedom, the US Supreme Court recognized that:

> It is the business of a university to provide that atmosphere which is most conducive to speculation, experiment, and creation. It is an atmosphere in which there prevail 'the four essential freedoms' of a university – to determine for itself on academic grounds who may teach, what may be taught, how it shall be taught, and who may be admitted to study.[32]

Note that the Supreme Court recognizes explicitly that the university can control the curriculum, which appears at first glance to be in direct conflict with the ability of the state to pass legislation to prohibit the teaching of CRT in the classroom.

Nevertheless, there are external factors that also have an impact on the curriculum colleges and universities may offer. Although the faculty own the curriculum, the higher education system functions under shared governance in which faculty, administration, and governing boards collaborate to identify institutional values, priorities, and strategic plans to serve their students. Decisions are to be made collaboratively and with input from all three parties carrying weight and respect. Recognizing that higher education enterprises operate under a broad level of autonomy, the impact of social and economic influences cannot be overlooked.

Public institutions of higher education rely heavily on state government subsidies to fund their operations. Each student they enrol and educate equates to a per diem of the state's share of instructional costs that flow into the institution's operating budget. The amount and frequency of these shares are controlled by elected officials whose agendas can shift based on the politics of the annual budget process. Most private institutions are tuition-dependent, meaning that they rely on the wants and needs of their students to fund their operating budgets through tuition dollars. While donations from alumni and corporate sponsors are helpful, the institution must attract, retain, graduate, and advance its students over their lifetime to remain solvent. Institutions are forced to offer the academic programmes students want and the job market demands to stay competitive in the enrolment management of a sustainable student body.

Now that we have a fundamental understanding of CRT and the system in which it operates, we can better explore the controversy surrounding CRT and its implications.

Opponents of CRT have issues with the concept's basic tenets and view them as potentially harmful. They interpret CRT as an attack on American nationalism and a lens that weakens the public trust needed for civil and civic engagement.[33] They cite the theory's academic foundations in Marxism and assume that CRT, by association, believes the ideals that the USA was founded on are evil and that white people should feel guilt for the actions of their forebears. Further, they describe CRT as the vehicle from which supporters have been given the creative licence to reimagine the history of the USA, giving more credence to the lived stories of marginalized people than documented truths provided by scholars of history.[34] The establishment of groups and applicable labels of 'victims and oppressors' is viewed as a hostile act that creates shame, guilt, and distress for those learning about these concepts.[35] Legislators have taken swift action to describe and limit access to a theory that, in their opinion, perpetuates racism and unrest. For example, Republican Senator Byron Donalds of Florida stated,

> Critical Race Theory is a warped ideology that seeks to divide Americans and relitigate the sins of the past by pinning White Americans against Black Americans, which is counterproductive and doesn't belong anywhere near our children. America's history regarding race is troublesome and deserves the proper attention, but we cannot allow for the degradation of American values and culture through so-called equity training. In the 21st century, we must teach and learn from our history and swear never to repeat it, but we cannot use our past to divide us, which Critical Race Theory will undoubtedly do.[36]

Those responding to Senator Donalds' statement may note that although his opinion is protected by freedom of speech, it does not mention the academic quality of CRT based on scholarly research, accountable inquiry, or healthy debate. Advocates of teaching CRT may suggest that the statement seeks to silence the process of academic freedom and further the anti-intellectual agenda of a group that is uncomfortable and potentially seeking simply to retain power.

CRT's detractors cite the recent racial incidents of violence that the United States has recently witnessed as correlated to the storytelling narratives of minority groups, which ignite outrage and actions that would have historically been labelled un-American. For example, the summer of 2020 was characterized by racial unrest in cities and on campuses in response to racially charged events such as the murder of George Floyd. Mr Floyd, a 46-year-old black man, was murdered while in police custody when a police officer kneeled on his neck, and he was observed by bystanders gasping for air. The events were caught on camera, and three officers were eventually charged with his killing. These events sparked riots across the country, which led to a violent confrontation with police, mass looting, and removal of national monuments that were viewed as symbols of the systematic racism present within the culture of the United States. Opponents of CRT see acting now to legally limit the theory's ability to be taught in schools as a means to create stability, restore order, and limit the voices that may continue or escalate these events. Of course, the challenge lies in identifying a causational relationship between CRT and these events.

The issue of the teaching and learning of CRT in the K-12 system, and more recently at the university level, has become a social and political hot button and an ethical dilemma for educators and administrators. As of July 2022, 42 states have introduced legislation prohibiting the teaching of CRT in K-12 classrooms, and 17 states have passed such legislation or imposed other measures to prevent schools from teaching CRT or related concepts.[37] Furthermore, 12 states now have laws on the books regulating how university professors can teach the concept of racism and sexism in their classrooms.[38]

For example, Iowa law currently prohibits public schools and universities from requiring coursework or training that suggests that the United States or the state of Iowa have been or are currently 'fundamentally or systematically racist or sexist'.[39] The broad and ambiguous laws prohibited instructors from establishing learning outcomes related to these concepts to determine students' grades. Moreover, the Socratic learning method is now at risk as it could lead to criminal behaviour if it were to cause students to feel discomfort or shame about studying these topics. As a result, faculty are now facing unprecedented pressure to limit their discussions on race and gender to keep their jobs and avoid breaking the law. CRT may seem overly esoteric, but these laws have implications for teaching significant events in US history. For example, students studying Jim Crowe laws, the Trail of Tears, and even diversity training could now be seen as a violation of some of these laws. What students have access to learn is now being determined by policymakers rather than educators.

The threat of the financial penalty schools may face for teaching CRT is happening at a time when higher education is facing historic enrolment and retention issues that have led to a decrease in revenue. Top-tier research institutions and Ivy League schools have large endowments to draw from and waitlists of prospective students to admit bridging the gap caused by declines in applicant numbers and cash flow. However, most tuition-dependent institutions in the USA are at the mercy of their prior years' budget strategies to weather this storm. Administrators and faculty are worried about the legal and economic impact of breaking these laws in the name of academic freedom. This could lead to additional financial stress organizationally and personally. Taking on expensive legal defences and lawsuits is considered high-risk activity and could be career-ending even for tenured faculty. Pursuing truth and justice within higher education has become less of an ethical issue and more of an issue of monetary expediency as institutions struggle to balance budgets.

The culture war described here has practical and ethical implications. The education of today's students has become limited based on the political and social agendas of political leaders and their constituents. How and what students learn about the history and the current ethos of diversity, racism, and social reform is now up for debate. Politicians now have a say in what students learn about their shared history through a prescriptive attempt to limit knowledge and a particular group's discomfort.

Now that we have a better understanding of CRT and the context in which it is applied, we can examine the ethics of teaching CRT through the lens of Rawls' concept of justice as fairness.

Let's begin by considering Rawls' central question: 'What would make for a just distribution of the social goods within a society?' To answer this question, let's consider Rawls' concepts of the original position and veil of ignorance. If we were to imagine ourselves designing an education system and did not know our place in the system, a rational person would most likely opt for a system that allowed *all* experiences to be heard. Wouldn't any rational person want to be represented and their experiences acknowledged by others? Now let's consider two primary principles of justice that all rational persons would agree to in the original position: the greatest equal liberty principle and the equal opportunity principle. Recall that the greatest equal liberty principle states that each person is to have an equal right to the most extensive basic liberty compatible with a similar liberty for others.[40] It would stand to reason that if the experiences of one group of Americans were acknowledged in the classroom, then the experiences of other groups should have the opportunity to express their experiences. CRT allows for the many stories and experiences of non-dominant groups to be heard.

Likewise, recall that the difference principle states that social and economic inequalities are to be arranged so that they are both: (a) to the greatest benefit of the *least* advantaged in a society, and (b) attached to offices and positions open to all under conditions of fair equality of opportunity.[41] The difference principle directly speaks to our case study in that the whole point of CRT is to give space for the stories and experiences of the least advantaged in society. In addition, in teaching CRT, educators can provide a fair and equal discussion of different perspectives in their classrooms.

Now let's consider Rawls' approach to ethics implications for policymakers. Rawls believes lawmakers should be constrained. Their chief purpose is to guarantee the rights of citizens. Rawls believed that the chief purpose of the social contract is to develop the principles of justice as a group of equal citizens – potential leaders and followers. After these principles are determined, the leader is obligated to protect them. This means that the leader's job is to allow for productive democratic debate and rational disagreement over morality rather than make judgments about goods and values because all citizens will already have access to a set of liberties that is wholly adequate. As applied to our case study, Rawls may argue that the United States already has agreed upon rights such as freedom of expression and academic freedom. Remember, to Rawls, a leader's role is primarily political and not moral. The leader is to ensure that all citizens continue to have access to their adequate set of liberties. Rather than prohibiting educators from discussing CRT in their classrooms, Rawls may argue that policymakers should be *safeguarding* their right to do so.

## FIVE COMPONENT ANALYSIS

Now, let's return to the Five Component Model of analysis to evaluate this situation (Figure 11.3). How would a leader apply Rawls' theory of justice as fairness to work towards CRT education policy?

The leaders in our case study are the US policymakers who are determining whether or not CRT can be taught in classrooms. As we noted above, Rawls' principle of equal liberties

outlines the leader's role: guarantee-
ing all citizens a wholly adequate set
of basic liberties. Moreover, Rawls
asserts that it is not the role of leaders
of democratic institutions to make
value judgments about these conceptions of the good, only to *protect*
basic liberties so that citizens have
the *freedom* to pursue the good. This
defines the leader's responsibility as
two-fold: distributing the material
and social goods the community
needs and providing the social and
political protections necessary for the
followers to flourish.

The followers in this case are the
faculty in schools throughout the
United States. Their role is to hold
the same space for the inquiry and
examination of ideas, allowing both
sides to be heard, accountable, and

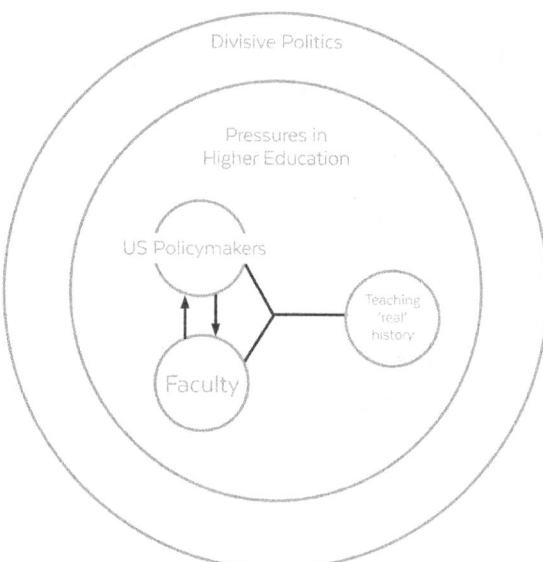

**Figure 11.3**    The Five Components of
Leadership Model applied to the
teaching of Critical Race Theory

respected in the process. Avoidance and suppression of knowledge fuel the fire of conflict as
people demand to speak and be heard. If these conversations and inquiries cannot happen
within the classroom, they will spill over into the media, where freedom of speech trumps academic quality in the headlines. Simply, if the types of conversations surrounding CRT cannot
occur in the college classroom, where can they occur?

In addition, educator followers may view CRT as a crisis within the normal cycle of the
social sciences where the previous theories on racism no longer apply and warrant further
examination to determine if a paradigm shift is warranted. The purpose of education is not
merely the accumulation of knowledge but also building the student's skill to think critically.
Likewise, developing new knowledge is a natural part of social theory development. Educators
opening up CRT to discussion is one way to resolve the tension and conclude its validity as an
academic theory.

Finally, educators may argue that looking at all sides of an issue is essential in the educational process of knowledge building. Students are free to accept or reject a theory based on
the evidence presented through the inquiry process. The educational process is inherently
uncomfortable as students are challenged to think about things they had not known or considered. All concepts are foreign at one point in a student's development, and each person
has the free will to assimilate new knowledge into their belief system or discard it. Seeking to
understand a point of view that is new or different is not the same as being forced to follow
it or discard it. Indeed, education at its best creates the space for that rigorous inquiry that
looks at the issues like CRT from multiple points of view in a professional venue that operates
with respect, accountability, and discernment. Educators examining the issues of gender and

racial inequality through the lens of CRT may lead to a more complete understanding of how the world functions and a means to create a more just and fair society. This is in keeping with Rawls' idea of setting up systems where the least advantaged in a society still have an opportunity to flourish.

The overarching goal shared by both the leader and the followers is to teach students 'real' history. At this point, a philosophical question also enters the discussion. If the person's world view aligns with objectivism – that is, the believe that there is only one true reality that is observable, stable, and measurable over time – then the studying CRT would hold no value as they do not accept the idea of multiple experiences and realities. Supporters of studying CRT in the classroom are more in line with the constructionist frame where reality is viewed as interpretative, and truth lies in the lived experience described by those who lived it. Regardless, Rawls' approach would allow CRT to be taught to both groups and embraced or disregarded by either. This is the main contention. Is history 'objective' or is it the experience of many people?

Rawls would have us ensure that all citizens are free to understand and make meaning of history and racial difference. To do so, the leaders and followers have to work together to both distribute social goods (in this case information) and safeguard citizens' ability to make meaning for themselves based on a fully informed understanding of historical justice and injustice. The challenge here is that leaders and followers often disagree upon the bounds of academic freedom as it pertains to diversity and racism as a part of American history. Creating space for truth and leaving room for discovering new knowledge may disrupt traditional views and perceptions about historical events.

The context for this leadership situation is the increasingly pressurized environment of higher education. Many are questioning the value of a college degree given the high cost of tuition. Likewise, many universities are at the mercy of state funding. This comes at a time in which higher education is employing far fewer tenured professors in exchange for part-time instructors. This deterioration of the tenure system diminishes academic freedom. Finally, more minority students are now perusing their college degree and demand that their voices be represented.

A final factor is the culture of divisive politics that is currently at the forefront of American culture. Nationalism saw a dramatic increase during the Trump presidency. The resurgence of the view that Americans must be loyal to 'America first' was solidified by President Trump when he issued an executive order on 22 September 2020 limiting diversity and inclusion training in the federal workplace, labelling such training as anti-American and stereotypical of race and gender.[42] This was set against a backdrop of protest of racial injustice, such as the murder of George Floyd and Breonna Taylor and the Black Lives Matter protests. However, the core values of democracy, diversity, freedom of expression, and pluralism still serve as the bedrock of American cultural values and norms and are central to Rawls' theory. Thus, Rawls' theory would view the limits placed on education, opinion, and speech as unethical and should be challenged for the benefit of justice as fairness appealing to the foundation of American cultural values and norms.

As we review each of the five components individually and as a system, we can see that the issues surrounding the teaching of CRT in higher education are deep and wide. While the philosophical and scientific merit of the theory can be argued, Rawls' theory would support the principles of academic freedom, freedom of speech, and freedom of opinion and, therefore, presentation and critical analysis of the CRT to today's students.

## SUMMARY AND CONCLUDING REMARKS

Initially, this chapter set out to explore the question, 'How can leaders and followers work together to create a just society?' Rawls offers the leaders some guidance in addressing this question. First, in understanding justice as fairness, Rawls makes the goal of leadership follower-centric. Using the theory of justice outlined by Rawls as an approach to ethical leadership compels leaders to work collaboratively with followers to ensure that the principles of justice that are developed provide the most comprehensive set of basic liberties to all citizens. Further, the leader's role is to provide the social and political safeguards necessary for citizens to maintain that adequate set of basic liberties. This goal is well-defined throughout Rawls' theory, and this provides guidance to the leader: work with followers toward this goal, within the immediate context that the community falls within, in accordance with the values and norms that shape that community.

So how can leaders and followers work together to create a just society? According to Rawls, leaders and followers must work together to guarantee the basic rights of those who cannot speak up for themselves. They also must have the presence of mind to realize that these rights are needed in order to have a society that makes success an option for all of its members.

### DISCUSSION QUESTIONS

1. What similarities do you see between Rawls' approach to leadership and other social contract theories, as outlined in Chapter 10?
2. Could a Rawlsian apply the Five Components Model to another culture that is not democratic by nature?
3. Is Rawls' reliance on rationality too much of a challenge for the theory to overcome?
4. Do you think that most individuals would agree with the two principles that Rawls claims would be developed in the original position?
5. What would be some basic liberties that leaders should protect for all citizens?

### ADDITIONAL RESOURCES

R. Talisse, *On Rawls*, Wadsworth Notes, Boston, MA: Cengage Learning, 2001.

This resource presents an in-depth basic introduction to John Rawls and his career and works.

R. Dworkin, 'What is equality? Part 2: equality of resources', *Philosophy and Public Affairs*, vol. 10, 1981, 283–345.

Dworkin's article on the concept of equality provides a good summary of the theory of equality of resources.

# NOTES

1. J. Rawls, *A Theory of Justice*, Cambridge, MA: Harvard University Press, 1971.

2. J. Rawls, '50 years after Hiroshima', *Dissent*, summer 1995. https://www.dissentmagazine.org/article/50 -years-after-hiroshima-2 (accessed 16 July 2022).

3. Rawls, '50 years after Hiroshima', 6.

4. J. Rawls, *Political Liberalism*, expanded edn, New York: Columbia University Press, 1993/2005.

5. J. Rawls, *The Law of Peoples*, revised edn, Cambridge, MA: Harvard University Press, 2001.

6. J. Rawls, *Justice as Fairness: A Restatement*, ed. E. Kelly, Cambridge, MA: Belknap Press, 2001.

7. W.J. Clinton, 'Remarks on presenting the Arts and Humanities awards', Washington, DC: The Administration of William J. Clinton, 1999. https://www.govinfo.gov/content/pkg/PPP-1999-book2/pdf/PPP-1999-book2 -doc-pg1624.pdf (accessed 16 July 2022).

8. T. Hobbes, *Leviathan*, ed. C.B. MacPherson, New York: Penguin, 1651/1985; J. Locke, *An Essay Concerning Human Understanding*, ed. R. Woolhouse, New York: Penguin, 1689/1997; and J. Rousseau, *On the Social Contract*, ed. D. Silver, trans. G.D.H. Cole, 1762/2003.

9. Rousseau, *On the Social Contract*.

10. I. Kant, *Critique of Judgment*, trans. W.S. Pluhar, Indianapolis, IN: Hackett, 1790/1987.

11. Rawls, *A Theory of Justice*, p. 92.

12. Kant, *Critique of Judgment*.

13. J. Rawls, *Collected Papers*, ed. S. Freeman, Cambridge, MA: Harvard University Press, 1999, p. 310.

14. Rawls, *A Theory of Justice*; and I. Kant, *Critique of Pure Reason*, ed. and trans. M. Weigelt, New York: Penguin, 1781/2007.

15. Rawls, *A Theory of Justice*, p. 266.

16. R. Greenleaf, *The Servant as Leader: Essentials of Servant Leadership*, in L.C. Spears and M. Lawrence (eds), *Focus on Leadership: Servant Leadership for the 21st Century*, New York: John Wiley, 2002.

17. Rawls, *A Theory of Justice*, p. 266.

18. Rawls, *A Theory of Justice*, pp. 216–17.

19. Rawls, *A Theory of Justice*, p. 266.

20. Rawls, *A Theory of Justice*, p. 12.

21. J. Rawls, 'Kantian constructivism in moral theory', *Journal of Philosophy*, vol. 77 no. 9, 1980, 515–72, p. 529.

22. S. Wong, 'Duties of justice to citizens with cognitive disabilities', *Metaphilosophy*, vol. 40 nos 3–4, 2009, 382–401, p. 386.

23. M. Nussbaum, 'Nature, functioning and capability: Aristotle on political distribution', *Oxford Studies in Ancient Philosophy* (supplementary volume), 1988, 145–84.

24. A. Rand, *The Objectivist Ethics*, Whitefish, MT: Literary Licensing, 2011.

25. C. Davis, 'Lily's place continuing to care for addicted babies', *Appalachia Health News*, West Virginia Public Broadcasting, 3 March 2016. http://wvpublic.org/post/lilys-place-continuing-care-addicted-babies#stream/ 0 (accessed 3 November 2022). See also Lily's Place homepage: http://www.lilysplace.org/ (accessed 3 November 2018).

26. The United Nations Declaration of Human Rights, https://www.un.org/en/about-us/universal-declaration -of-human-rights. See D.W. Black, 'Americas founders recognized the need for public education: democracy requires maintaining that commitment', *Time*, 22 September 2020. https://time.com/5891261/early -american-education-history/ (accessed 16 July 2022).

27. R. Growe and P.S. Montgomery, 'Educational equity in America: is education the great equalizer?' *The Professional Educator*, vol. 25 no. 2, spring 2003, 23–9; see also L.A. Cremin (ed.), *The Republic and the School: Horace Mann on the Education of Free Men*, New York, Columbia University Press, 1957, pp. 6–8.

28. Scholars have identified six basic principles of CRT, but we have limited the concepts here for simplicity. See *Britannica*, 'Basic tenets of Critical Race theory'. https://www.britannica.com/topic/critical-race-theory/Basic-tenets-of-critical-race-theory (accessed 16 July 2022).

29. For more on CRT, see R. Delgado and J. Stefanic, *Critical Race Theory: An Introduction*, 3rd edn, New York: New York University Press, 2017.

30. D.R. Euben, 'Academic freedom of professors and institutions', AAUP, May 2002. https://www.aaup.org/issues/academic-freedom/professors-and-institutions (accessed 16 July 2022).

31. Euben, 'Academic freedom'.

32. Euben, 'Academic freedom'.

33. National Review Editors, 'Republicans are right to push back against CRT', *National Review*, vol. 73 no. 14, 10 July 2021. https://www.nationalreview.com/2021/07/republicans-are-right-to-push-back-against-crt-in-the-classrooms/ (accessed 16 July 2022).

34. E. Pettit, 'The academic concept conservative lawmakers love to hate: how critical race theory became Enemy No. 1 in the battle against higher ed', *Chronicle of Higher Education*, vol. 67 no. 19, 12 May 2021. https://www.chronicle.com/article/the-academic-concept-conservative-lawmakers-love-to-hate (accessed 16 July 2022).

35. S.2346- Stop CRT Act. https://www.congress.gov/bill/117th-congress/senate-bill/2346/text (accessed 16 July 2022).

36. B. Donalds, 'Rep. Donalds cosponsors legislation to combat critical race theory', 14 May 2021. https://donalds.house.gov/news/documentsingle.aspx?DocumentID=233 (accessed 16 July 2022).

37. S. Swartz, 'Map where CRT is under attack', *Education Week*, 11 June 2021, updated 15 July 2022. https://www.edweek.org/policy-politics/map-where-critical-race-theory-is-under-attack/2021/06 (accessed 16 July 2022).

38. PEN America, 'Educational gag orders: legislative restrictions on the freedom to read, learn, and teach'. https://pen.org/report/educational-gag-orders/ (accessed 16 July 2022). See also PEN America, 'Index of educational gag orders'. https://docs.google.com/spreadsheets/d/1Tj5WQVBmB6SQg-zP_M8uZsQQGH09TxmBY73v23zpyr0/edit#gid=267763711 (accessed 16 July 2022).

39. B. McMurtie, 'Teaching about race? Be paranoid', *The Chronicle of Higher Education*, 17 September 2021. https://www.chronicle.com/article/be-paranoid-professors-who-teach-about-race-approach-the-fall-with-anxiety (accessed 16 July 2022).

40. Rawls, *A Theory of Justice*, p. 266.

41. Rawls, *A Theory of Justice*, p. 266.

42. Executive Orders, 'Executive Order on Combating Race and Stereotyping', 22 September 2020. https://trumpwhitehouse.archives.gov/presidential-actions/executive-order-combating-race-sex-stereotyping/ (accessed 16 July 2022).

# 12
# The common good

*Robert M. McManus*

## FRAMING QUESTION

What does the common good demand of leadership?

Figure 12.1    Timeline of major works on the common good in relation to the chapter case study

The concept of the common good has a long and expansive history in the study of ethics. Renowned scholars such as Aristotle, Thomas Aquinas, Niccolò Machiavelli, John-Jacques Rousseau, and Adam Smith, as well as contemporary philosophers, have all weighed in on the idea of the common good. The concept is most often expressed today through the idea of 'communitarianism' – a philosophy that emphasizes the individual's responsibility to the larger community and is championed by public intellectuals such as Robert Bellah and Amitai Etzioni.[1]

Despite its extensive and varied history – or perhaps because of this – the concept of the common good is not easily defined and is often contested. As we begin our discussion, it is important to point out that there are several potential meanings for the term 'the common good'. One scholar points out that there are at least four.[2] The first is the corporate good of a social group. A simple illustration is when a group acts in concert to achieve a common goal, such as when the players on a basketball team work together to win a game. The second use of the word is the sense of 'public welfare', such as when a town collects taxes to provide a police force to protect its citizens. The third usage of the term focuses on the shared interest in securing common conditions in which individuals are equal and free to pursue their own interests.[3] A manifestation of this use of the term can be found in American civil rights legislation, such as the integration of public schools. The term's fourth sense focuses on how human beings relate to each other. This use of the term views people as interdependent; as such, they reach their greatest fulfilment in cooperating with others and working towards a goal greater than themselves.[4] For example, we might experience this use of the word when we run a 5K to raise money to find a cure for cancer that we might never see in our lifetime. As we will see, we will touch on aspects of all these uses of the term in our case study at the end of the chapter. However, to begin our discussion, let's start with a general definition of the term 'common good' and fill in the details from there.

For our purposes, we will simply define the common good as something that benefits all of society, whereas an individual good only benefits a particular person or a certain group within society. It forces leaders to ask, 'What is the best thing to do for all of society?' Given this definition, you do not have to look very far to see examples of the common good. A strong economy, a fair and just legal system, and clean air and water are all tangible manifestations of the concept of the common good.[5]

As we have done in previous chapters, we will trace the intellectual roots of the concept under discussion and consider its major aspects, conclusions, and critiques. We will then consider how the idea relates to the Five Components of Leadership Model introduced in Chapter 1. We will conclude this chapter with an application of the common good to the Clean Air Act of 1970 and its amendments, as well as the Act's implications for global climate change.

## HISTORY

One of the first philosophers to address the idea of the common good was Plato in his treatise *The Republic*.[6] Plato believed 'the good' was an objective reality that all people naturally search for as they seek to fulfil their own happiness. Hence, for Plato, the individual good and the common good were closely tied together. As people come together to form communities, they naturally unite in their search for this objective good. However, Plato's student Aristotle more fully developed the concept of the common good and is more often identified as the idea's originator. In his book *Politics*, Aristotle argued that humans are 'political animals' and, as such, they can only find happiness by working together in a just community.[7] It is essential to keep in mind that, for Aristotle, the common good is more than simply the sum of individual parts: that is, it is something more than just the amalgamation of individuals, each seeking his or her own happiness. For Aristotle, happiness is created through community, and a just community logically provides an environment where all its members can most likely obtain happiness. Likewise, Aristotle believed that the common good was superior to the individual good. He states this clearly in his *Nicomachean Ethics*, where he claims: 'The attainment of the good for one person alone is, to be sure, a source of satisfaction; but to secure it for a nation and for its cities is nobler and more divine.'[8]

Two centuries later, the Roman statesman Marcus Tullius Cicero further developed the concept of the common good in his *De Re Publica*.[9] Like Aristotle before him, Cicero claimed that a community was not simply a collection of individuals but rather was 'a special assemblage of people in large numbers associated in agreement with respect to justice and a partnership for the common good'.[10] These early Greek and Roman philosophers laid the foundation for the common good's continued development, which saw its next incarnation within the early Roman Catholic Church.

One scholar notes, 'although the language of the common good is Aristotelian in origin. Its main development in history has been with Christian Theology.'[11] Influential Catholic theologians, such as Augustine of Hippo and Thomas Aquinas, built upon this Greek and Roman foundation of the common good applying it specifically to Christianity. In his book *The City of God*, Augustine argued that the ultimate good is God; thus, if all humanity were to seek God and worship Him and His goodness, it would be united in its quest for and achievement of the common good.[12] (Notice how Augustine seems to hold more of a Platonic view of the common good.) Aquinas built upon Augustine's argument of God as the source of all good, but he echoed more of Aristotle's view that the common good could only be achieved through community.[13] One Catholic scholar summarizes Aquinas' thinking in this regard:

> [For Aquinas] ... the good of each person is linked with the good shared with others in community, and the highest good common to the life of all is God's own self. For Thomas Aquinas, therefore, pursuing the common good carries out the Bible's double commandment to love God with one's heart, mind, and soul and to love one's neighbor as oneself.[14]

The Catholic teaching of the common good is still at the forefront of Catholic ethics today. The Second Vatican Council in 1962 reaffirmed the importance of the concept of the common good. It defined it as 'the sum of those conditions of social life which allow social groups and their individual members relatively thorough and ready access to their own fulfillment'.[15] Likewise, contemporary Catholic teaching regarding social justice invokes the common good when it emphasizes the idea that individuals and people working together can best achieve happiness in a just world; hence, the Church should work to ensure justice for the most disenfranchised and vulnerable members of society.[16]

Although Catholic teachings offer a vibrant theory and practice of the common good, the concept also has a long secular tradition. The idea surfaced throughout the Renaissance and Enlightenment as the thinking regarding constitutional republics evolved and matured; hence, the idea continues to shape our view of these systems of government even today. For example, Renaissance political philosopher Nicolló Machiavelli in his *Discourses on Livy* argued that the primary purpose of government is to secure the *commune benefizio*.[17] Enlightenment thinkers, such as Thomas Hobbes in his *Leviathan* and John Locke in his *Two Treatise on Government*, argued that humans are by nature individuals; thus, they are vulnerable. So they form communities for their own protection under the guise of the common good.[18] Later philosophers such as Jean-Jacques Rousseau, in his work *The Social Contract*, echo Machiavelli's assertion that the primary purpose of the state is to achieve the common good for its people.[19] Likewise, philosophers such as David Hume in his *A Treatise of Human Nature* and James Madison in the *Federalist Papers* maintain that the purpose of government is to create a just civil society for the common good.[20] Many of these philosophers and economists noted that defining 'the good' can become troublesome in a pluralistic society. Hobbes and Hume argued that nothing can be considered 'good' or 'bad' in and of itself; rather, it is how people react to something that defines it.[21] This thinking laid the foundation for the division between individualism and collectivism, as we will discuss later in this chapter.

In the field of economics, Adam Smith argued in his pivotal work *The Wealth of Nations* that the common good is an amalgamation of the individual good.[22] Smith represents a very different way of thinking about the idea of the common good in comparison to the early philosophers and religious thinkers who developed the concept. Smith argued that the common good is driven by the invisible hand of the market to ensure a maximum creation of wealth, which is the ultimate common good.

These intellectuals profoundly influenced Western thinking about the common good and how the concept was institutionalized through forms of government and economic systems throughout the world. However, these understandings of the common good present a more liberal pluralistic – or individualist – take on the concept of the common good in that they all emphasize the person's right to pursue his or her own happiness, as opposed to the individual's responsibilities to his or her community. For that, we turn to a more recent understanding of the common good – that proposed by communitarians.

The communitarian approach to the idea of the common good rose to its zenith in the 1980s with the work of public intellectuals such as Robert Bellah (*Habits of the Heart*), Robert Putnam (*Bowling Alone*), and Amitai Etzioni (*The Spirit of Community*); although other prominent scholars such as Charles Taylor, Alasdair MacIntyre, Michael Sandal, and Michael Walzer have made significant contributions to communitarian philosophy.[23] Communitarians argue that 'a person must be understood in the context of his or her community'.[24] Etzioni argues, 'if we consider society as composed of families, communities, national bonds of affection, identity, and shared values, we realize the importance of society in general, especially for the formulation of informal promotion of the good.'[25] As such, communitarians argue that 'the good' must be conceived of as social rather than purely individual.[26]

This is not to say that communitarians do not acknowledge individual rights. However, they point out that excessively individualistic societies, particularly in the West, 'have lost their equilibrium, and are heavily burdened with antisocial consequences of excessive liberty'.[27] Pollution, gun proliferation, and hate speech are just a few of these antisocial excesses. This is not to say that communitarians are hostile to the idea of individual freedom and autonomy. Indeed, many point out that some governments, particularly in the East, suffer from totalitarianism and authoritarianism in which individuals are forced to set aside their autonomy for the good of the group. Communitarians argue that these societies have gone too far in the other direction.[28] Instead, communitarians contend that there must be a balance between extreme individualism on one side of the spectrum and extreme universalism on the other. They call for a righting of the lack of balance on both sides of this continuum. They argue that a new golden rule should read: 'Respect and uphold society's moral order as you would have society respect and uphold your autonomy.'[29]

But how does one define 'community' or 'society' in the age of globalism? These terms take on an additional dynamic when one realizes that our individual and communal bonds now cross international borders through ecology, technology, politics, and trade. Communitarians argue that we must expand our idea of 'community' to consider our present cosmopolitan reality. Amitai Etzioni notes:

> There is a strong human tendency to include only the members of one's community, be it defined as family, village, or nation. However, justice may compel us to treat all human beings equally. Can particularistic obligations be justified in the face of such universal claims ... One tends to forget that nation-states are a relatively recent social construction, neither natural or divine. Indeed, a strong case can be made that, in this day and age, the more we separate community from state, the more peaceful the world may become.[30]

Other scholars further articulate this need by adapting Aristotle's original admonition to a global context: 'To secure the good for an interdependent world is nobler and more divine than to do so for a single neighborhood, city, or nation-state.'[31] A healthy natural environment, a reduced spread of communicable diseases, and the elimination of weapons of mass destruction are 'goods' that affect us all. As such, communitarians call for us to broaden our understanding of what constitutes one's community.[32]

## MAJOR CONCEPTS OF THE ETHIC OF THE COMMON GOOD

Now that we have an understanding of the history of the thinking about the common good, we can move on to some of the concept's major themes, applications, and criticisms.

### The Primacy of the Individual versus the Primacy of the Community

Which should we consider more important – the individual or the community? Philosophers have debated this question for millennia. The truth is, the West – particularly the United States – has always held these seemingly competing values in tension with one another. We can trace this tension back to democracy's birthplace in ancient Greece and specifically to Plato and Aristotle's competing approaches to leadership. For example, in his *Republic*, Plato argues that leaders are special; that is, they have a natural disposition to discern 'the Good, True, and Beautiful' better than the rest of us. These natural-born leaders are inherently better and wiser than their counterparts. Plato prescribes that societies identify these individuals when they are children and then set them apart to be trained for positions of leadership when they become adults. These Philosopher-Kings, as Plato labelled them, sit at the top of the hierarchy and rule those beneath them – such as the guardians (warriors) and producers (the rest of society) – in wisdom and benevolence.[33] Again, to Plato leaders are special; since they know the Good, they should define the common good for others.

In contrast, Aristotle thought that leaders were like almost everyone else. He thought that followers who had the chance to live and work under various types of leaders throughout their youth would know how to lead better when they were in such a position later in life. Since they would have learned what it was like to be a follower, they could act with empathy and justice when they became leaders. Aristotle refers to this as the 'life-cycle of leadership'.[34] Aristotle takes an obviously more communitarian approach to leadership. However, Aristotle took this one step further as it related to the common good. Remember, as we learned earlier, Aristotle believed that happiness could only be created through people working together in community. One scholar summarizes it this way: 'Plato and Aristotle present a vision of the common good that cannot simply be reduced to the sum of all private interests, but whose promotion is nonetheless conducive to those interests – virtuous, fulfilled citizens and harmonious communities are both consequences of the pursuit of the good life.'[35]

We have started with Plato and Aristotle because they represent two sides of a continuum representing the primacy of the individual and a command-and-control view of leadership versus the primacy of the group and a connect-and-collaborate side of leadership as seen throughout the study of philosophy and ethics. This continuum manifests itself through the years as scholars have sought to understand the common good. The implications for leadership can be best stated as a fundamental question: 'Should the common good be determined and shaped by the leaders for their followers, or should the common good be determined and shaped by the community of followers for each other?'[36]

The question of the primacy of the individual or the primacy of the group is not just a philosophical exercise; the answer has real-life implications. Voices on the political left and political right often share similar concerns as to the way the question is answered. Should the individual's rights be infringed upon for the common good? Societies worldwide, particularly in the West, have often grappled with this question and have usually settled on the primacy of the rights of the individual – or what is referred to as individualism or pluralistic liberalism. On the other hand, if there is a compelling threat to the larger community, societies create mitigating laws that permit a reasonable infringement upon these individual rights. This represents a more communitarian view. For example, many Western societies value individual freedom of speech, but it is still illegal to shout 'Fire!' in a crowded theatre when no such fire exists. Or consider the last time you went to the airport. Chances are you were searched or scanned before boarding the plane.[37] Most Western societies prohibit an unreasonable search, or a search that is not motivated by evidence of any wrongdoing. Conversely, in the case where there is a potential danger to others, as in our airport example, the common good may outweigh individual rights. This tension is difficult to balance, and adjustments are constantly required to ensure proper respect for both individual rights and the common good.

## The Costs and Benefits of the Common Good

It is important to point out that the ethic of the common good is not a matter of simple utilitarian ethics – that is, the greatest good for the greatest number of people. The grandfather of utilitarianism, Jeremy Bentham, argued that the very notion of society as distinct from an aggregate of individuals was a fiction.[38] Likewise, John Stuart Mill maintained that societal pressure to make individuals conform to a communal idea of a 'good' was nothing short of coercion.[39] The purpose of the common good is to benefit all of the community, not just the majority. The minority must also benefit from the common good. That is why the Catholic tradition of social justice and the common good pay special attention to the least advantaged in society. Justice must be the basis for defining the common good; otherwise, the concept could quickly devolve into what some of its detractors fear the most – that it be used simply as a rhetorical trope for the tyranny of the majority. The common good requires cooperation from all community members who will share the costs and benefits of the common good.

And there are costs associated with achieving the common good; indeed, some people may shoulder more of these costs than others, but all will reap the benefits. As we will see later in our case study, the core idea of the common good is that what affects one of us affects all of us. We all rely on fresh air, fresh water, and a healthy natural world to meet our most basic needs. This is true for the farmer, the stockbroker, and the coal miner. It is also true that each person may have to somewhat limit their personal happiness to achieve the greater good for themselves and the larger community. The farmer may have to limit the use of pesticides on her crops, which may mean a decreased harvest. The stockbroker may have to invest in companies with lower profit margins because of regulations designed to protect the environment. And the coal miner may have to learn a new trade in order to feed his family. Nevertheless, these individuals also benefit from the fresh air, clean water, and healthy natural world that these sacrifices protect. It is also incumbent upon the rest of the community to help care for those who may pay a higher price to help achieve the common good. Farmers who face decreased yields may need government subsidies to remain solvent. Companies investing in technology to help ensure a cleaner environment may need tax breaks to support their bottom line. And coal miners who can no longer mine for coal because of the move to cleaner alternative energy sources may need to receive training in other professions and trades to help them transition into new jobs. The common good is not free.

The common good is increasingly used to call for cooperation on some of the world's most pressing problems. This is the crux of the matter as it relates to leadership: leaders must learn to take responsibility for the common good and more fully consider the larger implications of their actions when making decisions for their followers and organizations and consider both current impacts as well as that on future generations. They must learn to ask not what is best for just themselves, their followers, and their organizations, but rather what is best for everyone. When faced with the question 'Are you your brother's keeper?' they must learn to respond, 'Yes, I am.'

## CRITIQUES OF THE COMMON GOOD

Now that we have a better understanding of the common good, it is important to consider its potential liabilities. For that, we will look at two major critiques of the idea: the belief that the common good is a fiction and the free rider problem.

### There Is no Such Thing as the Common Good

It should be noted that many eschew the very notion of a 'common good'. They argue that individuals can only determine the 'good' for themselves. Both libertarians and pluralistic liberals may fear that the idea of the common good may lead to governmental restrictions on individual liberties. Likewise, many libertarians and laissez-faire conservatives argue that societies prosper only when individuals are 'granted as much autonomy as possible'.[40] Ayn Rand was a twentieth-century intellectual who left an indelible mark on many people's thinking about the common good. Rand agreed with Bentham that the very idea of a common good was nothing more than a fiction. Her basic argument was that society is simply an amalgamation of individuals – nothing more. There is no such thing as 'society' or 'the tribe', as she calls it. As such, the concept of good or bad can only pertain to an individual. You cannot separate the good from those who will benefit from it. Rand writes:

> Only on the basis of individual rights can any good – private or public – be defined and achieved. Only when each man is free to exist for his own sake – neither sacrificing others to himself nor being sacrificed to others – only then is every man free to work for the greatest good he can achieve for himself by his own choice and by his own effort. And the sum total of such individual efforts is the only kind of general, social good possible.[41]

Rand believed that the term 'the common good' was merely a rhetorical tool used to force one person's idea of the good, or a particular group's idea of the good, on others. This leads to a power struggle to define what is good. The winners in this struggle inevitably impose their own idea of good onto the losers, which become, in her words, sacrificial animals. In fact, Rand maintains that the concept of the common good is the basis for all totalitarian regimes and dictatorships.[42] Many people still find Rand's objection to the common good compelling, and her criticism remains a powerful argument for many opposing the idea of the common good today, especially among those who hold to a capitalistic conservative world view and those with libertarian political views. In response to this criticism, some contemporary communitarians argue that these groups 'take an important truth, that freedom is essential to human dignity, and stretch it until it becomes a falsehood'.[43] On the other hand, communitarians also acknowledge that this criticism is, indeed, sometimes warranted.[44]

## The Tragedy of the Common Good: the Free Rider Problem

Another concept relevant to our discussion here and of particular interest to our case study later in this chapter is how one defines the term 'common'. The term 'the commons' refers to the idea that some assets are communal in that they do not belong to any one person but are available to everyone. Examples of the commons in the natural world include things such as the air we breathe, the rivers and oceans, and the wide variety of wildlife and ecosystems throughout our planet; whereas examples of commons that can be found in our social world include things such as city parks, libraries, and scientific research. The problem arises, however, when someone takes more than their fair share of these commons.

The ecologist and philosopher Garrett Hardin is often associated with this idea. In his article 'The tragedy of the commons', Hardin provides his readers with an example of what happens when someone takes more than their fair share of a commons.[45] He draws a picture of a pasture that is available to a group of ten ranchers. The pasture has enough grass to feed ten cows comfortably. So, each rancher can keep one cow on the land. But what happens if one rancher says, 'I'm going to keep two cows on the pasture'? Over time, the other cows will have about 10 per cent less food to eat, weighing about 10 per cent less and being about 10 per cent less productive. On the other hand, the rancher with two cows on the land receives almost twice the benefit he had with only one cow. When the other ranchers realize what is happening, they will say, 'Why shouldn't I benefit from having two cows on the land, too!' and each adds an extra cow to the pasture. If too many ranchers do this, the common pasture will be useless in no time and will cease to feed any cows. This is the tragedy of the commons. Hardin argues:

> Each man is locked into a system that compels him to increase his herd without limit – in a world that is limited. Ruin is the destination toward which all men rush, each pursuing his own best interest in a society that believes in the freedom of the commons. Freedom in a commons brings ruin to all.[46]

Economists refer to this as the 'free rider problem'. Thus, Hardin believes that the commons must be regulated by society to reduce individual freedom in an effort to promote the common good.

## FIVE COMPONENT ANALYSIS

As we have done in previous chapters, we now turn to the Five Component Analysis to better understand how the common good relates to the leadership process.

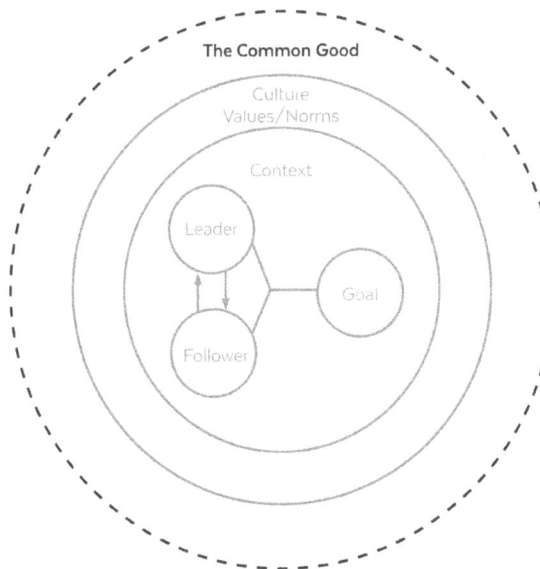

**Figure 12.2**    The Five Components of Leadership Model applied to the ethic of the common good

One could argue that the primary thesis of the book you hold in your hands is that it is not only important that leaders and followers work to reach a goal, but how leaders and followers reach that goal is equally important. The same is true when working for the common good. The common good affects all aspects of the Five Components of Leadership. It can be conceived as a 'superlayer' enveloping the other parts of the Five Components of Leadership Model, as shown in Figure 12.2.

Leaders and followers must work together to determine the common good and how the goal of the common good should be achieved. Suppose leaders simply impose their personal interpretation of the common good upon their followers. In that case, the critics of the common good may indeed be right to call such an act dictatorial and perhaps even tyrannical. On the other hand, if followers only seek their individual self-interests without concern for their fellow followers, leaders, and the communities they create, there is little hope of achieving a just environment to foster happiness – for the individual or the community. Instead, leaders and followers must work together to determine the common goal and the best means of achieving it.

Notice the two arrows between leaders and followers representing a mutual relationship between the two parties. In our case, these arrows represent the negotiation and reciprocal influence that must occur when defining the common good. This mutual influence is needed to prevent the abuse of power between leaders and followers and one party exerting a coercive influence over the other. Also, notice the lines connecting the leader and the followers to the goal. After leaders and followers have identified the common goal, they must also pursue the best means to achieve it. Again, this prevents one party's particular will from overpowering the other and ensures an equal commitment from both the leader and followers to achieving the agreed-upon common goal.

The common good forces leaders and followers to take a grander view of the goal, which is the creation of the common good. This notion is graphically represented here with the addition of a dotted circle encompassing the entire model. The common good takes into consideration all aspects of the Five Components of Leadership – the leaders, the followers, the goal, the environmental context, and the cultural values and norms. True, leaders and followers still work towards smaller goals, but these are better thought of as the means to achieve the larger goal, which is the common good.

The common good also affects the context because the situational factors dictate the specific common good to be achieved. Contingencies may drive leaders and followers to come together to address a pressing exigency. An example of this can be found in corporate social responsibility. The famed management professor Peter Drucker said, 'In the complex of organizations in which we live, the organizations – and that means the professionals that manage them – must surely take responsibility for the common weal.'[47] Most business professionals today realize that they cannot simply concentrate on creating wealth for their shareholders but must consider all of the stakeholders in a situation – employees, customers, communities, and the environment as well as shareholders. This is the kind of thinking that is needed to promote the common good and is becoming more of a standard in business, sometimes expressed in the phrase 'the triple bottom line – people, planet, and profit'. Likewise, those working in the public and non-profit sectors increasingly understand the intersections of globalization and the importance of looking outside of one's own tribe to create the common good in a globalized world. This intersectionality has particular relevance as we look to create the common good in an environment of competing cultural values and norms.

The common good requires us to embrace the broadest understanding of community in an effort to meet everyone's needs. This understanding presents perhaps the biggest challenge in achieving the common good. How does one achieve the common good in a pluralistic, multicultural world? Some would argue that such a goal is nothing more than wishful thinking. Others take a much more optimistic view. Arguing for the faith in the common good, one ethicist maintains that such a conviction '… is a matter of believing that the good of different persons in not so irreconcilably competitive as to make it incoherent to have the good of all persons as an end'.[48] It is with this hope that we turn to our case study.

## CASE STUDY: THE 1970 CLEAN AIR ACT AND THE COMMON GOOD[49]

In June 1962, ecologist and author Rachel Carson released her now famous book *Silent Spring*. In her book, Carson drew readers' attention to the perils facing the natural world. However, many Americans had personally witnessed many of the catastrophes Carson described in her book. The air quality in much of the United States during the mid-to-late twentieth century had become a toxic stew of chemicals such as lead, mercury, and sulphur dioxide due to leaded gasoline and pollution caused by factories and power plants. Disasters such as the Santa Barbara oil spill in California, the Cuyahoga River fire in Ohio, and the Love Canal toxic waste disaster in New York caught people's attention. Thick clouds of smog often blanketed cities such as New York and Los Angeles. However, the air in cities and small towns across the United States was also polluted with alarming levels of toxins.[50] Americans demanded that their legislators clean up the mess. More than 20 million Americans participated in the country's first Earth Day in 1970 to call for change.[51] In his 1970 State of the Union Address, President Nixon declared:

> Restoring nature to its natural state is a cause beyond party and beyond factions. It has become a common cause of all the people of this country ... Clean air, clean water, open spaces – these should once again be the birthright of every American. If we act now, they can be. We still think of air as free. But clean air is not free, and neither is clean water. The price tag on pollution control is high. Through our years of past carelessness, we incurred a debt to nature, and now that debt is being called ...[52]

In response, Congress passed the Clean Air Act of 1970 to stem the tide of pollution that had overwhelmed the country.

The Clean Air Act of 1970 (1970 CAA) was the culmination of several more minor and limited acts that Congress has passed over several decades.[53] However, the CAA was much larger in scope than the legislation preceding it. The Act established the federal government as the central authority to monitor and control air pollution and established several regulatory programmes to control its various sources. It also provided a mechanism for comprehensive federal and state regulations to limit emissions from 'stationary and mobile sources', such as factories, power plants, and vehicles.[54] The Nixon administration created the Environmental Protection Agency (EPA) and charged it with enforcing the Act. The 1970 CAA was enhanced by major amendments in 1977 and 1990 that expanded the scope of the original legislation and increased the EPA's power to create and enforce regulations in an all-out effort to clean up the country's air.[55]

It worked. Since the passage of the 1970 CAA and its amendments, the United States has lowered the levels of pollutants in the air by 78 per cent.[56] The Act has helped to reduce diseases caused or exacerbated by air pollution, such as lung and heart disease, resulting in millions of fewer deaths and increasing the life expectancy of those living in the United States.[57] The Act has been used to help repair the Earth's ozone layer, reducing cases of skin cancer. It has also helped to prevent the loss of IQ points in children due to lead exposure.[58] In short, the 1970 CAA has had a profoundly positive impact on human health. The 1970 CAA and its amendments have also helped improve the health of ecosystems. Air pollution has many adverse effects on the natural world. Poor air quality and the resulting acid rain damages plants and trees. It also harms natural habitats such as forests, streams, rivers, and oceans, thus harming animals, fish, and aquatic life while introducing toxins to the food chain.[59] By lowering the concentrations of toxins in the air, the 1970 CAA helped to improve the health of all living species.

As Nixon noted, clean air is not free. Regulations force industry and citizens to bear the cost of reducing emissions through new technology. However, the EPA recently conducted a cost–benefit analysis of the 1970 Clean Air Act and its 1977 and 1990 amendments and found that its benefits exceed its compliance costs by a factor of 30 to 1.[60] These benefits totalled an estimated $2 trillion in 2020 alone.[61] Many of these economic savings come in the form of fewer pollution-related illnesses, resulting in less money spent on medical treatments and lower work absenteeism.[62] So, although clean air is not free, the cost of polluted air is considerably higher. There are not only human costs to pollution, but there are also considerable financial costs.

Acknowledging the costs associated with air pollution drove innovation to produce cleaner and more efficient forms of energy. Likewise, regulators could provide an economic rationale to require industrial plants to emit fewer pollutants to contribute to the growth of the US economy.

However, we cannot view the CAA exclusively in the context of the United States; rather, we must view it in the larger context of global climate change. The Earth is warming because of the continued increase in fossil fuel consumption. These fossil fuels create an overabundance of greenhouse gases, specifically carbon dioxide – $CO_2$. Air pollution does not recognize national boundaries. The EPA tried to use the CAA to address the problem of climate change by regulating $CO_2$ emissions. In 2009, the EPA concluded that 'greenhouse gases in the atmosphere are reasonably anticipated to endanger the public health and welfare of current and future generations.'[63] They also determined that vehicles were responsible for more than a quarter of greenhouse gas emissions in the United States. In response, the EPA worked with the National Highway and Traffic Safety Administration to develop greenhouse gas and fuel economy standards for new vehicles, lowering the amount of greenhouse gases vehicles emit. The EPA attempted to also create and apply new standards for stationary emitters, specifically power plants, but the Supreme Court blocked their progress in 2022.

The main argument provided by Supreme Court's majority was that the 1970 CAA and its amendments targeted pollutants such as particles, ozone, lead, carbon monoxide, nitrogen dioxide, sulphur dioxide, and other toxic pollutants. However, it did not specifically apply to greenhouse gases such as carbon dioxide and other carbon emissions. The Supreme Court ruled that since Congress did not give the EPA the authority to address climate change, it could not use the power of the CAA to do so by limiting carbon emissions from sources such as power plants. The Court also took issue with the EPA's interventions having the potential to transform the United States economy, which is primarily dependent upon fossil fuels. Of course, there was significant dissent to the Court's ruling.[64]

In sum, the 1970 CAA and its amendments provided a way for the United States to improve air quality in the country, resulting in better health, a cleaner environment, and economic gains. However, the Supreme Court prevented the EPA from using the CAA to regulate carbon emissions from power plants. Next, we will consider the concept of the common good as it relates to the 1970 CAA. We will also address the controversies surrounding the 1970 CAA and the Supreme Court's refusal to allow the EPA to apply its authority to mitigate climate change.

The definition of the common good we have been using in this chapter is simply 'something that benefits all of society'. In contrast, an individual good only benefits a particular person or group within society. This definition forces leaders to ask, 'What is the best thing to do for all of society?' We all need clean air to be able to live healthy lives. This fact is as true for the coal miner as it is for the environmentalist. The CAA is a mechanism to help ensure clean air for everyone. But we can also apply other definitions of the common good to our case study.

As we saw earlier in this chapter, the concept of the common good has several meanings. The 1970 CAA relates well to the notion of the common good as a term to describe a social group working in concert to achieve a goal. It is noteworthy that politicians across the political spectrum, Republicans and Democrats, came together to pass the 1970 CAA. However, it was not just politicians who sought to clean up the air in the United States. Twenty million citizens, roughly 10 per cent of the population in the United States at the time, demonstrated on the first Earth Day and called upon their representatives to address the pollution plaguing the country.[65] If it were not for this collective action by *followers* pursuing a common goal, it is doubtful the United States would have been able to fix the pollution problem it had created.

Perhaps the definition of the common good that is most relevant to our case study applies to how the common good is used to promote public welfare. The 1970 CAA sought to reduce the harm to humans and the environment caused by air pollution. As we have seen, the Act was a remarkably successful tool in achieving this goal. Before the 1970 CAA, the air in the United States was a toxic stew of chemicals that had harmful effects on humans and the environment. As we saw earlier in our case study, the EPA was able to use the CAA to regulate emissions from stationary and mobile sources to significantly improve air quality across the United States, dramatically improving human health and the environment.

We can also apply a third use of the term to our case study, which focuses on securing common conditions in which individuals are equal and free to pursue their own interests. The Clean Air Act and the Administrative Procedures Act guarantee that every citizen has the opportunity to provide comment on any regulation the EPA proposes. The EPA publishes every proposed rule in the Federal Register to inform citizens and solicit feedback through public hearings.[66] The EPA works closely with stakeholders such as state and local governments, industries, communities, and environmental groups that may be affected by a proposed regulation. The EPA also hosts voluntary partnership programmes to help state and local governments, industries, and communities reduce pollution and greenhouse gases. Thus, the EPA and the Administrative Procedures Act help create an environment where all parties have a voice in the development of regulations. However, some parties may be constrained by rules designed to protect the common good.

The 1970 CAA is not without its detractors. The main criticisms are closely related to the criticisms of the common good highlighted earlier in this chapter. As Ayn Rand would say, there is no common good – good and bad can only be determined by the individual.

Those who oppose the Clean Air Act note that federal, state, and local governments and private industry must pay for the new technologies required to meet the CAA's air quality standards. This demand places a financial burden on taxpayers and businesses. However, the citizens and business owners bearing these costs can also enjoy their access to clean air and all the health and environmental benefits it brings. In addition, studies show that environmental costs usually amount to no more than 2 per cent of business costs.[67] This is a relatively small price to pay for clean air. Critics may also claim that the CAA imposes regulations that other countries do not have to follow, forcing manufacturers to go overseas, thus harming the United States' economy. However, the US gross domestic product has actually grown by 285 per cent since the passage of the CAA, and the air quality in the United States is remarkably better.[68] In addition, as we noted above, for every dollar spent on meeting the standards of the CAA, the United States actually saves 30 dollars. Clean energy also creates new jobs and is outpacing coal mining for job creation.[69] This trend is likely to increase with the passage of climate and energy provisions in the Inflation Reduction Act of 2022.[70] Those who attempt to force an either/or argument fail to acknowledge that the CAA has been good for both the environment *and* the economy. Finally, although it seems strange to have to state it, air does not belong to governments or businesses; it is truly a commons. It is a vital part of the natural world. After all, most living things need air to breathe; why should governments and businesses have the right to pollute it for their own economic gain? This relates to the next criticism of the CAA, the free rider problem.

The second major criticism of the CAA relates to the free rider problem, also discussed in this chapter. One of the unfortunate loopholes of the CAA is that the United States allowed previously built power plants to be 'grandfathered' into the new legislation. This means that outdated coal-burning power plants can continue to operate without the regulations imposed upon newer, cleaner energy facilities. To a certain extent, this is a legitimate concern. There are still power plants in operation that should have been shuttered decades ago. The power plants continue to pollute the environment and emit greenhouse gases and are beyond the reach of the EPA's enforcement of the CAA.

Likewise, different states have different laws, and some are much more environmentally friendly than others. However, air does not pay attention to arbitrarily drawn borders. Pollution from coal-burning power plants in Indiana and West Virginia makes its way to the eastern seaboard and beyond. Air polluted with the exhaust fumes from cars in Los Angeles makes its way to the Great Plains. In seeking to engage all stakeholders, the EPA has sometimes created different rules for different players. This predicament does open the EPA and the CAA up for criticism. However, the EPA has attempted to account for this by applying regional levels for air pollution that would account for states that emit a higher level of pollutants. Nevertheless, nobody can deny that the air in the United States is significantly cleaner now than it was before the act, regardless of states with less stringent regulations.

## FIVE COMPONENT ANALYSIS

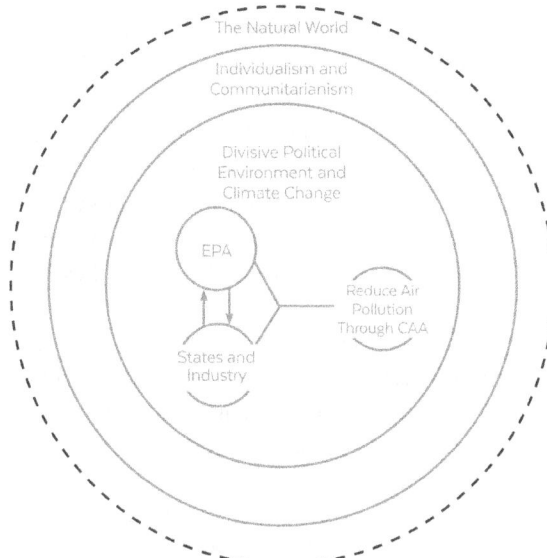

**Figure 12.3**      The Five Components of Leadership Model applied to the 1970 Clean Air Act and the common good

We now turn our attention to how McManus and Perruci's Five Components of Leadership relate to the 1970 Clean Air Act.

The 1970 Clean Air Act and its amendments required the United States to consider all of society in taking a grander view of the goal, in this case reducing air pollution. This is graphically represented in Figure 12.3 with the addition of a dotted circle encompassing the entire model and is labelled 'the natural world'. A healthy natural world is vital for leadership; it is the most basic context for all human interactions.[71] In this case, the EPA works with states and regions to set acceptable levels of air pollution, with the larger goal of reducing pollution throughout the country.

As we stated earlier, how leaders and followers reach the common good is as important as the goal itself. It is noteworthy that the EPA allows for public comment and works with states and industry to help minimize air pollution. Although it would be tempting for the EPA to set high goals and demand that industries and states meet these high goals, it is doubtful that any such unilateral action would be met with much compliance. Instead, by the EPA working with various stakeholders, it allows multiple groups to be a part of solving the problem of air pollution.

Note the arrows between leaders and followers representing a mutual relationship between the two parties. In our case study, these arrows represent the negotiation and reciprocal influence that must take place when agreeing to the goal and the means to achieve it.

The context for the Clean Air Act was the rise in pollution in the mid-to-late twentieth century and the current context of anthropomorphic climate change through the release of greenhouse gases. In the mid-to-late twentieth century, the federal government and the states, Republicans and Democrats, realized that they could not merely attempt to 'clean up their own backyard' if they were to address the air pollution problem throughout the country.

The cultural values and norms of the United States are particularly relevant to both the successes and the limitations of the Clean Air Act. The United States has traditionally held the concepts of individualism and communitarianism in tension.[72] In fact, one scholar goes as far as to characterize the United States as simultaneously holding two 'American Dreams' – one of the rugged individualist pulling himself up by his bootstraps and the other of a universal brotherhood of equality.[73] Although the Clean Air Act has been remarkably successful, significant factions in the United States still consider the Act and the EPA an instance of government overreach into the affairs of individuals and businesses. The CAA's detractors do not feel compelled to account for the consequences of their actions, which are still the cause of much of the pollution in the United States. Contrarily, many others more readily acknowledge their connection with the natural world, the communities in which they operate, and even their global interconnectedness. In fact, when the United States threatened to pull out of the Paris Agreement in 2016, many business leaders urged the United States to continue its participation.[74] These competing cultural values affect the leadership situation, specifically in regard to the CAA and global climate change. However, this exercise illustrates the importance of leaders considering the cultural values and norms in which they are embedded if they hope their initiatives will be successful.

Unfortunately, the Supreme Court prevented the EPA from using the 1970 CAA to mitigate climate change caused by $CO2$ and other greenhouse gases emitted by power plants. Had the Supreme Court ruled in the EPA's favour, the CAA could have been applied to yet another meaning of the term 'the common good' – one in which humans see themselves as interdependent and reach their greatest fulfilment in working towards a goal greater than themselves.[75] Global climate change jeopardizes the survival of species across the planet, not just in the United States.[76] It is to everyone's advantage to address global climate change. However, the Supreme Court's refusal to allow the EPA to use the 1970 CAA to address global climate change by regulating the greenhouse gases emitted by power plants threatens the EPA's ability to use the 1970 CAA as a tool to safeguard the public's health in regard to climate change. Electricity-producing power plants account for a quarter of greenhouse gas emissions in the United States.[77] In addition, the United States is historically the largest emitter of greenhouse gases and the second largest emitter at this point in history, second only to China.[78] If the United States and other governments throughout the world are to honour the ethic of the common good, they must seek ways to mitigate global climate change, even if this means that these governments must bear an economic cost.

Today, governments worldwide are realizing that they too must address global climate change on a planetary level if they hope to avoid massive climate destruction. Initiatives such as the Paris Agreement, in which 193 parties agreed to reduce their carbon emissions to mitigate global climate change, are evidence of this acknowledgment of our shared future and the ethic of the common good.

## SUMMARY AND CONCLUDING REMARKS

So, 'What does the common good demand of leadership?' According to the common good, leaders and followers must push themselves to consider more than what is merely beneficial for themselves and their organizations. They must also consider their actions' impact on everyone their organization touches. Rather than simply ask 'How will this benefit us?' leaders and followers must ask 'How will this benefit us and them?' To make this switch, leaders and followers must start expanding their view of 'stakeholders' and start thinking about how their organization impacts the world at large. The common good perspective can help leaders and followers see this bigger picture as being in their best interest.

Those who wish to see the work of the CAA continue, as well as those who hope to mitigate global climate change, would be wise to listen to the words of Amitai Etzioni when he says, 'No society can flourish without some shared formulation of the common good.'[79] The CAA provides evidence of what can be accomplished when leaders and followers work together to pursue a goal greater than themselves.

## DISCUSSION QUESTIONS

1. What are some other specific instances of the common good that you believe leaders would be wise to consider?
2. How compelling do you find the 'free rider' problem to be to the idea of the common good? What might be a way for leaders and followers to ensure all parties care for the commons?
3. How should leaders respond if their followers have competing ideas of what constitutes 'the good'?
4. The common good is considered one of the most controversial ethical positions. Can you think about when the idea of the common good may have been abused? When and where?
5. Is the ethic of the common good even worth pursuing if the idea can potentially be misused? Justify your answer.

## ADDITIONAL RESOURCES

R. Bellah, R. Madsen, W.M. Sullivan, A. Swidler and S.M. Tipton, *Habits of the Heart: Individualism and Commitment in American Life*, 3rd edn, Berkeley, CA: University of California Press, 1985/2017.

This book is often cited in the field of leadership studies and articulates the idea of communitarianism in a succinct and accessible manner.

A. Etzioni, *The Common Good*, Cambridge: Polity, 2004.

This book is scholarly work from a leading intellectual on the common good in which he presents the idea and addresses its detractors and critiques.

## NOTES

1. These great minds in the fields of philosophy, religion, government, economics, and ethics each have their unique interpretation and approach to the idea. Likewise, Asian traditions have their own distinctive approach to the concept of the common good that emphasizes harmony, whereas Western approaches tend to focus on the political and social implications of the concept. For example, see D. Solomon and P.C. Lo

(eds), *The Common Good: Chinese and American Perspectives*, Dordrecht: Springer, 2014. For the sake of simplicity and to focus our discussion, this chapter will focus on a Western conceptualization of the concept.

2.  P. Riordan, *A Grammar of the Common Good: Speaking of Globalization*, London: Continuum, 2008, pp. 59–60. Riordan notes, 'If the only possible use of common good talk were in the rhetoric of totalitarianism, then there would be little to be said in its favour. However, this exploration of the grammar of the common good shows that there are several possible and legitimate uses of the language' (p. 69).

3.  Some may refer to this as an 'individualist-instrumentalist' use of the term. See L. Honohan, *Civic Republicanism*, London: Routledge, 2002, p. 152.

4.  Riordan, *A Grammar of the Common Good*.

5.  M. Velasquez, C. Andre, T. Shanks and M.J. Meyer, 'The common good', The Markkula Center for Applied Ethics, Santa Clara University. https://www.scu.edu/ethics/ethics-resources/ethical-decision-making/the-common-good/ (accessed 3 November 2022).

6.  Plato, *Republic*, trans. G.M.A. Grube, revised by C.D.C. Reeve, 2nd edn, Indianapolis, IN: Hackett, 1992.

7.  Aristotle, *Politics*, trans. B. Jowett, Mineola, NY: Dover Publications, 1885/2000.

8.  Aristotle, *Nicomachean Ethics*, 1094b, in *Complete Works*, ed. J. Barnes, Cambridge: Cambridge University Press, 1984, vol. II, p. 1728. Aristotle's use of the word 'common' translates to something close to 'unified'.

9.  Cicero, *De Re Publica*, trans. C.W. Keyes, Cambridge: Loeb Classical Library, 1943.

10. Cicero, *De Re Publica*, Book 1 Chapter XXV.

11. Riordan, *A Grammar of the Common Good*, p. 7.

12. Augustine, *City of God*, trans. Henry Bettenson, London: Penguin Books, 1972/2003.

13. T. Aquinas, *The Summa Theologica*, trans. The Fathers of the English Dominican Province, New York: Benzinger Brothers, 1948/Reprint, Notre Dame, IN: Christian Classics, 1981.

14. D. Hollenbach, *The Common Good and Christian Ethics*, Cambridge: Cambridge University Press, p. 4.

15. Pastoral Constitution on the Church in the Modern World, *Gaudium et Spes*, Promulgated by His Holiness, Pope Paul VI, on 7 December 1965. http://www.vatican.va/archive/hist_councils/ii_vatican_council/documents/vat-ii_const_19651207_gaudium-et-spes_en.html (accessed 3 November 2022).

16. See Pontifical Council for Justice and Peace, Compendium of the Social Doctrine of the Church. http://www.vatican.va/roman_curia/pontifical_councils/justpeace/documents/rc_pc_justpeace_doc_20060526_compendio-dott-soc_en.html (assessed 3 November 2022).

17. N. Machiavelli, *Discourses on Livy*, trans. H.C. Mansfield and N. Tarcov, Chicago, IL: The University of Chicago Press, 1996; see also H. Waldemar, 'The common good in Machiavelli', *History of Political Thought*, vol. 31 no. 1, 57–85.

18. T. Hobbes, *Leviathan*, Mineola, NY: Dover Publications, 2006; and J. Lock, *Two Treatises on Government*, trans. Lewis F. Abbott, Manchester: Industrial Systems Research, 2009.

19. J. Rousseau, *The Social Contract*, trans. Maurice Cranston, New York: Penguin Putnam Inc., 1968.

20. D. Hume, *A Treatise of Human Nature*, Mineola, NY: Dover Publications, 2003; and A. Hamilton, J. Jay and J. Madison, *The Federalist Papers*, London: Penguin Books, 1987.

21. Riordan, *A Grammar of the Common Good*, p. 17.

22. A. Smith, *The Wealth of Nations*, New York: Random House, 1776/1994.

23. R. Bellah, R. Madsen, W.M. Sullivan, A. Swidler and S.M. Tipton, *Habits of the Heart: Individualism and Commitment in American Life*, 3rd edn, Berkeley, CA: University of California Press, 1985/2017; R.D. Putnam, *Bowling Alone: The Collapse and Revival of American Community*, New York: Simon and Schuster,

2000; and A. Etzioni, *The Spirit of Community: Rights Responsibilities and the Communitarian Agenda*, New York: Crown Publishers, 1993.

24. M.J. Sandal, *Liberalism and the Limits of Justice*, Cambridge: Cambridge University Press, 1982, p. 179.

25. A. Etizioni, *The Common Good*, Cambridge: Polity, 2004, p. 5.

26. C. Taylor, *Sources of the Self: The Makings of Modern Identity*, Cambridge, MA: Harvard University Press, 1989, p. 170.

27. A. Etzioni, *The New Golden Rule, Community and Morality in a New Democratic Society*, New York: Basic Books, 1996, p. xvii.

28. Etzioni, *The New Golden Rule*, p. xvii.

29. Etzioni, *The New Golden Rule*, p. xviii.

30. Etzioni, *The New Golden Rule*, pp. 4–5.

31. Hollenbach, *The Common Good*, p. 220.

32. Hollenbach, *The Common Good*, pp. 215–16.

33. Plato, *Republic*.

34. Aristotle, *Politics*.

35. A. Etzioni, 'The Common Good,' in M.T. Gibbons (ed.), *The Encyclopedia of Political Thought*, Hoboken, NJ: John Wiley and Sons, 2015. https://icps.gwu.edu/sites/g/files/zaxdzs1736/f/downloads/Common%20Good .Etzioni.pdf. (accessed 3 November 2022).

36. For further discussion regarding how leadership holds a tension between the individual's primacy and the community's primacy, see R. McManus and G. Perruci, *Understanding Leadership: An Arts and Humanities Perspective*, 2nd edn, New York: Routledge, 2020.

37. Riordan, *A Grammar of the Common Good*, uses examples such as these in his explanation of the common good.

38. Quoted in Etzioni, *The Common Good*, p. 7.

39. J.S. Mill, *On Liberty*, ed. D. Spitz, Norton Critical Edition, New York: W.W. Norton, 1975, p. 71.

40. Etzioni, *The New Golden Rule*, pp. 3–4.

41. A. Rand, *The Ayn Rand Column*, 2nd edn, Irvine, CA: Ayn Rand Institute Press, 1998, p. 91.

42. A. Rand, *Capitalism, The Unknown Ideal*, Centennial Edition, New York: Signet, 1986, p. 12.

43. Etzioni, *The New Golden Rule*, p. 11. Etzioni is quoting R.P. George, who is quoting P. Strobin, 'Right, fight', *National Journal*, vol. 27 no. 49, 1995, 3022.

44. Etzioni, *The New Golden Rule*; and Riordan, *A Grammar of the Common Good*.

45. G. Hardin, 'Tragedy of the commons', *Science*, vol. 162 no. 3859, 1968, 1243–8. http://science.sciencemag .org/content/sci/162/3859/1243.full.pdf (accessed 3 November 2022).

46. Hardin, 'Tragedy of the commons', 162.

47. P.F. Drucker, *Adventures of a Bystander*, New Brunswick, NJ: Transaction, 1997, p. 293.

48. R.M. Adams, *Finite and Infinite Goods: A Framework for Ethics*, Oxford: Oxford University Press, 1999, p. 378.

49. I extend my gratitude to Dr David J. Brown, Professor of Biology and Environmental Science at Marietta College, for his assistance in helping me research and write this case study.

50. See D. Davis, *When Smoke Ran Like Water: Tales of Environmental Deception and the Battle Against Pollution*, New York, Basic Books, 2002.

51. Earthday.org, 'The history of Earth Day'. https://www.earthday.org/history/?gclid=Cj0KCQjw2_OWBhDqA
    RIsAAUNTTGX62y9T651HYnNB3zjA7v_lAeaOtHDQDfGLaW5Xezf8U08DEnXglYaAsVeEALw_wcB
    (accessed 1 August 2022).

52. R. Nixon, 'Annual message to the Congress on the State of the Union', 22 January 1970. https://www
    .presidency.ucsb.edu/documents/annual-message-the-congress-the-state-the-union-2 (accessed 1 August
    2022).

53. United States Environmental Protection Agency, 'Evolution of the Clean Air Act', 2 December 2021. https://
    www.epa.gov/clean-air-act-overview/evolution-clean-air-act#:~:text=The%20enactment%20of%20the
    %20Clean,industrial)%20sources%20and%20mobile%20sources (accessed 1 August 2022).

54. United States Environmental Protection Agency, 'Evolution'.

55. United States Environmental Protection Agency, 'Evolution'.

56. United States Environmental Protection Agency, 'Progress cleaning the air and improving people's health',
    9 March 2022. https://www.epa.gov/clean-air-act-overview/progress-cleaning-air-and-improving-peoples
    -health#pollution (accessed 1 August 2022).

57. United States Environmental Protection Agency, 'Progress'.

58. United States Environmental Protection Agency, 'Progress'.

59. United States Environmental Protection Agency, 'Progress'.

60. United States Environmental Protection Agency, 'Clean Air Act overview: benefits and costs of the Clean Air
    Act 1990–2020 the Second Prospective Study', 12 August 2021. https://www.epa.gov/clean-air-act-overview/
    benefits-and-costs-clean-air-act-1990–2020-second-prospective-study (accessed 1 August 2022).

61. United States Environmental Protection Agency, 'Clean Air Act overview'.

62. United States Environmental Protection Agency, 2021, 'Clean Air Act Overview'. Also note, the EPA states:
    'The EPA report received extensive review and input from the Council on Clean Air Compliance Analysis, an
    independent panel of distinguished economists, scientists and public health experts established by Congress
    in 1991.'

63. Federal Register, 'Part V Environmental Protection Agency 40 CFR Chapter 1', 15 December 2009. https://
    www.epa.gov/sites/default/files/2021–05/documents/federal_register-epa-hq-oar-2009–0171-dec.15–09.pdf
    (accessed 1 August 2022).

64. See Supreme Court, *West Virginia et al. versus the Environmental Protection Agency et al.*, October term 2021.
    https://www.supremecourt.gov/opinions/21pdf/20–1530_n758.pdf (accessed 3 November 2022).

65. Earthday.org, 'The history of Earth Day'.

66. Earthday.org, 'The history of Earth Day'.

67. E. Goodstein, K. Sheeran, P. Dorman, J. Laitner and J. Isham, 'Climate policy and jobs: an update on what
    economists know', Economics for Equity and Environment, June 2010.
    https://www.biologicaldiversity.org/programs/climate_law_institute/global_warming_litigation/clean_air
    _act/pdfs/Goodstein_2010.pdf (accessed 8 August 2022).

68. United States Environmental Protection Agency, 'The Clean Air Act and the Economy', 22 February 2022.
    https://www.epa.gov/clean-air-act-overview/clean-air-act-and-economy (accessed 8 August 2022).

69. Environmental Defense Fund, 'In demand: clean energy, sustainability and the new American work force',
    January 2018. http://edfclimatecorps.org/sites/edfclimatecorps.org/files/edf_in_demand_clean_energy
    _sustainability_and_the_new_american_workforce.pdf?_gl=1*1ryd1ab*_ga*MTg2MjQ4MjU3My4xNjU
    5OTk5NDEx*_ga_2B3856Y9QW*MTY1OTk5OTQxMC4xLjEuMTY1OTk5OTQyOC40Mg..*_ga
    _Q5CTTQBJD8*MTY1OTk5OTQxMC4xLjEuMTY1OTk5OTQyOC40Mg (accessed 8 August 2022).

70. B. Lefebvre, K. Tamborrino and J. Siegel, 'Historic climate bill to supercharge clean energy industry', *Politico*, 7 August 2022. https://www.politico.com/news/2022/08/07/inflation-reduction-act-climate-biden-00050230 (accessed 8 August 2022).

71. R.M. McManus, 'Toward an understanding of the relationship between the study of leadership and the natural world', in B.W. Redekop, D. Ringling Gallagher and R. Satterwhite (eds), *Innovation in Environmental Leadership: Critical Perspectives*, New York, Routledge, 2018, pp. 97–115.

72. See R.M. McManus and G. Perruci, 'Leadership in a Western cultural context', in *Understanding Leadership: An Arts and Humanities Perspective*, 2nd edn, New York, Routledge, 2020, pp. 87–102.

73. W. Fisher, 'A motive view of communication', *Quarterly Journal of Speech*, vol. 56 no. 2, 1970, 131–9.

74. L. Rehrmann, 'Top companies urge White House to stay in the Paris Agreement', Center for Climate and Energy Solutions, 26 April 2017. https://www.c2es.org/press-release/major-companies-urge-white-house-to-stay-in-paris-agreement/ and https://www.c2es.org/wp-content/uploads/2017/04/business-letter-white-house-paris-agreement-final-04-26-2017-1.pdf (accessed 10 August 2022).

75. Riordan, *A Grammar of the Common Good*, pp. 59–60.

76. IPCC, *Climate Change 2022: Impacts, Adaptation, and Vulnerability*. Contribution of Working Group II to the Sixth Assessment Report of the Intergovernmental Panel on Climate Change [H.-O. Pörtner, D.C. Roberts, M. Tignor, E.S. Poloczanska, K. Mintenbeck, A. Alegría, M. Craig, S. Langsdorf, S. Löschke, V. Möller, A. Okem and B. Rama (eds)]. Cambridge: Cambridge University Press, 2022. https://www.ipcc.ch/report/ar6/wg2/ (accessed 8 August 2022).

77. United States Environmental Protection Agency, 'Sources of greenhouse gas emissions', 5 August 2022. https://www.epa.gov/ghgemissions/sources-greenhouse-gas-emissions (accessed 8 August 2022).

78. J. Friedrich, M. Ge and A. Pickens, 'This interactive chart shows changes in the world's top 10 emitters', *World Resources Institute*, 10 December 2020. https://www.wri.org/insights/interactive-chart-shows-changes-worlds-top-10-emitters (accessed 8 August 2022).

79. Etizioni, *The Common Good*, p. 2.

# SECTION II

In Section II, we now move on to specific leadership models that seem to lend themselves well to discussions of ethics and leadership. While the Greater Good ethical model demonstrated itself to be equally concerned with all five components leadership, our next chapter will start with a consideration of authentic leadership – a model that is decidedly focused on the individual leader over the other four components.

Our chapters in this section will address Authentic Leadership, Servant Leadership, Followership, Transformational Leadership, Adaptive Leadership, and Toxic Leadership. As we progress through this material, readers will note an expanding circle of concern – moving from a focus on the individual leader and that leader's core values, to broader concerns about followers, goals, context, and larger cultural values and norms. All the leadership models here have implications for the five components, but as editors, we asked ourselves, 'What seems to receive the most attention if we use this leadership model as a lens for a particular leadership situation?' As we engage in case studies, readers will have the opportunity to reflect on examples from culture, business, and political engagement in multiple locations throughout the world.

# 13
# Authentic leadership

*Phyllis H. Sarkaria*

## FRAMING QUESTION

How can I lead with integrity?

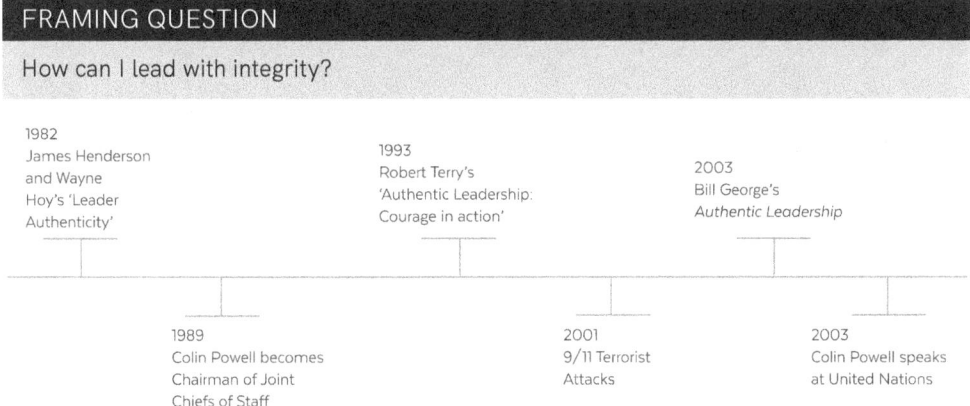

**Figure 13.1**   Timeline of major works on authentic leadership in relation to the chapter case study

Though relatively new compared to many other theories of leadership, the concept of authentic leadership has its origins in ancient Greece and Rome. Authenticity played a significant role in the teachings of early philosophers.[1] Shakespeare reflected their views in his play *Hamlet* when he penned the famous words for Polonius, 'To thine own self be true.' This statement highlights the importance of demonstrating one's ethics when leading and relating to others, yet it reflects only part of the concept of authentic leadership. Being 'authentic' – true to one's own personality, spirit, or character[2] – is not the same as being an authentic leader. Authentic leadership requires an understanding of self yet goes well beyond a focus that is 'all about me'. As time has passed, the idea of authentic leadership as a model for guiding and directing leaders has been refined.

In this chapter, we will examine the concept of authentic leadership. We will study the development of various theories and models relating to the idea, and focus on key concepts running throughout the literature on the topic, while introducing several of the scholars who have been pioneering the study of this approach to leadership. As we have done in previous chapters, we will then look at the critiques of authentic leadership and apply the Five

Components of Leadership Model to analyse the theory. We will end our time together with a case study that considers an internationally recognized military and political figure, former US Secretary of State Colin Powell.

Throughout the chapter, we will see how authentic leadership compels leaders to hold high ethical standards for their own behaviour, in the ways they relate to their followers, the means through which they pursue their goals, and the ways they influence the broader context surrounding them and the organizations in which they lead. In so doing, authentic leaders must be self-aware, practise balanced processing, maintain a personalized moral perspective, and seek transparency in their relationships with others. Perhaps the primary lesson we will learn in this chapter is that *truly* practising authentic leadership is challenging. Still, it is a worthy aspiration for leaders who want to set a high ethical bar for themselves and others.

## HISTORY

The contemporary study of authentic leadership can be traced back to 1982 when two researchers, James Henderson and Wayne Hoy, published findings on leadership authenticity, recognizing that social scientists had formerly focused more on the impact of *inauthentic* behaviour on organizations. They presented a perspective that authentic leaders accept responsibility for defining how leadership manifests itself because of who they are rather than allowing their title or position to determine *how they lead*.[3] Being guided by one's ethical core more than external forces is a fundamental premise of authentic leadership. The authors went on to develop a measure of authenticity based on statements that addressed, among other things, a leader's tendency to be more relational rather than operating 'by the book', a willingness to admit mistakes and acknowledge not having complete information, and acting in ways that were perceived as cooperative rather than manipulative. These common themes have subsequently continued to influence the literature on authentic leadership.[4]

A significant body of knowledge on authentic leadership was not explicitly developed for some time after Henderson and Hoy's work. Scholars Bruce Avolio, Fred Walumbwa, and Todd Weber recall the early years of the study of authentic leadership flowing from discussions of transformational leadership behaviours that were not necessarily genuine.[5] Other early researchers studying authentic leadership focused more on positive psychology and servant leadership, both of which share common elements with authentic leadership.[6] Servant and transformational leadership, discussed in more detail in Chapters 14 and 16, share some attributes with authentic leadership but have developed as specific and separate areas of leadership studies. Past research focuses more on the challenges of inauthentic behaviour and the benefits of positivity rather than measuring the impact of authenticity, a subtle but essential difference.

As a newer way of thinking about leadership, theories and models of authentic leadership are still being formed and defined. In 1993, Robert Terry described authenticity as 'action that is both *true* and *real* in *ourselves* and in the *world*'.[7] Terry underscored that action is at the heart of all leadership theories. For leadership to be authentic, he observed that self-knowledge and the context of the greater world in which the leader and the organization operate should factor into decisions on the appropriateness of specific actions. In his view, the intent is not sufficient to be authentic; a successful action is necessary. While these thoughts provided students of authentic leadership with some parameters to ponder, they also highlighted the challenges of defining authentic leadership because there are many subtleties and nuances to consider. In some ways, authentic leadership might be akin to how Supreme Court Justice Potter Stewart described pornography in his landmark 1964 opinion when he said, 'I know it when I see it.'[8] Indeed, authenticity can be as much about the followers' perception of the leader as it is about the internal motivations that drive the leader's behaviour.

Another decade passed before retired Medtronic CEO and Harvard Business School professor Bill George published a book titled *Authentic Leadership* that described the characteristics of authentic leaders.[9] George was concerned with an ethical gap he observed in corporate leadership after the failures of Enron, Arthur Anderson, WorldCom, and other large corporations. He felt it was necessary to highlight the organizational benefits of authentic leadership. More practical than theoretical, George's book brought the subject of authentic leadership out of the domain of academia and into the realm of popular thought. His ideas garnered widespread attention, leading to an interest in authentic leadership development programmes and further research into the impact of authentic leaders on their organizations and teams. Both academic and practitioner efforts, however, remained focused primarily on the ways authentic leaders influence their followers.

In 2005, *Leadership Quarterly* published a special issue that focused exclusively on authentic leadership.[10] Like Bill George's book, the *Leadership Quarterly* edition was published, at least in part, in response to concerns about corporate scandals derived from poor leadership and destructive business practices that ended up devastating employees, retirees, and investors.[11] Around this time, scholars began to define authentic leadership as requiring advanced moral development.[12] Building on transformational leadership and other leadership theories and models that emphasize ethics at their core, the definition of authentic leadership evolved to incorporate a distinctly ethical dimension.

Since that time, the theory of authentic leadership has continued to evolve. Some have questioned the validity of authentic leadership, arguing that it is aspirational to be authentic as a leader but that it may be an 'ideological, romantic version' of leadership.[13] Others have taken the position that the elements of the authentic leadership model are based on gender-biased views of leadership, resulting in women being seen as less authentic when they follow a similar model of leadership as men.[14] The ongoing debate regarding authenticity at work and how being authentic relates to authentic leadership has also heightened in the past decade and may create confusion around this leadership theory.

The ongoing discussion and development of authentic leadership are helpful to understand better this leader-centric theory that exists in relationship to others. William L. Gardner and his colleagues have contributed significantly to the further development of authentic leadership theory over the past decade and beyond. These scholars have observed that authentic leadership is an aspirational goal that leaders may work toward throughout their careers rather than a specific destination at which a leader arrives.[15] Studies of authentic leadership link its practice to positive results in organizations, making it attractive as a leadership theory.[16] At the same time, the theory has not yet matured. It continues to be assessed and augmented.

Now that we have a basic understanding of the history of authentic leadership and its ongoing evolution, let's look more closely at the foundational concepts of authentic leadership and how it is conceived today.

## MAJOR CONCEPTS OF AUTHENTIC LEADERSHIP

Like other models of leadership, authentic leadership seeks to identify the behaviours and traits that make leaders more effective. Authentic leadership shares some ideas with leader-centric models because self-awareness, understanding of one's values, and congruent behaviour are all critical aspects of the concept. Similar to transformational leadership, authentic leadership considers the traits and behaviours of leaders as they relate to and impact followers. The leader, follower, and context in which they interact are all inextricably intertwined.

With additional research and practical application of the concepts of authentic leadership, four primary attributes have come to define authentic leadership: awareness of self and others' perceptions of the leader; actively seeking information and alternative points of view before making decisions; consciously behaving in a way that is consistent with one's positive personal values; and acting transparently so that others see the congruence between the leader's actions and personal values.[17] These characteristics are closely related and interwoven. No single aspect is more important than another. Each influences an overall perception of authenticity and congruence between words and actions, contributing to the leader's credibility and trust.

### Self-awareness

Authentic leaders take time for reflection and seek to understand themselves and their motivations. Through heightened self-awareness, leaders can better regulate their actions and reactions, reducing impulsive, unpredictable behaviour and increasing trust and engagement within their work environment.[18] A number of graduate schools of business, including Harvard, Stanford, Dartmouth, and the University of Chicago, have identified self-awareness as a critical leadership capability that predicts effectiveness in managing others and success as a leader.[19] In fact, some suggest that self-awareness is more critical to leadership success than technical ability or intellect.[20] Self-aware leaders have a strong sense of identity and direction, whereas low self-awareness not only limits leaders but can 'impede organizational performance'[21] as those leaders make worse decisions, engaged in less coordination, and show less ability to manage conflict.[22] Nevertheless, self-awareness, while a crucial aspect of authentic leadership development, is not adequate on its own. Many skills and behaviours contribute to actual and perceived authenticity.[23] Knowing more about one's self is useful. How we behave in interactions with others ultimately demonstrates authenticity or lack thereof.

### Balanced Processing

By engaging in what the authentic leadership literature calls 'balanced processing', leaders demonstrate an openness to consider all relevant information objectively.[24] This behaviour demonstrates an unbiased interest in new ideas as the leader seeks out alternative views and opinions before making decisions. The idea is to consciously reflect on the information the leader may be lacking, recognizing that others may have vital insights from their perspective that the leader does not see. Balanced processing does not mean the authentic leader seeks to be proven wrong, but it does imply an openness to new ideas and information and a willingness to accept that the leader may not always be the one with all the answers. This humility leads us to consider authentic leadership's third common theme – the leader's values.

## Internalized Moral Perspective

Authentic leaders have a clear understanding of their values. They engage in introspection and actively seek to demonstrate these ideals to others. Authentic leaders draw upon a clear sense of purpose and 'inner system of belief'.[25] This begs the question, can a leader have clear but evil intent and still be considered authentic? Arguably by being clear as to what they stand for and transparent in their actions, it would be possible to be what one might call 'authentically evil'. However, the model that has evolved to define authentic leadership requires *positive* core values. Indeed, many scholars of authentic leadership believe an 'advanced level of moral development' is necessary for a leader to be truly authentic.[26] By understanding and communicating their values to others, authentic leaders can develop relational transparency with their followers.

## Relational Transparency

Authentic leaders are accountable for their actions, striving to be transparent in how their decisions and actions are consistent with their values. However, it is through their relationship with others that leaders can be perceived to be more or less authentic. Though leader-centric, the authentic leadership model highlights the interaction between the leader and followers as a measure of authenticity. Leaders who are self-aware and have clear motivations create greater transparency. The give-and-take in their relationships enhances this transparency, just as their openness to feedback influences their followers' perceptions of them and allows them to lead more authentically. Leaders cannot simply declare themselves authentic; instead, they must act in a way that others perceive as personifying their beliefs. Authentic leaders 'own' their successes *and* their mistakes, and they encourage followers to do the same. As Bill George has explained,

> Being authentic as a leader is hard work and takes years of experience in leadership roles. No one can be authentic without fail; everyone behaves inauthentically at times, saying and doing things they will come to regret. The key is to have the self-awareness to recognize these moments and listen to close colleagues who point them out.[27]

Engaging in these behaviours allows leaders to grow in wisdom and authenticity. This openness to feedback from followers also encourages more open communication because authentic leaders show through their actions that they value courageous followers that are willing to 'speak truth to power',[28] strengthening the bonds of trust and improving communication within their relationships. In this way, the authentic leadership model pairs well with the followership model discussed in Chapter 15.

Authentic leadership has been studied from different perspectives that all consider variations of these four core ideas. For example, Robert W. Terry identified 'seven Cs of authenticity', which include: consistency, concealment, correspondence, comprehensiveness, coherence, convergence, and conveyance.[29] Under Terry's model, leaders move from good intention to 'the embodiment of intention in the world',[30] acting in a way that matches words with actions and looks beyond a single action to consider how that decision will ripple through the organization. He cautions that authentic leaders must be mindful of the consequences of their actions and beware of rationalization, engaging in dialogue with followers to understand and gain greater insight, particularly when divergent opinions exist. Through openness to other perspectives, the leader can encourage the development of authenticity in followers by modelling appropriate behaviours and being receptive to the contributions of others. In such a way, authenticity is both given and received.

Bill George also framed authentic leadership in terms intended to be readily applicable by leaders. George identifies five dimensions of authenticity: purpose, values, relationships, self-discipline, and heart.[31] These dimensions are reflective of the four primary attributes mentioned above. George emphasizes that developing and applying these characteristics could result in a positive organizational culture, inferring that healthy cultures produce better outcomes than toxic cultures. Through this application of authenticity, leaders can connect with followers to increase follower engagement and loyalty to the common goal and organization. Even leaders who are hard on their followers can, through the same manner in which they challenge those individuals, convey that they are interested in the followers' success.[32]

More scholarly assessments have also echoed these four primary attributes.[33] One set of researchers determined that there was more to authentic leadership than 'being true to oneself' and sought to develop a tool for measuring behaviours and attitudes in the workplace.[34] The result of their research, the Authentic Leadership Questionnaire (ALQ), provided a validated measure for those seeking to be more authentic, classifying the characteristics under self-awareness, balanced processing, internalized moral perspective, and relational transparency. In many ways, these four measures have become the gold standard for assessing authentic leadership and providing a path for leadership development (Table 13.1).

**Table 13.1** Approaches to authentic leadership

| Seven Cs of authenticity (Terry, 1993) | Five dimensions of authenticity (George, 2003) | Authentic leadership questionnaire (Walumbwa et al., 2008) |
| --- | --- | --- |
| • Consistency | • Purpose | • Self-awareness |
| • Concealment | • Values | • Balanced processing |
| • Correspondence | • Relationships | • Internalized moral perspective |
| • Comprehensiveness | • Self-discipline | • Relational transparency |
| • Coherence | • Heart | |
| • Convergence | | |
| • Conveyance | | |

Authentic leadership has been defined in numerous ways. As research on the subject has matured, the definition of authentic leadership has emerged to reflect measures of self-awareness, balanced processing, internalized moral perspective, and relational transparency. Leaders who aspire to be more authentic in their work with others and seek to encourage new leaders to be more authentic can look to these measures to determine where growth opportunities exist. Further, scholars have suggested updates to the authentic leadership model to incorporate five processes by which authentic leaders influence positive follower outcomes.[35] These enhancements recognize that authentic behaviour by the leader alone is not sufficient to achieve positive results. Still, a higher level of scrutiny of authentic leadership brings to light the paradoxical nature of this model when moving from theory to application.

## CRITIQUES OF AUTHENTIC LEADERSHIP

There are a number of intervention-based training programmes available in the marketplace purporting to help organizations develop authentic leaders and assist individual leaders who wish to 'find' their authenticity.[36] Yet, as one scholar notes, 'there is little evidence-based research on whether these prescriptions or how-to strategies [are effective].'[37] Readings in the popular business press suggest that the term 'authentic leadership' is widely used but not necessarily well understood in the business world. Stanford professor of management Jeff Pfeffer has called authenticity 'misunderstood and overrated'.[38] Others have argued that the self-referential nature of authentic leadership makes it difficult, if not impossible, to know whether a person is acting in concert with their values.[39]

Experience with leaders who excuse poor behaviour through an 'excessive need to be me'[40] may turn individuals and organizations away from learning more about authentic leadership as a model for leadership. Further, the focus on authenticity has been mocked as damage control by corporations concerned about revelations of inappropriate leadership.[41] Comments like this tend to ignore the positive moral and ethical content that defines the character of authentic leadership.

Let us not confuse authenticity with authentic leadership. A leader might be true to himself and still not be an authentic leader. Boas Shamir and Galit Eilam tell the story of a junior military officer who had tried to influence a higher-ranking officer during wartime.[42] He failed, and the resulting action cost many in his unit their lives. Based on this experience and a sense that he should have pushed harder for a different result, the commander went on to justify unyielding and aggressive behaviour. He believed that had he been more forceful with his superior – more himself – lives might have been saved. The lessons he took from the experience convinced him that he had been right and should not compromise or accept alternative points of view. His inability to consider the situational nature of leadership caused him to be 'himself' in ways that were destructive to his relationships. Knowing one's self and acting accordingly does not excuse bad behaviour, narcissism, discriminatory acts, or a wide range of other poor leadership traits that may well represent a leader's true personality but are not 'authentic' as defined by authentic leadership theory. The misperception that authenticity is about being oneself without regard to moral values or self-control creates a challenge for those seeking to apply the authentic leadership model to their work as leaders. This tension to articulate what makes a leader 'real' could cause some to dismiss authentic leadership as non-substantive because of a lack of understanding.

It is also worth noting that women, people of colour, and others who approach leadership in non-traditional ways may be negatively impacted by expectations of gender and culturally specific behaviours within the work environment. For example, while men may be perceived positively when they exhibit characteristics consistent with transparency and vulnerability, women and others could be viewed as weak. This is a Catch-22 when norms in some workplaces continue to be defined by traditional white-male-dominated perspectives. Even the most diverse organizations are not always inclusive. Some argue that this reality ignores stereotypes that influence, often unconsciously, how individuals are perceived, reducing the potential effectiveness of authentic leadership as currently defined.[43]

Further, it has been observed that the inward-looking nature of authentic leadership theory's measure of self-awareness misses the opportunity to emphasize a strength often associated with a more feminine style of leadership: 'self in relation to others' rather than the individualized aspects of leadership.[44] As these differences are considered, the evolving nature of the authentic leadership model is beginning to acknowledge that authenticity is ultimately determined through the eyes of others rather than defined by the individual leader.

In addition to questions arising from greater awareness of diversity and inclusion, research over the past decade or more suggests that there is a clear moral component to authentic leadership.[45] Still, the connections have not been thoroughly studied to understand which values enhance authenticity. There could even be debate as to what constitutes a 'positive' purpose or value of a leader, and there remains some disagreement that pro-social behaviours are a requirement of authentic leadership.[46] While the measures contained in the ALQ[47] include high standards of ethical conduct, one might assert that an individual with nefarious goals who acts consistently with evil intent and inspires others to do the same is an authentic leader because of congruence between values and action. Such an argument, however, misses the insight into authentic leadership that the four primary attributes provide. These elements point to the need for a solid ethical core to engage in introspection and reflection to understand self and others. Even that perspective leaves open for discussion the question of whether authenticity is only evident in leaders with awareness, self-control, and accountability for living positive values.[48]

A potential dilemma is apparent in determining that positive values are a prerequisite of authentic leadership; however, the goal of the authentic leader is to be effective in relationships and interactions while still expressing the unique style and character that define her leadership.[49] Another way to think about this quandary is that it is not simply one particular act that matters, but rather the behaviours surrounding that act and the associated results within the larger context.[50]

Leaders who strive to be more authentic consistently scan the landscape of their relationships and results, learn from their experiences, and adjust as they move forward to increase alignment between values and outcomes. As these leaders gain insight into themselves, humility typically begins to play a more significant role in their interactions with others, further reflecting growth as a leader. While a desire for authenticity in relationships – work-related or otherwise – might be reason enough to focus on these areas for self-development, there are also specific ethical implications for the practice of authentic leadership. We now turn to consider the ethical implications of this theory more closely.

## ETHICAL IMPLICATIONS OF AUTHENTIC LEADERSHIP

Authentic leadership's emphasis on personal integrity and self-awareness carries an ethical implication for leaders as their followers look to them for guidance and direction. It is generally recognized that humans are fallible and perfect authenticity is not attainable;[51] however, when leaders endeavour to behave authentically, they are generally perceived as being more ethical, having more integrity, and being more trustworthy.[52] Researchers have identified a range of desirable outcomes when authentic leadership behaviours are demonstrated, including increased trust between leader and follower, greater follower work engagement, and improved well-being in the workplace. These results point, as well, to overall improved organizational performance.[53] This point is reinforced by scholars who have found a direct positive correlation between demonstrated self-awareness – an essential attribute of authentic leadership – and increased trust within organizations.[54] Transparent, authentic leaders can further increase trust when they seek others' input, disclose relevant information for decision-making, and reveal personal motives and thoughts that help others understand the positive moral and ethical development behind their words and actions.[55]

The perception of a leader as authentic creates a safe and trusting environment for followers to, in turn, be their authentic selves, thus creating a positive context for leaders and followers to work together.[56] Just as the presence of trust facilitates a positive culture, a lack of trust can cause followers to focus on self-protection instead of engaging with the leader to reach a common goal.[57] This self-protection may cause followers to justify poor behaviour or act unethically out of fear. Hence, authentic leadership may help create an ethical environment for leaders *and* followers where the 'right thing to do' is valued by all in the organization.

This brings us to the overall quality of relationships between all members of an organization. Thinking about these relationships provides more insight into how leaders can influence followers to reach their common goals.[58] Developing healthy, positive relationships through demonstrating authentic behaviours that reflect ethical congruence might point to ways that followers can support and influence one another when working together. While many underlying arguments of those studying authentic leadership are that authenticity leads to better performance,[59] the focus of authentic leadership has been primarily on positive impacts on individual followers, not necessarily on group dynamics. This is beginning to change. Recommended updates to the authentic leadership model suggest five specific actions that recognize the authentic leader's ability to inspire followers: serving as a positive behavioural role model; building connections with followers that enhance a feeling of belonging; bringing greater emotional positivity to interactions; facilitating follower efforts to achieve self-determination; and engaging in positive social exchanges that 'promote elevated levels of respect, positive affect, and trust';[60] though many of these influences may be extrapolated to broader results. As Bill George has noted, leaders who are open about their beliefs and willing to share their vulnerabilities empower their followers to ask for help and share their uncertainties in turn.[61] The openness and trust that flows from better knowledge of self and others that is congruent with a positive moral foundation can create a greater connection, leading to more ethical cultures and behaviour, thus strengthening team performance.[62] Additionally, ethical organizational cultures have been found to support authentic leadership development, further enhancing positive outcomes for leaders, followers, organizations, and their stakeholders.[63]

Increased trust, improved cooperation, and positive organizational culture would seem to suggest authentic leadership as an answer to many challenges that any organization may face. By applying the principles of authentic leadership to interactions with colleagues and within teams, one might assume similar positive organizational influences. This could be particularly impactful when the leadership team members demonstrate authenticity with one another.

## FIVE COMPONENT ANALYSIS

Greater clarity around what it means to be an authentic leader may be possible by stepping back to look beyond the leader-centric focus and consider the broader view within which leaders perform. Let's now examine authentic leadership using the Five Components of Leadership Model introduced in Chapter 1 (Figure 13.2). We will specifically concentrate on the first four elements of the model.

Authentic leadership theory begins with the individual leader who possesses a strong moral core and self-awareness and extends to what that leader brings to the followers, goals, context, and culture. This is reflected in how the leader's sense of self manifests through transparency and openness with followers. Because the authentic leader knows who she is and what she stands for, she is comfortable considering different points of view and is concerned with doing what is right for the people she leads.

Being authentic is not about perfection. Authentic leaders are fallible human beings. There is potential for any leader to disappoint followers or err in pursuit of a goal. Authentic

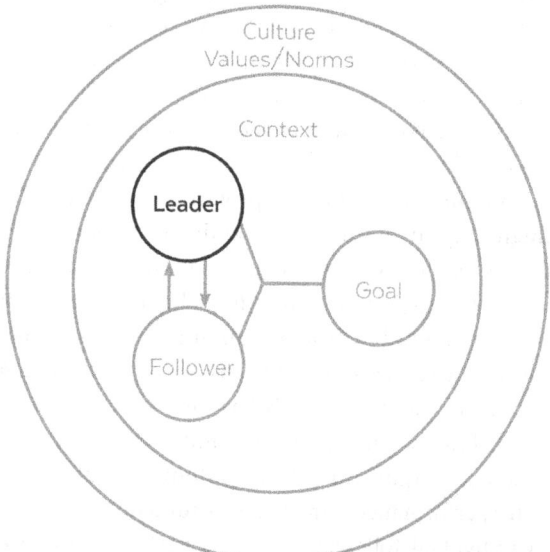

**Figure 13.2**   The Five Components of Leadership Model applied to authentic leadership

leaders genuinely desire to be better leaders, to connect with their followers, and to inspire positive outcomes. They recognize that no one is perfect, perhaps particularly themselves, and seek to improve themselves on an ongoing basis because of their sincere desire to live into their values.

Like servant and transformational leadership, there are explicitly ethical aspects of authentic leadership that exercise intrinsic influence on the leader and the leader's relationship with followers. Authenticity is not about following a formula for success but rather having a strong ethical core, aligning one's personal values with the organization's values, and sharing with followers how one's values are reflected in thought and action.

Such alignment is typically demonstrated externally through transparency and openness to new ideas. This behaviour allows leaders to work with followers in a unique partnership such that both leader and followers learn and grow. By modelling the attributes of authentic behaviour for followers, authentic leaders support the development of followers to become authentic in their interactions. Trust develops between leaders and followers to the benefit of the individuals and the organization as a whole, as authentic leaders foster the development of positive work environments that reflect their firm moral standards, transparency, and integrity.

From time to time, followers in any organization may feel pressure to 'do whatever it takes' to achieve a goal. Authentic leaders in such situations draw on knowledge of their values and awareness of their strengths and weaknesses to inspire others to deliver their best without compromising their ethics. This leads us to the way authentic leaders go about achieving goals.

There are challenges of 'knowing, showing, and remaining true to one's real self'[64] given pressures to conform and reach goals that, at times, seem unobtainable. Similarly, culture and environment can influence the ways these goals are achieved. Because authentic leader behaviour impacts organizational climate, authentic leaders can often affect goals, either directly or indirectly. The openness and transparency that exist between authentic leaders and their followers as they work toward goals worthy of their commitment are aspects of authentic leadership that can lead to more robust performance and better results.

Researchers have explored the impact of authenticity on team effectiveness and productivity, measuring a 59 per cent improvement in the performance of teams where leaders exhibit authentic behaviours.[65] Further, a study comparing the effect of authentic leadership and transformational leadership suggests that authentic leadership behaviours correlated with stronger group and organizational performance, showing greater influence over results relative to transformational leadership.[66] Yes, authentic leadership emphasizes a leader's values and ethics, and it also results in leaders and followers effectively achieving their goals.

A fundamental aspect of authentic leadership is the leader's ability and willingness to share feelings and information openly and appropriately. The authentic leader's actions and followers' perception of the leader's authenticity serves as a stimulus to the organizational climate and cultural norms. As organizations strive to lean into diversity and inclusion goals, the ability of all leaders and followers to be more genuine and transparent in their interactions will be a welcome progression. Situations faced by the leader and how the leader responds will continue to reflect the values and norms of leadership. Actions send a strong signal to followers as to what is and is not acceptable behaviour in the organization.

All organizations evolve to a certain extent. Within the organizational evolution, leaders may exercise positive influence to guide the culture. Authentic leaders help craft meaningful goals that support the aspirational culture and environment that develops as the organization's purpose is identified and pursued. Over time, transparency and trust demonstrated by the authentic leader can become the norm, and a healthy climate for accomplishing great things can evolve within the organization. As authentic leaders influence and are influenced by followers in the definition and pursuit of goals, they provide an example that can positively impact the immediate context and organizational culture.

Authentic leadership reflects the process through which leadership occurs and recognizes that leaders are continually developing and seeking to improve. As a result, the perception of authenticity may vary depending on the context or follower. A leader is not viewed as 'authentic' simply because she is determined to be so. The interconnected nature of leadership embodies how the environmental aspects of context exercise influence – and are influenced by – the leader's authenticity.

Challenges to the authentic leadership model and discussion of the five components of leadership as it pertains to authentic leadership exemplify the influence that leaders can have beyond those they directly lead, particularly when they are highly visible public figures. How leaders handle themselves in stressful situations can demonstrate integrity to moral principles and increase trust and credibility with constituents, or the leader's actions can come across as selfish and a poor model of leadership. Leaders may be considered either unifying or polarizing, depending on a particular follower's relationship with the leader. This raises the question of how some might see leaders as authentic while others view them negatively.

Considering the five components of leadership in a specific context is one way to test the defined boundaries of the authentic leadership model. Turning now to our case study, we will examine one such individual who rose to prominence through consistency and clarity of purpose and mission. He possessed a sincere commitment to personal values, aligned with the values and ideals of his country. This leader set an example of positive, authentic leadership through his words and actions. In a defining moment of his career, however, did he represent the self-aware, balanced, moral leader, or did he succumb to political pressure and lose his way?

## CASE STUDY: COLIN POWELL AND THE US DECISION TO INVADE IRAQ

Colin Powell lived to serve his nation. A dedicated professional soldier, diplomat, public servant, and philanthropist, Powell rose from modest circumstances to wield incredible influence on both the national and international stage. Born in New York to Jamaican immigrants, by his own admission he was not a particularly good student.[67] Enrolment in a Reserve Officer Training Corps (ROTC) programme during college gave him purpose, and he found inspiration and direction in the clearly defined goals and discipline of military life. Powell served two tours of duty in Vietnam and was injured in that conflict. Despite disillusionment about how the Vietnam War was handled, he pursued a career in the military, committed to influencing positive change from within.

Powell rose quickly through the ranks, recognized as a strong and capable leader. Whether interacting with the lowliest private in the army or with the senior-most levels of the government, he brought a distinctive ethic to his work that served the needs of his followers in keeping with his positive purpose, values, and mission. He has often been considered an excellent role model, demonstrating self-awareness and seeking others' ideas and input. He acted according to his values and openly discussed his values with those with whom he worked. At Powell's memorial, his long-time colleague and friend,

Richard Armitage, spoke of his boss with love and respect. Armitage observed that Colin Powell was a leader who viewed his role as being in service to others. He recalled Powell reminding his team that 'we all need to treat everyone with a little more kindness than we think they deserve because we don't know what's going on in their lives.'[68] This empathy and openness were consistent with Powell's moral perspective. His actions as a leader also incorporated many of the processes that encourage authentic followership: reaching out to those under his direction, even several levels lower, to understand their experience and perspective; connecting team members to the organizational identity and mission; developing followers' abilities to address moral challenges properly; and supporting the connection between behaviour at work and each person's sense of self.[69]

Serving more than 40 years in public life, Powell was the youngest one-star general at the time he attained that rank. He was also the youngest Chairman of the Joint Chiefs of Staff when named to the role. He achieved many other 'firsts' during his career. Rising through the ranks of the United States Army to the position of four-star general, Powell was named national security adviser under President Ronald Reagan, the first African American to hold the position. Under President George H.W. Bush, he was the first black Chairman of the Joint Chiefs of Staff and the youngest to serve in that role. He was also the first black Secretary of State, appointed by President George W. Bush.

Powell was committed to giving his country his best in these roles. He has been lauded for caring for those in his command and praised for a clear alignment between his values and actions. After retirement from military service, he focused on new ways to lead others consistent with his values. Powell got involved with the non-profit America's Promise, preparing new generations for leadership by building confidence and character in young people. The values he lived, supported by the message that a person's attitude is something they choose, came to be known as 'Powell's 13 Rules of Leadership':[70]

1. It ain't as bad as you think. It will look better in the morning.
2. Get mad, then get over it.
3. Avoid having your ego so close to your position that when your position falls, your ego goes with it.
4. It can be done.
5. Be careful what you choose: You may get it.
6. Don't let adverse facts stand in the way of a good decision.
7. You can't make someone else's choices. You shouldn't let someone else make yours.
8. Check small things.
9. Share credit.
10. Remain calm. Be kind.
11. Have a vision. Be demanding.
12. Don't take counsel of your fears or naysayers.
13. Perpetual optimism is a force multiplier.

Colin Powell's alignment between values and behaviours was a defining characteristic throughout his military and public service career. He was transparent about his faith, family's importance, and character's significance – actively seeking to do the 'right' thing. In a mid-career review of Powell's work, the Major General credited Powell with substantially raising morale and bringing care to his work, generating a sense of pride and common loyalty among those under his command.[71] Still, Powell saw himself as imperfect and continually strove to improve. His son, Michael, has spoken of his father's emphasis on the significance of humility and mutual respect. Michael recounted that his father had a genuine curiosity and interest in everyone he met, regardless of their level or station in life.[72] When his son followed him into public service and dealt with substantial challenges as chairman of the FCC, Powell encouraged Michael to push through the difficulties, recognizing that 'public service comes at a cost, if you are committed to doing the right thing'.[73]

The cost of public service was a price that Colin Powell experienced himself while serving as Secretary of State for the administration of George W. Bush. During confirmation hearings for Powell's appointment as Secretary of State, then-Senator Joe Biden recognized Powell's positive leadership. Biden referenced appreciation of the military who had benefited from Powell's service as Chairman of the Joint Chiefs of Staff, as well as the hopeful sense of those at the State Department who looked forward to having him in charge. Biden went on to observe, 'We know that when you tell us something, you mean it. We also know that you are very deft at not telling us what you do not want us to hear,' referring to Powell's 'legendary capability of being closed mouth'.[74] Powell responded, 'I promise that I will argue with you, I will debate with you, as I did in the past, but it will always be in the best spirit of cooperation to make sure we get the right answer for the American people.'[75] Throughout his prepared remarks, Powell espoused his commitment to values that supported democracy, fair and open trade, and commitment to collaboration towards a better relationship with the rest of the world.

Less than a year after his confirmation by the Senate in early 2001, the United States was violently attacked by terrorists through orchestrated events that would come to be known by the date they occurred, 9/11. With global sympathy and support for the USA high, the Bush administration prepared to invade Afghanistan in search of Osama bin Laden and the al-Qaeda terrorist organization he led. This was the terrorist organization responsible for the horrendous attacks on US soil. Colin Powell's military expertise and diplomatic prowess were crucial for developing the administration's position. However, he quickly found himself at odds with others in the Bush cabinet who sought to expand military action beyond Afghanistan and into Iraq.

Members of the Bush administration argued that Iraqi president Saddam Hussein was harbouring terrorists and developing weapons capabilities that were a threat to world stability. Powell counselled the president on the serious consequences of military action and expressed concern that non-military options had not been fully considered.[76] Nevertheless, when findings presented by US intelligence officials seemed to show the existence of weapons of mass destruction in Iraq, it was Secretary of State Powell who agreed to make a case for war at the United Nations (UN). Powell was unsuccessful in convincing the UN Security Council to back the United States in removing these suspected lethal weapons from Iraq. However, his words, and the conviction with which he offered them, rallied public support among Americans.

The USA invaded Iraq, captured and executed Hussein, and settled in for a long-term occupation of the country. Weapons of mass destruction were never found, and the intelligence community later debunked all prior claims. Powell's reputation was damaged, and his credibility among world leaders was called into question. Eventually, it was discovered that he had been misled and, perhaps, exploited precisely because of his character and trustworthiness.[77] This experience left Powell disillusioned. He left office at the end of Bush's first term, later referring to his appearance at the UN as a painful stain on his record.[78] Though he periodically used his stature and influence to support efforts he felt were aligned with his values, for the most part, Powell turned away from public life and focused on charitable efforts and family time.

## FIVE COMPONENT ANALYSIS

Examined using the Five Components of Leadership Model, Colin Powell seems to exemplify the measures of authentic leadership. Nevertheless, he was instrumental in swaying public opinion to support a war later determined to be unjustified. Examining more closely his role in moving the United States towards war in Iraq, we consider how his authenticity impacted the result. Was he unable to exhibit authentic leadership because the culture in which he operated limited his effectiveness?[79] Maybe he truly believed the intelligence reports and felt this was the best course forward. Or perhaps Powell was simply a fallible human being. Regardless of whether or not he was an authentic leader – which we will take up further in a moment – Colin Powell strongly influenced his followers, the goals they set together, the context in which those goals were pursued, and the culture that thrived under his leadership.

Our five-component analysis starts with the individual leader – Colin Powell (Figure 13.3). We then identify those he wished to influence – both US and international leaders. His goal was to influence decisions related to a growing consensus in the US executive branch about going to war in Iraq. The context of his work was the emotionally charged period shortly after 11 September 2001, when the United States experienced a terrorist attack with an even greater mortality rate than that of Pearl Harbor.[80] Among his personal values was a loyalty to the administration, which influenced how he addressed his responsibilities in the post 9/11 environment. The following paragraphs will consider this in detail.

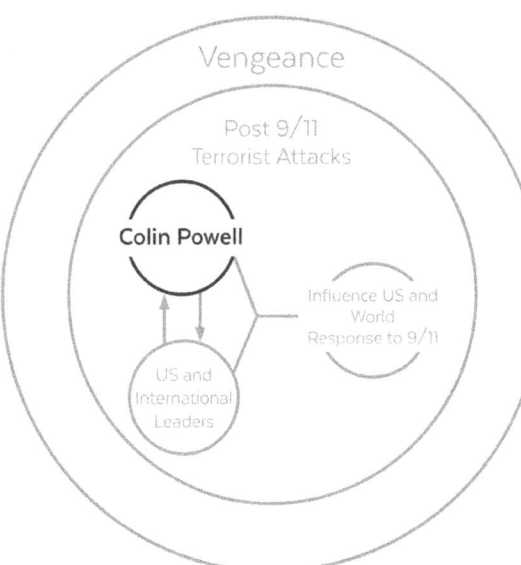

**Figure 13.3**  The Five Components of Leadership Model applied to the Colin Powell case study

Authentic leadership argues that leaders should act ethically while serving the needs of their followers in keeping with the leader's positive purpose, values, and mission. As already noted, introspection is required of authentic leaders to understand themselves. Interactions between leaders and followers impact their relationships. The authentic leader exercises influence on goals, the environment, and the overall culture. Ultimately, the authentic leader is accountable for the kind of culture that develops under his direction. Let's examine Powell a bit deeper in light of authentic leadership and the Five Components Model.

Though leader-centric, the authentic leadership model reflects leadership characteristics that recognize the interactive nature of the leader within the organizational culture as he relates with followers. Clarity of purpose and sufficient self-awareness to transparently work with and enable others to reach great heights reflect the leader's authenticity. Authentic leaders continually seek to do 'what's right for their constituency',[81] developing relationships that encourage others to be similarly ethically congruent, transparent, and balanced in decision-making and interactions.

Authentic leaders typically seek to understand their motivations to reduce unpredictable behaviour and appropriately share this self-knowledge with their followers. Knowing themselves and their inspiration allows these leaders to be more 'real' with followers. Throughout his career, those who worked in the organizations that Powell led saw him as worthy of their respect and loyalty. In these ways, he was clearly authentic as a leader.

Colin Powell had a reputation for humility and thoughtful consideration of many perspectives. He was viewed as highly credible because of the manner in which he interacted with people at all levels. Authentic leaders consider the means by which a goal is achieved. Even as he took on advocacy for invading Iraq, Powell repeatedly urged President Bush and his colleagues to fully consider non-military options before striking. He actively sought others' ideas and opinions. However, when presented with conflicting reports between the CIA and his own State Department, he chose to accept information that had been in the president's State of the Union address.[82]

Authentic leadership theory addresses the influence of authenticity on positive organizational outcomes, yet a leader can be authentic and still not achieve the 'right' results. Even the best leaders are still flawed humans.[83] How an authentic leader responds when faced with adverse outcomes attributable to his or her actions may further demonstrate that leader's authenticity. Powell's decisions were consistent with his values. He moved forward, believing the information he had been provided, and put his credibility on the line. Afterward, he was accountable for his actions, readily expressing regret and seeking to demonstrate greater alignment of values and actions.[84]

The authentic leader does not pretend to have the 'right' answers but instead continues to pursue answers that should have the most favourable long-term result for the organization (or government), adjusting and learning along the way. Powell shared this philosophy in his memoir:

No good idea succeeds simply because it is a good idea. Good ideas must have champions – people willing to believe in them, push for them, fight for them, gain adherents and other champions, and press until they succeed ... Bad ideas don't die simply because they are intrinsically bad. You need people who will stand up and fight them, put themselves at risk, point out the weaknesses, and drive stakes through their hearts.[85]

As Powell's '13 Rules' indicate, he believed strongly in sharing credit but was not one to publicly air dirty laundry. Perhaps he felt he had put himself at risk and pointed out weaknesses with respect to the invasion of Iraq. He may have wished that he had done more to 'drive a stake through the heart' of the plan. The misplaced loyalty to the goals of the administration he served resulted in greater influence on him than he was able to exercise on others at that moment. Some argue that Powell's loyalty undermined his effectiveness.[86] However, Colin Powell had a clear and consistent message on leadership throughout his career in the military and government. His words and actions were aligned with his moral compass, and he sought others' input rather than go it alone. These are crucial elements of authentic leadership.

Though Powell may be remembered by many as the person who falsely advocated for the invasion of a sovereign nation, he was open about his role in the Iraq debacle afterward, expressing regret that his instincts had failed him. The element of trust that was placed in him by US allies because of his authenticity worked against him in that case. Only in retrospect do we understand that Powell's moral compass led him to pursue private conversations with the president and others, arguing mightily for reason and care before taking action that would have far-reaching consequences.[87]

As Colin Powell turned to life as a private citizen, he continued to reflect on and write about his firmly held beliefs. Powell acknowledged that he was fallible and, as a man of faith, believed in grace. Through his stories of failure, perseverance, and learning, Powell continually demonstrated his fundamental efforts to align actions with values. This is, indeed, in keeping with the relational transparency and internalized moral perspective that are hallmarks of authentic leadership. Nevertheless, our case study highlights the fact that there are many factors at play in the process of leadership, and even the most authentic leader may not always be able to achieve their goal.

## SUMMARY AND CONCLUDING REMARKS

This chapter on authentic leadership began with the query: 'How can I lead with integrity?' Answering this question is the first step to becoming an authentic leader. As a first step, authentic leaders engage in self-examination and clarify those core values. By taking action in a way consistent with those values, they show integrity as a leader. Socrates taught that the unexamined life is not worth living. The authentic leader embraces examination of self and understanding of her authenticity; however, being 'real' is not sufficient on its own. Authentic leaders are not pursuing status or 'image' or focused on creating a specific persona. Rather, developing self-awareness grounded in a clear understanding of the moral fibre of one's self enables the leader to consciously act in ways that demonstrate the values that she holds dear.

So, 'How can I lead with integrity?' Authentic leadership goes beyond the leader's good intentions and requires combining intention and action to match the values of the organization where the leader works. For this to happen, leaders must engage in self-reflection, be open to other points of view, serve as positive role models, and invite followers to speak up when they believe the leader is not acting according to their publicly stated values. Ultimately, the true test of authentic leadership comes when a leader is under significant pressure. Such stress can help leaders clarify core values and test their faithfulness to those values, promoting the practice of authentic leadership.

## DISCUSSION QUESTIONS

1. Considering all aspects of authentic leadership, is an ethical component necessary to be an authentic leader? In other words, do you think it is possible to act congruently with a corrupt value system and still be considered an authentic leader? Why or why not?

2. Take a few minutes to reflect on your values. What value most clearly defines who you are and how you behave?

3. Considering the four major components of authentic leadership, which is most natural for you to demonstrate, and which do you find most challenging?

4. What accomplishment are you most proud of? Where have you 'blown it'? As you think about these two questions, consider how often you reflect on your actions and how frequently you ask others for feedback. How might engaging in greater self-reflection and increased pursuit of feedback improve your leadership?

5. How do we recognize 'authentic' leaders? Likewise, how do we respond to 'authentic' leaders who embrace values with which we disagree?

6. Much of the research into authentic leadership addresses the influence of authenticity on positive organizational outcomes. However, it is possible for a leader to be authentic and still not achieve the 'right' results. How might an authentic leader respond when faced with adverse outcomes attributable to his or her actions?

## ADDITIONAL RESOURCES

E.C. Dierdorff and R.S. Rubin, 'Research: we're not very self-aware, especially at work', *Harvard Business Review*, 12 March 2015.

This resource provides a succinct analysis of authenticity in the workplace.

W.L. Gardner, B.J. Avolio and F.O. Walumbwa (eds), *Authentic Leadership Theory and Practice: Origins, Effects and Development*, Bingley: Emerald Group Publishing, 2005.

This is a rich resource regarding the study of authentic leadership written for a scholarly audience.

B. George, *Discover Your True North*, Hoboken, NJ: John Wiley & Sons, 2015 and N. Craig, B. George and S. Snook, *The Discover Your True North Fieldbook: A Personal Guide to Finding Your Authentic Leadership*, Hoboken, NJ: John Wiley & Sons, 2015.

Bill George's updated guide for identifying purpose in leadership, along with the companion field book, are helpful for leaders interested in taking additional steps to become more authentic.

M. Heffernan, *Beyond Measure: The Big Impact of Small Changes*, New York: Simon & Schuster/ TED Books, 2015.

While not explicitly about authentic leadership, this book is a wealth of ideas and exercises for leaders who seek to increase their self-awareness, effectiveness, and connection with followers.

# NOTES

1.  For a history of the concept of authenticity, see S. Harter, 'Authenticity', in C.R. Snyder and S. Lopez (eds), *Handbook of Positive Psychology*, Oxford: Oxford University Press, 2002, pp. 382-94. Greek and Roman influences on authenticity are also mentioned in R. Riggio, 'What is authentic leadership? Do you have it?', *Psychology Today*, 22 January 2014. https://www.psychologytoday.com/blog/cutting-edge-leadership/ 201401/what-is-authentic-leadership-do-you-have-it (accessed 14 November 2021).

2.  *Merriam-Webster.com Dictionary*, s.v. 'authentic'. https://www.merriam-webster.com/dictionary/authentic (accessed 14 November 2021).

3.  J.E. Henderson and W.K. Hoy, 'Leader authenticity: the development and test of an operational measure', paper presented at the annual meeting of the American Educational Research Association, New York, 19-23 March 1982. http://files.eric.ed.gov/fulltext/ED219408.pdf (accessed 14 November 2021).

4.  This influence occurred despite Henderson and Hoy's authenticity assessment not being validated to confirm that it measured what it purported to measure.

5.  B.J. Avolio, F.O. Walumbwa and T.J. Weber, 'Leadership: current theories, research, and future directions', *Annual Review of Psychology*, vol. 60, 2009, 421-49.

6.  For more information, see P.A. Duignan and N. Bhindi, 'Authenticity in leadership: an emerging perspective', *Journal of Educational Administration*, vol. 35 no. 3, 1997, 195-209; and F. Luthans and B.J. Avolio, 'Authentic leadership: a positive developmental approach', in K.S. Cameron, J.E. Dutton and R.E. Quinn (eds), *Positive Organizational Scholarship: Foundations of a New Discipline*, San Francisco, CA: Berrett-Koehler, 2003, pp. 241-58.

7.  R. Terry, *Authentic Leadership: Courage in Action*, San Francisco, CA: Jossey-Bass, 1993, pp. 111-12. Emphasis in the original.

8.  378 US at 197 (Stewart, J., concurring).

9.  See also George's *True North* (2007), which expands on the concepts in *Authentic Leadership* (2003) with a focus on developing a personal leadership plan to be more authentic.

10. B.J. Avolio and W.L. Gardner, 'Authentic leadership development: getting to the root of positive forms of leadership', *The Leadership Quarterly*, vol. 16 no. 3, June 2005, 315-494. This special edition of *Leadership Quarterly* included Avolio and Gardner (2005), Cooper, Scandura, and Schriesheim (2005), and Gardner, Avolio, Luthans, May and Walumbwa (2005).

11. See D. Ackman, 'Worldcom, Tyco, Enron – RIP', *Forbes*, 1 July 2002. https://www.forbes.com/2002/07/01/ 0701topnews.html (accessed 14 November 2021).

12. See W. Gardner, B. Avolio and F. Walumbwa, 'Authentic leadership development: emergent trends and future directions', in W.L. Gardner, B.J. Avolio and F.O. Walumbwa (eds), *Authentic Leadership Theory and Practice: Origins, Effects, and Development*, Oxford: Elsevier Science, 2005, pp. 387-406. The authors pointed

out that leaders need a strong ethical core to engage in the introspection and reflection necessary to truly understand themselves and others.

13. See M. Alvesson and K. Einola, 'Warning for excessive positivity: authentic leadership and other traps in leadership studies', *The Leadership Quarterly*, vol. 30 no. 4, August 2019, 383–95.

14. See M.M. Hopkins and D.A. O'Neil, 'Authentic leadership: application to women leaders', *Frontiers in Psychology*, 15 July 2015. https://www.frontiersin.org/articles/10.3389/fpsyg.2015.00959/full (accessed 14 November 2021). N. Mantler, 'Women's authentic leadership development', *Integral Review*, vol. 16 no. 1, 2021, 215–24 also explores this topic in more detail.

15. See W.L. Gardner, E.P. Karam, M. Alvesson and K. Einola, 'Authentic leadership theory: the case for and against', *The Leadership Quarterly*, vol. 32. no. 6, December 2021. https://www.sciencedirect.com/science/article/pii/S1048984318307896 (accessed 17 September 2021).

16. See. E.P. Karam, W.L. Gardner, D.P. Gullifor, L.L. Tribble and M. Li, 'Authentic leadership and high-performance human resource practices: implications for work engagement', *Personnel and Human Resources Management*, vol. 35, 2017, 103–53, which outlines positive organizational outcomes of 'trust, work engagement, and workplace well-being' in greater detail (pp. 177–220). Further, Gardner et al., 'Authentic leadership theory', p. 15 describes 'desirable work outcomes including follower trust, leader and follower well-being, job satisfaction, employee voice, organizational commitment, work engagement, empowerment, organizational citizenship behavior, and employee, team, and organizational performance'.

17. See F.O. Walumbwa, B.J. Avolio, W.L. Gardner, T.S. Wernsing and S.J. Peterson, 'Authentic leadership: development and validation of a theory-based measure', *Journal of Management*, vol. 34 no. 1, 2008, 89-126. While included by numerous early scholars of authentic leadership in one form or another, the four primary attributes of authentic leadership are drawn primarily from the research and conclusions of Walumbwa et al. that resulted in the creation of a validated assessment of authentic leadership.

18. The following sources highlight the importance of self-awareness not for the sole purpose of being oneself but to promote alignment between the leader's values, feelings, thoughts, and behaviours. See M. Bamford, C.A. Wong and H. Laschinger, 'The influence of authentic leadership and areas of worklife on work engagement of registered nurses', *Journal of Nursing Management*, vol. 21 no. 3, 2012, 529-40; C.D. Cooper, T. Scandura and C.A. Schriesheim, 'Looking forward but learning from our past: potential challenges to developing authentic leadership theory and authentic leaders', *The Leadership Quarterly*, vol.16 no. 3, 2005, 475-93; Gardner et al., 'Authentic leadership development'; W. Gardner, C. Cogliser, K. Davis and M. Dickens, 'Authentic leadership: a review of the literature and research agenda', *The Leadership Quarterly*, vol. 22 no. 6, December 2011, 1120-45; and B. Tate, 'A longitudinal study of the relationships among self-monitoring, authentic leadership, and perceptions of leadership', *Journal of Leadership & Organizational Studies*, vol. 15 no. 1, 2008, 16-29.

19. See M. Showry and K.V.L. Manasa, 'Self-awareness – key to effective leadership', *IUP Journal of Soft Skills*, vol. 8 no. 1, March 2014, 15-26.

20. Showry and Manasa, 'Self-awareness'.

21. Showry and Manasa, 'Self-awareness', 23.

22. E.C. Dierdorff and R.S. Rubin, 'Research: we're not very self-aware, especially at work', *Harvard Business Review*, 12 March 2015.

23. C. Peus, J.S. Wesche, B. Streicher, S. Braun and D. Frey, 'Authentic leadership: an empirical test of its antecedents, consequences, and mediating mechanisms', *Journal of Business Ethics*, vol. 107 no. 3, 2012, 334-48.

The authors address the complex connection between self-awareness and other skills and behaviours in achieving authentic leadership.

24. For more information on balanced processing, see B. Avolio, W. Gardner, F. Walumbwa, F. Luthans and D. May, 'Unlocking the mask: a look at the process by which authentic leaders impact follower attitudes and behaviors', *The Leadership Quarterly*, vol. 15 no. 6, 2004, 801–23; B.J. Avolio, F.O. Walumbwa and C Zimmerman, 'Authentic leadership theory, research and practice: steps taken and steps that remain', in D. Day (ed.), *Oxford Handbook of Leadership and Organizations*, Oxford: Oxford University Press, 2014, pp. 331–56; Gardner et al., 'Authentic leadership development'; and Gardner et al., 'Authentic leadership'.

25. T. Pearce, *Leading Out Loud: Inspiring Change Through Authentic Communication*, San Francisco, CA: Jossey-Bass, 2003, p. 10.

26. Walumbwa et al., 'Authentic leadership: development and validation', 93.

27. B. George, 'The truth about authentic leaders', *Harvard Business School: Working Knowledge*, July 2016 [Web Log]. http://hbswk.hbs.edu/item/the-truth-about-authentic-leaders (accessed 14 November 2021).

28. For more information on the value of courageous followers to leaders, see I. Chaleff, *The Courageous Follower: Standing Up To and For Our Leaders*, San Francisco, CA: Berrett-Koehler, 2009.

29. See Terry, *Authentic Leadership*.

30. Terry, *Authentic Leadership*, p. 224.

31. B. George, *Authentic Leadership: Rediscovering the Secrets to Creating Lasting Value*, San Francisco, CA: Jossey-Bass, 2003.

32. B. George, 'Leadership styles: becoming an authentic leader', 28 August 2015 [Web Log]. http://www.billgeorge.org/page/leadership-styles-becoming-an-authentic-leader (accessed 14 November 2021).

33. For a more detailed examination of authentic leadership scholarship, see Avolio et al., 'Unlocking the mask'; B. Avolio and W. Gardner, 'Authentic leadership development: getting to the root of positive forms of leadership', *The Leadership Quarterly*, vol. 16 no. 3, 2005, 315–38; Cooper et al., 'Looking forward but learning'; Gardner et al., 'Authentic leadership development'; and Avolio et al., 'Authentic leadership theory'.

34. F.O. Walumbwa, B.J. Avolio, W.L Gardner, T.S. Wernsing and S.J. Peterson, 'Authentic leadership: development and validation of a theory-based measure', *Journal of Management*, vol. 34 no. 1, 2008, 89–126.

35. Karam et al., 'Authentic leadership and high-performance human resource practices', 112–16.

36. Course offerings range widely from training presented by organizations like The Authentic Leadership Institute to Harvard University. See http://www.authleadership.com and http://www.exed.hbs.edu/programs/ald/.

37. P.G. Northouse, *Leadership: Theory and Practice*, 7th edn, Los Angeles, CA: Sage, 2016, p. 208.

38. J. Pfeffer, *Leadership BS: Fixing Workplaces and Careers One Truth at a Time*, New York: HarperCollins, 2015, p. 85.

39. Alvesson & Einola, 'Warning for excessive positivity'.

40. For an excellent discussion of things leaders should stop doing to improve their leadership, see M. Goldsmith, *What Got You Here Won't Get You There*, New York: Hyperion, 2007, pp. 96–8.

41. E. Guthey and B. Jackson, 'CEO portraits and the authenticity paradox', *Journal of Management Studies*, vol. 42 no. 5, 2005, 1057–82.

42. B. Shamir and G. Eilam, 'What's your story?': a life-stories approach to authentic leadership development', *The Leadership Quarterly*, vol. 16 no. 3, 2005, 395–417.

43. Hopkins and O'Neil, 'Authentic leadership: application to women leaders'.

44. Hopkins and O'Neil, 'Authentic leadership: application to women leaders'.

45. See especially Gardner et al., 'Authentic leadership development'; and Walumbwa et al., 'Authentic leadership'.

46. Gardner et al., 'Authentic leadership theory'.

47. Walumbwa et al., 'Authentic leadership'.

48. While positive moral development has become a recognized measure of authentic leadership, Shamir and Eilam exclude morality, alternately defining authentic leaders as having a high level of integrity between belief and action. However, without a moral component, unethical leaders or those with nefarious goals could possibly manipulate perceptions of authenticity. See Shamir and Eilam, 'What's your story?'.

49. Gardner et al., 'Authentic leadership'.

50. Terry, who puts action at the heart of all leadership theories, explores the alignment of values and outcomes for authentic leaders in more detail. See Terry, *Authentic Leadership*.

51. Gardner et al., 'Authentic leadership theory'.

52. For more detail, see K.H. Mhatre, 'Rational persuasion and attitude change: the impact of perceived leader authenticity and perceived leader ability on target outcomes', doctoral dissertation, 2009, available from ABI/INFORM Global (Order No. 3355629).

53. Karam et al., 'Authentic leadership and high-performance human resource practices', 117–20 outlines positive organizational outcomes of 'trust, work engagement, and workplace well-being' in greater detail; while Gardner et al., 'Authentic leadership theory', 15 describe 'desirable work outcomes including follower trust, leader and follower well-being, job satisfaction, employee voice, organizational commitment, work engagement, empowerment, organizational citizenship behavior, and employee, team, and organizational performance.' For more on trust and team performance, see S. Ozham and A. Ceylan, 'Collective efficacy as a mediator of the relationship between authentic leadership and well-being at work', *International Business Research*, vol. 9 no. 6, March 2016, 17–30; B. Avolio, W. Gardner, F. Walumbwa, F. Luthans and D. May, 'Unlocking the mask: a look at the process by which authentic leaders impact follower attitudes and behaviors', *The Leadership* Quarterly, vol. 15 no. 6, 2004, 801–23; W. Zhu, D.R. May and B.J. Avolio, 'The impact of ethical leadership behavior on employee outcomes: the roles of psychological empowerment and authenticity', *Journal of Leadership and Organizational Studies*, vol. 11 no. 1, 2004, 16–26; M. Higgs and D. Rowland, 'Emperors with clothes on: the role of self-awareness in developing effective change leadership', *Journal of Change Management*, vol. 10 no. 4, December 2010, 369–85; S.M. Norman, B.J. Avolio and F. Luthans, 'The impact of positivity and transparency on trust in leaders and their perceived effectiveness', *Leadership Quarterly*, vol. 21 no. 3, 2010, 350–64; and S. Simsarian Webber, 'Leadership and trust facilitating cross-functional team success', *Journal of Management Development*, vol. 21 no. 3, 2002, 201–14.

54. See Norman et al., 'The impact of positivity'; and F. Erdem, J. Ozen and A Nuray, 'Relationship between trust and team performance', *Work Study*, vol. 52 nos 6/7, 2003, 337–40.

55. Norman et al., 'The impact of positivity' built on the theoretical work of Gardner et al. 'Authentic leadership development', linking authentic leadership behaviours and transparent communication with increased trust.

56. For a description of this result in more detail, see S. Ozham and A. Ceylan, 'Collective efficacy as a mediator of the relationship between authentic leadership and well-being at work', *International Business Research*, vol. 9 no. 6, March 2016, 17–30. Others have addressed different aspects of safety and trust leading to higher productivity and better outcomes for organizations. For examples, see A. Emuwa, 'Authentic leadership: commitment to supervisor, follower empowerment, and procedural justice climate', *Emerging Leadership Journeys*, vol. 6 no. 1, 2013, 45–65; S. Sinek, 'Why good leaders make you feel safe', TED, March 2014. http://

www.ted.com/talks/simon_sinek_why_good_leaders_make_you_feel_safe (accessed 14 November 2021); Henderson and Hoy, 'Leader authenticity'; and Tate, 'A longitudinal study'.

57. See Erdem et al., 'Relationship between trust and team performance'; and R.C Mayer and M.B. Gavin, 'Trust in management and performance: who minds the shop while the employees watch the boss?', *Academy of Management Journal*, vol. 48 no. 5, 2005, 874–88.

58. For more detail on the positive impacts on performance from authentic leadership, see H. Wang, Y. Sui, F. Luthans, D. Wang and Y. Wu, 'Impact of authentic leadership on performance: role of followers' positive psychological capital and relational processes', *Journal of Organizational Behavior*, vol. 35 no. 1, January 2014, 5–21.

59. See George, *Authentic Leadership*; Avolio et al., 'Unlocking the mask'; Gardner et al., 'Authentic leadership development'; and Gardner et al., 'Authentic leadership'.

60. Karam et al., 'Authentic leadership and high-performance human resource practices', 116.

61. B. George, *True North: Discover your Authentic Leadership*, San Francisco, CA: Jossey-Bass, 2007, p. 176.

62. Studies have suggested that knowing one's self and acting consistently with that insight leads to better team effectiveness. See Peus et al., 'Authentic leadership: an empirical test'.

63. M.P. Fladerer and S. Braun, 'Managers' resources for authentic leadership – a multi-study exploration of positive psychological capacities and ethical organizational climates', *British Journal of Management*, vol. 31, 2020, 325–43.

64. Gardner et al., 'Authentic leadership development'.

65. J. Politis, 'The relationship between team performance, authentic and servant leadership', *Proceedings of the European Conference on Management, Leadership & Governance*, 2013, 237–44. For more on greater team effectiveness resulting from authentic leadership behaviors, see Avolio et al., 'Unlocking the mask'; and Peus et al., 'Authentic leadership: an empirical test'.

66. Banks, McCauley, Gardner and Guler consider authentic leadership, building on the work of Boies, Fiset and Gill, who found that transformational leadership behaviours influence team outcomes by supporting trust in, and communication with, team members. G.C. Banks, K. Davis-McCauley, W.L. Gardner and C.E. Guler, 'A meta-analytic review of authentic and transformational leadership: a test for redundancy', *The Leadership Quarterly*, vol. 27 no. 4, August 2016, 634–52; and K. Boies, J. Fiset and H. Gill, 'Communication and trust are key: unlocking the relationship between leadership and team performance and creativity', *Leadership Quarterly*, vol. 26 no. 6, 2015, 1080–94.

67. C. Powell, *My American Journey*, New York: Random House, 1995.

68. 'Remembering Colin Powell: 1937–2021', CBS News, 5 November 2021, 59:37. https://www.youtube.com/watch?v=V7vdW_wlM4A (accessed 27 November 2021).

69. Karam et al., 'Authentic leadership and high-performance human resource practices', 112–16.

70. First appearing in *Parade* magazine in August 1989, the '13 Rules of Leadership' were later explained more fully in Colin Powell's memoir. See C. Powell, *It Worked for Me: In Life and Leadership*, New York: HarperCollins, 2012.

71. See J.J. Matthews, *Colin Powell: Imperfect Patriot*, Notre Dame, IN: University of Notre Dame Press, 2019.

72. 'Remembering Colin Powell: 1937–2021', 1:21:58–1:32:48.

73. 'Remembering Colin Powell: 1937–2021', 1:27:47.

74. US Senate, Committee on Foreign Relations, 2001, *Nomination of Colin L. Powell to be Secretary of State.* Hearing 107-14, 17 January 2001. Washington: US Government Printing Office. https://www.govinfo.gov/content/pkg/CHRG-107shrg71536/pdf/CHRG-107shrg71536.pdf (accessed 10 November 2022).

75. US Senate, Committee on Foreign Relations.

76. See E. Schmitt, 'Colin Powell, who shaped US national security, dies at 84', *The New York Times*, 18 October 2021. https://www.nytimes.com/2021/10/18/us/politics/colin-powell-dead.html (accessed 10 November 2022).

77. For more insights into this perspective, see J. Borger, 'Colin Powell's UN speech: a decisive moment in undermining US credibility', *The Guardian*, 18 October 2021. https://www.theguardian.com/us-news/2021/oct/18/colin-powell-un-security-council-iraq (accessed 4 December 2021).

78. 'Colin Powell', *20/20*, Series 27, Episode 1, ABC, 2 September 2005.

79. See A. Cavins, 'The ethics of authentic leadership: exposing limitations and refining core variables', *Journal of Biblical Perspectives in Leadership*, vol. 9, no. 1, Fall 2019, 266–85. https://www.regent.edu/acad/global/publications/jbpl/vol9no1/Vol9Iss1_JBPL_17_Cavins.pdf (accessed 1 December 2021). Cavins argues that the ability of leaders to apply the internalized moral perspective of authentic leadership relies on organizational cultures that are morally supportive. As a result, cultures that lack compatibility with the leader's personal values restrain an authentic leader from acting ethically.

80. The attack on Pearl Harbor precipitated US entry in the Second World War.

81. F. Luthans and B.J. Avolio, 'Authentic leadership: a positive developmental approach', in K.S. Cameron, J.E. Dutton and R.E. Quinn (eds), *Positive Organizational Scholarship: Foundations of a New Discipline*, San Francisco, CA: Berrett-Koehler, 2003, p. 248.

82. Borger, 'Colin Powell's UN speech'.

83. T.L. Price, *Understanding Ethical Failures of Leadership*, Cambridge: Cambridge University Press, 2006.

84. R. Siegel, *It Worked for Me: Interview with Colin Powell*, National Public Radio, 2012. https://www.npr.org/2021/10/18/1047117317/how-colin-powell-wanted-the-world-to-remember-him (accessed 10 November 2022).

85. Powell, *It Worked for Me: In Life and Leadership*, p. 279.

86. Matthews, *Colin Powell: Imperfect Patriot*.

87. Schmitt, 'Colin Powell, who shaped US national security, dies at 84'.

# 14
# Servant leadership

*Maribeth Saleem-Tanner*

## FRAMING QUESTION

How can leaders serve their followers and organizations?

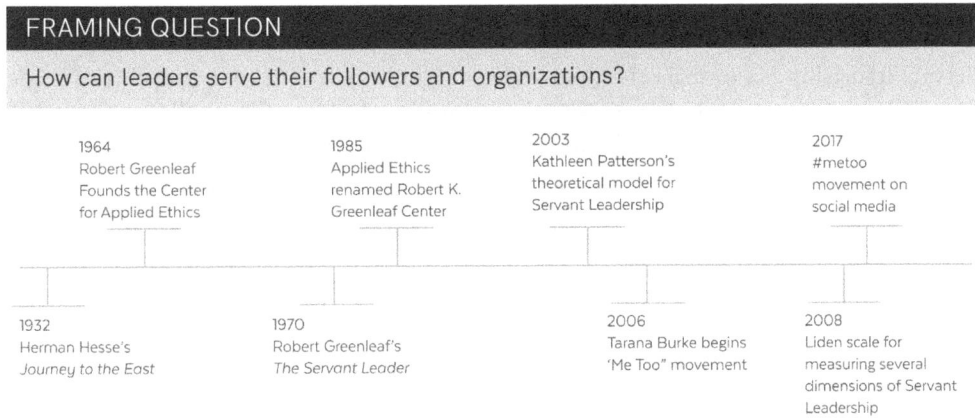

Figure 14.1    Timeline of major works on servant leadership in relation to the chapter case study

In an era where global interconnectedness, collaborative work teams, corporate social responsibility, and employee wellness are increasingly the norm in corporate culture, it can be difficult to appreciate just how much of a paradigm shift Robert K. Greenleaf's seminal essay 'The servant as leader' seemed to many at the time of its publication in 1970. It was a time, Greenleaf explains in the opening pages of his now iconic work, when 'A fresh, critical look is being taken at the issues of power and authority, and people are beginning to learn, however haltingly, to relate to one another in less coercive and more creatively supporting ways.'[1] To those reading Greenleaf's essay for the first time during the Nixon administration, in a country reeling from the Vietnam War, continuing racial tensions, and women campaigning for equal rights, the suggestion that the future of American corporate and institutional culture should move from hierarchy and authority towards inclusiveness and service was not an obvious or widely accepted conclusion.

In this chapter, we will begin by exploring the notion of servant leadership developed by Greenleaf, including historical and cultural examples that informed the model, as well as current academic research in the field. After discussing the evolution and key concepts of the model, our focus will turn to critiques and limitations of servant leadership in both theory and practice. Like the other chapters in this book, we will also consider how the Five Components of Leadership Model can be applied to servant leadership and conduct a case study. The case will examine the role of servant leadership in the #MeToo movement. Finally, we will offer additional resources for study and discussion questions. As the chapter progresses, readers will engage in a thoughtful analysis of how servant leadership, itself values-based, can be understood and applied in terms of both an individual and institutional ethical framework. Servant leadership can reshape relationships and power structures on all levels of society and engage both leaders and followers in active, ongoing work towards more caring, just, and participatory institutions and communities.

## HISTORY

Servant leadership as a formal concept in leadership studies traces its roots directly to a single twentieth-century author, Robert K. Greenleaf. However, the idea of the leader as servant has roots that spread deeply and widely throughout history and cultures, including in a variety of religious traditions. The writings of the ancient Chinese philosopher Confucius have a strong focus on the importance of relationships and the reciprocal care between elders/leaders and the younger/followers, as well as on the need for humility, care, altruism, and practice of reciprocity between leaders and followers within family and social structures.[2] In 'The servant as leader', Greenleaf cites his own interpretation of Confucian teachings, wherein the responsibility for the behaviour of followers rests heavily on the leader. A king is responsible for the well-being of his subjects and has a duty to create an environment in which those subjects can thrive and behave ethically. Confucian philosophy also places high value on the development of character, duty, and honour in leaders. This world view is similar to servant leadership and its emphasis on the importance of the individual leader as a force that shapes societies. The view also underscores that the quality of a society directly reflects the essential quality of its leaders, not simply the skills or capabilities of leaders, but personal attributes such as humility, care for followers, and knowledge.

Western audiences may be more familiar with the servant leadership of Jesus of Nazareth, who eschewed traditional hierarchy and political structures in favour of personal connection with his followers, serving as a friend and teacher rather than a lord and master. Ken Blanchard, who describes his Situational Leadership Model as 'a servant leadership model', believes 'Jesus exemplified the fully committed and effective servant-leader',[3] citing Jesus' words to his disciples in Matthew 20:27, 'Instead, whoever wants to be great among you must be your servant'. This belief, along with other examples in the Christian Bible, such as stories of Jesus healing social outcasts, interacting respectfully with children, and washing his disciples' feet, all speak to an inversion of traditional leader–follower relationships, as does Jesus' climatic action of self-sacrifice for the redemption of humanity.

Greenleaf's 'The servant as leader' essay argues that great leadership emerges only through a deep, authentic desire to serve. The idea is framed with the dramatic language of prophecy and supported by references to literature rather than social science research. This is not surprising given servant leadership's religious and philosophical underpinnings. Specifically, Greenleaf frames his definition of the servant leader with Hermann Hesse's short novel, *Journey to the East*, and French philosopher Albert Camus' exhortation to 'create dangerously'. Greenleaf directly credits Hesse's novel, first published in Germany in 1932, as the inspiration for his idea of the servant as leader. The story describes a group of men on a journey who cannot complete their quest after their servant, Leo, departs from the group. The end of the novel reveals that Leo was, in fact, the revered leader of the Order that had sponsored the group's journey and a man of great spiritual as well as positional power who chose to present himself to the group in the role of servant. This ideal of the leader as one who empowers, supports, and enables the work of a group through selfless service to followers is the essence of servant leadership. From Camus, Greenleaf draws a belief in the power of individual action and the primacy of motive and character in determining impact. What Camus calls 'hope', Greenleaf reinterprets as leadership: 'millions of solitary individuals whose deeds and works every day negate frontiers and the crudest implications of history. As a result ... each and every man, on the foundations of his own sufferings and joys, builds for them all.'[4]

While the tenets of servant leadership have strong philosophical and spiritual dimensions, the concept is solidly grounded in organizational leadership and has been widely applied in business and institutional settings. Greenleaf's personal and professional experiences shaped his interest in and insights on leadership, service, and ethics. As a person who spent his professional life in large institutions, Greenleaf based his writings and thinking on a framework wherein the organization is the primary unit of analysis. His upbringing in Indiana, influenced by the industrial economy and labour tensions around him, likely played a large part in his complex emotional and intellectual relationship with institutions and industry. He saw first-hand that industry could become either a force for community development or human exploitation, depending on the quality of leadership. Greenleaf's belief in the power of the individual to influence collective well-being and the importance of working for the common good also grew out of his life experiences, including his father's participation in community life and the Quaker religious tradition.

These early influences set Greenleaf's moral compass and influenced the mindset in which he began his career with AT&T in the 1920s. Throughout his 40-year tenure in management research, training, and development for the massive telephone company, Greenleaf observed first-hand the turbulent organizational and societal dynamics surrounding the Great Depression, the rise of labour unions, the war and post-war industrial era, and the social upheaval of the 1960s. In the 1960s and 1970s, after retiring from AT&T, Greenleaf built a thriving second career in organizational consulting and teaching, working with a variety of corporate and academic institutions. Greenleaf was keenly interested in what he perceived to be a loss of trust in institutions, which was a guiding theme in his writings and lectures throughout the 1960s and 1970s. In 1964, upon his retirement from AT&T, he brought together his interest in philosophy and business through the establishment of the non-profit Center for Applied Ethics in Indianapolis, Indiana; in 1985, it was renamed the Robert K. Greenleaf Center and still maintains headquarters in Indianapolis and an office in Atlanta, Georgia.

Several well-known authors, both popular and academic, have integrated Greenleaf's servant leadership concepts in their work in the last 40 years, among them Ken Blanchard and M. Scott Peck in the 1970s and 1980s, as well as Stephen Covey, Peter Senge, Margaret Wheatley, Larry Spears, and Kent Keith in the 1990s and 2000s.[5] The variety of thinkers influenced by this concept illustrates the flexibility of the servant leadership model, which can be applied to individual and institutional behaviours in various contexts.

Since the early 2000s, there has been a move by some scholars to formalize Greenleaf's concepts further. Dirk van Dierendonck's extensive review and synthesis of servant leadership literature in 2010 attempted to generalize six core servant leadership behaviours that are practised in any number of settings and reflected in a variety of literature on servant leadership: 'Servant-leaders empower and develop people; they show humility, are authentic, accept people for who they are, provide direction, and are stewards who work for the good of the whole.'[6] Over the past decade, the development of measurement tools has also sparked increased interest among organizational psychologists and other social scientists in defining and understanding the development, process, and outcomes of servant leadership as distinct from other leadership approaches studied through quantitative research.

## MAJOR CONCEPTS OF SERVANT LEADERSHIP

In 'The servant as leader', Robert K. Greenleaf clearly and eloquently poses the defining question for servant leadership in terms of both the motivations that should propel one towards servant leadership and also the outcomes that followers of the true servant leader should experience: 'The servant leader is servant first. It begins with the natural feeling that one wants to serve. Then conscious choice brings one to aspire to lead. The best test is: Do those served grow as persons; do they, while being served, become healthier, wiser, freer, more autonomous, more likely themselves to become servants?' Through unpacking this short, dense passage, we can begin to explore the shape and contours of modern servant leadership, as defined by Greenleaf.

### Integration of Service and Leadership

Much has been written on the semantic implications of the term 'servant leader'. As many have pointed out, it is mainly in the union of two terms that have traditionally been seen as opposites that the power and meaning of this model reside. When servant and leader are brought together as a whole, we are forced to rethink our assumptions about the purview of each of these roles and their status. At the same time, while 'servant leadership' holds both service and leading in a cohesive whole, Greenleaf highlights the primacy of service in the dynamic relationship between actions traditionally thought of as leading and those seen as serving. Peter Vaill describes it well when he explains, 'I think Greenleaf is saying that leadership is a special case of service; he is not saying that service is a special case of leadership.'[7]

The priority of service and the leader's goal to be of service to others distinctly set servant leadership apart from James MacGregor Burns' transformational leadership. While both models focus on the leader's personal characteristics, engagement of followers in creating a vision, and nurturing the leadership potential in others, the transformational leader mainly achieves this through the mechanism of inspiring, goal-setting, and role-modelling – a very different role than serving. Certainly, servant leadership can be understood as a kind of transformational leadership and has some shared outcomes with other types of transformational approaches. Both leadership mechanisms may create change in people, organizations, and values; however, the motivation behind and focus of each is distinct. A transformational leader aims to leverage followers' growth to optimize performance, while the servant leader, guided by altruism and humility, makes follower growth itself her or his main concern.[8]

In this frame, we can see servant leadership as inherently anti-hierarchical, both in execution and philosophy. There is no designation of specific duties, powers, or prestige that belongs to the leader rather than the servant. The servant leader does not receive or seek to receive adulation, glory, or credit for success, even as a means to inspire others. Rather, the servant leader seeks a leadership position only insofar as that position offers the most effective vantage point from which to support and nurture others. In business leadership, this reorganization or rejection of hierarchy is sometimes articulated as an inverted pyramid, whereby customers, and the front-line staff who interact with them, become positioned at the 'top' of the organizational structure, and management and policymakers are positioned at the bottom. Ken Blanchard articulates the impact of servant leadership in business in these terms:

> When you turn a pyramid upside down philosophically, who works for whom when it comes to implementation? You work for your people … [t]he difference is between who is responsible and who is responsive. With the traditional pyramid, the boss is always responsible, and the staff are supposed to be responsive to the boss. When you turn the pyramid upside down those roles get reversed. Your people become responsible and the job of management is to be responsive to their people … [the manager's] job is to help them win.[9]

## Choosing Servant Leadership

The 'conscious choice' described by Greenleaf is, therefore, a choice to take a position of leadership with the explicit aim of empowering followers to succeed. The desire to take on responsibility for the success of the group is what, in one sense, distinguishes servant leadership from other forms of service. While Dr Martin Luther King Jr famously opined 'Everybody can be great, because everybody can serve',[10] not everyone who serves takes on a leadership role. Leadership for servant leaders consists of accepting an obligation to do everything in one's power to ensure the good of followers. To reference back to the inspirational character from Hesse's *Journey to the East*, the great spiritual leader of the Order, Leo, chooses to accompany the part of travellers in the role of a servant. In this role, Leo tends to the travellers' needs, provides encouragement and entertainment, and makes sure they are able to continue; though by all rights, Leo could have easily – and perhaps effectively – taken the role of a guide or formal leader, simply telling the party where they needed to go and how. This example illustrates how the conscious choice to take on the role of servant leader is both a personal and a strategic decision. Servant leadership posits that authority, hierarchy, and coercive power – leading by force and position – may get things done in the short term, but it is collaboration, nurturing, caring, and investing in the growth of others – leading through service – that ultimately results in better long-term outcomes for individuals, institutions, and society alike.

## Outcomes for Followers

The long-term outcomes of servant leadership are the subject of Greenleaf's 'best test'. He describes the goal of this leadership approach as growth, well-being, and a perpetuation of leadership. In later writings, Greenleaf explained, 'I believe that caring for persons, the more able and the less able serving each other, is what makes a good society.'[11] Again, the complication of the leader–follower relationship, and a disruption of hierarchy, is key here; servant leadership is not simply the leader serving the follower indefinitely, but the creation of a reciprocal relationship in which parties on both sides of the dynamic – whether it be leader–follower, privileged–oppressed, or any other traditional dyad with a distinct power differential – fully participate in service, and so grow together towards a shared vision in which all can feel equal ownership and satisfaction.

This value of mutuality also supports the servant leadership approach's social justice goals. In the way that 'a rising tide lifts all boats', the more caring and inclusive leaders and their resulting institutions become, the better off all those affected by these leaders and institutions, including the traditionally disenfranchised or disempowered. If servant leadership is genuinely integrated into the culture of a group or institution, there can be no tolerance for the idea of winners and losers, those who benefit, and those who are left out. In this model, the enterprise of any institution is only successful insofar as all of those involved with the enterprise are considered essential to, and able to benefit from, the results. To put it another way, there is no question of whether the ends justify the means in servant leadership; in Greenleaf's words, 'means determine ends'.[12]

At some level, then, the means and ends of servant leadership are one and the same: to create a process by which all of those involved grow and benefit and work together towards a shared vision. From this follows Greenleaf's rule that all effective motivation in servant leadership is achieved through persuasion. The effective servant leader engages followers in creating a shared mission and vision and creates an environment in which all are motivated to work towards this mission because they have a personal, authentic commitment to the mission and vision and their well-being. As Greenleaf describes it, when workers are taken care of, nurtured, and actively engaged by their workplace, they develop a sense of purpose and vocation. Workers' motivation to help the company succeed, therefore, rests largely in their desire to continue being able to work there and be a part of the institution. The servant leader can, therefore, hold their followers accountable to high standards and excellence through a shared commitment to purpose and sense of mutual accountability rather than through coercion or fear.

The notion of motivation in the servant leadership model goes beyond a desire of followers for perks, a pleasant workplace, or professional development opportunities, grounded as it is in the ethic of service rather than self-interest. Greenleaf believes that internal motivation and a sense of calling, which he compares to the Buddhist concept of right livelihood in the noble

Eightfold Path,[13] is produced when the business itself becomes 'a serving institution – serving both producers [workers] and users [consumers]' through providing meaningful work and services or goods to these constituencies, respectively.[14] Within the institution, this is described as a 'people-building' versus 'people-using' approach.[15] A people-building institution may provide perks and incentives, but this is an added dimension of care for its people, not an ameliorative measure to keep people working in an unfulfilling or transactional people-using environment. This idea of the business as a servant institution has connections to current trends in employee wellness and diversity initiatives and, more deeply, in companies developing mission statements, decentralized decision-making structures, and social responsibility initiatives.

## Servant Leaders as Shapers of Culture

Servant leadership posits that as leaders can cultivate and practice servant behaviours consistently and intentionally, they will inspire and empower others to do the same. If servant leaders are successful, both they and their followers will make ethical choices, perpetuating a culture of service, care, and responsibility throughout their organizations. To put it in terms of reference to another model described in this book, followership, effective servant leaders create good followers, or in some articulations of followership dynamics, effective partners.

Kathleen Patterson describes one way to visualize the mechanism by which servant leadership operates to create this culture in terms of a progression through seven virtuous constructs. In Patterson's model, these virtues are characteristics of the servant leader, which are operationalized through the process of servant leadership. The root of this process is *agapao* love – the virtue through which leaders see their followers as whole, valuable people and prioritize their needs. From this root stems a sense of humility – valuing others rather than over-valuing the self – and altruism, or concern for the good of others. From this foundation, servant leaders can have faith in the future of people and organizations, which forms the basis for a guiding vision. Servant leaders also demonstrate trust in the abilities and potential of their followers and earn reciprocal trust by being transparent and behaving with integrity in all situations. All of these beliefs and resulting behaviours form the basis for true empowerment of followers, and a dedication to serving those followers, which sets the culture of service within effective servant leaders' organizations.

## CRITIQUES OF SERVANT LEADERSHIP

## Theoretical Concern: Varying Understandings of Servant Leadership

Robert Greenleaf was a prolific writer, addressing, re-addressing, and developing a variety of themes and applications of servant leadership throughout his essays and lectures. However, he never created a definitive list, model, or typology of servant leadership. In the decades since his death, many scholars have worked to distil his ideas into lists or themes.

Larry Spears compiled a list of 'Ten Characteristics of the Servant-Leader' drawn from Greenleaf's writings. His list includes: listening, empathy, healing and a desire for wholeness, awareness of self and others, reliance on persuasion rather than authority, conceptualization and ability to dream, foresight, stewardship, commitment to the growth of people, and a focus on building community.[16] Looking at this list in terms of themes, one finds items related to interpersonal interactions, including a desire to learn from followers (listening), a capacity to understand and appreciate followers as people (empathy), and intense compassion (healing and desire for wholeness). One also sees a set of characteristics about how the servant leader interacts with the environment. The servant leader commits to an honest assessment of reality, including thoughtful consideration of ethics and a willingness to own up to difficult or uncomfortable situations (awareness). They also eschew commanding in favour of consensus-building (persuasion), cultivate an ability to think long-term and develop a vision (conceptualization), and possess an ability to intuitively predict likely outcomes in various situations (foresight). Finally, the list includes a set of characteristics that define how the servant leader interacts with the institution in which they work, with a focus on sustainability and social good (stewardship), developing the potential of followers rather than simply maximizing outputs (commitment to the growth of people), and creating an ethos of care and interdependence among followers (building community).

Anne Fraker focuses more specifically on Greenleaf's discussions of the role of servant leadership in business ethics, communicated through his management training. She points out that Greenleaf seldom used the term 'ethics', believing that ethical behaviour resulted from individual courage rather than a formal code or belief system. However, Fraker points out that Greenleaf does distil some themes in his work that are connected to ethical behaviour and ethically sound institutions. Ethical business practices result from leaders with a commitment to service, including the strength to make the right choices, openness to knowledge, ability to understand past and present circumstances well enough to anticipate future issues (foresight), ability to sustain enthusiasm and inspiration (*entheos*), a sense of purpose, and an ability to laugh.[17]

More recently, social science research by Liden et al. focused on seven specific servant–leader behaviours that contribute demonstrably to positive outcomes for followers, such as increased engagement, increased organizational commitment, and increased organizational and community citizenship behaviours. These servant leader behaviours include: conceptual skills, emotional healing, putting followers first, helping followers grow and succeed, behaving ethically, empowering followers, and creating value for the community.[18]

These three examples illustrate one of the challenges of this model, which is the fact that, as Van Dierendonck explains in his extensive 2010 review of servant leadership literature, '[D]espite its introduction four decades ago and empirical studies that started more than ten years ago, there is still no consensus about a definition and theoretical framework of servant leadership.'[19] Without a clear, agreed-upon structure to understand this model, it becomes both difficult to study and also easy to dismiss as simply a restatement of transformational leadership theory with religious overtones. Those who try to build a coherent, comprehensive model of servant leadership based on Greenleaf's writings will find the task daunting.

G. James Lemoine Jr's 2015 prize-winning dissertation on servant leadership acknowledges this challenge. It addresses this lack of a consistent conceptual model by suggesting an updated definition of servant leadership:

> [As] influential behaviors, manifested humbly and ethically within relationships, oriented towards follower development, empowerment, and continuous and meaningful improvement for all stakeholders (including but not limited to those being led, communities, customers, and the leader, team, and organization themselves).[20]

This gives a useful and specific framework that may help focus understanding and future social science research.

Still, the concept's scope is far-reaching and touches on personal and spiritual development, organizational culture, business structures, and more. This has led, and will likely continue to lead, to many variations in scope and interpretation among those who claim to all be practising or defining servant leadership.

## Practical Concern Number One: Effectiveness

Beyond the limitations of the model's nonlinear historical development and broad scope, there are reasonable concerns about its effectiveness and practicality. Despite a growing body of research demonstrating effective positive outcomes, a common criticism of servant leadership is that it is ineffectual or weak and that servant leaders cannot successfully navigate situations with followers requiring structure and direction. The model has some answers to this critique, as effective servant leaders are required to possess foresight as well as an ability to direct followers through persuasion (rather than coercion). However, this can be a delicate balancing act between accountability and empowerment, and the method of leadership through persuasion can, in some cases, begin to either genuinely become or at least start to feel like manipulation. When the servant leader is perceived as manipulative, they lose critical bonds of trust, and perceptions of authenticity undermine the ability to lead effectively.

Also of concern is the conflict that can arise when individuals try to practise servant leadership within an institutional context grounded in hierarchical models of power. While servant leadership focuses on creating success for followers, an individual who practises it in an environment where it is not accepted or valued may set themselves and the followers who rely on that leader's support up for failure. Similarly, some express concern that the leader in the role of servant may create not empowerment but dependency among followers. It is of note here that the original inspiration for Greenleaf's servant leader, the character of Leo in Hesse's *Journey to the East*, at some point abandoned his party, who consequently were unable to complete their journey successfully without him.

## Practical Concern Number Two: Time

Another significant challenge of this model, acknowledged by Greenleaf himself, is the time required to implement it successfully. Particularly in institutional or social contexts where command and control leadership models have dominated, the transformation of both followers as individuals and also institutional structures must be a long-term process. When an institution or group must respond to an immediate crisis or opportunity, the time required to build bonds of trust or actively create relationships and solicit input may not be feasible. In cases such as these, the utility of servant leadership is limited.

## Practical Concern Number Three: The Role of the Individual

While we can speak about building servant institutions and shifting cultural values, the mechanism for these changes rests mainly on building specific kinds of relationships between individuals over time. Even Peter Drucker, who worked closely with Robert Greenleaf over many years, struggled with the focus of servant leadership on long-term personal transformation rather than on immediate effective action. As Drucker describes it, 'Bob [Greenleaf] was always out to change the individual, to make him or her into a different person. I was interested in making people do the right things, in their actions and behavior.'[21] One ethical dilemma that might arise from this situation is addressing a problem in which a follower has behaved contrary to institutional policy or norms or has put self-interest above institutional or societal goals. Suppose one believes that the follower's development as an individual is the responsibility of the servant leader. In that case, it might be best for the leader to spend time and energy trying to educate or persuade the follower to behave differently or develop a different value system. However, it may be more beneficial for the good of the institution, the goal, or even the other followers for the leader to take corrective action or administer consequences, even if that corrective action does not contribute to the growth and development of the individual who violated the policy or norm. In this case and others, in working towards the ideal of serving all followers well, the servant leader may well find her or himself in conflict between competing interests and needs.

## Practical Concern Number Four: Spoilers

A final consideration when looking to implement a servant leadership approach is the danger of what in peace negotiations are called 'spoilers' – those who have a personal interest in disrupting or preventing a successful outcome. Servant leadership rests on the assumption that all followers are valuable people, capable of contributing to the common good. There is little clear guidance in the servant leadership model for how to deal with those who might be actively working to undermine the institution's goals, sabotage the outcome, or hurt fellow followers. A dramatic example of this phenomenon is the 1995 assassination of Israeli prime minister Yitzhak Rabin by a militant Israeli nationalist who opposed peace negotiations with the Palestinians. Less significant examples happen daily in organizations, such as when a manager asked to implement a new policy makes their disdain of the policy known to subordinates or implements it haphazardly with the goal of having it deemed a failure and repealed. Servant leadership rests on the consent and active engagement of followers, and so is effective only to the degree of the desire and willingness of followers to participate in the process, behave ethically, and allow themselves to be served.

## FIVE COMPONENT ANALYSIS

With all that in mind, we will now turn our analysis, as in previous chapters, to applying the Five Components Model to servant leadership.

Years ago, I was invited to lead a supervision strategies workshop at a state-wide non-profit conference. We mainly talked about structures and strategies – how to monitor and manage staff and volunteers, communicate expectations and give effective feedback, and balance the time required to supervise people effectively with the time needed to get one's own work done. During the Q&A portion of the session, one of the attendees brought up a situation in which she was struggling to motivate an employee to improve her performance. In the course of addressing her question, I suggested creating regular times to meet with the employee to get updates on her work and offer feedback. I suggested that some of the weekly meeting be dedicated to learning more about the employee's goals, interests, and life outside of the office to establish a more supportive relationship. The workshop participant paused in taking notes, seeming to have a moment of insight.

'Right!' she exclaimed. 'I usually jump right into talking about tasks and keep the meeting focused on her performance. But you're saying I have to spend that time on small talk to make her feel like I care about her as a person.'

I thought about this for a moment, and then responded: 'Well, the key is that you actually do have to care about her as a person.' This exchange captures the essence of what sets servant leadership apart from other types of leadership, namely the authentic focus on the follower as the object of primary concern. Therefore, all of the components of the Five Components Model can be understood in servant leadership primarily in the context of how they affect the follower. This is represented in Figure 14.2 by the emphasis placed on the leader and the downward arrow pointing towards the follower.

While the leader and follower are represented as separate on the Five Components diagram, it is most appropriate in servant leadership to view them as two parts of the same whole since the leader–follower relationship is the crux of servant leadership. In the context of servant leadership, the arrows representing the interaction between leader and follower on the Five Components Model take on a deep, personal dimension, representing not only cooperation and exchange, but an

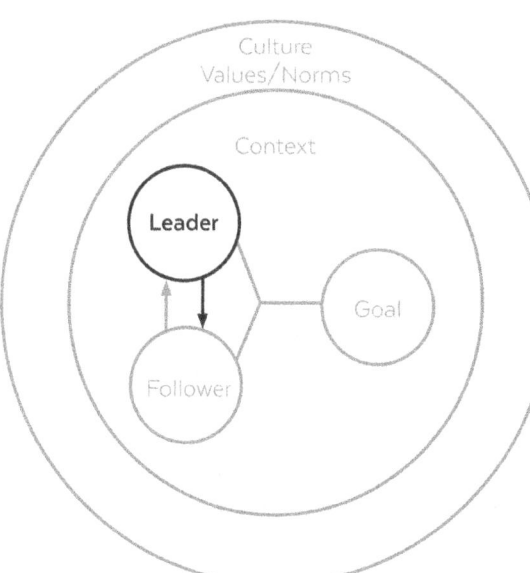

**Figure 14.2**     The Five Components of Leadership Model applied to servant leadership

ongoing relationship of mutuality, shared power, and genuine concern. The two-way arrow also represents the goal in servant leadership to have those served become servants themselves. Through a relationship with the servant leader, followers are both served and given opportunities to serve. This relationship has the power to impact institutions on a large scale, but it is enacted through an ongoing series of individual leader–follower interactions.

In understanding how the goal functions in servant leadership, one can return to Greenleaf's assertion that means determine ends. In this formulation of servant leadership, goal accomplishment is an organic result of the practice of servant leadership, because the leader uses the goal as a mechanism to facilitate followers' growth. This understanding runs counter to many common assumptions about the relationship between leadership and goals, but it is consistent with Greenleaf's assertion that servant leaders begin with an impulse to serve and then make a conscious choice to lead as a means of serving. To use another example from Greenleaf's writing, 'the work exists for the person as much as the person exists for the work.'[22] Put another way, 'the business exists as much to provide meaningful work to the person as it exists to provide a product or service to the customer.' In practice, goal setting in servant-led organizations functions as a collaborative process whereby the leader actively listens to the needs of followers and then sets goals based on their understanding of these needs. In practice, this could take the form of the servant leader facilitating a visioning process and then working actively to support followers in reaching it. This is in contrast to the theory of adaptive leadership, introduced in Chapter 17, where the goal is to give the work back to the people.

One question we may ask here is whether there might sometimes be worthwhile, noble, meaningful goals that do not inherently result in the growth of followers. Servant leadership posits that a successful servant leader can use almost any goal to facilitate the growth of those being served as long as that goal is achieved through a caring and nurturing process for all followers. This flexibility has contributed to servant leadership's popularity among business managers, who see the potential in this leadership practice to create mutually beneficial outcomes for workers and the organization to which those workers contribute. This aspect of mutually beneficial outcomes is at the core of Greenleaf's vision of servant institutions, whereby the practice of servant leadership within the institution implements a mandate of ethical, caring behaviour towards employees and stakeholders at all levels.

Because servant leadership deals so much with abstracts, values, principles, and relationships, context is more important here than in some other modes of leadership. In servant leadership, it is the responsibility of the leader to understand and navigate the elements of the environment that may impact the follower. The ability of the leader to skilfully navigate the context, anticipating and navigating challenges to support followers in reaching the goal is articulated in servant leadership terms as 'foresight'.

Servant leaders act upon, rather than within, the cultural circle in this model. Suppose we accept Greenleaf's formulation that the ultimate goal of servant leadership is to create more servant leaders. In that case, it is clear that in this dynamic, the leader doesn't respond to the current values and norms of the culture but instead works actively to create a culture of service and community through the promotion and practice of servant leadership. Greenleaf's vision of a world of 'servant institutions' is an example of what this leader-driven cultural change might look like. The case study Tanara Burke and the #MeToo movement that follows is another good example of the power of the servant leader to actively shape or reshape the cultural context in which leadership takes place.

## CASE STUDY: TARANA BURKE AND THE #METOO MOVEMENT

Robert Greenleaf describes his desire for a 'more serving society ... the climate that favors service, and supports servants', and believes 'the basics [of solving social problems] are the incremental thrusts of individuals who have the ability to serve and lead.'[23] If we believe Greenleaf's vision, a more serving society – one comprised of both servant leaders and servant institutions – has ethical behaviour embedded in its structures. If one's primary concern is for the well-being of people, then the choices that flow from that concern will necessarily be ethical choices within the limitations of the practical concerns noted above. Accepting that this serving society is a worthwhile goal how, on a practical level, can servant leadership most effectively be utilized to work toward a more service-oriented, and so more ethical, society? This is the question we take up through the lens of the Me Too movement and the organizing frame of the Five Components of Leadership Model. This case will illustrate a specific approach to servant leadership within the larger Me Too movement.

As the public face of a global movement, Tarana Burke isn't a typical example of a servant leader. Many of us are familiar with seeing servant leadership practised and discussed on the organizational level. But a closer look at Burke's journey to prominence, her stated goals, and her actions reveal how Burke's leadership is clearly grounded in the values of service and exemplifies the practice of servant leadership as conceived by Robert Greenleaf. Moreover, contrasting the original Me Too movement with the more well-known Hollywood-centred social media campaign, we gain insight into the ethical foundations of servant leadership. This case study explores servant leadership's roots in social justice and virtue ethics by examining Burke's approach of 'empowerment through empathy'[24] and comparing her example to other leadership styles.

More than a decade before the #MeToo began trending on Twitter, movement founder Tarana Burke started using the phrase 'Me Too' in her work to support young people of colour who had experienced sexual violence. An activist, writer, and non-profit executive, Burke focused her work at the individual and community level. Working in classrooms and rape crisis centres, camps, and after-school programmes, Burke led discussions, organized communities, and mentored youth, using the phrase as a call for solidarity, empathy, and support.

As she describes it in her memoir and interviews, Burke was as surprised as anyone when in October 2017, actress Alyssa Milano called for followers on Twitter to share using the hashtag #MeToo if they had experienced sexual violence. The response was overwhelming, with 1,595,453 posts appearing in the first week[25] and over 19 million uses of the hashtag within the first year[26] on Twitter alone. Burke and the original Me Too movement quickly gained national and global attention as the public became aware of her work in connection with the viral social media phenomenon. Tarana Burke was featured as a 2017 Person of the Year in *TIME Magazine*, attended the Golden Globes in 2018, and was awarded the Sydney Peace Prize in Australia in 2019.[27]

These public recognitions of Burke's work highlighted the far-reaching social impact of the Me Too movement. Speaking at UNC Wilmington in 2019, Burke explained that 'For millions of people – MILLIONS of people, the "Me Too" hashtag marked the first time in their lives that they had the space to share some of the deepest and darkest secrets. For hundreds of thousands, it was the start of a new, much-needed conversation about safety in our workplace, institutions, and communities.'[28]

At the same time that Burke rose in prominence on the national and international stage, widening the audience for and impact of her work, she also struggled with maintaining control of the narrative and direction of the movement.[29] Reflecting on the trajectory of the movement in a 2020 interview, Burke explained, '#MeToo has centered around pop culture and hype and not really around structures and systems that allow for sexual violence to be what it is.'[30] Burke's servant leadership approach resulted in a commitment to keeping her focus on healing, empowerment, and cultural change. Her story is a powerful example of servant leadership as social justice. Far from being a calculated technique to wield influence over followers or maximize profits, true servant leadership is an ethical commitment that defines not only leadership methods but also the very parameters of the leadership process, including defining the goal and the followers.

## UNDERSTANDING TARANA BURKE AS A SERVANT LEADER

To begin to unpack this rich and complex case, we'll examine Tarana Burke's leadership through the definition of servant leadership proposed by Eva et al. in an extensive 2018 review of existing literature on servant leadership:

> Servant leadership is a (1) other-oriented approach to leadership, (2) manifested through one-on-one prioritizing of follower individual needs and interests, and (3) an outward reorienting of their concern for self towards concern for others within the organization and the larger community. The above definition has three features that make up the essence of servant leadership, namely its motive, mode, and mindset.[31]

In examining Burke's stated motives for leadership, we see a clear parallel between her story and the prototypical leadership journey articulated by Greenleaf: 'It begins with the natural feeling that one wants to serve, to serve first. Then conscious choice brings one to aspire to lead.'[32] Burke grew up in a family that imparted a strong sense of her identity as a black woman and connected her to the legacy of the civil rights movement. She honed her identity as a leader through participation in 21st Century Youth Leadership Movement, where she later returned as staff.[33] Burke describes her motivation to serve based on the experiences she had of being nurtured as a teen, saying her participation in youth development programmes 'saved me and it helped shape my life … [then when] I got in that world, I saw what the needs were'.[34]

The experience of being drawn towards leadership by seeing needs – the nature of motive – is a critical determinant in servant leadership. Burke's leadership story also demonstrates a second key element of servant leadership, a focus on the well-being of followers rather than on an externally determined organizational or personal goal. Burke never consciously set out to secure a position of national scope. Instead, her work grew directly from her interactions with individual followers and her desire to address their needs. Her organization tells her story:

> Working in a youth program in Selma, Alabama, Burke encountered a Black girl who shared her story of sexual violence and abuse. Soon she found herself meeting dozens more. As a survivor herself, these were the stories with which she identified personally. Tarana realized that too many girls were suffering and surviving abuse without access to resources, safe spaces, and support.[35]

She set out to build up resources and support for individual survivors as a key element to a thriving future for the whole community since 'The servant leader understands that a healthy community is made up of healthy followers, whose needs are met so they can collectively work towards a better tomorrow.'[36]

Contrast this motivation and explicit focus on follower needs with the later origin of the social media hashtag #MeToo. In Actor Alyssa Milano's famous tweet, she states her intention to 'give people a sense of the magnitude of the problem'.[37] The context for her statement was ongoing media attention on disgraced producer Harvey Weinstein. While supporting survivors was certainly an implicit goal, the explicit goal was to bring attention to an issue and take advantage of a cultural moment in order to effectively influence public opinion and force accountability for perpetrators. Speaking to a reporter in the months after the tweet went viral, Milano embraced her role as a visible leader while also explaining that the outcome was more serendipitous than intentional: 'It was the perfect storm to happen and I feel really blessed I was the vessel, the messenger ... [i]t's very special, probably the greatest thing I've felt. I think the fact that it turned into a true movement was surprising. That was never my intention.'[38]

In contrast, Burke embodies the servant leader attributes of awareness, conceptualization, and foresight:

> I may not be on the front page of magazines or across the internet or what have you, but that's not necessarily as important. There's a way that having high visibility will make you believe that high visibility is the goal. It makes people pay attention to your message. So it does yield something. But I could have lived my whole life not being as visible as I am, and my work would still be important.[39]

That 'work' in Burke's case is explicitly the healing and wholeness of survivors of sexual assault. While awareness may be necessary to leverage resources, and accountability for perpetrators may be required to create safety, this awareness and accountability are not ends in themselves but mechanisms for healing and wholeness for survivors (followers). The goal is not media visibility for Burke or other survivors, or even specifically punishing abusers. In looking at Burke's movement through the framework of the Five Components of Leadership Model, the goal differs from that of the Hollywood version of the Me Too movement. It is more rightly defined as 'empowerment through empathy', which includes individual healing (goal), a commitment to community care (context), and a shift in culture towards an intolerance for sexual violence (values and norms) that creates long-term safety.[40] The followers of the original Me Too movement are not public figures or those with the power to prosecute crimes but the members of marginalized groups. The context of the work isn't Hollywood or the court of public opinion but the communities in which people live their day-to-day lives. Burke approaches her work with the belief that we can further society as a whole by focusing first on creating loving, joyful, and supportive communities free from fear and violence[41] where people (followers) can 'just be'.[42] Everything flows from the primary objective of supporting and growing individuals. To borrow Kae Reynolds's words, servant-leadership '… asserts that genuinely building up people's spirits and abilities also builds community; the formation and achievement of organizational objectives follow.'[43] To put it in Greenleaf's terms: the means determine ends.[44]

This comparison is in no way to denigrate Milano, who is herself a sexual assault survivor, nor to diminish the impact of her leadership or her contribution as an activist. Milano has clearly demonstrated courageous, effective, and ethical leadership. She even went on to partner with UNICEF to use her public visibility to bring help awareness to the stories of women and children worldwide who had experienced violence and sexual abuse. Rather, we compare these two leaders only to emphasize the distinctive nature of servant leadership. Leadership as 'a special case of service' always originates in a leader's connection to followers and their commitment to caring for people as individuals. Burke's approach to servant leadership is much more intentionally focused on specific survivors and their needs. To put it in Burke's own terms: 'I'm uncomfortable being the face of this thing; I didn't want to be a figurehead.' … 'now that I have [privilege], I'm trying to use it responsibly … [b]ut if it hadn't come along I would be right here, with my … Me Too shirt on, doing workshops and going to rape crisis centres … The work is the work.'[45] A thoughtful definition of 'the work' – as healing, empowerment, and wholeness – is the ethical foundation of servant leadership.

Social scientist and writer Christena Cleveland speaks of a 'hole' in servant leadership when the leader doesn't maintain an awareness of social justice. She explains that true servant leaders don't just care for the needs of followers, but take on the further responsibility of acting on the context, values, and norms in which the interaction between leader and followers takes place:

> All things being equal, servant leadership is a good idea. But in a world where all things are not equal – especially in matters of race, class, and gender – servant leadership has its limits … despite good intentions to serve, the leader retains the power. The inequality that often exists between the servant leader and the people being served remains unchanged.[46]

This is a lens through which to examine the differences between the Me Too movement of Tarana Burke, with its focus on healing, empathy, justice, and community, and the #MeToo of Hollywood. Speaking at Smith College in 2019, Burke explained that '#MeToo doesn't recognize Black, queer bodies – only white, able-bodied, beautiful celebrities.'[47] To put it in organizational terms, there is a difference between the servant leadership of a CEO staying after a company event to help move chairs alongside hourly workers versus the servant leadership of that same CEO in advocating to give custodial staff a raise and benefits, even if that move will cut into company profits.

Tarana Burke's Me Too movement is grounded in the power of a compelling vision and the conviction that servant leadership can – and must – disrupt patterns of exploitation to create true and lasting change:

> It is my job, I think, to amplify and elevate the voices of the most marginalized amongst us. I've always been really clear that I center Black women and girls. And that is not to the exclusion of anybody else. And, in fact, I try to explain to people is that you want that. You want a leader, a person who comes in with a vision that centers the most marginalized because it's the only way to ensure that everybody gets what they need.[48]

This centring of the leader's own community, and in this case specifically of marginalized communities, falls in line with Greenleaf's encouragement for servant-leaders to anchor their efforts within a sphere for which they can take full responsibility:

> All that is needed to rebuild community as a viable life form for large numbers of people is for enough servant-leaders to show the way, not by mass movements, but by each servant-leader demonstrating his own unlimited liability for a quite specific community-related group.[49]

The Hollywood-centred #MeToo movement certainly had positive aims – to draw attention to a widespread culture of sexual exploitation and abuse and to hold perpetrators to account. But a movement led by movie stars and with a specific goal of changing the culture of the entertainment industry and holding perpetrators to account will not ever extend the benefits of its work, the distribution of its social good, to those who are outside of its sphere of privilege. In Burke's words:

> #MeToo was a moment in history that elevated the Me Too movement, that amplified it and sent it off into the stratosphere and made it incredibly visible. But if we consider #MeToo the movement, then we will only define Me Too in the ways that the mainstream media has, then we will only ever be looking for who's the next case? Who's the next person who's going to get Me Too'd?'[50]

She goes on to explain,

> If we have a limited vision that the hashtag gives us, then we won't ever make the kind of progress that's necessary to actually look like we might end sexual violence. To get to a place where we have a generation of young people who are disgusted by it, who are programmed and socialized in such a way that they think about rape the way they think about murder. That can happen. That can absolutely happen. But it's not going to happen if we only focus on Matt Lauer in his summer home … [t]hat's not going to make it happen.[51]

All servant leadership is grounded in virtue ethics – the idea that a leader's motivation for leadership grows directly from their strong moral character and their deep, personal desire to serve others. Tarana Burke's leadership can clearly be traced to her commitment to service and healing. What makes this case especially interesting is Burke's explicit focus on marginalized followers and identification of healing and wholeness as ultimate, rather than proximate, goals. Burke's leadership of Me Too is notable for her refusal to compromise the well-being of her followers in service of personal power or social influence. This provides an excellent example of servant leadership that is justice-oriented and grounded firmly in care ethics (as explained in Chapter 6), which highlights the need for access to social goods to be thoughtfully extended throughout society to ensure equal access. Burke's courageous willingness to distance herself from the mainstream of #MeToo and commit herself to serve her community demonstrates how servant leadership, in its truest form, can require not just caring about people but also an unflinching consciousness of power dynamics (the context) and a willingness to truly subvert traditional hierarchies, even at the risk of diminishing the leader's power or influence.

It is important to emphasize that in seeking to practise servant leadership, leaders should keep in mind the proverbial advice to not let the perfect be the enemy of the good. Many leaders and researchers have, rightly, emphasized the practical benefits of servant leadership, even when practised in ways that stay firmly within traditional power structures.[52] Both research and logic support the idea that leaders can benefit from taking care of their followers,[53] and that organizational goals are well-served by investing in the well-being and sustainability of their workforce.[54] One may even argue that self-serving or performative uses of servant leader behaviours are inherently better than other methods that see people as disposable or as means to an end. Similarly, good leaders can achieve positive outcomes for both organizations and society using means that don't inherently or directly develop their individual followers in the short term. Tarana Burke's example should, though, remind us that servant leadership includes an opportunity – and perhaps an obligation – for the leader to not only care for their followers and achieve their goals but also to consciously exert influence on the larger values and norms of the society in which the leader-follower interactions take place and to move with intention toward a more just and loving future for all.

## FIVE COMPONENT ANALYSIS

In the case study presented here, Tarana Burke is the leader, and her followers are those marginalized sexual abuse survivors with whom she directly works. Their mutual goal is empowerment and supportive healing. This leadership dynamic is set within the larger #MeToo movement, a movement attempting to *change* the larger cultural norms of exploitation and marginalization.

Reviewing the case in terms of the Five Components Model shows us how each element of servant leadership has been enacted in the Me Too movement (Figure 14.3).

Tarana Burke, the leader highlighted in this case, used her steady support of marginalized people, specifically women and girls of colour, to propel a movement that eventually became nationally known for two simple words, 'me, too'. The followers in this dyad are the black women whose voices Burke amplified, not to the exclusion of other voices, but because centring those voices best met the needs of the followers. The goal, in this case, is the empowerment and supported healing of survivors through the empathy of others.

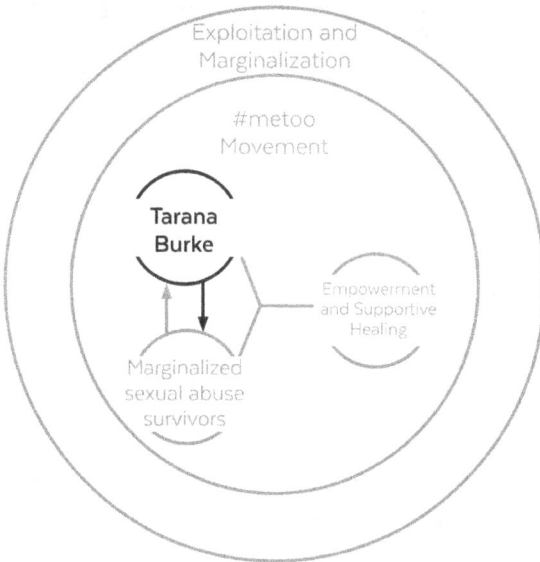

In considering the context within which survivors are supported, Burke made clear that the commitment to community care must be prioritized, not to create notoriety or influence, but in order to make a sustainable shift in the culture that allows women to be victimized in the first place. To heal survivors, it is necessary to heal the communities in which they are trying to survive. This commitment to community care is also informed by the values and norms associated with a shift to a culture that no longer tolerates marginalization, violence, or sexual assault or silences the voices of survivors.

**Figure 14.3**   The Five Components of Leadership Model applied to Tarana Burke and the Me Too movement

## SUMMARY AND CONCLUDING REMARKS

We began this chapter by asking: 'How can leaders best serve their followers and organizations?' According to servant leadership, the answer is simple and significant: taking care of them and helping create an environment in which those followers can grow into leaders. A better world will emerge when there is a shift in culture, away from exploiting followers and valuing profits and towards a nurturing environment that values people. This culture shift, whether in a corporation or a country, must involve a concerted effort by current servant leaders to strengthen the power of the leader–follower dyads in enough structures and institutions so that there can be a concerted effort across sectors to overcome challenges in the context and reshape cultural norms. This is a lofty goal, but we have seen in both academic literature and the case study that there are practical ways to work towards this long-term vision. Leaders must develop their ability to listen, empathize, and value their followers, respecting them not only as co-creators of success but also as human beings with inherent worth.

As a matter of personal practice, practitioners might consider developing their own capacity as servant leaders through activities and education that build their skills in listening, dialogue, consensus-building, facilitation, mentoring, and teaching. Time invested in reflection on one's own values and investment in spiritual and emotional development should also prove valuable in developing the skills required for servant leadership.

## DISCUSSION QUESTIONS

1. Which of the ethical models described in the first part of this book most closely aligns with the values of the servant leadership model?
2. Do you believe this type of leadership is realistic and practical? Can a leader truly possess all of the traits and characteristics Greenleaf identifies?
3. Is there any situation you can think of in which acting as a servant leader might not be ethical?
4. Are there any situations in which a leader might reasonably and ethically prioritize accomplishing a goal over developing followers?
5. Is it possible to truly practise servant leadership in an unstable or unsafe situation?
6. Can celebrities be servant leaders and be successful? Should we expect our celebrities to truly be 'servants'? If so, how would that look different than what we currently see?
7. The outcomes of servant leadership are primarily holistic and long term. How might a servant leader measure and judge success in their day-to-day work?
8. The very term 'servant leadership' can seem like a paradox or oxymoron. In what other ways does ethical leadership require leaders to challenge preconceived notions of 'leadership' as a phenomenon?
9. In what situations might a servant leadership model actually be a hindrance to achieving organizational goals? How could you resolve this as a leader?
10. How can leaders know when they have moved beyond 'persuasion' into 'manipulation'?

## ADDITIONAL RESOURCES

K.M. Keith, *The Case for Servant Leadership*, Indianapolis, IN: The Greenleaf Center, 2015.

This book serves as an accessible overview of the concept of servant leadership, including an appendix comparing it to other models of leadership as well as many examples.

K.R.C. Linden, A. Panaccio, J.D. Mueser, J. Hu and S.J. Wyane, 'Servant leadership: antecedents, processes, and outcomes', in D.V. Day (ed.), *The Oxford Handbook of Leadership and Organizations*, Oxford: Oxford University Press, 2014, pp. 357–79.

This source presents an overview of the development of servant leadership as a research area and a theoretical model.

The Greenleaf Center for Servant Leadership (http://www.greenleaf.org) offers workshops and resources, as well as an annual conference. The Center has also published a series of books with collections of essays, adapted chapters, and excerpted writings from a variety of contemporary thinkers.

# NOTES

1.  R. Greenleaf, 'The servant as leader: essentials of servant leadership', in L.C. Spears and M. Lawrence (eds), *Focus on Leadership: Servant Leadership for the 21st Century*, New York: John Wiley, 2002, p. 21.
2.  J. Riegel, 'Confucius', in E.N. Zalta (ed.), *The Stanford Encyclopedia of Philosophy*, summer 2013 edn. https://plato.stanford.edu/archives/sum2013/entries/confucius/ (accessed 12 November 2022).
3.  K. Blanchard, 'Foreword', in Spears and Lawrence, *Focus on Leadership*, p. xi.
4.  Camus quoted in Greenleaf, 'The servant as leader', p. 23.
5.  Robert E. Greenleaf Center for Servant Leadership, 'What is servant leadership?' https://www.greenleaf.org/what-is-servant-leadership/ (accessed 12 November 2022).
6.  D. van Dierendonck, 'Servant leadership: a review and synthesis', *Journal of Management*, vol. 37 no. 4, 2011, 1228–61, p. 1228. Originally published online, 2 September 2010.
7.  P. Vaill, 'Foreword', in R. Greenleaf, *The Power of Servant Leadership*, ed. L.C. Spears, San Francisco, CA: Berrett-Koehler, 1998, p. xii.
8.  K. Patterson, 'Servant leadership: a theoretical model,' unpublished manuscript, Servant Leadership Research Roundtable, Regent University School of Leadership Studies, August 2003. https://www.regent.edu/acad/global/publications/sl_proceedings/2003/patterson_servant_leadership.pdf (accessed 12 November 2018).
9.  K. Blanchard, 'Servant-leadership revisited', in L.C. Spears (ed.), *Insights on Leadership: Service, Stewardship, Spirit, and Servant-Leadership*, New York: John Wiley, 1997, p. 25.
10. M.L. King, 'The drum major instinct', in P. Holloran and C. Carson (eds), *A Knock At Midnight: Inspiration from the Great Sermons of Reverend Martin Luther King, Jr.*, New York: Time Warner, 1998, p. 182.
11. Greenleaf, 'The servant as leader', p. 17.
12. R. Greenleaf, 'Coercion, manipulation, and persuasion', in D. Frick and L. Spears (eds) *On Becoming a Servant Leader*, New York: John Wiley, 1996, p. 128.
13. R. Greenleaf, 'Business, ethics, and manipulation', in D. Frick and L. Spears (eds) *On Becoming a Servant Leader*, New York: John Wiley, 1996, p. 118.
14. Greenleaf, 'Business, ethics, and manipulation', p. 117.
15. R. Greenleaf, *Servant Leadership: A Journey into the Nature of Legitimate Power and Greatness*, 25th anniversary edn, Mahwah, NJ: Paulist Press, 2002, pp. 53–4.
16. L. Spears, 'Tracing the past, present, and future of servant leadership', in Spears and Lawrence, *On Becoming a Servant Leader*, pp. 4–8.
17. A.T. Fraker, 'Robert K. Greenleaf and business ethics: there is no code', in L. Spears (ed.), *Reflections on Leadership: How Robert K. Greenleaf's Theory of Servant Leadership Influenced Today's Top Management Thinkers*, New York: John Wiley, 1995, pp. 42–5.
18. R.C. Liden, A. Panaccio, J.D. Meuser, J. Hu and S.J. Wayne, 'Servant leadership: antecedents, processes, and outcomes', in D.V. Day (ed.), *The Oxford Handbook of Leadership and Organizations*, Oxford: Oxford University Press, 2014, pp. 357–79.
19. van Dierendonck, 'Servant leadership: a review and synthesis', p. 1229.
20. G.J. Lemoine, 'Closing the leadership circle: building and testing a contingent theory of servant leadership', Georgia Institute of Technology, unpublished dissertation, 2015, p. 3. https://smartech.gatech.edu/handle/1853/53862 (accessed 12 November 2022).
21. P. Drucker, 'Foreword', in Frick and Spears, *On Becoming a Servant Leader*, pp. xi–xii.
22. R. Greenleaf, *Servant Leadership*, Mahwah, NJ: Paulist Press, 1977, p. 142.

23.    Greenleaf, 'The servant as leader', p. 5.

24.    Me Too.org, 'Get to know us'. https://metoomvmt.org/get-to-know-us/tarana-burke-founder/ (accessed 12 November 2022).

25.    S. Modrek and B. Chakalov, 'The #MeToo movement in the United States: text analysis of early Twitter conversations', *Journal of Medical Internet Research*, vol. 21 no. 9, 3 September 2019. https://www.ncbi.nlm.nih.gov/pmc/articles/PMC6751092/ (accessed 12 November 2022).

26.    M. Anderson and S. Toor, 'How social media users have discussed sexual harassment since #MeToo went viral', Pew Research Center, 11 October 2018. https://www.pewresearch.org/fact-tank/2018/10/11/how-social-media-users-have-discussed-sexual-harassment-since-metoo-went-viral/ (accessed 12 November 2022).

27.    K.L. Alexander, 'Tarana Burke', National Women's History Museum, 2020. https://www.womenshistory.org/education-resources/biographies/tarana-burke (accessed 12 November 2022).

28.    W. Becker, 'Tarana Burke delivers emotional leadership lecture', *The Seahawk*, 30 September 2019. https://theseahawk.org/23750/news/taran-burke-delivers-emotional-leadership-lecture/ (accessed 12 November 2022).

29.    D. Watkins, 'Me Too founder on her healing memoir and creating change: "all of us contribute to rape culture"', Salon, 15 September 2021. https://www.salon.com/2021/09/15/tarana-burke-me-too-unbound-salon-talks/ (accessed 12 November 2022).

30.    N. Carroll, 'Tanara Burke on the power of empathy, the building block of the Me Too movement', *USA Today*, 19 August 2020. https://www.usatoday.com/in-depth/life/women-of-the-century/2020/08/19/tarana-burke-me-too-movement-19th-amendment-women-of-century/5535976002/ (accessed 12 November 2022).

31.    N. Eva, M. Robin, S. Sendjaya, D. van Dierendonck and R.C. Liden, 'Servant leadership: a systematic review and call for future research', *The Leadership Quarterly*, vol. 30 no. 1, February 2019, 111–32. https://www.sciencedirect.com/science/article/pii/S1048984317307774 (accessed 12 November 2022).

32.    Greenleaf, 'The servant as leader'.

33.    Carroll, 'Tanara Burke on the power of empathy'.

34.    Watkins, 'Me Too founder on her healing memoir'.

35.    Me Too.org. https://metoomvmt.org/get-to-know-us/tarana-burke-founder/.

36.    E.J. Russell, R.J. Maxfield and J.L. Russell, 'Discovering the self-interest of servant leadership, a grounded theory', *Servant Leadership: Theory and Practice*, vol. 4 no. 1, Spring 2017, 75–97. https://csuepress.columbusstate.edu/cgi/viewcontent.cgi?referer=&httpsredir=1&article=1039&context=sltp (accessed 12 November 2022).

37.    Milano's Tweet was published on 15 October 2017.

38.    See https://www.theguardian.com/culture/2017/dec/01/alyssa-milano-mee-too-sexual-harassment-abuse.

39.    C.R. Greenlee, 'Tanara Burke on the birth of #MeToo, letting Black girls "just be," and leaning on her faith', *Self*, 16 September 2021. https://www.self.com/story/tarana-burke-memoir (accessed 12 November 2022).

40.    Watkins, 'Me Too founder on her healing memoir'.

41.    See https://dailycollegian.com/2019/03/me-too-founder-tarana-burke-talks-community-leadership-and-activism/.

42.    Greenlee, 'Tanara Burke on the birth of #MeToo'.

43.    K. Reynolds, 'Servant-leadership: a feminist perspective', *The International Journal of Servant Leadership*, vol. 10 no. 1, 2016, 35–63.

44. Greenleaf, 'The servant as leader'.

45. E. Brockes, '#MeToo founder Tanara Burke: "you have to use your privilege to serve other people"', *The Guardian*, 15 January 2018. https://www.theguardian.com/world/2018/jan/15/me-too-founder-tarana-burke-women-sexual-assault (accessed 12 November 2022).

46. C. Cleveland, 'The hole in our servant leadership', *Christianity Today*, 26 October 2015. https://www.christianitytoday.com/ct/2015/november/hole-in-our-servant-leadership.html (accessed 12 November 2022).

47. A. Buyinza and R. Duke Wiesenberg, '"Me Too" founder Tanara Burke talks community leadership and activism', *The Massachusetts Daily Collegian*, 21 March 2019. https://dailycollegian.com/2019/03/me-too-founder-tarana-burke-talks-community-leadership-and-activism/ (accessed 12 November 2022).

48. Carroll, 'Tanara Burke on the power of empathy'.

49. Greenleaf, 'The servant as leader'.

50. Carroll, 'Tanara Burke on the power of empathy'.

51. Carroll, 'Tanara Burke on the power of empathy'.

52. J. Laub, *Leveraging the Power of Servant Leadership*, Basingstoke: Palgrave Macmillan, 2018.

53. Russell et al., 'Discovering the self-interest of servant leadership'.

54. Eva et al., 'Servant leadership: a systematic review'.

# 15
# Followership

*Stanley J. Ward*

## FRAMING QUESTION

How can followers partner with their leaders to do the right thing?

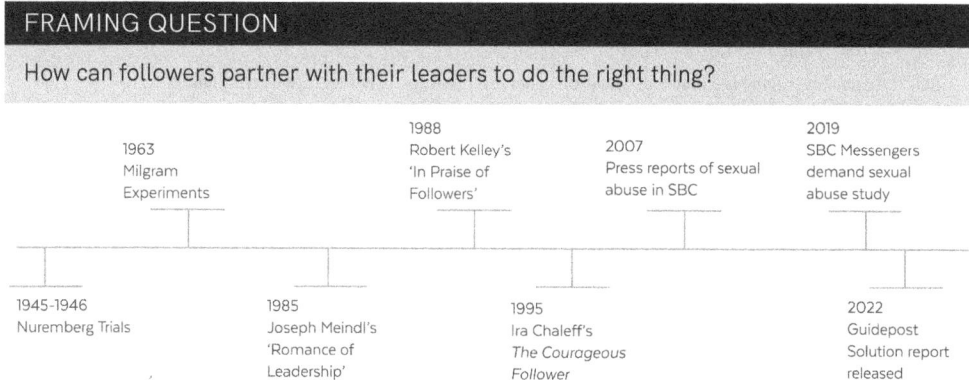

**Figure 15.1**    Timeline of major works on followership in relation to the chapter case study

For centuries, leaders have pondered what to do with followers, including how to relate to them. For example, in his advice to a young prince, Machiavelli infamously addressed whether it is better to be feared or loved by followers – while love is good, fear is more effective. The conclusion of those thoughts by Machiavelli and others often emphasized the idea that followers should be dominated or used as cannon fodder.[1]

Though followers were certainly considered, the primary concern was still leader-centric. As leadership studies continued to develop, this leader-centric perspective was shared by the 'great man' leadership model expressed in the nineteenth century.[2] In the twentieth century, leadership and organizational thinkers began to better appreciate the role – and power – of followers, which eventually led to 'followership' as a small but growing body of knowledge in the early twenty-first century. The followership concept contributes to a more robust understanding of leadership by challenging leader-centric models and empowering the role of followers. Empowered followers are a critical component of ethical leadership, though it is a role that includes risks for leaders and followers alike. All of this adds up to a renewed appreciation for the vital function of followers in an organization.

In our chapter, we will start by considering the development of followership in the twentieth century and its ongoing growth. After discussing key concepts and important contributors to the idea, we will consider critiques against 'followership' as a term for leadership studies. Like the other chapters in this book, we will also consider how the Five Components of Leadership Model analyses followership and conduct a case study. The case will consider the recent sex abuse scandal in the Southern Baptist Convention and what the case study can teach us about followership.

As the chapter progresses, readers will see how followership serves as an ethics-oriented leadership model for a variety of reasons. Among these reasons, and perhaps most important among them, is how followers can *remind* leaders of the core ethical principles of an organization and how followers can *refuse* to follow leaders who blatantly disregard ethical practices. This capacity to remind and refuse transforms followers from passive 'yes-people' to active partners in an organization's success.

## HISTORY

Mary Parker Follett's work demonstrates an early appreciation for the influence of followers. Read by business leaders in the 1920s and 1930s, Follett emphasized that both management and labour shared certain common concerns, and these concerns could serve as a focal point for the management–labour relationship. When businesses like Walmart or JCPenney call their employees 'associates', we still see her impact. Her power model for leaders was *co-active* and not *coercive*.[3] Like the Common Good discussed in Chapter 12, the shared concerns of management and labour became a crucial ethical foundation as the study of followership developed.

In the aftermath of the Second World War, the Western world realized the importance of assertive followers. The Nuremberg Trials (1945-46) judged influential actors from the Nazi regime who carried out the Holocaust or other war crimes. Some defendants claimed they could not be held responsible for their actions because they were merely following orders as faithful members of the Nazi party. The common plea was that these followers were not the ones who initiated the orders, and therefore they were not responsible for their actions. The tribunal rejected such claims, finding those who carried out the orders to be morally culpable. To clarify the moral obligations of followers, Nuremberg Principle IV states that 'The fact that a person acted pursuant to an order of his Government or a superior does not relieve him from responsibility under international law, provided a moral choice was in fact possible to him.'[4]

During the second half of the twentieth century, issues of followership received increasing attention. In 1963, a psychologist from Yale University, Stanley Milgram, wanted to better understand the Nuremberg defence of the Nazi followers. Just how much harm would a person be willing to do to another person in the name of obedience to authority? To answer his question, he created a famous series of 'education' experiments where participants were asked by a 'researcher' to administer an electrical shock to a 'learner' every time the learner got an answer wrong. For each wrong answer, the shock increased – until it reached possibly deadly levels.

The 'learner' was an actor who pretended to experience increasing levels of shock and would sometimes even beg the research participant to stop.[5]

During the 1980s and 1990s, additional appreciation for the power of followers can be seen in James R. Meindl's work. Meindl viewed leadership not as something independent from followers but actually a construction of followers.[6] He posited a 'romance of leadership' where followers made a 'fundamental attribution error' and attributed organizational results to individual leaders. Going even further, he later posited a 'social contagion' theory where the group prescribes what leadership is, so the individual leader could actually be taken out of the equation.[7] So with Meindl, we see the root of power more in the hands of the followers than in the hands of the leader.

Then, in 1988, Robert Kelley published a *Harvard Business Review* article that became an often-cited resource for followership: 'In praise of followers'. Kelley later followed the popular *HBR* article with a book, *The Power of Followership*. Recognizing the power of engaged followers, he explained that highly committed followers to the organization's mission would be powerful contributors. Similarly, engaged followers motivated by concerns contrary to the organization's mission could be highly destructive. He recognized that courageous followers were necessary to keep organizations ethical – an idea that Ira Chaleff's work would further develop in the twenty-first century. Likewise, Kelley's article suggested ways organizations could train for more effective followership and leadership. Additionally, organizations needed to change how they defined 'leadership' and 'followership' because these were temporary 'roles' in an organization, not a state of being.

Early in the twenty-first century, this new appreciation for the role of followers can be seen to coincide with growing complexities for leaders, such as globalization and the Internet. Another indication of a growing appreciation for leadership's complex and non-linear nature can be seen in books such as Margaret Wheatley's *Leadership and the New Science* and Ronald Heifetz's concept of 'adaptive leadership', well expressed in the title of his book, *Leadership Without Easy Answers*.[8] Multiple factors had to be considered for effective leadership in complex situations. Might followers have a crucial role to play in solving the 'wicked problems' confronting humanity?[9]

Two writers contributed substantially to the discussion of followership in the early twenty-first century: Ira Chaleff and Barbara Kellerman. Chaleff continued the discussion on courageous followers and added to it with a discussion on 'intelligent disobedience', which also reflected on the previously mentioned Nuremberg trials and the Milgram experiments.[10] Kellerman also developed a typology for followers and continued to challenge the primary emphasis on leaders themselves as a central force for 'leadership'. Recently, Kellerman has described a 'followership paradox'; while followers may be acting more, they often act alone or in uncoordinated efforts.[11] As a result: 'Emboldened followers make it hard for leaders to lead. Ineffectual followers make it easy to see why leaders usually remain in place, no matter how evidently inadequate. No wonder collective problems remain impervious to collective solutions.'[12]

For our purposes, we will consider followership as *a partnership between leaders and followers where both hold each other accountable for the success of the organization.*

## MAJOR CONCEPTS OF FOLLOWERSHIP

After reviewing the growing work around 'followership', this chapter will next consider the dynamics of leader–follower relationships, typologies of followers, and what happens when the leader–follower relationship breaks down: the whistle-blower and responding to toxic leadership. The hallmark concept of followership is a dynamic view of leader–follower relationships and understanding followers as partners in leadership interactions instead of seeing them as simply those who implement the leader's wishes. With that overview in mind, let's consider the dynamics of the leader–follower relationship.

### Dynamics of the Leader–Follower Relationship

#### Followers aren't so different from leaders

Robert Kelley memorably points out that the idea of followers as contributors is contrary to how many perceive followers. Followers are not simply 'sled dogs whose destiny is always to look at the rear end of the dog in front of them, but never to see the wider horizon or make the decisions of the lead dog'.[13] Instead, followership is an active mode of being in which followers can make decisions that have real consequences for both the organization and themselves. Especially in a knowledge-based economy, followers must be able to move into self-directed leadership.[14] Interestingly, the traits that make for great leaders are also associated with the traits that make for great followers.[15] Followership models point out that the status of 'leader' and 'follower' are actually mutable roles. In fact, the same person may play both roles, though in different work relationships. The mid-level manager would be a classic example – this manager is seen as a 'leader' by his direct reports and, likewise, is viewed as a 'follower' by his direct supervisor. Consequently, the chasm between 'leader' and 'follower' is not as great as one might suppose. In reality, the followership model is about developing 'leadership' skills in followers and recognizing that leader and follower titles are really roles instead of permanent conditions. With this in mind, some scholars call for followership that is about learning to think like a leader.[16]

So, in order to fully appreciate how followership and leadership are not so different, we need to try different terms. Perhaps a better term for empowered followers would be 'ownership'. Followers must own their personal responsibility for shaping the direction of a community or organization. For example, Avolio discusses psychological ownership as an important part of followership, arguing that more owners are needed as the external and internal demands on organizations increase and as even remote workers can make decisions and take actions that have a significant impact on the organization. The benefits of psychological ownership include a sense of place, a sense of self, and a sense of efficacy.[17] This sense of place, self, and efficacy can provide the strong presence necessary for followers to challenge toxic leaders.

Empowered followership, or ownership, can be expressed through courageous behaviours. Chaleff's discussion of courageous followership lists six examples of how followers must be courageous. His list of behaviours could just as easily be described as the behaviours of a courageous leader as much as of a courageous follower: assuming responsibility, serving, challenging, participating in transformation, taking moral action, and speaking to hierarchy.

And by no means does the courage of a follower abnegate courage for a leader. In fact, when followers take these courageous actions, leaders need similar courage to listen to their followers.[18] When we consider our case study of the Southern Baptist Convention scandal, a breakdown in the listening behaviours of leaders will be one noted contributing factor in the scandal.

## Active followers are empowered followers

When one considers the various typologies suggested for followers, one can see the traditional notion of followers as 'passive' and a status not accorded with praise. (For example, at this time, I know of no universities offering majors in 'followership' or proudly listing their students' 'followership' accomplishments.) Yet, when we consider follower typologies, followers are not merely passive recipients of the action. Consider Table 15.1. The organizing factors for these typologies often relate, at least in part, to the activity level of the follower. Readers will note that as the level of organizing factors increases, the followers' descriptive title also shows increased presence on the part of the follower and the increasing presence of terms that are considered positive.

**Table 15.1** Followership typologies

| Source | Organizing Factors | Types (ordered by increasing presence of organizing factors) |
|---|---|---|
| Abraham Zalesnik's (1965) 'The Dynamics of Subordinancy' | Dual axes of dominance–submission and activity–passivity | Impulsive subordinates; Compulsive subordinates; Masochistic subordinates; Withdrawn subordinates |
| Robert Kelley (1988) | Follower independence of thought; Extent of follower activity | Sheep; Yes People; Alienated; Effective Followers; Survivors |
| Ira Chaleff (1995) | Support or challenge for leaders | Implementers; Partners; Individualists, and Resources |
| Barbara Kellerman (2008) | Involvement/Engagement | Isolates, Bystanders, Participants, Activists, Die Hards |
| Rosenbach, Bitmann and Potter (2012) | X/Y axis of relationship initiative and performance initiative | Subordinates; Contributors; Politicians; Partners |

Perhaps the simplest typology we can offer here is 'good' versus 'bad' followers. Kellerman emphasizes activity in her discussion of 'good' versus 'bad' followers: (1) followers who do something are almost always preferred to those who do nothing; (2) good followers actively support good leadership (which Kellerman describes as effective and ethical leadership) and actively resist bad leadership (that which is ineffective or unethical). With an increasing appreciation for followers as actors whose decisions have consequences for both their leaders and their organizations, followers can be understood to have a growing importance as moral actors in their various settings. As a thought experiment, imagine how 'courageous followership' might have impacted the moral atrocities addressed in the Nuremberg trials. More engaged followers who possessed a strong moral compass and were willing to endure great personal risk could have mitigated some of the Holocaust's horrors. By reviewing the typologies listed here, readers will note that as followers become more active, they are also described in more favourable terms.

Why this growing emphasis on the empowerment of active followers? Part of it may come from an increasing distrust of leaders. Kellerman points out that the balance of power has shifted away from a leadership monopoly to more influence for followers, and some of that shift is because of a growing contempt for leaders.[19] So, healthy followership might just be the cure for failing leadership. A study of followership forces leadership practitioners to consider the wealth of follower types and their influence on the organization. The variety of follower-ship typologies demonstrates that followers cannot be lumped into one homogeneous and passive bundle, and their variety goes beyond sorting into only 'good' and 'bad' types.

## Followers are moral agents

Followership is critical because it allows those in a non-authoritative role to still have agency in their settings. Given Principle IV from the Nuremberg Trials, empowered followership skills are necessary because followers are morally culpable for their actions, even when fol-lowing orders. Ethical followers do not have the luxury of being passive. Bass explains that the opposite of leader is not 'follower' but rather the completely disengaged or apathetic, because both leaders and followers can be transformational when they are fully engaged and following something larger than themselves.[20] Chaleff's *Courageous Follower* also empha-sizes how followership is not a passive activity and illustrates the power of a leader–follower relationship based on mutual accountability to a higher purpose. In this case, the core of the leader–follower relationship focuses on the organization's purpose. This shared commitment to a common purpose empowers followers to take moral action when needed. In sum, leaders hold followers accountable for the organization's purpose, and followers are empowered like-wise to hold leaders accountable for following that same purpose.

Even more powerful than a shared sense of mission, a commitment to core values allows the follower to serve as a force for moral accountability. Values are a resource followers can use when they query and appeal to unclear or ill-advised directives from their leader.[21] In his discussion of the Milgram experiments, Chaleff notes that a distinguishing quality for those who disobeyed an order from an authority figure was a stronger sense of obedience to some-thing else, something higher.[22] When we view followers as active moral agents, the result of the Nuremberg trials makes more sense. While 'loyal Nazis' may have just been following orders, there are other values to be considered than simple 'obedience'. More to the point, obedience is a misappropriated value when the obedience is following orders to carry out genocide.

In his work specific to followership, Chaleff also suggests that followers should develop a variety of communication skills to best serve as a trusted voice for the leader. In his work on intelligent disobedience, Chaleff later says that followers who disobey must clarify *why* they do so and do so clearly, with a strong voice that does not use 'mitigating language'. His basic formula for the follower is to (1) understand the mission, (2) clarify the order as needed, (3) make a conscious choice, and (4) assume personal accountability for the choice.[23] Intelligent disobedience is not the same as 'civil disobedience'. Civil disobedience is intentionally disrup-tive and violates laws. Intelligent disobedience '[does] not flagrantly violate existing laws'.[24]

One of the ways that followers can be active moral agents is by serving as a 'whistle-blower'. Admittedly, the status of 'whistle-blower' represents a breakdown of trust in the organization. It could require the follower to break with the value of 'loyalty' or 'obedience' to take action on a higher value. In *Courageous Followers*, Chaleff points out that being a whistle-blower is not the same as courageous followership. One can take the corrective actions of a courageous follower without disavowing the leader. Likewise, one can be a whistle-blower motivated by something other than the organization's best interests.

The decision to become a whistle-blower is challenging because the action can have a great cost for both the organization and the whistle-blower. For example, Fred Alford uses the imagery of a 'scapegoat' and explains that the Greek word for such, *pharmakos*, can be translated as both 'poison' and 'cure'. The scapegoat/whistle-blower serves as both in an organization. The cure is that it puts our sins at a distance, but the whistle-blower can also be seen as a poison to their industry. Between one-half to two-thirds of whistle-blowers lose their jobs, and many are not able to find employment again in their industries.[25]

### Active followers can respond to toxic leaders

Perhaps one of the most positive outcomes of the model is the ability to recognize and respond appropriately to toxic leadership (Chapter 18). Jean Lipman-Blumen defines toxic leadership at its most basic level as those leaders who leave us worse than when they found us, or those who intentionally enhance themselves at the expense of others.[26] Why do we support such leaders? Lipman-Blumen explains that they give followers a sense of meaning, safety, and stability. When we review our discussion of followership so far, we can see a number of ways that active followers can serve as a check and balance against toxic leadership. Fundamentally, engaged followers are not just passive yes-people. Likewise, engaged followers do not simply disengage when they see leaders who threaten the organization or disregard core values. When they perceive a threat, followers can use their communication skills to speak up, remind leaders of the mission, and provide alternative decisions. When necessary, followers can practise intelligent disobedience. As a final step, active followers can serve as whistle-blowers – though often at great cost.

In conclusion of this section, if one forced me to identify a single outcome of the followership model, especially from an ethical perspective, the greatest outcome is that it demonstrates that 'good followers' are not simply those who take orders. Followership is not passive. From a consideration of 'ethical leadership', healthy followership is essential in an organization for two reasons: (1) its potential to empower good leaders; and (2) its potential to resist bad leaders.

Much of this chapter has considered how followers can respond to bad leaders and why followers should do so. However, we would be remiss not to pause for a moment and remind ourselves of the power of followership for supporting good leaders. In the same way that followers can be a check and balance for bad leadership, they are also a powerful dynamo for good leadership. Passive followers harm an organization – they do not resist bad leadership, and they do not support good leadership. Passive followership represents a threat to our organizations. Therefore, while leadership training is still essential for organizations, they would also do well to invest some of those resources in developing followers and training leaders on how to respond to followers. Likewise, organizations must invest in creating a culture that welcomes and empowers good followership. Kellerman puts it this way: 'we can't reduce the number of bad leaders unless we reduce the number of bad followers.'[27]

## CRITIQUES OF FOLLOWERSHIP

Followership is a powerful concept for organizations that wish to reinforce consistent ethical practices. Yet, it also has drawbacks as a concept. These drawbacks include theoretical concerns and practical concerns. Let's start our discussion of followership's challenges with a discussion of two theoretical challenges and then discuss practical concerns.

### Theoretical Challenge Number One: The Limits of Language

From a theoretical standpoint, the very term 'follower' may be one of the biggest obstacles for the followership model. To be a 'follower' can quickly become equated with being a passive recipient of the actions or commands of the leader. If one starts with the 'great man' model of leadership as an assumption, then the follower's role is minimized. Because of this, Joseph Rost suggests using the term 'collaborator' instead to recognize the active role that followers can play in organizations.[28] He suggests that the term 'follower' only reinforces the great-man leadership model. Similarly, in *Hard Times*, Kellerman notes that while follower seems to be the only obvious antonym for leader, people still use a variety of terms to express the idea: 'stakeholder, constituents, participants, subordinates, employees, group members, or team members'.[29] So, to really discuss followership as an ethical resource in organizations, we need to rely on terms inspired by Follet's work, like 'associate' and 'partner', or, at minimum, terms like 'engaged follower'. By redefining followership with more active and engaged language or finding new terms, we can view the follower role in an entirely new light. We must come to understand the follower as a partner who works with the leader, sometimes even holding the leader accountable, for the sake of the organization's missional success.

### Theoretical Challenge Number Two: The Hierarchical Nature of Organizations

Intuitively, not everyone can be a leader – so how do we understand organizational charts for 'empowered followers'? One suggestion from Gene Dixon is to change the chart from a top-down leader/follower relationship to viewing all members of the organization as leader–followers who exhibit different qualities in different contexts, with the hope that such a sense of organizational structure would call leader–followers to be more self-aware of how their work impacts both those to whom they report and those whom they manage. Such a construct would also recognize that titles like 'leader' and 'follower' are not permanent character traits but rather flexible roles.[30] For example, even CEOs often have a board that holds the chief executive accountable for specific results.

## Practical Concern Number One: Risks for Followers

Theoretical concerns are not the only possible shortcoming of the followership model. There are practical risks for both followers and leaders. An imminent concern for followership is related to the hierarchical nature of the organizations mentioned above. In this case, we consider the power difference between leaders and followers. Leaders have access to resources that followers lack. Because of the power difference between leaders and followers, followers depend upon functioning mechanisms like ethics hotlines. They need reinforcement from external resources if they are to take the difficult stand sometimes required.

Also, in an employment setting, followers generally depend on the income and other benefits that go with their job. How can they risk the repercussions of speaking up if to do so is to risk their livelihood? To go further, to speak up as a 'whistle-blower' can have dire consequences not just at that current place of employment, but for a worker's future in an entire industry. Another struggle for followership is that sometimes correcting bad leadership is not in the best interest of individual followers.[31] For example, if the employee benefits financially or in other ways because of poor leadership, what would inspire the follower to speak up?

## Practical Concern Number Two: Risks for Leaders

Leaders may also fear empowering followers because it can risk creating an antagonistic relationship between leaders and followers. The followership model might be perceived as a threat to organizations that depend on order, efficiency, or the authority of leaders. For followers to be genuinely empowered, leaders must relinquish a certain degree of control and be more open to critical feedback from subordinates. Leaders may thus be required to change their self-concepts about the nature of their power and status. So, training would be required for both leaders and followers. For followership to work, leaders and followers must take risks.

## ETHICAL IMPLICATIONS OF FOLLOWERSHIP

The real ethical power source for followership has two dimensions. First, it elevates how leaders view followers. No longer are followers seen as cannon fodder. Now they are partners for the leader's success and, even more importantly, for the organization's success and mission. Next, the power source for the follower himself is rooted in ethical concerns – either common concerns (where leader and follower have a shared set of values) or contrary concerns. With that in mind, here are some observations on followership as an ethical leadership model:

- Followership supercharges any leader–follower relationship where the leader and follower share common ethical concerns. In this case, the follower is a partner who can empower the leader to pursue those ethical concerns. When leaders seem to lose sight of those shared concerns, the followers can remind leaders to re-evaluate their actions.
- Followership gets tricky when the leader and follower operate under different ethical concerns. For example, a leader might be fully 'authentic' in his drive for success and pursue an implied social contract with investors (who expect the leader to report quar-

terly profits). At the same time, the follower may see these actions as actually taking advantage of others.

● What this means for followership is that it can be a leadership model to reinforce any of the ethical models we discussed in section one of our text. However, *how* followers show support for that ethical model will vary. For example, the concerns of an engaged follower who supports the common good might look different from an engaged follower who supports a social contract that rejects the notion of a 'common good'.

Thus, those who wish to be fully empowered followers and partners for their leaders would do well to have an ethical vocabulary. Empowered followers must also practise their communication skills to reinforce core values in the organization, redirect the leader when needed, and in the most extreme cases, resist the leader entirely.

## FIVE COMPONENT ANALYSIS

As with the other chapters, we now consider how the Five Component Model can help us understand the focus of our chapter on followership. Let's start our analysis with a riddle from one of my favourite comic books – *Usagi Yojimbo*. In a discussion with a fellow Samurai Warrior, Usagi considers a Bushido riddle:

> Which more exemplifies Bushido – a Samurai who serves a good and fair lord or one who faithfully serves a wicked lord?' Usagi answers (correctly): 'The one who is loyal to his evil lord, of course.' Loyalty is the first principle of Bushido.[32]

In the riddle's model of followership, we see two primary sources of authority: culture, as expressed through the tenets of the Bushido riddle; and the leader himself, no matter what his moral intent.

The Bushido riddle exemplifies the 'diehard' follower type mentioned by Kellerman. In this case, the Samurai follows the orders of his master – even if those orders are wicked and require the Samurai to sacrifice his own life. If we understand followership in purely passive terms, this would also be our view of followership in the Western world. However, when we discuss terms like 'courageous followers', 'intelligent disobedience', and 'good followers', we enter into a new understanding – one that promotes an ethical leadership model. Let's take a look at how each of the five leadership components is addressed by the followership described in the current chapter (Figure 15.2).

Shamir described followers as 'constructors' of leadership.[33] With his description, we see an emphasis on the relationship between leaders *and* followers instead of leaders *over* followers. So, we are moving away from a purely linear view of leadership. Additionally, although the model's title may feature the term 'follower', in reality, followership considers much more, such as the relationship between leader and followers, the goals, the organizational context, and the larger values that guide the organization. In this sense, the followership model provides a robust understanding of leadership (ironically, given the label 'followership'). Regarding the leader–follower relationship, the one essential component seems to be that the follower is responsible for assessing the leader and the goal, all within a larger context – that of an organization's purpose, values, and vision. Additionally, titles like 'leader' and 'follower' are not permanent states of being, but fluid and interchangeable roles, depending on the situation.

This is where the conversation about toxic leadership can come to play. Given that the follower is not seen as passive, the follower can be morally culpable for 'just following orders'. The moral dilemma of 'just following orders' was highlighted in the Nuremberg trials, when Nazi soldiers who helped carry out the Holocaust claimed they were not morally responsible for their actions precisely because they were following orders. One consequence of the

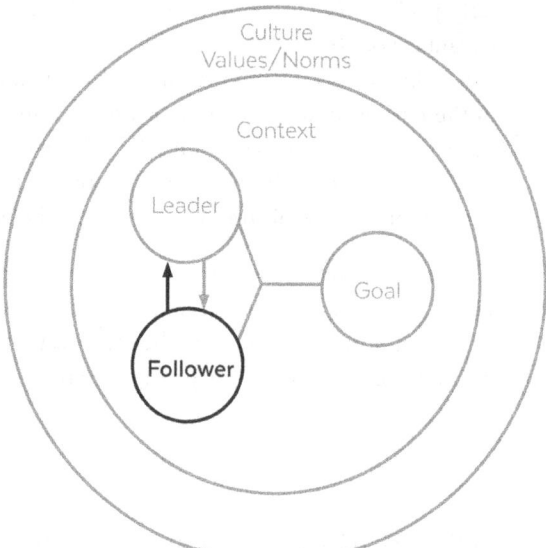

**Figure 15.2**    The Five Components of Leadership Model applied to followership

Nuremberg trials was that moral and, by extension, legal culpability extended beyond obedience to authority. So, a strong followership model that views followers as individually responsible agents can serve as a corrective force for toxic leadership.

To apply this back to the Five Component Model, both the leader's 'circle' and that of the follower are important. The follower partners with the leader for success. Both are accountable to something other than themselves – the purpose of the organization, or a higher ethical principle. This accountability was illustrated in the Milgram experiments (discussed earlier in the chapter) where participants refused to follow the orders of a so-called expert because the participant appealed to a higher moral code.

So what, then, are the practical interactions between follower and leader? Followership rightly reminds us that followers can decide whether to resist or support the leader. And that those choices themselves are not simply either/or. We might consider the extreme range of responses for followers to be outright disobedience at one end of the spectrum and unquestioning obedience at the other end. In most circumstances, healthy followership avoids these extremes.

For example, if the follower believes the leader is about to make a bad decision, the follower can provide support to the leader by questioning the current decision. Yes, it might look like resistance in the short term, but the overall motivation for questioning the leader's decision is to help the leader be successful in the long term. While the 'whistle-blower' option may seem to represent a complete breakdown between leader and follower – even then, the follower is motivated by a larger concern for the success or survival of the organization. In this case, the follower brings to light practices that hurt the organization's integrity.

The goal is still important, but simply accomplishing the goal is not the final measure of success. There is another concern that determines the goal's validity – namely, the values of the organization or the larger values of the culture. The goal should be consistent with this larger purpose. So, the circle representing the goal, while still important, should attract less of our notice.

From the leader's perspective, good followers may be those who simply crank out product – accomplishing goals. But suppose we see followership as a skillset for ethical leadership in an organization. In that case, the follower's responsibility for achieving the goal becomes much more nuanced. Followers must ask themselves if the goal is moral and evaluate how the goal is being achieved.

The context is also a powerful factor in the leader–follower dynamic because it is in this sphere that we can often find pressures that challenge healthy leader–follower relationships and may cause leaders to make unethical requests of their followers. These pressures can include the need to make sales quotas, industry trends, or regulations threatening the organization's ability to achieve its goals and prosper. Likewise, the environment also includes resources that can help a follower respond to unhealthy pressure from a leader. If there is a high demand for the skills of a follower, he can choose to work elsewhere. The follower can use those resources if the organization has an ethics hotline or HR process for addressing concerns. There may even be legal precedents to which a follower can appeal.

If we see the sphere of culture as the locus for things like 'values', 'purpose', and 'mission', then we quickly see the importance of culture for engaged followership. The real power source for followership is the ability of the follower to know those core values, to communicate them, and to act on them – even if it means refusing the leader's directives. When the follower looks to the cultural circle instead of an organizational chart, the follower's role suddenly does not seem so fixed. Leaders and followers are both in service to the purpose of the organization at minimum, and to even higher values based on larger cultural concerns like ethics and morality. The cultural spheres of concern provide the moral compass for the followership model. Because of this, the model should be understood as an ethical leadership model, where authority rests in something transcending the leader.

So, to return to our riddle of the wicked master, according to the typology suggested by Barbara Kellerman, the Samurai would be a 'diehard' follower, but he would not be a 'good' follower. Kellerman says good followers resist bad leaders. Thus, the courageous follower would need to start by expressing concern to his master, possibly practising intelligent disobedience. If that does not work, the follower would want to actively resist his master. Depending on the organization, this resistance could go as far as whistleblowing. For the Samurai to claim he was 'just following orders' from his wicked master would not remove him from moral culpability.

## CASE STUDY: THE SOUTHERN BAPTIST CONVENTION'S SEX ABUSE SCANDAL

During the twenty-first century, sexual abuse by clergy members gained media attention in the USA and abroad. Cases of mistreatment in the Roman Catholic Church began coming to light in the 1980s, with a growing body of reports so that by the early 2000s child sex abuse had become 'a major global story'.[34] In the early 2000s, journalists also began investigating abuse within Protestant churches. During this time, the Southern Baptist Convention also began a reckoning. At the time, it was the largest Protestant denomination in the United States. For both the Roman Catholic Church and the Southern Baptist Convention, the primary push for accountability came from church members rather than the hierarchy. This case study will examine followership's role in the Southern Baptist Convention's (SBC) decision to allow a full and independent investigation regarding how the Convention's executive leaders mishandled concerns about sexual abuse in member churches.

The SBC's over 15 million members make it the world's largest Baptist denomination and largest protestant denomination in the United States.[35] The SBC represents a tradition in Christian denominations that emphasizes local churches' autonomy rather than organizing them under a centralized and hierarchical leadership. That emphasis on autonomy makes it different from other ecclesiastical structures, such as those in the Roman Catholic, Anglican, or Presbyterian traditions. In the SBC, local churches make decisions about their own governance rather than confirming the decision with an outside authority.

Nonetheless, the local churches are still part of a larger corporate body that agrees to a particular confession of faith. That organizational body has an executive leadership team – thus, the Executive Committee of the Southern Baptist Convention. This unique dynamic relationship between the Executive Committee and the local church representatives makes this case interesting for those who study followership. As part of this dynamic between the Executive Committee and the member churches, the SBC hosts an annual convention. Member churches send voting representatives, called 'Messengers'. Their role is to vote on issues that impact the denomination. Messengers vote at the annual convention to determine the direction of the convention partnership. Topics include programme budgets, electing officers and trustees, receiving reports, passing resolutions, and voting on recommendations.[36] The SBC is organized around a cooperative funding programme where the member churches provide financial support for institutional agencies like seminaries as well as representatives like missionaries. The Messengers influence this process as well. This annual Messenger meeting occurs over two days. When the Messengers are not in session, the denomination's executive body provides administration for the convention.

By the early 2000s, a global awareness developed around the issue of sexual abuse by clergy and possible cover-ups by their hierarchy. During this time, a series of press stories uncovered abuses in the Roman Catholic Church. However, the problem was not limited to one particular faith or denomination. By 2007, the press began reporting similar issues in Protestant denominations, including the Southern Baptist Convention.[37] The convention president at the time announced that he would consider the possibility of creating a database to register sex offenders in SBC ministry. Some SBC Messengers advocated for a sex abuse database, but the convention did not take action. Ultimately, the executive leadership decided they did not have the authority to control hiring or firing in local churches due to the unique structure of the SBC with its loose association of autonomous churches. In 2015, the leadership also rejected calls for a sexual abuse education conference.[38]

The issue of sexual abuse in the SBC came to national attention again with the 2018 firing of Southwestern Baptist Theological Seminary president Paige Patterson over how he mishandled a rape case during his presidency at another SBC seminary, antagonizing the victim. Ten years previously, an individual had gone on record with concerns that he had covered up abuse. Patterson was a significant figure in the SBC, and his loss of status represented a considerable change in the status quo of the previous decade. In 2018 the SBC also launched a Sexual Abuse Advisory Study, and the Executive Committee chair, Mike Stone, said he wanted to address the issue as part of his tenure.[39]

During the 2018 convention, Messengers also voted to 'condemn all forms of abuse', and the Ethics and Religious Liberty Commission put together a report on sexual abuse in the convention. The 2019 report was met with resistance from legal counsel 'whose "over-riding concern" was about ascending liability'.[40] The Executive Committee also removed the word 'crisis' when referring to sexual abuse and expressed additional concerns about how the report could create liabilities for churches.[41]

The issue came to the forefront once again in 2019, as both *The Houston Chronicle* and *The San Antonio Express-News* published a series of articles highlighting sexual abuse in the SBC. The series was entitled 'Abuse of faith'. One of the issues was how offend-ers could move from one church to another because of the lack of a centrally organized authority that kept track of these individuals. The report also indicated cases where con-victed sex offenders were on church staff. The two papers created a hotline that over 400 people contacted, and after verifying concerns, they created a database of offenders. This was the first public database related to the original request of Messengers in 2007.

The sexual abuse crisis was again a topic at the 2019 convention meeting. The news-papers distributed copies of their abuse of faith series, and Messengers called for an independent investigation. This time, executive leadership supported this initiative. Convention president J.D. Greear and Executive Committee president Ronnie Floyd made public announcements. Delegates also changed bylaws, allowing the convention to 'disfel-lowship' churches with abusers on staff. In 2020 the denomination disfellowshipped one of its member churches for the first time over its decision to retain a clergy member who had been convicted of sexually abusing pre-teen girls in 2003.

Also in 2020, the Executive Committee expressed concerns about the investigation pro-cess as it addressed communication within the Executive Committee itself about sexual abuse. Executive Committee members expressed concerns about potential liabilities that could significantly harm the Convention. They decided to have the independent committee report back to the Executive Committee instead of a broader public audience. In other words, the leadership committee being investigated would have the results reported to itself instead of publicly making it available to the followers who called for the report.

Leadership within the convention was divided over how the Executive Committee han-dled concerns about abuse. In 2020 and 2021, Russell Moore, president of the Ethics and Religious Liberty Commission, published public letters accusing former Executive Committee heads Floyd and Stone of antipathy or active antagonism towards survivors and concerns about them co-opting the investigative process. In response, Moore was twice investigated by task forces appointed to investigate complaints against him.[42] He later resigned from his post in 2021.

At the 2021 convention, concerns over sexual abuse and how the Executive Committee handled the issue were again addressed by Messengers. This time they could use convention committee processes to return the matter to the forefront of the Convention. The Executive Committee was resistant to the idea of an independent investigation. Then-president Ronnie Floyd tried to prevent the motion from moving forward.[43] Eventually, the motion for an independent investigation passed by more than a two-thirds majority. Guidepost Solutions was later employed to provide an independent investigation of the Executive Committee and its handling of the situation.

In May of 2022, Guidepost Solutions published a damning report. The report's findings were a response to Messengers who called for 'an inquiry into the actions and decisions of Executive Committee staff and members' from 1 January 2000 to 15 June 2021 regarding 'abuse, mishandling of abuse, mistreatment of victims, patterns of intimidation of victims or advocates, and resistance to sexual abuse initiatives'.[44] The overall trend of the report was to highlight how a small group of executive leaders were resistant to addressing the issue and either ignored survivors or treated them with hostility. That resistance also included pushback on the Convention's Ethics and Religious Liberty Commission and the censorship of media within the Convention. The report also highlighted how a small group of Executive Committee members had maintained a secret list of suspected church predators for years. One of the primary drivers of this resistance was a concern for liability. When survivors contacted Executive Committee offices, lawyers advised the Executive Committee to 'say nothing and do nothing'.[45]

What began in 2008 as concerns about sexual abuse within the convention turned into an investigation of how the senior leadership mishandled those abuse situations. The full extent of the crisis, and the extent that executive leadership resisted addressing the issue, would not have become public knowledge without over a decade of persistent pressure from SBC members, their elected Messengers, outside media, and an external review.

## FIVE COMPONENT ANALYSIS

For the purpose of this case study, the SBC Executive Committee will be viewed as the 'leader' (Figure 15.3). The Committee was a group that provided oversight of the SBC between its annual conventions and was tasked with carrying out the will of its member churches. The Executive Committee was divided over leadership responsibilities towards preserving the institution and its reputation versus a 'spiritual fiduciary responsibility' to those who had been harmed.[46]

The division among these leaders illustrates how leaders manage a dual responsibility to the organizational

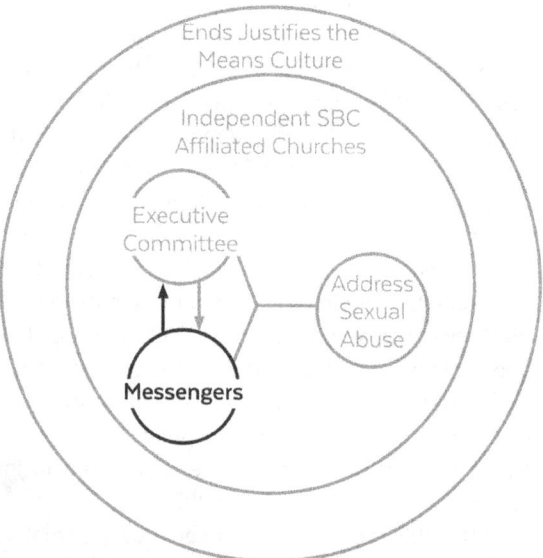

**Figure 15.3**  The Five Components of Leadership Model applied to the SBC case study

structures they serve and the stakeholders impacted by those organizations. Leaders of large organizations frequently face a kind of moral calculus that requires them to weigh choices between their organizations and the individuals affected by those organizations. They must often ask themselves, 'do the ends justify the means?' Some walk that tightrope well. Others do not.

The 'followers' in this case study are the Messengers who represented member churches of the SBC. Some of these followers began calling for reforms as early as 2008. Messengers continued to call for reforms for over 13 years. SBC abuse survivors and their advocates experienced years of resistance from the executive leadership group of their organization. Their patience and persistence should be the first takeaway from the case.

While their patience and persistence were necessary, that persistence alone did not appear to have been sufficient. The media attention, especially as developed by the *Houston Chronicle* and *San Antonio Express-News*, played such an important role that they were highlighted in the comments of then-president Greear, who commented, 'Advocates and journalists have faithfully filled the role of helping us to see things we can't unsee'. Through their work, a 'growing awareness within our denomination that the evangelical church has many areas for growth in how we prevent and care for abuse' developed.[47]

Some noteworthy followers also chose to leave the convention during that time. Notable examples are Beth Moore and Russell Moore (not related). Beth Moore was a popular women's speaker and author of numerous Bible studies who had been a lifelong member of the SBC. Both cited multiple issues in their final decision to break with the convention, and the mistreatment of women was primary, along with their own mistreatment. They illustrated the observation of Ira Chaleff that followers must sometimes have 'the courage to leave'.[48]

The most significant force for change and the most influential voice for these followers came from the independent, third-party review of Guidepost Solutions. When the integrity of the review process came into question, the Messengers were able to use the parliamentary procedures of the convention to move forward with a review that would not be under the purview of the Executive Committee.

The overall goal was agreed upon – addressing concerns about sexual abuse within the SBC. How to achieve that goal was an area of significant conflict. Survivors and their advocates wanted reforms that would bring public accountability for abusers and protect others from future abuse. The Executive Committee leadership focused on limiting liability for the organization rather than protecting its members from predatory clergy. Worse yet, leadership became antagonistic towards survivors and their advocates.

The corporate structure of the SBC itself seemed to cause some trepidation among the leadership. Member churches are considered autonomous and agree to cooperate with the SBC leadership. So, one of the challenges for the members was the lack of a top-down structure to enforce penalties for churches that did not address sexual abuse issues.[49] Public statements from those who resisted investigating abuse cases or keeping a public database of sexual predators often appealed to this lack of corporate authority over member churches.

On the other hand, other movements in the context of these events paralleled the efforts of Messengers calling for reform. In particular, these events occur during an era of increasingly active social media, the #MeToo and #ChurchToo movements, and investigative journalism regarding sexual abuse among the clergy of various denominations, private schools, ministries, and camps. No single organization, church, or parachurch ministry seemed to be immune. The 'Me Too' movement began in 2006 and by 2017 became a widespread social media movement with its use of the #MeToo hashtag (see Chapter 14). Between 1 October 2017 and 1 October 2018, the hashtag was used over 19 million times.[50] Soon after, the hashtag #ChurchToo appeared on social media. They were used by those who had been abused in church settings. Both social media and professional journalism combined with continuing to bring attention to the sexual mistreatment of women and others. As mentioned in the introduction to this case, the Roman Catholic Church had already been under scrutiny for decades before the issue was raised in the SBC. As in the SBC case, the push for reform came from lay members within the Roman Catholic Church rather than its leadership.[51]

One of the great struggles for mission-oriented organizations is to avoid falling into an 'ends justifies the means' kind of thinking. The argument goes that whatever we must do to get there is acceptable as long as the outcome is good. In other words, 'bad' deeds are acceptable as long as they get a 'good' result. Of course, one of the problems here is how we define a 'good' outcome. One might call this thought pattern an example of the 'dark side' of utilitarianism. This kind of thinking was a significant struggle across a number of Evangelical ministries as well as the SBC example. The argument essentially says that 'because of all the good things this leader/organization is accomplishing, we must not allow them to be discredited or questioned in any way.'

For example, before its involvement in the SBC crisis, Guidepost Solutions had previously investigated Ravi Zacharias International Ministries. They found that its board members were blind in their loyalty to Ravi Zacharias when he was accused of sexual misconduct. Part of this loyalty came because of the positive impact of Zacharias' preaching, teaching, and writing.[52]

As a second example, *The Rise and Fall of Mars Hill* podcast series by *Christianity Today* chronicled the story of Mark Driscoll – a charismatic pastor and church founder whose autocratic, and often toxic, leadership style was tolerated because of the church's apparent growth and success in bringing positive changes in the lives of its parishioners. Eventually, the church imploded when Driscoll became caught up in a public scandal.[53]

As an example from the SBC Guidepost Report, when former SBC president Johnny Hunt was credibly accused of sexually assaulting a woman, the counsellor warned the survivor and her spouse that they could not speak about the incident for fear that it would cause untold damage for the SBC church community.[54]

As a result of this kind of thinking, when SBC followers called for accountability or questioned some of these leaders, they were often met with hostility and treated as traitors to their cause – especially on social media. Notable examples included Russell Moore, Beth Moore, and numerous survivors of sexual assault who came forward. As pointed out by the Guidepost Report, which found 'patterns of intimidation of sexual abuse victims and advocates by Executive Committee Members'.[55] The report concluded:

> Overall, the legal advice focused on liability created a chilling effect on the ability of the EC to be compassionate towards survivors of abuse. Survivors were viewed through the lens of

potential plaintiffs threatening lawsuits rather than as individuals who had been harmed and were in need of care.[56]

Aside from the general recommendations already made in our chapter, three specific recommendations follow from the SBC case analysis. We will consider these recommendations one at a time.

Recommendation #1: Followers must beware of 'ends justify the means' leadership. Particularly troubling in the Guidepost Solutions report was how Executive Committee members treated those they believed to represent a liability to the organization. Likewise, bad actors were given more 'grace' than their victims out of concern for the possible larger consequences to the SBC should their crimes come to light.

As a subset of this recommendation, followers must beware of any religious leader who treats them as an 'implementer' instead of a 'partner', no matter how winsome the leader's personality or supposedly noble their cause. In a number of these cases, charismatic and authoritative leaders appealed to how public accountability would somehow harm the mission of their churches or convention. One might make exceptions here for some forms of military service – but even then, readers must remember the lessons of the Nuremberg trials and their personal moral responsibility.

Recommendation #2: Followership requires fortitude against both resistance and cynicism. It would be easy to read a case like this and make categorical statements like 'all religious leaders are hypocritical hucksters'. But such broad assessments would not be fair to the religious leaders from many traditions who exert themselves and make personal sacrifices to relieve human suffering and advance a message that they genuinely believe needs to be proclaimed. Many of these individuals would fall into the category of 'good' leaders who deserve support from their followers. One common struggle for followers is recognizing that leaders who do 'good' in one area may do 'bad' in another. That's why followers would be unwise to assume addressing an issue only once will be sufficient for organizational change – even when working with 'good' leaders. As pointed out by Chaleff, followers must 'maintain our own commitment, energy level, and hopeful outlook' despite resistance.[57]

Recommendation #3: For followers to correct their leaders, they need access to resources outside of the chain of command. That's why a third party can be especially helpful – whether it's an ethics hotline to an outside and independent body or the use of external media resources. Readers should take note of the various outside sources that also influenced how this case developed while followers were working on the inside of the system to draw attention to their concerns and make changes. Outside of the SBC and its own media agencies (which had been censored by executive leaders),[58] attention and pressure came from media reporting and bloggers. And to achieve a full accounting of the sexual abuse crisis, a third-party investigation was required.

In many of the abuse examples, churches tried to deal with the issue 'in-house' rather than involving outside authorities. One result was that perpetrators were able to continue illicit practices, and the victims were left without any recourse. Without the aid of an outside institution, power remained in the hands of the wrong people.

## SUMMARY AND CONCLUDING REMARKS

So how, then, can followers partner with leaders to do the right thing? I suggest four fundamental responses to the question. First, ethical followers should strive to be partners with good
leaders and to redirect or resist bad leaders. Second, ethical followers should access external
resources such as higher values and the organization's mission – and they can reinforce these
values by developing feedback loops that report when these values are being ignored or outright violated. Third, ethical followers should realize they have access to a range of responses
when they believe a leader is operating outside of what is appropriate. These followers have the
savvy to take responses that go beyond simple 'obedience' or 'disobedience'. Finally, ethical
followers should remember that they are morally culpable for their own actions, even if it
means direct disobedience to their leader's commands. For organizations to empower this
kind of followership, leaders will need to see corrective feedback from followers as an asset to
the organization as well as their own leadership success. And followers will require additional
training to understand and apply the full range of responses they can engage when they believe
their leader has abandoned the organization's core values.

Let us conclude our consideration of followership, especially 'ethical followership', with
a helpful quote: 'To lead others, a person must first know what it is to follow and then seek
willing agreement rather than coercion or trickery. The case must be just, both when we lead
and when we follow others, if the outcome is to be successful.'[59] The quote is helpful for our
summary and conclusions because: (1) it reminds us to consider the follower; (2) it calls for
a partnership, not domination by coercion or trickery; and (3) it challenges us to consider the
goal – is it just?

So, with the rise of followership we can change our understanding of leadership from
focusing primarily on a single person (the leader) to concentrating on the interactions between
leaders and followers (managers and subordinates) where they together create/develop
'leadership'.[60]

---

### DISCUSSION QUESTIONS

1. At what point should leaders expose an organization to legal or financial ruin when
   ethical concerns are involved? How can leaders resolve the conflict of interests? How
   can one sort out leader/follower roles in loose affiliations or flattened organizations?
2. What sources of influence can followers turn to when they are concerned for their
   leaders or organizations?
3. What are the advantages and disadvantages of removing the emphasis from individual leaders to looking at leader–follower interactions or group processes to understand leadership?
4. For effective followership to take place in an organization, what should be measured
   and how?

## ADDITIONAL RESOURCES

Barbara Kellerman, *Followership*, Boston, MA: Harvard Business Press, 2008.

Kellerman has much to say that challenges traditional, 'leader-centric' thinking. Her followership book is an excellent place to start in following her work and should be read alongside the work by Ira Chaleff, already discussed in this chapter.

G.J. Sorenson and G.R. Hickman, *The Power of Invisible Leadership: How a Compelling Common Purpose Inspires Exceptional Leadership*, Los Angeles, CA: Sage, 2015.

This is a good place for readers who want to understand better the power of purpose and values in guiding an organization should consult the literature on invisible leadership.

Jean Lipman-Blumen, *The Allure of Toxic Leaders*, Oxford: Oxford University Press, 2005.

Readers should also consult the literature on toxic leadership to fully appreciate the importance of empowered followers. Doing so will help followers recognize leadership that must be resisted and how to avoid following into its traps.

## NOTES

1.  There are certain 'classic' texts that 'well-read' leaders should get to know. Among those books are Machiavelli's *The Prince* and Sun Tzu's *The Art of War*. I wouldn't recommend these texts as guides to 'ethics', but they are helpful reminders that leadership is a practical skill and not just a thought exercise. Likewise, those texts might give readers insight into how the person 'across the table' is viewing them.

2.  See Thomas Carlyle's *On Heroes, Hero Worship and the Heroic in History*. It's another one of those 'classics'.

3.  As described by D.A. Wren and R.G. Greenwood, *Management Innovators: The People and Ideas that Have Shaped Modern Business*, New York: Oxford University Press, 1998. They also point out that Warren Bennis views Folletts' work as foundational for modern leadership writing.

4.  I. Chaleff, *Intelligent Disobedience: Doing Right When What You're Told to Do Is Wrong*, Oakland, CA: Berrett-Koehler, 2015, p. 65.

5.  For a complete discussion, see S. Milgram, *Obedience to Authority: An Experimental View*, New York: HarperCollins, 2009.

6.  J.R. Meindl, S.B. Ehrlich and J.M. Dukerich, 'The romance of leadership', *Administration Science Quarterly*, vol. 30 no. 1, March 1985, 78-102.

7.  J.R. Meindl, 'On leadership: an alternative to the conventional wisdom', in B.M. Straw and L.L. Cummings (eds), *Research in Organizational Behavior*, Greenwich, CT: JAI Press, 1990, pp. 59-203.

8.  See R. Heifetz, *Leadership Without Easy Answers*, Cambridge: MA: Harvard University Press, 1998; and R. Heifetz, *The Practice of Adaptive Leadership: Tools and Tactics for Changing Your Organization and The World*, Boston, MA: Harvard Business Press, 2009.

9. Wicked problems are those problems that lack a clear, technical solution. For a discussion of wicked problems and leadership, see K. Grint, *Leadership: A Very Short Introduction*, Oxford: Oxford University Press, 2010.

10. I. Chaleff, *The Courageous Follower: Standing Up To and For Our Leaders*, 3rd edn, San Francisco, CA: Berrett-Koehler, 2015; Chaleff, *Intelligent Disobedience*, p. 65.

11. B. Kellerman, *Hard Times: Leadership in America*, Stanford, CA: Stanford Business Books, 2015.

12. Kellerman, *Hard Times*, p. 282.

13. R.E. Kelly, 'Rethinking followership', in R. Riggio, I. Chaleff and J. Lipman-Blumen (eds), *Art of Followership*, San Francisco, CA: Jossey-Bass, 2008, p. 6.

14. R.G. Lord, 'Followers' cognitive and affective structures and leadership processes', in Riggio et al., *Art of Followership*, pp. 255-66.

15. For example, a 1955 study by Hollander and Webb indicated the same peers nominated as most desired leaders were also nominated as most desired followers. See B.M. Bass and R. Bass, *The Bass Handbook of Leadership: Theory, Research, and Managerial Applications*, 4th edn, New York: Free Press, 2008.

16. J. Maroosis, 'Leadership: a partnership in reciprocal following', in Riggio et al., *Art of Followership*, pp. 17-26.

17. B.J. Avolio and R.J. Reichard, 'The rise of authentic followership', in Riggio et al., *Art of Followership*, pp. 325-37.

18. Chaleff, *The Courageous Follower*.

19. Kellerman, *Hard Times*.

20. Bass and Bass, *The Bass Handbook of Leadership*.

21. Chaleff, *The Courageous Follower*.

22. Chaleff, *The Courageous Follower*.

23. Chaleff, *The Courageous Follower*, pp. 38, 43, 2.

24. Chaleff, *The Courageous Follower*; Chaleff, *Intelligent Disobedience*, p. 19.

25. Avolio and Reichard, 'The rise of authentic followership'.

26. J. Lipman-Blumen, 'Following toxic leaders: in search of posthumous praise', in Riggio et al., *Art of Followership*, p. 182.

27. B. Kellerman, *Bad Leadership: What It Is, How It Happens, Why It Matters*, Boston, MA: Harvard Business Review Press, 2004, p. 21.

28. J. Rost, 'Followership: an outmoded concept', in Riggio et al., *Art of Followership*, pp. 53-65.

29. Kellerman, *Hard Times*, p. 270.

30. G. Dixon, 'Getting together', in Riggio et al., *Art of Followership*, pp. 155-76.

31. Kellerman, *Bad Leadership*.

32. S. Sakai and U. Yojimbo, *The Dragon Below Conspiracy*, 4th edn, Seattle, WA: Fantagraphics Books, 2005, p. 66.

33. B. Shamir, P. Rajnandini, M.C. Bligh and M. Uhl-Bien (eds), *Follower-Centered Perspectives on Leadership*, Charlotte, NC: Information Age Publishing, 2007.

34. BBC, 'Catholic Church child sexual abuse scandal', BBC News, 5 October 2021. https://www.bbc.com/news/world-44209971 (accessed 13 November 2022).

35. Lifeway Research, 'Annual church profile statistical summary'. https://lifewayresearch.com/wp-content/uploads/2021/05/ACP_Summary_2020.pdf (accessed 13 November 2022).

36. About the SBC – SBC.net (n.d.). https://www.sbc.net/about/ (accessed 13 January 2022).

37. J. Avila, B. Van Gilder and M. Lopez, 'Preachers accused of sins, and crimes', ABC News, 13 April 2007. https://abcnews.go.com/2020/story?id=3034040&page=1 (accessed 13 November 2022).

38. Guidepost Solutions, LLC. *Final Report*, 15 May 2022, pp. 185ff. https://www.documentcloud.org/documents/22031737-final-guidepost-solutions-independent-investigation-report (accessed 13 November 2022).

39. G. Harris, 'Pastor Mike Stone, new SBC Committee Chairman, answers some probing questions', *The Christian Index*, 24 August 2022. https://christianindex.org/stories/pastor-mike-stone-new-sbc-executive-committee-chairman-answers-some-probing-questions,2447 (accessed 13 November 2022).

40. Guidepost Solutions, *Final Report*, p. 187.

41. Guidepost Solutions, *Final Report*, p. 187.

42. Religion News Service, 'Russell Moore to ERLC trustees, "they want me to live in psychological terror"', Religion News Service, 2 June 2021. https://religionnews.com/2021/06/02/russell-moore-to-erlc-trustees-they-want-me-to-live-in-psychological-terror/ (accessed 13 November 2022).

43. Guidepost Solutions, *Final Report*, p. 189.

44. Guidepost Solutions, *Final Report*, p. 48.

45. Guidepost Solutions, *Final Report*, p. 190.

46. Associated Press, 'A Southern Baptist panel has voted to open legal records to investigators of abuse', NPR, 5 October 2021. https://www.npr.org/2021/10/05/1043471111/southern-baptist-vote-sexual-abuse-records (accessed 13 November 2022).

47. D. Roach, 'SBC recalls "year of waking up" since abuse investigation', *Christianity Today*, 10 February 2020. https://www.christianitytoday.com/news/2020/february/sbc-waking-up-houston-chronicle-abuse-investigation.html (accessed 13 November 2022).

48. Chaleff, *The Courageous Follower*, pp. 159ff.

49. K. Shellnutt, 'Southern Baptists vote to name abuse as grounds for expelling churches', Christianity Today, 15 June 2019. https://www.christianitytoday.com/news/2019/june/sbc-annual-meeting-southern-baptist-vote-abuse.html (accessed 13 November 2022).

50. M. Anderson and K Toor, 'How social media users have discussed sexual harassment since #MeToo went viral', Pew Research Center, 11 October 2018. https://www.pewresearch.org/fact-tank/2018/10/11/how-social-media-users-have-discussed-sexual-harassment-since-metoo-went-viral/ (accessed 13 November 2022).

51. For an extended discussion of how followership pushed for reforms within the Roman Catholic Church, see chapter seven, 'Activists: voice of the faithful', in Barbara Kellerman's *Followership*, Boston, MA: Harvard Business Press, 2008.

52. D. Silliman, 'RZIM spent nearly $1M suing Ravi Zacharias abuse victim', Christianity Today, 23 February 2022. https://www.christianitytoday.com/news/2022/february/rzim-board-donor-money-guidepost-report-ravi.html (accessed 13 November 2022).

53. Christianity Today, 'The rise and fall of Mars Hill', podcast. https://www.christianitytoday.com/ct/podcasts/rise-and-fall-of-mars-hill / (accessed 13 November 2022).

54. Guidepost Solutions, *Final Report*, p. 153.

55. Guidepost Solutions, *Final Report*, p. 176.

56. Guidepost Solutions, *Final Report*, p. 192.

57. Chaleff, *The Courageous Follower*, p. 203.

58. Guidepost Solutions, *Final Report*, pp. 177–8.

59. Maroosis, 'Leadership'. Maroosis is quoting *The I Ching*.

60. Avolio and Reichard, 'The rise of authentic followership'.

# 16
# Transformational leadership

*Benjamin P. Dean*

## FRAMING QUESTION

How can leaders create positive change for themselves, their followers, and their organizations?

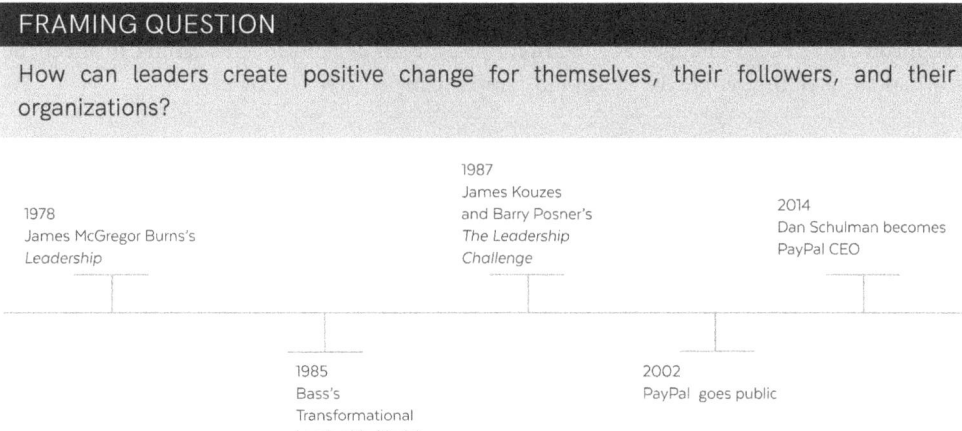

1978
James McGregor Burns's
*Leadership*

1985
Bass's
Transformational
Leadership Model

1987
James Kouzes
and Barry Posner's
*The Leadership
Challenge*

2002
PayPal goes public

2014
Dan Schulman becomes
PayPal CEO

**Figure 16.1**     Timeline of major works on transformational leadership in relation to the chapter case study

Transformational leadership represents one of the most positively regarded approaches to leadership today.[1] The fact that the transformational approach to leadership has been adopted in so many contexts and places suggests that leaders find it works and that followers tend to embrace leaders who use it. Transformational leadership broadly tends to produce positive results for leaders and followers. Leaders who demonstrate transformational leadership behaviours generally prove effective in influencing, motivating, and enabling others to achieve goals.[2] Indeed, research shows these factors constitute an effective overall organizational leadership approach.[3] In addition to the effectiveness of transformational leadership, much of the approach's popularity derives from its positive association with ethical behaviours, which positions transformational leadership within the broadly defined group of ethical or values-based leadership models. Values-driven leadership approaches, including transformational leadership, can thus increase leaders' effectiveness.[4]

This chapter begins by examining the different sources from which the transformational leadership approach emerged and how several different streams essentially have converged in this approach. Focusing on the essential aspects that characterise the transformational leadership approach, we will consider its key components and ethical implications. The chapter will compare transformational leadership with several other major approaches and will show the elements of transformational leadership that either overlap or contrast with the elements of those other approaches. The chapter will also address some of the limitations and challenges of transformational leadership. And as in previous chapters, we will analyse this leadership approach by applying the Five Components of Leadership Model.[5]

Transformational leadership in action becomes most apparent through leadership behaviours directed towards changing organizations and developing people in ways that achieve positive results for organizations and their people. To examine transformational leadership as applied in an organizational context, we will look at the transformational approach used by PayPal President and CEO Daniel Schulman, an organizational leader highly regarded as both effective and ethical. As we will see in that case study, one of the most significant ethical challenges a transformational leader may face arises from circumstances in which the leader recognizes that crucial changes are required because an organization is failing to meet the essential needs of the people on whom the company depends for its success.

## HISTORY

The modern concept of transformational leadership rests on the writings of James MacGregor Burns.[6] Burns articulated a concept of 'transforming' leadership, which he described as a process of social influence by which leaders and followers engage in the process of mutual change and development, raising each other to higher levels of morality and motivation.

Rather than reflecting one distinct theory, the transformational approach represents a collection of several theoretical models and overlapping sets of behaviours that describe what is now generally understood as 'transformational leadership'. Several constructs thus exist to articulate the transformational leadership approach. The work by Warren Bennis and Burt Nanus reflects one of these models.[7] Bennis and Nanus described a transformative approach to leadership as consisting of four behaviours of leaders seeking to transform organizations: presenting a clear vision of the future, shaping the understandings of followers into shared meanings, generating the followers' trust in a leader, and developing the followers' competence. Developing followers' awareness of their own competence involves leveraging their learning and creativity. Through those kinds of transformative behaviours, a leader genuinely focuses on followers and engages closely with them to inspire and develop them.[8]

Another well-known formulation of transformational leadership emerged from James Kouzes and Barry Posner.[9] They identified five leadership practices: modelling the way, inspiring a shared vision, challenging the process to achieve change, enabling others to act, and encouraging the heart through recognition and celebration. The components of Kouzes and Posner's description of transformational leadership overlap with some of Bennis and Nanus' elements. However, Kouzes and Posner included a more explicit emphasis on change and the processes required to achieve change.

Similarly, Philip Podsakoff and his colleagues described transformational leadership as six distinct dimensions: articulating a vision, providing an appropriate (role) model, fostering acceptance of group goals, expecting high performance, giving individualized support, and generating intellectual stimulation. Leaders using these kinds of transformational behaviours enhance their engagement with followers, which helps both leaders and followers to reach their goals.[10] These behaviours also help leaders to build trusting relationships with followers, which is an essential dynamic in the leader–follower relationship.[11]

The best-known formulation of transformational leadership, however, comes from a model derived by Bernard Bass.[12] Bass and his colleagues identified four key elements,[13] which are commonly listed as idealized influence (similar to charisma), inspirational motivation, intellectual stimulation, and individualized consideration.[14]

Table 16.1 provides a summary of these five main theoretical formulations or typologies that comprise the primary literature on transformational leadership.

**Table 16.1** Major typologies of transformational leadership

| Models and sources | Behaviours/components |
|---|---|
| 'Transforming' leadership by Burns (1978) | A process of mutual change and development by which leaders and followers raise each other to higher levels of motivation and morality |
| Transformational leadership by Bass (1985, 1997); Bass & Steidlmeier (1999); Bass & Riggio (2006) | • *Idealized Influence* – Functionally equates to charisma<br>• *Inspirational Motivation* – Manifests a leader's high expectations to instil in others a desire to exert greater efforts aimed at higher moral standards<br>• *Intellectual Stimulation* – Engages other mentally in ways that challenges them and may encourage more creativity and innovation, and<br>• *Individualized Consideration* – Reflects a leader's supportive actions towards a follower |
| 'Transformative' leadership by Bennis and Nanus (1985) | • Presenting a clear vision of the future<br>• Shaping the understanding of followers into shared meanings<br>• Generating the followers' trust in a leader, and<br>• Developing the followers' competence |
| Transformational leadership by Kouzes and Posner (1987, 2002) | • Modelling the way<br>• Inspiring a shared vision<br>• Challenging the process to achieve change<br>• Enabling others to act, and<br>• Encouraging the heart through recognition and celebration |
| Transformational leadership by Podsakoff et al. (1990) | • Articulating a vision<br>• Providing an appropriate (role) model<br>• Fostering acceptance of group goals<br>• Expecting high performance<br>• Giving individualized support, and<br>• Generating intellectual stimulation |

## MAJOR CONCEPTS OF TRANSFORMATIONAL LEADERSHIP

Even though these theoretical models of transformational leadership vary in their elements, the collections of behaviours that define elements of these respective constructs remain consistent enough that transformational leadership stands as a distinct approach to leadership that can be powerful and effective. Each of the various ways of conceiving this leadership approach shows that transformational leadership's defining behaviours are useful and practical in leading people and organizations. Although in a later section of this chapter we will examine some critiques of transformational leadership, we will also see that studies on the behaviours characterizing the transformational approach fairly consistently produce positive outcomes in a variety of settings.

As Bass's model comprises the most commonly recognized set of dimensions describing transformational leadership, we can apply the four main components of that model to examine the transformational leadership approach. Using this framework, we can also trace common themes and behaviours among the various formulations or typologies of transformational leadership.[15] These elements in Bass's model will be addressed separately in the following sections. The sections will look at the common themes reflected among the several ways of viewing the transformational leadership approach.

## Idealized Influence

Transformational leaders seek to inspire followers and encourage them to achieve goals reflecting higher purposes. Idealized influence constitutes a crucial component in Bass's model for analysing transformational leadership and centres on leaders serving as role models for followers.[16] The elements presented by Kouzes and Posner include a leader modelling the way. Likewise, the transformational leadership elements derived by Podsakoff et al. expressly describe leaders as providing appropriate role models to followers. Followers look to transformational leaders as exemplary role models.[17] According to Bennis and Nanus, this is a dynamic element by which leaders can build trust so others will follow them. This idealized influence component is sometimes referred to as 'charisma', which will be discussed later in more detail when we compare transformational leadership and charismatic leadership.

The effectiveness of transformational leadership depends on the leader's behaviours and how followers view and understand those behaviours. The effectiveness of transformational leadership also depends on the extent to which people trust the leader, allow themselves to be influenced by the leader, and are willing to embrace the leader as a model to follow. The followers' perceptions of the leader's behaviours prove to be crucial. Follower perceptions, especially followers' recognition of ethical behaviours, determine how much impact a transformational leader's behaviours will have. In a later section on the ethics of transformational leadership, we will address the implications of followers' understanding of a leader's ethical behaviours towards transformational goals.

## Inspirational Motivation

Transformational leaders communicate expectations and seek to motivate followers' performance towards achieving meaningful goals and accomplishing positive change. For Podsakoff et al. and for Kouzes and Posner, this element emerges as articulating and inspiring a shared vision. This overlaps with the element Bennis and Nanus described as presenting a clear vision of the future. The leader leverages this focus on a shared vision, according to Podsakoff et al., to inspire and motivate followers while articulating high-performance standards.

According to Bass, transformational leaders generate inspirational motivation by expressing high expectations of followers, instilling in others a desire to exert greater efforts, and giving meaning to work that seeks higher goals or standards.[18] From the perspective of Burns' early description of the transformational approach, such efforts may aim towards raising followers' moral standards.[19] This element of inspirational motivation, combined with the idealized influence, magnifies a leader's impact on followers because these two elements of transformational leadership merge into one compelling dynamic.[20] The studies of transformational leadership provide considerable evidence that this approach ties closely and positively with moral reasoning processes and leadership integrity. Studies such as these also provide evidence that transformational leaders hold greater capacity for moral reasoning and tend to display more leadership integrity. Motivating followers towards meaningful goals and positive change appears especially consistent with behaviours manifesting ethical leadership.

## Intellectual Stimulation

Intellectual stimulation mentally engages others in ways that challenge them and may enhance creativity and innovation.[21] Kouzes and Posner describe transformational leadership as challenging an existing process to achieve change. Such leaders, according to Bennis and Nanus, shape the mental understanding of followers to form shared meanings. Shared meanings increase cohesiveness among followers. According to Podsakoff et al., a transformational leader leverages intellectual stimulation to foster group acceptance of goals. Leaders can engage intellectual stimulation that encourages followers to move in new directions and thereby enhances followers' collective creativity and innovation.

## Individualized Consideration

Individualized consideration reflects a transformational leader's supportive actions directed towards a follower, including actions such as attending to followers' needs through two-way communication.[22] Burns saw this leadership approach as involving a process of mutual change in which leaders and followers develop each other and raise each other to higher levels of motivation and morality.[23] Podsakoff et al. identified the element as giving individualized support to followers. Bennis and Nanus observed that these leaders develop followers' competencies. Kouzes and Posner described transformational leaders as enabling others to act and recognizing and celebrating followers in ways that encourage the heart.

## TRANSFORMATIONAL LEADERSHIP DISTINGUISHED FROM OTHER LEADERSHIP APPROACHES

Transformational leadership shares important features with other major leadership approaches described in this book. Even so, transformational leadership remains sufficiently distinct to be recognizable from these other approaches. The present section will compare and contrast transformational leadership with other key approaches available to a leader: charismatic leadership, transactional leadership, servant leadership, visionary leadership, and authentic leadership.

## Charismatic Leadership

Transformational leadership shares many behaviours with charismatic leadership. How then can one distinguish the two approaches? According to one well-known set of elements defining the charismatic leadership model, a charismatic leader likely fits the following characteristics or behaviours: dominance, a strong desire to influence others, self-confidence, and a strong sense of moral values.[24] The last of those elements – a sense of moral values – potentially brings charismatic leadership into the broad group of ethical models, at least to the extent such leadership behaviours prove to be others-directed. How ethical is the leadership of a given charismatic leader will depend on that leader's underlying motivations and values.[25] However, this means that the positive influence exercised by charismatic and transformational leaders connects with followers through moral values, consequently permitting both approaches a claim to the broadly defined category of ethical leadership.[26]

The other elements of charismatic leadership – the strong desire to influence others and the dominant, self-confident behaviours – differ from the features defining transformational leadership, even if a given transformational leader displays some charismatic personality traits. It is possible one person could meet both sets of essential elements defining a transformational leader and a charismatic leader. The particular 'socialized' form of charisma, similar to what one should see in authentic transformational leadership, represents a more ethical form of charisma because in this form a leader is genuinely seeking to use influence and power on behalf of the group to serve the followers' and the organization's needs, which stands in contrast to a 'personalized' form of charisma that seeks primarily to serve the leader's own interests.[27]

## Transactional Leadership

In contrast to transformational leadership, transactional leadership involves much less emphasis on inspiration or vision. The transactional leader engages followers in a more tangible, fairly direct exchange of mutual benefits. A leader and a follower join in a kind of quid pro quo transaction by which the leader gains the loyalty or services of a follower by explicitly or implicitly promising to deliver benefits to the follower in return. Clear examples of a transactional leadership approach arise in political campaigns where a politician promises specific legislative outcomes and perhaps even patronage benefits for those political followers who support the leader's campaign and vote for that leader. Once elected to office, the political leader is expected to 'make good' on those campaign promises.

One may view transactional leadership not as an ethical leadership approach but as a values-neutral approach.[28] Transactional leadership mainly motivates others by appealing to a cost–benefit calculation and self-interest analysis. In that regard, the leader–follower relationship relies much more heavily on an economic rationale than an ethical basis. Because of transactional leadership's economic-type trade-offs, transactional leaders – in contrast to transformational leaders – tend to engage much less in personal interactions with followers once the parameters of the mutual exchange are established and set into motion. In transactional leadership, the leader rewards followers as long as they perform; followers continue to perform as long as leaders fulfil their end of the bargain. When the flow of mutual benefits stops, the leader–follower relationship begins to break down. Transactional leaders may even feel threatened by the active kinds of autonomous followership behaviours described in Chapter 15.

Conversely, the developmental nature and aims of transformational leadership suggest that a transformational leader, in contrast to a transactional leader, would likely welcome active followership behaviours (i.e. effective and meaningful involvement by followers). Motivation inspired by transformational leaders tends to induce more effort by followers in organizations than does the contingent rewards approach – the 'carrot or the stick' method – exercised by transactional leaders.[29] This developmental nature helps explain, as we saw earlier, how transformational leaders make a more substantial positive impact on people and organizations; transformational leaders, therefore, tend to be more effective over the longterm than transactional leaders.

While transactional leadership and transformational leadership consist of distinct elements, the elements can be conceived along a single continuum of leadership behaviours that place transactional leadership and transformational leadership at opposing ends.[30] This continuum is referred to as the 'full-range of leadership' model. Transformational and transactional leadership still represent two different forms of leadership, even though some overlap may occur among their characteristic behaviours.[31]

## Servant Leadership

Transformational leadership's emphasis on followers resembles the focus of another influential ethical leadership approach – servant leadership, which is discussed in detail in Chapter 14. Both transformational leadership and servant leadership leverage ethical means and ends to influence others positively. Both transformational and servant leadership seek to develop people individually and collectively and thus tend to increase followers' organizational commitment and engagement.[32] Nevertheless, the two leadership approaches still differ overall. While servant leaders exert influence mainly through satisfying followers' needs, transformational leaders exert influence mainly through satisfying their followers' perception of leaders' effectiveness.[33] Transformational leaders tend to be more directed towards the organization's collective goal,[34] whereas servant leaders appear comparatively more focused on the follower's needs.[35]

While most definitions of leadership, including transformational leadership, consider influence as an essential element, servant leadership more clearly shifts the attention to service that emphasises the needs of followers.[36] The loyalty of some servant leaders potentially lies more with the individual than with the organization, while the opposite would tend to apply to transformational leaders.[37] As we will see later when we discuss developing people, a transformational leader in an organization may have to struggle more in dealing with an ethical choice that requires a decision about whether to improve the capabilities and welfare of followers as individuals or of followers collectively for organizational benefit.

## Visionary Leadership

Transformational leadership encompasses a fundamental component that seeks to motivate followers by inspiring them. This encourages followers to see and focus on a clear vision. In this critical aspect, transformational leadership shares an essential dimension with a model of leadership known as visionary leadership. While ongoing research seeks to better define and provide more support for the visionary leadership approach, the best-known model is the one by Kouzes and Posner.[38] Tying visionary leadership with their concept of transformative leader behaviours (as described above), Kouzes and Posner observed that for a leader to help people and organizations change, a leader must be credible. This credibility allows people to embrace the leader's vision.

A potential criticism of visionary leadership also affects transformational and charismatic leadership. The three approaches may easily be conflated because they substantially overlap, especially in their dynamics of idealized influence. Yet, visionary leadership and transformational leadership remain distinguishable. In transformational leadership, however crucial the leader's credibility and trustworthiness in offering a vision, idealized influence constitutes only one element among several on which the effectiveness of a transformational leader's actions will depend. For this reason, the visionary leadership approach may offer less value to followers and organizations as compared with what transformational leadership and its several key dimensions can deliver to followers and organizations. Next, we will move to another leadership approach distinct from transformational leadership.

## Authentic Leadership

As its label suggests, authentic leadership focuses on the extent to which a leader is genuine with followers. (Authentic leadership is discussed in detail in Chapter 13.) Authentic leadership and transformational leadership are closely related but distinct approaches.[39]

Authentic leaders relate to others through behaviours that reflect a thorough understanding of one's values, specifically regarding the leaders' sense of who they are, where they want to go, and the right things to do.[40] For example, a manager in a supervisory position over a team may have serious concerns about whether the organization will provide sufficient resources to achieve production targets imposed on the team. In the dilemma of whether to be transparent about the resource problem ahead, we anticipate that an authentic leader might choose to be more open with team members about the problem and more forthcoming with relevant information to preserve trust and strengthen bonds within the leader–follower relationship.

Although transformational leadership may be somewhat preferred for organizational leadership,[41] work on authentic leadership as a theory began partly due to a perceived need to go beyond the defining aspects of transformational leadership. Taking at face value transformational leadership's characterizing components, one would assume that a transformational leader's motivations towards followers' welfare must be genuine and authentic. However, a leader could outwardly manifest transformational behaviours while hiding actual intentions and motivations that focused more on the leader's self-interest. Theories of transformational leadership thus began to emphasise an 'authentic' transformational leadership versus an inauthentic, 'pseudo-transformational' leadership.[42] So, a primary means of comparing authentic leaders with transformational leaders relates to how well transformational leadership serves as a reliable indicator of a leader's real intentions towards followers.[43] Bass, through his refinement of an 'authentic' form of transformational leadership, seems to have provided a glimpse into the importance of this additional ethical dimension insofar as a transformational leader must engage followers in a genuine relationship. In any event, transformational leadership and authentic leadership appear complementary, and thus a leader may benefit by drawing on the critical behaviours of both ethical leadership approaches.

## CRITIQUES OF TRANSFORMATIONAL LEADERSHIP

Having compared and contrasted transformational leadership with several other important approaches to leadership, we now need to address particular critiques of transformational leadership based on what some reviewers consider to be limitations of this approach. Even though transformational leadership has emerged as a well-established and broadly accepted approach to leadership, critics of this approach continue to raise challenges. We will identify three major criticisms.

### Overlap and Confusion between Transformational and Other Approaches to Leadership

Despite years of study, no single clearly established and uniformly accepted construct of transformational leadership exists. Even under Bass's theoretical development of transformational leadership – essentially the most well-established and best-known conceptualization – some controversy exists as to whether studies bear out its four dimensions as sufficiently distinct and verifiable. Those dimensions, as previously discussed, encompass idealized influence, inspirational motivation, intellectual stimulation, and individualized consideration. The components of idealized influence and inspirational motivation, for example, tend to merge when practised. Similarly, those same elements – idealized influence and inspirational motivation – may hold the weakest support from research studies on transformational leadership. Also, in practice, while one may observe a leader displaying behaviours that appear consistent with transformational leadership, one cannot be sure whether the leader's actual, hidden intentions or motives derive from authentic transformational leadership or pseudo-transformational leadership.

Another limitation of the transformational leadership model arises from its potential overlap and confusion with transactional leadership. A leader using either approach can be engaging, to some degree, in transactional exchanges for the mutual benefit of a leader and followers. As noted earlier, while some overlap of behaviours or similarities in actions may emerge in a given situation, the aims and actions of a transformational or transactional leader remain fundamentally different.[44] For example, even leaders who recognize the difference between transformational and transactional behaviours may default to basic exchange patterns with followers rather than proactively engage followers for their development and well-being.

A single leader can simultaneously engage with the same followers on different tasks accomplished through transformational interactions or transactional exchanges.

A similar limitation of the transformational leadership model arises from the overlapping behaviours and confusion with charismatic leadership. The transformational leadership and charismatic leadership approaches share a high level of interpersonal engagement with followers. This is illustrated by the strong ties of trust that followers form with a leader and that one can leverage into leadership influence. In both approaches – transformational and charismatic, leaders communicate expectations, inspire followers, and motivate them towards performance goals or higher standards. Although this accurately suggests that charismatic and transformational leadership can be conflated, the two are still not coextensive. Indeed, aside from idealized influence and inspirational motivation, the other components of transformational leadership – intellectual stimulation and individualized consideration – appear to extend beyond the defining characteristics of charismatic leadership. Conversely, as noted earlier, charismatic leadership displays certain elements that transformational leadership may not. So, we can meaningfully distinguish transformational leadership from charismatic leadership, as we can from transactional leadership, by focusing on fundamental differences between the approaches' underlying goals.

## Calling Followers to a Higher Ethical Level

For the reasons already noted, we can rightly view transformational leadership as an effective and ethical approach to leading people and organizations. But even if transformational leadership behaviours are useful and effective in achieving results, what makes the transformational leadership behaviours ethical in terms of the outcomes it achieves? This question has stimulated considerable debate.[45] The answer emerges from at least three sources: the inherent nature of those behaviours that define transformational leaders, the positive outcomes such leadership aims to accomplish, and the ability of followers to recognize and understand the ethical aspects of transformational leadership actions. As seen in the studies cited earlier, transformational leadership does bear a close connection with moral reasoning and leadership integrity, both within a leader and as perceived by a follower. Such studies further suggest that leaders whom followers identify as engaging in transformational leadership also tend to be leaders whom followers identify as being ethical in their leadership behaviours.

A particular ethical aspect of the debate revolves around whether one can accurately characterise transformational leadership as an approach that calls followers to a 'higher level of motivation and morality'.[46] Considering studies that focus on the leader–follower dynamics and that describe the idealized influence component of transformational leadership, followers are likely to affirm and adopt the behaviours of those leaders with whom the followers personally identify. By logical extension, followers similarly would be likely to affirm and emulate ethical behaviours manifested by those leaders whom followers describe as transformational. In these respects, transformational leadership's manifestations of moral reasoning ability and leadership integrity can likewise inspire followers towards higher ethical standards and goals.

## Transformational Leadership's Potential 'Dark Side'

As noted, a potential problem arises to the extent leaders who appear transformational may hide intentions or motivations rooted in self-interest. This was a key reason why some researchers began distinguishing an authentic transformational leadership from a less authentic, *pseudo*-transformational leadership.[47] The main difference between authentic transformational leaders and pseudo-transformational leaders is the leader's intentions and moral/ethical values, regardless of the leader's outward behaviours.[48] The pseudo-transformational view of leadership suggests that the strong bonds formed through transformational leadership (or similarly through charismatic leadership) with followers could be abused by a leader. This possibility of a leader deceiving followers about his or her real intentions or motives suggests a need to consider the possibility of less ethical results emanating from what may appear on the surface to be transformational leadership behaviours.

The transformational leader's core capacities for creating a vision and inspiring the members of an organization may similarly carry the potential for achieving unethical purposes.[49] This dynamic by no means limits itself to transformational leadership; one can observe the same problem occurring in negative forms of charismatic leadership. Leaders who exercise influence over followers through unhealthy interpersonal relationships and influence can become manipulative and destructive for followers. In the most severe manifestations, such leaders descend below a values-neutral, amoral leadership standard into unethical forms of leadership, variously identified as 'dysfunctional leadership', 'toxic leadership',[50] or the 'dark side' of leadership.[51] Others have referred to 'destructive leadership', described as the systematic and repeated behaviours of a leader who violates the legitimate interests of followers and the organization.[52]

We see that a leader can leverage those defining elements that enable transformational or charismatic leadership to be both effective and ethical, or they can exploit leadership influence in ways that are effective yet unethical. However, a clear division between these two models would arise when the motives of the charismatic leader bend towards motivations and values reflecting more self-interest than concern for followers. Indeed, as suggested earlier, the potential for a leader's likely self-focused, 'personalized' use of influence is even more acute in a charismatic leadership approach. A charismatic leader, for example, can continue motivating followers by appealing to moral values that the leader appears to embrace, but does not embrace in reality. History records numerous instances of charismatic cult leaders inspiring a group of devout followers and motivating them towards an idealistic vision of the future. However, when the enterprise has spun out of the leader's control, such leaders have chosen to destroy their followers rather than yield power. One of the most dramatic instances of such abuse of influence was by the cult leader Jim Jones, who became infamous for directing the Jonestown mass suicide. Even in such a tragically dysfunctional scenario where a charismatic leader has exploited others for narcissistic reasons or self-serving ends, one might somehow still consider the leader's behaviours to be effective and useful for achieving that unethical leader's purposes.

In contrast, authentic transformational leaders characteristically focus on the needs and welfare of followers and their collective good rather than on the leader's self-interest.[53]

Logically, the necessary elements defining transformational leadership should preclude an authentic transformational leader from applying leadership influence tied to a personal motive or self-interest that conflicts with the interests or values of his or her followers.[54] Moreover, when the leadership behaviours depart from a positive approach to people, those behaviours begin to define a fundamentally different and substantially less ethical way of leading people – that is, a pseudo-transformational version, in contrast to an authentic version, of transformational leadership.

## ETHICAL IMPLICATIONS OF TRANSFORMATIONAL LEADERSHIP

We have expressly described transformational leadership as a predominantly ethical form of leadership. This section addresses in more depth its ethical dynamics and implications.

### Ethical Dynamics of Transformational Leadership

Given transformational leadership's defining elements, as identified earlier, we know that this approach relies on leaders engaging in ethical behaviours that inspire, motivate, and encourage people towards higher purposes and goals. Based on four overarching dynamics of transformational leadership, we have observed that transformational leaders characteristically engage in ethical behaviours that integrate the following: (a) inspiring pursuit of meaningful goals, higher purposes, and positive change; (b) engaging in moral reasoning; (c) relying on strong leader–follower relationships; and (d) developing people through encouragement and support.

We noted above the components of transformational leadership that such leaders inspire the pursuit of meaningful goals, higher purposes, and positive change. Research affords evidence that transformational leaders seek to inspire and empower people towards higher levels of motivation and morality.[55] Studies show that leadership through ethical behaviours tends to produce positive outcomes for organizations, including higher job satisfaction, more innovation, and better performance.[56] Other studies have demonstrated that the effectiveness of transformational leadership relates significantly to its ethical qualities. For example, when a transformational leader's behaviours reflect consistency and fairness, followers tend to evaluate that leader as acting ethically.[57]

Similarly, followers' perceptions of the transformational leader's integrity constitute another crucial aspect affecting whether followers view the leader's actions as ethical. Indeed, followers' trust depends significantly on the integrity a leader displays.[58] A study showed that leaders who demonstrated strong patterns of transformational leadership were perceived as displaying the most integrity.[59] Furthermore, as perceived leader integrity increases, so do certain critical leadership and organizational effectiveness markers. The same study on leader integrity indicated that the best way to explain why some leaders were perceived as having low integrity arose from the evidence that those leaders only infrequently displayed or expressed their ideals – one of the defining elements of transformational leadership.

A further study showed that leaders who are perceived as being more transformational in their leadership behaviours tend to have more capacity for exercising moral reasoning than leaders who are not seen as transformational.[60] That study looked at followers' perceptions of transformational leadership behaviours and asked employees how often their managers displayed specific behavioural characteristics of transformational leadership. These evaluations were then analysed against scores each of the managers attained on a test of moral reasoning ability. Managers who scored highest on a moral reasoning test exhibited more transformational leadership behaviours than those who scored lower on moral reasoning. The researchers in that study concluded that leaders with a capacity for more complex moral reasoning tend to pursue goals beyond self-interest and seek the collective good.

Another study examined transformational leadership behaviours as perceived by followers, but this time focused on the moral reasoning capacity of the *followers*. This study showed that followers' perceptions of transformational leadership depend on the followers' ability to identify and interpret ethical issues.[61] The effectiveness of transformational leadership, therefore, depends not just on the behaviours of the leader but also on whether followers can recognize, appreciate, and respond to the ethical aspects of a leader's transformational actions. Followers who recognize and understand the ethical nature of the transformational leader's behaviours appear more willing to embrace and emulate such a leader as a role model. These results indicate that for leaders to be fully effective in their transformational leadership behaviours, leaders must consider the extent to which followers can perceive and understand those behaviours.[62]

## Developmental Change as an Ethical Focus of Transformational Leadership

Leaders who effectively use influence can serve as active change agents.[63] Leaders are vital in developing people and organizations because they have the opportunity to serve as active agents of change – transformation – by influencing people and circumstances in ways that significantly affect human development and well-being for individuals and groups.[64] As observed in the analysis of the four main components of transformational leadership, such leaders focus on developing people and themselves.[65] They actively engage with followers in ways that assist followers in grappling with the challenges of change and personal growth.[66] They also emphasise the need to develop people and positively impact them by encouraging and supporting them – individually as persons and collectively within organizations.[67] Leadership's natural social context and its human impact suggest that leaders should be dedicated to guiding a process that requires reconciling the uniqueness of human cultural diversity and individual human rights with the universal value of promoting global human opportunities.[68] For these reasons, one can hardly overestimate the importance of leaders having a well-grounded moral view of what constitutes 'good' outcomes, especially in regard to developing people, their organizations, and their communities, and what constitutes ethical influence in achieving those results.[69]

Despite transformational leadership's potential limitations, it remains accurate to describe the approach as a powerful and inherently ethical way for leaders to influence followers. Leaders inevitably face dilemmas in seeking to act ethically while also addressing conflicting demands placed on them.[70] Leaders bear significant responsibility for driving change in organizations and society and can profoundly impact the lives of individuals. For example, when a new CEO comes into a company, the employees naturally brace for change – anticipating that some of them might be hurt due to the changes that the new CEO initiates. Yet we can see in the various ways already described that ethical leaders – including transformational leaders – work for the benefit of followers, even to the extent possible while accomplishing organizational goals. *Transactional* leaders in a limited exchange may do the same, but transformational leaders go further by exerting intentional efforts to transform and develop the people, individually and collectively. Authentic transformational leaders (as Bass described them) genuinely focus on the growth and development of people and strongly emphasise an ethic of developing and supporting them.[71] From an ethical standpoint, transformational leaders legitimately exercise influence from a foundation of genuine concern for developing followers and from an authentic motivation to inspire and support followers in developing them to their fullest potential.[72] At the ethical core of transformational leadership, there resides a 'development ethic' that can be viewed as grounded in moral philosophy.

The moral dimension that underlies leadership's ethical imperative fundamentally flows out of the leader's concern for human value.[73] The leader's – particularly the transformational leader's – focus on developing people represents a crucial ethical mandate. This is why transformational leadership is so significant morally; it moves beyond most other leadership approaches in using influence purposefully to drive change and achieve goals that will enhance (versus impair) the human development of followers. A leader who undertakes transformational behaviours to influence people and build organizations essentially creates a moral obligation to be responsible for protecting human value and developing people through that process.[74] These developmental aims and purposes that underlie transformational leadership spotlight leaders' moral responsibilities and practical impact on people, organizations, and communities.

In sum, we can logically conclude that transformational leadership fundamentally constitutes an ethical approach to leadership because of the inherent moral dimensions of its characteristic behaviours, such as inspiration, encouragement, development, and support of followers. We also recognize transformational leadership's positive ethical nature in view of such leaders' efforts at balancing results for organizations with developmental outcomes for the people who comprise those organizations. Even so, other ethical leadership approaches reflect similar others-focused behaviours and purposes. This suggests that in the next section we need to consider the distinguishing aspects of transformational leadership and compare them with the positive ethical behaviours embedded in other leadership approaches, but especially with the positive behaviours of other ethical leadership approaches.

## FIVE COMPONENT ANALYSIS

Transformational leadership's central focus on the quality of the relationship between a leader and a follower is a major reason this approach is so widely recognized and accepted.[75] Transformational leadership readily fits within the view of leadership as a process by which leaders and followers develop a relationship and work towards a goal(s) within a context shaped by culture.[76] Accordingly, we may also view transformational leadership and its distinguishing dynamics through the lens of the Five Components Model that serves within this book as our broad framework for analysing the various leadership approaches. We turn now to the five components to consider how each relates to the transformational leadership approach.

By applying the Five Components of Leadership Model, we see that the most important aspects of transformational leadership are the leader, follower, and the goal, as well as the relationship between the leader and follower and their means of achieving the goal (Figure 16.2). The other components – cultural values and organizational context – do bear on transformational leadership's effectiveness.[77] However, this conceptual analysis emphasises the leader, follower, and goals because those components relate more directly to the behaviours that define transformational leadership and determine its effectiveness.

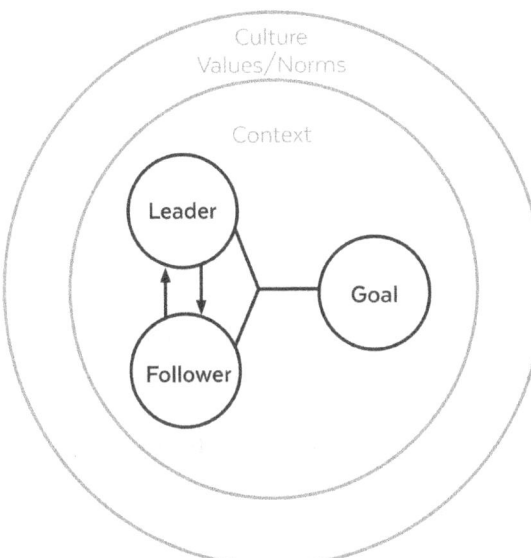

**Figure 16.2** The Five Components of Leadership Model applied to transformational leadership

As we specifically analyse the leader component of the model and tie this leader component to our overview of moral philosophies, we can recall how focusing on the leader as a person requires us to consider applications of moral virtues. Transformational leadership's view of a leader–follower relationship encompasses a mutual development exchange. This includes looking at a leader's own development.[78] This exchange affirms the crucial roles of leaders and followers. This exchange depends on what values (i.e. what virtues) the leader personally embraces and how he or she externally manifests those values within his or her relationships of trust and influence with followers. Especially in regard to transformational leaders, we see how important authentic transformational leadership is for understanding the leader's values that underlie efforts to transform and develop one's followers and of the actual 'goodness' of his or her intentions in seeking to inspire and motivate followers towards particular goals. Further, regarding this focus on the transformational leader individually, we can see how Kant's philosophy emphasizing the leader's moral duty also strongly relates to what obligations a transformational leader owes followers in inspiring, motivating, and developing them.

From our discussion of transformational leadership so far, we have seen that such leaders actively build relationships with followers, which strongly ties the leader component within the Five Components Model to the follower component.[79] Ethical leaders engage followers in ways that assist others in grappling with the challenges of change and personal growth.[80]

Transformational leadership's significant emphasis on followers means that our analysis most directly explores a leader's role in developing others.[81] As James MacGregor Burns originally articulated the concept, leaders who engage in this distinctive approach to leadership seek to engage with followers in a *mutual* process of social influence in which both parties are *positively changed* and developed.[82] We have also seen that transformational leaders emphasise the need to develop people affirmatively and impact them positively – supporting them both as individuals and collectively within organizations.[83] Accordingly, we understand that authentic transformational leaders engage followers individually and collectively. Such leaders employ ethical means to inspire and motivate their followers and encourage them to achieve meaningful goals, higher purposes, and positive change.

Because of transformational leadership's priority on developing followers as individuals and collectively, we have already observed how ethical issues arise concerning the practical effects of the leader–follower relationship on followers. This means that the leader–follower relationship inherently raises significant ethical issues involving a leader's treatment of followers, especially a leader's sense of justice and fairness towards followers as individuals and as groups. As we may observe regarding the development of followers, John Rawls's moral philosophy of distributive justice specifically seeks to achieve a person's human development by ensuring access to the resources and social goods that allow every person to meet a threshold of human functioning and human capability.

In addition to the leader and follower components, we can also direct our analysis towards goals, another critical factor among the Five Components. Goals remain essential within transformational leadership. For the analysis of a leadership approach emphasizing goal achievement, a leader might tend to apply his or her leadership influence in ways ethically guided towards utilitarian results, seeking 'good' outcomes for the greatest number of people involved. Recall those studies showing that leaders who demonstrate transformational leadership behaviours generally prove effective in influencing, motivating, and enabling others to achieve goals.[84] While it remains accurate to say that transformational leaders seek to be and generally are effective organizational leaders, authentic transformational leadership behaviours genuinely focus on developing people to their fullest human capability and encouraging them to work together to achieve higher purposes. Such ethical behaviours and higher purposes logically would include aiming for the higher-purpose outcomes envisioned by that organization in which leader and follower interact.

As discussed earlier, transformational leadership involves a mutual exchange process that drives *how* development is accomplished. In an organizational context, achieving objectives necessarily involves relating to followers collectively, so the human development dynamic tends to be collective.[85] In this dynamic of relating to followers collectively, a transformational leader may sense a need to adopt utilitarian ethical standards by which he or she hopes to achieve organizational goals while also accomplishing the greatest degree of human development for the largest number of organizational members.

By definition, within the Five Components Model of analysis, cultural norms and values operate to shape the given context. The model analyses leadership as applied within a specific context and as shaped by cultural norms and values. As the model indicates, all leadership influence necessarily draws its application and meaning from the particular context in which leadership and followership are exercised. Cultures may be organizational or national. As noted from the outset of this chapter, transformational leadership's broad acceptance across different cultures suggests that transformational leadership tends to be effective within a myriad of different contexts. All five components of the model relate to transformational leadership. However, compared with the model's leader, follower, and goal components, the other components – the context component and the cultural values/norms component – seem to bear less directly on the behaviours that characterise a transformational leader.

Transformational leadership's effectiveness and appeal may not be tied to particular cultures. This observation regarding culture also appears consistent with Bass' observation that transformational leadership's effectiveness tends to cross the boundaries of culture.[86] However, does not necessarily mean that various applications of transformational leadership would look the same or that transformational leadership would always be the leadership approach of choice in all contexts and cultures. For example, one might logically predict that transformational leadership, with its emphasis on building strong leader–follower relationships, would be an unlikely leadership preference in a highly directive or authoritarian context or a culture manifesting a wide power-distance gap between leaders and followers. For those reasons, and in view of research showing transformational leadership is widely embraced, the model's contextual and cultural values/norms components appear to produce comparatively less effect on transformational leadership outcomes than the other components.

So far, we have examined in considerable detail the core elements of transformational leadership and have described the characteristic behaviours of a transformational leader. We have also analysed these leadership elements and behaviours against the template of the Five Components Model to understand how transformational leaders apply their leadership influence in ethical ways and how their priorities align within the framework of those five components. This chapter next considers these concepts as applied to an actual case.

## CASE STUDY: TRANSFORMATIONAL LEADERSHIP OF DANIEL SCHULMAN, PRESIDENT AND CEO OF PAYPAL

Daniel Schulman has served since 2014 as the president and CEO of PayPal. This innovative company forever changed the online financial services industry by bringing digital payments and money transfers into the mainstream.[87] Under Schulman's direction, PayPal has continued to push forward against competitors and has prospered.[88] PayPal's first-quarter earnings in 2021 hit a record, and revenues increased 31 per cent from the previous year.[89]

Some of Schulman's most innovative initiatives have focused on PayPal's investment in its employees.[90] In 2017 PayPal created an employee relief fund to help employees through unexpected financial events. Even without such events, PayPal employees were in need, barely meeting essential expenses from one pay check to the next.[91] When PayPal further investigated its employees' financial health, the company found hourly wage earners struggling to make ends meet, even though workers were being paid what the company considered fair wages at or above market rates.[92] For example, average wages for a PayPal customer service representative in Omaha, Nebraska, were just under $17 per hour, which was well above the state's minimum wage yet well below a living wage for a sole provider in that area.[93] 'I thought the market would take care of this,' Schulman said.[94] The situation at PayPal was not an anomaly, as one in eight Americans was reported to live below the poverty line in 2019, before the Covid-19 pandemic.[95]

PayPal also embraced the concept of *net disposable income* as a new metric for assessing employee financial well-being.[96] For many employees, the money left over after taxes, insurance premiums, and essential living expenses was 4–6 per cent. But that was not enough. According to Schulman, the goal should be that every employee receives a net disposable income (NDI) of at least 20 per cent of total pay.[97] To help struggling PayPal employees, in 2019, Schulman announced an Employee Financial Wellness initiative. Through that programme, PayPal:

- raised employee wages where needed,
- lowered employee healthcare premiums,
- created a means for employees to gain equity in the company,
- developed a financial education programme for employees, and
- encouraged long-term saving by employees.[98]

By the end of 2020, the NDI figure at PayPal had reached 16 per cent and still was increasing.[99]

PayPal's human capital investment has been paying off in various ways for the company, including through greater employee effectiveness. For example, PayPal already has saved millions of dollars in staffing costs due to reduced turnover, partly due to employees not having to find ways to earn more.[100] However, Schulman's leadership has accomplished far more than just profitability for PayPal. Schulman's leadership ethos prioritises employees because the foundation of a great company, says Schulman, is having the best employees.[101] 'We have responsibilities,' he said. 'And I think that responsibility starts with the wellbeing of our employees.'[102] When a company takes care of its employees, he said, they are more likely to go above and beyond what is expected.[103] Schulman and other business partners have called on other business leaders to conduct their own financial-wellness surveys of employees.[104]

Schulman also sought to 'democratize financial services' so that managing and moving money could be accessible and affordable for all citizens, not just the affluent.[105] Schulman also has worked with minority businesses and communities to close a significant racial gap in the nation's wealth.[106] He has been a strong advocate for building a better economy through a broader view of capitalism – an upgraded capitalism in which a company is accountable to multiple stakeholders.[107] Schulman stated that over the long run, if a company takes care of its employees, it will be taking care of its customers, and if a company does that, it naturally takes care of its shareholders.[108]

Schulman's leadership has contributed to a business trend that has increased multiple stakeholder accountability by companies over recent years.[109] In August 2019, the CEOs of more than 180 companies, including JPMorgan, Walmart, and Mastercard, joined PayPal in the Business Roundtable to provide a voice within the business community.[110] In an open letter, the CEOs expressed the need for moving away from an economic perspective of companies as existing solely for the benefit of shareholders.[111] Schulman demonstrated that effective, ethical behaviours by a single transformational leader could influence other organizational leaders to build more accountable and inclusive firms and industries and thereby contribute to a more robust economy and more cohesive society.[112]

Due to Schulman's sustained and effective leadership efforts at PayPal, he was recognized for three consecutive years as one of *Fortune*'s top-20 businesspeople of the year. He also received visionary awards from the Council for Economic Education in 2017 and the Financial Health Network in 2018 for promoting a better-informed society through economic and financial literacy.[113] In 2021, *Fortune* magazine listed Schulman among the World's 50 Greatest Leaders.[114]

## FIVE COMPONENT ANALYSIS

In this case study, Daniel Schulman at PayPal serves as an example of transformational leadership. Schulman's leadership effectiveness suggests that a transformational approach to leadership can work well even in a highly competitive environment such as the financial services industry. We can see that Schulman reflects the characteristic actions of a transformational leader: idealized influence, inspirational motivation, intellectual stimulation, and individualized consideration.[115]

We can also probe more deeply into the ethical aspects of transformational leadership by examining Schulman's leadership example in light of the Five Components Model. This chapter's discussion indicates that three components of the Five Components Model appear most important in characterizing and analysing the transformational leadership approach. These components – *leader*, *follower*, and *goals* – most strongly drive and shape the efforts of a transformational leader like Schulman (Figure 16.3).

First, considering the *leader* component, we can reasonably expect that leadership priorities and behaviours such as those displayed by Schulman at PayPal will naturally emerge and distinguish that person as an authentic transformational leader. Much of Schulman's actions as a leader manifested not just a desire to achieve financial growth for PayPal but emerged from a genuine concern for the long-term welfare of the company's people. We see Schulman's willingness to assume responsibility for the welfare and growth of those

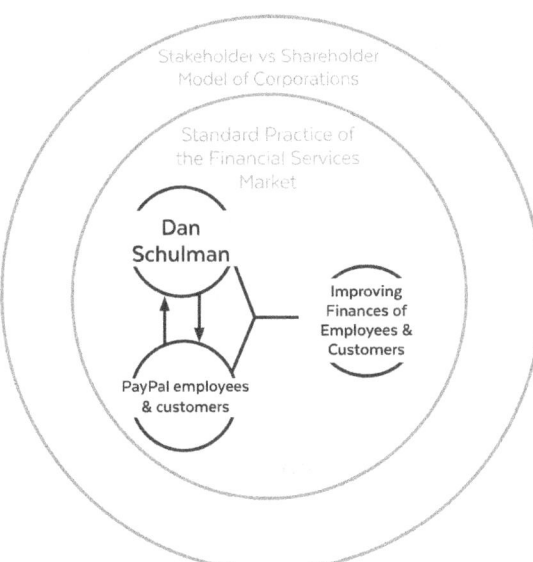

**Figure 16.3**     The Five Components of Leadership Model applied to Daniel Schulman and the PayPal case study

people within his sphere of leadership influence and to exert influence in creative ways that develop employees and enhance their well-being.[116]

Integrating another of the five components – the *follower* – one can expect a transformational leader to relate to followers by acting consistently with the ethical values he or she expresses. In Schulman's relationship with followers, his actions were well-grounded in the ethical values he envisioned and articulated to followers. Schulman became an inspirational and motivational voice for fair treatment of PayPal employees. Through creative initiatives and human capital investments, Schulman purposefully pursued meaningful transformation that developed and improved PayPal employees' financial health and future opportunities. Even more broadly, he was a visionary advocate for positive change and expanded opportunities for millions of disadvantaged people in society, people with little or no affordable access to financial tools and limited knowledge about how to use them.[117]

In prioritising employees, Schulman expressly followed an ethos that ultimately helps develop a great company.[118] Popular press articles often refer to a CEO or prominent person as a transformational leader because the person catalysed change (whether positive or not). This change substantially transformed the nature or direction of the organization or some part of it. Efforts at organizational change alone – however substantial – may fall short of the actions that fully characterise a transformational leader, as such leaders are described in this chapter. Schulman, however, not only achieved positive change for PayPal as a company, but he also used his leadership influence to achieve positive development of the organization's people, individually and collectively.

As noted earlier, Schulman initially believed that so long as PayPal was paying above the legal minimum wage within a given jurisdiction, free-market forces would ultimately achieve a living wage for an employee and his or her family, but such was not what PayPal's investigation revealed.[119] This suggests Schulman began from a fairly conventional sense of a company's minimum ethical duty towards its employees, a duty that essentially was tied to PayPal's legal obligations. More accurately, Schulman has expressed concerns for employees' financial welfare, even before the Covid-19 pandemic and despite PayPal's above-market wages, suggesting he was a leader who had embraced something more than just a basic moral duty within the employment relationship and a minimal level of corporate responsibility towards employees. Apart from Schulman's example, one can readily imagine organizational leaders and financial decision-makers expressing a more austere, owner-dominant ethical perspective: 'Our company has complied with the laws, so we've met our obligation towards employees. How that amount of pay impacts an employee's welfare is purely a private matter and is no "business" of the company or its executives and owners.' Implicitly, the organization's legal obligation effectively defines and limits any ethical duty to employees and frees the organizational leaders from assuming any concern or responsibility for employee welfare beyond the work itself. This minimalist view of duty could prevail even if legal compliance did not preclude a company from embracing a higher ethical standard in providing for employees and attempting to do more for their welfare.

Although at the outset Schulman had relied on economic forces to provide systemically for employees and to fulfil adequately any ethical duty towards employees, the perspective of his ethical responsibility to employees expanded. As a transformational leader, Schulman recognized and responded to a need he recognized among followers. He and PayPal then took an ethical step forward by creating the employee relief fund. From knowledge PayPal gained from engaging employees in the relief initiative, Schulman also launched the investigation that resulted in his deeper awareness of employee financial needs – needs that went well beyond those he initially had perceived. Again, Schulman, as a leader, responded in a way that promoted followers' financial and personal development and visibly demonstrated a genuine concern for their long-term well-being.

The third among the five components emphasises the transformational leader's *goals*. Schulman's leadership of PayPal has proven highly effective in expanding the business and accomplishing the company's financial goals.[120] Early on, Schulman also adopted as a critical goal for PayPal to create new financial tools for the millions of Americans who are underserved by the US financial system.[121] In seeking to grow PayPal as an organization and to achieve its company goals, Schulman set and prioritised followers' financial health and well-being achieved through an array of beneficial changes. Schulman achieved his specific goal of improving the financial health of followers, notably by implementing the Employee Financial Wellness programme and by creating and applying the NDI metric to ensure measurable progress towards the goal of at least 20 per cent NDI for each PayPal employee. He also contributed to people's broader well-being by developing their knowledge and capabilities, encouraging them in their productive potential, and expanding savings for future opportunities.[122]

In those ways, Schulman's approach was authentically transformational for the company and its people. His actions manifested ethical behaviours that used idealized influence through which he accomplished positive change. Schulman inspired and enabled followers towards goals of greater financial security and motivated and encouraged them to increase saving and investing for the future. He imparted inspirational motivation to engage and retain PayPal employees and persuade the company's directors and shareholders of the long-term benefits. Schulman integrated intellectual stimulation of followers through financial education and instruction for employees on the importance of saving and building equity (i.e. gaining equity in the company). His leadership behaviours also reflected individualized consideration for the financial health and well-being of each individual working for PayPal. Further, Schulman extended his sphere of leadership influence to inspire and motivate the CEOs and organizational leaders of other companies towards more caring concern for their own people and better ethical treatment of employees in need. In Schulman's example of transformational leadership, we can observe how his actions reinforced his idealized influence and inspirational motivation of followers even beyond PayPal employees and strengthened the relationships of leadership trust Schulman achieved through acts of caring concern.[123]

Viewing Schulman's transformational leadership interactions with PayPal employees at a deeper level, we can see how a dynamic ethical interplay emerged, especially between the components of leader and follower. As predicted by the research on transformational leadership, this dynamic generated a mutual developmental benefit for leader and follower.[124] On one side, we can see how Schulman's ethical leadership perspective progressively developed through his interactions with PayPal employees. Schulman as a leader continued to engage with PayPal employees through an increasing series of ethical responses. On the other side, although no facts indicate that PayPal employees expected the company to provide financial relief, they acquired financial knowledge for their long-term benefit. They also gained personal experience with a company and its key leader proving his ethical commitment to the employees' development and well-being. We can see in such ethical engagement how both the leader and the follower advanced through this dynamic of mutual development, including moral development.

Having examined the elements and dynamics applied in the case study and analysed them through the lens of the Five Components Model, we are ready to answer the framing question with which we launched this chapter: 'How can leaders create positive change for themselves, their followers, and their organizations?' It is accurate to conclude that in our case study Dan Schulman's priorities, values, and actions as a transformational leader achieved positive change and meaningful development for PayPal employees, individually and collectively, and thus valuable change and growth for PayPal as an organization. Likewise, practising authentic transformational leadership can serve as a path for other leaders to answer this question.

## SUMMARY AND CONCLUDING REMARKS

We began this chapter on transformational leadership with a question: 'How can leaders create positive change for themselves, their followers, and their organizations?' The answer starts with a duty to engage in ethical leadership behaviours grounded in a moral obligation towards others. Transformational leadership comprises not only an effective approach to leadership across various contexts but also represents an ethical approach to leadership that emphasises the importance of strong leader–follower relationships for achieving collective goals.

The leadership principles and dynamics summarised here offer strong support that transformational leaders crucially inspire, motivate, and stimulate others towards higher goals. Transformational leaders also demonstrate genuine concern for followers and a development ethic towards the people and organizations for whom such leaders hold responsibility. These observations suggest a related question: What behaviours inspire leaders and followers to grow as persons and bring about positive change? In contrast with transactional leaders, transformational leaders would not be satisfied with relationships in which leaders only engage with followers to reward or punish them for performance. Instead, these leaders find ways to challenge the assumptions of their followers, connect with them as individuals, and inspire them to action – all while somehow embodying the core values of their mutual organizational and cultural contexts. To become this kind of leader, one must value long-term development as much as immediate performance. Moreover, one must demonstrate the ability to clearly communicate core values and live them consistently in credible ways that enhance mutual trust and development.

Drawing from the preceding conceptual discussion, the actual case of Daniel Schulman at PayPal illustrates even more clearly how the ethical grounding of a transformational leader can manifest in action. The case study shows how transformational leadership behaviours can use positive change to achieve successful outcomes for a company and its employees. Schulman exemplifies the ethical motivations and actions of an authentic transformational leader, including the sense of responsibility such a leader bears towards those within his or her sphere of leadership influence. The case shows at the same time how transformational leadership proves highly effective both in developing successful organizations and people.

## DISCUSSION QUESTIONS

1. How does a transformational leader's use of the charisma element make a difference in the performance of team or organization members?
2. Considering that some observers have questioned transformational leadership's nature as a fundamentally ethical approach to leadership, what are the distinctive behaviours that support the view that authentic transformational leadership constitutes ethical leadership?
3. What situations or circumstances might arise that could put a transformational team leader into a dilemma where he or she has to choose between achieving team effectiveness and organizational goals, on the one hand, or promoting the welfare and development of team members, on the other hand? Would the team leader's decision to emphasise one choice over the other necessarily make the leader's actions any more or less moral or ethical?
4. What practical implications or effects emerge for followers from the reality that a given organizational leader can be either displaying an ethical, 'authentic' transformational leadership or a less ethical, 'pseudo' form of transformational leadership? Would it ever be possible for an authentically transformational leader to display a leadership 'dark side'?
5. What are some of the similarities and differences in behaviours that characterise transformational and servant leaders?
6. What does it mean that in a transformational leadership approach a leader and a follower tend to engage in mutual change and development? What might an example of such mutual change and development look like?
7. Considering that Daniel Schulman, president and CEO of PayPal, initiated changes and achieved goals for the company's business growth and financial success, should these facts be sufficient to conclude that Schulman fully meets the leadership behaviours that characterise an authentic transformational leader? Assuming one concludes that Schulman does exemplify an authentic transformational leader, what additional vital facts support that conclusion?

## ADDITIONAL RESOURCES

B. Bass and B.J. Avolio, The Multifactor Leadership Questionnaire. https://www.mindgarden.com/16-multifactor-leadership-questionnaire.

The MLQ survey is the most typically used instrument for analysing transformational and transactional leadership.[125] Adaptations of the MLQ also are in use.[126]

J. Kouzes and B. Posner, LPI: Leadership Practices Inventory. http://www.leadershipchallenge.com/professionals-section-lpi.aspx.

This is another tool for measuring and evaluating transformational leadership. It follows Kouzes and Posner's model and uses a survey instrument known as the leadership practices inventory (LPI).[127]

> P.M. Podsakoff, S.B. MacKenzie, R.H. Moorman and R. Fetter, 'Transformational leader behaviors and their effects on followers' trust in leader, satisfaction, and organizational citizenship behaviors', *The Leadership Quarterly*, vol. 1 no. 2, June 1990, 107–42.
>
> The authors of this study developed a third tool for evaluating transformational leaders, the GTI.[128] The GTI was designed as a short and practical measure compared to the longer MLQ and LPI.[129]

# NOTES

1. J. Lee, J. Cho and R. Pillai, 'Does transformational leadership promote employee perceptions of ethical leadership?: a moderated mediation model of procedural justice and power-distance orientation', *Journal of Leadership, Accountability & Ethics*, vol. 17 no. 6 2020, 88–100.

2. R.J. House and R.N. Aditya, 'The social scientific study of leadership: *Quo vadis?*' *MANAGE Journal of Management*, vol. 23 no. 3, 1997, 409–743.

3. For example, see J.J. Hater and B.M. Bass, 'Superiors' evaluations and subordinates' perceptions of transformational and transactional leadership', *Journal of Applied Psychology*, vol. 73 no. 4, 1988, 695–702. See also B.M. Bass and B.J. Avolio, *Improving Organizational Effectiveness Through Transformational Leadership*, Thousand Oaks, CA: Sage, 1994.

4. M.K. Copeland, 'The impact of authentic, ethical, transformational leadership on leader effectiveness', *Journal of Leadership, Accountability & Ethics*, vol. 13 no. 3, 2016, 79–97.

5. R.M. McManus and G. Perruci, *Understanding Leadership: An Arts and Humanities Perspective*, 2nd edn, New York: Routledge, 2020.

6. J.M. Burns, *Leadership*, New York: Harper & Row, 1978.

7. W.G. Bennis and B. Nanus, *Leaders: The Strategies for Taking Charge*, New York: Harper Business, 1997.

8. Bennis and Nanus, *Leaders*, pp. 202–3.

9. J.M. Kouzes and B.Z. Posner, *The Leadership Challenge: How to Get Extraordinary Things Done in Organizations*, San Francisco, CA: Jossey-Bass, 1987; J.M. Kouzes and B.Z Posner, *The Leadership Challenge*, San Francisco, CA: Jossey-Bass, 2002.

10. P.M. Podsakoff, S.B. MacKenzie, R.H. Moorman and R. Fetter, 'Transformational leader behaviors and their effects on followers' trust in leader, satisfaction, and organizational citizenship behaviors', *The Leadership Quarterly*, vol. 1 no. 2, June 1990, 107–42.

11. Podsakoff et al., 'Transformational leader behaviors'.

12. B.M. Bass, *Leadership and Performance Beyond Expectations*, New York: Free Press, 1985.

13. See Hater and Bass, 'Superiors' evaluations and subordinates' perceptions'; and Bass and Avolio *Improving Organizational Effectiveness*.

14. B.J. Avolio, D.A. Waldman and F.J. Yammarino, 'Leading in the 1990s: the four I's of transformational leadership,' *Journal of European Industrial Training*, vol. 15 no. 4, 1991. https://doi.org/10.1108/03090599110143366.

15. See Bass, *Leadership and Performance*; B.M. Bass and P. Steidlmeier, 'Ethics, character, and authentic transformational leadership behavior', *The Leadership Quarterly*, vol. 10 no. 2, 1999, 181–217; B.M. Bass and R.E. Riggio, *Transformational Leadership*, Mahwah, NJ: L. Erlbaum Associates, 2006.

16. Bass and Avolio, *Improving Organizational Effectiveness*.

17. Bass and Riggio, *Transformational Leadership*; M.E. Brown and L.K. Treviño, 'Socialized charismatic leadership, values congruence, and deviance in work groups', *Journal of Applied Psychology*, vol. 91 no. 4, July 2006, 954–62.

18. Bass and Avolio, *Improving Organizational Effectiveness*.

19. Burns, *Leadership*.

20. See B.M. Bass and B.J. Avolio, *Full Range Leadership Development: Manual for the Multifactor Leadership Questionnaire*, Palo Alto, CA: Mind Garden, 1997; see also B.M. Bass, 'Does the transactional-transformational leadership paradigm transcend organizational and national boundaries?' *American Psychologist*, vol. 52 no. 2, 1997, 130–39.

21. Bass and Avolio, *Improving Organizational Effectiveness*.

22. Bass and Avolio, *Full Range Leadership Development*.

23. Burns, *Leadership*.

24. R.J. House, *A 1976 Theory of Charismatic Leadership*, Working Paper Series, Toronto University, October 1976. https://eric.ed.gov/?id=ED133827 (accessed 4 July 2022). Also see R.J. House, *The Theory of Charismatic Leadership: Extensions and Evidence*, Philadelphia, PA: Reginald H. Jones Center, Wharton School, University of Pennsylvania, 1993; F.J. Yammarino and B.J. Avolio, *Transformational and Charismatic Leadership: The Road Ahead*, 10th anniversary edn, Bingley: Emerald, 2013.

25. Bass and Avolio, *Improving Organizational Effectiveness*.

26. Ethical leadership viewed herein as a broad category or group of leadership models, is distinguished from the specific model or construct labeled as 'ethical leadership'. See M.E. Brown, L.K. Treviño and D.A. Harrison, 'Ethical leadership: a social learning perspective for construct development and testing', *Organizational Behavior and Human Decision Processes*, vol. 97 no. 2, 2005, 117–34. Brown, Treviño, and Harrison defined the 'ethical leadership' construct as a leader's 'demonstration of normatively appropriate conduct through personal actions and interpersonal relationships, and the promotion of such conduct to followers through two-way communication, reinforcement, and decision-making' (p. 120).

27. M.E. Brown and L.K. Treviño, 'Leader–follower values congruence: are socialized charismatic leaders better able to achieve it?' *Journal of Applied Psychology*, vol. 94 no. 2, 2009, 478–90.

28. Bass, *Leadership and Performance*; see also Bass and Avolio, *Full Range Leadership Development*.

29. Bass, *Leadership and Performance*. See also B.M. Bass, *Transformational Leadership: Industrial, Military, and Educational Impact*, Mahwah, NJ: Lawrence Erlbaum, 1998.

30. Bass and Avolio, *Full Range Leadership Development*.

31. Bass and Avolio, *Full Range Leadership Development*.

32. D. van Dierendonck, 'Servant leadership: a review and synthesis', *Journal of Management*, vol. 37 no. 4, July 2011, 1228–61; D. van Dierendonck and I. Nuijten, 'The servant leadership survey: development and validation of a multidimensional measure', *Journal of Business and Psychology*, vol. 26 no. 3, September 2011, 249–67.

33. D. van Dierendonck, D. Stam, P. Boersma, N. de Windt and J. Alkema, 'Same difference? Exploring the differential mechanisms linking servant leadership and transformational leadership to follower outcomes', *The Leadership Quarterly*, vol. 25 no. 3, June 2014, 544–62.

34. A.G. Stone, R.F. Russell and K. Patterson, 'Transformational versus servant leadership: a difference in leader focus', *Leadership & Organization Development Journal*, vol. 25 no. 4, June 2004, 349–61.

35. van Dierendonck et al., 'Same difference?'.

36. van Dierendonck et al., 'Same difference?'.

37. J. Parolini, K. Patterson and B. Winston, 'Distinguishing between transformational and servant leadership', *Leadership & Organization Development Journal*, vol. 30 no. 3, May 2009, 274–91.

38. Kouzes and Posner, *The Leadership Challenge*.

39. K.P. Merlini, C. Albowicz and P.G. Merlini, 'A transformational and an authentic leader walk into a bar: who feels included?', *Journal of Leadership, Accountability & Ethics*, vol. 16 no. 3, 2019, 96–108.

40. B. George, *Authentic Leadership: Rediscovering the Secrets to Creating Lasting Value*, San Francisco, CA: Jossey-Bass, 2004; B. George, *Discover Your True North*, Hoboken, NJ: Jossey-Bass, 2015.

41. Merlini et al., 'A transformational and an authentic leader walk into a bar'.

42. Bass and Steidlmeier, 'Ethics, character'.

43. K.W. Parry and S.B. Proctor-Thomson, 'Perceived integrity of transformational leaders in organisational settings', *Journal of Business Ethics*, vol. 35 no. 2, January 2002, 75–96.

44. Bass and Steidlmeier, 'Ethics, character'.

45. Parry and Proctor-Thomson, 'Perceived integrity'.

46. Burns, *Leadership*.

47. Bass and Riggio, *Transformational Leadership*; Bass and Steidlmeier, 'Ethics, character'.

48. Parry and Proctor-Thomson, 'Perceived integrity'.

49. Parry and Proctor-Thomson, 'Perceived integrity'.

50. J. Lipman-Blumen, *The Allure of Toxic Leaders: Why We Follow Destructive Bosses and Corrupt Politicians – and How We Can Survive Them*, Oxford: Oxford University Press, 2006.

51. J.A. Conger, 'The dark side of leadership', *Organizational Dynamics*, vol. 19 no. 2, September 1990, 44–55.

52. S. Einarsen, M.S. Aasland and A. Skogstad, 'Destructive leadership behaviour: a definition and conceptual model', *The Leadership Quarterly*, vol. 18 no. 3, June 2007, 207–16.

53. A. Christie, J. Barling and N. Turner, 'Pseudo-transformational leadership: model specification and outcomes', *Journal of Applied Social Psychology*, vol. 41 no. 12, December 2011, 2943–84.

54. Bass and Riggio, *Transformational Leadership*.

55. Burns, *Leadership*. Also see M.Z. Hackman and C.E. Johnson, *Leadership: A Communication Perspective*, 6th edn, Long Grove, IL: Waveland, 2013.

56. Lee et al., 'Does transformational leadership promote employee perceptions'; see also Merlini et al., 'A transformational and an authentic leader walk into a bar'.

57. Lee et al., 'Does transformational leadership promote employee perceptions'.

58. R.B. Shaw, *Trust in the Balance: Building Successful Organizations on Results, Integrity, and Concern*, San Francisco, CA: Jossey-Bass, 1998.

59. Parry and Proctor-Thomson, 'Perceived integrity'.

60. N. Turner, J. Barling, O. Epitropaki, V. Butcher and C. Milner, 'Transformational leadership and moral reasoning', *Journal of Applied Psychology*, vol. 87 no. 2, 2002, 304–11.

61. A.M. Naber and R.G. Moffett, 'Follower moral reasoning influences perceptions of transformational leadership behavior', *Journal of Applied Social Psychology*, vol. 47 no. 2, February 2017, 99–112.

62. Naber and Moffett, 'Follower moral reasoning'.

63. P.F. Buller, J.J. Kohls and K.S. Anderson, 'The challenge of global ethics', *Journal of Business Ethics*, vol. 10 no. 10, October 1991, 767–75.

64. B.P. Dean, 'Emerging leadership ethics in an interdependent world: human capabilities development as a global imperative for moral leadership', in N.S. Huber and M.C. Walker (eds), *Emergent Models of Global Leadership*, College Park, MD: International Leadership Association, 2005, pp. 17–33.

65. Bass and Steidlmeier, 'Ethics, character'.

66. J.B. Ciulla, *Ethics, The Heart of Leadership*, Westport, CT: Quorum Books, 1998; R.A. Heifetz, *Leadership Without Easy Answers*, Cambridge, MA: Harvard University Press, 1994.

67. Bass and Riggio, *Transformational Leadership*.

68. A. Safty, *Leadership and Global Governance*, Irvine, CA: Universal Publishers, 2003.

69. Dean, 'Emerging leadership ethics'.

70. Einarsen et al., 'Destructive leadership behaviour'.

71. Bass and Steidlmeier, 'Ethics, character'.

72. B.J. Avolio, B.M. Bass, and D.I. Jung, 'Re-examining the components of transformational and transactional leadership using the Multifactor Leadership', *Journal of Occupational and Organizational Psychology*, vol. 72 no. 4, December 1999, 441–62. See also Bennis and Nanus, *Leaders*.

73. R.N. Kanungo and M. Mendonca, *Ethical Dimensions of Leadership*, Thousand Oaks, CA: Sage, 1996. See also R. Bergman, 'Why be moral? A conceptual model from developmental psychology', *Human Development*, vol. 45 no. 2, April 2002, 104–24.

74. Kanungo and Mendonca, *Ethical Dimensions*.

75. Bass and Riggio, *Transformational Leadership*.

76. See McManus and Perruci, *Understanding Leadership*, p. 15.

77. Compare, e.g. Lee et al., 'Does transformational leadership promote employee perceptions', observing that the relation between transformational leadership and procedural justice was stronger for followers from cultures with a lower power-distance orientation.

78. McManus and G. Perruci, *Understanding Leadership*.

79. For further discussion of the crucial role of followers as viewed through the Five Components Analysis, see Chapter 15, which addresses how followers can crucially impact ethical leadership behaviours and reviews the emerging body of knowledge relating to followership.

80. Ciulla, *Ethics*; and R.A. Heifetz, *Leadership Without Easy Answers*.

81. See McManus and Perruci, *Understanding Leadership*.

82. Burns, *Leadership*.

83. Bass and Riggio, *Transformational Leadership*.

84. House and Aditya, 'The social scientific study of leadership'.

85. Even considering individualized consideration as a critical component of transformational leadership, an organizational leader's focus on and interactions with members tend to be collective and, to that extent, somewhat less individual. This dynamic could constitute another difference between transformational leadership and other leadership approaches, such as servant leadership (as further discussed within this chapter in the comparison of transformational leadership and servant leadership).

86. Bass, 'Does the transactional-transformational leadership paradigm transcend'.

87. 'Daniel Schulman', *Fortune*, 2019. https://fortune.com/businessperson-of-the-year/2019/daniel-schulman/ (accessed 30 December 2021).

88. 'Daniel Schulman', *Fortune*, 2019.

89. 'Dan Schulman', *Fortune*, 2021. https://fortune.com/worlds-greatest-leaders/2021/dan-schulman/ (accessed 30 December 2021).

90. 'Dan Schulman', *Fortune*, 2021.

91. S. Balogh, 'PayPal workers were struggling to make ends meet; CEO Dan Schulman vowed to change that', *SHRM*, 2021. https://www.shrm.org/executive/resources/articles/pages/paypal-ceo-helps-workers-with-finances.aspx (accessed 27 December 2021). This article by Balogh was originally published in *Business Insider*.

92. Balogh, 'PayPal workers were struggling'; 'Dan Schulman', *Fortune*, 2021; TED Business, *How We Can Actually Pay People Enough – with Paypal C.E.O. Dan Schulman*, 2020. https://www.ted.com/talks/ted_business_how_we_can_actually_pay_people_enough_with_paypal_ceo_dan_schulman (accessed 27 December 2021]; PayPal, 'A financial health moon shot: PayPal president and C.E.O. Dan Schulman on barefoot innovation podcast', *PayPal Newsroom*, 2021. https://newsroom.paypal-corp.com/2021–06–10-A-Financial-Health-Moonshot (accessed 30 December 2021).

93. Balogh, 'PayPal workers were struggling'.

94. TED Business, *How We Can Actually Pay People Enough*.

95. Balogh, 'PayPal workers were struggling'.

96. TED Business, *How We Can Actually Pay People Enough*.

97. TED Business, *How We Can Actually Pay People Enough*.

98. M. Fitzgerald, 'PayPal C.E.O. says investing in low-level employees will drive shareholder returns', *CNBC*, 2020. https://www.cnbc.com/2020/11/12/paypal-ceo-investing-in-low-level-workers-drives-shareholder-returns-.html (accessed 30 December 2021); TED Business, *How We Can Actually Pay People Enough*.

99. Balogh, 'PayPal workers were struggling'; 'Dan Schulman', *Fortune*, 2021; TED Business, *How We Can Actually Pay People Enough*.

100. Balogh, 'PayPal workers were struggling'.

101. Balogh, 'PayPal workers were struggling'; TED Business, *How We Can Actually Pay People Enough*.

102. Balogh, 'PayPal workers were struggling'.

103. TED Business, *How We Can Actually Pay People Enough*.

104. Balogh, 'PayPal workers were struggling'.

105. Fitzgerald, 'PayPal C.E.O. says'.

106. A.R. Sorkin and others, 'PayPal invests in racial equality', *The New York Times*, 28 October 2020, section Business. https://www.nytimes.com/2020/10/28/business/dealbook/paypal-invests-in-racial-equality.html (accessed 30 December 2021).

107. PayPal, 'A financial health moon shot'.

108. TED Business, *How We Can Actually Pay People Enough*.

109. Balogh, 'PayPal workers were struggling'.

110. R. Feloni, '181 C.E.O.s of public companies, including Apple, JPMorgan Chase, and Walmart, have declared a company's purpose is to serve more than just shareholders', *Business Insider*, 2019. https://www.businessinsider.com/business-roundtable-ceos-say-companies-must-serve-more-than-shareholders-2019–8 (accessed 27 December 2021).

111. Balogh, 'PayPal workers were struggling'; see also Feloni, '181 C.E.O.s of public companies'.

112. See Balogh, 'PayPal workers were struggling'; see also Feloni, '181 C.E.O.s of public companies'.

113. Financial Health Network, 'Dan Schulman: paying it forward', *Financial Health Network*, 2020. https://finhealthnetwork.org/podcast/episode-1-paying-it-forward/ (accessed 30 December 2021).

114. 'Dan Schulman', *Fortune*, 2021.

115. See Avolio et al., 'Leading in the 1990s'.

116. See Balogh, 'PayPal workers were struggling'; see also TED Business, *How We Can Actually Pay People Enough*.

117. Financial Health Network, 'Dan Schulman: paying it forward'; Fitzgerald, 'PayPal C.E.O. says'; Sorkin, 'PayPal invests in racial equality'.

118. See Balogh, 'PayPal workers were struggling'; see also TED Business, *How We Can Actually Pay People Enough*.

119. See Balogh, 'PayPal workers were struggling'.

120. 'Dan Schulman', *Fortune*, 2021.

121. Fitzgerald, 'PayPal C.E.O. says'.

122. TED Business, *How We Can Actually Pay People Enough*.

123. See Shaw, *Trust in the Balance*.

124. Burns, *Leadership*.

125. Bass and Avolio, *Full Range Leadership Development*.

126. See e.g. S. Xirasagar, M.E. Samuels and C.H. Stoskopf, 'Physician leadership styles and effectiveness: an empirical study', *Medical Care Research and Review*, vol. 62 no. 6, 2005, 720–40.

127. B.Z. Posner and J.M. Kouzes, 'Development and validation of the leadership practices inventory', *Educational and Psychological Measurement*, vol. 48 no. 2, April 1988, 483–96.

128. Podsakoff et al., 'Transformational leader behaviors'.

129. S.A. Carless, A.J. Wearing and L. Mann, 'A short measure of transformational leadership', *Journal of Business & Psychology*, vol. 14 no. 3, Spring 2000, 389–406.

# 17
# Adaptive leadership

*Stephen C. Trainor*

## FRAMING QUESTION

How should both leaders and their followers adapt their thinking to solve complex challenges?

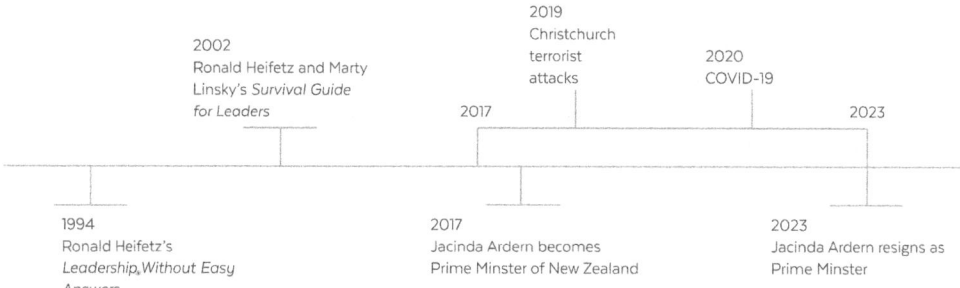

**Figure 17.1** Timeline of major works on adaptive leadership in relation to the chapter case study

Albert Einstein famously observed, 'Problems cannot be solved with the same mindset that created them.'[1] His fundamental premise that a change in thinking is the key to solving the most challenging and complex problems serves as the organizing principle of the subject for this chapter: the adaptive leadership framework. Adaptive leadership provides a path for leaders to frame problems while supporting and mobilizing their followers to adapt to change.

Much has changed in the world since Einstein argued for a new way of thinking about problems. However, the challenges facing individuals, organizations, and societies today are no less serious, and the stakes still include survival. In fact, the interrelated and increasingly globalized nature of the world has resulted in new categories of challenges, the most vexing of which are termed 'wicked' problems. Such problems are considered wicked because they are incredibly difficult, if not impossible, for any single organization or solitary leader to solve.[2] Prolific management theorist Peter Drucker goes even further to suggest that the challenges of the twenty-first century cannot be solved by implementing more sophisticated economic, political, or managerial plans and policies.[3] Instead, Drucker argues that future problems are rooted in outdated assumptions about how things ought to work and can only be solved when leaders and followers begin to think differently.[4] Adaptive leadership provides a simple operating framework for leaders and followers better suited for today's complex problems.

As we have done in the previous chapters, we will first examine the history of adaptive leadership, apply the theory to a five-component analysis, and finally examine how the theory works in the context of a specific case study – in this instance, the leadership of Jacinda Ardern. Ardern became New Zealand's prime minister in 2017 and was the youngest prime minister to serve New Zealand in more than 150 years.[5] From this case study we suggest that youth and gender, along with other aspects of diversity (and a host of less traditional attributes of leadership) may advance a different leadership paradigm where adaptive leadership is an inherent capability rather than a response to the tension presented by the problems leaders face

## HISTORY

Abraham Kaplan observed, 'Give a small boy a hammer, and he will find that everything he encounters needs pounding.'[6] While history shows us that leaders have always sought better ways to master the art of solving problems, it also demonstrates that our perspective on the nature of problems is often limited. The adaptive leadership framework, first described by Harvard University lecturer Ronald Heifetz in the 1994 book *Leadership Without Easy Answers*, suggests that it isn't merely about finding a way to solve problems, but a different and more effective way to think about solving problems.[7] As the book's title implies, adaptive leadership emerged from the personal stories of leaders who were increasingly frustrated in their struggle and inability to solve organizational problems, or at least their dissatisfaction with the generally accepted approach to problems that seemed different than those they had been conditioned to solve.[8] A closer study of the framework highlights the connections between crucial leadership and management thinking shifts and the past century's associated social, political, economic, and technological trends.[9] The most influential of those ideas, trends, and connections are described below.[10]

Problem-solving has always been a critical concern of organizational leadership, but the leader's approach to that role has changed over time.[11] One of the earliest modern sources on leadership and problem-solving is Frederick Winslow Taylor's study of work and the ensuing field of scientific management.[12] This problem-solving approach shifted management's focus from the external challenges of securing capital and resources to an internal focus on efficiency and workers' productivity.[13] At the same time, the 'Great Man' and trait-based views of leadership suggested that the primary job of leaders was to make decisions and solve organizational problems through a dispassionate process of analysis and design.[14] The primary assumptions of this early management perspective were that problems had predictable, rational, and technical solutions and that only certain types of leaders possessed the ability to deal with those problems effectively. As this approach to management expanded and industry grew, so too emerged the first studies about how to cultivate analysis and rational decision-making and specialized schools of management and business where this curriculum was taught.[15] This approach to organizational management and problem-solving contributed much to the dramatic growth of Western industry and society in the early twentieth century. However, by the Second World War, the mechanistic and leader-centric paradigms of problem-solving proved incapable of dealing with the challenges of expanding scale, scope, and impact.[16]

A new form of management thinking emerged from research that began in the Great Depression and became prominent during the massive expansion of industrial power in the United States during the Second World War. In stark contrast to the deterministic and rational scientific management methods, the human relations perspective confirmed that the person was a key variable in organizational problem-solving.[17] Research conducted prior to and during the Second World War studied the relationships between leaders and followers and discovered significant effects on group dynamics and organizational performance.[18] The follower was no longer merely a tool that leaders applied to a problem but part of a unique social system and a direct and vital participant in the problem-solving process.[19] Leadership theory in this period sought the right conditions and behaviours whereby leaders effectively motivated followers toward the goal. However, human relations theory also challenged leaders to consider, for the first time, the effects of their actions on followers as they shaped organizational systems to solve complicated problems. For example, the classic Hawthorne studies of group dynamics sought to understand how leaders could make work groups more productive but discovered that leaders merely paying attention to workers influenced their motivation and productivity.[20] By mid-century, it was clear that leaders were no longer merely managing a mechanism of people and machines but responsible both for the roles of followers in problem-solving and performance and, for the first time, for fostering an ethical imperative related to the follower's well-being.[21]

As the operating environment for many organizations expanded in the post-war period, so did the need for effective problem-solving. A new leadership perspective emerged that highlighted the interconnections and relationships of the organizational environment.[22] The organization was no longer viewed as a static entity but a dynamic, evolving, and almost-living organism.[23] While the leader remained at the centre of the organization, leadership and problem-solving was increasingly dependent, or contingent, on other factors like technology and communication systems and organizational and social structures that made the world smaller and expanded the nexus of problem-solving to the internal and external environments.[24] The changing circumstances increased both the scale of considerations and the scope of responsibilities that factored into bigger, more complicated problems leaders were expected to solve.

The explosive impact of information technology in the 1960s and 1970s contributed to an even different wave of thinking about leadership and an equally dramatic shift in the problems that organizational leaders faced. The leader's responsibilities in the information age expanded well beyond the confines of traditional organizations and industries to include larger interconnecting systems and an array of entities with a stake in the system. Along with the change in scope and scale of responsibility, approaches to leadership, like transformational, authentic, and servant leadership, focus less on roles and activities and more on purposes and forms of leadership that produce results in an expanding system.[25] The objective to subjective shift in leadership thinking is a dramatic transformation that sets a higher bar for both leadership perspective and performance, as well as new mindsets and skillsets to deal with the growing complexity of leadership.[26] When we think of leaders in the information age, the image is no longer just of an executive directing an industrial operation from the corner office, but also includes images of people and purposes beyond the traditional organization.

In this era, leaders and leadership exist everywhere. They range from aid workers helping to bring clean drinking water to a remote community, to front-line healthcare and safety workers battling an unknown global health crisis, to businesses facing an unknown future of global supply chains while reinventing the very nature of how work gets done. In each case, leadership extends beyond traditional walls to focus not only on problems of complicated logistics, production, and data processes but increasingly on complex interdependencies that make up intangible attributes, like quality, effectiveness, and satisfaction, as well as broader public goods, such as health, safety, sustainability, and even happiness.

Unlike earlier times when leaders faced predictable, manageable tasks and plans, information-age leaders must respond to a growing number of intangibles they are incapable of solving with the expertise and knowledge they alone possess.[27] Adult development theorist, Robert Kegan, describes the situation as leaders being 'in over their heads'.[28] In response to the increasing complexity of life, work, and intersecting challenges, adaptive leadership offers a radically different approach from traditional problem-solving. Leaders activate, mobilize and leverage the interconnecting systems of people, knowledge, culture, and capabilities to enable the learning needed for adaptive challenges. Adaptive leadership rejects the classical, technical, and mechanical solutions, like Taylorism, and recognizes that leaders need more metaphorical tools than just a hammer. They need a more extensive toolbox and other frameworks like vertical development, leadership agility, and complexity leadership theory, which have emerged with a similar focus on helping leaders raise the bar of their thinking to meet the needs of the evolving context.[29]

## MAJOR CONCEPTS OF ADAPTIVE LEADERSHIP

The previous section highlighted the dramatic shifts in management thinking and approaches to problem-solving that bring us to a world where previous perspectives and practices seem trite at best. We now turn to adaptive leadership, which is the practice of mobilizing and supporting the people who tackle complex challenges.[30] While leaders have always concerned themselves with solving problems and seeking opportunities, many leaders struggle in an increasingly turbulent environment. This new environment is punctuated by macro trends like globalization, climate change, human rights, demographic shifts, technological innovation, political polarization, global pandemics, and the potential for superpower conflict.[31] On the one hand, this turbulence might be a product of wickedly unsolvable problems, discussed previously, or it may be that the modern world is one where the pace, size, and nature of problems have expanded beyond the current capability of leaders, technologies and organizational initiatives.[32] Whatever the reason, this capability gap, also known as an 'adaptive challenge', demands more of leaders than traditional approaches to problem-solving can deliver. Two assumptions about leadership help to explain this capability gap. The first assumption is that an increasing number of problems and crises lack simple, straightforward solutions. The second assumption is that many leaders do not recognize that they must change their thinking to build the adaptive capacity needed to recognize and solve those problems.[33] Or, as former US Secretary of State George Shultz observed, 'There are problems you can solve, and problems you can only work at.'[34]

A familiar saying is that solving a complex problem is often like 'building a bridge while you cross it'. This metaphor exemplifies how very different the problems leaders face today are from those leaders have been trained to expect and prepared to solve. Instead, leaders in a complex world need a different way of thinking, being, and acting.[35] For example, community service leaders very often find themselves in situations of simultaneously 'building and crossing' this metaphorical bridge. While many community leaders come to their role with a passion for serving and meeting needs like nutrition, housing, safety, and healthcare, they soon experience the broad impact of increased political division and regulatory bureaucracy that prevents their mission of 'just helping people'.[36] To be successful in complex environments such as this, leaders must realize the need for new knowledge, abilities, and relationships. For instance, effective community leaders must often exercise political influence or networking skills with business and governmental organizations.[37] These and other activities are inherently risky because they are outside the individual's core capability of helping and supporting. The leader's need for partners and collaborators diminishes their ability to control their impact on the mission.[38] However, the upside to building and crossing the bridge simultaneously is the possibility of seeing progress and emerging problems in a new light and accomplishing a previously unimaginable goal. The metaphor of 'building and crossing' simultaneously serves as an example of the distinctions in leadership thinking and activities of adaptive leadership that help solve complex adaptive challenges and achieve high-risk goals.

Central to the practice of adaptive leadership are a series of key distinctions of thinking, or leadership paradigms, and corresponding activities closely associated with adaptive leadership (Table 17.1). These distinctions and activities form the core of adaptive leadership and set this approach apart from more traditional models and theories of leadership presented in the text. Thus termed a 'framework', adaptive leadership operates on the idea that leaders first need a distinctive shift in thinking, or mindset, before they can learn and adopt new practices and activities to address the world's complex challenges. The key idea within Table 17.1 is that mindset shapes and drives skillset. In other words, a change in leader perspective enables the work of adaptive leadership. While the work of Heifetz and colleagues presents these and other ideas in greater detail, the following paragraphs highlight six of the most important distinctions and the associated activities of adaptive leadership.[39]

**Table 17.1** Keys to adaptive leadership

| Leadership distinction | Adaptive activity |
| --- | --- |
| The illusion of the broken system | Get on the balcony |
| Technical problems are the problem | Identify the adaptive challenge |
| Authority isn't leadership | Give the work back to the people |
| What's precious and essential vs. expendable? | Protect leadership voices from below |
| Live in disequilibrium | Regulate distress |
| Leadership is an improvisation | Run experiments and learn fast |

## Get on the Balcony

While surveys of leaders from around the globe consistently list dealing with change as one of the most critical challenges they face, the reality is that few deal with it effectively.[40] One of the biggest reasons for this shortfall is a narrow and outdated belief that organizational problems result from deficiencies in people, structure, or process rather than impacts and interactions manifested within a system or in the environment. Adaptive leadership characterizes this mindset as the illusion of a broken system.[41] Central to this illusion is the belief that there are simple fixes to most leadership challenges. Thousands of books and articles on leadership and management are published each year in an effort to provide simple, predictable, and actionable leadership solutions and support. The simplicity and action approach results in a lack of understanding of the full nature of important challenges and a failure to see profitable opportunities and adapt to new realities.

Adaptive leaders deal with this distinction by getting on the balcony to separate themselves from present thinking and gain a fuller understanding of the situation.[42] This figurative (and sometimes literal) activity shows how a change in a leader's perspective affects how one views the problems they face. It might be as simple as seeking input from someone outside of a leader's direct reports, or it could involve a physical move, like a strategic offsite meeting to create time and distance from the everyday activities of leadership. In professional athletics, coaches often move higher in the stadium to see the entire playing field. Adaptive leaders engage in this activity to help them see the broader operational and system context. A move to the balcony and a shift in perspective also helps leaders recognize where followers (and even themselves) may be struggling and who may be better suited to deal with new and complex problems.[43]

## Identify the Adaptive Challenge

The critical shift to the balcony is necessary for another important reason. The adaptive leadership framework contends that most leadership failures are due to adaptive challenges being treated as technical problems.[44] The adaptive leadership framework suggests that technical problems differ from adaptive challenges because leaders rely on known solutions, current capabilities, and expert insights to solve them. In contrast, adaptive challenges lack definition and typically extend beyond the organizations' boundaries and the leaders' capabilities to solve them alone.[45] While stability, predictability, and efficiency are common and desirable organizational needs, the tendency to misidentify technical problems and pursue simplistic actions results in unanticipated and undesirable costs. Outright failure aside, organizations waste precious time and resources in fruitless searches for simple, technical solutions when they should be learning and developing the capacity to think and act differently.[46] Leaders who move to the balcony see past this illusion and position themselves to identify the adaptive challenge, the second critical adaptive leadership activity.[47] This adaptive activity is a critical shift in leadership perspective from expert decision-maker to the role of explorer and diagnostician, searching for clues and causes.

## Give the Work Back to the People

Traditional thinking about leadership holds that formal role authorities and organizational structures and systems are designed to handle most challenges and keep the business running. As the COVID-19 pandemic and subsequent global supply chain breakdowns demonstrated, complexity can quickly bring leaders, organizations, and even entire societies to a standstill. Specific roles, remits, or political mandates do little to resolve the volatility and ambiguity of adaptive challenges. This key leadership distinction highlights the mindset that formal position and authority are not a substitute for leadership when facing a need to learn and adapt. Instead, adaptive challenges require considerably more of leaders than traditional roles, structures, or processes will ever provide.[48] While formal authority structures promote order and protection and operate well for technical challenges with known solutions, the rigidity of authority breaks down rapidly in the face of unravelling complexity and expanding uncertainty. To make matters worse, leaders often double down on existing authority, processes, and structure to deal with instability and risk (and the fear of loss within the organization) rather than opening up and expanding opportunities to learn and leverage new capabilities.

Adaptive leaders respond to this complexity by stretching the limits of authority and shifting organizational control beyond the 'corner office' to explore aligning values, assumptions, and capabilities with the organization's core purpose and evolving needs.[49] The adaptive activity that helps leaders mobilize for change and optimize the system is to give the work back to the people.[50] Adaptive leaders recognize that players in other positions, closer to (and even further from) the action possess unique insights, relevant experience, and proximity to solve the challenge better. Rather than hold tight the reins of rigid authority structures, leaders look outward (forward, sideways, backward) for differing perspectives and for others who are capable of seeing evolving needs and discovering threats and opportunities headed for the organization.[51]

## Protect Leadership Voices from Below

While the risks associated with technical challenges and change tend to be programmatic and financial, the actions and outcomes of adaptive work frequently include individual, professional, and reputational risks as well.[52] Consequently, another essential leadership distinction when facing complexity is to clarify what is really at stake and what is fully intended. Adaptive leaders help others see what is precious and essential versus expendable in their culture and organization.[53] When faced with change and the risk of operating in an ambiguous or volatile environment, it is normal to fear losing things familiar and important to us.[54] In the face of danger to what is known, the human reaction to complexity leads to resistance and avoidance that limits action and minimizes perceived loss.[55] What is actually needed for adaptive work is space, time, and direction to learn, relearn, and unlearn. Adaptive leaders do this by shining a bright light on capabilities and core values while encouraging ways to reshape culture (expectations, norms, and behaviours) and structures that stand in the way of future success. In other words, adaptive leaders help followers understand the current context, embrace change, and navigate towards an uncertain future together.[56] One crucial way to uncover dysfunctional norms and behaviours is by protecting (and promoting) leadership voices from below.[57]

Adaptive leaders seek out marginalized, minority, and other diverse voices and build a bigger, more inclusive perspective to inform, align, and mobilize the team even further.[58] Adaptive leaders recognize that it is not enough to say they welcome the perspectives of others; they must act to remove fear and barriers and promote participation and engagement of all players, especially by amplifying and echoing the voices of the marginalized and overlooked. Building a bigger chorus of voices expands the range of activity and empowers people across the organization to speak, share, and solve local problems with strategic implications.

## Regulate Distress

Addressing the fear of loss and marginalization of voices that often accompanies the revolving door of organizational change enables people to focus on important decisions and take essential actions in complexity. However, focus and action alone are not enough to facilitate real adaptive work. The limited uncertainty and risk associated with technical problems create a baseline (and manageable) level of distress for people. In contrast, adaptive challenges compile an array of intersecting variables, unknowns, and risks, which contributes to the stress of more significant duration and intensity.[59] Even before the COVID-19 pandemic, increased levels of stress and the impact on health and performance were one of the biggest concerns of business leaders.[60] For instance, a typical hospital emergency department is staffed with specially trained healthcare workers who operate according to well-designed protocols and shift work schedules designed to mitigate the stress of treating serious injury. The emergence of a global pandemic brought complexity and disruption on an unimaginable scale to a health system designed to address technical and complicated health challenges efficiently. Weeks and months of protocols and exposure to suffering, death, and personal risk led to waves of distress that impacted the entire healthcare industry.

To deal with distress, adaptive leaders distinguish what it means to live in the disequilibrium of adaptive work rather than avoiding the situation. While it sounds like something unpleasant, disequilibrium is a state of tension where higher stress promotes deeper learning and growth needed for change.[61] Adaptive leaders accomplish this by regulating distress, which describes applying (or managing, in most situations) just enough pressure in the system to maintain momentum towards the goal without reaching levels of stress that harm people or undermine organizational capabilities.[62] Similar to setting the temperature of an oven to create the conditions for ingredients to combine and change state, regulating distress promotes the conditions for people to learn and enables the synergy needed to employ new capabilities and accomplish adaptive work. Unfortunately, the stress levels for adaptive work pose risks for followers if not fully understood and effectively managed.[63] One way adaptive leaders regulate distress is by addressing the context of stress and 'creating a holding environment' or the conditions where new learning, practice, failure, and conflicts are safely addressed, rather than spilling over and impacting other parts of the organization.[64]

## Run Experiments and Learn Fast

While technical problems have finite and well-practised solutions, adaptive challenges unfold in real-time and at varying pace. Consequently, adaptive leaders share a different mindset that allows them to acknowledge – and even welcome – conflicting perspectives and different approaches to time, distance, and other contextual factors associated with adaptive work.[65] In other words, while traditional authority produces largely scripted actions, adaptive leadership is an improvisation that happens in real time.[66] That distinction enables leaders to see the future, not in straight lines or tidy boxes, but as it happens in an interacting system of experiments and tests.[67] In the face of complexity, leaders often need to go 'off book' in order to manage the adaptive work and distress of others in real time.[68] However, just as professional jazz musicians apply methods and practices to improvise a song, adaptive leaders do not just 'wing' their approach to adaptive challenges. Within the structure of the holding environment, they apply the core practices of adaptive leadership, methodically run experiments, and learn fast to assess how their assumptions hold up in the real world.[69] Whereas linear approaches to problem-solving and change often have predetermined steps and predictable end states, adaptive leadership is an iterative and ongoing process where leaders observe, interpret, and design experiments and interventions, over and over, with the goal of learning and increasing capacity in an organization.[70] While every jazz performance is unique, it relies on common keys, tempo, and a shared vision. Likewise, adaptive leaders rely on core capabilities and share principles and practices to explore, experiment, and exploit new learning in complexity.

Another way that adaptive leaders improvise their work is by seeing themselves as a system operating within a more extensive organizational system.[71] A leader has unique needs, values, loyalties, and perspectives like any other person. However, we often forget that leaders and followers alike are embedded in an organizational system with its own array of needs, values, and loyalties.[72] Just the thought of systems within systems and the many interactions between and among players underscores the complexity and demands of adaptive leadership. Adaptive leaders make sense of complexity by regularly changing perspective, moving from the balcony to the dance floor where the work occurs, and then returning to the balcony to assess what has changed.[73] Shifting between the balcony and the dance floor helps leaders see the larger system, the interactions among people, as well as their own influence on the action.[74] A leader who stays in one place cannot see the complex interactions and outcomes that result from systems interacting with and influencing other systems.

The resulting flow of distinctions and actions by adaptive leaders may seem recursive, but the framework is neither scripted nor sequential, like a stepwise model. Instead, adaptive leadership consists of perspectives and practices that evolve and interact constantly and are applied and adapted uniquely. Consequently, before putting the framework into practice and evaluating its effectiveness, it is important to broaden our understanding by highlighting theoretical and practical critiques and ethical considerations of the adaptive leadership framework.

# CRITIQUES OF ADAPTIVE LEADERSHIP

Adaptive leadership first came to prominence in 1994 with the publication of *Leadership Without Easy Answers*. The framework has played a uniquely influential, if not unorthodox, role in the leadership literature ever since. The framework's enduring influence is a function of the grounded approach it takes, presenting volumes of cases and compelling examples illustrating how the various concepts and practices of adaptive leadership bring about relevant change for real people. This makes the framework especially accessible and widely appealing (unlike much of traditional management and leadership theory). However, those same factors that present practical appeal also bring criticism from more traditional practitioners and academic scholars. As a result, the framework has a distinct set of fans and supporters, as well as its share of critics. The following paragraphs offer the most common critiques of the adaptive leadership framework.

## Theoretical Disconnect

The practical examples and activities found in adaptive leadership work on the assumption that the concepts are generalizable to the larger framework.[75] The authors accomplish this by drawing heavily on consultation, interviews, and observations of organizational leaders, especially those who expressed frustration with problems that prevented them from achieving goals and objectives. While the concepts hold face validity, the overall validity of adaptive leadership suffers because the larger framework is not grounded in theory or the product of a testable model of organizational behaviour.[76] While the authors argue that the framework has empirical foundations, which means there is evidence to support their arguments, they also acknowledge that they have not yet developed the framework into an empirical theory.[77] The reader is left to judge the merits of the framework on the weight of historical cases and anecdotal examples alone. The authors cite several influences on the development of adaptive leadership, such as evolutionary biology, systems theory, service orientation, and psychiatry, but the framework has limited connections to other research or relevant theory.[78] Some concepts of adaptive leadership (such as moving to the balcony) have received recognition and are cited in other leadership models and by leadership scholars, but little more has occurred.[79] In the present chapter, we have attempted on our own to make connections between the thinking and the actions of leaders doing adaptive work. In the end, adaptive leadership remains conceptually attractive after more than twenty-five years because it highlights the challenges that real leaders face. In contrast, other theoretical leadership models often struggle to bridge the gap from theory to practical relevance.

## Leader-centric

At the start of this chapter, we discussed how perspectives on leadership have shifted from the 'great man' or trait-based approaches to the interactional and systems approaches to leadership.[80] While research still considers characteristics of leaders and individual outcomes, the focus of the field has largely moved beyond the person, or the role, to the activity and outcomes of leadership interactions.[81] At a conceptual level, adaptive leadership highlights a similar shift. It focuses on the activity of leadership as a means to solve adaptive challenges. However, most of the literature on adaptive leadership presents the concepts and describes the activities through a leader-centric lens.

The authors suggest that adaptive leadership exists anywhere, but much of the framework is oriented towards traditional leaders in organizational settings.[82] In fact, the prescriptive set of adaptive activities seems, at times, more like a checklist for leaders to enact than a conceptual framework about how leadership works.[83] While clearly not the intent of the authors, this unintended bias may limit the ability to transmit these critical ideas about distinctions, shifting mindsets, and adaptive activities to those who do not see themselves as leaders in the traditional sense, and others who reject the perspectives of traditional leaders as biased and privileged. Regardless of how narrow the voice and perspective of adaptive leadership may appear, the framework calls out the broader purpose and service of leaders everywhere to improve conditions and engage people to solve complex challenges and achieve goals.[84]

## Practical Limitations

Management scholar Peter Senge suggests 'practicing a discipline is different from emulating a model', and a framework like adaptive leadership must have utility to be of real value for those who practice the discipline of leadership.[85] As a framework developed from real-world cases and the experiences of actual leaders, adaptive leadership offers a set of tools and practices and multiple examples to illustrate central components and outcomes. However, a shortcoming of adaptive leadership is the absence of deeper conceptual definitions, more precise descriptions of the interrelationships to which it refers, and more complete explanations of outcomes associated with the framework.[86] Similar to the theoretical disconnect, leaders risk misinterpretation or misapplication of the adaptive activities without greater clarity and conceptual precision.[87] The authors try to compensate for this problem by providing numerous examples of leaders using the concepts in a variety of situations, but a good set of descriptions and explanations would add practical value to this framework.

Another hazard of this conceptual gap is that some readers, not seeing a coherent whole in the framework, may focus on certain aspects that resonate or seem relevant to the problem at hand to the exclusion of other aspects of the framework. Selecting and applying individual components may offer a practical impact at the moment and contribute to significant shifts in a leader's approach to problem-solving. However, it may also lead to 'partial learning' where leaders grasp one or two key adaptive activities but fail to integrate the broader concepts of the framework, leaving themselves at risk in other essential areas.[88] The lack of integration between ideas and actions may result in greater emphasis on specific behaviours and activities at the expense of other distinctions that provide the conceptual power of adaptive leadership. Without that conceptual foundation, adaptive leadership risks becoming just another problem-solving tactic.

# ETHICAL IMPLICATIONS OF ADAPTIVE LEADERSHIP

Adaptive leadership has much to say about what is wrong with leadership but even more to say about what is right and what can be better if leaders embrace the thinking and actions of the framework. Does that make the framework an ethical approach to leadership? In some ways, yes, and in other ways, it depends. Like other models in this text, adaptive leadership suggests a significant shift away from leader behaviours and styles to the very character of leadership itself. In fact, authors using adaptive leadership do not write about the framework in an abstract sense (a prior critique) but speak directly to leaders and for leaders – instructing, guiding, and motivating them to tackle the complex challenges in their world. While other approaches like transformational and authentic leadership focus on the leader's values, adaptive leadership speaks to the normative purpose of leadership itself, which is creating conditions where people thrive and achieve shared aspirations and goals.[89] From these claims, one might conclude that adaptive leadership has an ethical foundation.

So, what does it mean to thrive, and how is that ethical? The authors of adaptive leadership clearly state that thriving is much more than attaining personal or material success; instead, it is about improving the well-being of people's lives, whether in an organization, a community, or a society at large.[90] In addition to improving well-being, adaptive leaders assume personal and professional risk by taking on adaptive challenges, both of which highlight a distinct ethical perspective of serving others for the common good, as discussed in Chapter 12.[91]

Adaptive leadership argues that it would be wrong for a leader to pursue selfish values or seek personal gain, but it also assumes that leaders have a sense of what is right from where they stand on the balcony.[92] How are we to know if a leader's pursuits are ethical, and how does a leader ensure their perspective is right? While the framework assumes a leader's motives are pure, leaders must confirm their intentions by asking themselves what is non-negotiable in support of their values.[93] This outcomes-based ethical orientation uses three basic assessments to help adaptive leaders view the impact of their actions: (1) the harm it might cause others; (2) the risk it poses to self and personal values; and (3) the rationalizations, or explanations used to justify it.[94] While adaptive leadership does not offer a measure or test of goodness to judge a leader's values, it assumes that leaders are self-knowing and fully reflective. This approach may not guarantee ethical behaviour, but it provides a way for leaders to self-assess the ethics of their actions.

Another question of ethics emerges in the methods and practices of adaptive leadership. The specific focus on the ethics of an action is a strong point of adaptive leadership. However, the framework's lack of conceptual clarity (a prior critique) may create conditions of 'motivated blindness' where people have a vested interest in ignoring the ethical concerns of an act or 'overvaluing outcomes', where people see the ends of surviving an adaptive challenge as justifying the means.[95] Vague terminology and lack of clarity may create enough space for leaders to see how surviving and thriving justifies things that could be ethically questionable.

For instance, adaptive leadership places immense value on the distinction between authority and leadership, but is it ethical to encourage leaders to 'exceed their authority'?[96] The framework highlights the importance of pushing oneself and the organization beyond the status quo but offers little insight into ethical considerations of ignoring the authority limits granted to leaders. While the framework assumes pure motives, the lack of clarity around ethical considerations might suggest resistance, disobedience, and rationalizing the ends to justify the means. The ethical exercise of authority and responsibility build trust in an organization, and leaders who disregard the limits of authority may erode the very trust they seek to generate.

Another potential ethical issue surrounds the framework's concept of 'disequilibrium'. Living in disequilibrium is an essential distinction of adaptive leadership that seeks to establish the conditions necessary to learn and change. While the framework makes it clear that heightened stress facilitates learning and growth in critical areas, there may be ethical concerns with encouraging leaders to 'turn up the heat'.[97] The framework describes how pressure and distress move people into the zone of discomfort and learning but offers little insight into what methods and limits of inducing stress are healthy and which produce harm. Without offering more specifics, the framework's recommendation to 'adjust the heat ... and test how far you can push people to stimulate the changes you believe are necessary' could produce adverse outcomes or lead to lasting harm.[98]

Finally, the distinction that leadership is an improvisation shows how scripts do not bind leaders. Instead, they have the flexibility to shape and influence complex situations to encourage adaptive work. However, this distinction leads to questions about the ethical considerations of taking risks and running experiments in an organization. Adaptive leaders observe, interpret, and intervene to gather the knowledge and feedback needed to learn. However, the framework does not discuss the ethical limits to testing and experimentation, given the natural human fear of loss and distress in response to change. In fact, the framework suggests that in certain situations, if it is 'the only way to get people on board', it is acceptable for leaders to calm followers' fears by suggesting that an experiment is actually a 'solution'.[99]

Concerns and issues like these are increasingly important in a world where collaboration and relationships between leaders and followers are essential to success, but where most organizational structures are hierarchical and working relationships are still based on impersonal transactions. The adaptive leadership framework seeks better relationships but does not provide a concrete collaborative means to reconcile differences in values and practices between leaders and followers. The framework encourages leaders to 'give the work back to the people', but that very act assumes a change in the leader's privileged status of defining the challenge, the goal, and the means.[100] Connections with other leadership approaches, such as how leaders ethically empower followers or when leaders share authentic values and shortcomings to build greater trust and respect, may mitigate some of the ethical concerns. The framework may gain ethical strength by building bridges between other theories and approaches that close the gap in some of the ethical concerns and practical shortcomings of adaptive leadership.

The adaptive leadership framework closes with a discussion on the leader's purpose and heart.[101] For a leader to survive and thrive, the framework argues that they must not 'lose heart', or sacrifice their innocence, curiosity, and compassion, which the authors suggest are the attributes that make each of us distinctly human.[102] The authors continue to stress that without a focus on purpose and heart, leaders are susceptible to 'cynicism, arrogance, and callousness that can be rationalized in ways to protect the leader instead of serving others'.[103] The attributes of heart and the impacts on character taken up by adaptive leadership show distinct connections to virtue ethics, presented in Chapter 4, as well as self-awareness for authentic leadership, presented in Chapter 13. Additional connections to other theories and concepts of ethics, like virtue, duty, and utility, would strengthen adaptive leadership's conceptual and practical value.

## FIVE COMPONENT ANALYSIS

As in other chapters of this text, we now turn to the Five Components of Leadership Model to help integrate and synthesize the learning about adaptive leadership. Adaptive leadership emerged in response to the experiences and needs of real leaders in actual organizations.[104] The framework was not designed in a psychology lab and was not proposed as a grand theory of human behaviour. Instead, it is offered as a prescriptive framework that leaders use to solve actual problems they face. In a similar fashion, the Five Components Model describes leadership as a process where 'individuals come together and develop a relationship with a purpose in mind'.[105]

As you can see in Figure 17.2, the context is the most important aspect of adaptive leadership. This context, however, affects all other aspects of the Five Components Model. The leader alone must 'get on the balcony' and move back and forth to the dance floor to sufficiently survey the landscape to understand the actual gaps and what those gaps mean. In today's complex world, leaders can ill afford to miss the strategic gaps and opportunities they face and must rely on group strategies and teamwork to actively move between the balcony and the dance floor. Leaders who change perspective and leverage the capabilities of their teams as 'early warning sensors' gain a much better understanding of the multiple dimensions of a situation. They have a distinct purpose for this movement. Moving to the balcony is a critical first step to finding and assessing the gaps that exist in the leadership situation addressed by the model.

According to the adaptive leadership framework, the most common failure of leadership is when leaders misidentify adaptive challenges as technical problems. A second key concern is when leaders 'lose heart' or become overconfident and arrogant in their ability to solve an organization's problems when, in fact, they do not have all the answers.[106] Without 'heart', or character and humility, leaders become unable (or unwilling) to truly see the challenges they face and thus rely on technical solutions instead of adaptive ones.

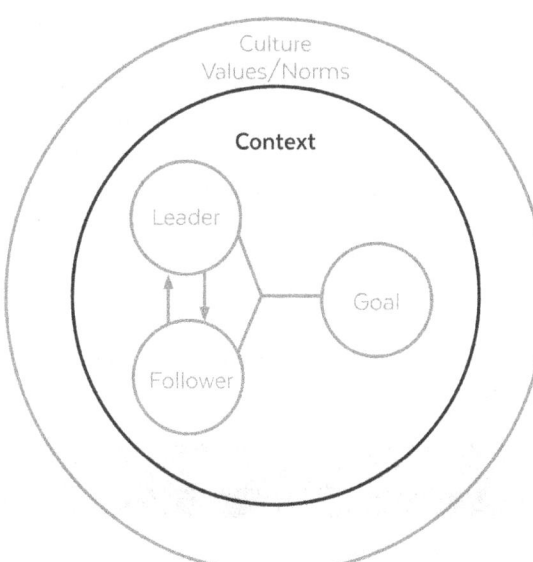

**Figure 17.2**    The Five Components of Leadership Model applied to adaptive leadership

While 'getting on the balcony' is a leader-centric act, that does not mean adaptive leadership focuses on the leader's efforts alone. One of the chief responsibilities of the leader is to engage followers to assess and address the situation. A leader with 'heart' understands that traditional authority and expertise alone will never solve an adaptive challenge, so they seek ways to 'give the work back to the people' to close the existing capability gaps.[107]

Leaders often speak of empowering followers, and this model requires that leaders do exactly that. Adaptive leadership encourages leaders to let go of a desire to control the situation and instead allow followers to own the process. Conversely, the framework can be especially challenging for followers who seek clarity from a leader – instead, followers are expected to step into the tension and stress of learning. To accommodate and manage the stress that followers experience because they lack a clear solution, the leader creates a 'holding space' where followers are able to work through the uncertainty of adaptive challenges.

Adaptive leadership is not about solving technical problems with linear solutions. Rather, it is a different choice about how to solve challenging problems that lack clear answers. What makes this approach special is the ability to view adaptive challenges in a new light and see alternatives hidden by traditional, technical problem-solving methods. To access these new insights and alternatives, adaptive leaders 'run experiments and learn fast' and often go 'off book' or improvise their work in response to emerging circumstances.[108] Thus, the goal is not only accomplishing an objective but also how that objective is achieved.

The leader moves between the balcony and dance floor to assess and understand the gaps, but eventually, they must also consider the context to make sense of the adaptive challenge. In many ways, the context is what demands adaptive leadership. While adaptive leadership addresses the leader, follower, and goal triad, the context dictates when adaptive leadership is needed. Something in the environment has changed that makes the old way of doing things no longer effective, requiring leaders and followers to find a different answer.

Even when leaders see the gaps and understand the adaptive challenge, there is no guaranteed easy solution. Adaptive work is hard, complex, takes time, and demands change. Sometimes there is a change of perspective, quite often a change in plans, and almost always a change in organizational culture. To help their followers understand what is truly essential, adaptive leaders shape culture by highlighting important values, 'protecting leadership voices from below', and eliminating dysfunctional norms that prevent progress.[109] As a result of this more egalitarian leadership orientation, highly authoritarian cultures and rigid hierarchies may struggle with the adaptive leadership framework.

With the framework fully explored, we will now apply adaptive leadership's methodology and ethical implications to a specific case study.

## CASE STUDY: JACINDA ARDERN – A NEW MODEL OF ADAPTIVE LEADERSHIP

With a thorough understanding of the adaptive leadership framework and the Five Components of Leadership Model as our guide, this next section applies a case study of adaptive leadership. The adaptive leadership framework emerged from the stories and experiences of the leader-centric era where expertise, achievement, charisma, and strength of personality dominated. This powerful identity helped leaders control information, direct strategy, and propel traditional business models to greater power and influence. Nevertheless, the disruptions of the information age revealed a critical blind spot in leadership as the spread of information, access to knowledge, and technological advances disrupted (and even destroyed) many industry giants. From the ashes of this struggle emerged a new framework built from the experiences of leaders who, despite years of preparation, practice, and positioning, struggled against the overwhelming power of an increasingly volatile, uncertain, complex, and ambiguous (VUCA) world.

The adaptive leadership framework assumes that complex challenges are not solved by pedigree, expertise, or long-suffering effort but with open interaction, collective foresight, and inclusive collaboration.[110] Adaptive leadership does more than try to explain or describe how leadership works. Instead, this framework offers new ways of thinking – or mindsets – and very different actions – or skillsets – to learn and lead in a VUCA world.

This case study takes a slightly different approach. It highlights a leader who grew up in a world dominated by adaptive challenges and personally experienced systems already struggling to address complex social, political, environmental, and economic challenges. Rather than focusing on a past leader who embodies the tension and transformation of adaptive leadership, such as Nelson Mandela, this case study introduces Jacinda Ardern, former prime minister of New Zealand, as an exemplar of learning and leading in an increasingly complex and rapidly changing world.

Jacinda Ardern was born in 1980 into a middle-class family in the rural town of Murupara on the North Island of New Zealand. She is of a generation born into and fully raised in the global information age. She is an example of leadership emergence, a critical assumption of modern leadership theory such as Adaptive Leadership. In 2017, at the age of 37, Jacinda Ardern became prime minister of New Zealand. She became the youngest female elected head of government in the world and only the second head of state to give birth while serving in office.[111] Her emergence, rather than transformation, as an adaptive leader distinguishes Jacinda Ardern from traditional political leaders and is emblematic of the intrinsic and inclusive value of adaptive leadership.

## FIVE COMPONENT ANALYSIS

Let's look at Ardern's work as an adaptive leader through the lens of the Five Components of Leadership Model (Figure 17.3).

In our case study, Jacinda Arden is our leader. Her followers, of course, are the citizens of New Zealand. The leader and the citizen's both have the common goal of 'good governance'. Arden and her followers were able to accomplish this goal within the context of building a coalition government and influenced by the larger cultural value of unity.

The Five Components of Leadership Model's focus on context helps introduce the complex web of social, economic, and familial influences on Ardern's growth and development. New Zealand is an interesting and exotic land filled with rich natural resources and beauty and an equally interesting history that contributes to unique societal values based on the ideals of fairness and freedom.[112] While New Zealand's political, social and religious groups have approached those ideals differently, the basic perspective and shared understanding of caring for all individual New Zealanders and enabling all groups to flourish plays an important, if not essential, role in Jacinda Ardern's world view and leadership style.

Ardern's rural, conservative, and religious upbringing might have predisposed her to a more traditional political and social mindset and approach to leadership. Yet, while her family practised a conservative religion with distinct gender norms and values, Jacinda was not lacking in strong female role models, with both maternal and paternal grandmothers active in political campaigning.[113] Jacinda's father, Ross Ardern, served in law enforcement for more than 30 years and greatly influenced Ardern's

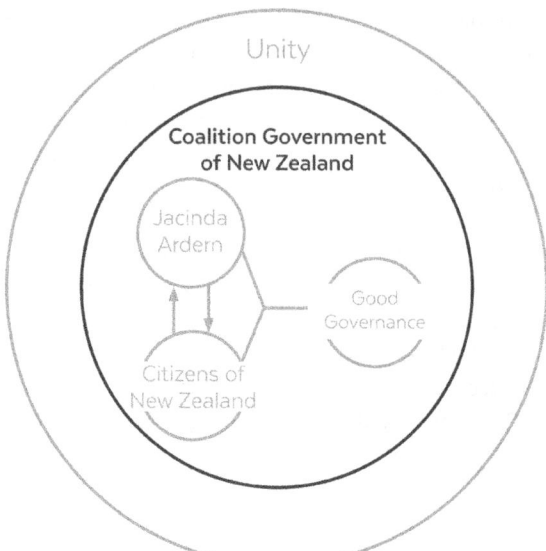

**Figure 17.3**   The Five Components of Leadership Model applied to Jacinda Arden's leadership of New Zealand

growth and development with his work as a skilled administrator and humanitarian during regional disaster relief efforts. He was commended for his patient and skilled conflict negotiations that averted troubling and dangerous situations, which helped shape Jacinda's core values of empathy and humility.[114] In these and many other ways, Jacinda Ardern benefited from an upbringing that included many contrasts, such as conservatism and social justice, achievement and compassion, humanitarianism and public safety.[115] This context shaped a set of principles and beliefs that enabled Ardern to feel and manage the tensions between idealism and pragmatism as well as authority and inclusion more effectively than many other political leaders.[116]

When effective, the context of politics is the collaborative and generative integration of competing ideas and values in service of shared goals and purposes. However, politics have become deeply polarized, zero-sum games played by highly skilled operatives.[117] The context and practice of politics have regressed to a competition for power and control, which leads to very different norms and practices. The tension of competing ideas has been replaced by a political gulf that seems unbridgeable. The dominant approach is from politicians who claim the power or ability to solve big problems and meet expansive needs. This expert mindset suggests there is a simple 'fix' to an illusory 'broken system'. As appealing as that message may be, events around the globe reveal how ineffective and potentially dangerous this polarizing leadership style can be.[118]

In contrast, adaptive leadership suggests a trip to the balcony to gain a new perspective on the system. Jacinda Ardern's motivation to enter politics was driven by strong moral and personal values that helped her see the political system in a new light. Her ability to hold two conflicting or opposing ideas simultaneously is one way adaptive leaders move to the balcony and understand the complexity of the context and the nature of adaptive challenges. Adaptive leadership suggests that moving to the balcony is often driven by internal growth and maturity when leaders begin to self-author personal values and principles.[119] Jacinda Ardern's leadership style embraces the tension of an idealist core value to better the lives and livelihoods of all New Zealanders, along with a humble and pragmatic acknowledgment that no simple or individual pathway exists. She is guided by an internal compass of practices and principles, or things that are precious and essential in life. Those principles of governing are compassion, empathy, responsibility, and courage.[120]

Jacinda Ardern emerged to political leadership equipped with these principles and an ability to adapt and communicate comfortably and authentically, which are essential capabilities of modern leadership, regardless of context. Moreover, those attributes also work remarkably well when a crisis inevitably hits, as it did when Andrew Little resigned as Labour Party leader less than two months before the election of 2017. This last-ditch effort to avert a massive drubbing from the ruling National Party thrust Jacinda Ardern onto the political stage and gave her access to a new audience and a different balcony.[121]

Through her rise in the Labour Party, Jacinda Ardern had opportunities to observe other leaders and gain multiple political perspectives, all the while holding onto her purpose. What set her apart from others was a belief that New Zealand governance wasn't broken, but it needed different perspectives and more humane guiding principles. This combination of mindset and skillset helped Jacinda Ardern diagnose the adaptive challenges of politics and chart a new and different path to leading New Zealand.

Jacinda Ardern's first press conference as a candidate demonstrated her unique combination of humility, authenticity, and innovation that immediately changed the direction of the election.[122] Adaptive leaders recognize that leadership is an improvisation and possess both the humility to accept not being the expert and the courage to run experiments and learn fast. Jacinda Ardern stepped into a leadership vacuum and addressed uncertainty and fear by acknowledging the challenge, welcoming the opportunity, and declaring that her campaign would be characterized by 'relentless positivity'.[123] As an adaptive leader, she didn't have all the answers and wasn't completely prepared for the challenge, but she articulated the principles that would guide the work at hand.

Campaigning on four core needs for all New Zealanders (a place to live, food to eat, clothing to wear, and something to hope for), the Labour Party edged ahead of the National Party in the final polls; however, the election outcome was different. The ruling National Party held the lead over the Labour Party in the final results. However, the Parliamentary form of government in New Zealand often leads to no party with an outright majority. A coalition of parties is generally required to form a government; in this case, the National Party was assumed to lead that coalition.[124] Instead, Jacinda Ardern literally moved between different levels of the Parliament building to help create new perspectives by engaging not one but two coalition partners to form a government like none before in New Zealand politics.[125]

The stunning election outcome and ensuing coalition government placed Jacinda Ardern in an uncharted political position. She was both the leader of the Labour Party and a member of a political coalition made up of three very different political perspectives. Rather than polarization, Ardern created a new governing dynamic by moving between parties and engaging all in shared goals for New Zealand. Others may have dug into positions and possibly forfeited the opportunity to create something new. The result was not the brilliant display of Labour programmes and agendas but a slow and steady creation of sustainable improvements built on cooperation and collaboration from three very different political perspectives.[126]

However, another factor placed Ardern in new personal and political territory. Three months into her new government, Jacinda Ardern announced she was pregnant. Upon delivering her daughter, she made coalition partner Winston Peters acting prime minister during her maternity leave.[127] Ardern provided a powerful model for women of New Zealand and around the globe. However, she also demonstrated the adaptive mindset that authority is not leadership, and the work of adaptive leadership ultimately belongs to the people. In these actions, she helped dismantle myths about heroic leadership and elevated the concept of governing as the basis for political leadership. Meaning and values matter when dealing with adaptive challenges. Ardern's ability to communicate and model what is most precious would matter even more when New Zealand faced an unthinkable tragedy.

In 2019, in Christchurch, New Zealand, an attack on two different mosques resulted in the death of 51 Muslim worshipers and injury to more than 40 others. Like so many other mass shootings, this tragedy is a function (or even a direct result) of the change and challenge in an increasingly VUCA world. However, the leadership response to the human tragedy on this day differed from the approach many leaders take in a crisis. The natural response to a crisis and adaptive challenge is the search for certainty among feelings of fear and loss. More often than not, traditional leadership uses strong language and demonstrations of power and action to calm the fear and anguish of loss. However, Ardern's first words in response to the Christchurch attacks laid out a very different response to this crisis. Her first message was, 'They are us', which acknowledged that the suffering of Muslims in Christchurch was the suffering of all New Zealanders.[128] By including all of New Zealand in this experience, Ardern didn't minimize the tragedy of the Muslim community. Instead, her words and actions, such as when wearing a headscarf to meet with victims of the attack, demonstrated her desire to model how to live in the tensions and disequilibrium of adaptive challenges, in this case, where safety and protection coexist with openness and compassion.

But is it not enough for leaders to merely live or survive in a VUCA world. The imperative is to thrive amidst the tension and challenge of adaptive learning. By contrast, the response to terrorist attacks in many other nations has focused almost entirely on a technical solution: increased security and identifying individuals or groups as targets of retaliation and anger. In complexity, a technical mindset and 'either/or' solutions lead to narrowed thinking and unilateral action, whereas managing tensions and seeking multiple perspectives promotes an array of possible actions. Ardern invited all New Zealanders to take responsibility for healing the nation after the Christchurch tragedy and created a space where others helped solve the complexity of safety and belonging. She appealed to the community's shared vision and took several actions to make progress on the goals of safety and compassion. One of those actions was privately pressuring coalition partners to support significant changes in New Zealand's gun laws. Only after that pressure led to progress did she confirm publicly that 'Our gun laws will change.'[129] Adaptive leaders understand the importance of managing tension and applying pressure to protect core values and the people closest to the challenges. Jacinda Ardern's skilful application of communication and political pressure in this crisis achieved a policy change, but more importantly, it enabled the goals of safety and openness to be mutually supported.

In a hallmark characteristic of complexity, just as New Zealanders were beginning to feel safe and open again, a new and even bigger challenge emerged in the form of a global pandemic. On 30 January 2020, the World Health Organization declared the COVID-19 virus a global public health emergency and two days later Prime Minister Ardern took action and announced a travel ban from mainland China. Ardern and her administration began implementing what would be one of the strictest and most comprehensive set of protocols in the fight against the pandemic. Around the globe, nations and political leaders struggled to adapt to this unseen enemy and deal with the complex challenge and disruption to systems, institutions, and entire industries. The rules, expertise and practices of supply and logistics, healthcare, and even travel no longer worked and leaders accustomed to expert knowledge and command and control had little to no effect on unfolding events. That lack of effect that plagues traditional leadership is because adaptive challenges require expanded perspective, new learning, different voices, and experimentation. While other leaders floundered in response to the crisis, Jacinda Ardern learned, experimented, and cast the widest net possible gain perspective, knowledge, and speed in order to stay ahead of the spreading virus and prevent it from gaining a foothold in New Zealand.

Relying on the core principles of care, transparency and commitment that helped guide her response, Jacinda Ardern launched a simple four-level alert model that engendered trust in New Zealanders and enabled swift actions and flexible decision-making based on the latest information and science.[130] Even in Ardern's announcement of the new system, it's easy to see the capabilities and mindsets of adaptive leadership as she said, 'I'm speaking directly to all New Zealanders today, to give you as much certainty and clarity as we can as we fight COVID-19.'[131]

While other leaders promised the impossible, Ardern promised the certainty and clarity of direct communication and the best possible information. By giving people a handhold to navigate in complexity, she invited all New Zealanders to trust one another and work together to solve this problem. Owing to some natural 'immunity' as a small, relatively isolated island nation, Ardern and her team rallied the nation around a set of practices that were the most stringent in the world at that time.[132] And less than five months from first taking action, New Zealand had the lowest transmission rate of any democratic state in world and attained a daily milestone of zero new active cases.[133]

At a time when political division in other countries led to battles over vaccines and individual freedoms, New Zealanders achieved one of the highest vaccine rates and maintained one of the lowest transmission and death rates in the world. While many leaders would be quick to take the credit and claim a political win, Jacinda Ardern did what adaptive leaders do, she invited others to join her in the continued fight against COVID by thanking here 'team of five million' and tempered expectations by refocusing on the long-term health and wellness of all New Zealanders by saying, 'we may have won a few battles but we have not won the war.'[134]

Ardern's adaptive leadership is in full display as she includes others in the journey and helps them hold onto a broader perspective of the challenge and a longer view of the future.

This case highlights the practical application of learning and leading because adaptive leaders do more than just encourage and inspire others; they actively create and sustain the environment where the adaptive work takes place. Sometimes this means they surface and address conflicting values, and other times they create structure and protection where experiments are run, and new solutions are created. What is true is that the work of leadership occurs across all five components of leadership: leader, follower, goal, context, and culture, and the highest, best work of leadership is to seek out from among those factors where new learning will help the organization thrive.

Jacinda Ardern provides a uniquely refreshing example of empathetic and compassionate governance in a world where cold-hearted pragmatists and cut-throat power-dealers mark politics. Moreover, she proves that diplomacy and courage are not only the domain of traditional political leaders. Ardern said, 'I never went into politics for the sport of politics, I went into it because it's a place where you can make really positive change', which has become a 'tonic for those who have lost faith in politics'.[135] A restored faith in politics and the global COVID-19 pandemic led the Labour Party to 50.01 per cent of the party vote in the 2020 national elections and the largest political victory in more than 50 years.[136] This overwhelming mandate and widespread support from the New Zealand people might have emboldened a more traditional politician to settle scores and proclaim a bold agenda of action. Instead, in victory, Jacinda Ardern described the challenge and the opportunity of adaptive leadership in the world of politics. She said,

> We are living in an increasingly polarised world, a place where more and more people have lost the ability to see one another's point of view. I hope that [in] this election, New Zealand has shown that … as a nation, we can listen and we can debate …. Elections aren't always great at bringing people together, but they also don't need to tear one another apart.[137]

By the end of 2022, Jacinda Ardern and the Labour Party, like many other post-pandemic leaders, faced an increasingly critical public over lingering pandemic effects, unmet policy expectations and growing economic and social challenges. The wave of support and unity had evaporated and in January 2023, Jacinda Ardern announced her resignation as Prime Minister. Unlike many politicians who seek every possible way to cling to power, Jacinda Ardern made her exit after going to the balcony one more time and sharing,

> I'm leaving, because with such a privileged role comes responsibility. The responsibility to know when you are the right person to lead and also when you are not.[138]

The adaptive leadership framework addresses the tension of learning in response to changing circumstances, but it also grounds this learning from an ethical perspective of virtue, care, and authenticity. Each of these perspectives has been covered in detail in this project and demonstrate how leadership and ethics intersect in the modern, complex world. In this chapter, we have shown an exemplar of leadership and ethics in Jacinda Ardern. She embodies the ethical principles of a competent and caring prime minister in crisis and a kind and decent human being in the practice of politics.[139] While such attributes seem out of place in the traditional and messy world of politics, the adaptive leadership demonstrated by Jacinda Ardern might just be what the world needs to build bridges across the complex economic, national security, climate and philosophical gaps that teams, organizations and nations must address in order to survive and thrive. We hope that through this case study others will be inspired to approach politics and leadership with the mindsets and skillsets of adaptive leadership.

## SUMMARY AND CONCLUDING REMARKS

To conclude this chapter, let us return to the framing question, 'How should both leaders and their followers adapt their thinking to solve complex challenges?' Adaptive leadership offers us three major changes in how organizations view leadership. The first change occurs between leaders and followers, as leaders realize they can only solve these unfamiliar problems by shifting responsibility from the centralized manager to those closest to the problems. The second change emerges in the practices and behaviours of leaders who no longer directly deal with the problem at hand but, nonetheless, still bear responsibility for the organizational outcomes. The third change is a shift of organizational focus, from internally held goals and culture to the dynamic interplay between goals, culture, and the external environment that holds the keys to unfamiliar problems and opportunities.[140] To prepare leaders and followers for these changes in thinking, organizations will benefit by helping leaders learn how to 'go to the balcony' when problems arise. They must also provide the resources that leaders and followers can use to navigate the uncertainty and manage the inevitable stress of adaptive learning and organizational transformation.

Ultimately, the adaptive leadership framework is a set of choices: tested practices and relevant principles to guide leaders who need to build more agile, resilient, and sustainable organizational capacity. The challenges facing today's leaders demand abilities far greater than any leader has alone. Like Jacinda Ardern, most organizational leaders must attend to many things at once, often managing in the present and leading into the future. Like the idea of simultaneously crossing and building a bridge, leaders must adapt and execute in real-time, develop 'next practices' while excelling at today's best practices, and invent novel ways to manage old problems.[141] Perhaps the case study of Jacinda Ardern demonstrates that the next era of leadership is not driven by technology, culture, or societal forces but by the developmental transformation that a new generation of leaders is bringing to organizations. And for the world to survive and thrive, we might just see more youthful, empathetic, and passion-driven leaders like Jacinda Ardern take up the mantle of adaptive leadership.

## DISCUSSION QUESTIONS

1.  What are the most common technical challenges facing you, your organization, or your community, and is an adaptive challenge likely to emerge? Where is an adaptive challenge least likely to occur? How might your thinking about adaptive challenges be

flawed?

2. Given what you understand about adaptive leadership, what are some of the most important considerations when facing adaptive challenges?
3. In your view, what makes the practice of adaptive leadership most difficult?
4. Adaptive challenges often present higher risks and greater potential rewards. How might expectations or ethical standards be used to guide the decisions and actions of leaders?
5. One of adaptive leadership's principles is to engage the people closest to the challenge. What factors and assumptions influence organizations to seek out external experts while overlooking the internal wisdom and experience closest to the problem?
6. Another aspect of adaptive leadership involves 'turning up the heat' or inducing stress to promote learning in the face of an adaptive challenge. What ethical and practical concerns do you see with this practice, and how else might learning and growth be promoted without leaders adding external pressure to a situation?

## ADDITIONAL RESOURCES

R.A. Heifetz and D. Laurie, 'The work of leadership', *Harvard Business Review*, vol. 79 no. 11, 2001, 131–40.

The authors make the case that the business of leadership is to solve problems, but many of the problems no longer have easy answers. The authors argue that the work of leadership is to help followers deal with both a changing environment and the demanding work of change.

R.A. Heifetz, A. Grashow and M. Linsky, 'Leadership in a (permanent) crisis', *Harvard Business Review*, vol. 87, July–August 2009, 62–9.

In this special *Harvard Business Review* issue on Leadership in the New World, the authors of the Adaptive Leadership Framework suggest that crises like the global economic downturn in 2008 provide even more evidence that traditional approaches to leadership are no longer relevant in a complex, globalized world.

R.A. Heifetz, A. Grashow and M. Linsky, *The Practice of Adaptive Leadership: Tools and Tactics for Changing Your Organization and the World*, Boston, MA: Harvard Business School Publishing, 2009.

This text is a comprehensive overview of the adaptive leadership framework and a resource book for leaders to practice and reflect on the journey to becoming an adaptive leader.

S.D. Parks, *Leadership Can be Taught: A Bold Approach for a Complex World*, Boston, MA: Harvard Business School Press, 2005.

This text provides an overview and assessment of the teaching and learning method associated with the Adaptive Leadership course offered at the Harvard Kennedy School of Government.

# NOTES

1.  The original quote by Albert Einstein in 1946 was written as part of the debate on the development of thermonuclear weapons published in the *Russell-Einstein Manifesto of 1955*. 'A new type of thinking is essential if mankind is to survive and move toward higher levels.'

2.  See H.W. Rittel and M.M. Webber, 'Dilemmas in a general theory of planning', *Policy Sciences*, vol. 4 no. 2, 1973, 155–69. The idea of 'wicked problems' was first addressed in the context of systemic social policy issues that, because of interdependencies and uncertainties, were beyond the capability of any one individual, programme, or institution to solve.

3.  P.F. Drucker, *Management Challenges for the 21st Century*, New York: Harper Business, 1999, p. x.

4.  Drucker, *Management Challenges*, p. xi.

5.  S. Vani and C. Harte, *Jacinda Ardern: Leading with Empathy*, London, OneWorld Publications, 2021, p. 8.

6.  A. Kaplan, *The Conduct of Inquiry: Methodology for Behavioral Science*, 4th edn, New Brunswick, NJ: Transaction Publishers, 2009, pp. 28–9. Abraham Kaplan's 'law of the instrument' critiqued a narrow-minded, parochial approach to behavioural science problem-solving.

7.  R.A. Heifetz, *Leadership Without Easy Answers*, Cambridge, MA: The Belknap Press, 1994.

8.  Heifetz, *Leadership Without Easy Answers*, pp. 16–27. Ronald Heifetz developed the Adaptive Leadership framework after listening to the stories of executives attending programmes at Harvard University.

9.  E. Schein, *Organizational Culture and Leadership*, 3rd edn, San Francisco, CA: Jossey-Bass, 2004; C. Argyris, *Overcoming Organizational Defenses: Facilitating Organizational Learning*, Boston, MA: Allyn & Bacon, 1990; P.M. Senge, *The Fifth Discipline: The Art and Practice of the Learning Organization*, New York: Doubleday, 1990; R. Kegan and L. Laskow Lahey, *Immunity to Change: How to Overcome It and Unlock Potential in Yourself and Your Organization*, Boston, MA: Harvard Business Press, 2009; R. Martin, 'How successful leaders think', *Harvard Business Review*, vol. 85 no. 6, 2007, 60–67; P.F. Drucker, *Managing In a Time of Great Change*, New York: Talley Books/Dutton, 1995; and Drucker, *Management Challenges*.

10. For descriptions of the major trends influencing leadership in organizations, see Drucker, *Managing In a Time of Great Change*; Drucker, *Management Challenges*; Kegan and Laskow Lahey, *Immunity to Change*; Martin, 'How successful leaders think'; Argyris, *Overcoming Organizational Defenses*; Senge, *The Fifth Discipline*; T.W. Malone, *The Future of Work: How the New Order of Business Will Shape Your Organization, Your Management Style and Your Life*, Boston, MA: Harvard Business School Press, 2004; P.F. Drucker, *The Age of Discontinuity: Guidelines to Our Changing Society*, New York: Harper & Row, 1969; and P.F. Drucker, *Managing in the Next Society*, New York: Truman Tally Books, 2002.

11. H. Mintzberg, *The Nature of Managerial Work*, New York: Harper & Row, 1973.

12. G. Morgan, *Images of Organization*, Thousand Oaks, CA: Sage Publications, 1997, p. 22.

13. Drucker, *Management Challenges*, p. 136.

14. Drucker, *Management Challenges*, pp. 136–7; Heifetz, *Leadership Without Easy Answers*, pp. 16–19.

15. D. Van Fleet and D. Wren, 'History in today's business school', *Accounting Historians Journal*, vol. 9, no.1, 1982, p. 29. https://egrove.olemiss.edu/aah_journal/vol9/iss1/7 (accessed January 2022).

16. Morgan, *Images of Organization*, pp. 26–7.

17. M. Anteby and R. Khurana, *A New Vision*, 2007. https://www.library.hbs.edu/hc/hawthorne/anewvision.html#e (accessed 4 September 2017). See Anteby and Khurana's essay for an introduction to the dramatic impact of The Hawthorne Studies on changes in organizational research and leadership.

18. The American Soldier Studies, a four-volume series of research conducted for the US Army, is considered by many to be the foundation of modern understanding of group dynamics and leadership, as well as many core theories of social psychology and social science research methods. See S.A. Stouffer et al., *The American Soldier: Adjustment During Army Life*, New York: Science Editions, 1965.

19. Anteby and Khurana, *A New Vision*.

20. Anteby and Khurana, *A New Vision*.

21. Anteby and Khurana, *A New Vision*.

22. Morgan, *Images of Organization*, pp. 31–7. Morgan describes the notion of 'sociotechnical systems', a term that originated in the Tavistock Institute in England, highlighting the interdependencies between the work, the people, and the environment. This early work contributed to the fields of organizational design and contingency theories of leadership that took hold in the 1960s.

23. Morgan, *Images of Organization*, p. 33.

24. Morgan, *Images of Organization*, p. 56. Contingency approaches to organization and leadership theory emerged in the 1950s and 1960s in response to research that showed how organizational variables interacted in a dynamic environment to influence performance and outcomes.

25. B.J. Avolio, 'Pursuing authentic leadership development', in N. Nohria and R. Khurana (eds), *Handbook of Leadership Theory and Practice*, Boston, MA: Harvard Business Press, 2010, pp. 739–68.

26. See R. Kegan and L. Lahey, *Immunity to Change: How to Overcome It and Unlock the Potential in Yourself and Your Organization*, Cambridge, MA: Harvard Business School Publishing, 2009, Kindle loc. 547; J.G. Berger, *Changing on the Job: Developing Leaders for a Complex World*, Stanford, CA, Stanford University Press, 2012, pp. 18–19; B. Joiner and S. Josephs, *Leadership Agility: Five Levels of Mastery for Anticipating and Initiating Change*, San Francisco, CA, Jossey-Bass, 2007, pp. 5–6.

27. D. Kahneman, *Thinking, Fast and Slow*, New York: Macmillan, 2011; Argyris, *Overcoming Organizational Defenses*; Drucker, *Management Challenges*; Senge, *The Fifth Discipline*; Kegan and Laskow Lahey, *Immunity to Change*.

28. R. Kegan, *In Over Our Heads: The Mental Demands of Modern Life*, Cambridge, MA: Harvard University Press, 1994, p. 5.

29. See Berger, *Changing on the Job*; Joiner and Josephs, *Leadership Agility*; N. Petrie, 'Vertical leadership development – part 1: developing leaders for a complex world', White Paper, Center for Creative Leadership, November 2013. https://www.ccl.org/articles/white-papers/vertical-development-culture-beats-strategy/ (accessed 15 January 2022).

30. R.A. Heifetz, 'Anchoring leadership in the work of adaptive progress', in F. Hesselbein and M. Goldsmith (eds), *The Leader of the Future 2: Visions, Strategies and Practices for the New Era*, San Francisco, CA: Jossey-Bass, 2006, pp. 75–6.

31. World Economic Forum, *Insight Report: The Global Risks Report 2017*, 12th edn. https://www.weforum.org (accessed 25 February 2017); Drucker, *Management Challenges*.

32. K. Lawrence, *UNC Executive Development White Paper: Developing Leaders in a VUCA Environment*, 2013. https://www.execdev.unc.edu (accessed 25 February 2017). The modern leadership environment is often increasingly volatile, uncertain, complex, and ambiguous. The term 'VUCA' has been used to describe both the environment and the kinds of challenges that emerge from this sort of environment. VUCA was initially used to describe the operational military environment, but it is often used to describe the context and challenges many organizational leaders face today.

33. Heifetz, *Leadership Without Easy Answers*, p. 2; Heifetz, 'Anchoring leadership in the work of adaptive progress', 76–7.

34. Quoted in G. Hamel and B. Breen, *The Future of Management*, Boston, MA: Harvard Business Press, 2007, p. 38.

35. Berger, *Changing on the Job*, p. 2.

36. P. Auspos and M. Cabaj, 'Complexity and community change: managing adaptively to improve effectiveness', The Aspen Institute Roundtable on Community Change, 24 September 2014, vi. https://www.aspeninstitute .org/publications/complexity-community-change-managing-adaptively-improve-effectiveness/ (accessed 8 September 2017).

37. Auspos and Cabaj, 'Complexity and community change', vi.

38. R.A. Heifetz and M. Linsky, *Leadership on the Line: Staying Alive Through the Dangers of Leading*, Boston, MA: Harvard Business School Press, 2002, pp. 2, 13.

39. Heifetz and Linsky, *Leadership on the Line*; Heifetz, *Leadership Without Easy Answers*; R.A. Heifetz, A. Grashow and M. Linsky, 'Leadership in a (permanent) crisis', *Harvard Business Review*, vol. 87 no. 7/8, 2009, 62–9.

40. W.A. Gentry, R.H. Eckert, S.A. Stawiski and S. Zhao, *The Challenges Leaders Face Around the World: More Similar Than Different*, Greensboro, NC: Center for Creative Leadership, 2016.

41. Heifetz et al., 'Leadership in a (permanent) crisis'.

42. Heifetz et al., 'Leadership in a (permanent) crisis'.

43. Heifetz, 'Anchoring leadership in the work of adaptive progress', 76–7. For example, consider how Kennedy handled the Cuban missile crisis. See M.T. Hansen, 'How John F. Kennedy changed decision making for us all', *Harvard Business Review*, 22 November 2013. https://hbr.org/2013/11/how-john-f-kennedy-changed -decision-making (accessed 8 September 2017).

44. Heifetz, 'Anchoring leadership in the work of adaptive progress', 77; Heifetz and Linsky, *Leadership on the Line*, p. 14.

45. Heifetz et al., 'Leadership in a (permanent) crisis'; Heifetz, *Leadership Without Easy Answers*; Heifetz, 'Anchoring leadership in the work of adaptive progress'.

46. Kegan and Laskow Lahey, *Immunity to Change*; Heifetz, *Leadership Without Easy Answers*; Heifetz, 'Anchoring leadership in the work of adaptive progress', 75.

47. Heifetz et al., 'Leadership in a (permanent) crisis'.

48. Heifetz et al., 'Leadership in a (permanent) crisis'.

49. Heifetz et al., 'Leadership in a (permanent) crisis'.

50. Heifetz et al., 'Leadership in a (permanent) crisis', 77.

51. Heifetz et al., 'Leadership in a (permanent) crisis'.

52. Heifetz et al., 'Leadership in a (permanent) crisis'.

53. Heifetz et al., 'Leadership in a (permanent) crisis', 78.

54. Kegan and Laskow Lahey, *Immunity to Change*.

55. Kegan and Laskow Lahey, *Immunity to Change*.

56. Heifetz et al., 'Leadership in a (permanent) crisis'.

57. Heifetz et al., 'Leadership in a (permanent) crisis'.

58. Heifetz et al., 'Leadership in a (permanent) crisis'.

59. Heifetz et al., 'Leadership in a (permanent) crisis', 80.

60. J. Pfeffer, *Dying for a Paycheck: How Modern Management Harms Employee Health and Company Performance – And What We Can Do About It*, New York, HarperCollins, 2018, pp. 2–3.

61. Heifetz et al., 'Leadership in a (permanent) crisis'; Heifetz, *Leadership Without Easy Answers*.

62. Heifetz, 'Anchoring leadership in the work of adaptive progress'.

63. Heifetz, 'Anchoring leadership in the work of adaptive progress'.

64. Heifetz et al., 'Leadership in a (permanent) crisis'.

65. Martin, 'How successful leaders think'.

66. Heifetz, 'Anchoring leadership in the work of adaptive progress', 80.

67. Heifetz, 'Anchoring leadership in the work of adaptive progress', 79.

68. Heifetz et al., 'Leadership in a (permanent) crisis'; HBR Spotlight on Leadership Lessons from the Military, 'You have to lead from everywhere: interview with Admiral Thad Allen, USCG (Ret.)', *Harvard Business Review*, November 2010, 76–9, pp. 77–8.

69. Heifetz, 'Anchoring leadership in the work of adaptive progress', 79.

70. Heifetz et al., 'Leadership in a (permanent) crisis'.

71. Heifetz et al., 'Leadership in a (permanent) crisis'.

72. Heifetz et al., 'Leadership in a (permanent) crisis'.

73. Heifetz et al., 'Leadership in a (permanent) crisis'; and Heifetz, *Leadership Without Easy Answers*.

74. Heifetz et al., 'Leadership in a (permanent) crisis'.

75. R. Angelmar, G. Zaltman and C Pinson, 'An examination of concept validity', in M. Venkatesan (ed.), *Proceedings of the Third Annual Conference of the Association for Consumer Research*, Chicago, IL: Association for Consumer Research, 1972, pp. 586–93, p. 586.

76. S.D. Parks, *Leadership Can Be Taught: A Bold Approach for a Complex World*, Boston, MA: Harvard Business School Press, 2005, p. 251; and P.G. Northouse, *Leadership: Theory and Practice*, 7th edn, Thousand Oaks, CA: Sage, 2015, p. 275.

77. Heifetz, *Leadership Without Easy Answers*, pp. 7–8.

78. Heifetz, *Leadership Without Easy Answers*, p. 4; and Heifetz et al., 'Leadership in a (permanent) crisis'.

79. Parks, *Leadership Can Be Taught*, p. 251; and M. Uhl-Bien, R. Marion and B. McKelvey, 'Complexity leadership theory: shifting leadership from the industrial age to the knowledge era', *The Leadership Quarterly*, vol. 18 no. 4, 2007, 298–318, p. 300.

80. Uhl-Bien et al., 'Complexity leadership theory', 298.

81. Uhl-Bien et al., 'Complexity leadership theory', 298.

82. Heifetz and Linsky, *Leadership on the Line*, p. 236.

83. Heifetz and Linsky, *Leadership on the Line*, p. 5.

84. Heifetz and Linsky, *Leadership on the Line*, p. 236; and Heifetz et al., 'Leadership in a (permanent) crisis'.

85. Senge, *The Fifth Discipline*, p. 11.

86. Parks, *Leadership Can Be Taught*, pp. 251–2; and Northouse, *Leadership*, p. 276.

87. Northouse, *Leadership*, p. 276.

88. Parks, *Leadership Can Be Taught*, pp. 251–52.

89. Heifetz, 'Anchoring leadership in the work of adaptive progress', pp. 81–2.

90. Heifetz et al., 'Leadership in a (permanent) crisis', Kindle loc. 98.

91. Parks, *Leadership Can Be Taught*, p. 256.

92. Heifetz, 'Anchoring leadership in the work of adaptive progress', 83.

93. Heifetz et al., 'Leadership in a (permanent) crisis', Kindle loc. 7418.

94. Heifetz et al., 'Leadership in a (permanent) crisis', Kindle loc. 7418.

95. M.H. Bazerman and A.E. Tenbrunsel, 'Ethical breakdowns', *Harvard Business Review*, April 2011, 58–66, p. 63.

96. Heifetz et al., 'Leadership in a (permanent) crisis', Kindle loc. 8246.

97. Heifetz et al., 'Leadership in a (permanent) crisis', Kindle loc. 8261.

98. Heifetz et al., 'Leadership in a (permanent) crisis', Kindle loc. 8273.

99. Heifetz et al., 'Leadership in a (permanent) crisis', Kindle loc. 8168.

100. Heifetz et al., 'Leadership in a (permanent) crisis', Kindle loc. 6321.

101. Heifetz et al., 'Leadership in a (permanent) crisis', Kindle loc. 8046.

102. Heifetz and Linsky, *Leadership on the Line*, pp. 225–6.

103. Heifetz and Linsky, *Leadership on the Line*, pp. 225–6.

104. Heifetz, *Leadership Without Easy Answers*, p. 7.

105. R.M. McManus and G. Perruci, *Understanding Leadership: An Arts and Humanities Perspective*, New York: Routledge, 2015, p. 17.

106. Heifetz et al., 'Leadership in a (permanent) crisis'.

107. Heifetz et al., 'Leadership in a (permanent) crisis'.

108. Heifetz et al., 'Leadership in a (permanent) crisis'; and HBR Spotlight, 'You have to lead from everywhere'.

109. Heifetz et al., 'Leadership in a (permanent) crisis'.

110. Heifetz, *Leadership Without Easy Answers*, p. 2.

111. Vani and Harte, *Jacinda Ardern*, p. 357.

112. D.H. Fischer, *Fairness and Freedom: A History of Two Open Societies*, Oxford: Oxford University Press, 2012, p. 5.

113. Vani and Harte, *Jacinda Ardern*, pp. 169–70.

114. Vani and Harte, *Jacinda Ardern*, p. 67.

115. Vani and Harte, *Jacinda Ardern*, p. 11.

116. Vani and Harte, *Jacinda Ardern*, p. 11.

117. D. Shapiro, 'The power of the civic mindset: a conceptual framework for overcoming political polarization', *Connecticut Law Review*, 2021, 447. https://opencommons.uconn.edu/law_review/447 (accessed 18 November 2022).

118. Shapiro, 'The power of the civic mindset', 447.

119. Berger, *Changing on the Job*, pp. 40–41.

120. Vani and Harte, *Jacinda Ardern*, p. 13.

121. Vani and Harte, *Jacinda Ardern*, p. 278.

122. Vani and Harte, *Jacinda Ardern*, p. 287.

123. Vani and Harte, *Jacinda Ardern*, p. 285.

124. Vani and Harte, *Jacinda Ardern*, p. 339.

125. Vani and Harte, *Jacinda Ardern*, p. 342.

126. Vani and Harte, *Jacinda Ardern*, p. 372.

127. Vani and Harte, *Jacinda Ardern*, p. 370.

128. Vani and Harte, *Jacinda Ardern*, p. 411.

129. Vani and Harte, *Jacinda Ardern*, p. 413.

130. Vani and Harte, *Jacinda Ardern*, p. 462.

131. Vani and Harte, *Jacinda Ardern*, p. 463.

132. Vani and Harte, *Jacinda Ardern*, p. 464.

133. Vani and Harte, *Jacinda Ardern*, p. 470.

134. Vani and Harte, *Jacinda Ardern*, p. 470.

135. Vani and Harte, *Jacinda Ardern*, p. 11.

136. Vani and Harte, *Jacinda Ardern*, p. 487.

137. Vani and Harte, *Jacinda Ardern*, p. 489.

138. J. Diaz, 'New Zealand's Jacinda Ardern is resigning, Is there a lesson for other politicians?' National Public Radio, January 22, 2023. https://www.npr.org/2023/01/22/1150051375/new-zealand-jacinda-ardern-resigning-takeaways-politicians (accessed 15 June 2023).

139. Vani and Harte, *Jacinda Ardern*, p. 493.

140. Heifetz, 'Anchoring leadership in the work of adaptive progress', 74–5.

141. R.A. Heifetz and D. Laurie, 'The work of leadership', *Harvard Business Review*, vol. 79 no. 11, 2001, 131–40, p. 133.

# 18
# Toxic leadership

*Stanley J. Ward and Robert M. McManus*

## FRAMING QUESTION

What qualifies as 'toxic' leadership?

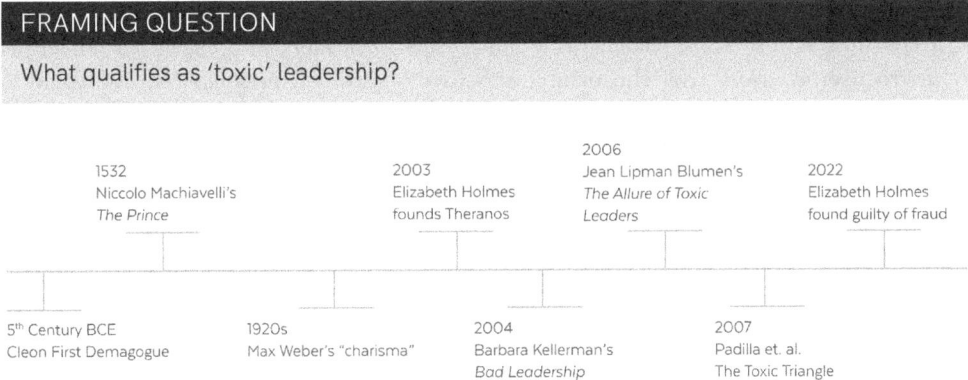

**Figure 18.1**  Timeline of major works on toxic leadership in relation to the chapter case study

The chapters on leadership up to this point have considered leadership models that exhibited positive ethical qualities. This chapter will address leadership's dark side, sometimes called 'toxic leadership'. The term 'toxic' has become part of the regular discourse in Western culture. In 2018, the *Oxford English Dictionary* recognized 'toxic' as its word of the year because of its increasing frequency of usage to describe not only physical or chemical toxicity but also relationships, politics, workplaces, and culture.[1] Being 'toxic' has become a common term for any unhealthy relationship or an especially negative person. We hope this chapter clarifies this term in the context of leadership for the benefit of organizations, individual leaders, and those who follow them. After reading this chapter, readers will be able to recognize toxic leaders better, understand what empowers these leaders, and distinguish between various kinds of destructive leaders. We hope that by the end of the chapter, and after having read the other chapters of our text, readers will have enough information and insight to create action plans to minimize the damage from toxic leaders for themselves, their organizations, and their communities.

So what exactly is 'toxic leadership'? The term *toxicon pharmakon* was a Greek concept describing the arrows that archers had dipped into poison. These instruments of war did not just cause pain – they were meant to be especially deadly. Likewise, a toxic leader is much more than one who is simply rude or generally negative. Toxic leaders are not just bosses that you 'love to hate'. Rather, they embody a leadership style that unleashes destruction like poisoned arrows fired into a crowd.[2] Thus, one can interchangeably use terms like 'toxic leaders' and 'destructive leaders'.

One significant voice in the conversation around toxic leaders and toxic leadership is Jean Lipman-Blumen. She is a long-time contributor to leadership studies, a recipient of the International Leadership Association's Lifetime Achievement Award, and the author of the Pulitzer Prize nominated *The Connective Edge: Leading in an Interdependent World*. We will reference her multiple times in our conversation around toxic leadership in part because of her work to also understand the followers of these leaders. Lipman-Blumen defines the toxic leader as follows:

> Here, we shall use 'toxic leaders' as a global label for leaders who engage in numerous *destructive behaviors* and who exhibit certain *dysfunctional personal characteristics* ... [They] must inflict some reasonably serious and enduring harm on their followers and their organizations. The intent to harm others or to enhance the self at the expense of others distinguishes seriously toxic leaders from the careless or unintentional toxic leaders, who also cause negative effects.[3]

Put simply, toxic leaders leave us worse off than when they found us. Sometimes it is because of their lack of skill, and other times it is because of their malice. The question for us is, 'Why do we seem to welcome these leaders armed with poisoned arrows?' – especially when they prove indiscriminate with their targets! Why do we not run them off at first sight?

By this point in our text, we know that leadership is about more than simply leaders alone, and we don't want to fall into the fundamental attribution error of laying all the responsibility for toxic leadership at the feet of these leaders (though they certainly should bear the majority of the blame).[4] Bad followers resist or derail good leaders, but as our chapter progresses, we shall discover that toxic leaders seem to attract toxic followers and vice-versa.

As our chapter proceeds, we will discover that all five components of the Five Components of Leadership Model deserve our attention if we wish to recognize, prevent, or avoid toxic leadership. Along the way, we will see examples of a variety of 'bad' leaders – some who are incompetent, some who are malicious, and some who created a divided response about whether they are toxic to their organizations or a hero. Besides the work of Lipman-Blumen, we will also draw upon Barbara Kellerman's observations about bad leaders and Padilla et al.'s discussion of a toxic triangle that includes the leader, the followers, and their environment. Our discussion of the five components will expand upon those three to consider the impact of goals on toxic leadership. We will also understand the 'environment' to include both context and culture. But before we address the five components, we need to understand better how charismatic leadership can contribute to toxicity and identify symptoms to watch for. We will also pay special attention to how followers get caught up in toxic 'leadership' (a phenomenon that goes well beyond the individual leader). Then our case study will examine a recent example of toxic leadership: Elizabeth Holmes and the rise and fall of Theranos.

## HISTORY

In the early twentieth century, Max Weber first brought the concept of 'charisma' to conversations about leadership. 'Charisma' was originally a theological term associated with a 'divine gift' that these leaders possessed. That gift separated the leader from the rest of common humanity. These leaders often rose to power during times of crisis. In his observations of these leaders, Weber noted a kind of narcissism alongside their other character qualities.[5] Later research observed that those who followed these leaders experienced a kind of transcendence simply by being linked to the charismatic leader in some way.

While charismatic leadership is associated with positive leadership styles such as transformational leadership, charisma is a double-edged sword. In the early twentieth century, Sigmund Freud observed a genuine difference between leaders who were prized by seeming to fulfil their followers' fantasies versus those leaders who focused their followers on more transcendent goals.[6] Additionally, Padilla et al. note that 'while not all charismatic leaders are destructive … destructive leaders are typically charismatic.'[7]

For example, consider the first Greek Demagogue – Cleon. Democratic government rooted its authority in the *demos*, or people, versus the individual *autos*, the self, of the autocracy. One who took advantage of this reliance on the populous was a 'demagogue'. This kind of leader appealed directly to the people outside of traditional systems. The first recorded example of this type of leader was Cleon in Athens. As described by the fifth-century BCE writers Thucydides and Aristophanes, he rejected his aristocratic contemporaries and enflamed the masses to gain short-term objectives for himself. Similar concerns can be seen during the Roman era with those who rejected the rise of Julius Caesar. During the development of democracy in the United States of America, framers also feared what could happen if too much power were placed in the hands of a popular individual, so they intentionally limited the powers of the presidency.[8]

Part of what makes these leaders so attractive is the grand vision they offer us.[9] Just as Cleon was able to appeal to the masses, modern destructive leaders connect with their followers by offering an appealing vision of the future or an explanation for the current reality and the struggles experienced by their followers. The problem is that these visions are actually 'grand illusions'.

For example, consider the rapid rise and fall of Liz Truss in 2022 as the prime minister of the United Kingdom and the economic impact of her brief tenure. During her six weeks in office, she offered a free-market economy plan that would supposedly spur growth and restore England's economy. But rather than providing a practical strategy for the United Kingdom's future, her vision ignored some fundamental economic principles. As a result, the British pound declined and sent markets tumbling. Truss quickly had to reverse course. She fired the Chancellor of the Exchequer, and when her party continued to suffer declines in public opinion along with internal strife, she resigned.[10] Thus, she became the shortest-serving prime minister in Great Britain's history. She also illustrated how destructive leaders can sometimes 'flame out' when their charisma takes them beyond their competence.

In the most egregious cases of toxic vision casting, these charismatic and destructive leaders offer us a paradisal vision. By being part of their chosen few, followers can experience a utopia and possibly even enter immortality. Consider the Jonestown massacre – which represented the largest number of American civilians to die outside of natural events before the 11 September 2001 terrorist attacks. Jim Jones led the People's Temple movement and was a civil rights activist. Over time, Jones's leadership became increasingly cult-like, and he eventually convinced his followers to leave the USA and establish a commune in Jonestown, Guyana. What was supposed to be a paradise for Jones' followers became a mass grave when he ordered them to drink flavour-aid mixed with cyanide (this is also the story behind the phrase 'drinking the Kool-Aid'). Over 900 people died. Jones took his own life as well.[11]

When discussing charismatic leaders, we also need to consider what it means for a leader to be a narcissist. The Greek myth of Narcissus tells the story of a young man who fell in love with his own image. Thus, the narcissist is one who is in love with themselves. The American Psychological Association defines narcissism as 'excessive self-love or egocentrism'.[12] Some would say that a measure of narcissism is necessary for leaders to have the self-confidence needed to tackle inevitable challenges. The problem with pathological narcissism is that it tends to 'leave damaged systems and relationships' in its wake.[13] Qualities of the narcissist include 'an inflated sense of their own importance', and 'a deep need for excessive admiration and attention' along with 'troubled relationships and a lack of empathy for others'.[14] Narcissistic leaders are often paradoxical in that they demonstrate tremendous arrogance while at the same time feeling inferior. They have an insatiable need for recognition and feeling superior, partly caused by their internal emptiness.

As a result, the narcissistic leader 'is more concerned about her own self-worth, appearance, and/or ability to be admired and respected than about the well-being and success of her organization or colleagues'.[15] To address such leaders requires 'timely inquiry and response to strange or disturbing behavior' that is repeated in order to detoxify the organization.[16] These leaders are motivated primarily 'by their own egomaniacal needs and beliefs, superseding the needs and interests of the constituents and institutions they lead'.[17] Regarding the ethics of narcissistic leadership, it is 'immoral when it leads to exploitation of others, expectations of undeserved special favors without reciprocation, indifference, and lack of empathy for others'.[18]

## MAJOR THEMES OF TOXIC LEADERSHIP

Recognizing and addressing toxic leaders can be difficult. First, their charisma is such that we naturally want to follow them. The 'success' of these leaders is part of what makes them so challenging to address. Consider the coach with a winning record who berates his players. At what point does he cross the line from 'authoritarian' and 'tough' to 'abusive' and 'toxic'?

For example, coach Bobby Knight was a remarkably successful basketball coach who was equally known for his angry outbursts, such as throwing a chair onto the court during a game in 1985. The Indiana University president eventually fired him for his behaviour patterns after numerous accusations of physical intimidation and angry outbursts, which continued after the university's board issued a 'zero tolerance policy' for that behaviour. Students protested his departure, and over 8,000 attended a final pep rally in his honour.[19] His example is relevant here because what one person views as a 'toxic leader' may be another person's 'hero'.[20]

A second difficulty in recognizing a truly 'toxic' leader is that all leadership creates change, and this change can be painful. So how do organizations or followers recognize the difference between acceptable and unacceptable amounts of pain? We need some sort of rubric to help us sort this out because some measure of toxicity can be present in even the best of leaders, as observed by Lipman-Bluman's observation that 'even exemplary leaders have some toxic chinks'.[21] There is some real murkiness here, which is why followers and trustees of organizations should also keep in mind the spectrum of leadership behaviours: Super Functional and Positive, Highly Functional and Positive, Functional and Non-Toxic, Dysfunctional and Toxic, Extremely Dysfunctional and Highly Toxic.[22]

Part II of our textbook has followed the general trend in leadership studies where much of the emphasis on leadership education is on the positive. Barbara Kellerman said we should study bad leadership in the same way that a pathologist studies disease. For those who wish to recognize, or possibly even 'diagnose', toxic leadership, there are symptoms to watch for. We will examine some of these symptoms in our chapter.

## Watch for Leaders Who Increase their Own Power at the Expense of their Followers

Toxic leaders function like parasites. They are good at taking without giving anything of real value in return.[23] They develop relationships with their followers where the leader increases in power at the expense of the followers. Lipman-Bluman provides examples of what this can look like. In some cases, the leaders intentionally deceive followers into increasing the power of the leader and limiting the ability of followers to stand on their own. Perhaps the clearest example of such behaviour is when the leader proclaims, 'Only I can save you.'[24]

Another way toxic leaders may enrich themselves at the expense of their followers is when they fail to nurture successors. Toxic leaders cling to power beyond their appointed time, 'with the occasional exception of [transferring power to] blood kin'.[25] We can see a stark example of this in Francois 'Papa Doc' Duvalier and his son, Jean-Claude, also known as 'Baby Doc'. They ruled Hatti from 1957 to 1986. Francois served as president of Hatti from 1957 to 1971. He was elected democratically as a populist candidate and later grew increasingly autocratic in his administration, using violence to silence even suspect dissenters. In 1964 he declared himself 'president for life' and remained in power until his death. He was then succeeded by his 19-year-old son, Jean-Claude, who ruled in a similar manner until he was ousted in 1986.

A less egregious example of this failure in succession planning is the concept of 'founder's syndrome', when an organization's founder holds onto their power and influence in such a way that it hurts the organization. Founders often have a special status in their organizations, and as a result, the organization gives undue preference to the personal wishes of the founder. Another cause can be seen when founders hand-pick a board of close friends and family instead of looking for the most qualified trustees with needed expertise for oversight.

Another way toxic leaders can empower themselves at the expense of their followers is through a 'kiss up, kick down' behaviour pattern. In this behaviour, leaders exude all their charms towards those they believe to have higher status. These leaders often experience promotions or other benefits because of their interpersonal skills with people of influence. On the other hand, these same leaders often blame, berate, belittle, and in other ways make life miserable for those not deemed as valuable to their personal goals.[26]

## Watch for Leaders Who Transform Followers into Lesser Versions of Themselves

Toxic leaders often leverage in-group versus out-group dynamics, highlighting those 'for us' versus those 'against us'. [27] To be like the leader is to be special. To generate this unique identity, toxic leaders can be transformational in the worst sense. This could include 'playing to the basest fears and needs of the followers' as well as setting them against each other. Or, they may treat their followers well while convincing them that the other side must be hated, overcome, and, eventually, destroyed.[28] In contrast, non-toxic leaders offer a vision 'designed to help humankind' rather than only the chosen few.[29] One way readers can evaluate this for themselves is to ask who benefits from following this leader. The smaller the circle that benefits, and the more like the leader they must be to do so, the greater likelihood that a leader is generating a potentially toxic 'in-group'.

## Watch for Leaders Who Are Willing to 'Burn It All Down'

The desire to destroy a person or organization rather than see it succeed without the leader is an even more destructive variation of the parasitic leader. While some leaders are content simply to enrich themselves at the cost of others, these leaders protect themselves by 'structuring the costs of overthrowing them as a trigger for the downfall of the system they lead, thus further endangering followers and non-followers alike'.[30] If they cannot benefit from the resources of their followers, they make sure no one else will. Recall the story of Jim Jones, who convinced his followers to commit mass suicide. The context of this action was that their commune was under investigation, and Jones' personal guard killed some investigators. Realizing that his movement had come to an end, Jones made that an end for everyone.[31]

## Watch for Leaders Who Offer a Vision that Is Too Good to Be True

Unlike a healthy form of leadership that asks followers to face the facts of reality, these leaders offer their followers illusions of safety and security, often with the implied promise that the cost for these things will be minimal to the followers. Indeed, Lipman-Blumen observes that when we try to live 'too safely', we put ourselves at risk of embracing toxic leaders,[32] and especially authoritarian ones. Additionally, their visions are so grandiose that they are not practical.[33]

Non-toxic leaders offer us an achievable reality that includes difficulties along the way. For example, in US president Kennedy's proclamation that the USA would send a human to the moon and return them safely, he famously said:

> We choose to go to the moon. We choose to go to the moon in this decade and do the other things, not because they are easy, but because they are hard, because that goal will serve to organize and measure the best of our energies and skills, because that challenge is one that

we are willing to accept, one we are unwilling to postpone, and one which we intend to win ...[34]

In our current era of social media and practically limitless information outlets, 'disinformation' or 'misinformation' has become an especially effective tool for toxic leaders to spread their vision for the world. The problem, of course, is that their vision of reality is based on falsehoods and conspiracy theories.[35]

## Watch for Leaders Who Believe the Rules Don't Apply to Them

Manfred Kets de Vries admits that all leaders have some degree of narcissism (a belief in their uniqueness or special ability) to function well.[36] While this high sense of self-confidence is needed to push past the significant obstacles that leaders inevitably face, unbound narcissism can lead to such feelings of entitlement that they pursue power and prestige at all costs. What can make this personal exceptionalism so destructive is that, to an extent, it is true. There is a unique drive that inspires these individuals. Leaders have tremendous appetites, and their appetite helps drive them to success.[37] The problem with toxic leaders is that what they hunger for is not in the best interests of their followers, and without some moderating influence, we are left to the mercy of these appetites.

## Watch Yourself

And while readers are watching out for signs of toxic leadership, they would also do well to 'watch themselves' in three particular senses of the phrase. First off, given that narcissistic leaders often have a higher opinion of themselves than they deserve, some authentic self-awareness is needed to keep oneself from inadvertently falling into the patterns of toxic leadership. As leaders become more aware of their actions and the real consequences of those actions, they gain an internal compass that helps them to course correct more quickly. In the second sense, one must 'watch themselves' in the sense of watching their own back around these leaders. Remember – recognizably toxic leaders are wrecking balls that have no problem causing chaos and damage to their organizations and the people around them. Third, remember that toxic leaders rely on their followers to enrich themselves and maintain their power. Readers must be self-aware of how they follow those who lead them. What motivates their followership? How do they treat those outside of the perceived 'in-group'?

## The Toxic Triangle

Before considering toxic leadership in terms of the five-component model, we must recognize that three dimensions have already been highlighted by Padilla et al. as a 'toxic triangle' involving leaders, followers, and their environment.[38] Their work examined how these three factors reinforce each other, as illustrated by Fidel Castro. Castro ruled Cuba as one of the longest-serving dictators in history for over 50 years. As a charismatic leader, he came to power after a revolution at the end of 1958. He promised his followers a vision of democracy and a better life – all the while suppressing any opposition. Once the middle class realized that

Castro's promise of democracy was false, many fled the island, leaving Castro with followers who either benefited personally from their allegiance with him or those too poor and disempowered to resist him. He was able to rise to power during the reign of a corrupt and ineffective government. He maintained his power with a constant narrative about outside threats, and there was no external system to which he was accountable. Padilla warns readers to watch out for the three elements of the 'toxic triangle': destructive leaders who are charismatic but narcissists with a thirst for personal power; susceptible followers who conform to the leader's toxic behaviour or collude with the leader to serve their personal ambitions; and conducive environments marked by instability, perceived threat, and a lack of checks and balances.[39]

## FIVE COMPONENT ANALYSIS

We will now use the five components of leadership to help us better understand toxic leadership and appreciate that the issue is about so much more than individual leaders. With that understanding, we can then consider ways to respond to toxic leadership when we see it. Our discussion will expand on the model of the toxic triangle. Note in Figure 18.2 that toxic leadership specifically implicates the leader, the followers, and the context, but the goal and the cultural values and norms may also have a role to play in toxic leadership.

This is probably what we think of first with 'toxic leadership' – individual leaders who are just as dangerous for their organizations as a poison-tipped arrow. Sometimes that danger is because of incompetence, and other times it is because of the leader's ethical failures. Barbara Kellerman offers a helpful typology here. Sometimes leaders are ineffective because they 'fail to produce desired change'. Other times leaders are unethical because they fail 'to distinguish between right and wrong'.[40] In her list of 'bad' leaders, the first three are ineffective. The last four are unethical (Table 18.1).

At this point, readers should consider how both character and competence are needed for 'good' leaders.

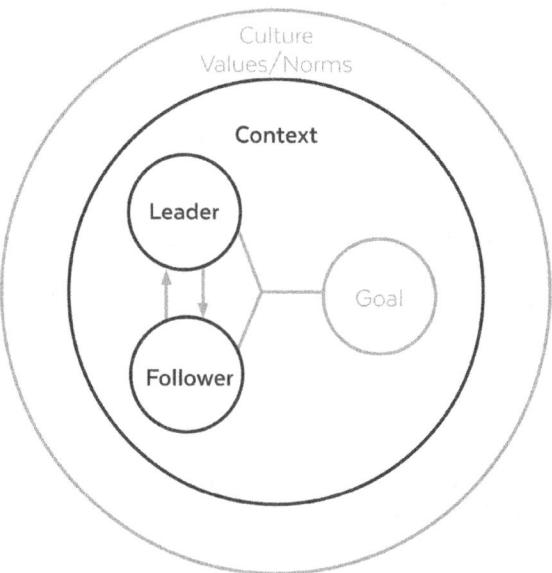

**Figure 18.2**   The Five Components of Leadership Model applied to toxic leadership

We want to hire people of character who also are competent. If we hire leaders of character who lack the competence required for the challenges at hand, we have ineffective leaders. If we hire competent leaders who lack character, they will

Table 18.1 Kellerman's typology of bad leadership

| Ineffective types | Incompetent | Lacking in needed skill or drive to create needed positive change |
| | Rigid | While capable, they still do not make needed adaptations to create positive change |
| | Intemperate | A leader who lacks needed self-control and is often accompanied by followers who accommodate the behaviour |
| Unethical types | Callous | Leaders who ignore or minimize the legitimate needs of members in the organization |
| | Corrupt | Leaders who excessively put self-interest ahead of public interest |
| | Insular | Leaders who disregard or downplay the good of 'outsiders' |
| | Evil | Leaders who cause real harm by committing atrocities |

use that competence to wreck the organization. And regarding character, toxic leaders can be spotted by a preference for appearing moral rather than actually being such.[41]

Earlier, we mentioned the concept of 'demagogue' from the classical world. This type of toxic leader first arose during the origins of Western civilization and continues to prove a threat. For example, during the twentieth century, the world watched Adolf Hitler embody the archetype of a demagogue as he transformed a minor political party into an autocratic regime, all the while appealing to the needs and fears of the masses. At a minimum, the demagogue could be seen as exhibiting the 'Insular' type described by Kellerman, and as in the case of Hitler, would be typed as 'Evil'.

In Padilla et al.'s discussion of 'destructive leadership', they highlight five qualities that work together in these leaders: charisma, the power that is focused on the benefit of self rather than looking towards the benefit of others ('personalized' versus 'socialized' power), narcissism, a world view filled with hate for the 'other' that legitimizes violent acts, and negative life themes that often originate in childhood. For Padilla et al., no one quality is sufficient for truly destructive leadership, and when all five of these qualities are present, destruction is inevitable.[42]

It should be no surprise that toxic leadership can easily occur when there is a deficiency of courageous followers. As we saw in Chapter 15, followers have real power. They can empower either 'good' leaders or 'bad' ones. A recurring plot in folklore and mythology is the 'tempter' who offers something that looks good at first and yet ends up having devastating consequences for those who take the temptation. In many ways, this is also the experience for the followers of toxic leaders. More to the point, the susceptibility of followers to the many temptations offered by toxic leaders empowers these leaders.

After the Second World War, researchers began considering what could make people susceptible to a leader like Hitler. As early as the 1950s, researchers began identifying how people could be vulnerable. As we have stated before, much of the toxic leader's power derives from their relationship with their followers. Followers become convinced that this leader can meet their needs. Lipman-Bluman connects Maslow's hierarchy of needs with rationalizations that followers can make that end up empowering toxic leadership (Table 18.2).

**Table 18.2** Follower rationalizations that support toxic leaders

| Physiological needs (hunger, thirst, etc.) | By submitting to the leader, followers believe their most basic needs will be met |
|---|---|
| Safety needs (protection from danger) | Challenging the toxic leader may appear too fraught with danger or the situation is so bad that it's worth putting up with the bad leader. Belief that the leader is too strong to overcome |
| Need for belonging, love, self-esteem (acceptance and approval) | Other people think the leader is great, so I should go along with them. I can't resist the leader alone |
| Cognitive needs (knowledge & understanding, finding meaning) | Too much uncertainty around who would/could replace the leader. I can't trust my understanding of the situation, so I need the leader |
| Aesthetic needs (need for order) | We need the leader to put things in order |
| Need for self-actualization (self-fulfillment) | I must give up other things I want in order to replace the leader |
| Need for transcendence | I have all the basics, but I still feel like something is missing. Maybe this leader can help me find it |

*Source:* Lipman-Bluman, *Allure of Toxic Leaders*, p. 130.

As illustrated by the case of Hitler and the observations of Weber, Kellerman, Lipman-Blumen, and Padilla et al., followers are especially susceptible to demagogues during times of crisis and instability – as these leaders offer appealing solutions to their problems and a path forward that seems desirable. Some personality types may be more susceptible to demagoguery and toxic leadership than others – especially those prone to extreme responses and want a leader who does the same. In these earlier examples of follower motivation, the toxic leader taps into legitimate felt need to gain power. In other cases, the follower's motivations may be such that they choose to empower leaders, even though they know those leaders are toxic. Sometimes, it may be in the follower's favour to create/empower toxic leaders or, worse yet, to topple good leaders. Contrary to the parasitic leader who appears to be good yet damages followers and organizations, the parasitic follower attaches themself to a leader for their own purposes – either enabling bad leaders or sometimes even tempting good leaders to stray.[43] Thus, the case for reducing the number of bad followers goes beyond 'ethics' into simple pragmatism, as replacing a toxic worker can have a greater impact on a company than hiring a superstar employee, as these toxic workers not only cause harm by their individual actions, but they can also influence others to do the same.[44]

Padilla et al. divide followers into two groups: the colluders and the conformers. Conformers go along with the leader because of their unmet needs and immaturity. Regarding unmet needs, they also observe that 'the most impoverished countries in the world … are also ruled by the most corrupt governments.'[45] Colluders are those who actively empower destructive leaders. These followers find that the destructive leaders' world views and agendas overlap with their own, and they hope to achieve their own ambitious goals through this leader's success.

As noted earlier, low self-esteem often goes with narcissism, and it also appears in followers susceptible to toxic leadership. Padilla et al. explain that followers with low self-esteem connect with charismatic leaders because they want to become 'more desirable'.[46] These followers feel that they lack the ability to impact their environment meaningfully, so they look to an external champion who can do it for them.

Other necessary follower qualities for the toxic triangle include low maturity, ambition, and overlapping values and beliefs. Followers with low maturity are more likely to concede to the directions given by their leaders – even if those directions seem immoral. The Stanley Milgram experiments demonstrated how those who typically followed the rules were most capable of committing immoral behaviours when directed by someone in authority. Additionally, a clear sense of differentiated self – an identity separate from that of the leader – was necessary to resist destructive leaders. Whereas in some cases, followers fail to resist bad leaders because they are conformers, the colluders follow toxic leaders because of the follower's ambition. Followers perceive this toxic leader as a way to get ahead and achieve their own goals – doubly so when there is an overlap of core beliefs and values. One practical result: malicious leaders tend to attract malicious followers.[47]

While goals can certainly be outright unethical and, therefore, toxic, there are frequent cases where the culpability of a goal in contributing to toxic leadership is not so obvious. Ordonez, Schweitzer, and Golinsky pointed out that goals are not value-neutral and can lead to a toxic culture. When not appropriately set, the authors identify issues, including a rise in unethical behaviour, the neglect of those issues not directly related to the goal, and even poor risk management. All of this can harm the overall culture of an organization.[48] The authors pointed to the Enron scandal of the early 2000s as one example of this. The previous edition Ethical Leadership: A Primer, included a case study on Wells Fargo that also demonstrated the negative impact of goal setting if it is not counterbalanced with the measurement of other core principles in the organization. Recommendations to prevent goals from leading to toxicity include measuring goals by more than 'just the numbers' with an emphasis on both what gets done and how it gets done.[49] In sum, the goals of our organizations have both a human cost and a material cost. For leadership to be 'ethical', it must consider both.

Given how psychological health plays a role in a leader's toxicity, the overall psychological health of one's context is also an issue. For example, when psychological health issues are rising in a pandemic, one might expect to see additional rises in toxic leadership behaviours. The problem here is that the context impacts both leaders and followers, so the context contributing to a leader's toxicity may also contribute to weakening effective followers. Conversely, toxic followers may make good leaders ineffective or even tempt them to abandon their sense of mission and pursue short-term gains that will cost the organization in the long run. The term 'toxic workplace' has also seen its share of attention in recent years. Toxic workplaces generally refer to the kinds of relationships that co-workers have with each other as well as the productivity of the workplace. Where a person works can impact their likelihood of behaving ethically.[50]

Note that these leaders come to power in the context of uncertainty and instability. For example, Liz Trust came to power after the fall of Prime Minister Boris Johnson, who lost power after multiple scandals. Likewise, Hitler's rise to power occurred during the turbulent years after the First World War and during the Great Depression, which devastated Germany's economy.

Besides instability, a lack of checks and balances also sets these leaders up for abusing their power. As pointed out by J.M. Burns, the US Founding Fathers intentionally limited the powers of the executive leader.[51] In Federalist Paper 47, James Madison quotes Montesquieu, saying:

'When the legislative and executive powers are united in the same person or body' says he, 'there can be no liberty, because apprehensions may arise lest *the same* monarch or senate should *enact* tyrannical laws, to *execute* them in a tyrannical manner.' Again 'Were the power of judging joined with the legislative, the life and liberty of the subject would be exposed to arbitrary control, for *the judge* would then be *the legislator*. Were it joined to the executive power, *the judge* might behave with all the violence of *an oppressor*.'[52]

While putting more power into the hands of an individual can create a greater speed for responding to emergencies, it also gives that person the ability to overreact or enact a malicious or incompetent agenda of their choosing. When putting power into the hands of a leader, one must consider both the character and competence of the leader, as well as the trends of human nature. As also pointed out by Padilla et al., when people perceive a serious eternal threat, they are more likely to give this power to the leader. The external threat does not have to be real. A perceived threat is sufficient for destructive leaders to gain more power. In our current age of so-called 'disinformation', this is especially troubling.

We certainly seem to be in a time where there is increasing awareness of 'toxicity', as illustrated by the *Oxford English Dictionary*'s decision to make 'toxic' the word of the year for 2018. Recent years have continued to see toxic behaviours by leaders, such as Elizabeth Holmes at Theranos. Likewise, we have observed the impact of toxic followers, such as the political backlash facing Boris Johnson after he attended parties organized by his followers during the COVID-19 lockdowns of 2020 and 2021. During the so-called 'Great Resignation' of 2022, toxic corporate culture was identified as the top predictor of people leaving the workplace. It was ten times more likely to be the cause than compensation.[53]

Regarding culture, readers should consider an organization's culture as the intersection of belief and behaviour. Further, when it comes to behaviours, 'what gets rewarded gets repeated'. Because of this, organizations must reflect on how they might be unintentionally rewarding toxic behaviours in leaders or followers. In our current era, the rise of social media and its cultural impact seems to illustrate how what gets rewarded is repeated. Note how social media algorithms are designed to prioritize what people pay attention to, and the AI does not make any moral judgment. As a result, the most shocking or incendiary remarks often get the most followers and attention – effectively incentivizing toxic language or bombastic claims for those who wish to be influencers.

Additionally, in their discussion of the Toxic Triangle, Padilla et al. observed that culture with a high need for security, resistance to ambiguity, group loyalty that emphasizes in-groups versus out-groups, and giving undue privilege to high-status individuals are all cultural factors that empower destructive leaders. Their work parallels the observations of Lipman-Blumen.

Now that we know a bit more about toxic leadership and what to look for, let's examine a particular instance of toxic leadership. For that, we turn to our case study.

## CASE STUDY: ELIZABETH HOLMES AND THERANOS[54]

In 2003, Elizabeth Holmes dropped out of Stanford and founded Theranos, a medical diagnostic testing company. She was 19 years old. By 2014, she was named one of the wealthiest women in America, with an estimated worth of 4.5 billion USD. Two years later, her net worth was less than zero. By 2018, Theranos was forced to close its doors, and Holmes was facing federal fraud charges. So, what went wrong? This case study will examine Elizabeth Holmes' rise and fall and the closure of Theranos as an example of toxic leadership.

Reading about Holmes and Theranos is like studying a cautionary tale of toxic leadership, with all the elements highlighted earlier in this chapter. It would be easy to lay all the blame for the failure of Theranos at the feet of its founder, Holmes. And indeed, she is ultimately to blame. But to truly understand what went wrong, we must delve deeper into the Theranos story.

The name 'Theranos' is a combination of the words 'therapy' and 'diagnosis'. Holmes had the vision to create a device that could detect myriad diseases from a drop of capillary blood drawn from a finger prick. This idea was revolutionary. Medical testing usually requires ampules of blood to be drawn venially. Disease testing is conducted by experts in sophisticated laboratories and run on large-scale industrial diagnostic equipment. Holmes had hoped to change all that with her invention of the Edison – a machine about the size of a microwave oven that could automatically test for a variety of diseases through a single drop of blood. It was a worthy goal and, if achieved, would have been hailed as a breakthrough in modern medicine. Early testing and diagnosis can save millions of lives, and Holmes proposed that her invention could do just that. The only problem was that her invention didn't work, but few people knew the truth in the early days of Theranos.

Between 2004 and 2013, Holmes raised more than 400 million USD from investors in Theranos. The company was valued at close to 10 billion USD during that time. There is no doubt that Holmes possessed what Max Weber termed 'charisma'. Holmes was charming and enigmatic. She had a captivating persona and told a compelling story of her desire to save lives after watching her uncle pass from cancer when she was a child. Part of her persona included a letter that she had written to her father when she was nine in which she wrote, 'Dear Daddy, what I really want out of life is to discover something new, something that mankind didn't know was possible to do.'[55] She wore all black all the time, in a seeming homage to another tech titan, Steve Jobs. Holmes surrounded herself with wealthy and influential investors such as former US Secretaries of State Henry Kissinger and George Shultz, General James Mattis, publisher Rupert Murdoch, and a host of Silicon Valley venture capitalists. She graced the cover of *Fortune*, *Forbes*, and *Inc.* magazines and was considered the youngest female self-made billionaire. Her followers found her enchanting. Many women saw her as a role model. She was even identified as a Woman of the Year by *Glamour* magazine. She was a captivating figure, especially in the tech world, which men have historically dominated. The problem was not that Holmes was charismatic; the problem was that she used that charisma to deceive investors and, ultimately, the public who trusted Theranos and their faulty technology to diagnose their diseases.

Let's return to Jean Lipman-Blumen's definition of a toxic leader from earlier in the chapter. She defines toxic leaders as those who 'engage in numerous destructive behaviors and who exhibit certain dysfunctional personal characteristics … [They] must inflict some reasonably serious and enduring harm on their followers and their organizations.' Holmes seems to fit Lipman-Blumen's definition of a toxic leader well.[56]

First, lets us consider Theranos' patients. The evidence indicates that Holmes knew full well that the Theranos technology didn't work. Nevertheless, she sold her idea to drugstore giant Walgreens, which then opened medical testing sites in their stores. Most patients in the United States cannot request their own lab work. However, Holmes lobbied the state of Arizona to allow patients to order their own lab tests without the oversight of a medical professional. This change in law meant that patients could request Theranos to test them for more than 200 diseases, although the Food and Drug Administration (FDA) had only approved the Edison to test for *one* disease – herpes. When patients would arrive at Walgreens to have their blood tested, many were told that their blood had to be drawn venially and sent to Theranos for testing. Theranos had led these patients to believe their blood could be tested with a simple finger prick. Although this was false, the harm induced was relatively minor. However, a more significant and concerning issue was that Theranos diluted many of the blood samples from these patients or did not follow other proper testing protocols. This practice led to inaccurate test results for patients. False information of this kind can be life-threatening and certainly falls under Lipman-Bluman's criterion of toxic leaders causing 'serious and enduring harm'.

Likewise, we can apply Lipman-Blumen's criterion for a toxic leader to Holmes and her leadership of Theranos as an organization. Holmes raised more than 400 million USD in her time at Theranos. Investors believed in her and her technology. However, their faith in her was based on lies. Those interested in investing in Theranos were deceived when visiting the facility. Technicians would take a sample of their blood via a finger prick. The sample was loaded into the Edison, but then the potential investors would be offered a tour of the facility. When the investors left the room, a technician would retrieve the sample and run the tests on commercially available machines. The investors would return to their results, never realizing that they had been duped. A reporter from *The Wall Street Journal* finally caught on to Holmes and the deception at Theranos in 2015. After the newspaper article was released, the FDA released a report calling a critical component of Theranos' blood testing procedure, their proprietary 'nanotainer', an 'uncleared medical device' and cited other concerns with the company. The following year, regulators threatened sanctions against the company. Theranos was forced to void two years of blood tests and was sued by multiple parties. The company laid off many of its employees and ultimately folded. The Securities and Exchange Commission charged Holmes with 'massive fraud' in which she 'exaggerated or made false statements about the company's technology, business, and financial performance'. Holmes was later found guilty and sentenced to prison. In short, Holmes ultimately caused the demise of Theranos, resulting in the loss of investment and livelihood for its stakeholders. Here is another example of Holmes' meeting Lipman-Bluman's criteria.

Thus far, we have focused on Lipman-Blumen's definition of toxic leadership and have applied it to Elizabeth Holmes. However, we can also use Barbara Kellerman's typology in our analysis. Recall that Kellerman defines two types of 'bad leaders' – those who are ineffective and those who are unethical. Holmes ultimately falls into both of these categories. First, she acted unethically by defrauding investors and lying to them and the public. Holmes was corrupt because she 'lied to a degree that exceeded the norm and put her own self-interests ahead of the public interests'.[57] One might also consider meeting Kellerman's definition of 'callous' in that she did not seem to show any concern for the patients who would receive the faulty results produced in her labs or for her investors losing their money. Finally, Holmes may also be termed 'ineffective' because she failed to bring her ideas to fruition. She had a dream of creating a breakthrough medical technology; unfortunately, that was all it ever was – a dream. By the time the public learned of Holmes' deception and false claims, patients had committed their health into her hands, employees had lost their jobs, and investors had lost millions of dollars. Thus, Holmes seems to fit a variety of Kellerman's typologies for a 'bad leader'.

We would be remiss if we did not examine other aspects of the leadership process, particularly the followers in this case. Holmes did not act alone. Perhaps the best way to understand followers' role in the Theranos saga is to return to Padilla et al. and their idea of 'colluders' and 'conformers'. First, let's begin with colluders. Toxic leaders do not act alone, and neither did Holmes. Her chief colluder was Ramesh 'Sunny' Balwani, the President and Chief Operating Officer of Theranos when Holmes was CEO. Balwani and Holmes also had a romantic relationship. First-hand accounts refer to Balwani as an omnipresent force at Theranos. Those inside Theranos saw Balwani as the 'enforcer'. He monitored emails between employees, and he was instrumental in helping to create a culture of fear and secrecy that hid the lies at the company's roots. Those who disagreed with Holmes or raised questions about the veracity of the technology were often 'disappeared' by Balwani – meaning, they were quickly and unceremoniously fired.[58] Balwani has been described as having an 'aggressive, in-your-face management style [that] projected an air of menace. He was haughty and demeaning toward employees, barking orders and dressing people down.'[59] Padilla et al. refer to the colluder's ambition, similar world views to the leader, and their bad values as the reasons for the colluder follower's complicity. These descriptors seem to fit Balwani, who was tried and convicted of 12 counts of fraud for his work at Theranos. Balwani was certainly not Holmes' only colluder, but he does exemplify this kind of follower well.

Investors and the employees at Theranos were also part of Holmes' follower group, but most of them played the role of conformers. By all accounts, Holmes was a charismatic figure who could charm investors and employees. Holmes served as a role model to many women in the tech industry and as one of the first 'self-made' female billionaire entrepreneurs. She presented a compelling vision of a product that would allow access to early disease detection and ownership of one's health information, which she referred to as a basic human right. Many people positively responded to Holmes' charismatic personality and vision. Unfortunately, they did so without critically examining Holmes' claims. Padilla et al. say that conformer followers often follow toxic leaders to meet their unmet needs. Likewise, Lipman-Blumen argues that followers often stick by toxic leaders because they offer them a grand vision and fulfil their need to feel special. No doubt, anyone caught up in Elizabeth Holmes' orbit felt special. Many lauded her as one of the most important inventors of a century, compared to the likes of Steve Jobs and Archimedes. To be associated with Holmes at her zenith was to share in that glow – investor and employee alike.

Who is to say why any of Holmes' followers chose to follow; what is important is that some didn't. Toxic leaders would be wise to remember that the followers ultimately brought Holmes and Theranos down. Although Holmes could sell the Theranos lie for more than a decade, other followers within the company ultimately blew the whistle on the deception. Many of these followers had been attempting to sound the alarm in Theranos, but they had systematically been silenced. People throughout the company knew that Theranos' technology didn't work. Those who raised the issue with Holmes were either ignored, side-lined, or fired. Eventually, a few courageous followers turned to the media and regulators to expose the deception. This decision was not easy. One scientist, Ian Gibbons, took his own life when faced with the repercussions of daring to suggest that Theranos' technology didn't work. Another follower, Tyler Shultz, an intern at the company, revealed to his grandfather – a board member at Theranos – the fraud happening at the company. His grandfather refused to believe him at the time. Other followers, such as former lab technician Erika Cheung, was one of the few whistleblowers to alert regulators that Theranos was misrepresenting data. Theranos attorneys hounded her. There was Dr Adam Rosendorff, the Theranos lab director whose testimony featured prominently in Holmes' fraud trial. Finally, there was John Carreyrou, the reporter at *The Wall Street Journal*, who broke the Theranos story and exposed Holmes' deception. For their bravery, these followers suffered a maelstrom of intimidation from lawyers, public scrutiny, and a mountain of legal fees. However, their courageous followership brought the truth to light and sent Holmes to prison. So, followers played both positive and negative roles in the Theranos story. The focus on followers also illustrates that leadership is untimely *a process* and about more than just a single person.

Lastly, we must consider the context and culture that allowed Holmes and her lie to flourish for so long. The environment is the third component of Padilla et al.'s toxic triangle. The authors suggest that environments conducive to toxic leadership include instability, a perceived threat, poor cultural values, and a lack of checks and balances.[60] All of these were present at Theranos.

Holmes and Balwali set about to create a common enemy of LabCorp and Quest Diagnostics, their chief competition in the medical testing industry. When John Carreyrou, *The Wall Street Journal* reporter, exposed their deception, he became the company's enemy. Carreyrou and these established companies were cast as the evil foes set upon Theranos' destruction. When Theranos finally received FDA approval for *one* test on their Edison machines, Holmes and Balwani led the Theranos employees in a collective 'fuck you' to Quest Diagnostics. They also led the employees in a similar chant for John Carreyrou. Holmes cast herself as the public's saviour from the greedy medical testing industry. Holmes's 'invention' was supposed to be a disruptor. Indeed, it was a noble goal. Had it worked, her dream may have led to the early detection of disease and could have made healthcare more efficacious and affordable. However, the desire for the dream to be 'real' led many people to look past the falsehoods of Holmes' claims and only focus on the potential good – and potential money – to be created by such a dream.

To doubt the veracity of Holmes' claims was to invite accusations of disloyalty and narrow thinking, along with the possible loss of employment or litigation. The culture of the company was plagued by mistrust. Employees were required to sign non-disclosure agreements and were organized into silos to prevent them from knowing what other departments were doing. One journalist commented, 'What exactly happens in the machine is treated as a state secret. And Holmes's description of the process is comically vague.'[61]

The US military wanted to test Theranos technology in the field, but Theranos turned down the lucrative offer because they wanted to control access to the prototypes. In hindsight, this caginess was designed to hide the truth from investors, employees, and the public that Holmes' invention was nothing but a pipe dream. Requests for information were met with excuses that Theranos was protecting their 'trade secrets' and they were attempting to prevent their competitors from stealing their technology. The truth was, there was no such secret technology. This culture of mystery certainly contributed to Holmes' ability to keep the Theranos secret for as long as she did.

However, there were also problematic issues within the broader culture of Silicon Valley. Tech start-up culture is known for its secrecy, and non-disclosure agreements are standard. Many companies avoid going public to be able to withhold information that they would be required by law to provide if they were a publicly held company, such as submitting quarterly earnings statements. The practice of 'fake it until you make it' is all too common in Silicon Valley. Indeed, Holmes named her technology after Thomas Edison, who was known to exaggerate and lie about his own technological marvels. Overexaggerated claims and flashy ad campaigns that sell form without substance seem part and parcel of the culture of tech start-ups and Silicon Valley. That culture may be unethical but may cause limited harm when selling the newest gadget. However, when dealing with a patient's health, the stakes are much higher.

There is also a strong mythos of 'the founder' in Silicon Valley – the lore of the self-made 'man' rising against all odds to beat the system. Consider Steve Jobs, Bill Gates, Elon Musk, Jeff Bezos, Mark Zuckerberg, and the 'pantheon' of tech giants. The tale of the brilliant college dropout pursuing a dream and starting a multi-billion-dollar business out of their garage is powerful in the American consciousness. It fails to consider the overwhelming number of tech companies that fold or those 'brilliant' college dropouts who fail to 'change the world'. As one economist put it, 'Data doesn't sit in minds as much as stories.'[62] Unfortunately, for those investing in Holmes and Theranos, the fiction was more persuasive than the facts.

## FIVE COMPONENT ANALYSIS

Let's place our case study on the Five Components of Leadership Model. In this instance, the leader is Elizabeth Holmes, the founder and CEO of Theranos (Figure 18.3). The followers are the investors and the employees of Theranos. The goal was to develop breakthrough technology in the field of medical testing. The context was tech start-up culture, which is plagued by exaggeration, and – in this case – a preponderance of outright lies and fraud. The cultural values and norms are the American founder mystique and the myth of the 'self-made man'. As you can see, the focus on the leader, follower, and context comports with Padilla et al. and their identification of the destructive leaders, susceptible followers, and conducive environments highlighted in their toxic triangle.

We might also consider the goal as part of our discussion. As we have stated, Elizabeth Holmes' goal was a noble one. However, the way she went about attempting to achieve that goal was anything but ethical. Would we be so harsh on Holmes had she actually obtained her goal and Theranos found a way to make her dream a reality? Perhaps. But we should think twice about this. It was just this sort of thinking that allowed Holmes' fraud to thrive for so long. She believed her ends would justify her means. Theranos is a morality tale that raises many ethical issues discussed throughout this text. Here are just a few of the ethical considerations: Kantian ethics would call upon the categorical imperative and argue that lying is wrong regardless of the outcome; virtue ethicists would say that Holmes lacked the virtue needed to be an ethical leader; care ethics would say that Holmes should have put Theranos' patients' needs for reliable results and her investor's savings

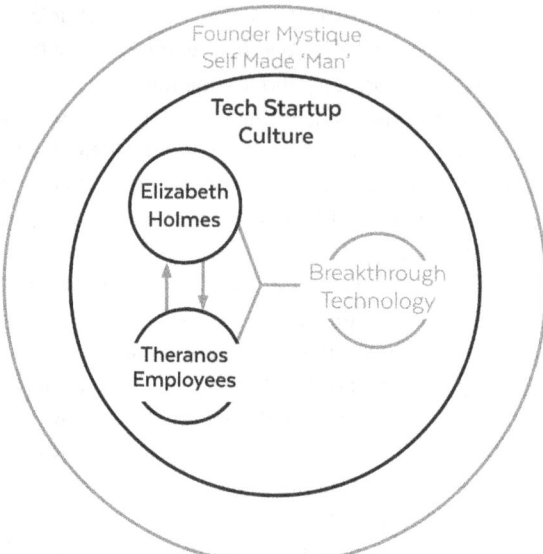

Figure 18.3    The Five Components of Leadership Model applied to the Theranos and Elizabeth Holmes case study

at the centre of her decision-making; even ethical egoism would argue that Holmes should have considered what was best in her *long-term* interest – something that the guilty verdict she received convicting her of fraud and her ultimate prison sentence indicates that she failed to consider.

The Five Components Model also shows us that we cannot lay the blame for toxic leadership entirely at the feet of the leader. Holmes did not act alone. Many followers – both colluders and conformers – aided and abetted her deception. They may have had various reasons for doing so, including their own selfish ambition or simply a desire to be a part of something greater than themselves. Some followers were surely oblivious to Holmes' deception. Others were most likely not. In the end, only a few dared to come forward and blow the whistle on the fraud occurring. As we saw in the chapter on followership, leadership cannot happen without followers – toxic leadership or otherwise.

Before we are too quick to judge Holmes and her colluding and conforming followers, we must also consider the context that played a role in this morality tale. We are all guilty of contributing to a culture that values charisma and form over substance. Many of us buy into the magic that is Silicon Valley and the larger American mythos of the 'self-made man' either knowingly or unknowingly. The Holmes and Theranos story can serve as a cautionary tale for all of us to consider how we may contribute to toxic leadership and apply the lessons learned in this chapter to the leadership processes in which we find ourselves.

## SUMMARY AND CONCLUDING REMARKS

In our discussion of 'toxic' or 'destructive' leaders, we've noted that while these charismatic leaders may be the *'sine qua non'* that is a requirement for toxic leadership, it's not just the leaders alone. Leaders, followers, and their contexts all work together to reinforce the leader's power.

Recognizing these leaders can be difficult because (thankfully) not every destructive leader is a Hitler. While our chapter has highlighted disturbing and notable abuses of power and cult leadership, such as that of Jim Jones or the cult-of-personality and authoritarian leadership of 'Papa Doc' and 'Baby Doc' Duvalier, not all forms of toxic leadership are so egregious. Some of these leaders cause destruction through their clumsy incompetence. Others cause destruction by their focused malice. Either way, their behaviours work like poisoned arrows that are fired into the crowd of their followers and their organization's stakeholders. Moreover, these leaders can make (poor) use of the power that *we* have given to them. We seem to have more patience and sympathy for those whose destructive tendencies may overlap with our own values. And if these leaders appear to be 'successful' in goals that we consider worthy, we may label them as 'heroes' instead of 'villains'. Rather than saying we expect 'too much' or 'too little' from our leaders, perhaps we would do well to turn the spotlight on ourselves. When thinking about toxic leadership, we encourage readers to return to our Followership chapter and consider in what ways do we expect 'too much' or 'too little' of our followership of charismatic leaders and how we support or challenge them.

So how, then, are we to recognize truly 'toxic' leaders? From our chapter, there appears to be a list of 'do's' and 'don'ts'.

### Do:

- Consider the costs associated with their work in both material and human terms;
- Examine what the leader uses to inspire cooperation from followers;
- Weigh how the leader uses or 'uses up' the organization to advance their own agendas.

### Don't:

- Evaluate the leader on their goal-achievement alone;
- Allow a leader's charisma to distract from assessing their character;
- Succumb to simple 'in-group' vs. 'out-group' thinking.

### DISCUSSION QUESTIONS

1. How can we help leaders who are prone to toxicity?
2. How does one recognize when leadership has become 'toxic' in real-time?
3. What could make followers more resilient against toxic influences?
4. Given the negative impact that toxic followers can have on their good leaders and workplaces, what do you think makes it so difficult to replace these workers?

## ADDITIONAL RESOURCES

'The Rise and Fall of Mars Hill' (2021).

This podcast series examines what toxic leadership can look like in a religious setting, tracing the phenomenal growth and eventual decline of a Church with worldwide satellite locations, including how social media both empowered a toxic leader and helped bring about his downfall.

Robert J. Sutton's *The No Asshole Rule* (2009) and Adam Grant's *Give and Take* (2014).

These books offer readers practical advice on recognizing leaders and co-workers who take from their organizations much more than they give. And they provide readers with suggestions on how to manage these difficult relationships.

Various media outlets have chronicled the Theranos story in documentary and dramatized format.

# NOTES

1. Oxford Languages, 'Oxford word of the Year 2018'. https://languages.oup.com/word-of-the-year/2018/ (accessed 15 January 2022).

2. J. Lipman-Bluman, *The Allure of Toxic Leaders: Why We Follow Destructive Bosses and Corrupt Politicians – and How We Can Survive Them*, New York: Oxford University Press, 2005.

3. Lipman-Bluman, *Allure of Toxic Leaders*, p. 18.

4. For more on how we assign credit to 'leadership' as cause for certain results, see J.R. Meindl, S.B. Ehrlich and J.M. Dukerich, 'The romance of leadership', *Administrative Science Quarterly*, vol. 30 no. 1, March 1985, 78–82.

5. A summary of Weber's work on charismatic leaders, along with further development of the concept, can be found in B. Bass and R. Bass, *The Bass Handbook of Leadership: Theory, Research, and Managerial Applications*, 4th edn, New York: Free Press, 2008.

6. See Freud, 1922, in Bass and Bass, *The Bass Handbook of Leadership*.

7. A. Padilla, R. Hogan and R.B. Kaiser, 'The toxic triangle: destructive leaders, susceptible followers, and conducive environments', *The Leadership Quarterly*, vol. 18 no. 3, 2007, 176–94, p. 180.

8. See James MacGregor Burns' discussion of the founding fathers in J.M. Burns, *Leadership*, New York: HarperCollins, 1978; and discussion in B. Kellerman, *Bad Leadership: What It Is, How It Happens, Why It Matters*, Boston, MA: Harvard Business School Press, 2004.

9. J. Lipman-Blumen, 'Toxic leadership: when grand illusions masquerade as noble visions', *Leader to Leader*, Spring 2005, 29–36.

10. D. Victor, 'What happened with Liz Truss in Britain? A guide to the basics', *The New York Times*, 20 October 2022. https://www.nytimes.com/2022/10/20/world/europe/uk-politics-liz-truss.html (accessed 18 November 2022).

11. For a variety of primary and secondary sources on the story of Jim Jones and Jonestown, see https://jonestown.sdsu.edu/.

12. American Psychological Association, 'Narcissism', 2022. https://dictionary.apa.org/narcissism (accessed 18 November 2022).

13. S.A. Rosenthal and T.L. Pittinsky, 'Narcissistic leadership', *The Leadership Quarterly*, vol. 17 no. 6, 2006, 613–53, p. 618.

14. Mayo Clinic, 'Narcissistic personality disorder', 2022. https://www.mayoclinic.org/diseases-conditions/narcissistic-personality-disorder/symptoms-causes/syc-20366662 (accessed 18 November 2022).

15. A. Goldman, *Transforming Toxic Leaders*, Stanford, CA: Stanford University Press, 2009, p. 137.

16. Goldman, *Transforming Toxic Leaders*, pp. 102–3. So how does one recognize such patterns? I suggest a general rule of thumb for such behaviours. Once is an accident. Twice is a concern. Three times is a trend. Trends must be addressed.

17. Rosenthal and Pittinsky, 'Narcissistic leadership', p. 629.

18. Bass and Bass, *The Bass Handbook of Leadership*, p. 232.

19. *The Indianapolis Star*, 'Bob Knight: former Indiana University basketball coach', Indystar.com, updated 2008. https://web.archive.org/web/20100419194719/http://www2.indystar.com/library/factfiles/people/k/knight_bob/knight.html (accessed 18 November 2022).

20. Lipman-Blumen, *Allure of Toxic Leaders*.

21. Lipman-Bluman, *Allure of Toxic Leaders*, p. 6.

22. A. Goldman, *Transforming Toxic Leaders*, Stanford, CA: Stanford Business Books, 2009.

23. M.F.R. Kets de Vries, 'Coaching the toxic leader', *Harvard Business Review*, April 2014. https://hbr.org/2014/04/coaching-the-toxic-leader (accessed 18 November 2022).

24. Lipman Bluman, *Allure of Toxic Leaders*.

25. Lipman-Bluman, *Allure of Toxic Leaders*, p. 19.

26. For an extensive discussion of this pattern and how people can respond in the workplace, see R.I. Sutton, *The No Asshole Rule: Building a Civilized Workplace and Surviving One That Isn't*, New York: Grand Central Publishing, 2010.

27. Kets de Vries, 'Coaching the toxic leader'.

28. Lipman-Bluman, *Allure of Toxic Leaders*, p. 19.

29. Lipman-Bluman, *Allure of Toxic Leaders*, p. 10.

30. Lipman-Bluman, *Allure of Toxic Leaders*, p. 19.

31. Another tragic example of this can be seen in the story of David Koresh and the Brand Davidian compound he led until 1993 when the group immolated itself rather than surrender to the FBI.

32. Lipman-Blumen, *Allure of Toxic Leaders*, p. 16.

33. Padilla et al., 'The toxic triangle'.

34. J.F. Kennedy, 'Address at Rice University on the nation's space effort', 12 September 1962. https://www.jfklibrary.org/learn/about-jfk/historic-speeches/address-at-rice-university-on-the-nations-space-effort (accessed 18 November 2022).

35. For more discussion on this point, see the Pew Research Center's webpage on 'misinformation'. https://www.pewresearch.org/topic/news-habits-media/media-society/misinformation/ (accessed 18 November 2022).

36. Kets de Vries, 'Coaching the toxic leader'.

37. B. Kellerman and T. Pittinsky, *Leaders Who Lust: Power, Money, Sex, Success, Legitimacy, Legacy*, Cambridge: Cambridge University Press, 2020.

38. Padilla et al., 'The toxic triangle'.

39. Padilla et al., 'The toxic triangle'.

40. Kellerman, *Bad Leadership*, pp. 33–4.

41. S. McClean, S.H. Courtright, T.A. Smith and J. Yim, 'Stop making excuses for toxic bosses', *Harvard Business Review*, 19 January 2021. https://hbr.org/2021/01/stop-making-excuses-for-toxic-bosses (accessed 18 November 2022).

42. Padilla et al., 'The toxic triangle'.

43. Kellerman, *Bad Leadership*; and Lipman-Bluman, *Allure of Toxic Leaders*.

44. M. Housman and D. Minor, 'Toxic workers', Working Paper, 16–057, Harvard Business School, November 2015. https://www.hbs.edu/ris/Publication%20Files/16-057_d45c0b4f-fa19–49de-8f1b-4b12fe054fea.pdf (accessed 18 November 2022).

45. Padilla et al., 'The toxic triangle', 183.

46. Padilla et al., 'The toxic triangle', 183.

47. Padilla et al., 'The toxic triangle'.

48. L.D. Ordóñez, M.E. Schweitzer, A.D. Galinsky and M.H. Bazerman, 'Goals gone wild: the systematic side effects of over-prescribing goal setting', *The Academy of Management Perspectives*, vol. 23 no. 1, 1 February 2009, 6–16. https://journals.aom.org/doi/abs/10.5465/amp.2009.37007999 (accessed 18 November 2022).

49. NDDCEL Staff, 'Science of setting goals: what works and what backfires', Notre Dame Deloitte Center for Ethical Leadership, 2022. https://ethicalleadership.nd.edu/news/getting-goals-right/ (accessed 14 January 2022).

50. Housman and Minor, 'Toxic workers'.

51. Burns, *Leadership*.

52. A. Hamilton, J. Madison and J. Jay, 'Separation of powers', 47: 327–31, *The Federalist*, ed. J.E. Cooke, Middletown, CN: Wesleyan University Press, 1961. https://press-pubs.uchicago.edu/founders/documents/v1ch10s14.html (accessed 17 November 22).

53. D.S. Zweig, C. Sull and B. Zweig, 'Toxic culture is driving the great resignation', *MIT Sloan Management Review*, 11 January 2022. https://sloanreview.mit.edu/article/toxic-culture-is-driving-the-great-resignation/ (accessed 10 February 2022).

54. Many journalists have documented the Elizabeth Holmes and Theranos story. This case study calls upon many of these, including J. Carreyrou, *Bad Blood: Secrets and Lies in a Silicon Valley Startup*, New York: Alfred A. Knopf, 2019; HBO documentary films, *The Inventor: Out for Blood in Silicon Valley*, 2019, directed by Alex Gibney; *The Dropout*, 2019, podcast, hosted by Rebecca Jarvis, ABC News.

55. This was a letter that Elizabeth Holmes often referred to and was even referenced with the judge during her fraud trail.

56. Lipman-Bluman, *Allure of Toxic Leaders*, p. 18.

57. Kellerman, *Bad Leadership*, p. 120.

58. Carreyrou, *Bad Blood*, p. 77.

59. Carreyou, *Bad Blood*, pp. 68–9.

60. Padilla et al., 'The toxic triangle'.

61. K. Auletta, 'Blood, simpler: a woman's drive to upend medical testing', *The New Yorker*, 8 December 2014. https://www.newyorker.com/magazine/2014/12/15/blood-simpler#:~:text=What%20exactly%20happens%20in%20the,which%20is%20then%20reviewed%20by (accessed 22 November 2022).

62. Quote by Dan Ariely, behavioral economist, in HBO documentary films, *The Inventor: Out for Blood in Silicon Valley*.

# 19
# Conclusion

*Robert M. McManus, Stanley J. Ward and Alexandra K. Perry*

Once again, we return to our central question in this book – 'What is ethical leadership?' Recall that in Chapter 1 we proposed a two-pronged answer to this question: (1) ethical leadership is the practice of leaders using various approaches of ethics to make ethically sound decisions, and (2) using one's position of leadership to bring about positive change. If you were hoping for this book to provide you with a universal prescription to ensure ethical leadership in all situations, you were – no doubt – disappointed. *We would expect that any book that thoroughly explored the scope of ethical leadership would be equally disenchanting.* We hope that by now readers realize there is no single approach to ethics or leadership that answers the question 'What is ethical leadership?' in every situation. Rather, we encourage readers to see themselves as leaders who are developing the tools for handling complex leadership issues with a variety of ethical concerns. To borrow an oft-used observation, 'If your only tool is a hammer, then everything looks like a nail.' As an alternative, we want our readers to access a full suite of tools to help them make sound decisions and lead ethically, a good set of which can be found in this book's approaches to ethics and leadership. To that end, allow us to provide you with one more set of tools for your toolbox – several guidelines that will help you work through the ethical dilemmas you may face.

## PRACTICAL ETHICAL GUIDELINES

Below we have assembled several practical ethical guidelines to help leaders apply what they have learned in this book to their particular situations.[1] Although these guidelines may serve as helpful strategies for determining the ethical implications of a potential decision, we encourage readers to be mindful that they must apply these guidelines with a mastery of the more in-depth material available throughout this text for the guidelines to be useful.

### Common Sense

Many people have observed the irony that, despite its name, common sense is remarkably rare. Perhaps they're right. Nevertheless, leaders can use this guideline when faced with an ethical dilemma simply by asking themselves, 'Does this decision make sense?' Note that this question may require you to consider many of the ethical theories we have examined in this book, such as utilitarianism, egoism, ethics of care, and others.

However, a word of caution is in order when using this guideline: the leader asking this question may only be considering the *short-term consequences* of an action and fail to consider an action's *long-term implications*. It might 'make sense' to fudge the numbers on a report in the short term, but the organization may suffer from the leader's short-term thinking in the long run. The leader's actions may result in the leader and followers ultimately failing to reach their goal. Not to mention, such an action is just plain wrong. This guideline is also sometimes referred to as the 'smell test'. If something doesn't smell right, don't do it. Applying such a test could save leaders a great deal of trouble.

## One's Best Self

Another simple guideline that can help leaders make sound decisions is considering how their actions may affect their self-concept. To apply this guideline, leaders might ask themselves: 'Do my actions represent me at my best?' 'Can I look myself in the mirror knowing what I know?' 'Am I proud of myself for what I did or said?' Considering ethical theories such as virtue ethics, Kantianism, and justice as fairness would prove helpful in attempting to answer such questions, as would authentic leadership. Indeed, we could all stand to keep these questions in mind whether we are in a leadership position or not. Another word of caution, however: human beings are capable of remarkable self-deception and rationalization. Although this guideline may be helpful, realize that it is not fool proof.

## Public Disclosure

The guidelines that we have considered thus far would pair well with the public disclosure guideline. This guideline forces leaders to think about the consequences their actions may have upon their reputations. When using this guideline, leaders might ask themselves, 'Would I be comfortable with others knowing of my action or decision?' Leaders might make more ethical choices if they thought their behaviours would be featured on the front page of the *New York Times* or the local news. Another way to frame this guideline is the 'Grandma test'; leaders should ask themselves, 'Would my grandmother approve of my actions?' Many of the ethical theories and approaches to leadership presented in this book could help one consider the answer to this question: virtue ethics and toxic leadership are just two that spring to mind.

## Ventilation

Perhaps the most straightforward guideline we can offer to help leaders make ethical decisions is to seek other people's opinions about a potential course of action. Leaders must listen to their followers and other stakeholders to see how their potential decisions may affect them. Obtaining input from others may help reveal the unseen ethical consequences of a leader's decision.

For example, consider a supervisor who considers giving a bonus to a direct report for their exemplarily work on a project. It certainly may be in the supervisor's preview to do this; still, the supervisor may fail to consider all the other people who put in just as much time and effort on the same or another unrelated project. Imagine how the other employees would feel if they heard that their co-worker was the only one who received a bonus! If the supervisor had taken the time to listen to others involved in the project, they might have learned that many people were worthy of recognition and reward. Then they could have applied Rawls' idea of justice as fairness, social contract theory, or even adaptive leadership to determine the best course of action. Sometimes actions that may seem insignificant or even positive at first glance may have unseen consequences. Seeking input from others may help ward off decisions that may ultimately carry adverse ethical outcomes.

## Test of a Purified Idea

Many ethical missteps are caused by leaders assuming an idea or an action is ethical because someone in a position of authority deems it to be so. Such ideas or actions are considered to be 'purified'. Perhaps a lawyer or an accountant told the leader something was legal, but they did not consider a higher threshold for an action's morality.

For example, one of the editors of this book was a part of Title IX training at his educational institution. (Title IX is a law that prohibits sex-based discrimination for schools that receive funding from the United States government.) The editor asked the attorney providing the training about the law's implications for the institution's LGBTQ+ students. The federal government did not consider LGBTQ+ students covered by the law at the time. The attorney responded, 'Title IX does not cover them [LBGT+ students]; you can do anything with them that you want.' The editor was appalled by the callousness of the attorney's response. The implication was that if an action was legal, it was ethically permissible. Although it might have been *legal* at the time to discriminate against LGBTQ+ people, it certainly was not ethical. To their credit, the organization that hired the lawyer who made the offending comment discontinued its relationship with that particular attorney. The federal government has also since mandated the law to be applied LGBTQ+ students. The test of a purified idea reminds leaders to evaluate ideas for their ethical implications critically. It also warns leaders that, in the end, *they* are the ones who will have to answer for their actions. The chapter on followership featured in this text vividly illustrates this fact.

## The 'Big Four'

The 'big four' guideline also helps leaders critically evaluate their decisions and consider their ethical implications. The 'big four' refers to the significant factors of decision-making that may have negative ethical implications: greed, speed, laziness, and haziness.

Greed is probably one of the most tantalizing ethical traps. There is a good reason the love of money is referred to as 'the root of all evil'. Bribes, kickbacks, and corruption are a few of greed's more flamboyant manifestations. However, greed can take on much more subtle – and therefore insidious – forms, such as when a company sells a product it knows to cause harm to increase profits. Consider the now-infamous case of the tobacco industry's long-standing knowledge of the damage its products had upon human health while continuing to sell their products and increasing levels of nicotine to foster addiction.[2] In general, leaders need to be wary of any behaviours that have the potential to place profits over people.

Likewise, speed can also get leaders into trouble, such as when they cut corners to accomplish a goal. What student hasn't been tempted to plagiarize a paper or cheat on a test the night before an assignment is due? Alternatively, consider a more deadly instance in which speed led to a poor decision, such as NASA's Challenger space shuttle disaster. NASA's leadership team failed to heed the engineers' warnings about the effect launching in record-low temperatures could have upon the shuttle's O-ring seals because of the leadership team's desire to launch on time. Their desire for speed cost seven astronauts their lives.[3]

'Haziness' is the third in our line-up. The term refers to a person failing to understand the whole situation before acting. All leaders must make decisions with limited information, but consider how so many problems could be avoided if leaders just took a bit more time to understand the situation more thoroughly before acting. The classic example of haziness is the 'the fog of war'. The term is used to encapsulate the uncertainty of information pervasive in battle. Lack of information, however, does not give leaders a pass for their poor decisions or unethical actions. People succumb to much more mundane manifestations of this ethical trap every day. Leaders would be wise to ask, 'Do I have all the information I need to make this decision?' If the answer is 'no', perhaps they should wait a bit to see if the fog clears.

Finally, laziness is the last of the 'big four'. Moral laziness is a term for failing to consider how our actions may run contrary to our values. Think of the many times we have all driven our car to run a quick errand, thereby contributing to global warming when we just as easily could have walked or ridden our bicycle. Or think about the last time you picked up a cheap t-shirt on a whim and failed to consider the sweatshop workers who received pennies for their labour. Many of our everyday decisions have ethical implications, but it takes vigilance to be mindful of them and thereby truly live by our values. *That is why the information contained in this book is so crucial for leaders to master.*

These are just a few practical guidelines to help leaders make ethical decisions (Table 19.1). They are best used in conjunction with each other to help thoughtfully consider all sides of an issue. Hopefully, the information you gleaned from this book will become second nature, and you can call upon it to apply such guidelines every day.

**Table 19.1** Practical ethical guidelines

| Concept | Questions to consider |
| --- | --- |
| Common sense | 'Does this decision make sense in the long-term as well as the short-term?' |
| One's best self | 'Can I look myself in the mirror knowing what I know?' |
| Public disclosure | 'Would I be comfortable with others knowing of my action or decision?' |
| Ventilation | 'Have I considered asking other people their opinions about a potential action or decision?' |
| Test of a purified idea | 'Have I critically evaluated this idea for its ethical implications, regardless of what someone in a position of authority may say?' |
| The 'big four': greedy, speedy, hazy, lazy | 'Am I putting profits over principles?' 'Am I sacrificing my ethics for expediency?' 'Do I have all the information I need to make an ethical decision?' 'Have I considered all my options to make the most ethically informed decision?' |

# REVIEW

Review is the mother of learning. As we conclude our text, let's spend some time reviewing the work we've done so far in order to internalize it. After that, we can get to yet another question, and this is the one that should be at the heart of any educational endeavour – 'So what?' We will do that here by first summarizing the content of our chapters on ethics and leadership. Then we will make some general observations based on those summaries. Finally, we will dig into the 'so what' for our text with the hope that we can provide our readers with some final insights that will last even longer than the tables and figures we developed to help readers synthesize and remember key content for each chapter.

As we come to the conclusion of *Ethical Leadership: A Primer*, we offer Table 19.2 as a helpful aid to sort through information that might be new to most of our readers. In our book, we have attempted to describe ethical leadership by examining how a variety of ethical models highlight various pieces of the five components of leadership. The table provides an overview of the ethical models we considered in Section I – starting with the framing question, highlighting how those models draw attention to various pieces of the Five Components Model, and listing the accompanying case example.

**Table 19.2** Summary of ethics models

| Model | Framing question | Emphasis | Case example |
|---|---|---|---|
| Kantianism | 'What is the moral duty of leaders and follower?' | The Goal, regardless of the Context | Meta and protecting children |
| Utilitarianism | 'How do leaders create the greatest good for the greatest number?' | Both the Goal and the Context | Smithsonian's *Enola Gay* exhibit |
| Virtue Ethics | 'What is virtuous leadership?' | The Leader | The USAF cheating scandal |
| Ethical Egoism | 'What is self-interested leadership?' | The Leader | NCAA NIL rights |
| The Ethics of Care | 'What obligations do leaders have to care for followers?' | The Leader | Heart valves for IV drug users |
| Universal Ethics | 'How can universal standards guide leaders and followers in any context?' | Universal Values and Norms | Indigenous land rights in Brazil |
| Cultural Relativism | 'How do culture and context impact leadership?' | Cultural Values and Norms | Facebook and language moderation in Myanmar |
| Divine Command Theory | 'What does The Divine require from leadership?' | The Divine's Values and Norms as well as The Divine's Commands applied in the Context | International Justice Mission |
| Social Contract Theory | 'What obligations do leaders and followers have toward each other?' | Leaders, Followers, and Goal | Higher Education |
| Justice as Fairness | 'How can leaders and followers together create a just society?' | The connections between leaders, followers, and goals | Critical Race Theory |
| The Common Good | 'What is the best thing to do for all of society?' | All five components | The Clean Air Act |

Likewise, Table 19.3 provides a list of the leadership models we considered in Section II, the framing question for each model, the leadership component(s) emphasized, and the case example for each chapter.

**Table 19.3** Summary of leadership models

| Model | Framing question | Emphasis | Case example |
|---|---|---|---|
| Authentic leadership | 'How can I lead with integrity?' | Leaders | Colin Powell's values |
| Servant leadership | 'How can leaders serve their followers and organizations?' | Leaders serving followers | Tarana Burke #MeToo |
| Followership | 'How can followers partner with their leaders?' | Followers partnering with leaders | The Southern Baptist sex abuse scandal |

| Model | Framing question | Emphasis | Case example |
|---|---|---|---|
| Transformational leadership | 'How can leaders and followers transform each other and their organizations?' | Leaders and followers with a transforming goal | Dan Schulman's leadership at PayPal |
| Adaptive leadership | 'How can leaders and followers respond to adaptive challenges?' | Adaptive challenges in the context | Jacinda Ardern's leadership of New Zealand |
| Toxic leadership | 'What qualifies as "toxic" leadership?' | Leaders, followers and context | Elizabeth Holmes and Theranos |

## NOW FOR SOME OBSERVATIONS

We would like to offer some observations made at the end of the writing process. Once the editors had assembled all the material for these chapters, three themes revealed themselves: (1) how ethical and leadership models seem to pair with each other; (2) what seems to be required for ethical leadership, and (3) specific behaviours for promoting ethical leadership.

### How the Models Pair With Each Other

One fascinating finding occurred as we developed the visual representation of the five components of leadership for each ethical model. These models often 'paired' themselves with similar or inverted areas of emphasis. These similarities became the final organizing scheme for the order of chapters. For students who want to understand better the nuances of these different models, we suggest they pay attention to the similarities and differences of these pairings (Table 19.4). While all models of ethical leadership may ask a fundamentally similar question – 'What is the right thing to do?' – the nuanced differences in how these models frame the question – and where they seem to focus on the five components of leadership – is worth noting.

**Table 19.4** Models with mutual areas of concern

| Leadership component | Ethical models | Leadership models |
|---|---|---|
| The leader | Egoism and virtue ethics, justice as fairness, social contract, care ethics | Authentic leadership, servant leadership |
| The follower | Justice as fairness, social contract | Followership |
| The goal | Justice as fairness, social contract, utilitarianism, Kantianism | Transformational leadership |
| The context | Utilitarianism | Adaptive leadership |
| Cultural values and norms | Universal ethics, cultural relativism, divine command theory | |
| All components | The common good | Toxic leadership |

## Distribution of components and emphasis

When first thinking about 'ethical leadership', it is easy to slip into the mindset that it is all about the individual leader, and that if individual leaders can simply develop enough strength and personal character, everything will take care of itself. If our analysis of the ethical models is correct, then ethical and effective leadership will require leaders to tap into components that go far beyond themselves. Also, note how four of the six leadership models looked beyond the individual leader for their primary emphasis. This observation is consistent with how the last few decades of leadership studies have continued to push academics to see leadership as something larger than simply individual leaders or the 'great people' of history.

## Egoism, virtue ethics, ethics of care, authentic leadership, and toxic leadership

What an irony that egoism, virtue ethics, ethics of care, and authentic leadership all emphasize the same component. At first glance, it can appear that these models are pointing in opposite directions. However, all of these models emphasize a leader's self-awareness. For egoism, the leader must be reflective enough to determine what is genuinely in the leader's long-term self-interest. A virtue approach that explicitly emphasizes the leader's virtues requires self-awareness that can accurately assess the leader's strengths and weaknesses as compared to what the leader might imagine those virtues to be. This emphasis on a self-aware leader is also at the heart of authentic leadership. Authentic leadership emphasizes being true to oneself in a manner that could parallel well with egoism, as well as an emphasis on living consistently with core values, which correlates with virtue ethics. Likewise, toxic leadership emphasizes the leader while highlighting all the potential *foibles* of egoism, a leader's *lack* of virtue, and caring *only* for their self-interests. And it is no surprise that Table 19.4 places these approaches to ethics and leadership on the same line.

## Kantianism, utilitarianism, and transformational leadership

Kant focused on an immutable goal – the 'leader's duty always to do what is right' no matter the consequences. In a different manner, utilitarianism also emphasizes the goal, but with a specific assessment of the consequences of that goal. As we now reflect on Transformational Leadership and note its emphasis on the goal as well, we can note that it is also concerned with the consequences of the goal – transforming both the organization and the members of that organization toward 'higher levels of motivation and morality,' as James MacGregor Burns would say.[4]

## Utilitarianism and adaptive leadership

Both of these models look to the context of a leadership event. In the case of utilitarianism, it considers the impact of the leaders, followers, and goal upon the context. In the inverse of this, adaptive leadership recognizes how the context impacts leaders, followers, and goals.

## Universal ethics, cultural relativism, and divine command

These are the ethical approaches that often ignite the 'culture wars'. And as we consider some of the different claims from these ethical models, we can understand why there could be tension between adherents to these different ethical positions. Those claiming to follow a 'universal ethic' are attempting to root themselves in a tradition that respects religion yet does not look towards religion as an ultimately authoritative source. Instead, it often looks towards the values of a secular and Western model of liberal 'freedom-granting' values. Cultural relativism also appreciates religious values, but it places different religious systems on an equal footing, asking 'What can we learn?' from each system, rather than claiming one system is 'right'. In contrast, divine command theories are founded upon a particular religious tradition and look both towards the divine and how the will of the divine has been expressed in written tradition. Nonetheless, all three models value reason's role in applying their various claims. Thus, you might see why those holding to these particular ethical traditions might run into conflict with each other.

### The common good

In our analysis of ethical leadership, the common good seemed to work almost like a 'super-layer' over the top of our whole schema. We need to be careful with that representation – especially in light of the concept of 'culture wars' mentioned above. We believe that the common good is distinct among the ethical models because it is equally concerned with the leader, followers, goal, context, and cultural norms – striving to find actions that benefit all those layers of the model. Additionally, although toxic leadership concentrates on the leaders, follower, and context, as we say in the Chapter 18, the context and overall culture may also have on effect on toxic leadership.

## Requirements for Ethical Leadership

After considering the various questions asked by our chapters and the answers provided, we observed a few components that seem to be a *sine qua non* for ethical leadership.

First, humility expressed as a realistic sense of self – both strengths and weaknesses. Humility shows up in a number of chapters as an essential quality for leadership. In virtue ethics, we saw how humility was prized in Hinduism, Buddhism, Judaism, Christianity, and Islam as well as how the Greek tradition warned against hubris. It was also a necessary characteristic for dealing with the challenges of cultural relativism. Additionally, we can argue that humility is beneficial for applying the leadership models in our text. For example, those who wish to practise servant leadership must accurately assess their genuine motives for leadership. That self-awareness must be applied to determine how both the leader and follower are impacted by their mutual goals to practise transformational leadership. For authentic leadership, that self-awareness is the fundamental trait required. For adaptive leadership to take place, the leader must give up the desire to be the 'problem solver' and allow followers to do the work. Regarding followership, without humility, leaders will not be willing to receive honest feedback from followers who act as 'partners' and not just 'implementers'.

Second, while practically impossible to make decisions utterly free of self-interest, ethical awareness often calls the leader to something beyond self-interest. Note how often the emphasis on an ethical or leadership model was on the followers, the goal, the context, or the culture instead of just the leader. One could even argue that the humility we just discussed is necessary for leaders to appreciate the lack of leader-centricity in these models. Certainly, what leaders do matters – but for them to operate effectively as ethical leaders, they must assess themselves in light of how they impact the other spheres of the Five Components Model. Even something as leader-centric as egoism requires leaders to be aware of their impact on the other spheres – and to assess how that impact is or is not in the leader's self-interest. We suggest that for leaders to be genuinely ethical, they must be accountable to something outside of themselves. Our discussion of ethics and the five components of leadership confirms this.

## ACTION STEPS FOR ETHICAL LEADERSHIP

So, if we take these observations from our text and once again think about the five components of leadership, we can understand the journey of the ethical leader. It begins with the self-awareness that leads to an accurate assessment of the self and one's place in the world. This awareness also considers how one relates to others and their impact on others as they work together to achieve a common goal. Then the perspective continues to broaden by reflecting on how their work together impacts the context in which they work to reach their goals. Finally, one considers how these factors correspond with or challenge the prevailing values and norms of the culture. Such self-awareness is the journey of a lifetime, so we now suggest some practical action steps readers can take on their journey as ethical leaders.

Note how we framed each of our chapters with reflective questions. Asking such questions is not just an activity for academics. Rather, these questions are intended to promote self-awareness. As you strive to be an ethical leader, consider it to be a journey that works from the inside out and a mix of self-aware thinking with self-aware action. (So once again, we return to the definition of leadership as *purposeful interaction*.)

Finally, we leave you with a few challenges to consider as you develop your own ethical leaderships. First, we invite you to take the time to assess yourself as a leader. Which ethical models or leadership models are your default? How would you benefit from drawing on additional models?

Next, when trying to lead others ethically, we invite you to ask these questions of your peers and followers. Try questions like, 'How do we promote the greatest good for the greatest number? How can followers partner with leaders in this situation? How can we work together to transform our organization?' By using these questions to frame your goals and interactions with others, you can purposefully move yourself and your organization to consider how specific ethical frameworks and leadership models impact your work.

Finally, studying and teaching leadership with case examples has become standard practice. Use these case studies and stories when you want to educate and inspire those you work with and continue to look for more examples that can help you and others continue to understand the implications of these ideas better.

## SUMMARY AND CONCLUDING REMARKS

In our introduction to the book, we mentioned the need to connect ethical thinking and ethical doing. One can still 'ace' an ethics exam in the classroom by cheating. So, the real test of an ethics class is not how students do on a classroom exam or essay but rather how they act ethically in day-to-day life. So while our book has encouraged readers to look beyond the scope of the individual leader, we will now return to considering their personal leadership.

### Sacrifice and Ethical Leadership

One of the editors was recently studying great American leaders such as George Washington, Abraham Lincoln, and Dr Martin Luther King, Jr. He observed the overwhelming sadness that seemed to saturate their time as leaders – particularly Abraham Lincoln and Dr King's assassinations. His professor paused the class discussion and commented with a soft and slightly trembling voice, 'If you really want to know where you are ready to be a leader, you have to know where you are ready to suffer.'

On a similar note, we are convinced that the real test of our ethics, or 'values', is what we are willing to suffer to maintain those values. In other words, for a thing to truly have 'value', we must be willing to pay something in exchange. We saw multiple examples of how businesses should have made financial sacrifices to meet the various standards of the ethical models in our text. We saw cases where individuals may have to forego personal advantages that may have been allowable by law to benefit a larger population. To behave ethically, both secular and religious adherents need to find a way to accommodate each other, and to do so will require a willingness to bypass philosophical purity. The humility necessary for cultural relativism will require leaders to abandon the comfort of adhering to the faultlessness of their own cultural assumptions and accede where others are correct. Leaders who genuinely want partners in their organizations will have to share their power with others and, in some cases, drop their defences so they can receive critical feedback from their followers.

As with our text, leadership studies often use case examples to help illustrate a point. And numerous stories about ethical leadership or character-based leadership feature the tales of individual leaders. While some of our case studies may have drawn attention to and celebrated those who have made difficult decisions at personal or organizational cost, we also recognize that numerous leaders make intentional decisions that have personal costs daily – sometimes *great* personal costs – and they do so without fanfare. Instead of 'no guts, no glory', it's 'all guts and still no glory'. No wonder humility showed up in our earlier analysis of themes for ethical leadership.

Consequently, a fundamental question for knowing where you are ready to be an ethical leader is to ask yourself, 'For what am I willing to suffer?' If you want an ethical organization, ask your team, 'For what are we willing to suffer?' To the extent that you and your organization can have that conversation genuinely, you have taken a positive step forward. We must remember that ethical leadership is about using ethical theories and models to facilitate ethical decision-making and for leaders to use their leadership positions to create positive change. We now call you and ourselves to rise to both of these challenges.

## DISCUSSION QUESTIONS

1. Which of the ethical models resonated most with you and why?
2. Which of the leadership models resonated most with you and why?
3. What do you view to be the most significant obstacles to ethical leadership?
4. How can you apply the insights of this book in your leadership roles?
5. For what are you willing to suffer to be an 'ethical leader'?

## ADDITIONAL RESOURCES

J.B. Ciulla (ed.), *Ethics, the Heart of Leadership*, 2nd edn, Westport, CT: Praeger, 2004.

This compilation is often referenced when studying leadership and can be a helpful next step in a journey of thinking about the connections between leadership and ethics.

T.L. Price, *Leadership Ethics: An Introduction*, Cambridge: Cambridge University Press, 2008.

Price's book is an introduction to ethical theories and their relevance to leadership, emphasizing psychology and Kantianism.

L. Fisher Thornton, *7 Lenses: Learning the Principles and Practices of Ethical Leadership*, Richmond: Leading in Context, 2013.

This book offers readers a short and practical guide to ethical decision-making.

C.E. Johnson, *Meeting the Ethical Challenges of Leadership: Casting Light or Shadow*, 6th edn, Los Angeles, CA: Sage, 2018.

Johnson's book introduces ethical theories and models and their relevance to leadership and focuses on the implications of unethical leadership's 'dark side'.

## NOTES

1.  These guidelines are often used to help leaders consider the ethical implications of their decisions. However, we are grateful to the following for assembling these guidelines: A.B. Carroll, J.A. Brown, and A.K. Buchholtz, *Business & Society: Ethics, Sustainability & Stakeholder Management*, 10th edn, Boston, MA: Cengage Learning, 2018, pp. 237–9.

2.  The Truth Initiative, '5 ways tobacco companies lied about the dangers of smoking cigarettes', 21 December 2017. https://truthinitiative.org/research-resources/tobacco-prevention-efforts/5-ways-tobacco-companies -lied-about-dangers-smoking (accessed 5 July 2022).

3.  A.S. Teitel, 'What caused the Challenger disasters', History.com. https://www.history.com/news/how-the -challenger-disaster-changed-nasa (accessed 5 July 2022).

4.  J.M. Burns, *Leadership*, New York: HarperCollins, 1978, p. 20.

# INDEX